T0350728

National Bureau of Economics
Conference Report

Europe and the Euro

Edited by **Alberto Alesina and Francesco Giavazzi**

The University of Chicago Press

Chicago and London

ALBERTO ALESINA is the Nathaniel Ropes Professor of Political
Economy at Harvard University, visiting professor at the Innocenzo
Gasparini Institute for Economic Research (IGIER), Bocconi
University, and a research associate of the National Bureau of
Economic Research. FRANCESCO GIAVAZZI is professor of economics
at Bocconi University, visiting professor at the Massachusetts Institute
of Technology, and a research associate of the National Bureau of
Economic Research.

The University of Chicago Press, Chicago 60637
The University of Chicago Press, Ltd., London
© 2010 by the National Bureau of Economic Research
All rights reserved. Published 2010
Printed in the United States of America

19 18 17 16 15 14 13 12 11 10   1 2 3 4 5
ISBN-13: 978-0-226-01283-4 (cloth)
ISBN-10: 0-226-01283-2 (cloth)

Library of Congress Cataloging-in-Publication Data

Europe and the euro / edited by Alberto Alesina and Francesco
  Giavazzi.
        p. cm. — (National Bureau of Economic Research conference
  report)
     Includes proceedings of the National Bureau of Economic
  Research conference, held Oct. 2008.
     Includes bibliographical references and index.
     ISBN-13: 978-0-226-01283-4 (alk. paper)
     ISBN-10: 0-226-01283-2 (alk. paper)
     1. Euro—Congresses. 2. Euro area—Congresses. 3. Monetary
  policy—European Union countries—Congresses. 4. European
  Union countries—Economic integration—Congresses. 5. Economic
  and Monetary Union—Congresses. I. Alesina, Alberto. II. Giavazzi,
  Francesco. III. Series: National Bureau of Economic Research
  conference report.
    HG925.E87 2009
    332.4'94—dc22

                                                          2009025748

Relation of the Directors to the
Work and Publications of the
National Bureau of Economic Research

1. The object of the NBER is to ascertain and present to the economics profession, and to the public more generally, important economic facts and their interpretation in a scientific manner without policy recommendations. The Board of Directors is charged with the responsibility of ensuring that the work of the NBER is carried on in strict conformity with this object.

2. The President shall establish an internal review process to ensure that book manuscripts proposed for publication DO NOT contain policy recommendations. This shall apply both to the proceedings of conferences and to manuscripts by a single author or by one or more co-authors but shall not apply to authors of comments at NBER conferences who are not NBER affiliates.

3. No book manuscript reporting research shall be published by the NBER until the President has sent to each member of the Board a notice that a manuscript is recommended for publication and that in the President's opinion it is suitable for publication in accordance with the above principles of the NBER. Such notification will include a table of contents and an abstract or summary of the manuscript's content, a list of contributors if applicable, and a response form for use by Directors who desire a copy of the manuscript for review. Each manuscript shall contain a summary drawing attention to the nature and treatment of the problem studied and the main conclusions reached.

4. No volume shall be published until forty-five days have elapsed from the above notification of intention to publish it. During this period a copy shall be sent to any Director requesting it, and if any Director objects to publication on the grounds that the manuscript contains policy recommendations, the objection will be presented to the author(s) or editor(s). In case of dispute, all members of the Board shall be notified, and the President shall appoint an ad hoc committee of the Board to decide the matter; thirty days additional shall be granted for this purpose.

5. The President shall present annually to the Board a report describing the internal manuscript review process, any objections made by Directors before publication or by anyone after publication, any disputes about such matters, and how they were handled.

6. Publications of the NBER issued for informational purposes concerning the work of the Bureau, or issued to inform the public of the activities at the Bureau, including but not limited to the NBER Digest and Reporter, shall be consistent with the object stated in paragraph 1. They shall contain a specific disclaimer noting that they have not passed through the review procedures required in this resolution. The Executive Committee of the Board is charged with the review of all such publications from time to time.

7. NBER working papers and manuscripts distributed on the Bureau's web site are not deemed to be publications for the purpose of this resolution, but they shall be consistent with the object stated in paragraph 1. Working papers shall contain a specific disclaimer noting that they have not passed through the review procedures required in this resolution. The NBER's web site shall contain a similar disclaimer. The President shall establish an internal review process to ensure that the working papers and the web site do not contain policy recommendations, and shall report annually to the Board on this process and any concerns raised in connection with it.

8. Unless otherwise determined by the Board or exempted by the terms of paragraphs 6 and 7, a copy of this resolution shall be printed in each NBER publication as described in paragraph 2 above.

Contents

Acknowledgments

It was an honor to be invited by Martin Feldstein to organize a National Bureau of Economic Research (NBER) conference on "Europe and the euro" on the occasion of the tenth anniversary of the European Central Bank. For the past thirty years, Marty, in his role as president of the NBER, has encouraged leading economists to do high-quality empirical research, informed by economic theory, with relevance for policymakers. A key guarantor of the quality of this research is the NBER conferences at which economists from academia, the public sector, and the private sector gather to discuss their work. The resulting NBER conference volume is a lasting record of the conference and an influential outlet for the chapters presented there. We are particularly pleased that Marty participated in the conference and contributed to this volume with a discussion.

Special thanks are due to Carl Beck, Lita Kimble, and Helena Fitz-Patrick from the NBER and to Parker Smathers from the University of Chicago Press, as well as to the Innocenzo Gasparini Institute for Economic Research (IGIER) and Bocconi University, which hosted the conference, and to Corriere della Sera, who hosted the conference dinner. The local organization would not have been possible without the dedication of Ornella Bissoli at the IGIER.

Introduction

Alberto Alesina and Francesco Giavazzi

Ten years into the euro experience, one can evaluate the extent to which the single currency has met its promises. This volume brings together the first comprehensive collection of essays that help make such an assessment.

This introduction does two things: first, we lay out what we think we learned from reading these chapters; then, we go one more step. The conference from which this volume is drawn took place in the midst of the financial crisis (in October 2008), but the chapters had been written long before. Thus, the issues raised by the crisis are touched on only marginally in these chapters. We address some of the lessons for the euro from the crisis in the second part of this introduction.

One issue that has emerged from the conference is that there are benefits from membership in the euro area as well as challenges. In tranquil times, the benefits (and costs) are sizeable, and many chapters discuss them in a variety of different ways. But in a crisis, the benefits appear to be magnified.

Will the Euro Survive?

Is there a chance that the euro area might fall apart? This is the question addressed in chapter 1 by Barry Eichengreen. One can start asking what the answer to this question would have been before the 2007 to 2010 crisis and what it could be now. Before the crisis exploded, one might have been

Alberto Alesina is the Nathaniel Ropes Professor of Political Economy at Harvard University, visiting professor at the Innocenzo Gasparini Institute for Economic Research (IGIER) at Bocconi University, and a research associate of the National Bureau of Economic Research.

Francesco Giavazzi is professor of economics at Bocconi University, visiting professor at the Massachusetts Institute of Technology, and a research associate of the National Bureau of Economic Research.

worried that countries such as Italy and Portugal that were doing so poorly could have succumbed to the temptation to exit to be able to use competitive devaluations to get out temporarily from stagnation. Inside the euro, both countries would have needed large real wage adjustment to restore a balance between nominal wage growth, productivity, and inflation. The possibility of either country abandoning the euro seemed rather remote, but the current Italian interior minister had expressed that view a few years back when not in office—and at some point, the issue was publicly debated in Portugal. Nevertheless, Eichengreen concludes that before the crisis, the event of a major country exiting and of EMU breaking down was highly unlikely in the medium run, and we agree. The crisis—perhaps paradoxically—has strengthened the euro area. Countries with traditionally weak currencies have realized that without the anchor of the euro, they would have experienced a spiral similar to that of developing countries: a speculative attack, a balance-of-payments crisis, interest rates jumping through the roof, and so forth.

The Euro and Structural Reform

The main reason why continental Europe—that is, most of the countries that now form the euro area—in the past twenty years has been unable to keep up with growth in the United States—and also in the United Kingdom and in the Nordic countries—is its reluctance to reform. Has the euro provided new stimulus for economic reform? Or as the evidence sometimes suggests, has euro membership produced "reform fatigue," in the sense that after having painfully met the Maastricht criteria, euro member countries have taken a break from reform?

Two chapters in the volume provide evidence on this question. In chapter 2, Alesina, Ardagna, and Galasso investigate whether the adoption of the euro has facilitated the introduction of structural reforms, defined as deregulation in the product markets and liberalization and deregulation in the labor markets. They find that the adoption of the euro has been associated with an acceleration of the pace of structural reforms in the product market. As for the labor market, the evidence is more complex. Reforms in the primary labor market have proceeded very slowly everywhere, and the euro does not seem to have generated much of an impetus here. On the other hand, in many countries—including many euro ones, such as France, Italy, and Spain—new forms of labor contracts have been introduced based on temporary agreements between employers and workers. The authors also explore whether the euro has brought about wage moderation: they find evidence of wage moderation in the run-up (1993 to 1998) of euro membership but not afterward. In chapter 3, Bugamelli, Schivardi, and Zizza further pursue this question from a different angle and find that productivity growth has been relatively stronger in those countries and sectors that relied more on competitive devaluations to regain price competitiveness before the euro was adopted. This finding is confirmed when the authors analyze firm-level data from the Italian manufacturing sector. They find that low-tech businesses, which arguably benefited most from devaluations, have been restructuring more since the adoption of the euro. Restructuring has entailed a shift of business focus from production to upstream and downstream activities, such as product design, advertising, marketing, and distribution, and a corresponding reduction in the share of blue-collar workers.

These results run contrary to our prior and challenge the view that entry into the euro has produced "reform fatigue." They are encouraging for Europe, suggesting that at least in some parts of the economy—though probably less so in the labor market—firms have responded to the macroeconomic constraint imposed by the single currency and the single monetary policy by accelerating the pace of restructuring. These observations also bring to center stage issues of sequencing of labor market and product market reforms, as discussed in Blanchard and Giavazzi (2003). Further work is needed to test this proposition, but these two chapters strongly suggest that the euro might have accelerated the creation of new firms (or newly restructured firms) and the destruction of older ones—those that used to rely on the temporary breath afforded by competitive devaluations. If this is true, aggregate statistics—for instance, on the pace of productivity growth—could be misleading, as they might reflect a shift in composition: an acceleration of firms exiting and entering. It would be important to extend the work of Bugamelli, Schivardi, and Zizza by using firm-level data to investigate whether their findings also apply to other countries that were previously characterized by high inflation and repeated devaluations.

Business-Cycle Convergence

Another debate that took place while the euro was being designed was whether the single currency would induce convergence or divergence in the economic performance of member countries. The argument in favor of convergence was simple: a single monetary policy means no more idiosyncratic nominal shocks and thus one less reason for divergent economic cycles. The fiscal rules introduced with the Stability and Growth Pact added to this argument by limiting the size of idiosyncratic fiscal shocks. On the opposite side, increased economic integration (reduced transport costs, harmonized regulation, higher mobility of capital and labor) would have induced specialization. As countries, or regions, specialized in specific industries, they would have been subject to industry-specific shocks: this would have resulted in more, not less, macroeconomic divergence. The two mechanisms may refer to different time horizons: specialization takes time, while more synchronized nominal shocks were almost instantaneous with the creation of the European Monetary Union (EMU). The verdict remains open.

Chapter 4 by Giannone, Lenza, and Reichlin investigates the changes induced by the single currency on the business cycles of member countries. The authors produce forecasts of gross domestic product (GDP) per capita of each euro member country, conditional on their per-EMU structure and the observed path of euro area-wide growth. They find that in the first ten years, business cycles have hardly changed. In those countries that started from similar initial conditions in terms of real activity in the 1970s (Germany, France, Italy, Holland, Austria, and Belgium), business cycles are very similar, and no significant change can be detected since 1999. For the other countries (Spain, Portugal, Ireland, Finland, and Greece), there is a lot of uncertainty, and not much can be said—but in this group as well, no clear change since the EMU can be identified. This finding has a remarkable implication. Countries that benefited from a large reduction in real interest rates after joining the euro, such as Italy, have not shown output growth rates that are significantly different from countries that have faced smaller idiosyncratic shocks, such as Germany or Belgium. Moreover, although the costs of the elimination of exchange rate adjustments and of independent monetary policy are likely to have been different across countries, this factor does not appear to have magnified asymmetries.

The chapter also asks whether the single currency has affected the euro area-wide business cycle. The authors forecast euro area growth conditionally on the pre-EMU structure and on the observed path of U.S. GDP growth. They find that since 1999, growth has been lower than what could have been predicted on the basis of historical experience and U.S. observed developments. The gap between U.S. and euro area GDP per capita level has been 30 percent on average since 1970, and there is no sign of catching up or of further widening. Thus, the introduction of the euro does not appear to have significantly changed the historical transatlantic linkages. In spite of the relevant changes in the macroeconomic environment (the Great Moderation, German reunification, the euro area inception), the relationship between the U.S. and euro area real economic activity has remained stable.

The Euro and Infra-European Trade

The extent to which cycles are correlated is related, among other factors, to trade between member countries. The effect of currency unions on trade has received a large amount of attention since a very provocative paper by Rose (2000). This author finds an extremely large effect of currency unions on trade: these findings used evidence from existing unions, which, for the most part, involved small countries linked to large ones. A large literature has attempted to explain away the apparently unreasonably large effects found by Rose, with an uneven amount of success. In chapter 5, Frankel finds a 15 percent increase in trade over just seven years (1999 to 2006): this is small compared to the large effects found by Rose when studying other currency unions—and Frankel goes thorough the possible explanations for this difference—but the effect is by no means negligible. The question is whether a 15 to 20 percent increase in intraeuro area trade is big or small. Without the Rose paper, most observers (us included) would have concluded that 15 percent in just seven years is quite a sizeable number. Obviously, it pales relative to Rose's number, but one should also consider that euro area countries were already quite integrated before the euro: further increases in trade of 200 or even 300 percent—the numbers found by Rose in other currency unions—are thus unlikely.

How the increase in intraeuro area trade affects the correlation of business cycles among euro member countries is an issue that remains to be explored.

Financial Integration

Could it be that the lack of stronger effects of the euro on business cycles is the result of the slow pace of financial integration? Two chapters in the volume address this question. In chapter 6, Kashyap and Gropp ask to what extent the single currency has created a single market in banking services. They go about it in a novel way by proposing a test of integration based on convergence in banks' profitability. They find evidence of convergence for listed banks (where an active market for corporate control is likely to work) but not for unlisted banks. They conclude that the banking market in Europe appears far from being integrated—in contrast to the United States, where the profits of both listed and unlisted commercial banks seem to converge, and high-profit banks see their profits driven down quickly. Incomplete banking integration could be one reason why the euro has had almost no effect on business cycles so far.

Chapter 7 by Alberto Giovannini focuses on a different and often overlooked aspect of financial integration: whether the euro area has a single integrated market for securities. The chapter explains what a single integrated market for securities entails, why efficient arrangements to deliver securities to a counterparty (posttrading) are essential for such a market to function properly, and why we do not have it yet. The chapter reflects on the political economic reason why this has not happened and suggests a path for future policy actions.

Fiscal Policy in the Euro Area

In chapter 8, Antonio Fatás and Ilian Mihov investigate the evolution of fiscal policy in the euro area. They do not present yet another discussion of the pros and cons of the Stability and Growth Pact but instead discuss the cyclical behavior of fiscal policy in the euro area from the point of view of the sustainability of fiscal stance, its cyclical behavior, and the behavior of discretionary fiscal maneuvers. As a useful benchmark, they look at the fiscal policy of the United States. Given that reliable fiscal data are annual for most countries, and given the short life of the euro, it is quite difficult to discuss with much confidence this important subject, simply because we did not have enough time to evaluate cyclical patterns. The potentially large recession that is impending as we write (November 2008) may provide a very important observation in this respect. One of the most interesting conclusions of this chapter is that fiscal policy in the European Union has been mildly procyclical. That is, it has *not* been used as a stabilizing tool. This is either because automatic stabilizers have not functioned too well or because discretionary spending has gone up in good times and perhaps has gone down in bad times because of the Stability and Growth Pact. This is in contrast with the United States, where the properties of fiscal policy seem more countercyclical. In our view, these results are driven by the fact that several EU countries made a fiscal effort to be admitted into the euro area. Then, in 2000 to 2001, when their economies were doing relatively well, rather than accumulating surpluses—as an appropriate fiscal policy requires—these countries relaxed. Not having the constraint imposed by acceptance in the euro area, their government started spending again. Whether this is a one-time event or a permanent procyclical bias of some European government remains to be seen. Certainly, those governments that have been fiscally irresponsible in the more recent and more distant past will pay the price with less fiscal flexibility in the current recession.

Are Financial Supervision and the Lender-of-Last-Resort Function Sound Enough?

The decentralized structure of euro area supervision and of the lender-of-last-resort function has long been a source a concern. When the European Central Bank (ECB) was being designed, the influential paper "The European Central Bank: A Bank or a Monetary Policy Rule" (Folkerts-Landau and Garber 1992) vividly made the point that the new institution was not really a central bank; rather, it resembled an automaton, programmed to set interest rates on the basis of some rule. Critics used to say that in order to turn the ECB into a real central bank, a crisis was needed—provided the crisis was not too serious; otherwise, it might take away the ECB altogether. The crisis has now happened, and it is more serious than anyone could have imagined. How has the ECB performed in the crisis?

Although chapter 9 by Cecchetti and Schoenholtz was completed halfway through the crisis, it addresses a number of issues related to financial supervision and liquidity provision. In the area of liquidity provision as a lender of last resort, the authors give high points to the bank's management of the crisis so far. In August 2007, the ECB boosted liquidity supply early and aggressively to counter the sharp increases in funding rates as banks turned cautious and alternative private sources of funding shut down. In order to deliver liquidity effectively, the ECB utilized the broad flexibility that it enjoys with respect to assets that it may accept as collateral or may acquire outright, including a variety of asset-backed securities. Some actions by the Federal Reserve came with a lag and were inspired by the ECB.

Cecchetti and Schoenholtz also discuss other, potentially more troubling aspects of the euro area stability framework. In contrast to liquidity matters that lie clearly within the ECB's mandate, solvency matters are addressed exclusively by national institutions, which may have different views about what constitutes a systemic threat and about how and when public resources should be employed. The fact that there is no euro area fiscal agent means that burden sharing across nations would be a challenge should a large (truly European rather than national) institution become unstable. Similarly, the decentralized structure of banking supervision—national supervision authority placed with different institutions, depending on the country—could create potentially dangerous incentive problems. These would not disappear by simply delegating the responsibility for supervision of national central banks—as some of the interviews on which the Cecchetti Schoenholtz chapter is based clearly demonstrate.

Has the Crisis Altered the Incentive to Join EMU?

In the final two chapters of the volume, we return to the longer-term issues addressed by Barry Eichengreen in chapter 1: how long will it take for all twenty-seven nations of the EU to adopt the euro, and has the crisis of 2007 to 2010 altered the incentives to join the EMU? To begin, misgivings about the euro in countries that were already in the union have completely disappeared. While several politicians—in Italy, but also in France and Spain—had complained about the straightjacket of the euro and the ECB policy before the crisis, since the summer of 2007, those voices have been silenced. The widespread feeling in Italy, for instance, is that without the euro, this country could have taken an Argentinean-style route of wild depreciation and currency attacks to the old lira. At the same time, countries that had decided to stay out of the union are reconsidering the wisdom of their decision. Some countries such as Iceland that are not even members of the European Union are starting the membership process for the sole reason of being able to one day adopt the euro. Two chapters in the book reconsider the decision by Sweden and the United Kingdom not to join. Although these chapters were written before the crisis, some of the findings are suggestive of why the crisis may have altered the incentives faced by these countries.

In chapter 10, Söderström finds that in Sweden, the exchange rate to a large extent has acted to destabilize rather than to stabilize the economy, pointing to the potential risks of an independent monetary policy. In chapter 11, Di Cecio and Nelson, studying the UK experience, make a similar point, suggesting that euro membership would eliminate shocks to the uncovered interest rate parity condition, which they identify as a major source of exchange rate variation.

So far in Sweden, the issue has been muted, because since the start of EMU, the exchange between the krona and the euro has remained remarkably stable—so stable that one could have argued whether the Riksbank was really targeting domestic inflation. But since the crisis erupted, the krona has depreciated in a few months by almost 10 percent against the euro. This has confronted Sweden with a difficult policy choice: either raise interest rates to stabilize the krona-euro exchange rate (thus avoiding the costs identified in chapter 10) or lower rates to avoid financial trouble and a possible recession.

It is interesting that Denmark, Sweden, and the United Kingdom reacted to the crisis by moving in opposite directions. Sweden and the United Kingdom have given up on exchange rate stability and have lowered rates, whereas the Danish central bank has intervened heavily in the foreign exchange market and has been forced to raise interest rates from 5 percent to 5.5 percent—a full 1.75 points higher than the ECB's rate—in an attempt to stabilize the exchange rate.

As a result, a renewed debate about the benefits of euro membership has opened up in Denmark: some argue that the country should run a new referendum on the euro. Even Iceland now speaks about the benefits of the euro, although this country is not even a member of the European Union. We read that diplomats from Iceland are making discreet inquires in Brussels about accession, and a poll conducted in October 2008 found that approval for EU membership among Icelandic citizens has increased from 48.9 percent to 68.8 percent in one year.

Willem Buiter and Anne Sibert (2008) argue that Iceland is only an extreme case of a more general phenomenon—a small country with its own currency and with banking sectors too large to be bailed out by national authorities. Others are Denmark, Sweden, and Switzerland. The United Kingdom is larger, and according to Buiter and Sibert, also enjoys "minor-league legacy reserve currency" status (2). But some of the arguments apply to the United Kingdom as well. In fact, a renewed debate about euro area membership has started in the United Kingdom, too.

Similar problems have manifested themselves in Central and Eastern Europe. In Hungary, almost all mortgages are denominated in Swiss francs or in euros; currency depreciation has triggered a series of personal and banking failures. Thus, the country is struggling between the desire to stabilize the exchange rate and the need to provide liquidity to the economy. Recently, the International Monetary Fund suggested that several countries in Central and Eastern Europe should consider adopting the euro, even without a seat on the board of the ECB. The reaction of euro member countries has been cautious. But this is another sign that during a crisis, the umbrella of the euro seems especially valuable.

In summary, there is no doubt in our mind that the crisis of 2007 to 2010 has altered the incentives to join the euro. It has also provided the countries that are already members with reasons to be more cautious about enlargement. The euro's second decade promises plenty of interesting developments.

References

Blanchard, O., and F. Giavazzi. 2003. Macroeconomic effects of regulation and deregulation in goods and labor markets. *Quarterly Journal of Economics* 118 (3): 879–907.

Buiter, W., and A. Siebert. 2008. The Icelandic banking crisis and what to do about it. CEPR Policy Insight no. 26. London: Center for Economic Policy Research. Available at: www.cepr.org.

Folkerts-Landau, D., and P. Garber. 1992. The European Central Bank: A bank or a monetary policy rule. NBER Working Paper no. 4013. Cambridge, MA: National Bureau of Economic Research, March.

Rose, A. 2000. One money, one market: Estimating the effect of common currencies on trade. *Economic Policy* 15 (30): 7–45.

1

The Breakup of the Euro Area

Barry Eichengreen

1.1 Introduction

The possibility of the breakup of the euro area was already being mooted, even before the single currency existed.[1] These scenarios were then lent new life five or six years on, when appreciation of the euro against the dollar and problems of slow growth in various member states led politicians to blame the European Central Bank (ECB) for disappointing economic performance.[2] Highly placed officials, possibly including members of the governing council of the German central bank, reportedly discussed the possibility that one or more participants might withdraw from the monetary union.[3] How seriously should we take these scenarios? And how much should we care? How significant, in other words, would be the economic and political consequences?

The conclusion of the author is that it is unlikely that one or more members of the euro area will leave in the next ten years and that the total dis-

Barry Eichengreen is the George C. Pardee and Helen N. Pardee Professor of Economics and Political Science at the University of California, Berkeley, and a research associate of the National Bureau of Economic Research.

I thank Alberto Alesina, Martin Feldstein, Jan Fidrmuc, Francesco Giavazzi, and Joao Nogueira Martins for comments. I also thank Mark Hallerberg for help with data and Jeffrey Greenbaum for research assistance. Financial support was provided by the Coleman Fung Risk Management Center at the University of California, Berkeley.

1. See, for example, Garber (1998) and Scott (1998).

2. Appreciation of the euro against the dollar (and against Asian currencies pegged to the dollar) first occurred in 2002 to 2004. In June 2005, Italian Welfare Minister Roberto Maroni declared that "the euro has to go" and called for the reintroduction of the lira. The then prime minister Silvio Berlusconi followed by calling the euro "a disaster."

3. Bundesbank president Axel Weber dismissed as "absurd" reports that he had taken part in such a meeting (Expatica 2005, 1).

integration of the euro area is more unlikely still.[4] The technical difficulties of reintroducing a national currency should not be minimized. Nor is it obvious that the economic problems of the participating member states can be significantly ameliorated by abandoning the euro, although neither can this possibility be dismissed. And even if there are immediate economic benefits, there may be longer-term economic costs and political costs of an even more serious nature. Still, as Cohen (2000, 180) puts it, "In a world of sovereign states . . . nothing can be regarded as truly irreversible." Policy analysts should engage in contingency planning, even if the contingency in question has a low probability.

The remainder of this chapter considers such scenarios in more detail. While it is widely argued that the technical and legal obstacles to a country unilaterally reintroducing its national currency are surmountable, it will be argued here that the associated difficulties could in fact be quite serious. To be sure, there are multiple historical examples of members of monetary unions introducing a national currency. It has also been suggested that the legal problems associated with the redenomination of contracts can be overcome, as they were when the ruble zone broke up or when Germany replaced the mark with the reichsmark in 1923/1924. But changing from an old money to a new one is more complicated today than it was in Germany in the 1920s or in the former Soviet Union in the 1990s. Computer code must be rewritten. Automated teller machines must be reprogrammed. Advance planning will be required for the process to go smoothly, as was the case with the introduction of the physical euro in 2002. Moreover, abandoning the euro will presumably entail lengthy political debate and the passage of a bill by a national parliament or legislature, also over an extended period of time. Meanwhile, there will be an incentive for agents who are anticipating the redenomination of their claims into the national currency, followed by depreciation of the latter, to rush out of domestic banks and financial assets, precipitating a banking and financial collapse. Limiting the negative repercussions would be a major technical and policy challenge for a government contemplating abandonment of the euro.

The economic obstacles revolve around the question of how debt servicing costs, interest rate spreads, and interest rate-sensitive forms of economic activity would respond to a country's departure from the euro area.[5] A widespread presumption is that departure from the euro area would be associated with a significant rise in spreads and debt-servicing costs. But

4. Note that I have violated the first rule of forecasting: give them a forecast or give them a date, but never give them both. The point is that over horizons longer than ten years, so many things could change that forecasting becomes prohibitively difficult. But I will later turn to the question of long-term developments.

5. There is also the question of whether other EU member states would retaliate against a country reintroducing and depreciating its national currency with trade sanctions—considered later.

further reflection suggests that the consequences will depend on why a country leaves. (The defector could conceivably be a Germany, concerned with politicization of ECB policy and inflationary bias, rather than an Italy, facing slow growth and an exploding public debt.) They will depend on whether credible alternatives to the ECB and the Stability and Growth Pact are put in place at the national level (whether national central bank independence is strengthened and credible fiscal reforms are adopted at the same time that the exchange rate is reintroduced and depreciated). It seems likely that there would be economic costs but that these could be minimized by appropriate institutional reforms.

The political costs are likely to be particularly serious. The Treaty on European Union makes no provision for exit. Exit by one member would raise doubts about the future of the monetary union and would likely precipitate a further shift out of euro-denominated assets, which would not please the remaining members. It might damage the balance sheets of banks in other countries with investments in the one abandoning the euro. Diplomatic tension and political acrimony would follow, and cooperation on nonmonetary issues would suffer. The defector would be relegated to second-tier status in intra-European discussions of nonmonetary issues. And, insofar as they attach value to their participation in this larger process of European integration, incumbents will be reluctant to leave.

The chapter starts by describing scenarios, revolving around high unemployment and high inflation, under which euro area participants may wish to leave. The immediately subsequent sections then evaluate the economic, political, procedural, and legal obstacles to doing so. An empirical section provides evidence on the realism of the exit scenarios by using survey data from the Eurobarometer and on the economic barriers by using data on the impact of euro adoption on commercial credit ratings. Following that is a discussion of reforms that might attenuate dissatisfaction with the operation of the single currency. A coda immediately preceding the conclusion discusses the implications of the 2008 financial crisis in Europe for the arguments of this chapter.

1.2   Scenarios

Different countries could abandon the euro for different reasons. One can imagine a country like Portugal, suffering from high labor costs and chronic slow growth, reintroducing the escudo in an effort to engineer a sharp real depreciation and to export its way back to full employment. Alternatively, one can imagine a country like Germany, upset that the ECB has come under pressure from governments to relax its commitment to price stability, reintroducing the deutschemark in order to avoid excessive inflation.

These different scenarios would have different implications for whether defection implies breakup—that is, for whether one country's leaving reduces the incentive for others to remain. In the case of Portuguese defection, the residual members might suffer a further loss of export competitiveness, while in the event of German exit, they might find their competitiveness enhanced. Specifically, if other countries are similarly experiencing high unemployment associated with inadequate international competitiveness, then Portugal's leaving will aggravate the pain felt by the others and may lead them to follow suit—but Germany's leaving may have no, or even the opposite, effect. Similarly, if discomfort with the inflationary stance of ECB policy is shared by other countries, then Germany's leaving, by removing one voice and vote for price stability, may heighten the incentive for others to do likewise.

More generally, if the country that leaves is an outlier in terms of its preferences over central bank policy, then its defection might better enable the remaining participants to secure an ECB policy more to their liking, in which case the likelihood of further defection and general breakup would be reduced. Disagreements over the stance of policy being an obvious reason why a participating member state would be disaffected, one might think that the defector would automatically be an outlier in terms of its preferences over central bank policy. But this is by no means certain: countries whose preferences differ insignificantly from those of other members could choose to defect for other reasons—for example, in response to an exceptionally severe asymmetric shock, or because of disagreements over noneconomic issues.[6]

And if the country that leaves is small, this would be unlikely to much affect the incentives of other members to continue operating a monetary union that is valued primarily for its corollary benefits. The contribution of the euro to enhancing price stability would not be significantly diminished by the defection of one small member.[7] The impetus for financial deepening ascribed to the single currency would not be significantly diminished.[8] If Portugal left the euro area, would the other members notice? Even if it used its monetary autonomy to engineer a substantial real depreciation, would its euro area neighbors experience a significant loss of competitiveness and feel serious pain?

On the other hand, if Germany defected, the size of the euro area would decline by more than a quarter. This would imply significant diminution of the scale of the market over which the benefits of the euro were felt in terms of increased price transparency and financial deepening. Countries balancing these benefits against the costs of being denied their optimal national

---

6. These issues were analyzed in an influential early article by Alesina and Grilli (1993).

7. The literature on price transparency and the euro is reviewed by Mathä (2003).

8. On the stimulus to the development of European financial markets, see Bishop (2000) and Biais et al. (2006). On the corollary benefits of monetary union more generally, see Mongelli and Vega (2006).

monetary policy might find themselves tipped against membership. Defection by a few could then result in general disintegration.

In practice, a variety of asymmetric shocks could slow growth and raise unemployment in a euro area member state and create pressure for a real depreciation. The shocks that have attracted the most attention are those highlighted in Blanchard's model of rotating slumps (Blanchard 2006). The advent of the euro has brought credibility benefits to members whose commitment to price stability was previously least firm and whose interest rates were previously high.[9] Enhanced expectations of price stability have brought down domestic interest rates, bidding up bond, stock, and housing prices. Foreign capital has flooded in to take advantage of this convergence play. The cost of capital having declined, investment rises in the short run, and as households feel positive wealth effects, consumption rises as well. The capital inflow has as its counterpart a current account deficit. In the short run, the result is an economic boom, driven first and foremost by residential construction, with falling unemployment and rising wages.

But once the capital stock adjusts to the higher levels implied by the lower cost of capital, the boom comes to an end. Unless the increase in capital stock significantly raises labor productivity (which is unlikely insofar as much of the preceding period's investment took the form of residential construction), the result is a loss of cost competitiveness. The country then faces slow growth, chronic high unemployment, and grinding deflation, as weak labor market conditions force wages to fall relative to those prevailing elsewhere in the euro area. The temptation, then, is to leave the euro zone so that monetary policy can be used to reverse the erosion of competitiveness with a "healthy" dose of inflation.

This particular scenario has attracted attention, because it suggests that the tensions that could eventually result in defections from the euro area are intrinsic to the operation of the European Monetary Union (EMU). It suggests that the intra-euro-area divergences that are their source are direct consequences of the monetary union's operation. This story tracks the experience of Portugal since the mid-1990s—first boom, then overvaluation, and finally slump. There are signs of similar problems in Italy, where the difficulties caused by slow growth are compounded by the existence of a heavy public debt, and in Spain, which experienced many of the same dynamics as Portugal. The implication is that Greece and Slovenia (and future EMU members such as Estonia and Latvia) will then follow.[10]

9. Benefits that in some sense reflect the operation of the barriers to exit are described later.

10. One can also argue that Greece and Slovenia will have learned from the problems of Portugal, Spain, and Italy, and that they will take preventive measures—aggressively tightening fiscal policy, for example, to prevent capital inflows from fueling an unsustainable construction-led investment boom and leading to a consequent loss of competitiveness. In this view, the negative shocks experienced by the first cohort of convergence economies may not be felt by their successors.

1.3   Economic Barriers to Exit

But would reintroducing the national currency and following with a sharp depreciation against the euro in fact help to solve these countries' competitiveness and debt problems? The presumption in much of the literature is negative.[11] A country like Italy—where slow growth combines with high inherited debt/gross domestic product (GDP) ratios to raise the specter of debt unsustainability (that it would become necessary to restructure the debt or for taxpayers and transfer recipients to make inconceivable sacrifices)—might be tempted to reintroduce the lira as a way of securing a more inflationary monetary policy and of depreciating away the value of the debt, but doing so would result in credit rating downgrades, higher sovereign spreads, and an increase in interest costs, as investors anticipate and react to the government's actions. A country like Portugal—where high real wages combine with the absence of exchange rate independence to produce chronic high unemployment—might be tempted to reintroduce the escudo as a way of securing a more expansionary monetary policy and of pushing down labor costs, but doing so will only result in higher wage inflation, as workers anticipate and react to the government's actions. Estimates in Blanchard (2006) suggest that Portugal would require a 25 percent real depreciation in order to restore its competitiveness.[12] It is not clear that workers would look the other way if the government sought to engineer this through a substantial nominal depreciation. Observers pointing to these effects conclude that exiting might not be especially beneficial for a country with high debts or high unemployment. To the contrary, the principal obstacle to exiting the euro area in this view is that doing so may have significant economic costs.

Yet, one can also imagine circumstances in which reintroducing the national currency might constitute a useful treatment. Assume that Portuguese workers are prepared to accept a reduction in their real wages, but they confront a coordination problem: they are willing to accept a reduction only if other workers or unions accept a reduction, perhaps because they care about relative wages.[13] Under these circumstances, there will be a reluctance to move first, and wage adjustment will be suboptimally slow. Then, a monetary-cum-exchange rate policy that jumps up the price level, reducing real wages across the board, may be welfare enhancing; this is the so-called "daylight savings time" argument for a flexible exchange rate. Importantly, in the circumstances described here, there will be no incentive for individual workers or unions to push for higher wages to offset the increase in prices. The

11. See, for example, Gros (2007).
12. Absent further divergences in productivity growth.
13. Or perhaps it is because the aggregate rate of growth, from which everyone benefits, depends on the national average level of costs. One can imagine still other formulations of this coordination problem. A survey is Cooper (1999).

lower real wages obtained as a result of depreciating the newly reintroduced currency deliver the economy to the same full-employment equilibrium that would have resulted from years of grinding deflation, only faster.

Note the assumption here: whatever caused real wages to get out of line in the first place is not intrinsic to the economy, so the problem will not recur. Thus, the Portuguese example contemplated here is described under the assumption that real wages have fallen out of line for reasons extrinsic to the operation of the economy—for example, irrational exuberance on the part of workers in the run-up to Stage 3 of the Maastricht process, something that will not recur. If, on the other hand, real wages are too high because of the existence of domestic distortions—for example, the presence of powerful trade unions that exclusively value the welfare of their employed members—then it is implausible that a different monetary-cum-exchange rate policy will have an enduring impact.

There are similar counterarguments to the view that a country like Italy that reintroduced the lira in order to pursue a monetary-cum-exchange rate policy that stepped down the value of the debt would necessarily be penalized with lower credit ratings and higher debt-servicing costs. Sovereign debt is a contingent claim; when debt is rendered unsustainable by shocks not of the government's own making, and the source of those shocks can be verified independently, there are theoretical arguments for why investors will see a write-down as excusable.[14] Even when the country's debt problem is of its own making, credible institutional and policy reforms—strict legal or constitutional limits on future budget deficits, stronger independence to insulate the central bank from pressure to help finance future debts—may reassure the markets that past losses will not recur. The fact that the debt burden has been lightened similarly makes it look less likely that prior problems will be repeated. There is ample evidence from history that governments that default, either explicitly by restructuring or implicitly by inflating, are able to regain market access by following appropriate institutional and policy reforms. The mixed findings of studies seeking to identify a reputational penalty in the form of higher interest rates are consistent with the view that this penalty can be avoided by countries that follow up with institutional and policy reforms, reassuring investors that the experience will not be repeated. The implication is that the cost in terms of reputation may not be a prohibitive barrier to exit.

How applicable is this scenario to countries like Italy? It is hard to argue that Italy's heavy debt burden is due to factors not of its own making. Italy does not have a reassuring history of guarding the central bank's independence or of adopting budgetary procedures and institutions that limit free-rider and common-pool problems. Whether exiting the euro area and reintroducing the lira would therefore result in credit rating downgrades

---

14. See, for example, Grossman and Van Huyck (1998).

and increases in spreads sufficient to deter any such decision is an empirical question.[15]

The other economic barrier to exit cited in this connection is that a country that abandoned the euro and reintroduced its national currency might be denied the privileges of the single market. A country that reintroduced its national currency at levels that stepped down its labor costs by 20 percent might be required to pay a 20 percent compensatory duty when exporting to other members of the European Union, reflecting concerns that it was unfairly manipulating its currency and solving its economic problems at the expense of its neighbors. Whatever the compensatory tariff, collecting it would require the reestablishment of customs posts and border controls, adding to transactions costs. Other states might seek to tax foreign investment outflows on the grounds that the defector was using an unfair monetary-cum-exchange rate policy to attract foreign direct investment. In this climate of ill will and recrimination, they might seek to limit the freedom of movement of its citizens.

But it is not clear that other member states could or would respond in this way. Sweden, Denmark, the United Kingdom, and all but one of the new member states have their own national currencies, yet they are not denied the privileges of the single market. If Germany, Italy, or Portugal decided to join their ranks, it is not clear that it could be treated any differently under European law. To be sure, the United Kingdom, Sweden, the Czech Republic, Hungary, and Poland do not presently participate in the Exchange Rate Mechanism II (ERM-II), and therefore there are no formal restrictions on the currencies' fluctuation. It can be objected that these countries anchor their monetary policies by inflation targeting, which frees them of accusations that they are manipulating their currencies relative to the euro. But a country like Germany that left the euro area out of dissatisfaction with the ECB's inflationary bias would presumably do likewise.[16] Even a country abandoning the euro because it saw a need to step up the price level as a way of addressing debt and unemployment problems might then adopt inflation targeting as a way of avoiding reputational damage. In turn, this could insulate it from accusations that it was continuing to manipulate its currency. Countries can remain EU member states in good standing and enjoy all the privileges associated with that status without adopting the euro. To be sure, most of the new members have not adopted the euro, because they do not yet meet the preconditions laid down by the Maastricht Treaty, where there is a presumption that this status is purely transitional. The United Kingdom, for its part, negotiated a derogation permitting it to remain outside the ERM and to retain sterling indefinitely as a condition for agreeing to the Maas-

15. More on which is discussed later.
16. Or, who knows—they could also adopt a two-pillar strategy targeting inflation and a monetary aggregate.

tricht Treaty. An Italy or Portugal that abandoned the euro would enjoy no such derogation. Would it then have to joint the ERM-II? But Sweden, alluding to the British precedent, announced unilaterally that it would not enter the ERM or follow a fixed schedule for adopting the euro. Is it clear that a Sweden that never entered the euro area should be treated differently, in terms of its access to the single market, than an Italy that left it?

1.4   Political Barriers to Exit

More generally, a country that abandoned the euro and reintroduced its national currency because of problems of inadequate international competitiveness, high unemployment, and slow growth might suffer political costs by being relegated to second-class status in negotiations over other issues. One interpretation of the process of monetary integration that culminated in the advent of the euro is that monetary integration is a stepping stone to political integration, which is the ultimate goal of the architects of the European Union. As the point was once put by Jacques Delors, "Obsession about budgetary constraints means that the people forget too often about the political objectives of European construction. The argument in favor of the single currency should be based on the desire to live together in peace."[17] Like the European Union's blue flag with twelve yellow stars, the single currency is a visible symbol that fosters a sense of Europeanness among the continent's residents. As suggested by the theory of neofunctionalist spillovers (Haas 1958), the existence of the euro and the European Central Bank generates pressure for a more powerful European Parliament to hold the ECB democratically accountable for its actions.[18] A country that unilaterally abandons the euro, something for which there is no provision in the Treaty on European Union, would deal a setback to these larger political ambitions. It would signal that it did not attach high value to the larger process of political integration.

On both grounds, such a country would be unlikely to be regarded as a respected interlocutor in discussions of how to push the process forward. An Italy that abandoned the euro would have a diminished role in discussions of how to strengthen the powers of the European Parliament. It would have less sway in discussions of how to revise and ratify the European constitution. Other member states would be less likely to grant it a seat at the table in discussions of whether to formulate a common foreign policy or to create a European army. For better or worse, the common European position on such issues has grown out of discussions among a core of countries centered on France and Germany that first develop a common position and then sell it to the other members. For a country like Italy that has participated

17. Cited in Prior-Wandesforde and Hacche (2005, 23).
18. See section 1.5.

in this larger process of European integration from the foundation of the European Economic Community half a century ago, precisely as a way of elevating itself to the status of a first-tier European country, these political costs would be substantial. In turn, this constitutes a major barrier to exit.

What about Germany? If Germany abandoned the euro out of dissatisfaction with excessively inflationary ECB policies, this would significantly diminish the prospects for political integration. Germany would be indicating that it regarded the experiment with a supranational institution with real powers—in this case, the power to make monetary policy—as a failure. The idea that Germany would then cede to other supranational institutions at the EU level the power to make its security policy, its foreign policy, or its fiscal policy, these being three of the key prerogatives of a sovereign state, would become less plausible. Germany has always been a strong proponent of the larger European project. Reflecting memories of World War II, it continues to feel limits on its ability to formulate an assertive foreign policy, to maintain a standing army, and to deploy troops abroad; at a basic level, its interest in political integration is to regain a foreign policy voice in the context of an EU foreign policy. And without German support, European political integration is unlikely to display the same momentum.

Given this, Germany will presumably attempt to fix the problems it perceives with the ECB in order to salvage its vision of political integration rather than concluding that further integration is infeasible and abandoning the euro—or at least it will invest more in seeking to fix perceived problems than another member state with a weaker commitment to the larger European process. It will choose voice and loyalty over exit, complaining publicly about the inflationary stance of ECB policy and lobbying to change it, precisely in order to demonstrate that supranational European institutions can work and that its integrationist vision is still viable. This is not to deny that there could come a point where the German government and its constituents conclude that voice and loyalty have failed. But this argument does suggest that Germany may be prepared to suffer with a monetary policy not to its liking and that it will work to change that policy, rather than abandoning the euro, for longer than other member states less committed to the larger process.

Not everyone will agree that a monetary union process that adds to momentum for political integration is desirable on these grounds. Some would argue that the European Union should concentrate on economic integration while shunning aspirations of political integration. For them, if a failure of monetary union means a failure of political union, then the latter is not a cost.[19] But for influential political elites, political integration

---

19. This is not to say that the opponents of political union necessarily see the failure of monetary union as desirable, as the latter may have other benefits, including the impetus it provides to economic integration.

remains a valued goal. For them, exits from the euro area that set back its progress would be a significant cost.

1.5   Procedural Barriers to Exit

A final set of barriers to exit are the technical and legal obstacles to reintroducing the national currency. Take the case where a country suffering from inadequate competitiveness and high unemployment reintroduces its national currency in order to depreciate it against the euro. It would be straightforward for it to pass a law stating that the state and other employers will henceforth pay workers and pensioners, say, in lira. With wages and other incomes redenominated into the national currency, it would become politically necessary to redenominate the mortgages and credit card debts of residents into the national currency as well; otherwise, currency depreciation would have adverse balance-sheet effects for households, leading to financial distress and bankruptcies. But with mortgages and other bank assets redenominated, bank deposits and other bank balance-sheet items would also have to be redenominated in order to avoid destabilizing the financial sector. With government revenues redenominated into the national currency, not just public-sector wages and pensions but also other government liabilities—notably the public debt—would have to be redenominated to prevent balance-sheet effects from damaging the government's financial position.

The idea that redenomination has to be comprehensive to limit financial distress is a lesson of Argentina's exit from convertibility in 2001.[20] It is also an implication of the literature on dollarization, where it is argued that partial dollarization creates scope for destabilizing balance-sheet effects. It is better either to be fully dollarized (or euroized, in the present example) or to dedollarize (or de-euroize) by redenominating claims in the national currency (see, for example, Levy Yeyati and Ize [2005] and Levy Yeyati [2006]).[21]

20. Note that across-the-board redenomination, while insulating domestic banks from destabilizing balance-sheet effects, might create problems for foreign banks, which saw their euro-denominated investments, say, in Italian government bonds redenominated into lira and then saw this currency depreciate against the euro. This is another reason why other euro area countries would not welcome exit by an incumbent seeking to restore competitiveness by reintroducing and depreciating its national currency.

21. Argentina's experience also sheds light on another approach to exiting the euro area that has occasionally been proposed—namely, reintroducing the national unit as a parallel currency. Italy would not have to leave the euro area or eliminate its euro circulation in order to reintroduce the lira, according to this scheme; it could simply reissue the lira and allow it to circulate side by side, along with the euro. The Argentine provinces did something similar in 2001 when they experienced serious difficulties in financing their current expenditures: they issued very short-term notes that circulated as quasi currency ("Patacones," in the case of the province of Buenos Aires). The problem with this approach is that absent trade restrictions, it will have no effect on the prices of goods and services on local markets; it will simply drive out a corresponding number of euros via trade deficits. This is what happened in Argentina: the more Patacones were issued, the more peso-denominated bank deposits were liquidated. Similarly,

Technically, nothing prevents the legislature from passing a law requiring banks, firms, households, and governments to redenominate their contracts in this manner. But in a democracy, this decision will require discussion. And for it to be executed smoothly, it will have to be accompanied by planning. Computers will have to be reprogrammed. Vending machines will have to be modified. Payment machines will have to be serviced to prevent motorists from being trapped in subterranean parking garages. Notes and coins will have to be positioned around the country. One need only recall the planning that preceded the introduction of the physical euro in 2002.

The difference between the transition to the euro and the transition back to national currencies is that in the first instance, there was little reason to expect subsequent changes in exchange rates and thus little incentive for currency speculation, while in the second case, such changes would be viewed as virtually inevitable. In 1998, the founding members of the euro area agreed to lock their exchange rates at the then-prevailing levels at the beginning of 1999. This precommitment effectively ruled out efforts to depress national currencies designed to steal a competitive advantage prior to the locking of parities in 1999. In contrast, if a participating member state now decided to leave the euro area, no such precommitment would be possible. Pressure from other member states would be ineffective, by definition. And the very motivation for leaving would presumably be to change the parity.

Market participants would be well aware of this fact. Households and firms anticipating that domestic deposits would be redenominated into lira, which would then lose value against the euro, would shift their deposits to other euro area banks. In the worst case, a system-wide bank run could follow. Investors anticipating that their claims on the Italian government would be redenominated into lira would presumably shift into claims on other euro area governments, leading to a bond market crisis. If the precipitating factor was parliamentary debate over abandoning the lira, it would be unlikely that the ECB would provide extensive lender-of-last-resort support. And if the government was already in a tenuous fiscal position, it would not be able to borrow in order to bail out the banks and buy back its debt. This would be the mother of all financial crises.

Presumably, the government would respond with a "corralito," Argentine style, limiting bank withdrawals. It would suspend the operation of the bond market, although this might be of limited effectiveness insofar as the same bonds and derivative instruments based on them are also traded on other national markets. But all this would almost certainly be costly in terms of

---

the more lira are issued, the greater the extent to which they will dominate the domestic circulation, until the point comes where only lira circulate domestically, and the parallel currency approach dissolves into the simple substitution of the domestic unit for the euro, after which exchange rate depreciation presumably follows. And seeing this outcome coming, holders of euro-denominated claims will flee Italian banks and markets in advance, precipitating the same kind of financial crisis.

output and employment. It would be hard to keep production going while the financial system was halted in its tracks; this is a clear lesson of Argentina's 2001/2002 crisis.

When the ruble zone broke up in the 1990s and new national currencies were introduced, the successor states of the former Soviet Union were able to limit the destabilizing financial consequences because their banking and financial systems were not well articulated, so limits on deposit withdrawals and other forms of arbitrage were relatively effective. They could limit the substitution of foreign for domestic assets by imposing or simply retaining exchange controls, an option that is not available to EU members with commitments to the single market. They could seal their borders to provide time to stamp old currencies or swap old currencies for new ones. Firms did not have computerized financial accounts and inventory-management systems. Europe today is a more complicated place. All this means that the technical obstacles to exit may be greater than in the past. While these technical obstacles may be surmountable, they pose greater challenges than in earlier instances where monetary unions broke up.

The same lesson is evident in the breakup of the Czechoslovak monetary union in 1993.[22] The Czechs and Slovaks agreed to political separation as of January 1, 1993, but initially kept their monetary union in place in order to minimize dislocations to trade and economic activity. It was clear from the start, however, that politicians in both countries were actively contemplating exit. The monetary arrangement signed in October 1992 establishing the Czech-Slovak currency union in fact made provision for exit (unlike the Treaty on European Union). The union could be abandoned (equivalent to exit, given that there were only two participants) if a member ran an excessive budget deficit, if it suffered excessive reserve losses, if there were excessive capital flows from one republic to the other, or if the monetary policy committee was deadlocked.[23] Although the Czech and Slovak Republics initially agreed to maintain a common currency for a minimum of six months, the markets did not find this agreement credible; they expected that the Slovak authorities would push for a much looser monetary policy and that their Czech counterparts would not accept the consequent high inflation. The result was a flight of currency and deposits from Slovakia to the Czech Republic. Given their divergent preferences and the market's lack of confidence in the monetary union, the authorities decided in favor of monetary separation. The demise of the monetary union was announced on February 2, just five weeks after it had commenced operation, and separate national currencies were quickly introduced. Czechoslovak banknotes were

22. See Fidrmuc, Horvath, and Fidrmuc (1999).
23. Under the provisions of the agreement, the Czechoslovak central bank was dissolved and replaced by a Czech National Bank and a National Bank of Slovakia. The common monetary policy was made by simple majority vote of a six-member committee made up of the governors and two senior officials from the two banks.

stamped and then replaced with new national banknotes. During this period, no currency was allowed to be transferred or exported abroad.[24]

This case suggests that monetary separation is technically feasible under some circumstances. Some of the technical problems of introducing a national currency were solved by stretching out this process over time. Old Czechoslovak banknotes were stamped during the second week of February, but the process of introducing the new Czech and Slovak banknotes was finally completed in August. The problem of adjusting vending machines and parking garages was addressed by allowing old Czechoslovak coins to continue to circulate in both countries for up to six months.

But the circumstances that made this possible were quite different from those in the euro area today. The commercial banking system was only just getting up and running in the Czech Republic and Slovakia. The authorities adopted elaborate clearing mechanisms to limit withdrawals from and strains on their respective banking systems. Trading of shares in then-Czechoslovak companies acquired as a result of the voucher privatization got underway only in May 1993—that is, three months after exit from the monetary union. Thus, there was limited scope for arbitrage between national banking systems and securities markets. There were few institutional investors in a position to shift large financial balances from one successor state to the other.

Moreover, in the period leading up to the monetary separation, extensive capital controls were already in place. These slowed capital flight from the Slovak Republic, in particular, where the new currency was expected to weaken, but they did not halt them. Payments between the two republics were halted completely at the beginning of February while the details of the separation were ironed out. This protected the banking system, especially in the Slovak Republic, from capital flight.

Finally, the fact that the old Czechoslovak currency disappeared at the end of the six-month transition eased the process of dissolving the currency union. In the case of an individual member exiting from the euro area, in contrast, the euro would continue to circulate in the rump euro zone (whose size would presumably be considerable). Were Italy, for example, to exit the euro area, stamp the euro area banknotes of residents or replace them with new Italian banknotes, and impose restrictions on capital flows for the period of the currency exchange, Italian residents would be able to simply hold onto their euro cash and coins and then export them once the restrictions were lifted. This would make operations designed to exchange Italian residents' euro banknotes for the new national currency—as opposed to injecting new national currency notes in addition to existing euro banknotes—considerably more difficult.

---

24. Although there was apparently some movement of unstamped banknotes from Slovakia to the Czech Republic during the period when stamping took place, because borders were not sealed to individual foreign travel.

The need for extraordinary measures is also the clear lesson of the breakup of earlier monetary unions, such as that of the successor states to the Austro-Hungarian Empire.[25] Austria, Hungary, and the other ethnic regions of the empire all successfully introduced national currencies following World War I. Previously, they had operated a formal monetary union, with control of the circulation vested in the Austro-Hungarian bank in Vienna. The component parts of the empire constituted a free-trade zone, and both real and financial integration were extensive. At the same time, like EMU today, the constituent states (Austria and Hungary) decided on separate budgets while contributing to some of the expenditures of the union.

Ethnic demands for autonomy boiled up during World War I. Vienna, occupied elsewhere, lost the capacity to assert its control over non-Austrian parts of the empire. Other regions held back food supplies, disrupting the operation of the internal market. Czechs and other ethnic groups withdrew from the military alliance, siding with the Allies. With the armistice, the Czechs, Poles, and Hungarians declared their political independence and sought to establish and defend their national borders. They also abandoned prior restraints on their fiscal policies, partly owing to postwar exigencies and partly in reflection of the value they now attached to political sovereignty. Importantly, however, the Austrian crown remained the basis for the monetary circulation throughout the former empire. This was awkward for separate sovereign nations that did not share in the seignorage and that experienced asymmetric shocks and suffered from chronic fiscal and financial imbalances.

Starting with Czechoslovakia and the Kingdom of Serbs, Croats, and Slovenes (Yugoslavia), one successor state after another left the monetary union and introduced a national currency. Typically, this involved first announcing that only stamped Austrian banknotes would be acceptable in transactions. Stamping (either overprinting with an ink stamp or adding a physical stamp) had to be conducted carefully, with a high level of uniformity, to discourage forgery. At the same time the currency was stamped, a portion was withheld as a capital levy (as a way of transferring desperately needed resources to the government). In Hungary, for example, 50 percent of tendered notes were withheld as a forced loan. In Czechoslovakia, the 50 percent tax was applied to current accounts and treasury bills when these were redenominated in stamped crowns. In turn, this created an incentive to withhold currency from circulation if there were prospects of using it in other countries where stamping had not yet taken place. Thus, there was an incentive for capital flight not unlike that which might afflict an inflation-prone country today that chose to opt out of Europe's monetary union.

Stamping was therefore accompanied by the physical closing of the country's borders and the imposition of comprehensive exchange controls. Individuals were prohibited from traveling abroad, and merchandise trade was

25. See also Dornbusch (1992) and Eichengreen (2007).

halted. The capital levy, equivalent to depreciation of the new currency against the old one, could also precipitate a run on the banks, as it did in Czechoslovakia. In Austria, which could observe Czechoslovakia's earlier experience, bank securities and deposits were frozen at the outset of the transition. Again, avoiding serious financial dislocations required closing the borders, banning foreign travel, halting merchandise trade, and imposing draconian exchange controls while the conversion was underway. The feasibility of similar measures today is dubious.

Finally, what about a country, say, Germany, that might wish to leave the euro area because other governments had successfully pressured the ECB to run inflationary policies? The procedural difficulties in this case would be less. Here, the expectation would be that the deutschemark, once reintroduced, would appreciate against the euro. There would be no incentive to flee German banks and financial markets but rather an incentive to rush in, given this one-way bet on appreciation. The challenge for Germany would thus be massive capital inflows in the period when exit from the euro area was being discussed. The result would be inflation, a booming stock market, and soaring housing prices.[26] Soaring asset valuations are less uncomfortable than collapsing ones, but the financial dislocations would still be considerable.

These uncomfortable financial consequences would in turn constitute a disincentive to contemplate exiting. Germany faced similar problems in the 1960s, when it was widely anticipated that the deutschemark would be revalued against the dollar. But at that point in time, it was able to impose capital controls to limit inflows. Germany reimposed controls in 1960 to 1961, the period prior to the first revaluation of its currency. In mid-1970, the country then imposed discriminatory minimum reserve requirements against non-resident bank deposits and from May 1971 required prior authorization for the sale of money-market paper and certain fixed-interest securities to foreigners. Similar responses would be difficult in the context of the single market (assuming, as seems plausible, that Germany would still wish to preserve its single market obligations).[27]

---

26. The symmetry between buying and selling attacks on currencies is the subject of Grilli (1986).

27. The closest precedent for exit by a strong-currency country of which I am aware was the possibility that Luxembourg might exit from its monetary union with Belgium in 1993. The European Monetary System (EMS) crisis of that year had led to currency devaluation by a number of participating countries, and in the summer, Germany and the Netherlands considered the possibility of unilaterally exiting from the ERM rather than facing pressure to inflate along with Belgium, France, and the others. At this point, the authorities in Luxembourg evidently contemplated following the deutchemark and the guilder rather than the two francs, which would have required them to break their monetary union with Belgium. In fact, Luxembourg had established a protocentral bank (the Luxembourg Monetary Institute) a decade earlier, in 1983, when the Belgians had unilaterally realigned without engaging in prior consultations with their monetary union partner. (Ironically, the prime minister of Luxembourg at the time was Pierre Werner, commonly regarded as one of the fathers of the euro.) From the early 1980s, Luxembourg also evidently maintained a stock of coins and banknotes

This case can, in fact, be argued both ways on procedural grounds. It can be argued that Germany could insulate its economy from the impact of the capital inflows loosed by its reintroduction of the deutschemark, because German interest rates would be lower than foreign interest rates, and the risk premia associated with investing in Germany would be lower as well. Thus, the Bundesbank would be able to sterilize the inflows associated with its reintroduction of the national currency.

Goodhart (2008)—in a note written partly in response to the present chapter—questions the relevance of this German exit scenario. He observes that the ECB enjoys statutory independence. It has a mandate to pursue price stability. Its board is made up of professional central bankers who have internalized arguments for the value of low inflation. Changing the status quo and exposing the ECB to effective political pressure would require amending the international treaty that established the ECB and the euro— something that Germany could veto. European politicians can posture all they want. They can take whatever measures they wish to elevate the visibility of the Eurogroup of finance ministers. But their statements and actions are unlikely to weaken the ECB's commitment to price stability. And if Goodhart is right, the German exit scenario has a vanishingly small probability.

1.6   Legal Barriers to Exit

Even if there is agreement that the transition would be smoothed by redenominating all Italian debt contracts into lira, there is the question of what exactly constitutes an Italian debt contract. Not all such contracts are between Italian debtors and Italian creditors, are issued in Italy, and specify Italian courts for adjudicating disputes. Italian companies issue bonds abroad and borrow from foreign banks. Foreign multinationals sell bonds in Italy. Foreigners hold the bonds of Italian governments. A further complication is that contracts are not simply being redenominated from one Italian currency to another; rather, they are being redenominated from a European currency to an Italian currency. Foreign courts might therefore take EU law as the law of the currency issuer (Italy) and invalidate the redenomination of certain contracts.

Mann (1960) argues that when a case involves two competing currencies, the courts should apply the law specified in the contract. For instruments

for the contingency that it might have to exit from its monetary union with Belgium. (See former prime minister Juncker's interview with Agence Presse France, summarized at: http://news .bbc.co.uk/2/hi/business/1677037.stm.) The implications for the present argument are unclear, because Belgium ultimately did not devalue against the guilder and the deutschemark in 1993. Whether Luxembourg, with its open-capital markets and highly developed financial system, in fact could have smoothly broken its monetary link with Belgium is at a minimum an open question. What is revealing, however, is that Luxembourg chose to destroy its stock of national notes and coins in 2002 when the physical euro came into existence.

such as Italian government bonds issued domestically, this is Italian law. But foreign laws govern a variety of other Italian financial instruments, such as corporate bonds issued abroad. And in some cases, no explicit choice of law is specified in the contract. For example, this is the case for loans by German banks to Italian corporations or for purchases of parts in Germany by Italian manufacturing firms. Italian courts would presumably rule in favor of the redenomination of all loans to Italian borrowers, including those from German banks, but German courts might rule against redenomination. And there are few precedents to guide the courts' decision in such circumstances.[28] This opens the door to litigation and to an extended period of uncertainty.

Still, Argentina's dealings with its creditors suggest that the government of a country altering its currency arrangements is in a relatively strong position. While that case also gave rise to litigation in a variety of venues, it did not force the redollarization of previously pesified contracts or force other compensation to aggrieved creditors. But cases involving suits against Italian debtors in the courts of other European countries and in the European Court of Justice could be messier. And the Italian government would be loath to disregard their judgments insofar as it attached value to the country's other links with the European Union.

1.7 Evidence

Since 2002, the Eurobarometer has conducted annual surveys of public opinion regarding the euro in the participating member states. Here, I analyze answers to the following question: "In your opinion, for [COUNTRY], is the adoption of the euro advantageous overall and will it strengthen us for the future, or rather the opposite, disadvantageous overall and will it weaken us?" Figure 1.1 shows the pattern of responses from the most recent survey at the time of writing. Evidently, the euro is least popular, as measured here, in low-income euro area member states (Greece, Portugal) and in slowly growing economies (Italy and again Portugal) but also in the Netherlands (where concerns are disproportionately over inflation—see figure 1.2).

Table 1.1 shows regressions of the share of the population, by country and year, that views the euro as disadvantageous. The dependent variable, a logit transformation of this share, is regressed on inflation and growth in the current year.[29] The results are consistent with the notion that higher

---

28. Technically, the country in which delivery is physically taken (where the transaction is physically completed) should be the one whose law governs international contracts. In the present instance, this would be German law if the Italian company's truck drives to Stuttgart to pick up parts at the German factory, but it would be Italian law if the German company's truck is used to transport the parts to the Italian assembly plant.

29. One can imagine more sophisticated specifications, but the limited amount of data available do not really permit their estimation.

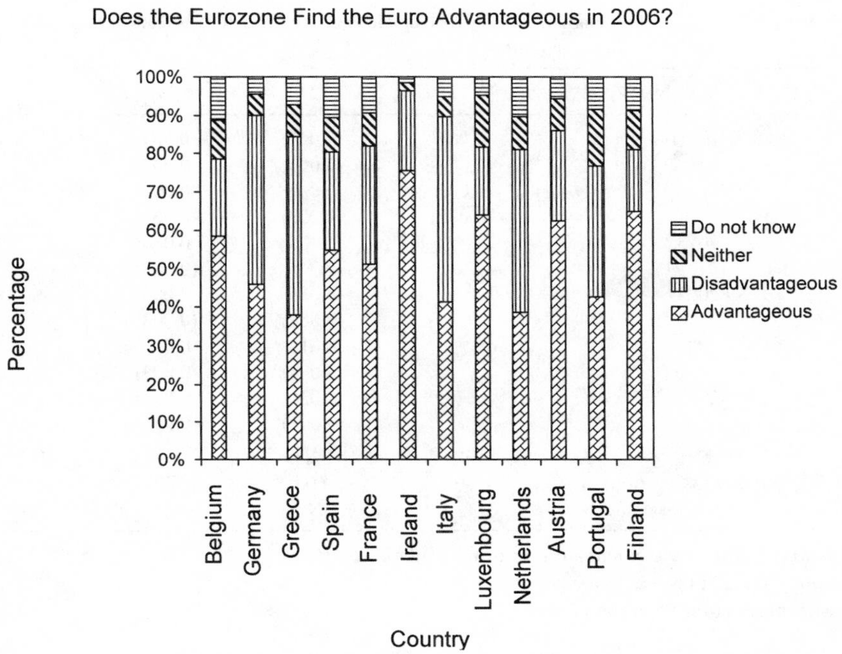
Does the Eurozone Find the Euro Advantageous in 2006?
100%
90%
80%
70%
60%
50%
40%
30%
20%
10%
0%
Percentage
Do not know
Neither
Disadvantageous
Advantageous
Belgium
Germany
Greece
Spain
France
Ireland
Italy
Luxembourg
Netherlands
Austria
Portugal
Finland
Country

Fig. 1.1 Public opinion by country

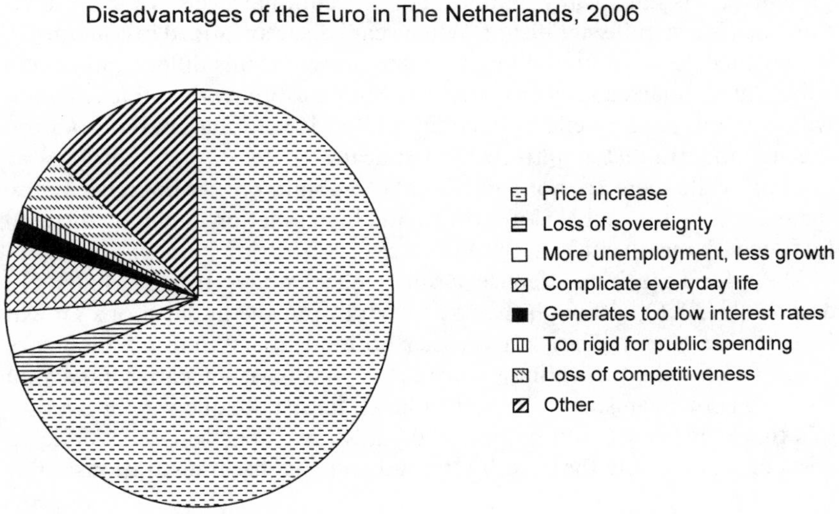
Disadvantages of the Euro in The Netherlands, 2006
Price increase
Loss of sovereignty
More unemployment, less growth
Complicate everyday life
Generates too low interest rates
Too rigid for public spending
Loss of competitiveness
Other

Fig. 1.2 Survey responses in the Netherlands

Table 1.1   Determinants of negative opinions of the euro, 2002 to 2006 (standard
                   errors in parentheses)

Variable	(1)	(2)	(3)
Inflation	0.005	0.007[a]	0.004[a]
	(0.003)	(0.003)	(0.002)
Growth	−0.005[a]	−0.007[a]	0.001
	(0.002)	(0.002)	(0.001)
2003		0.003	0.006[a]
		(0.008)	(0.003)
2004		0.015	0.008[a]
		(0.008)	(0.003)
2005		0.015	0.012[a]
		(0.008)	(0.003)
2006		0.026[a]	0.013[a]
		(0.008)	(0.003)
R^2	0.12	0.028	
Observations	60	60	60
Random effects	N	N	Y

Source: Eurobarometer and author's own calculations.
Note: Constant term estimated but not reported.
[a]Significant at the 95 percent level.

inflation raises dissatisfaction with the euro, while higher growth reduces dissatisfaction. In the basic regression on pooled data, in column (1), the growth term is statistically significant at conventional levels, while the inflation term is not quite significant. When year effects are added in column (2), the coefficients on both the inflation and growth terms differ significantly from 0 at standard confidence levels. When we estimate the same equation with random country effects in column (3), it is the inflation term but not the growth term that is statistically significant.

Thus, while there are not enough data to obtain precise point estimates, there are indications that slow growth and high inflation could fan dissatisfaction with membership in the euro area.[30]

The second empirical exercise has in fact been undertaken by Hallerberg and Wolff (2006), although they do not draw out the implications for exit from the euro area. They test whether both membership in the monetary union and fiscal reforms that reduce deficit bias have a negative impact on sovereign borrowing costs. Thus, they speak at least obliquely to the hypothesis that a country could minimize any adverse impact on debt-servicing costs of abandoning the euro by strengthening its fiscal institutions. They

30. It is also possible to analyze the individual survey responses in order to see how sentiment toward the euro varies with education, gender, urbanization, and so forth. See Jonung and Conflitti (2008).

estimate panel regressions with country fixed effects for ten EU member states, where the dependent variable is the yield on ten-year government bond rates relative to the corresponding German yield, and the period covered is 1993 to 2005. This spread is regressed on the difference in the budget deficit between country i and Germany and the difference in the public debt/GDP ratio between country i and Germany. Control variables include a measure of market liquidity and a measure of global risk aversion. The key explanatory variables are then dummy variables for membership in the euro area and for the strength of fiscal institutions, which are entered by themselves and interacted with the deficit measure.[31]

The authors follow Von Hagen (1992) in arguing that deficit bias reflects a common-pool problem: special interests benefiting from additional public spending fail to internalize the implications for the deficit and therefore for the government's borrowing costs. They argue that this bias can be minimized by assigning authority over the budget to a single individual, the finance minister, who will have a greater tendency to internalize such effects. They operationalize this idea by constructing an index measuring the ability of the finance minister to affect the budget. They also consider a survey-based measure of the structure of the budget process and a synthetic measure that relies not on delegation but on fiscal targets for countries where the ideological distance between coalition partners is large and therefore where delegation is unlikely to be effective.[32] Results are similar for the alternative measures, so I discuss the most straightforward ones—those for delegation of authority to the finance minister—here.

Higher debts and deficits increase spreads, although the effects are small. The effect of EMU is also evident: an increase in the deficit by 1 percent of GDP raises the spread by 4 basis points for a noneuro area country but only by 1.5 percent for a euro area member. An increase in the finance minister's powers from Portuguese to Austrian levels reduces the spread by 2 to 4 basis points; it also reduces the impact of an increase in the deficit by 1 percent of GDP by 2 basis points. These results are consistent with the hypothesis that EMU and strengthened budgetary procedures are alternative ways of strengthening fiscal discipline.[33] They suggest that countries exiting the monetary union can avoid higher interest costs if they put in place efficient bud-

31. In addition, the EMU variable is interacted with the measure of market liquidity and with the debt ratio.

32. In addition, they consider a measure of the degree of the legislature or the parliament over the budget (Lienert's [2005] parliamentary index). However, it is possible to raise questions about the relevance of this particular measure to the issues at hand. Hence, I do not consider it further in what follows.

33. The assumption underlying this interpretation is that the smaller impact of deficits on spreads in euro area countries reflects the disciplining effect of the monetary union—that deficits will not persist or that larger deficits now will be followed by smaller deficits later—rather than assuming myopia on the part of governments or that the latter will receive a debt bailout from their partners in the event of fiscal difficulties.

getary procedures that mitigate common-pool problems. At the same time, the size of the effects is small. Just 4.5 additional basis points for a euro area country whose deficit grows from 0 to 3 percent of GDP makes one wonder whether these estimates are picking up the full effect or if something else is going on. One explanation for why economic policies and institutions do not have a larger impact on spreads is that the ECB carries out open market operations in the bonds of all its members, regardless of the strength of their policies and institutions; this does not force spreads to equality but may limit differentials.[34]

I further investigated the robustness of these results by analyzing the impact of EMU and fiscal institutions on sovereign credit ratings. This involves analyzing their impact on three credit rating measures: Fitch's, Standard and Poor's, and an average of the two rating agencies. In the interest of space, here I report the results using the average of the two ratings as the dependent variable.[35] The country sample and period are essentially the same as in the Hallerberg and Wolff study, as the analysis is constrained by the availability of their indices of fiscal measures. One difference here is the use of quarterly data: the fiscal measures are available at a quarterly frequency, and the credit ratings can be sampled at the end of each quarter. Another difference is that I look at the absolute level of credit ratings, not ratings (or spreads) relative to Germany (and not the strength of fiscal institutions relative to Germany).[36]

I start with a simple panel regression of the credit rating(s) on the measure of fiscal institutions (in column [1] of each table). Year fixed effects are then added (column [2]), and if these are jointly significant, they are then included in the remaining regressions. Column (3) adds country effects (using the Hausman test to choose between fixed and random effects). Column (4) adds the entire vector of macroeconomic and financial variables. The empirical specification follows Christensen and Solomonsen (2007), who estimate empirical models of credit ratings; the main difference here is the addition of interaction effects for euro area countries, plus the use of total debt rather than public debt (following Hallerberg and Wolff [2006]). Finally, I incorporate improvements in the measures of fiscal arrangements developed by the authors since the appearance of their earlier working paper.[37] Specifically,

---

34. More precisely, the ECB assigns the short-term sovereign debt instruments of all euro area member governments to the same (highest) liquidity category, implying the lowest haircut when accepting them as collateral. Because the ECB mainly accepts short-term instruments in its market operations, it is these on which spreads should show the strongest tendency to converge. Spreads on the longer-term instruments considered by Hallerberg and Wolff are then freer to vary, although they will still be affected by the term-structure relationship. See Buiter and Sibert (2005).

35. The additional results for Fitch and S&P separately are available on request. The Fitch and S&P letter scores are both converted to a numerical score ranging from one to twenty-one.

36. As a result, I have an additional set of country observations for Germany itself.

37. And that were kindly made available by Mark Hallerberg.

I employ three measures of fiscal arrangements: "Strong finance minister" (a measure of the power of the finance minister during budget negotiations in the cabinet and with Parliament), "Index S2" (the authors' synthetic measure that relies not on delegation to a strong finance minister but on fiscal targets for countries where the ideological distance between coalition partners is large), and "Fiscgov" (the authors' survey-based measure of the degree of centralization of the budgetary process). All three measures are scaled so as to vary from 0 to 1, with larger values indicating arrangements better suited for resolving common-pool problems.

The results found in tables 1.2 through 1.4 are broadly consistent with those using spreads as the dependent variable.[38] All three measures of the centralization of fiscal policymaking are positively associated with the rating agencies' measures of credit quality. This remains the case, except for Index S2, when a wide range of controls are included in the estimating equation. Macroeconomic and financial conditions generally affect ratings in the expected direction, although their effects are not always significant at conventional confidence levels. Inflation, unemployment, large current account deficits, and high debts lower ratings. So far, so good.

Evidence on whether adopting the euro attenuates the impact of macroeconomic and financial imbalances on credit ratings is mixed. Consistent with the hypothesis, the negative effects of inflation and unemployment on credit ratings are attenuated by participation in the monetary union. Countries with large current account deficits suffer less in terms of credit rating if they are members of the monetary union. The one uncomfortable result is that the interaction of the EMU dummy with the debt ratio (general government-consolidated gross debt as a percentage of GDP) is negative, not positive as anticipated under the maintained hypothesis. This coefficient is 0 in the final column, where the lagged dependent variable is included (as seems to be preferred by the data), which makes the result somewhat less perplexing. Sensitivity analysis—dropping countries one by one—reveals that these anomalous results are driven by Belgium. Without the observations for this one country, one obtains a negative and significant coefficient on the debt/GDP ratio and a smaller positive and significant coefficient on the debt/GDP ratio interacted with EMU. This is not entirely surprising in that Belgium has long had a relatively high credit rating, despite its very high government debt, for reasons that are not entirely clear.

One interpretation of these results is that any increase in debt-servicing costs experienced by a country like Portugal that is abandoning the euro can be neutralized by reforming fiscal institutions to delegate more authority to

---

38. I adopt the same variable names as Hallerberg and Wolff for ease of comparison, except that I refer to the squared deviation of real GDP per capita from trend as "trend deviation" (or simply "deviation") as opposed to "sustainability" to avoid confusion with debt sustainability.

Table 1.2   **Effect of EMU and fiscal institutions on credit ratings (Strong finance minister measure of fiscal institutions)**

	(1)	(2)	(3)	(4)	(5)
Strong Finance	2.5358	2.3411	2.6822	0.8813	0.1640
Minister	(0.474)***	(0.520)***	(0.187)***	(0.244)***	(0.079)**
Real GDP per				−0.00005	−0.00002
capita				(0.00002)**	$(7.97 * 10^\wedge -6)^*$
Trend deviation				$1.50 * 10^\wedge -10$	$3.81 * 10^\wedge -10$
				$(1.09 * 10^\wedge -9)$	$(3.46 * 10^\wedge -10)$
Debt (% of GDP)				−0.0235	−0.0042
				(0.0105)	(0.0034)
Inflation				−0.3068	−0.0368
				(0.0372)***	(0.0136)***
Unemployment				−0.0227	−0.0066
rate				(0.0156)	(0.0049)
Export growth				−0.0215	−0.0017
(year to year)				(0.0064)***	(0.0020)
Current account				0.0379	0.0277
deficit < 4%				(0.127)	(0.040)
EMU				−0.7083	−0.1579
				(0.2598)***	(0.0833)*
Real GDP per				0.00004	0.00001
capita * EMU				(0.00003)*	$(8.32 * 10^\wedge -6)^*$
Trend deviation				$-1.50 * 10^\wedge -10$	$-3.96 * 10^\wedge -10$
* EMU				$(1.10 * 10^\wedge -9)$	$(3.49 * 10^\wedge -10)$
Debt (% of GDP)				−0.0148	−0.0006
* EMU				(0.0053)***	(0.0017)
Inflation * EMU				0.4160	0.0379
				(0.048)***	(0.017)**
Unemployment				0.0340	0.0065
* EMU				(0.013)***	(0.004)
Export growth				0.0156	−0.0017
* EMU				(0.0083)*	(0.0026)
Current account				−0.2702	−0.0433
deficit * EMU				(0.1222)	(0.0387)
Lagged dependent					0.9181
variable					(0.015)***
Constant	17.964	17.941	17.871	20.813	1.8503
	(0.316)***	(0.504)***	(0.122)***	(0.378)***	(0.332)***
Year fixed effects	No	Yes	No	No	No
Country fixed effects	No	No	Yes***	Yes***	Yes**
N	462	462	462	462	451
R^2	0.0587	0.0587	0.0587	0.4863	0.9949

***Significant at the 1 percent level.
**Significant at the 5 percent level.
*Significant at the 10 percent level.

Table 1.3   **Effect of EMU and fiscal institutions on credit ratings (Index S2 of fiscal institutions)**

	(1)	(2)	(3)	(4)	(5)
Index S2	2.5638	2.1848	3.3274	0.4829	0.1317
	(0.619)***	(0.659)***	(0.272)***	(0.328)	(0.106)
Real GDP per capita				−0.00006	−0.00002
				(0.00003)**	(8.04 * 10^−6)**
Trend deviation				2.16 * 10^−10	3.99 * 10^−10
				(1.11 * 10^−9)	(3.48 * 10^−10)
Debt (% of GDP)				−0.0231	−0.0040
				(0.0107)**	(0.0033)
Inflation				−0.3633	−0.0434
				(0.0364)***	(0.0137)***
Unemployment rate				−0.0147	−0.0054
				(0.0156)	(0.0049)
Export growth (year to year)				−0.0228	−0.0017
				(0.0065)***	(0.0021)
Current account deficit < 4%				0.0786	0.0352
				(0.128)	(0.0398)
EMU				−0.7523	−0.1577
				(0.2664)***	(0.0849)*
Real GDP per capita * EMU				0.0001	0.00002
				(0.00002)**	(8.38 * 10^−6)*
Trend deviation * EMU				−2.53 * 10^−10	−4.12 * 10^−10
				(1.12 * 10^−9)	(3.51 * 10^−8)
Debt (% of GDP) * EMU				−0.0155	−0.0008
				(0.0054)***	(0.0017)
Inflation * EMU				0.4668	0.0436
				(0.0480)***	(0.0171)**
Unemployment * EMU				0.0318	0.0062
				(0.013)**	(0.004)
Export growth * EMU				0.0175	−0.0015
				(0.0084)**	(0.0026)
Current account deficit * EMU				−0.2826	−0.0455
				(0.1237)**	(0.0388)
Lagged dependent variable					0.9213
					(0.015)***
Constant	18.071	18.028	17.622	21.120	1.8080
	(0.376)***	(0.546)***	(0.163)***	(0.419)***	(0.340)***
Year fixed effects	No	Yes	No	No	No
Country fixed effects	No	No	Yes***	Yes***	Yes*
N	462	462	462	424	414
R^2	0.0360	0.0360	0.0360	0.4651	0.9950

***Significant at the 1 percent level.
**Significant at the 5 percent level.
*Significant at the 10 percent level.

Table 1.4   **Effect of EMU and fiscal institutions on credit ratings (Fiscgov measure of fiscal institutions)**

	(1)	(2)	(3)	(4)	(5)
Fiscgov	4.7004	4.5864	4.2989	2.2219	0.2477
	(0.518)***	(0.531)***	(0.306)***	(0.340)***	(0.115)**
Real GDP per capita				−0.00004	−0.00002
				(0.00002)	(7.92 * 10^−6)**
Trend deviation				−3.57 * 10^−10	3.50 * 10^−10
				(1.06 * 10^−9)	(3.47 * 10^−10)
Debt (% of GDP)				−0.0183	−0.0038
				(0.0102)	(0.0034)
Inflation				−0.2533	−0.0400
				(0.0345)***	(0.0126)***
Unemployment rate				−0.0327	−0.0070
				(0.0151)**	(0.0049)
Export growth (year to year)				−0.0213	−0.0019
				(0.0062)***	(0.0020)
Current account deficit < 4%				0.0219	0.0297
				(0.122)	(0.0398)
EMU				−0.6714	−0.1677
				(0.2507)***	(0.0828)**
Real GDP per capita * EMU				0.00003	0.00001
				(0.00003)	(8.30 * 10^−6)*
Trend deviation * EMU				3.17 * 10^−10	−3.69 * 10^−10
				(1.07 * 10^−9)	(3.50 * 10^−10)
Debt (% of GDP) * EMU				−0.0128	−0.0004
				(0.0051)**	(0.0017)
Inflation * EMU				0.3691	0.0416
				(0.046)***	(0.017)***
Unemployment * EMU				0.0423	0.0071
				(0.013)***	(0.0041)*
Export growth * EMU				0.0142	−0.0015
				(0.008)*	(0.0026)
Current account deficit * EMU				−0.2616*	−0.0445
				(0.1184)	(0.0387)
Lagged dependent variable					0.9133
					(0.015)***
Constant	16.200	16.047	16.488	19.565	1.8667
	(0.3842)***	(0.540)***	(0.222)***	(0.434)***	(0.331)***
Year fixed effects	No	Yes	No	No	No
Country fixed effects	No	No	Yes***	Yes***	Yes**
N	462	462	462	462	451
R^2	0.1517	0.1517	0.1517	0.5196	0.9949

***Significant at the 1 percent level.
**Significant at the 5 percent level.
*Significant at the 10 percent level.

the prime minister, by addressing concerns over the common-pool problem, and by reassuring investors that exit will not result in a loss of fiscal discipline. The financial disincentive may not, therefore, be an insurmountable obstacle to abandoning the euro.

One reason for questioning these results is that the impact of debts and deficits—euro adoption and fiscal institutions notwithstanding—are suspiciously small in these regressions, as in the earlier work of Hallerberg and Wolff on interest rate spreads.[39] One worries that for whatever reason, these results are not picking up the entire effect of fiscal conditions, current and prospective, on credit ratings. But the fact that the rating agencies do not dramatically differentiate between fiscally messy Belgium and Italy and fiscally responsible Finland and Ireland is widely commented on—just as it is noted that markets differentiate between them relatively little in terms of interest rate spreads. If there is an anomaly, in other words, it would appear to be in the behavior of investors and rating agencies rather than in the econometrics.

In addition, one worries that ratings fail to reflect differences in current fiscal conditions among euro area countries, not because the euro represents a commitment to get one's fiscal house together in the not-too-distant future, but rather because fiscally profligate governments can expect a debt bailout from their euro area partners. At the same time, the prospects for a bailout can be questioned. And even if the mechanism making for rosier future prospects is a bailout rather than fiscal reform, this does not change the argument that a potential benefit of euro area membership is an easier fiscal ride. One worries that in a more turbulent environment (out of sample), the results might differ—although it is not entirely clear why the Lucas critique would apply in this context. Finally, to the extent that fiscal rules are endogenous (to the extent that they reflect the same political pressures that lead to large observed deficits), it may be naive to think that a country abandoning the euro because of chronic deficit problems will then be able to turn around and strengthen its policy-making institutions. That said, it is interesting to observe that Italy succeeded in significantly strengthening the ability of the finance minister to affect the budget following the 1992 crisis that ejected it from the Exchange Rate Mechanism of the European Monetary System and presumably weakened the disciplining effect of EMU on its budget.[40]

Finally, it is possible to compare these results with Standard & Poor's own exercise (S&P; 2005). Standard & Poor's considered the impact of a country leaving the euro area in 2006 using its own proprietary model (which

39. Thus, an increase in the debt ratio from 50 to 100 percent of GDP is expected to lower a country's credit rating by just one notch, say, from A to–A. This small effect is a widely commented-on phenomenon (see, for example, Buiter and Sibert [2005]), although here it applies not just to euro area but also to noneuro area countries.

40. The same was true, inter alia, of Spain and Finland, according to the indices of Hallerberg and Wolff (2006).

similarly regresses ratings on a range of indicators intended to capture political, economic, and financial conditions). It was assumed that a country leaving the euro area was able to successfully depreciate the real exchange rate, restoring it to the average level prevailing in the 1990s—something that had the effect of improving ratings, other things equal. But it was also assumed that interest rates on government debt rose by 100 basis points. Thus, the conclusion was that leaving the euro area would have relatively little effect on ratings for lightly indebted countries that had suffered significant deteriorations in competitiveness but would have a significant negative effect on heavily indebted members whose competitiveness losses had been limited (Greece, Italy, Portugal, Spain, and Belgium). The main difference from the exercise in this chapter is that S&P assumed no further change in current or expected future fiscal policies and procedures. Its analysis does not contradict the point that significant fiscal reform could offset the impact on ratings of abandoning the euro; it simply does not consider the possibility.

1.8   Reforms to Avert a Breakup

If one wishes to minimize the likelihood of breakup, then what kind of reforms are needed? Here, there is no magic potion, only the standard measures pointed to by the literatures on optimum currency areas (OCA) and the democratic accountability of economic policymakers.[41]

Measures to further enhance labor mobility within the euro area are a first set of reforms pointed to by OCA theory.[42] Regulations to ensure that French ski resorts extend equality of treatment to instructors trained in other European countries—and more generally, the removal of residual barriers to the mutual recognition of technical credentials, the portability of pensions, and the receipt of social services—will relieve the pressure that countries with depressed labor markets otherwise feel to do something, anything, including reintroducing the national currency, to address their unemployment problem. Concretely, the European Union has made some progress in the requisite direction, making qualifications more transparent and transferable by creating a standard portfolio of documents (the

41. An earlier attempt to ask these same questions is found in Cohen (2000).

42. These are supplemented by measures to enhance the flexibility of real and nominal wages. The ECB (2007) argues that real wages remain less flexible in the euro area than in the United States and that the degree of wage bargaining centralization and percentage of employees organized in trade unions—factors likely to condition the extent of such flexibility—have remained largely unchanged. At the same time, there has been a reduction of wage minima affecting young people and the implementation of subminimum wage regulations for youths in some euro area countries, which some would argue has enhanced wage flexibility in certain segments of the labor market. Such arguments would suggest that further reforms along similar lines would make it easier for countries suffering shocks requiring downward wage adjustment to cope with the single currency. This would appear to be the ECB's own view (see the same reference).

"Europass"), removing many remaining administrative and legal barriers to mobility, coordinating cross-border social security provisions through the introduction of a European health insurance card, and making occupational pension rights more portable.

Note, however, some uncomfortable implications of this advice. Facilitating labor mobility within the monetary union implies reinforcing barriers to immigration, legal and illegal, from outside the union. Australia allows citizens of New Zealand to work freely in its country, and vice versa, but only New Zealand permits the relatively free immigration of citizens of Fiji.[43] Customs and immigration officials in Australia spend much of their time repatriating illegal Fijian immigrants entering through New Zealand, straining the arrangements designed to ensure integration of the two national labor markets. In the European context, limiting the strains on the labor markets of the countries on the receiving end of the labor flow and hence the political fallout may require limiting immigration from outside the union. Among other things, this may mean limiting labor mobility from North Africa and the Middle East, regions where earnings differentials vis-à-vis the European Union are large and where the efficiency effects of freer labor mobility would be especially pronounced.[44] Harsh treatment of undocumented immigrants from these countries may also create strains with their governments, which would not be helpful for a European Union that is trying to encourage democratic values and market-oriented economic development in what is sometimes referred to as "Wider Europe."

One can even imagine differential treatment of workers from EU member states that have and have not adopted the euro. Allowing, indeed encouraging, workers to relocate freely within the monetary union would become more uncomfortable politically if workers from member states outside the euro area were also permitted to freely migrate to relatively prosperous euro area member states. One can imagine political pressure to situate the immigration ring-fence at the borders of the euro area, not at the borders of the European Union itself. In the short run, this would create problems for the Schengen Agreement, which has been implemented by Denmark and Sweden, as well as most euro area member states.[45] In the longer run, it is likely to create strains between EU members inside and outside the fence and to disrupt the operation of the single market. The idea that euro area member states would only take measures to further enhance labor mobility among themselves if there was also a credible barrier against immigration from tiny, prosperous Denmark is not especially compelling, but one can imagine such concerns becoming serious if and when, say, Turkey is admitted to the European Union.

43. For whose foreign policy it has traditionally borne responsibility.
44. For arguments to this effect, see Rodrik (2002) and Bhagwati (2003).
45. And, by Norway and Iceland.

Measures to enhance the countercyclical use of fiscal policy are the other reforms pointed to by the literature on optimum currency areas. European countries are uncomfortable with their loss of monetary autonomy, because having tied the monetary hand behind their backs, they have little scope for using fiscal policy countercyclically. Inherited debt ratios are high, which means that increasing deficit spending in slowdowns threatens rating downgrades and increases in borrowing costs. The Stability and Growth Pact, whatever the practice, in principle limits the scope for discretionary fiscal policy and even automatic stabilizers in countries close to or exceeding its 3 percent of GDP threshold for excessive deficits. To be sure, for countries like Portugal, where the problem is excessive labor costs and inadequate competitiveness, expansionary fiscal policy to boost aggregate demand is beside the point; the imperative is to cut labor costs, and using fiscal policy might only slow the inevitable adjustment while threatening debt sustainability. Still, one can imagine a variety of other countries suffering negative aggregate demand shocks that can be offset by temporary increases in budget deficits that would benefit from greater freedom to use fiscal policy in countercyclical fashion.

For them, reforms of the Stability and Growth Pact that encourage governments to run budgets close to balance or even in surplus in good times so that they can allow deficits to widen in bad times would make life with the euro more comfortable.[46] My own view is that reform of the Stability and Growth Pact should encourage changes in fiscal institutions and procedures that work to solve common-pool and free-rider problems and thereby contain deficit bias in good times.[47] The alternative, where the European Commission and Council agree to fines and sanctions against countries

46. To be clear, I am not arguing that the 3 percent ceiling is too low but rather that it leaves inadequate room for countercyclical policy, because deficits are excessive in good times. There are too many alternative reform proposals for these to be usefully surveyed here. See Fischer, Jonung, and Larch (2007) for a survey of alternatives.

47. On fiscal decentralization as a source of common-pool problems, see Rattso (2003) and Eichengreen (2003). My own scheme for reform is as follows. The rationale for the pact is that deficits today may imply deficits tomorrow and that chronic deficits will force the ECB to provide an inflationary debt bailout. But not all deficits are equally persistent. Chronic deficits are a danger only where countries fail to reform their fiscal institutions. Countries with large unfunded pension liabilities, such as Greece and Spain, will almost certainly have deficits down the road. Where workers are allowed to draw unemployment and disability benefits indefinitely, deficits today signal deficits tomorrow. Countries that have not completed privatizing public enterprise, such as France, are similarly more likely to find future fiscal skeletons in the closet. Where revenue-sharing systems that allow states and municipalities to spend today and to be bailed out tomorrow, central governments will almost certainly suffer chronic deficits. Thus, the pact should focus not on fiscal numbers, which are arbitrary and easily cooked, but on fiscal institutions. The Council of Ministers could agree on an index of institutional reform, say, with 1 point each for privatization, pension reform, unemployment insurance reform, and revenue-sharing reform. It should then authorize the European Commission to grade countries accordingly. Those receiving 4 points would be exempt from the Stability and Growth Pact guidelines, as there is no reason to expect that they will be prone to chronic deficits. The others, in contrast, would still be subject to warnings, sanctions, and fines.

whose deficits are deemed excessive, assumes a level of political solidarity—a Europe in which different nationalities view themselves as members of a common polity, such that a majority of members can impose fines and sanctions against a renegade minority—that does not exist and that is unlikely to exist for the foreseeable future. In the absence of deeper political integration, in other words, a stability pact with anything resembling the current structure is unlikely to be enforceable.[48]

The same conclusion applies to proposals to strengthen the operation of the monetary union by supplementing it with a European system of fiscal federalism. A system of temporary transfers among member states or an expanded EU budget where contributions and expenditures are keyed to a member state's relative economic situation could provide an alternative to a national monetary policy as a buffer during periods of cyclical divergence.[49] Economic activity would be more stable, because intracountry transfers would render demand more stable. But making such transfers effective would require significant expansion of the EU budget, especially insofar as the majority of that budget is tied up in agricultural subsidies and ongoing transfers to relatively low-income member states. And again, significantly increasing the share of tax revenues that member states pay to the European Union and whose disposition is then decided by the member states as a group would require a level of political solidarity that does not exist.

Another way of thinking about this is that fiscal federalism is an insurance pool through which members of the monetary union that are temporarily better off assist their brethren who are temporarily worse off—participants require a system of collective self-help if they are going to willingly expose themselves to the vicissitudes of monetary union. Rodrik (1996) has made an argument like this to explain why more open economies have larger governments—their citizens are willing to expose themselves to the risks of trade openness only if they can count on help from their stronger neighbors in the event of a temporary worsening of their economic situation due to international competition. The analogy here is that countries suffering temporary unexpected economic costs as a consequence of their participation in the monetary union would accept the latter only if they can temporarily

48. This argument has a long lineage; see, inter alia, Kindleberger (1973) and Eichengreen (1997). As De Grauwe (2006) puts it, while the European Commission decides when a country's deficit is excessive and when its government must therefore cut spending and raise taxes, it is the national government that must implement those tax increases and spending cuts and that will be rewarded or punished for doing so by its constituents. In contrast, the commission cannot be replaced, except in the event of dereliction of duty. In effect, the commission—and therefore the Stability and Growth Pact—lacks democratic legitimacy. It will continue to lack such legitimacy until European political integration proceeds further and results, inter alia, in direct election of the commission.

49. Early influential statements of this view were Inman and Rubinfeld (1992) and Sala-i-Martin and Sachs (1992).

expect transfers from their neighbors to buffer the effects. The difference is that Rodrik's argument applies to citizens of the same country, whereas the present argument concerns transfers between sovereign states. One suspects that the citizens of different countries will be less enthusiastic about giving money to one another; lacking a common national identity, they lack the requisite political solidarity, absent significant steps toward political integration at the European level.[50] The European Union is made up of diverse national identities, and absent a sense of European identity, resistance to such transfers may be considerable.[51] At the level of the European Union, there is also the question of whether a system of interstate taxes and transfers could be agreed on for a subset of member states—those participating in the monetary union—without the active involvement of noneuro area members.

A similar implication flows from the observation that the risk of a breakup could be reduced by enhancing the democratic accountability of the ECB. The modern literature on monetary policy distinguishes a central bank's operational independence and democratic accountability. A central bank should have the independence to select and implement its tactics independent of political pressures, but in choosing the objectives at which those tactics are directed, it should be answerable to the polity. National central banks ultimately answer to national legislatures, which have the power to alter their statutes in the event that those responsible for the formulation of monetary policy are perceived as pursuing objectives inconsistent with their mandate—where the latter is decided by the polity as a whole.[52]

But in Europe, there is no euro area or EU government that can act as an effective counterweight to the ECB.[53] The powers of the European Parliament are limited relative to those of national parliaments and legislatures.

50. In addition, Rodrik's premise and central result have been questioned by Alesina and Wacziarg (1998), who argue that the actual association is between government spending and country size, with small countries both spending more on public consumption and being more open to trade.

51. Thus, authors such as Alesina, Baqir, and Easterly (1999) show that more diverse political jurisdictions are less likely to provide public goods, including coinsurance against shocks, to their residents.

52. Some authors (for example, Alesina and Tabellini [2007, 2008]) argue that the need for democratic accountability of independent agencies like the ECB can be overstated. They argue that EU member states have shown themselves prepared to accept limited democratic accountability for such institutions as the price for policy efficiency, pointing not just to the ECB but also to the case of the European Commission. My own view is that the effort to draft a European constitution (including the Nice Summit that preceded the constitutional convention and the Brussels Summit that followed it) point to a deep and abiding desire in Europe for the adequate democratic accountability of such institutions.

53. Accountability can be defined and provided in different ways; see, in the context of the ECB, Bini-Smaghi (1998), Buiter (1999), Issing (1999), and De Haan and Eijffinger (2000). By referring here to *democratic* accountability, I attempt to distinguish accountability of policymakers to democratically elected politicians from other mechanisms for accountability—for example, accountability to the public through the mechanism of public opinion, achieved through the release of voting records and board minutes.

The Parliament holds hearings at which the president of the ECB delivers a statement and answers questions but cannot threaten to replace the president in the event of disagreement over objectives. The mandate of the ECB is a matter of international treaty, signed by the governments of the member states, and cannot be altered by the Parliament. Altering it requires the unanimous consent of the member states, which would be a formidable obstacle in practice.[54] This means that the ECB is less democratically accountable than the typical national central bank. In turn, this leaves less cope for the European polity to influence its objectives. In the event of serious disagreement, political groups that object to how the central bank chooses to operationalize its mandate are likely to choose exit over the relatively ineffective option of voice.[55]

Making voice more attractive would require giving the European Parliament more power to refine the institution's mandate and replace the president and perhaps other members of the board in the event of serious disagreement over objectives.[56] But there was a reluctance to significantly enhance the powers of the European Parliament during the constitutional convention process of 2003/2004, reflecting majority sentiment against creating anything resembling a European government. And even limited steps in that direction were resisted by the French and Dutch electorates in their referenda on the draft constitution. This is a reminder that monetary union without political union is problematic.[57] Because the latter is not likely to change anytime soon, collapse of the former cannot be dismissed out of hand.

1.9   Coda: The 2008 Financial Crisis

The financial crisis that spread from the United States to Europe in 2008 suggested yet another scenario for the breakup of the euro area.[58] The crisis led to suggestions that a country experiencing a severe banking crisis and incurring high costs of bank recapitalization might feel impelled to abandon the euro. If such costs were to exceed the fiscal capacity of the state, a govern-

---

54. De Haan and Eijffinger (2000) observe that the power of the European Parliament to alter the ECB statute is quite limited. They state that they "would prefer that, in the case of the statute of the ESCB, the European Parliament should have the final say and thus could act as a real parliament" (402), but they don't explain how to bring this about.

55. In principle, there are alternatives to democratic accountability, as previously noted. But given the difficulty of modifying the central bank's statute or ousting members of its board, reflecting the treaty-based nature of its structure, it can be argued that these provide an inadequate substitute.

56. Alternatively, and less desirably in my view, this power could be delegated to another political body such as the Eurogroup (the group of finance ministers of the members of the euro area).

57. As emphasized by De Grauwe (2006).

58. As readers who have gotten to this point will have inferred, most of the present chapter was drafted prior to those events.

ment and its central bank might resort to the inflation tax to augment that fiscal capacity. Levying the inflation tax at the national level presupposes the existence of a national currency. Hence, a state in these dire straits might feel impelled to abandon the euro and to reintroduce its national unit.

The basic issue is familiar to aficionados of the literature on monetary union: it is the feasibility of monetary union without fiscal union. The European Union has only a relatively small budget—less than 2 percent of EU GDP—much of which is tied up in the Structural Funds and Common Agricultural Policy. There is no federal fiscal mechanism for transferring resources to a member state suddenly confronted with high bank recapitalization costs. At the same time, economic and financial integration (as cemented by the price transparency afforded by the adoption of a common currency) has led some countries to specialize in the production of financial services. They have grown very large formal and shadow banking systems that in extreme circumstances may require a large public capital infusion in order to survive. In the absence of federal fiscal arrangement, a member of the monetary union, prevented from resorting to the inflation tax, may lack the public resources adequate to carry this out. Countries like Belgium, where the value of short-term bank liabilities approached three times GDP in mid-2008, illustrate the point.

The height of the crisis saw considerable discussion of this scenario: "For Europe, this is more than just a banking crisis," Munchau (2008) wrote. "Unlike in the US, it could develop into a monetary regime crisis. A systemic banking crisis is one of those few conceivable shocks with the potential to destroy Europe's monetary union. The enthusiasm for creating a single currency was unfortunately never matched by an equal enthusiasm to provide the correspondingly effective institutions to handle financial crises. Most of the time, it does not matter. But it matters now. For that reason alone, the case for a European rescue plan is overwhelming." Evans-Pritchard (2008) made a similar point: "Who in the eurozone can do what Alistair Darling has just done *in extremis* to save Britain's banks, as this $10 trillion house of cards falls down? There is no EU treasury or debt union to back up the single currency. The ECB is not allowed to launch bail-outs by EU law. Each country must save its own skin, yet none has full control of the policy instruments. . . . This is a very dangerous set of circumstances for monetary union. Will we still have a 15-member euro by Christmas?"

The answer depends in part on the arithmetic. On a monetary base of €1.35 trillion, the euro area would take in roughly €100 billion by running an inflation rate of 15 percent; this assumes that an interest elasticity of demand for base money is one-half and that inflation feeds through into interest rates one for one.[59] From this should be deducted the additional interest payments that would have to be paid on the previously existing public debt as a result

59. Readers can prorate this country by country as they wish.

of abandoning the euro; the estimates in section 1.7 suggest that this might amount to an additional 10 basis points. On €6 trillion of euro area debt, this would add $6 billion to debt-servicing costs. While the resulting revenue is not inconsequential, it pales in comparison with the roughly €2.5 trillion of aggregate tax receipts in the euro area.[60]

More important, however, would be the other adverse financial effects. The analysis of previous sections suggests that the banking-crisis-leads-to-serious-discussion-of-euro-abandonment scenario would play out as follows. The decision to reintroduce the national currency would require the passage of a law. It would also require the redenomination into that currency of domestic bank liabilities, public debt, mortgage and credit card debts, and wage contracts. The relevant legislation would be complex, and in a democracy, crafting and passing it would take time. Meanwhile, knowing what was coming—depreciation of the new national unit against the euro, the involuntary conversion of domestic assets into the new national unit, and their depreciation against euro-denominated assets—there would be an incentive to engage in asset substitution. This is precisely the banking crisis scenario previously described.

It might be objected that the country was already in the throes of a banking crisis—why worry about creating a problem that already exists? But the expectation that other domestic financial assets would be involuntarily redenominated and then devalued against the euro would surely cause additional capital flight. In response, bond markets would have to be shut down. The stock market would have to be shut down. This policy response would require not just a bank holiday of nonnegligible length but also a financial holiday—all markets would have to be closed for a nonnegligible period.[61] This would have high costs for the efficiency of resource allocation and the reputation of the country's financial markets.

Meanwhile, there exist a number of alternative approaches to dealing with the challenge of bank recapitalization. Most obviously, governments could agree to share the costs. Typically, banks whose liabilities are a multiple of GDP have large cross-border operations and multinational ownership. In Belgium, for example, the banks with such large short-term liabilities are not solely owned by Belgians. Fortis was so highly leveraged because it had purchased Dutch Amsterdam-Rotterdam Bank operations, impelling the

---

60. It also is small relative to the €1.5 trillion that euro area members devoted to recapitalization of their banking systems in mid-October 2008, at the height of the financial crisis.

61. One can also imagine resorting to the parallel-currency scenario previously discussed. Euros would still be used for most transactions, while the parallel domestic unit would be used to recapitalize banking system. Banks (and other eventual holders) could then exchange the new parallel currency for euros as they wished on the foreign exchange market. The parallel domestic currency would presumably quickly begin to trade at a discount. The "bad" money would promptly begin driving out the "good" one. In other words, there would be additional capital flight on the part of those holding euro-denominated claims. This approach would similarly seem to lead ultimately to the imposition of a moratorium on all financial transactions.

Dutch to help with the bailout. Similarly, Belgium, France, and Luxembourg cooperated in recapitalizing Dexia, a heavily Belgium-based mortgage lender. In the longer run, euro area countries and EU members more generally could agree on formal cost-sharing rules.

Alternatively, recapitalization might be done without resorting to public funds. Buiter (2008) has suggested an across-the-board debt equity conversion in reverse order of seniority: to resolve the crisis, existing debt would be involuntarily converted into equity, possibly preferred. Zingales (2008) advocates prepackaged bankruptcy: banks entering into this procedure would have old equity holders wiped out and their existing long-term bonds and commercial paper converted into equity. To protect the shareholders of solvent institutions against expropriation, they would be allowed individually to decide whether to buy out debt holders at the face value of their debt. If access to ECB credit was limited to banks that had undergone this procedure, solvent banks with no need for ECB funds would not undergo the procedure, but others would.

Third, recapitalization could be carried out using already-available fiscal resources. It is not obvious that 10 percent of GDP, which is what it typically takes to resolve a banking crisis, is beyond the fiscal capacity of European states. Adding 10 percent of GDP to the public debt at a 2 percent real interest rate makes for two-tenths of a percent of GDP of additional debt service. One should add ancillary costs—notably, higher interest rates on outstanding debt and crowding out of private investment—but these numbers are still not unreasonable.

Be this as it may, if the euro area survives the stresses roiling financial markets in the latter half of 2008—a series of events that are increasingly referred to as the most serious financial crisis of our lifetimes—then the hypothesis of this chapter can be said to have passed its ultimate test.

1.10   Conclusion

The possibility that an incumbent member of the euro area might reintroduce its national currency cannot be excluded. The European Union is still an entity whose residents identify themselves as citizens of nation states. Differences in national history and identity imply differences in preferences over monetary policy. Monetary union by its nature entails compromises and trade-offs. Member states must agree on a common monetary policy that in some cases is not any nation's optimum. By choosing to remain members, countries trade off the costs of a suboptimal monetary policy against other benefits.

Where there are compromises and trade-offs, it is possible that changes in circumstances may lead to a change in commitments. A country that experiences an asymmetric shock may find the costs of following policies determined by the majority of participating member states, while tolerable previously, to now be prohibitive. A country that sees its monetary union partners appointing less inflation-averse central bankers to the ECB board may similarly decide that the costs of accepting the common policy, while previously tolerable, are now prohibitively high.

How formidable are the obstacles to withdrawing? Economically, it is not clear which way the arguments cut. A country contemplating exit in order to obtain the kind of real depreciation needed to address problems of chronic slow growth and high unemployment would be deterred if it thought that its efforts to engineer a real depreciation would be frustrated by the inflationary response of domestic wages and prices, or if it thought that leaving the monetary union would significantly raise its debt-servicing costs. But if the defector strengthens the independence of its central bank and the efficiency of its fiscal institutions, then it is at least conceivable that these negative economic effects would not obtain.

In contrast to some other authors, I have argued that the technical and legal difficulties of reintroducing the national currency, while surmountable, should not be underestimated. But the political domain is where the most serious obstacles to withdrawing reside. A country that withdraws from Europe's monetary union would be seen as disregarding its commitments to other euro area members. Such a country would not be welcomed in the meetings where the future architecture of the European Union is discussed and where policy priorities are decided. Insofar as member states value their participation in these political discussions, they would incur significant costs. The "insofar" in the preceding sentence is of course an important caveat. Be that as it may, my own assessment is that the high value that member states attach to the larger European project would prevent them from exiting from the monetary union, except under the most extreme circumstances.[62]

Would defection by one country cause the general disintegration of the euro area? As with many things economic, the answer is, "it depends." For other countries experiencing the same economic problem, there might be a strengthened incentive to follow. If Italy left, owing to inadequate competitiveness and slow growth, and depreciated its national currency against the euro, other euro area members suffering from inadequate competitiveness and slow growth would feel greater discomfort and a greater temptation to follow. If Germany left, owing to high inflation, and allowed its national currency to appreciate against the euro, then other euro area members that were similarly uncomfortable with the rate of inflation would experience still higher import prices and again would be more tempted to follow suit.

But if economic problems in the defecting country were the converse of those of its partners in the monetary union, then the opposite conclusion might obtain: the rump union could be rendered more cohesive. Similarly,

---

62. This is a specific application of the general conclusion drawn by Cohen (2000) that monetary unions have tended to be stable when they are interwoven into a fabric of related ties.

if the country exiting the union had different preferences, independent of differences in national economic circumstances, its departure might make it easier for the remaining members to agree on a policy more to their liking and render the residual union more cohesive. The first set of effects is likely to be of negligible importance if the departing country is small but of greater significance if it is large. The second set of effects would be independent of country size insofar as ECB policy is decided on the basis of one country, one vote.

The analysis here has focused on scenarios for the next ten years. What about longer horizons? The longer the euro survives, the less likely it would seem that a participating country would see reintroducing its national currency as a logical treatment for its economic ills. Markets adapt to the single currency, rendering attempts to tamper with it correspondingly more costly. Expectations adapt to its existence: having no first-hand experience with alternatives, residents take the existence of a European currency as the normal state of affairs and come to regard the reintroduction of a national currency as beyond the pale. Notwithstanding the fact that it experienced a very severe asymmetric shock in the form of Hurricane Katrina and was disappointed by the assistance it then received from its partners in the U.S. currency union, the state of Louisiana did not contemplate abandoning the dollar and introducing its own currency, even though a sharp depreciation might have been appropriate for addressing some of its economic problems.[63]

At the same time, other developments could make the breakup of the euro area more likely. There could be a diplomatic and political falling out, say, over foreign policy. In a world of dirty bombs and terrorist cells, a member state could experience an asymmetric shock of sufficient magnitude that a dramatic real depreciation was seen as essential and the costs of abandoning the euro were trivial in comparison. The possibilities are endless.

References

Alesina, A., R. Baqir, and W. Easterly. 1999. Public goods and ethnic divisions. *Quarterly Journal of Economics* 114 (4): 1243–84.

Alesina, A., and V. Grilli. 1993. On the feasibility of a one-speed or multispeed European Monetary Union. *Economics and Politics* 5 (2): 145–66.

Alesina, A., and G. Tabellini. 2007. Bureaucrats or politicians? Part I: A single policy task. *American Economic Review* 97 (1): 169–79.

———. 2008. Bureaucrats or politicians? Part II: Multiple policy tasks. *Journal of Public Economics* 92 (3/4): 426–47.

63. One can object that high labor mobility between Louisiana and neighboring states obviated the need for such a response, but one can also argue that after nearly two centuries of currency union, leaving the dollar area was inconceivable in any case.

Alesina, A., and R. Wacziarg. 1998. Openness, country size and government. *Journal of Public Economics* 69 (3): 305–21.

Bhagwati, J. 2003. Borders beyond control. *Foreign Affairs* 82 (January/February): 98–104.

Biais, B., F. Declerc, J. Dow, R. Portes, and E.-L. von Thadden. 2006. *European corporate bond markets: Transparency, liquidity, efficiency.* London: Center for Economic Policy Research.

Bini-Smaghi, L. 1998. The democratic accountability of the European Central Bank. *Banca Nazionale del Lavoro Quarterly Review* 51 (205): 119–43.

Bishop, G. 2000. The euro bond market: Developments and implications for monetary policy. Paper presented at the European Central Bank seminar, 5–6 May, Frankfurt, Germany.

Blanchard, O. 2006. Adjustment within the euro: The difficult case of Portugal. Massachusetts Institute of Technology, Department of Economics. Manuscript, November.

Buiter, W. 1999. Alice in Euroland. *Journal of Common Market Studies* 37 (2): 181–209.

———. 2008. More and different: Including a debt-equity swap for the financial sector. Willem Buiter's Maverecon blog, *Financial Times*. September 21. Available at: www.ft.com/maverecon.

Buiter, W., and A. Sibert. 2005. How the eurosystem's treatment of collateral in its open market operations weakens fiscal discipline in the eurozone (and what to do about it). Unpublished manuscript. Available at: http://www.nber.org/~wbuiter/sov.pdf.

Christensen, L., and T. Solomonsen. 2007. New Europe: Mind the ratings. Danske Bank, Market Research Department. Manuscript, March.

Cohen, B. 2000. Beyond EMU: The problem of sustainability. In *The political economy of European monetary unification,* ed. B. Eichengreen and J. Frieden, 179–204. Boulder, CO: Westview.

Cooper, R. 1999. *Coordination games.* Cambridge: Cambridge University Press.

De Grauwe, P. 2006. On monetary and political union. Catholic University of Leuven, Department of Economics. Manuscript, May.

De Haan, J., and S. Eijffinger. 2000. The democratic accountability of the European Central Bank: A comment on two fairy-tales. *Journal of Common Market Studies* 38 (3): 393–407.

Dornbusch, R. 1992. Monetary problems of post-communism: Lessons from the end of the Austro-Hungarian empire. *Weltwirtschaftsliches Archiv* 128 (3): 391–424.

Eichengreen, B. 1997. On the links between monetary and political integration. *Swiss Political Science Review* 3 (1): 127–33.

———. 2003. Institutions for fiscal stability. PEIF Working Paper no. 14. University of California, Berkeley, Institute of European Studies, Political Economy of International Finance, October.

———. 2007. Su generis EMU. University of California, Berkeley, Department of Economics. Manuscript, December.

European Central Bank. 2007. Developments in the structural features of the euro area labour markets over the last decade. *Monthly Bulletin,* January, 63–76.

Evans-Pritchard, A. 2008. Who is going to bail out the euro? *Telegraph* (London). October 10. Available at: http://www.telegraph.co.uk.

Expatica. 2005. Euro collapse report "absurd": Bundesbank chief. *Expatica.* June 1. Available at: http://www.expatica.com.

Fidrmuc, J., J. Horvath, and J. Fidrmuc. 1999. Stability of monetary unions: Lessons from the breakup of Czechoslovakia. *Journal of Comparative Economics* 27 (4): 753–81.

Fischer, J., L. Jonung, and M. Larch. 2007. 101 proposals to reform the Stability and Growth Pact: Why so many? A survey. European Economy Economic Paper no. 67. Brussels: European Commission, January.

Garber, P. 1998. Note on the role of TARGET in a stage III crisis. NBER Working Paper no. 6619. Cambridge, MA: National Bureau of Economic Research, June.

Goodhart, C. A. E. 2008. Is the euro sustainable? London School of Economics, Financial Markets Group. Manuscript, March.

Grilli, V. 1986. Buying and selling attacks on fixed exchange rate systems. *Journal of International Economics* 20 (1/2): 143–56.

Gros, D. 2007. Will EMU survive 2010? CEPS Commentary. Brussels: Center for European Policy Studies, January.

Grossman, H., and J. van Huyck. 1988. Sovereign debt as a contingent claim: Excusable default, repudiation and reputation. *American Economic Review* 78 (5): 1088–97.

Haas, E. 1958. *The uniting of Europe.* Stanford: Stanford University Press.

Hallerberg, M., and G. B. Wolff. 2006. Fiscal institutions, fiscal policy and sovereign risk premia. Discussion Paper no. 35/2006. Frankfurt: Deutsche Bundesbank.

Inman, R., and D. Rubinfeld. 1992. Fiscal federalism in Europe: Lessons from the United States experience. *European Economic Review* 36 (2/3): 654–60.

Issing, O. 1999. The eurosystem: Transparent and accountable or "Willem in euroland." *Journal of Common Market Studies* 37 (3): 503–19.

Ize, A., and E. Levy Yeyati. 2005. Financial de-dollarization: Is it for real? IMF Working Paper no. 05/187. Washington, DC: International Monetary Fund.

Jonung, L., and C. Conflitti. 2008. Is the euro advantageous? Does it foster European feelings? Europeans on the euro after five years. European Economy Economic Paper no. 313. Brussels: European Commission.

Kindleberger, C. P. 1973. *International economics.* 5th ed. Homewood, IL: Richard D. Irwin.

Levy Yeyati, E. 2006. Financial dollarization: Evaluating the consequences. *Economic Policy* 21 (45): 61–118.

Lienert, I. 2005. Who controls the budget: The legislature or the executive? IMF Working Paper no. 05/115. Washington, DC: International Monetary Fund.

Mann, F. A. 1960. *Money in international public law.* Leyden: Hague Academy of International Law.

Mathä, T. 2003. What to expect of the euro? Analysing price differences of individual products in Luxembourg and its surrounding regions. Paper presented at the 43rd Congress of the European Regional Science Association. 27–30 August, Jyväskylä, Finland.

Mongelli, F. P., and J. L. Vega. 2006. What effects is EMU having on the euro area and its member countries? ECB Working Paper no. 599. Frankfurt: European Central Bank, March.

Munchau, W. 2008. The case for a European rescue plan. *Financial Times.* October 8. Available at: http://www.ft.com.

Prior-Wandesforde, R., and G. Hacche. 2005. European meltdown? Europe fiddles as Rome burns, *Macro: European economics.* HSBC Global Research Report. London: The Hongkong and Shanghai Banking Corporation, July.

Rattso, J. 2003. Fiscal federalism or confederation in the European Union: The challenge of the common pool problem. Norwegian University of Science and Technology, Department of Economics. Manuscript, September.

Rodrik, D. 1996. Why do more open economies have bigger governments? NBER Working Paper no. 5537. Cambridge, MA: National Bureau of Economic Research, April.

————. 2002. Feasible globalizations. NBER Working Paper no. 9129. Cambridge, MA: National Bureau of Economic Research, August.

Sala-i-Martin, X., and J. Sachs. 1992. Fiscal federalism and optimum currency areas: Evidence for Europe from the United States. In *Establishing a central bank: Issues in Europe and lessons from the US,* ed. M. Canzoneri, V. Grilli, and P. Mason, 195–227. Cambridge: Cambridge University Press.

Scott, H. 1998. When the euro falls apart. *International Finance* 1 (2): 207–28.

Standard and Poor's. 2005. *Breaking up is hard to do: Rating implications of EU states abandoning the euro.* London: Standard and Poor's.

Von Hagen, J. 1992. Budgeting procedures and fiscal performance in the European Communities. European Economy Economic Paper no. 96. Brussels: European Commission.

Zingales, L. 2008. Why Paulson is wrong. *Economists' Voice* 5 (5): art. 2.

Comment   Martin Feldstein

I'm pleased to be a discussant of Barry Eichengreen's chapter about whether the euro and the European Economic and Monetary Union (EMU) will survive.

Before turning to the substance of this interesting chapter, I should say something regarding the views about the euro that I expressed before its launch a decade ago (Feldstein 1992, 1997, 2007). Contrary to what many people think, I did not express doubts about whether the EMU could be launched or whether it could survive. My concern in those papers was that the single currency would have undesirable long-term economic and political effects, including higher average unemployment in the euro zone and a weakening of the political alliance between Europe and the United States. I shall not pursue those ideas here.

Barry has given us a careful and balanced analysis of the possibility that one or more members of the EMU will leave the monetary union in the coming decade. He concludes that one country leaving in the next ten years is unlikely, and a complete breakdown of the EMU during that period is even less likely. He notes that it is difficult to predict beyond ten years but suggests that a political marriage that lasts ten years is likely to keep going.

I will begin by discussing Barry's analysis and then go beyond his framework to consider two other reasons why one or more members of the EMU might choose to abandon the euro.

The draft that Barry circulated at the conference was dated May 2008,

Martin Feldstein is the George F. Baker Professor of Economics at Harvard University and president emeritus of the National Bureau of Economic Research.

This is a comment on a paper with the same title presented by Barry Eichengreen at National Bureau of Economic Research Conference in Milan, Italy, on October 17, 2008 (revised November 2008).

indicating that he prepared these remarks well in advance of the meeting. But as he noted in his presentation, the current financial and economic crisis may provide a severe test of the strength of the monetary union. However, nothing Barry said in his presentation makes me think that he changed his mind because of the current situation. I'll return to that at the end of my remarks.

The potential exit of an EMU member is not just a hypothetical question. The interest rate differentials among the ten-year government bonds of the EMU countries show that financial markets consider it a real possibility. The interest rate on the German bond is the lowest. But the ten-year government bonds of Greece and Portugal pay over 100 basis points more than German bonds, and even Italian bonds pay nearly 100 basis points more—indicating that the markets think there is a risk that during the next decade, those countries will not be able to pay in euros—either because they are insolvent, or because they have left the EMU.

Barry's analysis proceeds along two basic tracks. First, he considers whether it could be in a country's rational self-interest to leave the EMU. Second, he considers the barriers—technical, legal, and political—that might cause it to stay in the EMU, even if the government of that country thought it would be desirable to leave.

I will start with the latter issues. Barry notes that many previous currency unions or single currency states have broken up (the Austro-Hungarian empire, the Soviet Union, the Czech-Slovak split). But he then goes on to argue that those splits occurred either at a much earlier time in history, when financial systems were simpler, or in countries with simpler financial systems. He also notes that the exit by one EMU country might not be by mutual agreement, adding treaty complications. But in the end, he concludes that splitting a country out of the EMU would be possible, although the leaver would have a diminished political status in the European Union.

Having set those issues aside, I can focus on why a country might decide to leave the EMU. Of course, countries don't decide. Political leaders decide. I will come back to that important distinction.

Rational Optimal Policy

I will start as Barry does by asking whether it could be in a country's interest to leave the EMU. Barry focuses on the desire of a country to pursue a different monetary policy. He notes that a country with slow growth, high unemployment, and a large trade deficit—he gives Greece, Italy, and/or Portugal as current examples—might be tempted to leave in order to ease monetary conditions and to devalue its currency. Barry explains why that might be a foolish decision, because leaving the euro zone might lead to higher real interest rates and higher inflation.

Conversely, a country that wants a tougher monetary policy—that could be Germany, if some future majority in the European Central Bank (ECB) is less concerned about inflation than Germany is at that time—could leave the EMU in order to pursue a tighter policy. Barry explains the risks of that strategy—particularly, the capital inflow that might occur—but recognizes that the economic consequences for a strong country leaving the EMU would be less adverse than for a weak-currency country.

Although the problem of a one-size-fits-all monetary policy is the most obvious reason for a country to want to leave the EMU, it is not the only one.

The Stability and Growth Pact that limits fiscal deficits could be another reason why a country might want to leave the EMU. In a serious downturn, a country may wish to pursue a traditional Keynesian policy of fiscal stimulus. Although the Stability and Growth Pact may be elastic enough to permit some of that stimulus, a country may feel constrained from acting as aggressively as it wants. It is certainly possible that the current downturn—especially if it becomes very deep and very long—will provide a fiscal challenge to EMU solidarity that has not occurred during the past decade.

It is of course also possible that a substantial number of countries will decide at some future tome to pursue a very expansionary fiscal policy and that the Economic and Financial Affairs Council (ECOFIN) will choose to allow that because of a significant economic downturn. A country that is opposed to such large fiscal deficits and that sees itself hurt by the resulting rise in euro interest rates and by the induced change in the value of the euro might feel that it would rather pursue a tighter fiscal policy in order to avoid those exchange rate and interest rate consequences and would leave the EMU in order to do so.

The current financial crisis raises another problem—the lack of a clear national lender of last resort. It remains to be seen how willing the ECB will be to provide national central banks with the volume of euros needed to be a full lender of last resort. If a country sees its banks failing because the national bank cannot create as much currency as it would have been able to before the EMU, that would be a further reason for a country to consider leaving the EMU.

There is one additional reason that might apply to leaving the European Union as well as the EMU. As of now, taxation is a national responsibility within the European Union. Income redistribution among the EU countries is thus relatively limited. But there is frequent discussion in some circles that this should be a matter for the European Union, opening the way to substantial income redistribution. High-income countries might find this reason enough to want out.

Although each of these four reasons—monetary, fiscal, lender of last resort, and taxation—might be enough to cause a country to want to leave the EMU, Barry might of course be able to explain in each case that doing so would be a mistake. But the economic officials in the EMU countries might not understand the economy as well as Barry does, or they may have a quite different view of what drives inflation, exchange rates, and other key variables. We certainly know that thinking about those key relations has changed substantially, even in the United States, during the past few decades. So, officials might be provoked by any of these four reasons to believe that withdrawing from the EMU would be helpful, even if the majority of economists at the conference would disagree.

Threats

But for a moment, let's assume that the government officials fully understand the adverse consequences of leaving the EMU and do not want to do so. These officials may nevertheless not like the way policy is going in the EMU—monetary policy at the ECB or fiscal policy because of an inadequately (or excessively) permissive ECOFIN. That may cause the country to threaten that it will leave the EMU if policy is not changed. That is clearly a substantial risk if the country is Germany or France. But even if it is one of the smaller countries, it might be a serious threat, because it could be seen as the beginning of an unraveling of the EMU. So, either type of country could make the threat in hopes that the threat would be enough to cause their EMU colleagues to agree to their desired change in policy.

The risk of course is that the other countries may not be intimidated. The threatening country would then have to choose between accepting a humiliating defeat or leaving the EMU.

Decisions of Politicians

Finally, I want to return to the idea that policy decisions are made by individual politicians or groups of politicians who are motivated by their own self-interest rather than by a pure interest in the national well-being. Democratic procedures are of course supposed to align the self-interest of politicians and the well-being of at least a majority of the public. But that only works in a complex area such as economic policy if the public is sufficiently wise, technically sophisticated, and farsighted.

If not, and this is certainly a more reasonable description, a politician could make the case for a policy that would help him or her or his or her party to get elected, even if it is not in the long-run national interest.

Here's an example of how self-interested politicians could lead to an EMU withdrawal by building on existing voter attitudes. A recent official Eurobarometer survey indicated that 95 percent of respondents in the twelve euro countries believe that the EMU has raised prices (Lane 2006). In Italy, it was 97 percent, and in Germany, 91 percent. If at some future time inflation is rising rapidly, it might occur to some political group to argue that if they are elected, they will bring down prices or inflation by taking the country in question out of the EMU.

Or, to take a different example, what if the current economic downturn and financial crisis becomes very severe, producing very high unemployment? It is certainly possible that some politicians will argue out of a mixture of conviction and self-interest that if elected to a position of control, they would take their country out of the EMU, permitting the combination of easy money, fiscal deficits, and lender-of-last resort assistance to banks to revive the economy.

It is important in this context that the support for the EMU, and even for the European Union, is generally very weak. For example, when the Eurobarometer recently asked French respondents how attached they are to the European Union, only 16 percent said that they are "very attached." In contrast, 56 percent of that group said they are very attached to France as a nation.

Barry's chapter reports a similar lack of support for the EMU among respondents in many countries. When asked in the 2006 Eurobarometer survey whether they thought EMU membership had been to the advantage of their country, only 40 percent of Italians said yes. The proportion was similar in Portugal and even smaller in the Netherlands and Greece. In Germany, it was only about 45 percent. Only four countries showed really substantial belief—more than 60 percent—that EMU membership had been advantageous: Ireland, Luxembourg, Austria, and Finland.

Similarly, when asked whether they had confidence in the ECB, only 44 percent of Italians said yes.

In short, after a decade of experience with membership in the EMU, the public support for EMU is weak at best. A political leader or political party could use this weak support to promote its political power by promising to withdraw the country from the EMU or by saying that they will threaten to withdraw if the other member countries do not agree to their proposed policy changes.

The currently developing economic crisis may provide a significant test of these temptations.

References

Feldstein, M. S. 1992. Europe's monetary union: The case against EMU. *Economist.* June 13.
———. 1997. The political economy of the European Economic and Monetary Union: Political sources of an economic liability. *Journal of Economic Perspectives* 11 (4): 23–42.
———. 2007. EMU and international conflict. *Foreign Affairs.* November/ December.
Lane, P. R. 2006. The real effects of European Monetary Union. *Journal of Economic Perspectives* 20 (4): 47–66.

The Euro and Structural Reforms

Alberto Alesina, Silvia Ardagna, and Vincenzo Galasso

2.1 Introduction

One of the arguments in favor of the introduction of the common currency area in Europe was that it would have pressured member countries to improve their macroeconomic policy and pursue "structural reforms," the latter being defined as labor and product markets' liberalization and deregulation. Has it worked? Have members of the euro area had a better policy performance after adopting the common currency?

High-inflation countries have gained a sound monetary policy with the adoption of the common currency and the European Central Bank. The euro does not have any direct implication for fiscal policy,[1] but its adoption was accompanied first by the imposition of converge criteria on budget deficits and public debt and then by the Stability and Growth Pact (SGP), which established some rules about deficits. For some high-debt countries (e.g., Italy, Belgium, and Greece), the threat of being left out served as an incentive to initiate fiscal adjustments. However, once the euro was intro-

Alberto Alesina is the Nathaniel Ropes Professor of Political Economy at Harvard University and a research associate of the National Bureau of Economic Research. Silvia Ardagna is assistant professor of economics at Harvard University. Vincenzo Galasso is associate professor of economics at Bocconi University.

Prepared for the National Bureau of Economic Research and conference on "Europe and the Euro," October 17 and 18, 2008. We thank Olivier Blanchard, Francesco Caselli, Francesco Giavazzi, Guido Tabellini, Silvana Tenreyro, and our discussant Otmar Issing for very useful comments. We also thank Carlo Prato and Roberto Robatto for excellent research assistantship.

1. One possible indirect channel is through an interest rate effect caused by very large public debt of some (large) countries, but this effect is likely to be small.

duced, the threat of exclusion vanished,[2] large deficits reappeared in several member countries, and the SGP was widely violated: chapter 8 in this volume by Fatas and Mihov discusses fiscal policy in the euro area. In this chapter, we focus on structural reforms.

Why should joining the common monetary area accelerate and facilitate structural reforms? We can think of a few sound economic arguments and some wishful thinking. On the former (and more solid) ground, more competition due to the single market might increase the cost of regulation in the product markets. The protection of insider firms and workers would become more costly and more visible to consumers and voters. For example, imagine a country that protects a national airline at the expense of a low-cost one that flies in the rest of the union: the costs for the travelers and taxpayers would be large and obvious. This would also weaken the insiders of the protected national airline, from union workers to pilots to managers accumulating losses at the expenses of taxpayers. Of course, this argument presupposes that the euro per se is a necessary condition for having a truly common market, a point which requires discussion. Second, the elimination of strategic devaluations shuts down a (possibly temporary) adjustment channel for a country losing competitiveness. In the product market, this means that firms and their organizations may demand deregulation of the market for inputs such as nontradable services, energy, and transportation to contain costs. Also, if real wage growth is out of line with productivity, a nominal devaluation is not available any more as a solution (or a palliative). This creates incentives for countries to free their labor markets from regulations that create obstacles for real wage adjustments and labor mobility and flexibility. In fact, those who were skeptical about the introduction of the euro (see Obstfeld [1997], for instance) raised precisely the issue of real wage adjustment and labor market rigidities: the elimination of those was seen as a condition difficult to implement but necessary for the euro to survive. It is interesting to note that the pre-euro economic debate focused much more on labor market reforms and much less, or not at all, on product markets, while in reality, as we will see later, the latter markets were liberalized first.

The wishful thinking part was the rhetoric often too common in Europe, according to which any step toward integration is "by definition" good and brings about all sorts of wonderful achievements for the continent. More seriously, many commentators viewed the adoption of the euro as essentially a political move, a step toward some sort of United States of Europe. Jacques Delors is quoted as saying, "Obsession about budgetary constraints means that the people forget too often about the political objectives of the

---

2. See chapter 1 by Barry Eichengreen in this volume on the low probability of a collapse of the euro system.

European constitution. The argument in favor of the single currency should be based on the desire to live together in peace."[3]

When we started this research project, we were rather skeptical that we would find any effect of the euro on structural reforms. English-speaking countries such as the United States, New Zealand, the United Kingdom, and Ireland had started major deregulation processes way before the birth of the euro; some Nordic countries (in and out of the euro area) had followed more recently as a result of poor economic performance in the 1990s; and some laggards such as Greece, Belgium, Italy, France, and Germany were struggling to keep the pace. The euro did not seem to have much to do with this timing. Much to our surprise, the empirical results were different. We uncovered significant correlations between the speed of adoption of structural reforms in the goods market and the adoption of the euro. With respect to labor markets, the picture is more nuanced and complex. We find no evidence that the adoption of the euro has accelerated labor market reforms in the primary market. This result does not imply that *no* labor market reforms have occurred in Europe but rather means that the adoption of the euro has not accelerated reforms. However, in several countries in Europe, we now have a secondary market of labor with temporary and much more flexible contracts. (See Bertola [2008] for an assessment of the role of the euro on labor market outcomes.) We still do not have good data on a comparable international basis to examine the evolution of the markets. Indirectly, however, one could look at whether nominal wages have reacted more or less to past inflation and whether there has been wage moderation and therefore a smaller second-round inflationary effect. We find that in countries preparing to enter the euro during the period from 1993 to 1998, there have indeed been signs of substantial wage moderation and a slowing down of the adjustment of nominal wages to past inflation. This is likely to have been part of the macroeconomic efforts to meet the criteria to enter the monetary union. After the adoption of the euro, wage moderation seems to have lost some steam, perhaps as a result of "fatigue." However, in certain countries such as Germany, wage moderation continued until recently. In others, such as Italy and France, the evidence is mixed.

We also investigated the sequencing of goods and labor market reforms. The former have generally come sooner than the latter. This important issue has been raised by Blanchard and Giavazzi (2003) and empirically investigated by Fiori et al. (2007). Our results show that the deregulation of labor markets is made easier by product market deregulation. However, there are features of the labor market that seem to be useful preconditions for product market deregulation: namely, the reduction of firing costs, and even more,

3. See Eichengreen (chapter 1 in this volume) for the original citation. See Alesina and Perotti (2004) for a criticism of EU rhetoric.

the existence of unemployment benefits. This makes sense, as the deregulation of product markets implies labor reallocations across firms and sectors, which require some labor market flexibility; any may lead, at least in the short run, to higher unemployment.

We should be clear from the start that we are considering a handful of countries: eleven original members of the euro area (all but Luxembourg), a few EU but not euro members, and the remaining Organization for Economic Cooperation and Development (OECD) countries. We are also looking at a one-shot event: the introduction of the euro. It is possible that a certain timing of reforms across countries may lead to a spurious correlation that happens to coincide with the adoption of the euro.[4] Or, it may be possible that it is not the euro per se but the membership in the European Union that creates incentives for product market deregulation, and there are simply not enough countries that are members of the European Union but not members of the monetary union to identify this difference.

Finally, the decision to adopt the euro is clearly not exogenous, and we try to address issues of endogeneity. The recent literature on currency areas (Alesina and Barro 2002; Alesina, Barro, and Tenreyro 2002) offers insight about instruments that may have led to the decision of adoption. One should be aware, however, that various countries adopted the euro for different reasons. In some cases, it was done mostly for anchoring purposes (e.g., in Italy), while in other cases, the intention was to be at the core of the European integration process (e.g., in France and Germany). In fact, one theme of the pre-euro debate amongst economists was, what is the benefit for Germany? There seemed to be no big economic gains for this country, which seemed to provide the service of being an anti-inflation anchor without receiving an obvious benefit in return. However, the benefit was political. To put it differently, the decision was partly dictated by noneconomic factors, hard to capture with an instrument.

We are not the first to investigate the relationship between the adoption of the euro and structural reforms. The International Monetary Fund (2004) suggests that belonging to the European Union accelerates the reform process in the product market but has no conclusive effect on the labor market. Yet, this paper fails to disentangle the effects of the adoption of the euro and of the European single market (ESM). Hoj et al. (2006) provide supporting evidence to these results. They find a positive effect of the ESM on product market reforms—particularly in the transportation and telecommunication sectors—but no impact on the labor market. However, they do not directly test for the effects of the euro. Duval and Elmeskov (2005) instead investi-

---

4. For instance, some directives of the European Commission regarding some sectors decided in the mid-1990s implied actions to be taken in 1998 and 2000 for all members of the European Union. This timing coincided with the adoption of the euro. Note, however, that these directives do not apply only to EMU countries but to all the EU countries. Nevertheless, this timing may imply some spurious correlation.

gate this issue using a database of OECD countries in which they analyze large structural reforms in the labor and product market. Stacking together these (different) reform measures, they conclude that a lack of monetary autonomy, which is defined as belonging to the European Monetary Union (EMU) or to other fixed-exchange rate regimes,[5] can have a negative, significant impact of the probability of undertaking large structural reforms, but only in large economies. In a database of 178 countries on a longer, yet less-recent, time span (1970 to 2000), Belke, Herz, and Vogel (2005) obtain different results. They find that a higher degree of monetary authority independence, as measured by an index of exchange rate flexibility, has a positive impact on an overall index of reform effort, especially in the financial and banking sectors. They find no robust evidence for an index of market regulation in the sample of OECD countries.

This chapter is organized as follows. In section 2.2, we discuss the rationale for which the euro might favor structural reforms. Section 2.3 presents our results on product market deregulation. Section 2.4 discusses results on labor market reforms, while the last section contains the conclusion.

2.2   Structural Reforms and the Euro

2.2.1   Why Should the Euro Matter?

The adoption of the euro and the implementation of structural reforms in the labor and product markets seem at first glance to be two largely unrelated events. However, the euro has always been portrayed as the final stage of a process of economic integration among the country members of the European Union that involved more trade, more labor, and capital mobility: in a word, fewer restrictions on the mobility of goods, services, and people. To achieve this goal, the introduction of the ESM in 1992 established a legal framework to increase trade and competition in the European Union and allowed the European Commission to rule against state aid or against monopolistic practices to all EU members. Thus, it seems quite plausible that the ESM would have had an effect on product and labor market reform. But the subsequent adoption of the euro did not have direct legal effects on competition policies. Did it have economic implications on them?

Several commentators have discussed various reasons why the adoption of the euro may facilitate, or on the contrary, create obstacles to the adoption of structural reforms.

On the proreform side, one may argue that entrance into the EMU acts as an external constraint that pushes countries to reform. By relinquishing the control of the monetary policy to an external authority (the ECB), mem-

---

5. For instance, Austria is classified under a de facto fixed-exchange regime with the deutsche-mark, even before the EMU.

ber countries become unable to use their monetary policy to accommodate negative shocks. This might have created incentives to liberalize the labor and product market in order to rely more heavily on market-based adjustments that take place through changes in prices and wages (Bean 1998; Duval and Elmeskov 2005).

A single currency may also increase price transparency and therefore facilitate trade. A larger European market increases competition and makes it more difficult for domestic monopolists to protect their rents. It is certainly true that Europe does not have a truly common market in every sector, especially in the service sector, where domestic protection, direct or indirect, is still widespread. Yet, the degree of competition and integration in the European product market has largely increased in the last two decades. To the extent that a larger common market makes it more difficult for local monopolists to dominate local markets, this might have created pressures to deregulate product markets. Yet, is this the result of the euro increasing the trading opportunities across member countries, or is it simply the impact of the ESM? In the empirical analysis, we try to disentangle these two effects.

The question of whether a monetary union is necessary for a common market and whether it reduces trade barriers across countries and facilitates commerce in goods, services, and financial assets has recently received much attention following a provocative paper by Rose (2000). This paper found that monetary unions have an extremely large effect on trade amongst members. Critics argued (amongst other things) that most monetary unions in Rose's sample involved very small countries and that the effects would have been much smaller in the euro area, an issue which chapter 5 by Frankel and Stein in this volume tackles.[6] According to their chapter, the adoption of the euro appears to have facilitated trade among member countries, even though the order of magnitude of this effect is on a different scale relative to Rose (2000) and seems more realistic. Research applied to Canada and the United States showed that trade between Canadian provinces, even ones that were thousands of miles apart, was easier than trade between U.S. states and bordering Canadian provinces, suggesting that a single currency matters for trade.[7]

Note that these proreform arguments based on the role of trade imply that most action should take place in the tradable sector, where competition becomes stronger, rather than in the nontradable service sector. But firms in the tradable sector may react to an increase in competition by translating this pressure upstream onto the intermediate goods producers—and hence only on the service sector—and onto the labor market (see Nicoletti and Scarpetta 2005).

6. Alesina and Barro (2002); Alesina, Barro, and Tenreyro (2002); Persson (2001); Thom and Walsh (2002); and Tenreyro (2007) address theoretically and empirically a host of issues relating the effect of monetary unions on trade.
7. See, for instance, McCallum (1995).

The economic literature also provides some arguments suggesting that the euro may hinder structural reforms. Saint-Paul and Bentolila (2000) argue that under the EMS, the up-front cost of structural reforms may increase. Some labor market reforms may have positive long-term effects but entail a negative short-term impact in terms of higher unemployment. For this reason, several commentators have favored a two-handed approach: structural reform on the supply side, accompanied by expansionary aggregate demand policies. Under the euro, this two-handed policy may be more difficult, because aggregate demand is more constrained at the national level, and monetary policy is in the hands of the ECB. A similar argument may apply to pension reforms. They may provide long-term savings for the social security funds but may also imply short-term budget deficits, which may violate the limits imposed by the Stability and Growth Pact.

Obstfeld (1997), in his early and wide-ranging review of the pros and cons of the euro, emphasized that the euro would eliminate a major channel of adjustment to macroeconomic shocks—namely, a nominal devaluation of the exchange rate—to regain competitiveness by reducing real wages for given (rigid) nominal wages. He suggested that this might put pressure on the unions to be more flexible about allowing adjustments to nominal and real wages and argued that this was a necessary condition for the euro to survive. The pessimists argued that unions would not be so flexible in Europe and that on the contrary, they would fuel political momentum against the euro project, leading to its collapse.

Reality turned out to be more creative than economists' predictions. There have certainly been complaints and political rumblings against the euro, mainly in countries that felt they were especially in need of devaluation, as chapter 1 by Barry Eichengreen in this volume documents, but the euro has not collapsed and does not seem even close to doing so. Sure enough, the political battle with the unions for labor market reforms in many countries is still in place, and the next few years may be critical.

Because in many European countries the labor unions have effectively become unions of old workers, public employees, and pensioners (in Italy, for instance, the majority of union members are retired), it should not come as a surprise that they tolerated or even endorsed the introduction of temporary job contracts, in which young, entry-level workers would be hired without much or any protection at low wages and could be fired at will by the employers. In exchange, they kept a very high degree of protection for older workers in the traditional labor markets. Spain, Italy, and France are prime examples.[8] In Italy, around a third of the newly created jobs are temporary contracts, and in Spain, the percentage reaches 50 percent. In the

---

8. See Saint-Paul (1996, 2000) for an early discussion of reforms that avoid touching the interests on incumbent workers and focus only on new entrants and also for a comparison of French and Spanish early reform attempts.

short run, this has worked in terms of increasing employment. In the last ten years in Europe, about 18 million jobs have been created—just as many as in the United States. But in the medium run, lacking further reforms, this situation may become explosive, because such a two-tier market might be unsustainable.

One may argue that as these temporary workers became a large minority of the workforce, they will put pressure on the workers in the traditional sector to abandon some of their privileges, creating a momentum in favor of deregulation of the entire labor market.[9] However, there is another possibility. These temporary workers may demand to enter the traditional labor market, with all its implied protection and rules against firing. If all these workers are simply shifted into the traditionally rigid labor market of union-protected elderly workers, Europe will move back ten years. In summary, labor markets in several European countries are then in a precarious position: half-baked reforms have created a two-tier labor market that is economically inefficient and politically unsustainable.

Finally, this discussion relates to issues of sequencing of reform; that is, is it more politically feasible to move first with product market deregulation or with labor market deregulation? Blanchard and Giavazzi (2003) argued that European countries should first deregulate the product market, claiming that this would make labor market reforms easier. The reasoning is that product market regulation creates rents, which are enjoyed both by incumbent firms and by labor unions. Unions would strenuously oppose labor market reforms that reduce their rents. Product market reforms would curtail rents, reducing the benefits for the unions from the status quo in the labor market and thus reducing their opposition to labor market reforms.

The argument is compelling, and as we will see next, European countries have indeed moved faster on product market liberalizations than on labor market ones. There is, however, one important caveat. Deregulation of product markets sometimes implies closures or reductions in size of incumbent firms in favor of new entrants, and more generally, reallocation of labor force from firm to firm and sector to sector. This process of "creative destruction" generates temporary unemployment. In countries in which firing is costly, if not virtually impossible, this process is difficult. In this respect, the elimination or reduction of firing costs is then a prerequisite in order for product market liberalization to work. The elimination of firing costs requires some well-designed system of unemployment compensation, but not all European countries have this—a case in point being Italy. Inefficiencies in the system of unemployment compensation give the unions ammunition to defend existing jobs and oppose restructuring. So in this respect, a labor market reform that reduces firing costs and introduces unemployment compensation systems seems like a prerequisite for a well-functioning product market

9. See Saint-Paul (1999) for a formalization of this argument.

deregulation. Denmark is an example of a country in which labor market reforms have moved exactly in this direction.[10]

2.2.2   When Do Reforms Occur?

In addition to the adoption of the euro, other factors may create incentives for governments to adopt structural reforms. On the one hand, one needs to take such factors into account as controls, and they are interesting in their own right. One commonly held view is that governments reform when they are in a crisis and when they have their backs against the wall. For the case of fiscal reforms, one can easily identify a crisis as a runaway deficit, and in fact, Alesina, Ardagna, and Trebbi (2006) show evidence consistent with this hypothesis. Using a large sample of OECD and developing countries, they show that fiscal adjustments and stabilization of inflation are more likely to occur when this kind of macroeconomic imbalance degenerates into a crisis of runaway (hyper) inflation or of very high budget deficits.[11] The case of structural reforms is more complicated. The lack of reforms may lead to a slow decline that does not degenerate into a sudden crisis. However, when the decline, evaluated in terms of prolonged periods of low growth, begins to become front page news, then reform blockers may lose some of their political clout. Recent discussions of relative decline in Europe (and particularly of Italy) may be leading in that direction.[12] However, the recent financial crisis may have generated a political movement in some countries against deregulation and in favor of a return to easy and long-term state intervention. At the time of this writing (October 2008), it is hard to predict how much the tides will move toward reregulation.

Much has also been written about the political cycle and reforms.[13] Conventional wisdom suggests that governments should not introduce reforms close to elections and that in general, liberalizing and/or fiscally conservative reforms lead to electoral losses. Thus, if a government has a chance of introducing reforms, it ought to do so soon after it is appointed, for two possible reasons: first, to take advantage of the honeymoon period, and second, because the short-term costs of reforms will be gone before the next election. We examine the timing of reforms in relation to the electoral cycle, and we do find some evidence that reforms tend to occur at the beginning of a new term. As for the likelihood that the reforming government will lose the next election, one has to maintain a healthy dose of skepticism with

10. See, for instance, Alesina and Giavazzi (2006) for some discussion of the Danish case and the applicability to other European countries.

11. See Alesina and Drazen (1991) and Drazen and Grilli (1993) for models consistent with this hypothesis, and see Drazen and Easterly (2001) for empirical evidence. See also Drazen (2000) for an extensive discussion of the political economy of stabilization policies.

12. See Alesina and Giavazzi (2006) for a recent discussion of potential European decline due to insufficient reforms.

13. See Alesina, Roubini, and Cohen (1997) for work on the political business cycles, and see Brender and Drazen (2005) for a political budget-cycle model.

regard to conventional wisdom. For instance, Alesina, Perotti, and Tavares (1998) show that governments that engaged in sharp fiscal adjustments have often been reappointed.

2.3   Product Markets: The Evidence

2.3.1   The Data on Regulation

We use yearly data on twenty-one OECD countries (Australia, Austria, Belgium, Canada, Switzerland, Germany, Denmark, Spain, Finland, France, the United Kingdom, Greece, Ireland, Italy, Japan, the Netherlands, New Zealand, Norway, Portugal, Sweden, and the United States), covering a maximum time span from 1975 to 2003. The data come from a variety of different sources. In the next sections, we describe the regulatory, macroeconomic, and political data; the appendix includes the exact definition and source of each variable we use in the empirical analysis.

We use time-varying measures of regulation for seven nonmanufacturing industries in twenty-one OECD countries for the period from 1975 to 2003. The data have been collected by Conway and Nicoletti (2007) from both national sources (by means of specific surveys) and published sources and are described in detail by Nicoletti and Scarpetta (2003). The regulatory indicators measure, on a scale from 0 to 6 (from least to most restrictive), restrictions on competition and private governance in the following industries: electricity and gas supply, road freight, air passenger transport, rail transport, post, and telecommunications (fixed and mobile).

The summary index of regulation includes information on entry barriers, public ownership, the market share of the dominant players (in the telephone, gas, and railroad sectors), and price controls (in the road freight industry). Entry barriers cover legal limitations on the number of companies in potentially competitive markets and rules on vertical integration of network industries. The barriers to entry indicator takes a value of 0 when entry is free (i.e., a situation with three or more competitors and with complete ownership separation of natural monopoly and competitive segments of the industry) and a value of 6 when entry is severely restricted (i.e., situations with legal monopoly and full vertical integration in network industries or restrictive licensing in other industries). Intermediate values represent partial liberalization of entry (e.g., legal duopoly, mere accounting separation of natural monopoly and competitive segments). Public ownership measures the share of equity owned by central or municipal governments in firms of a given sector. The two polar cases are no public ownership (a value of 0 for the indicator) and full public ownership (a value of 6 for the indicator). Whenever data are available (i.e., telecoms, air transport), intermediate values of the public ownership indicator are calculated as an increasing function of the actual share of equity held by the government in the dominant firm. In some cases (e.g., the energy industries), a simpler scale is used, pointing to full or majority control by the government (a value of 6), various degrees of mixed public/private ownership (intermediate values), and marginal public share or full private ownership (a value of 0).

The construction of the indicators by the OECD involved the following steps. First, they separated indicators for barriers to entry, public ownership, and market share of new entrants, and price controls were created at the finest available level of industry disaggregation (e.g., mobile and fixed telephony). Second, they aggregated indicators at the industry level, taking simple averages or revenue-weighted averages (when aggregating horizontal segments of industries, such as mobile and fixed telephony). Third, they computed the index of overall regulation by averaging, in each of the seven industries, the indicators of barriers to entry, public ownership, market share of new entrants, and price controls.

Here, we used simple averaging of the indices to reach the level of industry aggregation for which macroeconomic data (value added, labor costs, and employment) are available. More specifically, we have aggregated the regulation indices for the seven sectors in three broader sectors: energy (electricity and gas), communication (telecommunications and post), and transportation (airlines, road freight, and railways).

In our benchmark regressions, we use the regulatory indicator REG, which includes all dimensions except public ownership. In the sensitivity analysis, we also consider three other indicators of regulation: the overall indicator, including all the regulation dimensions; one indicator that summarizes barriers to entry (comprising legal restrictions and vertical integration); and one indicator that includes only public ownership information.

In the augmented regressions, we introduced two additional sectors: retail and professionals. Data on regulation in these two sectors in twenty-one OECD countries are available only for two years: 1996 (for professionals) or 1998 (for retail) and 2003. These regulatory indicators range from 0 to 6 (from least to most restrictive). In the retail sector, they capture three components: barrier to entry, operational restrictions, and price control. For the professionals, indicators measure entry regulations and conduct regulations in four sectors: accounting, architecture, engineering, and legal services. For a detailed description, see Conway and Nicoletti (2007).

2.3.2   The Macroeconomic and Political Data

The economic data on value added, labor costs, and total employment at the country-sector-year level for the period from 1975 to 2003 come from the OECD STructural ANalysis (STAN) database for industrial analysis, revision 3 (ISIC rev. 3). This database covers both services and manufacturing sectors for the OECD countries. The macroeconomic data for the non-manufacturing sectors for which we have indices of regulation are available at the following level of industry aggregation: (a) electricity, gas, and water;

(b) communications and posts; and (c) transport and storage. From now on, we will name the sectors defined in (a), (b), and (c) as energy, communications, and transport, respectively. We merge the data from the STAN data set with the database containing the regulation indices. As mentioned previously, because data on value added, labor costs, and total employment are not available for each single industry for which regulation indices exist, we mapped the industry-level regulatory indicators into the nonmanufacturing aggregates covered by the STAN database.

Macroeconomic data at the country-year level are from the OECD *Economic Outlook* number 80 database. Finally, the Database of Political Institutions (DPI) of the World Bank, compiled by Beck et al. (2001) and updated in 2004, contains all the political variables employed in the analysis.

2.3.3   Patterns of Product Market Deregulation

Beginning in the late 1970s, OECD countries have initiated a broad-based process of deregulation. They were not all starting from the same initial position, however. Generally speaking, Anglo-Saxon countries (the United States, in particular) were less regulated than continental European countries, and they started to deregulate early: the United States and the United Kingdom in the early 1980s, New Zealand in the late 1970s, and Ireland in the late 1980s. In the last two decades, there has been convergence: the difference in the degree of regulation of product markets (at least for the sector for which we have data) is lower now than it was in the early 1980s. The laggards are catching on.

In what follows, we divide the countries into three groups: (a) those that adopted the euro (the EMU group); these countries are Austria, Belgium, Finland, France, Germany, Ireland, Italy, the Netherlands, Portugal, and Spain; (b) those that are part of the European Union but did not adopt the euro (the European single market group, or ESM); these countries are Denmark, Sweden, and the United Kingdom; and (c) those that are not in the European Union and obviously do not have the euro; these countries are Australia, Canada, Japan, New Zealand, Norway, Switzerland, and the United States.

Figure 2.1 shows that all sectors have deregulated—communications more than any other and energy less than any other. Figure 2.2 shows that non-EU countries have deregulated less, but as we said before, they were starting from a much lower average level of regulation. The single market group has deregulated most, but in the period from 1999 to 2003, the EU countries have picked up momentum, having done very little until then, especially given their high initial level of regulation. With the exception of Ireland, very few EU countries did much in terms of deregulation in the 1980s, so leaving Ireland out, the pattern for the EU countries would be even more skewed toward the recent period. The ESM group includes the

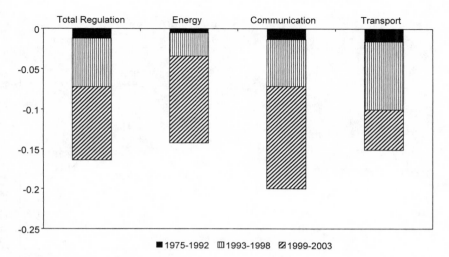

Fig. 2.1   Deregulation by sector

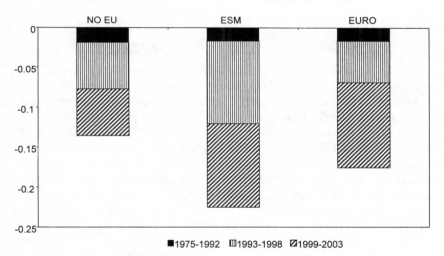

Fig. 2.2   Product market deregulation

United Kingdom, which started deregulation early, as did other English-speaking countries, and also includes Nordic countries, which have deregulated quite a lot, and this shows in these pictures. Figure 2.3 shows some pattern of convergence in the deregulation process: since 1999, the countries that deregulated more were clearly those that had higher degrees of regulation until the mid-1990s.

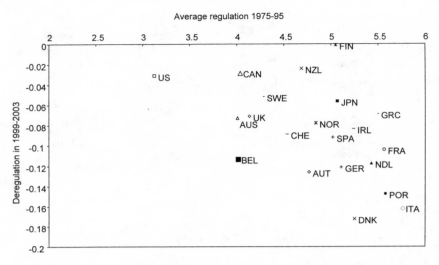

Fig. 2.3   Convergence in regulation

2.3.4   The Euro and Product Market Reforms: Benchmark Specifications

All our regressions in this section and in the tables discussed in the next sections are estimated with generalized least squares, allowing for heteroschedasticity of the error term; they include the lagged value of the left-hand side variable, as well as country, sector, and time dummies. Sensitivity analysis confirms that all the results are robust to controlling for country-sector-specific dummies, time trends, and country-specific time trends.

In table 2.1, we estimate our basic specification of the level of regulation (measured by the indicator variable REG). The first three columns include data on the three sectors of transportation, energy, and communications; columns (4) through (6) also include the two additional sectors: retail and professionals. We measure the impact of the single market program and of the euro on regulation with the dummy variables ESM and EMU. Specifically, ESM is an indicator variable equal to 1 from 1993 onward for all countries that belong to the European Union (i.e., Austria, Belgium, Denmark, Germany, Finland, France, Greece, Ireland, Italy, the Netherlands, Portugal, Spain, Sweden, and the United Kingdom) and equal to 0 otherwise. The indicator variable EMU is equal to 1 from 1999 onward only for those countries of the European Union that have adopted the euro (i.e., Austria, Belgium, Germany, Finland, France, Greece, Ireland, Italy, the Netherlands, Portugal, and Spain) and equal to 0 otherwise.

Column (1) shows that both the single market and the euro have accelerated deregulation: the coefficients of ESM and EMU are negative (equal to −0.064 and −0.18, respectively) and statistically significant at the 5 percent

Table 2.1   The euro and product market reforms

	Three Sectors			Five Sectors		
	REG (1)	REG (2)	REG (3)	REG (4)	REG (5)	REG (6)
REG(–1)	0.94	0.93	0.95	0.93	0.93	0.95
	(109.60)***	(107.19)***	(104.66)***	(112.17)***	(108.13)***	(104.96)***
ESM	–0.06			–0.06		
	(–2.28)**			(–2.05)**		
EMU	–0.18			–0.15		
	(–5.28)***			(–4.83)***		
ESM*ENERGY		0.02	0.01		0.03	0.01
		(0.61)	(0.23)		(0.70)	(0.24)
ESM*COMMUNICATIONS		–0.03	–0.03		–0.03	–0.03
		(–0.81)	(–0.81)		(–0.72)	(–0.74)
ESM*TRANSPORT		–0.16	–0.15		–0.16	–0.15
		(–4.35)***	(–4.05)***		(–4.32)***	(–4.02)***
ESM*RETAIL					–0.26	–0.27
					(–2.07)**	(–2.54)**
ESM*PROFESSIONAL					0.22	0.24
					(2.74)***	(2.87)***
EMU*ENERGY		–0.43	0.04		–0.43	0.11
		(–9.07)***	(0.49)		(–8.95)***	(1.23)
EMU*COMMUNICATIONS		–0.28	0.02		–0.29	0.06
		(–5.74)***	(0.31)		(–5.79)***	(0.86)
EMU*TRANSPORT		0.11	0.46		0.11	0.50
		(2.39)**	(6.26)***		(2.35)**	(6.98)***
EMU*RETAIL					0.52	0.85
					(4.16)***	(5.75)***
EMU*PROFESSIONAL					–0.09	0.29
					(–1.14)	(2.94)***
EMU*REG(–1)			–0.12			–0.14
			(–6.24)***			(–7.34)***
Observations	1,764	1,764	1,764	1,802	1,802	1,802

Notes: Generalized least squares regressions allowing for heteroschedasticity of the error term and including country, sector, and time dummies. *T*-statistics in parentheses.

REG: indicator of regulatory impediments to product market competition, excluding public ownership; ENERGY, COMMUNICATIONS, TRANSPORT, RETAIL, and PROFESSIONAL: sectorial dummy variable that equals 1 for the corresponding sector; ESM: dummy variable equal to 1 from 1993 onward for the countries that enter the European Union's single-market Program; EMU: dummy variable equal to 1 from 1999 onward for the countries that enter the EMU. Columns (1) through (3) include the following three sectors: ENERGY, COMMUNICATIONS, and TRANS-PORT. Columns (4) through (6) include all five sectors in our database: ENERGY, COMMUNICATIONS, TRANSPORT, RETAIL, and PROFESSIONAL. See also the appendix for the exact definition of the variables.

***Significant at the 1 percent level.

**Significant at the 5 percent level.

level or better. Interestingly, the adoption of the euro has had a larger (about three times as large) impact on regulation than that of the single market program, and for a country that participated in the single market and adopted the euro, our estimates imply that the level of regulation decreased by about –0.25 points.

In column (2), we check whether these results hold for each sector in our sample. The adoption of the euro was especially important for energy and communications, while the single market was key for transportation and had no statistically significant effect in the energy and communications sectors.[14]

Finally, we investigate whether the effect of the single market program and the adoption of the euro depends on the initial level of regulation by adding the variables ESM*REG(–1) and EMU*REG(–1) to the specification of column (2). The effect of the single market is independent of the level of regulation: the coefficient of the interaction term between the single market dummy and the level of regulation lagged one is not statistically significant, both in a specification in which we exclude the variable EMU*REG(–1) and in one in which we include it. (Results are not shown but are available upon request.)

On the contrary, column (3) shows that the effect of the euro was larger when the initial level of regulation was larger, reemphasizing the process of convergence mentioned previously. Note that in column (3), the coefficients of the dummy variable EMU in the energy and communication sectors become positive but insignificant (see column [3]). However, the magnitude of the coefficients of the variables EMU*ENERGY and EMU*COMMUNICATION and of EMU*REG(–1) imply that for each value of REG(–1) observed in the energy and communications sectors, adopting the euro is always associated with deregulation.

The last three columns of table 2.1 reestimate the specifications of columns (1) through (3) in the sample in which the two additional sectors, retail and professionals, are also included. The estimates show that the single market, not the euro, was important for the retail sector and that the professionals sector has not been deregulated at all.

Finally, the regulatory variable that we are using (REG) looks at all aspects of regulation, except the one of public ownership. Results hold when we use the indicator of regulation that only measures barriers to entry and vertical integration and the more general indicator that also looks at public ownership.

Summarizing, the introduction of the euro has contributed to structural reforms in the product markets. This effect is above and beyond the effect of membership in the European Union from 1993 onward. Moreover, deregulation was stronger in EMU country-sectors with higher initial levels of regulation. This may give some prima facie and indirect support to the idea that deregulation was most needed once countries could not rely on exchange rate devaluations to boost competitiveness. In fact, the more heav-

14. We also checked whether the countries that deregulated after the adoption of the euro in the years following 1999 had experienced a delay in deregulation because they were too busy achieving the target criteria to join the monetary union. More specifically, we tested what happened to EU countries in the run-up to the euro during the period from 1993 to 1999. We did not find any evidence of an effect of postponement.

ily regulated (and less productive and competitive) country-sectors may have been those suffering the most from the loss of competitive devaluations and hence the ones that were forced to liberalize the most. In the next section, we investigate this idea in more detail.

2.3.5 Why Should the Euro Matter? Empirical Evidence

One of the reasons why a country joining the EMU may want to adopt structural reforms is that the competitive devaluation channel is not available anymore as a tool (or a palliative) to regain competitiveness.[15] In table 2.2, we explore this idea. Lacking competitiveness indicators at the country-sector-year level for the period from 1975 to 2003 for the energy, communications, and transport sectors, we measure competitiveness with variables varying only along the country-year dimension. We use two different indicators: the growth rate of the Consumer Price Index (CPI) relative to competitors at $t-1$—COMPET1 (-1)—and the growth rate of the export goods deflators relative to competitors at $t-1$—COMPET2(-1). We include the linear and quadratic terms to capture for possible nonlinearities; we add the interaction term of the competitiveness indicators and the EMU dummy variable to investigate whether the loss of exchange rate devaluation as a policy instrument to boost competitiveness leads to structural reforms. The coefficients of the variables COMPET1(-1) and COMPET2(-1) and their squares are not statistically significant at conventional critical values, suggesting that deregulation reforms do not generally occur in countries that are losing competitiveness. However, this is not true for countries that adopted the euro. In fact, the interaction terms of the competitiveness indicators and the EMU dummy variable are negative and statistically significant at the 5 percent level, suggesting that for EMU countries, the higher the growth rate of CPI and export goods deflators relative to competitors at $t-1$, the larger the decrease of the regulatory index. Finally, in columns (3) and (6), we control for the number of devaluations that countries that adopted the euro experienced in the period from 1979 to 1993. Our idea is that only countries that de facto used the exchange rate as a tool to regain competitiveness should suffer from its loss and liberalize markets. The variable N. OF DEVALU-ATIONS FROM 1979–1993 is equal to 5 for France, 1 for Belgium, 7 for Italy, and 3 for Ireland. It is equal to 0 otherwise. For the EMU countries, the more devaluations a country did from 1979 to 1993, the larger the decrease of the regulatory index (but the coefficient is statistically significant only at the 10 percent level).

Two caveats are worth mentioning. First, we are treating our competitiveness indicators as exogenous. While this clearly may not be the case, note that

---

15. Chapter 3 by Bugamelli, Schivardi, and Zizza in this volume presents some microeconomic evidence suggesting that sectors that have gone through deeper transformations and that enjoyed more productivity gains are exactly those that benefited more from pre-1999 devaluation.

Table 2.2   The euro, product market reforms, and competitiveness

	Three Sectors			Five Sectors		
	REG (1)	REG (2)	REG (3)	REG (4)	REG (5)	REG (6)
REG(−1)	0.95	0.94	0.95	0.95	0.94	0.95
	(101.60)***	(92.94)***	(104.17)***	(101.85)***	(93.51)***	(104.47)***
ESM*ENERGY	0.00	0.00	0.01	0.00	0.00	0.01
	(0.12)	(0.08)	(0.23)	(0.10)	(0.02)	(0.24)
ESM*COMMUNICATIONS	−0.03	−0.02	−0.03	−0.03	−0.02	−0.03
	(−0.84)	(−0.65)	(−0.83)	(−0.75)	(−0.52)	(−0.76)
ESM*TRANSPORT	−0.16	−0.15	−0.15	−0.16	−0.15	−0.15
	(−4.37)***	(−3.89)***	(−4.05)***	(−4.31)***	(−3.82)***	(−4.02)***
ESM*RETAIL				−0.27	−0.26	−0.27
				(−2.44)**	(−2.18)**	(−2.52)**
ESM*PROFESSIONAL				0.23	0.22	0.24
				(2.71)***	(2.76)***	(2.87)***
EMU*ENERGY	0.23	0.20	0.03	0.31	0.28	0.10
	(2.38)**	(1.92)*	(0.30)	(3.42)***	(3.05)***	(1.10)
EMU*COMMUNICATIONS	0.14	0.12	0.02	0.19	0.17	0.06
	(1.95)*	(1.56)	(0.28)	(2.76)***	(2.41)**	(0.84)
EMU*TRANSPORT	0.56	0.54	0.44	0.61	0.59	0.49
	(7.37)***	(6.66)***	(6.06)***	(8.43)***	(8.09)***	(6.84)***
EMU*RETAIL				1.01	0.95	0.85
				(6.73)***	(5.99)***	(5.83)***
EMU*PROFESSIONAL				0.51	0.46	0.27
				(4.91)***	(5.08)***	(2.74)***
EMU*REG(−1)	−0.18	−0.17	−0.11	−0.20	−0.19	−0.13
	(−7.94)***	(−7.08)***	(−5.51)***	(−9.62)***	(−9.56)***	(−6.79)***

	(1)	(2)	(3)	(4)	(5)	(6)
COMPET1(−1)	−0.11			−0.10		
	(−0.96)			(−0.86)		
COMPET1²(−1)	−0.57			−0.56		
	(−0.55)			(−0.53)		
EMU*COMPET1(−1)	−2.76			−2.64		
	(−2.81)***			(−2.78)***		
COMPET2(−1)		0.05			0.05	
		(0.38)			(0.36)	
COMPET2²(−1)		−0.15			−0.06	
		(−0.11)			(−0.04)	
EMU*COMPET2(−1)		−1.97			−1.96	
		(−2.77)***			(−2.78)***	
N. OF DEVALUATIONS FROM 1979–1993			0.02			−0.01
			(3.46)***			(−1.89)*
EMU* N. OF DEVALUATIONS FROM 1979–1993			−0.02			−0.01
			(−1.83)*			(−1.33)
Observations	1,680	1,572	1,764	1,717	1,609	1,802

Notes: Generalized least squares regressions allowing for heteroschedasticity of the error term and including country, sector, and time dummies. *T*-statistics in parentheses.

REG: indicator of regulatory impediments to product market competition, excluding public ownership; ENERGY, COMMUNICATIONS, TRANSPORT, RETAIL, and PROFESSIONAL: sectorial dummy variable that equals 1 for the corresponding sector; ESM: dummy variable equal to 1 from 1993 onward for the countries that enter the European Union's single-market program; EMU: dummy variable equal to 1 from 1999 onward for the countries that enter the EMU; COMPET1: growth rate of the CPI relative to competitors; COMPET2: growth rate of the export goods deflators relative to competitors; N. OF DEVALUTIONS FROM 1979–1993: number of devaluations that a country that belonged to the European Monetary System did from 1979 to 1993. See also the notes to table 2.1 and the appendix for the exact definition of the variables.

***Significant at the 1 percent level.

**Significant at the 5 percent level.

*Significant at the 10 percent level.

here, we are not really interested in the effect of competitiveness on regulation but instead on its differential effect among EMU and other countries. Hence, even if the competitiveness indicators were not exogenous, it is not clear why the bias in our estimates should differ among EMU and other countries. Second, the coefficient of the variable EMU*REG(–1) remains negative and statistically significant, as in table 2.1, suggesting that: (a) our competitiveness indicators are not capturing the loss of competitiveness, and hence the need of reforms, very well when the exchange rate instrument cannot be used anymore; (b) the euro is important for structural reforms in product markets for other reasons beyond the fact that the competitive devaluation channel is not available anymore; (c) what we are identifying as a euro effect is just picking up the impact of some omitted variable; and (d) any combinations of (a), (b), and/or (c).

2.3.6   Other Determinants of Product Market Reforms

In this section, we investigate other possible determinants of product market reforms. We also check that accounting for other critical elements that drive reforms does not alter the results we discussed so far on the effect of the euro on the deregulation of product markets.

We begin by testing whether various variables that measure the macroeconomic conditions of each sector matter. Specifically, in table 2.3, we include the sectors' value added, labor expenses, and total employment at time $t – 1$, measured as a share of country's total value added, labor expenses, and total employment at time $t – 1$. Blanchard and Giavazzi (2003) suggest that in the short run, product markets' deregulation reforms generate costs for both incumbent firms and their workers. Hence, incumbents tend to oppose such reforms. When rents are lower, however, resistance to deregulation falls, as the incumbents' short-term losses can be easier outweighed by the future benefits of deregulation. Results in table 2.3 support this argument. In fact, we find that regulation decreases when value added and labor costs of the sector fall—that is, when the sector's rents decrease. We also find that product markets are deregulated in country-sectors-years with lower employment. Hence, in less labor-intensive sectors, governments can meet less resistance and can more easily implement deregulation measures. In columns (4) through (6), we also investigate whether there are differential effects between EMU and non-EMU countries relative to the effects of value added, labor costs, and employment on regulation, but on this score, we found no differences between EMU and non-EMU countries.

Second, in table 2.4, we augment the specifications of table 2.3 with several macroeconomic and political controls. We investigate the crisis hypothesis, the role of the countries' fiscal conditions, the timing of reforms in relation to the electoral cycle, the interaction between reforms in the product and labor markets, and the effect of reforms occurring in trading partners' countries. All variables are measured at time $t – 1$, both to allow for the

Table 2.3   **Other determinants of product market reforms (sectors indicators)**

	Three Sectors			Five Sectors		
	REG (1)	REG (2)	REG (3)	REG (4)	REG (5)	REG (6)
REG(−1)	0.94	0.93	0.93	0.94	0.93	0.93
	(84.13)***	(75.86)***	(73.56)***	(84.06)***	(75.82)***	(73.43)***
ESM*ENERGY	−0.02	−0.02	−0.03	−0.02	−0.03	−0.03
	(−0.52)	(−0.59)	(−0.71)	(−0.52)	(−0.66)	(−0.73)
ESM*COMMUNICATIONS	−0.05	−0.06	−0.12	−0.05	−0.06	−0.12
	(−1.36)	(−1.65)*	(−2.70)***	(−1.35)	(−1.66)*	(−2.76)***
ESM*TRANSPORT	−0.18	−0.18	−0.20	−0.18	−0.18	−0.20
	(4.25)***	(−4.02)***	(−4.28)***	(−4.26)***	(−4.07)***	(−4.34)***
EMU*ENERGY	0.27	0.19	0.19	0.15	0.07	0.05
	(2.48)**	(1.73)*	(1.65)*	(1.20)	(0.51)	(0.36)
EMU*COMMUNICATIONS	0.13	0.09	0.13	0.00	−0.04	−0.06
	(1.68)*	(1.13)	(1.55)	(0.02)	(−0.30)	(−0.45)
EMU*TRANSPORT	0.59	0.54	0.54	0.32	0.28	0.05
	(7.08)***	(6.40)***	(5.95)***	(1.70)*	(0.97)	(0.20)
EMU*REG(−1)	−0.19	−0.18	−0.17	−0.19	−0.18	−0.17
	(−7.46)***	(−6.80)***	(−6.56)***	(−7.50)***	(−6.78)***	(−6.25)***
COMPET1(−1)	−0.06	−0.04	0.03	−0.06	−0.04	0.02
	(−0.45)	(−0.27)	(0.22)	(−0.47)	(−0.29)	(0.16)
COMPET1²(−1)	−0.81	−0.85	−0.50	−0.75	−0.77	−0.44
	(−0.71)	(−0.71)	(−0.40)	(−0.66)	(−0.64)	(−0.36)
EMU*COMPET1(−1)	−2.63	−2.52	(2.49	−2.79	−2.72	−2.37
	(−2.19)**	(−2.05)**	(1.93)*	(−2.31)**	(−2.20)**	(−1.81)*
VA(−1)	2.13	−0.64	−0.42	1.80	−1.33	−0.57
	(2.24)**	(−0.44)	(−0.29)	(1.86)*	(−0.88)	(−0.38)
LABOR EXPENSES(−1)		3.43			3.87	
		(2.03)**			(2.24)**	
TOT. EMPLOYMENT(−1)			4.90			4.45
			(2.06)**			(1.85)*
EMU*VALUE ADDED(−1)				5.57	7.03	3.32
				(1.64)	(1.75)*	(0.75)
EMU*LABOR EXPENSES(−1)					−1.80	
					(−0.27)	
EMU*TOT. EMPLOYMENT(−1)						6.90
						(1.08)
Observations	1,383	1,282	1,158	1,383	1,282	1,158

Notes: Generalized least squares regressions allowing for heteroschedasticity of the error term and including country, sector, and time dummies. *T*-statistics in parentheses. REG: indicator of regulatory impediments to product market competition, excluding public ownership; ENERGY, COMMUNICATIONS, TRANSPORT, RETAIL, and PROFESSIONAL: sectorial dummy variable that equals 1 for the corresponding sector; ESM: dummy variable equal to 1 from 1993 onward for the countries that enter the European Union's single-market program; EMU: dummy variable equal to 1 from 1999 onward for the countries that enter the EMU; COMPET1: growth rate of the CPI relative to competitors; COMPET2: growth rate of the export goods deflators relative to competitors; N. OF DEVALUATIONS FROM 1979–1993: number of devaluations that a country that belonged to the European Monetary System did from 1979 to 1993; VA: value added at the sectorial level; LABOR EXPENSES: labor costs or compensation of employees at the sectorial level; TOT. EMPLOYMENT: total employment at the sectorial level. See also the notes to table 2.1 and the appendix for the exact definition of the variables.

***Significant at the 1 percent level.

**Significant at the 5 percent level.

*Significant at the 10 percent level.

Table 2.4   Other determinants of product market reforms (countries indicators)

	Three Sectors			Five Sectors		
	REG (1)	REG (2)	REG (3)	REG (4)	REG (5)	REG (6)
REG(–1)	0.92	0.91	0.92	0.89	0.86	0.87
	(75.89)***	(68.51)***	(68.30)***	(55.21)***	(49.64)***	(48.67)***
ESM*ENERGY	–0.02	–0.02	–0.02	0.02	0.05	0.03
	(–0.35)	(–0.44)	(–0.54)	(0.28)	(0.80)	(0.54)
ESM*COMMUNICATIONS	–0.05	–0.06	–0.11	0.00	0.02	–0.07
	(–1.22)	(–1.46)	(–2.44)**	(0.02)	(0.43)	(1.06)
ESM*TRANSPORT	–0.18	–0.18	–0.19	–0.15	–0.11	–0.15
	(–3.97)***	(–3.83)***	(–3.94)***	(–2.55)**	(–1.88)*	(–2.30)**
EMU*ENERGY	0.23	0.15	0.15	0.11	0.01	–0.03
	(2.10)**	(1.32)	(1.26)	(0.85)	(0.06)	(–0.24)
EMU*COMMUNICATIONS	0.12	0.07	0.13	0.03	–0.04	0.02
	(1.47)	(0.87)	(1.45)	(0.27)	(–0.36)	(0.18)
EMU*TRANSPORT	0.58	0.52	0.52	0.49	0.43	0.39
	(6.55)***	(5.96)***	(5.57)***	(4.84)***	(4.31)***	(3.66)***
EMU*REG(–1)	–0.17	–0.16	–0.16	–0.14	–0.12	–0.11
	(–6.63)***	(–5.94)***	(–5.82)***	(–4.64)***	(–3.99)***	(–3.57)***
COMPET1(–1)	–0.16	–0.15	–0.12	–0.06	0.01	0.03
	(–1.21)	(–1.05)	(–0.83)	(–0.35)	(0.06)	(0.15)
COMPET1^2(–1)	0.13	0.25	0.39	0.37	0.50	0.38
	(0.11)	(0.21)	(0.32)	(0.27)	(0.33)	(0.26)
EMU*COMPET1(–1)	–2.66	–2.50	–2.44	–2.62	–2.66	–2.47
	(–2.15)**	(–2.00)**	(–1.87)*	(–2.01)**	(–2.02)**	(–1.80)*
VA(–1)	2.52	–0.58	–0.75	2.43	–1.54	–2.30
	(2.51)**	(–0.39)	(–0.48)	(1.98)**	(–0.77)	(–1.12)
LABOR EXPENSES(–1)		3.89			5.70	
		(2.20)**			(2.20)**	
TOT. EMPLOYMENT(–1)			6.40			8.29
			(2.49)**			(2.41)**
CRISIS(–1)	–0.06	–0.06	–0.06	–0.09	–0.08	–0.10
	(–2.30)**	(–2.36)**	(–2.27)**	(–2.65)***	(–2.48)**	(–2.78)***
PR. SURPLUS/GDP(–1)	0.65	0.61	0.63	0.66	0.59	0.48
	(2.05)**	(1.82)*	(1.84)*	(1.70)*	(1.41)	(1.12)
RIGHT GOV.(–1)	–0.01	–0.02	–0.02	–0.01	–0.02	–0.02
	(–0.83)	(–0.96)	(–1.01)	(–0.52)	(–0.83)	(–0.75)
CENTER GOV.(–1)	–0.07	–0.08	–0.07	–0.10	–0.11	–0.12
	(–1.84)*	(–2.07)**	(–1.71)*	(–1.86)*	(–2.08)**	(–1.97)**
ELECTION YEAR(–1)	–0.02	–0.03	–0.03	–0.02	–0.02	–0.02
	(–1.52)	(–1.75)*	(–1.76)*	(–0.98)	(–1.10)	(–1.02)
REG. TRADING PART.(–1)	0.06	0.06	0.05	0.07	0.08	0.08
	(2.07)**	(1.88)*	(1.69)*	(1.94)*	(2.08)**	(2.08)**
UNEMPL. BENEF.(–1)				–0.33	–0.28	–0.38
				(–2.19)**	(–1.78)*	(–2.35)**
EMPLOY. PROTECTION(–1)				0.04	0.07	0.02
				(1.01)	(1.67)*	(0.41)
Observations	1,301	1,211	1,119	984	919	835

Notes: Generalized least squares regressions allowing for heteroschedasticity of the error term and including country, sector, and time dummies. *T*-statistics in parentheses. CRISIS: dummy variable equal to 1 when the output gap (defined as the difference of actual output to potential) is below the ninetieth percentile of the output gap empirical density; PR. SURPLUS/GDP: primary deficit as a share of GDP; RIGHT GOV.: dummy variable that equals 1 if the government is led by a right-oriented party; CENTER GOV.: dummy variable that equals 1 if the government is led by a center-oriented party; ELECTION YEAR: dummy variable that equals 1 if (parliamentary or presidential) elections were held during that year; REG. TRADING PART.: average of the value of the indicators REG for the trading partners; UNEMPL. BENEF.: unemployment benefit replacement rate for low-income workers in their first year of unemployment; EMPLOY. PROTECTION: summary indicator of the stringency for employment protection legislation. See notes to table 2.3 and the appendix for the exact definition of all the variables included in the regressions.

***Significant at the 1 percent level.

**Significant at the 5 percent level.

*Significant at the 10 percent level.

fact that it may take some time until governments react to macroeconomic events and to reduce the possibility of reverse causality in our estimates. Several results are worth noting. First, the results on EMU shown thus far are robust to the inclusion of the additional control variables. Second, we find evidence that deregulation reforms occur in country-years in which the output gap (defined as the difference of actual output to potential) is below the ninetieth percentile of the output gap empirical density (equal to –3.4 percent). This gives some support to the crisis hypothesis—namely, that reforms are more likely to occur in bad times. Third, the higher the primary deficit as a share of gross domestic product (GDP), the lower the level of regulation, indicating that reforms' blockers may be less powerful when they feel that public finances are also in trouble and that liberalizing the economy can help both in boosting growth and possibly in reducing the likelihood of further increases in taxes or cutting in spending. Fourth, we find some evidence that product market reforms happen at the beginning of the political term (right after an election), but this result is not particularly robust to specification changes. Fifth, deregulation in trading partners fosters deregulation at home. This result is consistent with the evidence in Hoj et al. (2006).

Finally, we looked into the interaction between labor market reforms and product market reforms. Specifically, our estimates show that an increase in unemployment benefits leads to lower regulation in product markets, while a decrease in the employment protection index is associated with less regulation of product markets (but the coefficient is significant at the 10 percent level only in column [5]). Product market liberalization reforms seem easier to implement if workers receive some kind of protection in the form of social insurance. As mentioned earlier, workers of the incumbent firms are more likely to become unemployed and lose in the short run from deregulation. Hence, they can be more willing to bear the short-run costs once the generosity of unemployment benefits increases than they otherwise would. Fiori et al. (2007) find that labor market reforms do not Granger-cause product market reforms. However, their labor market indicator is the principal component of unemployment benefits and employment protection. Results in table 2.4 show that the two variables have opposite effects on regulation in product markets. Hence, considering a combination of the two variables may prevent one from detecting any effect of labor market regulation on product market regulation.

2.3.7   Endogeneity of Euro Membership

The decision to join the EMS and especially to adopt the euro is of course not an exogenous variable. In order to investigate this issue, we have reestimated table 2.1 using an instrumental variable procedure. First, we have estimated with a probit model the probability that a certain country adopts the euro. The choice of the right-hand side variable is based upon the gravity literature on trade and the literature on currency unions.[16] The specification, described in detail in Alesina, Ardagna, and Galasso (2008), is meant to capture that: (a) countries that trade more with each other should be more likely to choose to be part of the same common currency area; (b) the higher the correlation of the business cycle frequency (output and prices), the more likely it is that two countries will choose to join the union; and (c) the higher past inflation, the more likely it is that a country will join the union. In fact, the more two countries trade with each other, the more they benefit from a common currency. The more correlated are their business cycles, the lower the costs of a simple monetary policy. Finally, a history of high inflation makes a monetary anchor especially effective. We find support with regard to EMU for the first two effects but not for the third.[17] This is not surprising, as the monetary anchor argument certainly did not apply to low-inflation members (e.g., Germany and France).

We then use the estimated probability of joining the union as an instrumental variable (IV) for table 2.1. The results, shown in Alesina, Ardagna, and Galasso (2008), indicate that the coefficients of interests on EMU in column (1) of table 2.1 are generally robust to this IV procedure. We have investigated all the specifications of table 2.1 with various degrees of success. In some cases, the IV results remain significant, while in some cases, the standard errors are too big for statistical significance. As we discussed in the introduction, we are not convinced that the decision of whether to enter the euro area was exogenous only (or mainly) to economic variables. Political consideration seemed crucial, and therefore it is hard to measure with an instrument the decision of whether to join.

2.4   Labor market: The Evidence

2.4.1   The Data

In order to investigate the determinants of labor market regulation, we consider two time-varying measures for twenty-one OECD countries for the period from 1985 to 2003. These two measures capture the degree of employment protection related to the firing decisions and the level of insurance provided to the unemployed, respectively. Data on the former measures are coded and collected by the OECD and described in the OECD *Employment Outlook* (2004). The latter data are also collected at the OECD and are described in the OECD *Benefits and Wages* (several issues); because original data are available only for odd years, data for even years have been obtained by linear interpolation.

---

16. See Alesina, Barro, and Tenreyro (2002), in particular.
17. Also, Rose (2000) finds a significant and negative impact of the inflation rate on the probability of joining a currency union.

The indicator on employment protection ranges from 0 to 6 (from least to most restrictive) and measures the restrictions placed on the firing processes by both labor legislation and collective-bargaining agreements. This index includes an assessment of the legislative provisions, as well as the enforcement dimension, as they provide a measure of the judicial practices and court interpretations of legislative and contractual rules. This indicator is also provided separately for regular and temporary workers.

For the regular workers, the indicator on the employment protectory regulation has three main components: (a) difficulty of dismissal—that is, legislative provisions setting conditions under which a dismissal is justified or fair; (b) procedural inconveniences that the employer may face when starting the dismissal process; and (c) notice and severance pay provisions. The index also provides a measure of the regulation of fixed-term contracts and temporary work agencies. This is intended to measure the restrictions on the use of temporary employment by firms with respect to the type of work for which these contracts are allowed and their duration. The employment legislation for regular contracts constitutes the core component of the overall summary index of employment protective legislation (EPI) strictness that we use.

The indicator on the level of insurance provided to the unemployed represents the unemployment benefit replacement rate for low-income workers in their first year of unemployment. This is measured by the average replacement rate—that is, the ratio of the unemployment benefit to the last wage—for a worker that earns 66 percent of average worker earnings.

2.4.2   The Euro and Labor Market Reforms

As for the product market, all our regressions are estimated with generalized least squares, allowing for heteroschedasticity of the error term, and include the lagged value of the left-hand side variable and country and time dummies.

In table 2.5, we consider the generosity of the unemployment benefits, as defined earlier, to be a measure of labor market regulation. In column (1), we start from the basic specification, with tests only for the effects of the European single market and of the euro. We then add the interaction of EMU with the lagged value of the dependent variable (column [2], our measures of competition (column [3]), and additional possible explanatory variables encountered in the literature, such as economic crisis and fiscal and political variables (column [4]). Finally, columns (5) and (6) report the results of the regressions that include the effects of the lagged variable of regulation in the product market, the alternative variable of regulation in the labor market (EPL), and the level of unemployment benefits in the trading partners. The results show that while the ESM had no impact on this measure of labor market regulation, the introduction of the euro led to an increase in the generosity of the unemployment benefit. No other variable shows

Table 2.5   The euro and unemployment benefits

	UNEMPLOYMENT BENEFIT (1)	UNEMPLOYMENT BENEFIT (2)	UNEMPLOYMENT BENEFIT (3)	UNEMPLOYMENT BENEFIT (4)	UNEMPLOYMENT BENEFIT (5)	UNEMPLOYMENT BENEFIT (6)
UNEMPL. BENEF.(-1)	0.93 (38.57)***	0.93 (38.58)***	0.94 (38.49)***	0.93 (36.90)***	0.93 (36.02)***	0.93 (35.80)***
ESM	0.00 (1.43)	0.00 (1.42)	-0.01 (-1.44)	0.00 (0.77)	0.00 (0.62)	0.00 (0.78)
EMU	0.01 (2.03)**	0.01 (1.35)	0.01 (1.62)	0.01 (2.00)**	0.01 (2.35)**	0.01 (2.29)**
EMU*UNEMPL. BENEF.(-1)		-0.01 (-0.45)				
COMPET(-1)			-0.01 (-0.63)			
COMPET1^2(-1)			-0.04 (-0.26)			
EMU*COMPET1(-1)			-0.11 (-1.27)			
CRISIS(-1)				0.00 (0.23)	0.00 (0.23)	0.00 (0.34)
PR. SURPLUS/GDP(-1)				0.04 (1.18)	0.03 (0.76)	0.03 (0.76)
RIGHT GOV.(-1)				0.00 (0.12)	0.00 (0.48)	0.00 (0.32)

CENTER GOV(–1)				–0.01	–0.01	–0.01
				(–0.99)	(–0.91)	(–1.11)
ELECTION YEAR(–1)				0.00	0.00	0.00
				(0.16)	(0.05)	(0.15)
EMPLOY. PROTECTION(–1)				0.00	0.00	0.00
					(0.46)	(0.52)
UNEMPLOYMENT BENEFIT TRADING PARTNERS(–1)					–0.10	–0.10
					(–2.29)**	(–2.39)**
PMKT REGULAT(–1)					0.00	0.00
					(1.38)	(0.45)
PMKT REGULAT(–2)						0.01
						(1.59)
Observations	378	378	360	366	362	362

Notes: Generalized least squares regressions allowing for heteroschedasticity of the error term and including country, sector, and time dummies. *T*-statistics in parentheses. UNEMPLOYMENT BENEFIT TRADING PARTNERS: average of the value of the indicator UNEMPL. BENEF. for the trading partners; PMKT REGULAT: country average value of the sectorial indicator REG. See notes to tables 2.3 and 2.4 and the appendix for the exact definition of all the variables included in the regressions.

***Significant at the 1 percent level.

**Significant at the 5 percent level.

any explanatory power, with the exception of the level of unemployment benefits in the trading partners, which presents a puzzling result, however, as more unemployment benefits in trading partners is associated with less unemployment benefits in the home country.

When using the degree of EPL as a measure of labor market regulation, as in table 2.6, we do not find any effect of EMU—or any other plausible explanatory variable—on labor market reforms. More generally, we found that this index of labor market reform moved much less than that of product market, as shown in figure 2.4.

2.4.3   Additional Evidence

The indicator of labor market reform used in the previous section may give an overly narrow view of the evolution of labor markets in Europe. These indicators of flexibility refer only to the primary labor market. But two other factors, related to each other, have changed. One has been the development of a vast labor market in several countries based on temporary contracts with very few, if any, of the rigidities of the primary labor market. For instance, much of the increase in employment reported in France, Italy, and Spain has occurred in this secondary market. The second change is that in the last ten or fifteen years, several European countries seem to have experienced a substantial amount of wage moderation. In table 2.7, we investigated whether the adoption of the euro has contributed to achieving wage moderation in these seemingly unreformed labor markets. This is of course important as an indicator of second-round effects: that is, whether inflationary shocks get a second-round boost from wage increases. This table shows that the countries that joined the EMU in 1999 have experienced a significant increase in wage moderation in the period leading up to the common currency: that is, between 1993 and 1999. After this period, there is no evidence of an additional effect of euro adoption on the degree of wage moderation. These results are consistent with the fact that in preparation for EMU membership, many countries had to put their houses in order. This meant inflation reduction and fiscal rigor (in areas including public salaries).

More specifically, in column (1) of table 2.7, the dependent variable is the growth of nominal wages. On the right-hand side, in addition to the lagged dependent variable, we have lagged inflation and our variables capturing simple market membership and EMU membership. The former (but not the latter) has a negative and statistically significant coefficient, indicating, at least at first sight, an effect of simple market membership on wage moderation. However, in column (2), we show that this result is driven by the countries' membership of the simple market and their preparation to join the EMU and attempts to achieve convergence criteria. In fact, we added a dummy for EMU countries in the run-up to the euro (1993 to 1998) and

Table 2.6   The euro and employment protection

	EMPLOYMENT PROTECTION (1)	EMPLOYMENT PROTECTION (2)	EMPLOYMENT PROTECTION (3)	EMPLOYMENT PROTECTION (4)	EMPLOYMENT PROTECTION (5)	EMPLOYMENT PROTECTION (6)
EMPLOY. PROTECTION(-1)	0.93	0.92	0.93	0.92	0.92	0.92
	(31.35)***	(31.08)***	(31.51)***	(30.70)***	(30.77)***	(30.68)***
ESM	-0.01	-0.01	-0.02	0.00	0.00	0.00
	(-0.97)	(-0.95)	(-1.07)	(0.28)	(0.24)	(0.24)
EMU	-0.01	0.04	0.00	-0.02	0.00	-0.01
	(-0.66)	(0.79)	(0.04)	(-0.89)	(0.23)	(-0.26)
EMU* EMPL. PROTECT.(-1)		-0.02				
		(-1.13)				
COMPET1(-1)			0.00			
			(0.06)			
COMPET1²(-1)			0.17			
			(0.34)			
EMU*COMPET1(-1)			0.51			
			(0.94)			
CRISIS(-1)				-0.01	-0.01	-0.01
				(-0.91)	(-0.46)	(-0.46)
PR. SURPLUS/GDP(-1)				0.00	-0.01	-0.01
				(0.01)	(-0.07)	(-0.08)
RIGHT GOV.(-1)				-0.01	-0.01	-0.01
				(-1.45)	(-0.99)	(-1.00)
CENTER GOV.(-1)				0.00	0.00	0.00
				(0.16)	(0.11)	(0.12)
ELECTION YEAR(-1)				0.00	0.00	0.00
				(0.51)	(0.37)	(0.38)
UNEMPL. BENEF.(-1)					-0.13	-0.13
					(-1.58)	(-1.53)
EMPL. PROTECT. TRADING PARTNERS(-1)					0.03	0.03
					(1.46)	(1.46)
PMKT REGULAT(-1)					-0.01	0.00
					(-0.47)	(0.20)
PMKT REGULAT(-2)						0.00
						(0.07)
Observations	373	373	355	362	362	362

Notes: Generalized least squares regressions allowing for heteroschedasticity of the error term and including country, sector, and time dummies. *T*-statistics in parentheses. EMPL. PROTECT. TRADING PARTNERS: average of the value of the indicator EMPL. PROTECT. for the trading partners. See notes to tables 2.3, 2.4, and 2.5 and the appendix for the exact definition of all the variables included in the regressions.

***Significant at the 1 percent level.

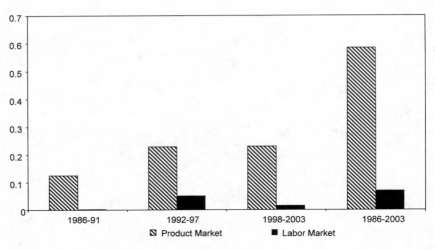

Fig. 2.4   Deregulation in product and labor markets

Table 2.7   The euro and wage moderation

	NOMINAL WAGE GROWTH (1)	NOMINAL WAGE GROWTH (2)
NOMINAL WAGE GROWTH LAGGED	0.48	0.47
	(10.43)***	(10.12)***
LAGGED INFLATION	0.22	0.24
	(3.69)***	(3.91)***
ESM	−0.01	
	(−2.50)**	
EMU 1993–1998		−0.01
		(−2.90)***
EMU 1999–2003	0.00	−0.01
	(0.89)	(−1.50)
EU-NO EMU 1993–2003		−0.01
		(−1.33)
Observations	508	508

Notes: Generalized least squares regressions allowing for heteroschedasticity of the error term and including country, sector, and time dummies. *T*-statistics in parentheses. See notes to table 2.1 and the appendix for the exact definition of all the variables included in the regressions.
***Significant at the 1 percent level.
**Significant at the 5 percent level.

another one after they adopted the single currency. As this column shows, the pre-euro dummy variable has a significant negative coefficient. Meanwhile, the coefficient on the posteuro period is insignificant. We also investigated possible differential effects between EMU and non-EMU countries relative to the effects of (lagged) inflation, but we found no differences.

2.5 Conclusions

Our statistical analysis suggests that the adoption of the euro has had a significant effect in promoting the adoption of product market reforms, at least in some sectors.

There are three possible interpretations of the results. One is that it is simply a coincidence: some countries decided to reform right at the end of the 1990s, and this time period happened to coincide with the adoption of the euro. The second interpretation is that the euro did indeed have an effect in promoting liberalization by eliminating the palliative of competitive devaluations. Firms found themselves losing competitiveness and became more vocal in demanding liberalization in sectors that were providing intermediate goods and services (including nontradable ones) in order to keep their costs low. A third story, related to the second, is that the euro did not matter that much economically per se but that it was used as a political tool by reformers to argue that countries belonging to the euro area needed structural reform; in other words, the euro was used as a justification to promote a product market reform agenda.

One should be worried about the possibility of spurious correlations because of the relatively small number of countries involved in the tests; however, the results do appear quite robust to a battery of econometric tests. It is hard to entirely disentangle the role of actual economic pressures introduced by the euro and the political rhetoric associated with it, but certainly, the results of our econometric exercise have moved us from our prior assumptions toward believing that the euro might indeed have had an effect, if not in promoting, at least in weakening the opposition to product market reforms. Future work should take some further steps toward trying to disentangle these three alternatives. One step in this direction would be to focus on where the political and economic pressure to liberalize certain sectors came from.[18]

The adoption of the euro does not seem to have had much of an effect in promoting labor market reforms, at least in the primary labor market sector: in general, labor markets have proceeded more slowly and tentatively than product markets. However, a secondary labor market with temporary labor contracts has grown in a few countries that did not reform the primary labor market. In addition, the run-up to euro adoption has led to some wage moderation. This timing has led us to consider the question of whether product market reform should indeed precede labor market liberalization. We find that regulation decreases when value added and labor costs of the sector fall (i.e., when a sector's rents decrease) and that product markets are

18. Interestingly, energy, the sector that was mostly affected by the introduction of the euro, was found by Barone and Cingano (2008) to be the service sector whose liberalization has the most beneficial effects on the growth rate of the downstream manufacturing sectors.

deregulated in country-sectors-years with lower employment. Hence, in less labor-intensive sectors, governments can meet less resistance and can more easily implement deregulation measures. However, we also find that product market deregulation is easier to implement when unemployment subsidies are more generous and is more difficult to implement when there are higher firing costs, which interfere with market reallocations. Therefore, the type of labor market policies more prone to facilitating product market reforms are those in which the workers are protected with unemployment subsidies but specific jobs are not, making the (re)matching between firms and workers easier. Labor market reforms are multidimensional in nature and are often quite complex and difficult to capture with one macroindicator. Also, several countries in the euro area have two separate markets: the traditional and highly regulated market, and a second, much more flexible one based on temporary contracts. Further investigation into the role of the euro in promoting labor market reform is an excellent topic for future research.

Appendix
Data Sources and Definitions

Our data set includes yearly data on twenty-one OECD countries (Australia, Austria, Belgium, Canada, Switzerland, Germany, Denmark, Spain, Finland, France, the United Kingdom, Greece, Ireland, Italy, Japan, the Netherlands, New Zealand, Norway, Portugal, Sweden, and the United States) from 1975 to 2003. Following is a list of variables used in our regressions, with their definitions and sources.

REG: Aggregation of the OECD summary indicator of regulatory impediments to product market competition, excluding public ownership, in three or five broad sectors: energy (electricity and gas), communication (telecommunications and post), and transportation (airlines, road freight, and railways); and retail and professionals. Data on regulation for professionals are only available in 1996 and 2003 and for retail in 1998 and 2003. (Source: Conway and Nicoletti [2007] and Nicoletti and Scarpetta [2003].)

ENERGY, COMMUNICATIONS, TRANSPORT, RETAIL, and *PRO-FESSIONAL:* Sectorial dummy variable that equals 1 for the corresponding sector.

European single market (*ESM*): Dummy variable that equals 1 for the countries that enter the European Union's single market program after its implementation in 1993.

EMU: Dummy variable that equals 1 for the countries that enter the EMU after its implementation in 1999.

EMU*"variable" (e.g., "energy"): Interaction between EMU and the corresponding variable.

ESM*"variable" (e.g., "energy"): Interaction between single market and the corresponding variable.

*COMPET*1: Indicator of lack of competitiveness at the country-sector-year level for the period from 1975 to 2003 for the energy, communications, and transport sectors, measured as the growth rate of the CPI relative to competitors at $t - 1$. (Source: OECD *Economic Outlook* number 80.)

*COMPET*2: Indicator of lack of competitiveness at the country-sector-year level for the period from 1975 to 2003 for the energy, communications, and transport sectors, measured as the growth rate of the export goods deflators relative to competitors at $t - 1$. (Source: OECD *Economic Outlook* number 80.)

N. OF DEVALUATIONS FROM 1979–1993: Number of devaluations that a country that belonged to the European Monetary System did from 1979 to 1993.

VA: Value added for the three sectors: energy (electricity, gas, and water), communications (communications and posts), and transport (transport and storage). It measures the sector contribution to national GDP, calculated as the difference between production and intermediate inputs. (Source: OECD STAN database for industrial analysis, revision 3 [ISIC rev. 3].)

LABOR EXPENSES: Labor costs or compensation of employees in the three preceding sectors. It includes wages and salaries of employees paid by producers, as well as supplements such as contributions to social security, private pensions, health insurance, life insurance, and similar schemes. (Source: OECD STAN database for industrial analysis, revision 3 [ISIC rev. 3].)

TOT. EMPLOYMENT: Total employment in the preceding three sectors. (Source: OECD STAN database for industrial analysis, revision 3 [ISIC rev. 3].)

CRISIS: Dummy variable equal to 1 when the output gap (defined as the difference of actual output to potential) is below the ninetieth percentile of the output gap empirical density (equal to –3.4 percent). (Source: OECD *Economic Outlook* database.)

PR. SURPLUS/GDP: Primary deficit as a share of GDP. (Source: OECD *Economic Outlook* database.)

RIGHT GOV.: Dummy variable that equals 1 if the government is led by a right party or coalition; that is, parties that are defined as conservative, Christian democratic, or right wing. (Source: Database of Political Institutions [DPI] of the World Bank, compiled by Beck et al. [2001].)

CENTER GOV.: Dummy variable that equals 1 if the government is led by a center party or coalition; that is, parties that are defined as centrist or whose position can best be described as centrist—for example, party advocates strengthening private enterprise in a social-liberal context. (Source: Database of Political Institutions [DPI] of the World Bank, compiled by Beck et al. [2001].)

ELECTION YEAR: Dummy variable that equals 1 if (parliamentary or presidential) elections were held during that year. (Source: Database of Political Institutions [DPI] of the World Bank, compiled by Beck et al. [2001].)

REG. TRADING PART.: Average of the value of the indicators REG for the trading partners. (Source: Conway and Nicoletti [2007]; Nicoletti and Scarpetta [2003]; and OECD STAN database for industrial analysis, revision 3 [ISIC rev. 3].)

UNEMPL. BENEF.: Unemployment benefit replacement rate for low-income workers in their first year of unemployment. This is measured by the average replacement rate—that is, the ratio of the unemployment benefit to the last wage for a worker that earns 66 percent of average worker earnings. (Source: OECD *Benefits and Wages.*)

EMPLOY. PROTECTION: OECD summary indicator of the stringency for employment protection legislation for all contracts, defined as the average of values for the indefinite contract (regular) workers and the fixed-term contract (temporary) workers. (Source: OECD, *Employment Outlook 2004.*)

UNEMPLOYMENT BENEFIT TRADING PARTNERS: Average of the value of the indicator UNEMPLOYMENT BENEFIT for the trading partners. (Source: OECD *Benefits and Wages* and OECD STAN database for industrial analysis, revision 3 [ISIC rev. 3].)

PMKT REGULAT. (−1 and −2): Country average value (lagged one and two periods) of the sectorial indicator REG.

EMPL. PROTECT. TRADING PARTNERS: Average of the value of the indicators EMPLOYMENT PROTECTION for the trading partners. (Source: OECD *Employment Outlook 2004* and OECD STAN database for industrial analysis, revision 3 [ISIC rev. 3].)

POPULATION1SH: The share of the population of a country over the total population in the eleven EMU countries. (Source: Tenreyro [2007].)

AREA1SH: The share of land mass of a country over the total land mass in the eleven EMU countries. (Source: Tenreyro [2007].)

PRMSE: The correlation shocks in prices of a country relative to the other eleven EMU countries. (Source: Tenreyro [2007].)

YRMSE: The correlation shocks in output of a country relative to the other eleven EMU countries. (Source: Tenreyro [2007].)

BORDER: The number of the eleven EMU countries with which a country shares borders. (Source: Tenreyro [2007].)

COMLANG: The number of the eleven EMU countries with which a country shares a common language. (Source: Tenreyro [2007].)

COLONY: The number of the eleven EMU countries with which a country was ever in a colonial relationship. (Source: Tenreyro [2007].)

*LPASTINLFWDI*1: Lagged value of the average over a five-year period of the inflation rate in a country, measured using the GDP deflator. (Source: World Development Indicator database.)

*LAGINFLDEVEU*11: Lagged value of the difference between the inflation rate in a country—measured using the GDP deflator—and the average inflation in the other eleven EMU countries. (Source: World Development Indicator database.)

*LPASTINFLDEVEU*11: Lagged value of the average over a five-year period of the difference between the inflation rate in a country—measured using the GDP deflator—and the average inflation in the other eleven EMU countries. (Source: World Development Indicator database.)

*LAGINFLWDI*1: Lagged value of the inflation rate in a country, measured using the GDP deflator. (Source: World Development Indicator database.)

LPASTLNTRADE: Lagged value of the average over a five-year period of the nominal sum of import and export that a country had with the other eleven EMU countries. (Source: OECD STAN Bilateral Trade Database.)

LAGLNRTRADE: Lagged value of the real sum of import and export that a country had with the other eleven EMU countries. (Source: OECD STAN Bilateral Trade Database.)

LPASTLNRTRADE: Lagged value of the average over a five-year period of the real sum of import and export that a country had with the other eleven EMU countries. (Source: OECD STAN Bilateral Trade Database.)

LAGLNTRADE: Lagged value of the nominal sum of import and export that a country had with the other eleven EMU countries. (Source: OECD STAN Bilateral Trade Database.)

References

Alesina, A., S. Ardagna, and V. Galasso. 2008. The euro and structural reforms. NBER Working Paper no. 14479. Cambridge, MA: National Bureau of Economic Research, November.

Alesina, A., S. Ardagna, and F. Trebbi. 2006. Who adjusts and when? The political economy of reforms. *IMF Staff Papers* 53 (special iss.): 1–49.

Alesina, A., and R. Barro. 2002. Currency unions. *Quarterly Journal of Economics* 117 (2): 409–36.

Alesina, A., R. Barro, and S. Tenreyro. 2002. Optimal currency areas. In *NBER macroeconomics annual 2002,* ed. M. Gertler and K. S. Rogoff, 301–55. Cambridge, MA: MIT Press.

Alesina, A., and A. Drazen. 1991. Why are stabilizations delayed? *American Economic Review* 81 (5): 1170–88.

Alesina, A., and F. Giavazzi. 2006. *The future of Europe: Reform or decline.* Cambridge, MA: MIT Press.

Alesina, A., and R. Perotti. 2004. The European Union: A politically incorrect view. *Journal of Economic Perspectives* 18 (4): 26–48.

Alesina, A., R. Perotti, and J. Tavares. 1998. The political economy of fiscal adjustments. *Brookings Papers on Economic Activity, Macroeconomics:* 197–266. Washington, DC: Brookings Institution.

Alesina, A., N. Roubini, and G. Cohen. 1997. *Political cycles and the macroeconomy.* Cambridge, MA: MIT Press.

Barone, G., and F. Cingano. 2008. Service regulation and growth: Evidence from OECD countries. Bank of Italy Working Paper no. 675. Rome: Bank of Italy.

Bean, C. 1998. The interaction of aggregate-demand policies and labor market reform. *Swedish Economic Policy Review* 5 (2): 353–82.

Beck, T., G. Clarke, A. Groff, P. Keefer, and P. Walsh. 2001. New tools and new tests in comparative political economy: The database of political institutions. *World Bank Economic Review* 15 (1): 165–76.

Belke, A., B. Herz, and L. Vogel. 2005. Structural reform and the exchange rate regime: A panel analysis for the world versus OECD countries. IZA Discussion Paper no. 1798. Bonn, Germany: Institute for the Study of Labor.

Bertola, G. 2008. Labor markets in EMU: What has changed and what needs to change. CEPR Discussion Paper no. 7049. London: Center for Economic Policy Research.

Blanchard, O., and F. Giavazzi. 2003. The macroeconomic effects of labor and product market deregulation. *Quarterly Journal of Economics* 118 (3): 879–909.

Brender, A., and A. Drazen. 2005. Political budget cycles in new versus established democracies. *Journal of Monetary Economics* 52 (7): 1271–95.

Conway, P., and G. Nicoletti. 2007. Product market regulation in non-manufacturing sectors of OECD countries: Measurement and highlights. OECD Economics Department Working Paper no. 530. Paris: Organization for Economic Cooperation and Development.

Drazen, A. 2000. *Political economy in macroeconomics.* Princeton, NJ: Princeton University Press.

Drazen, A., and W. Easterly. 2001. Do crises induce reform? Simple empirical tests of conventional wisdom. *Economics and Politics* 13 (2): 129–57.

Drazen, A., and V. Grilli. 1993. The benefits of crises for economic reform. *American Economic Review* 83 (3): 598–607.

Duval, R., and J. Elmeskov. 2005. The effects of EMU on structural reforms in labour and product markets. OECD Economics Department Working Paper no. 438. Paris: Organization for Economic Cooperation and Development.

Fiori, G., G. Nicoletti, S. Scarpetta, and F. Schiantarelli. 2007. Employment outcomes and the interaction between product and labor market deregulation: Are they substitutes or complements? IZA Discussion Paper no. 2770. Bonn, Germany: Institute for the Study of Labor.

Hoj, J., V. Galasso, G. Nicoletti, and T.-T. Dang. 2006. The political economy of structural reform: Empirical evidence from OECD countries. OECD Economics Department Working Paper no. 501. Paris: Organization for Economic Cooperation and Development.

International Monetary Fund (IMF). 2004. Fostering structural reforms in industrialized countries. In *World economic outlook: Advancing structural reforms,* ed. IMF, 24–148. Washington, DC: IMF, April.

McCallum, J. 1995. National borders matter: Canadian-U.S. regional trade patterns. *American Economic Review* 85 (3): 615–23.

Nicoletti, G., and S. Scarpetta. 2003. Regulation, productivity and growth: OECD evidence. *Economic Policy* 18 (36): 9–72.

———. 2005. Product market reforms and employment in the OECD countries. OECD Economics Department Working Paper no. 472. Paris: Organization for Economic Cooperation and Development.

Obstfeld, M. 1997. Europe's gamble. *Brookings Papers on Economic Activity,* Issue no. 2: 241–317.

Persson, T. 2001. Currency unions and trade: How large is the treatment effect? *Economic Policy* 16 (33): 335–48.

Rose, A. 2000. One money, one market: Estimating the effect of common currencies on trade. *Economic Policy* 15 (30): 7–45.

Saint-Paul, G. 1996. Exploring the political economy of labor market institutions. *Economic Policy* 11 (23): 265–315.

———. 1999. Assessing the political viability of labor market reform: The case of employment protection. CEPR Discussion Paper no. 2136. London: Center for Economic Policy Research.

———. 2000. *The political economy of labour market institutions.* Oxford: Oxford University Press.

Saint-Paul, G., and S. Bentolila. 2000. Will EMU increase eurosclerosis? CEPR Discussion Paper no. 2423. London: Center for Economic Policy Research, April.

Tenreyro, S. 2007. On the trade impact of exchange rate volatility. *Journal of Development Economics* 82 (2): 485–508.

Thom, R., and B. Walsh. 2002. The effect of a currency union on trade: Lessons from the Irish experience. *European Economic Review* 46 (6): 1111–23.

Comment   Otmar Issing

This chapter by A. Alesina, S. Ardegna, and V. Galano—in short, AAG—is indeed a triple-A contribution. It addresses an important aspect of the European Monetary Union (EMU) and brings together economics and political considerations to explain policy choices. The authors go the hard way of detailed empirical work, scrutinize a myriad of data, and remain careful in their interpretation.

To start with, EMU in the end was a political decision. Economists around the world were more or less skeptical. Their fundamental concern was an obvious lack of flexibility in the economies of potential member states, and as a consequence, in the future monetary union. For example, on February 9, 1998, 155 German academic economists published an open letter entitled "The Euro Is Coming Too Early"—the main reason being the lack of flexibility in labor markets (and insufficient progress in consolidating

Otmar Issing is the president of the Center for Financial Studies at the University of Frankfurt and a former member of the executive board of the European Central Bank.

public finances).[1] And it was in the first weeks after the establishment of the European Central Bank (ECB) when I received a letter by Milton Friedman saying, "Dear Otmar, congratulations on an impossible job. You know I am convinced, monetary union in Europe is doomed to fail."

In short, a clear majority of economists pointed to the fact that a monetary union with the envisaged large membership—eleven countries finally to start on January 1, 1999—would be far from fulfilling the criteria of an optimal currency area (OCA). But, the project of monetary union, the ambition to be allowed to participate, and after entry, the need to adapt to the new framework of a single monetary policy—"one size fits all"—and the removal of the tool of national monetary policy and changes in the exchange rate of the national currency strengthened structural reforms and fiscal consolidation.

The conditions for entry enshrined in the Maastricht treaty—at least formally—referred only to nominal variables. The discipline exerted by these criteria in some cases came late, but all in all, it was timely enough. The threat of not being in at the start of EMU unleashed unexpected forces, including the sphere of fiscal policy—admittedly with grave exemptions as regards public debt levels.[2]

But what about structural reforms, progress toward greater flexibility in product and labor markets? The authors identify two layers of a potential impact of EMU.

One is (dis)qualified by AAG as "wishful thinking"—the rhetoric that "any step toward integration is 'by definition' good and brings about all sorts of wonderful achievements for the continent." Strange as it might sound for an economist, this "philosophy" of integration—or what it may be called—played for some time an important political role under the label of the "monetarist" position. This was based on the expectation that once the exchange rate was fixed irreversibly, the rest would adjust in a mysterious way.

The other line of argument refers to the fact that monetary union eliminates the option of strategic devaluations, or more generally of adjusting policy rates to national cyclical conditions, and therefore enforces pressure for enhancing the flexibility of labor markets and wage bargaining.[3]

In this context, AAG mention that not surprisingly, the pre-euro debate initially focused on labor market reforms. The effect on product markets comes mainly from increasing costs of regulation due to stronger competition.

1. See Issing (1996).
2. Issing (2008).
3. A few authors argued that the disappearance of the exchange rate risk would lead to a higher demand for protectionism and thereby weaken the incentives for structural reforms. See Calmfors (2001).

To what extent are the criteria of OCA endogenous? What is the impact of EMU on concrete steps for more flexibility in product and labor markets?

Here, AAG are confronted with a tremendous identification problem. The authors concentrate their empirical study at a one-shot event—the introduction of the euro. The difficulties to isolate this effect from the rest of the environment are obvious—and fully recognized by the authors:

1. The process of globalization has created incentives for reforms worldwide.

2. The introduction of the euro is not just exogenous. Countries discussed pros and cons and adapted to the common currency for different reasons, which could have also affected incentives for structural reforms.

3. The effect of the introduction of the euro preceded the start of EMU. As soon as it became a common conviction that EMU would begin as agreed in Maastricht on January 1, 1999, risk premia in foreign exchange markets started to decline, and preparation for participation reached a decisive phase.

4. The observation period still is rather short—further impact might be in the pipeline.

5. Finally, and most importantly: is it possible to disentangle the effect of participation in the single market from the introduction of the euro?

The main result of their empirical study can be summarized in two sentences:

1. The adoption of the euro had a significant effect in promoting the adoption of product market reform, especially in some sectors. Here, one is tempted to argue that the impact should rather be in general terms (i.e., comprise structural reforms on a broad macrolevel). So, are sectoral reforms more due to sectoral specifics than to the introduction of the euro?

2. For labor market reform, the euro did not have much of an effect. Here, one may caution a bit. For example, the euro may have contributed to the major labor market reforms that were implemented in Germany in 2004 and early 2005.

The authors are also convinced that the sequencing of reforms should follow this pattern.

I will not try to evaluate the statistical method applied, nor to go through the myriad of details. While the data are impressive, it would help if the authors could try to consolidate their results.

The AAG chapter sets a landmark in extracting information from their model on an issue of highest importance for the functioning of EMU. Overall, their results are consistent with those of other studies. In the meantime, the European Commission has published its "EMU@10" special report (2008). Its summary concludes:

The evidence is not very conclusive, but it is clear that on balance the single currency has had little positive effect on the pace of structural reform[4]. . . . Consistent with these findings, the analysis . . . indicates that euro-area countries have on average been less forthcoming in implementing the structural policy recommendations made to them by the EU under the Broad Economic Policy Guidelines (BEPGs)—a Treaty-based tool for economic policy coordination—in the period 2000–2005. In particular, progress in the cross-border integration of services has been more muted than expected, which is particularly problematic. It is in this area especially that price rigidities persist. This has been recognised by . . . the European Commission, which in turn has led to intensified surveillance of national structural policies in the euro area in the framework of the Lisbon Strategy for Growth and Jobs, which was revamped in 2005. (22)

A paper by Pelkmans, Montoya, and Maravelle (2008) shows that product market reforms do help to "lubricate" adjustment processes in the euro area.[5]

Where Is EMU Going?

Notwithstanding the remaining lack of flexibility, especially in labor markets, the single monetary policy has worked with great success—certainly better than even the optimists had expected. This result might trigger a new discussion on the relevance of the OCA criteria. Financial integration might have played a role. Consumption smoothing and risk sharing should have contributed to the functioning of EMU.

On the other hand, significant challenges are ahead. Countries that continuously have lost competitiveness inside the euro area are confronted with heavy adjustment problems, and the slowdown of growth will reveal the lack in ambition on structural reforms throughout the euro area. The costs of the current financial crisis for the real economy will to a large extent depend on the flexibility of labor and product markets—in particular, on (downward) flexibility of labor costs and prices. In my book *The Birth of the Euro* (2008), the title of the last chapter, "Europe at the Crossroads," is a kind of short-cut message. The there-is-no-alternative (TINA) to structural reforms hypothesis remains true if the coherence of the area is to be preserved and the functioning of the single monetary policy guaranteed. The alternative is anything but promising: increasing tensions—economically and politically—with far-reaching consequences.

---

4. Duval and Elmeskov (2006) see no acceleration of reforms in EMU. A slowdown in reforms in 1999 to 2004 relative to 1994 to 1998 is reported by Duval (2006).
5. Pelkmans, Montoya, and Maravalle (2008).

References

Calmfors, L. 2001. Unemployment, labor market reform, and monetary union. *Journal of Labor Economics* 19 (2): 265–89.

Duval, R. 2006. Fiscal positions, fiscal adjustment and structural reforms in labour and product marets. In *Proceedings from the ECFIN workshop, "The Budgetary Implications of Structural Reforms,"* ed. S. Deroose, E. Flores, and A. Turrini, 169–204. Brussels: European Commission.

Duval, R., and J. Elmeskov. 2006. The effects of EMU on structural reforms in labour and product markets. ECB Working Paper no. 596. Frankfurt: European Central Bank.

European Commission. 2008. EMU@10: Successes and challenges after 10 years of economic and monetary union. Special issue, *Quarterly Report on the Euro Area* 7, no. 2.

Issing, O. 1996. Europe: Political union through common money? IEA Occasional Paper no. 98. London: Institute of Economic Affairs.

———. 2008. *The birth of the euro.* Cambridge: Cambridge University Press.

Pelkmans, J., L. A. Montoya, and A. Maravalle. 2008. How product market reforms lubricate shock adjustment in the euro area. European Economy Economic Paper no. 341. Brussels: European Commission.

3

The Euro and Firm Restructuring

Matteo Bugamelli, Fabiano Schivardi,
and Roberta Zizza

3.1 Introduction

One of the main drivers of European integration was the idea that a more integrated European economy would promote economic efficiency, allowing countries to fully exploit their competitive advantages, fostering factor mobility and increasing allocational efficiency (European Commission 1993). The euro was a crucial milestone along this path. Ten years after its launch, we can start to assess the effects of such a radical institutional change. In this chapter, we focus on whether the introduction of the euro—narrowly defined as the end of competitive devaluations—has induced significant changes in the productive structure of the euro area (EA) member states.[1]

When the euro was introduced in 1999, the European productive structure was sharply differentiated across member states, with a group of southern countries specialized in traditional, low human capital activities. Firms in these countries took advantage of recurrent devaluations to cope with international competition, especially from the low-wage economies. The

Matteo Bugamelli is at the Bank of Italy. Fabiano Schivardi is at the University of Cagliari and at EIEF. Roberta Zizza is at the Bank of Italy.

Prepared for the National Bureau of Economic Research (NBER) conference on "Europe and the Euro," October 17 and 18, 2008. We have benefited from discussions and comments from Alberto Alesina, Andrea Brandolini, Paola Caselli, Francesco Giavazzi, Francesca Lotti, Marco Magnani, Gianmarco Ottaviano, Daniela Puggioni, Paolo Sestito, and seminar participants at the Bank of Italy and NBER conference. The views expressed here are our own and do not necessarily reflect those of the Bank of Italy.

1. Competitive devaluations are in principle a possible option, even in the posteuro era. Nevertheless, the euro has put an end to the possibility of trade advantages with respect to the rest of the EA, which accounts for a significant fraction of exports for all members. Further, as the euro is a stronger currency, the risk of sharp devaluations is lower.

basic idea underlying our analysis is that the end of competitive devaluations should have had differential effects by country and sector. For one thing, before the introduction of the euro, countries had adopted different strategies in terms of devaluation vis-à-vis the deutschemark (DM; Giavazzi and Giovannini 1989). Second, in some sectors, competition is mainly in prices, so changes in the terms of trade are a fundamental determinant of performance; in other sectors, product differentiation is more pronounced, so prices are just one factor of competitiveness, alongside product quality, brand name, technological content, and so forth. Our initial hypothesis is that the euro should have been a greater shock for the sectors competing mostly in prices and the countries that made a more intense use of competitive devaluations. We therefore expect that restructuring has been more intense in these country-sectors.

We analyze restructuring along two dimensions. First, we consider whether there has been a reallocation of factors away from the sectors that presumably had relied more heavily on devaluations (between-sectoral reallocation process). Second, we consider to what extent the reallocation has occurred within sectors. As the recent body of literature on trade and productivity has shown (Melitz 2003; Bernard, Jensen, and Schott 2006a), most of the productivity gains from trade opening are achieved via the reallocation of production from less to more efficient firms within the same sector.

The between-sectoral analysis is based on standard techniques of convergence/divergence of productive structures. We find very weak support for the proposition that the euro has induced a reallocation of activities between sectors. Specifically, Krugman dissimilarity indices show that intersectoral reallocation in the posteuro era has been almost nil for most of the EA countries and modest for the rest. Although a finer sectoral classification might give a somewhat different picture, we think it is plausible that a substantial process of reallocation should be visible, even using the twenty-two two-digit manufacturing sectors of the Nomenclature générale des Activités économiques dans les Communautés Européennes (NACE) revision 3 classification system.[2]

We then move on to consider whether there is evidence of within-sectoral reallocation. Ideally, one would like to test this hypothesis directly with firm-level data. Unfortunately, such data are not available at the cross-country level. Our analysis is therefore based on sectoral data and on indirect mea-

2. The end of competitive devaluation is not the only channel through which the euro could have stimulated factor reallocation. A trade integration channel within the EA countries must also be acknowledged. The benefits from the use of a common currency—lower transaction costs, no exchange rate risk, better price and cost transparency—are expected to enhance openness to trade and investment, as well as to foster competition. Indeed, since the launch of the euro, bilateral trade among EA members has expanded far more rapidly than trade with other EU countries (European Commission 2008; Baldwin 2006; de Nardis, De Santis, and Vicarelli 2008). Our results suggest that these channels too have had little impact on sectoral reallocation.

sures of restructuring—in particular, productivity growth. We follow the approach introduced by Rajan and Zingales (1998). We rank countries by how heavily they relied on devaluations, considering both nominal and real devaluation vis-à-vis the DM over the 1980 to 1998 period. We classify sectors according to how important devaluations were for competitiveness using a series of indicators of the sectoral skill content, with the idea that low-skill content implies more price competition. An alternative ranking is to look directly at the importance of emerging economies in world trade in each sector. The variable we track is China's export share. The interaction between the country-level devaluation measure and the sectoral skill content measure constitutes the indicator of how much a country-sector should have been affected by the euro.

We find clear support for the hypothesis that the euro has induced relatively strong intrasectoral restructuring. Productivity growth has been fastest in the sectors with low-skill content and in the countries that had relied more on competitive devaluations. This result is robust to a series of checks. In particular, to address potential omitted-variable bias, we not only include country and sector dummies but also a control group of countries that are broadly similar to the EA countries, except for adoption of the euro—namely, Denmark, Sweden, and the United Kingdom. We also show that our results are not driven by some underlying autocorrelated process independent of the euro. Moreover, restructuring seems to have had little negative effect on employment. The exception is when we rank sectors according to the Chinese export share, in which case a clear negative effect on employment emerges. Note that this is only a within-country and sector comparison, so it does not allow us to draw conclusions on aggregate growth differentials between the countries or the sectors. All we can say is that *relative to the country and sector averages,* the productivity growth differential between low- and high-skill sectors was higher in a high-devaluation country than in a low-devaluation one.

To obtain direct evidence on the restructuring process, we then turn to firm-level evidence from Italian manufacturing. We first review a series of forty in-depth interviews with entrepreneurs conducted by researchers at the Bank of Italy in 2007, in the spirit of the National Bureau of Economic Research (NBER)/Sloan "pin factory" project (Borenstein, Farrell, and Jaffe 1998). The interviews offer soft evidence on the restructuring process. They suggest that since the adoption of the euro, firms have shifted their business focus from production to upstream and downstream activities, such as research and development (R&D), product design, marketing, and distribution. These activities in fact can procure a certain degree of market power and enable firms to escape the pure cost competition. Moreover, the shift is more dramatic in traditional low-tech activities, in line with the aggregate evidence. Finally, it emerges that restructuring is an ongoing process, not a single episode with a beginning and an end.

The insights from the interviews are corroborated by the hard, quantitative evidence provided by a database of manufacturing firms representative of the population of firms with at least fifty employees. First, the cross-sectional dispersion in both productivity and profitability has increased steadily since 1999, as one would expect during restructuring episodes. And there is a marked decline in the share of blue-collar workers, consistent with the thesis that firms are shifting the focus away from production. The lower the technological content of the sector, the sharper the decline. Interestingly, in the pre-euro era, the opposite was the case: low-tech firms used devaluations to recoup price competitiveness and intensified their reliance on low-skilled workers. We do not find that job flows intensified after the introduction of the euro; the restructuring process seems to entail a reallocation of workers within rather than between firms.

To close the circle, finally we consider whether the restructuring firms actually perform better than the others, regressing value added and productivity growth on indicators of restructuring at the firm level derived from ad hoc questions on the importance of trademarks and of changes in the mix of goods produced. We also include the share of blue-collar workers. The results confirm that the firms that undertook restructuring recorded higher growth rates, both in value added and in productivity.

A number of papers are considering the effects of the euro on member countries ten years after its inception. Alesina, Ardagna, and Galasso (see chapter 2 in this volume) show that the common currency has contributed to building political consensus for restructuring in the product markets—markedly through liberalization in the energy and communication sectors—but not in the labor market. Bertola (2007) finds an association between the euro adoption and the improvements in terms of employment and equilibrium unemployment. Our work is more broadly related to the growing body of literature that considers the effects of international competition on national productive structure (Chen, Imbs, and Scott 2007). The paper closest to our sectoral analysis is that of Auer and Fischer (2008) on the effects on U.S. industry of import penetration from emerging economies. They also find that the U.S. sectors most exposed to competition from emerging countries recorded higher productivity growth, as well as lower price inflation. The same result on productivity is found by Bugamelli and Rosolia (2006) on Italian data. Using U.S. firm-level data, Bernard, Jensen, and Schott (2006a) find that industries' exposure to imports from low-wage countries is correlated positively with the probability of plant death and negatively with employment growth. In a companion paper, Bernard, Jensen, and Schott (2006b) show that a reduction of inbound trade costs is positively associated with industry productivity (TFP), the probability of plant death, the probability of entry of new exporters, and export growth by incumbent exporters. For Italy, Bugamelli, Fabiani, and Sette (2008) show that greater exposure to Chinese export penetration has diminished the pace of firms' output price increases.

The rest of this chapter is organized as follows. In section 3.2, we describe the data and perform the between-sector analysis. Section 3.3 explains the econometric approach to test for within-sector reallocation and discusses the results. Section 3.4 deals with the firm-level evidence for Italian manufacturing firms, and section 3.5 concludes.

3.2   Cross-Sectoral Reallocation

In this section, we analyze the productive structure of the EU member countries and its evolution over time; given the need for a sufficiently long period after the introduction of the euro and data availability, we focus on the EU15 countries—that is, the eleven that adopted the euro on its inception (Austria, Belgium, Finland, France, Germany, Ireland, Italy, Luxembourg, the Netherlands, Portugal, and Spain) plus Greece (entered the EA in 2002), in addition to Denmark, Sweden, and the United Kingdom, which have not adopted the euro. Following Bertola (2007), the three non-EA countries constitute the control group.[3] Despite its evident shortcomings, this is the best control group available.[4] We assess whether the introduction of the euro has induced a reallocation of production between sectors, and if so, whether the intersectoral change has been more dramatic in the countries that had previously made greater use of competitive devaluations. The main data source we rely on in this and the next section is the March 2008 release of the European Union Level analysis of Capital, Labor, Energy, Materials, and Service Inputs (EU KLEMS) database (Timmer, O'Mahony, and Van Ark 2007). The manufacturing sector's share of value added in 2005 stood at around 20 percent for most countries, with lower values in France, Denmark, Greece, and Luxembourg. Following the secular decline in manufacturing, the share decreased somewhat between 1998 and 2005 in most countries;

3. Bertola (2007) uses a diff-in-diff approach to test the effects of the euro on income dispersion.

4. Ideally, the control group should have more than three countries in order to avoid idiosyncratic country patterns affecting the results. However, what is really crucial is that the control group (non-EA members) is comparable with the treatment group (EA members). As EU membership involves many factors not available to the econometrician (laws, regulation, etc.), a control group with only EU countries should provide the best guarantees in terms of similarity (Baldwin 2006), whereas including non-EU countries seems more problematic. One could also object that the treatment is not fully exogenous, as in principle, the three noneuro members could have deliberately opted out in order to not preclude future competitive devaluations. This does not seem to be the case, however. For example, in the context of the assessment made by HM Treasury on the case for the United Kingdom to join the euro zone, Buiter and Grafe (2003) conclude that monetary independence has not been instrumental to maintain (or regain) competitiveness; indeed, "the UK exchange rate during the 1990s and until well into 2002 has been a source of competitive misalignment" (35).

Ireland and the United Kingdom experienced the most pronounced downsizing of the sector.

From now on, we concentrate on manufacturing, as the effects we are considering work through the terms of trade and so are important mostly for tradeable goods. Data on value added, employment, and capital stock for the manufacturing sector are available for all EU15 countries, with a breakdown into twenty-two industries corresponding as a rule to the two-digit NACE classification. Southern countries such as Italy, Greece, and Portugal still have a large share of their value added in traditional sectors, such as textiles, apparel, leather goods, and footwear. The other countries concentrate their production in more technologically advanced sectors: machinery in Germany (but in Italy, too), chemicals in a host of countries (Belgium, France, Germany, the Netherlands, Ireland, and the United Kingdom), and radio, television, and communication equipment in the Nordic countries (Finland and Sweden, in particular).

In order to facilitate the comparison of productive structures among countries and over time, we first characterize sectors by their skill, R&D, and information and communication technology (ICT) intensity, and then we group them into intensity classes. Figures are computed from U.S. data, which we use in the regression analysis to avoid problems of endogeneity. Skill intensity is proxied by hours worked by high-skilled persons—defined as those with at least a college degree—as a share in total hours; R&D intensity is R&D expenditure over value added; ICT intensity is the ratio of ICT capital stock to the total capital stock, both in real terms.[5]

As table 3.1 shows, the machinery and the electrical and optical equipment sectors exhibit the highest ICT content; together with "other transport equipment," they spend a relatively higher fraction of their value added on R&D and employ relatively more-skilled persons. As a rule, traditional sectors (producing food, textiles, leather, and wood products) are characterized by low values of the three indicators. Intensity classes (low, medium low, medium high, high) are then defined according to quartiles in the distribution of each indicator (see table 3A.1 in the appendix for the matching of sectors into skill, ICT, and R&D categories). A glance at the value added shares broken down by skill content in 1998 and 2005 (figure 3.1) suggests that sectoral modifications were modest in the period. Only in Finland and Sweden has reallocation toward high-skill activities been substantial; Ireland stands out as the country where high-skill activities are prominent; if anything, Italy and Spain have increased their share in low-intensity activities.

To address sectoral modification in a more synthetic way, we apply standard techniques of convergence/divergence of productive structures. In

5. The ICT and skill intensity have been derived from EU KLEMS; R&D intensity comes from the OECD STAN database.

Table 3.1   **ICT, R&D, and skill intensities in the U.S. and China's world market share by sector of economic activity**

Sector (NACE code in parentheses)	ICT intensity	R&D intensity	Skill intensity	Chinese share
Food products and beverages (15)	0.06	0.01	0.16	0.03
Tobacco products (16)	0.06	0.01	0.27	0.02
Textiles (17)	0.05	0.01	0.10	0.09
Wearing apparel, dressing (18)	0.05	0.01	0.14	0.16
Leather, leather products, and footwear (19)	0.05	0.01	0.09	0.20
Wood and products of wood and cork (20)	0.04	0.01	0.08	0.03
Pulp, paper, and paper products (21)	0.10	0.02	0.17	0.01
Printing, publishing, and reproduction (22)	0.10	0.02	0.34	0.01
Coke, refined petroleum products, and nuclear fuel (23)	0.05	0.06	0.31	0.05
Chemicals and chemical products (24)	0.12	0.14	0.41	0.02
Rubber and plastics products (25)	0.04	0.03	0.15	0.06
Other nonmetallic mineral products (26)	0.07	0.02	0.14	0.05
Basic metals (27)	0.06	0.02	0.14	0.03
Fabricated metal products (28)	0.06	0.02	0.12	0.05
Machinery, n.e.c. (29)	0.18	0.06	0.16	0.02
Office, accounting, and computing machinery (30)	0.16	0.42	0.49	0.03
Electrical machinery (31)	0.16	0.12	0.21	0.04
Radio, television, and communication equipment (32)	0.16	0.22	0.36	0.05
Medical, precision, and optical instruments (33)	0.16	0.36	0.38	0.03
Motor vehicles, trailers, and semitrailers (34)	0.14	0.13	0.20	0.00
Other transport equipment (35)	0.14	0.24	0.33	0.12
Manufacturing, n.e.c.; recycling (36, 37)	0.09		0.16	0.09
Correlation matrix				
ICT intensity	1.0	0.7	0.6	−0.3
R&D intensity		1.0	0.8	−0.1
Skill intensity			1.0	−0.3
Chinese share				1.0

Source: Based on EU KLEMS, OECD STAN, and United Nations data. Year: 1998.
Note: "n.e.c." = not elsewhere classified.

particular, we calculate bilateral dissimilarity indices based on value added shares, broken down by industry and by skill, R&D, and ICT intensity according to the classification in table 3A.1. Dissimilarity between country A and country B is captured by the following index, á la Krugman:

$$(1) \qquad \text{Dis}_{AB} = \left(\frac{1}{2} \sum_i |a_i - b_i| \right),$$

where *a* and *b* are the corresponding shares. The index ranges from 0 (perfect similarity) to 1 (perfect dissimilarity). The productive structure of each country is compared with that of the EA, net of the country's own economy for EA members only; indices are calculated for 1998 and 2005. Table 3.2 shows that within the EA, the most highly dissimilar countries—apart from

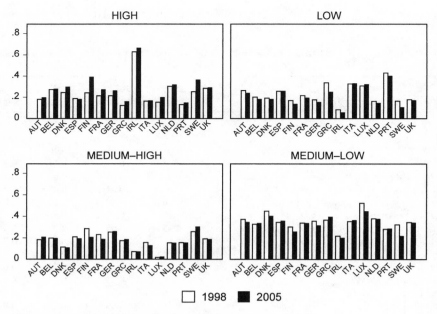

Fig. 3.1 Share of value added by skill content
Source: Our elaborations on EU KLEMS data.

Table 3.2	Krugman dissimilarity indices vis-à-vis the euro area							
	Skill intensity		ICT intensity		R&D intensity		NACE	
	1998	2005	1998	2005	1998	2005	1998	2005
Euro area								
Austria	0.06	0.06	0.07	0.04	0.06	0.07	0.15	0.11
Belgium	0.06	0.03	0.10	0.13	0.07	0.06	0.20	0.19
Finland	0.10	0.15	0.11	0.20	0.16	0.19	0.31	0.39
France	0.02	0.03	0.05	0.03	0.06	0.05	0.11	0.11
Germany	0.08	0.10	0.14	0.14	0.16	0.17	0.20	0.19
Greece	0.13	0.11	0.26	0.21	0.27	0.24	0.36	0.37
Ireland	0.42	0.42	0.21	0.18	0.35	0.34	0.47	0.47
Italy	0.13	0.19	0.11	0.12	0.09	0.13	0.16	0.21
Luxembourg	0.26	0.23	0.30	0.27	0.18	0.17	0.34	0.34
The Netherlands	0.13	0.11	0.12	0.14	0.12	0.11	0.21	0.24
Portugal	0.21	0.20	0.18	0.19	0.24	0.26	0.28	0.29
Spain	0.03	0.09	0.09	0.13	0.08	0.14	0.12	0.15
Noneuro area								
Denmark	0.13	0.11	0.07	0.03	0.06	0.06	0.18	0.19
Sweden	0.09	0.21	0.10	0.18	0.09	0.15	0.15	0.28
United Kingdom	0.07	0.05	0.05	0.07	0.06	0.06	0.14	0.15

Source: Based on EU KLEMS and STAN OECD data.

Note: Dissimilarity indices are calculated for each country with respect to the EA, net of the country itself for EA members.

Ireland and Luxembourg, which are exceptionally small—are the southern countries still specialized in low-skill activities. There is no sign of a uniform tendency toward either convergence or divergence: some countries increased and others decreased their similarity with the rest of the area. This is clear from figure 3.2, where we take an average of the indicators and plot the value for 2005 against that for 1998. Countries above (below) the 45degree line are those diverging from (converging to) the EA average sectoral structure. In line with previous evidence of very limited sectoral modification for almost all countries, we find little convergence/divergence; if anything, there is a slight tendency toward heterogeneity.

We also evaluate for each country the dissimilarity index between 1998 and 2005 to assess the extent of intersectoral change over the period. Irrespective of the sectoral breakdown, the extent of sectoral reallocation proves to be fairly modest (table 3.3). The dissimilarity index never goes beyond the first half of its range. The countries that changed their structure most are Sweden and Finland, followed by Greece.

It is interesting to see whether the degree of intersectoral reallocation, though mild, is related to competitive devaluations. We construct two mea-

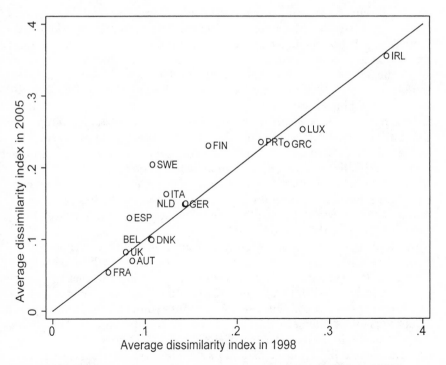

Fig. 3.2   Dissimilarity index with respect to euro area average: 1998 and 2005

Table 3.3   **Krugman dissimilarity indices, 1998 to 2005**

	Skill intensity	ICT intensity	R&D intensity	NACE
United Kingdom	0.01	0.02	0.02	0.06
The Netherlands	0.02	0.02	0.04	0.06
Belgium	0.02	0.02	0.02	0.04
Spain	0.02	0.03	0.05	0.07
Italy	0.03	0.05	0.04	0.07
Portugal	0.03	0.04	0.03	0.06
Ireland	0.04	0.09	0.04	0.11
Austria	0.05	0.04	0.04	0.07
Denmark	0.06	0.04	0.04	0.09
Germany	0.06	0.03	0.07	0.07
France	0.06	0.06	0.06	0.10
Luxembourg	0.07	0.06	0.05	0.10
Greece	0.08	0.09	0.13	0.14
Finland	0.15	0.16	0.16	0.20
Sweden	0.16	0.19	0.18	0.27

Source: Based on EU KLEMS and STAN OECD data.

Note: Countries are ordered according to the indices based on skill intensity.

sures of devaluation, nominal and real (DEVNOM and DEVREAL, respectively), calculated as the cumulated difference between January 1980 and December 1998 of the logarithm of each country's nominal/real effective exchange rate as a deviation from that of Germany. In principle, a negative sign indicates a depreciation relative to the DM; the absolute number refers to the intensity of the cumulative depreciation or appreciation. But for ease of interpretation, we invert the signs so that a higher value of the indicator reflects more intensive resort to competitive devaluations. Table 3.4 reports the values for DEVNOM and DEVREAL. The difference between the two (ΔP) is the cumulated change in relative producer prices. Both the nominal and the real indicators have been computed with respect to sixty-two countries, including the main emerging and developing economies. Both their exchange rates and their producer prices have entered the indicator, with a weight computed on the basis of trade flows (see Finicelli, Liccardi, and Sbracia (2005) for the methodology).

We find that when devaluation is measured in nominal terms (figure 3.3), the countries relying most heavily on devaluations are those most specialized in low-skill activities. This positive relationship vanishes when we consider devaluation in real terms. We also find some weak evidence that countries relying more heavily on devaluations exhibit relatively more pronounced signs of intersectoral reallocation, as shown by figure 3.4, where we plot the dissimilarity index between 1998 and 2005 (reported in the first column of table 3.3) against real devaluation; this evidence does not depend

Table 3.4   **Nominal and real measures of devaluation and price changes**

	DEVNOM	DEVREAL	ΔP
Austria	0.227	0.079	0.148
Belgium	0.408	0.187	0.222
Denmark	0.408	−0.042	0.450
Finland	0.432	0.109	0.323
France	0.479	0.068	0.411
Germany	0.000	0.000	0.000
Greece	1.945	0.086	1.859
Ireland	0.660	0.071	0.589
Italy	0.768	0.067	0.701
Luxembourg	0.408	0.187	0.222
The Netherlands	0.185	0.167	0.018
Portugal	1.366	−0.196	1.562
Spain	0.864	0.150	0.715
Sweden	0.893	0.099	0.794
United Kingdom	0.490	−0.230	0.720

Source: Bank of Italy's calculations. (See Finicelli, Liccardi, and Sbracia [2005].)

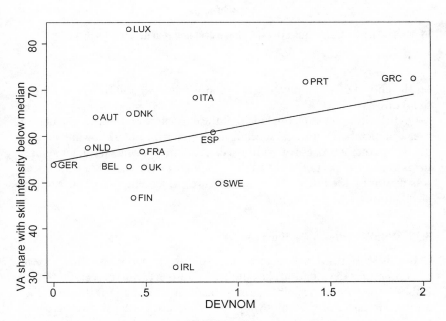

Fig. 3.3   Size of low-skill activities and devaluation in nominal terms

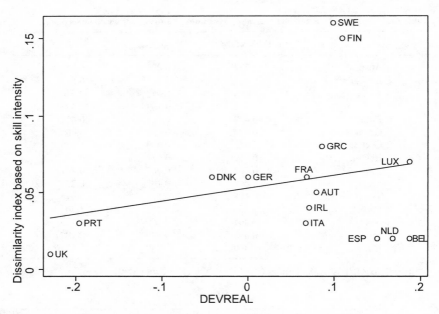

Fig. 3.4   Dissimilarity index (by skill intensity) and real devaluation

on the choice of the indicator (nominal versus real and different sectoral breakdowns).

On the whole, we can conclude that the euro has not induced a structural break in member countries' specialization patterns. Let us now move on to assess whether a process of within-sectoral restructuring characterized EA firms in the first part of this decade, and in particular, whether this process was driven by the introduction of the euro, which eliminated competitive devaluations.

3.3   Within-Sectoral Reallocation

In this section, we use sectoral data to test the hypothesis that the end of competitive devaluations has induced a restructuring process in the EA firms. We begin by describing the empirical approach and the data and then move on to the results. Finally, we perform a series of extensions and robustness checks.

3.3.1   The Empirical Approach and the Data

We test the effects of the euro on within-sectoral restructuring using sectoral data from different countries. Ideally, one would like to use direct measures of reallocation, such as job creation and destruction, entry, exit, and so forth. Unfortunately, such measures can only be constructed from firm-level data and so are not available for a cross-section of countries.[6] Accordingly, we use an outcome variable that should be closely related to reallocation (i.e., productivity growth). In fact, if reallocation and restructuring bring about productivity increases,[7] then the country-sectors that restructured more should have recorded a higher growth rate of productivity. We measure productivity as real value added per hour worked. We also consider growth in employment (more precisely, the number of hours worked) growth: in fact, productivity increases might have been due simply to a reduction in the employment level, connected with the exit of the less-productive plants and workers, the reorganization of production, and offshoring. Descriptive statistics by country for the outcome variables are provided in table 3A.2 in the appendix.

We follow the approach introduced by Rajan and Zingales (1998) in their paper on the effects of financial development on growth. The idea is to exploit both cross-country and cross-sectoral variability to test the effects of the euro on productivity growth. First, we determine how heavily the various countries had relied on devaluations (DEV_i): we expect that the greater this reliance, the stronger the effects of the euro. Second, we propose a measure S_j of how important devaluations were for sectoral competitiveness before the euro: in some sectors, competition is mainly price competition, so movements in the terms of trade are a fundamental determinant of performance; for others, product differentiation may be more pronounced, so prices could be just one in a series of other factors in competitiveness, such as product quality, brand name, and technological content. If the euro has had any effect in terms of restructuring, we expect it to be strongest in the country-sectors that relied more intensively on competitive devaluations, as measured by the interaction between the country and the sectoral indicators, $DEV_i * S_j$. We can test our argument through the following regression:

$$(2) \qquad \Delta \ln y_{ij9805} = \alpha_0 + \alpha_1 DEV_i * S_j + \alpha_2' \mathbf{X}_{ij} + DC_i + DS_j + u_{ij},$$

where $\Delta \ln y_{ij9805}$ is average yearly productivity growth in country i and sector j between 1998 and 2005, $\mathbf{X}_{ij}$ are additional controls, and DC_i and DS_j are country and sector dummies, respectively. Our prediction concerns the coefficient α_1: if $\alpha_1 > 0$, then the higher the country-sector reliance on devaluations, the stronger the effects of the euro on productivity; $\alpha_1 = \delta^2 \Delta \ln y_{ij} / \delta DEV_i \delta S_j$.

---

6. See Davis, Haltiwanger, and Schu (1996) for an overview of a large body of literature developed in the 1990s regarding sectoral reallocation. Bartelsmann, Scarpetta, and Schivardi (2005) compute sectoral statistics of reallocation for nine OECD countries, but their time span stops at the end of the 1990s at best.

7. The literature on productivity growth decomposition has identified various sources of productivity increases related to reallocation and restructuring; see Foster, Haltiwanger, and Krizan (2001) for a survey.

One important feature of this approach is the inclusion of both country and sector dummies. Country dummies ensure that the results are not driven by specific country characteristics that might potentially be related to the devaluation measure: rather, we use within-country differences in sectoral growth rates to identify the parameters of interest. The same applies to sectors: we do not compare different growth rates of productivity across sectors, as these might be dictated by sectoral characteristics potentially related to the variables we use to classify them. As such, this approach is robust to the main criticisms of the cross-country regressions with aggregate data, such as omitted-variable bias and reverse causality.[8]

Although the inclusion of country and sector dummies controls for the most likely omitted-variable problems, one could still argue that we might just be capturing an underlying process that would have occurred even without the euro. For example, the intensifying competition from emerging countries might have forced restructuring regardless. Such a process might have been more pronounced precisely in those countries and sectors that relied more on competitive devaluations, potentially more vulnerable to such competition. This is indeed a very serious concern. To address it, we take the three countries that did not adopt the euro as a control group and compute the effect of the interaction for the EA in deviation from non-EA countries. Formally, our regression framework is represented by:

$$(3) \qquad \Delta \ln y_{ij9805} = \beta_0 + \beta_1 DEV_i * S_j + \beta_2 EA_i * DEV_i * S_j + \beta_3' X_{ij} + DC_i + DS_j + u_{ij},$$

where EA_i is a dummy equal to 1 for the EA countries. In this specification, the coefficient β_2 measures the deviation of the EA effect from that of the non-EA countries, β_1. The idea is that the latter countries did not give up the possibility of devaluing but are similar to the EA countries from an economic point of view, because as members of the EU, they are subject to identical foreign trade rules, with the exception of the exchange rate. Differences in the degree of restructuring according to the interaction term can therefore be attributed to the euro. As discussed previously (see note 4), this control group is probably the best available, although it can be criticized both for its small size and its not necessarily random selection. To make sure that our results are not totally dependent on the control group, we also estimate equation (2) on EA members only—that is, considering the absolute effect rather than the deviation from the control group. In this case, we are not controlling for potential confounding factors. However, we still control for fixed country and sectoral attributes so that these estimates allow us to assess the extent to which our results depend on the control group.

---

8. Reverse causality could occur if productivity growth were persistent and if sectors with low productivity growth were determining the devaluation pattern before the euro. In this case, the correlation would actually be because productivity growth causes DEV. However, if anything, this should bias our estimates downward, inducing a negative correlation between DEV and productivity growth.

In terms of the country-level indicator, we want to capture the reliance on competitive devaluations. From the theoretical standpoint, it is unclear whether real or nominal devaluation is the relevant variable. Consider a country that kept a fixed nominal exchange rate with the DM but gained competitiveness by curbing price rises. For it, the euro should not represent much of a change, as the exchange rate was already stable, and using real devaluation might overstate its reliance on devaluations. On the other side, consider a country with relatively rapid price inflation that used devaluations to limit the effects on competitiveness. For such a country, appreciation was already under way before the euro, and using the nominal exchange rate would overstate the reliance on devaluations. These examples suggest that the ideal indicator should consider real devaluations that were due to changes in the nominal exchange rate. To capture this, in our basic specification, we introduce both the nominal exchange rate and the degree of relative producer price inflation in order to allow for potentially different dynamics of the two components of the real exchange rate. We test whether the coefficients of the two variables are opposite in sign and equal in absolute value, in which case the real exchange rate can be used directly.

For the sectoral indicators, we assume that price competition is more relevant in activities with a low human capital content (i.e., in which low-skilled workers are prevalent). The products of low-skill activities are likely to compete more in price than in quality relative to high-skill products. For a sector with low human capital content, the end of devaluations should have represented a stronger incentive to restructure; other things being equal, these sectors should have recorded higher productivity increases. Our main indicator is thus the skill content at the sectoral level. Following Rajan and Zingales (1998), in order to avoid endogeneity problems, we use the U.S. measure on the assumption that skill content is largely a technological characteristic, so the measure computed for the United States also applies to other countries. This assumption is particularly suitable for the EA countries, whose level of development is comparable to the United States. In accordance with our interpretation, we use sectoral low-skill intensity—that is, (1-skill intensity). This makes it easier to read the regression results.

We also experiment with other measures of sectoral dependence on devaluation. Following the same reasoning as before, high-R&D activities should also compete less on price and more on quality and technological content, reducing the price sensitivity of demand and hence the effects of exchange rate movements. Low-R&D activities should be characterized by greater price elasticity of demand, intensifying the response to terms of trade movements. We also use ICT intensity on the assumption that this is related to technological content. As before, we define sectors in terms of low-R&D and ICT intensity: (1-R&D content) and (1-ICT intensity), again computed for U.S. sectors.

Underlying our approach is the idea that in low human capital activities, the end to competitive devaluations has deprived EA countries of an instrument for meeting the competition from low-wage emerging economies. An alternative way to rank sectors, then, is to look directly at the importance of those economies in world trade. We take the most important of them, China, and compute its share of world exports in 1998. In this case, we are testing whether restructuring has been more intensive in countries that had relied on devaluations more heavily and in sectors where China's export share was larger.

The bottom part of table 3.1 reports the correlation coefficients between the sectoral indicators. As expected, the correlation between the first three indicators is high, ranging from 0.6 to 0.8. That between China's world market share and the others is negative. That is, the Chinese share is inversely related to the human capital content of production, but correlation is low in absolute terms: −0.3 with ICT and skill intensity and −0.1 with R&D intensity, suggesting that to see China simply as a low human capital good exporter might be to miss some important features of its economy.

We also run the same regression for EA countries in the period before the introduction of the euro. The assumption is that at that time, the competitive pressures were mitigated by competitive devaluations. In this case, we expect no particular difference between the study and the control group. In the language of the policy evaluation literature, we make sure that we are not simply capturing preexisting trends and that the euro did indeed induce a structural break.

3.3.2   Results

Our main regression is based on equation (3), where the outcome is average annual productivity growth for the period from 1998 to 2005. In addition to sectoral and country dummies, we include the log of the initial value of the dependent variable, and to control for any country-sector trend, its growth rate in the period from 1995 to 1998. Moreover, unless otherwise stated, to avoid endogeneity problems, we weight observations according to sectoral employment in 1998. We run weighted regressions for two reasons. First, accounting for the importance of the sector gives an estimated coefficient representative of the population effect. Second, sectoral data could suffer from measurement error, which is likely to be negatively correlated with the size of the sector itself. In particular, mismeasurement of employment or value added in some small sectors might have a powerful impact on the estimates.[9] Finally, all standard errors are computed using the White robust correction.

Table 3.5 reports the results of estimating equation (3) when the sectoral dependence on devaluations is gauged by low-skill intensity. Panel A shows

---

9. For example, in 1998, the "office, accounting and computing machinery" sector only had 1,500 employees in Austria, 800 in Belgium, and 300 in Greece; the "leather, leather products and footwear" sector only had 1,300 employees in Ireland.

Table 3.5   **Low-skill intensity and devaluations**

	(1)	(2)	(3)	(4)	(5)
	A. Productivity growth				
DEV * SK * EA	1.17**	1.01**	0.71	1.50***	0.55**
	(0.56)	(0.40)	(0.50)	(0.53)	(0.26)
DEV * SK	−0.64	−0.41*	−0.23	−0.66**	
	(0.50)	(0.23)	(0.37)	(0.31)	
ΔP * SK * EA	−1.05**				
	(0.45)				
ΔP * SK	0.58				
	(0.37)				
$\ln(\text{prod}_{98})$	−0.05***	−0.05***	−0.05***	−0.05***	−0.05***
	(0.01)	(0.01)	(0.01)	(0.02)	(0.01)
Δprod_{9598}	0.16**	0.16**	0.07	0.09	0.11*
	(0.07)	(0.08)	(0.08)	(0.11)	(0.06)
Observations	321	321	321	321	256
R^2	0.54	0.53	0.37	0.43	0.51
	B. Employment growth				
DEV * SK * EA	−0.19	−0.06	−0.06	−0.11	0.07
	(0.23)	(0.24)	(0.27)	(0.31)	(0.13)
DEV * SK	0.24	0.07	0.10	−0.03	
	(0.19)	(0.19)	(0.21)	(0.25)	
ΔP * SK * EA	0.12				
	(0.23)				
ΔP * SK	−0.16				
	(0.19)				
$\ln(\text{emp}_{98})$	0.01***	0.01***	−0.01**	0.01*	0.01***
	(0.00)	(0.00)	(0.00)	(0.00)	(0.00)
Δemp_{9598}	0.21***	0.20***	0.29***	0.16*	0.17**
	(0.07)	(0.07)	(0.10)	(0.08)	(0.07)
Observations	323	323	323	323	258
R^2	0.71	0.71	0.50	0.63	0.65

Note: DEV is the indicator of nominal devaluation (DEVNOM) in column (1) and of real devaluation (DEVREAL) in all other columns, computed over the period from 1980 to 1998; SK is low-skill intensity; EA is a dummy equal to 1 for the euro area countries; ΔP is the relative growth rate in producer prices (see the main text for details); $\ln(\text{prod}_{98})$ ($\ln(\text{emp}_{98})$) is initial productivity (employment), and Δprod_{9598} (Δemp_{9598}) is productivity (employment) growth in the 1995 to 1998 period. Outcome growth rates are computed for 1998 to 2005 in all columns except column (4), where it is computed for 2002 to 2005. All regressions are weighted with the sectoral employment, apart from that in column (3), which is unweighted. Robust standard errors in parentheses.

***Significant at the 1 percent level.

**Significant at the 5 percent level.

*Significant at the 10 percent level.

the estimates for productivity growth. The first column includes the interaction of skill intensity both with nominal devaluation (DEVNOM) and with relative producer price inflation (ΔP). The estimates for the control group are not significantly different from 0, in line with the idea that for these countries, the euro has not brought a structural break. Relative to the control group, the EA countries that had devalued more before the euro show relatively sharper productivity growth in low-skill-intensive sectors, while the reverse holds for the interaction with producer price inflation. The two coefficients are opposite in sign and very similar in absolute value (1.17 versus –1.05), and we fail to reject the hypothesis that one is equal to the negative of the other. We interpret this as an indication that while our earlier questions concerning the best measure of devaluation may be important in principle, in practice, real devaluation is a sufficient statistic for our purposes. We therefore concentrate on it in the other columns.

In column (2), we give the basic specification, with the interaction term constructed with the real exchange rate (DEVREAL). For the three non-EA countries, we find a negative coefficient, significant at 10 percent. This implies that productivity in sectors with less skill intensity grew relatively less when the real devaluation vis-à-vis the DM in the 1980 to 1998 period was greater. The interaction with the EA dummy gives a positive coefficient (1.01), significant at 5 percent (standard error equal to 0.40): compared to the control group, among the EA countries, productivity growth has been stronger when the real devaluation in the 1980 to 1998 period was greater and the sectoral skill intensity was lower. The other controls have the expected sign; in particular, productivity growth is positively serially correlated and displays mean reversion.

To evaluate the magnitude of the effects, we use the growth differential, defined as:

$$GD \equiv \beta_2(DEV_{75} - DEV_{25}) * (S_{75} - S_{25}),$$

where DEV_{75} is the value of DEV for the country at the seventy-fifth percentile of the distribution (Spain), and DEV_{25} is the value at the twenty-fifth percentile (France); S_{75} is the sector at the seventy-fifth percentile of the skill distribution (other nonmetallic mineral products), and S_{25} is the sector at the twenty-fifth percentile (other transport equipment). The variable GD measures how much more productivity grew in a low-skill sector (namely, at the seventy-fifth percentile of the skill distribution) compared to a high-skill one (at the twenty-fifth percentile) in a country that relied heavily on devaluations (at the seventy-fifth percentile) compared to one that did not (at the twenty-fifth percentile). For $\beta_2 = 1.01$, the growth differential is 1.7 percent—a sizeable effect—equal to the median yearly productivity growth and just below the mean (2.1 percent). It is important to note that this is only a within-country and sector comparison, so it does not allow us to draw conclusions on growth differential between the countries or the sectors. For example, it might well be that average productivity growth in Spain has been lower than in France: this would be captured by the country dummy. Similarly, average productivity growth in low-skill-intensity sectors might have been lower than in high-intensity ones. All we can say is that *relative to the country and sector averages,* the productivity growth differential between low- and high-skill sectors was higher in Spain than in France.

We then perform a series of robustness checks of this basic result. In column (3), we repeat the exercise without weights. The estimate of the coefficient drops to 0.7, and the standard error increases slightly so that the *p*-value is equal to 0.16. This indicates that the weighting scheme is important to obtain a significant coefficient, suggesting that the results have to be taken with due caution. Still, the value is positive and the *p*-stat reasonably low.

One could argue that firms require some time to adjust to the change of regime brought about by the euro. Moreover, even if restructuring started early on, such processes might take some time to result in productivity gains. According to this interpretation, one should find that the effects of restructuring are more visible in the latter part of the posteuro period, so we repeat the exercise and calculate productivity growth for the 2002 to 2005 period.[10] The coefficient does increase substantially—to 1.5—and is significant at 1 percent, lending support to the view that the effects of the euro on European firms did take some time to become appreciable. In fact, if we run the exercise for the 1998 to 2002 period (unreported), we get a substantially lower coefficient (0.36) that is not significantly different from 0 (standard error equal to 0.26).

As argued previously, a possible criticism relates to the control group, only made up of three countries. In column (5), we run regression (2) only for the EA countries. In this case, we are not controlling for potential confounding factors; still, given that both sector and country dummies are included, we are controlling for fixed attributes on both levels. We find a positive and significant coefficient, although smaller, in accordance with the fact that the effect was negative for the control group. According to this estimate, the growth differential is 0.96 percent. This allows us to exclude the possibility that our results are simply driven by some idiosyncratic characteristics of the control group: within the EA countries, productivity grew faster in exactly those country-sectors that are most likely to be hit by the introduction of the fixed-exchange rate regime.

As observed earlier, one might expect that productivity growth has been achieved through downsizing and offshoring, in which case it should go hand in hand with a reduction in employment. In panel B, we repeat the exercise and use employment growth as the dependent variable. Contrary to this proposition, we find no clear relation between our interaction mea-

---

10. To maximize comparability with the other regressions, we use the same initial value and pre-euro growth rate as we do for the other columns. Results are unchanged if we use the log of productivity in 2002 and the growth rate in the 1998 to 2002 period.

Table 3.6   Low-R&D intensity and devaluation

	(1)	(2)	(3)	(4)
	A. Productivity growth			
DEV * RD * EA	1.51**	0.62	1.63**	1.01***
	(0.59)	(0.52)	(0.73)	(0.36)
DEV * RD	−0.43	−0.08	−0.52	
	(0.34)	(0.39)	(0.37)	
$\ln(\text{prod}_{98})$	−0.06***	−0.06***	−0.06***	−0.05***
	(0.01)	(0.01)	(0.02)	(0.01)
Δprod_{9598}	0.16**	0.07	0.10	0.11*
	(0.08)	(0.08)	(0.11)	(0.06)
Observations	306	306	306	244
R^2	0.56	0.38	0.46	0.54
	B. Employment growth			
DEV * RD * EA	0.36	0.05	0.48	0.18
	(0.30)	(0.24)	(0.43)	(0.19)
DEV * RD	−0.27	−0.09	−0.43	
	(0.20)	(0.17)	(0.31)	
$\ln(\text{emp}_{98})$	0.01***	−0.01**	0.01**	0.01***
	(0.00)	(0.00)	(0.00)	(0.00)
Δemp_{9598}	0.22***	0.29***	0.19**	0.17**
	(0.07)	(0.10)	(0.09)	(0.07)
Observations	308	308	308	246
R^2	0.71	0.50	0.64	0.65

Note: DEV is the indicator of real devaluation (DEVREAL), computed over the period from 1980 to 1998; RD is low R&D intensity; EA is a dummy equal to 1 for the EA countries; $\ln(\text{prod}_{98})$ ($\ln(\text{emp}_{98})$) is initial productivity (employment), and Δprod_{9598} (Δemp_{9598}) is productivity (employment) growth in the 1995 to 1998 period. Outcome growth rates are computed for 1998 to 2005 in all columns except column (3), where it is computed for 2002 to 2005. All regressions are weighted with the sectoral employment, apart from that in column (2), which is unweighted. Robust standard errors in parentheses.
***Significant at the 1 percent level.
**Significant at the 5 percent level.
*Significant at the 10 percent level.

sure and employment growth. The coefficient of the interaction is generally negative but is small in absolute value and not significantly different from 0. According to this finding, restructuring does not seem to have had a downside in terms of job losses.

These basic patterns are confirmed when using R&D and ICT intensity as sectoral indicators of the importance of devaluations.[11] In table 3.6, we report the results for the R&D indicator. As before, the coefficient of the interaction is positive and significant, again with the exception of the

11. As for skill intensity, the specification with DEVNOM and ΔP confirms that DEVREAL is a sufficient statistic for our purposes. Accordingly, that specification is not reported.

unweighted regression. The effect increases in the second subperiod and still holds when computed on the EA countries only. The growth differential implied by the estimate in column (1) is similar in magnitude to that using skill intensity (1.6 percent productivity growth increase per year). Again, no clear effect on employment emerges—if anything, there is some evidence of a positive impact.

Similar results hold for ICT intensity, although the estimates tend to be less precise. The growth differential is 1.2 percent per year (table 3.7). With this indicator, we get a significant coefficient also in the unweighted case, while no evidence of a stronger effect in the second subperiod emerges. The employment regressions again suggest no effect of the interaction term.

Table 3.7   **Low-ICT intensity and devaluation**

	(1)	(2)	(3)	(4)
A. Productivity growth				
DEV * ICT * EA	1.64*	2.78**	1.35	0.83
	(0.91)	(1.34)	(1.37)	(0.51)
DEV * ICT	−0.66	−1.24	−0.68	
	(0.58)	(0.99)	(0.95)	
$\ln(\text{prod}_{98})$	−0.06***	−0.05***	−0.06***	−0.05***
	(0.01)	(0.01)	(0.02)	(0.01)
Δprod_{9598}	0.16*	0.07	0.09	0.10*
	(0.08)	(0.07)	(0.12)	(0.06)
Observations	321	321	321	256
R^2	0.53	0.37	0.42	0.50
B. Employment growth				
DEV * ICT * EA	0.29	−0.38	0.49	0.06
	(0.57)	(0.64)	(0.65)	(0.35)
DEV * ICT	−0.32	0.01	−0.56	
	(0.39)	(0.46)	(0.48)	
$\ln(\text{emp}_{98})$	0.01***	−0.01**	0.01*	0.01***
	(0.00)	(0.00)	(0.00)	(0.00)
Δemp_{9598}	0.21***	0.30***	0.16**	0.17**
	(0.06)	(0.10)	(0.08)	(0.07)
Observations	323	323	323	258
R^2	0.71	0.50	0.63	0.65

Note: DEV is the indicator of real devaluation (DEVREAL), computed over the period from 1980 to 1998; ICT is low ICT intensity; EA is a dummy equal to 1 for the EA countries; $\ln(\text{prod}_{98})$ ($\ln(\text{emp}_{98})$) is initial productivity (employment), and Δprod_{9598} (Δemp_{9598}) is productivity (employment) growth in the 1995 to 1998 period. Outcome growth rates are computed for 1998 to 2005 in all columns except column (3), where it is computed for 2002 to 2005. All regressions are weighted with the sectoral employment, apart from that in column (2), which is unweighted. Robust standard errors in parentheses.

***Significant at the 1 percent level.

**Significant at the 5 percent level.

*Significant at the 10 percent level.

Findings are somewhat different when the sectoral indicator is the export share of China (table 3.8). In this case, the productivity estimates tend to be less clear-cut. First, they are only significant for the baseline specification and for the unweighted one. The effect disappears when we exclude the control group, suggesting that these results are to be treated with even more caution than the others. In any case, according to the baseline specification, the growth differential is 0.5 percent, where the sectors at the twenty-fifth and seventy-fifth percentiles are chemicals and chemical products and rubber and plastic products, respectively. More interestingly, a negative effect on employment emerges. In the basic specification, we get a coefficient

Table 3.8   Chinese export share and devaluation

	(1)	(2)	(3)	(4)
A. Productivity growth				
DEV * CH * EA	1.34**	1.52**	0.98	0.27
	(0.67)	(0.70)	(1.19)	(0.38)
DEV * CH	−1.06**	−0.82	−0.97	
	(0.48)	(0.52)	(1.10)	
$\ln(\text{prod}_{98})$	−0.06***	−0.05***	−0.06***	−0.05***
	(0.01)	(0.01)	(0.02)	(0.01)
Δprod_{9598}	0.16*	0.07	0.09	0.11*
	(0.09)	(0.08)	(0.12)	(0.06)
Observations	321	321	321	256
R^2	0.53	0.36	0.42	0.49
B. Employment growth				
DEV * CH * EA	−1.77**	−1.01	−1.75**	−0.39*
	(0.69)	(0.67)	(0.77)	(0.23)
DEV * CH	1.38**	1.11***	1.22*	
	(0.64)	(0.41)	(0.71)	
$\ln(\text{emp}_{98})$	0.01***	−0.01**	0.01*	0.01***
	(0.00)	(0.00)	(0.00)	(0.00)
Δemp_{9598}	0.21***	0.29***	0.16**	0.19***
	(0.06)	(0.10)	(0.08)	(0.07)
Observations	323	323	323	258
R^2	0.73	0.51	0.64	0.65

Note: DEV is the indicator of real devaluation (DEVREAL), computed for the period from 1980 to 1998; CH is China's world export share; EA is a dummy equal to 1 for the EA countries; $\ln(\text{prod}_{98})$ ($\ln(\text{emp}_{98})$) is initial productivity (employment), and Δprod_{9598} (Δemp_{9598}) is productivity (employment) growth in the 1995 to 1998 period. Outcome growth rates are computed for 1998 to 2005 in all columns except column (3), where it is computed for 2002 to 2005. All regressions are weighted with the sectoral employment, apart from that in column (2), which is unweighted. Robust standard errors in parentheses.

***Significant at the 1 percent level.
**Significant at the 5 percent level.
*Significant at the 10 percent level.

of –1.77, significant at 5 percent. The implied growth differential is –0.6 percent.

As a final check, we run the same regressions as before for the period over which we computed the devaluation indicators: 1980 to 1998. This is to make sure that we are not just capturing some underlying autocorrelated process that was already operating before the euro.[12] To save on space, we report only the main specification with DEVREAL. There is no support for this hypothesis (table 3.9). Neither the effect for the control group nor the deviation for the EA countries is significant for productivity or for employment for any of the sectoral indicators. This further substantiates the argument that our results really are capturing a specific effect of the euro, not some other concomitant factor.

All in all, these regressions suggest that the end of competitive devaluations has had a positive impact on productivity growth in those countries and sectors that had presumably relied more on them. Moreover, there does not appear to be any downside in terms of jobs: reallocation does not seem to have come at the expense of employment growth. A clear exception to this is the regression using the Chinese export share. This analysis begs the question of how productivity growth was achieved—that is, how restructuring occurred. We tackle this issue in the next section.

3.4   Firm-Level Evidence of Restructuring: The Case of Italian Manufacturing

In this section, we turn to firm-level evidence on the response to the euro, drawn mostly from a survey of Italian manufacturing firms run by the Bank of Italy (INVIND). Restricting attention to Italy clearly limits the generality of the results, but Italy is an interesting case, as it had relied heavily on competitive devaluations and is specialized in traditional, low-tech activities, which according to the evidence set out previously should have been most severely affected by the introduction of the common currency. We first review some insights from a series of case studies and then consider the time series evolution of various measures of reallocation activities. Finally, we study the correlation between restructuring and performance at the level of the firm.

3.4.1   Case Studies

In the spring of 2007, the Bank of Italy conducted in-depth interviews with entrepreneurs and chief executive officers of some forty Italian firms, mostly in the manufacturing sector. Like the NBER/Sloan "pin factory" project (Borenstein, Farrell, and Jaffe 1998), the survey involved long inter-

---

12. The inclusion of lagged growth in the regressions should already account for this.

Table 3.9   Preregressions

	SKILLS		R&D		ICT		CHINA	
	PROD. (1)	EMP. (2)	PROD. (3)	EMP. (4)	PROD. (5)	EMP. (6)	PROD. (7)	EMP. (8)
DEV * SECT * EA	-0.11	-0.13	0.05	0.00	0.29	0.09	0.20	0.08
	(0.09)	(0.10)	(0.10)	(0.12)	(0.19)	(0.19)	(0.19)	(0.42)
DEV * SECT	0.07	0.08	-0.01	0.02	-0.10	-0.04	-0.11	-0.12
	(0.05)	(0.06)	(0.05)	(0.07)	(0.10)	(0.10)	(0.11)	(0.18)
$\ln(\text{prod}_{80})$	-0.03***		-0.03***		-0.03***		-0.03***	
	(0.00)		(0.00)		(0.00)		(0.00)	
Δprod_{7080}	0.40***		0.40***		0.40***		0.40***	
	(0.02)		(0.03)		(0.02)		(0.02)	
$\ln(\text{emp}_{80})$		-0.00***		-0.00***		-0.00***		-0.00***
		(0.00)		(0.00)		(0.00)		(0.00)
Δemp_{7080}		0.69***		0.69***		0.69***		0.69***
		(0.06)		(0.06)		(0.06)		(0.05)
Observations	293	302	278	287	293	302	293	302
R^2	0.96	0.85	0.96	0.85	0.96	0.85	0.96	0.85

Note: DEV is the indicator of real devaluation (DEVREAL), computed for the period from 1980 to 1998; SECT is the sectoral indicator, indicating low-skill intensity in columns (1) and (2), low-R&D intensity in columns (3) and (4), low-ICT intensity in columns (5) and (6), and China's world export share in columns (7) and (8); EA is a dummy equal to 1 for the EA countries; $\ln(\text{prod}_{80})$ $(\ln(\text{emp}_{80}))$ is initial productivity (employment), and Δprod_{7080} $(\Delta\text{emp}_{7080})$ is productivity (employment) growth in the 1970 to 1980 period. Outcome growth rates are computed for 1980 to 1998. All regressions are weighted with sectoral employment. Robust standard errors in parentheses.

***Significant at the 1 percent level.

views (between two and four hours). The interviewers, always researchers at the Bank of Italy, followed a set schema, but most of the interview was left for the entrepreneurs to elaborate freely. The main goal was to assess whether the firms were restructuring, and if so, in what forms. Of course, forty interviews cannot be statistically representative. The aim was to understand what forces were driving the process and how firms were responding, in order to guide subsequent quantitative analysis, among other things. The main findings were summarized in an internal report by Omiccioli and Schivardi (2007) on which this section is based; the report has not yet been made public for confidentiality reasons.

One clear insight from the interviews is that success stories are invariably based on some degree of market power. Entrepreneurs are generally very clear that given the growing role of low-wage countries in the world trade, competition based on production costs is rapidly becoming unsustainable, so the production of homogeneous, undifferentiated goods is less and less viable. All the firms that were surviving or even prospering in the globalized economy offered products that had a certain degree of differentiation and thus escaped pure cost competition. The challenge is to build up and maintain such market power.

The experiences reviewed were highly differentiated in a number of dimensions—by product, firm size, and the entrepreneur's personal history. But all the cases of successful restructuring had one feature in common: the firms had invested in activities not directly involving production. These activities may be classed as:

- Upstream: product creation (R&D, design) and brand establishment (advertising, marketing).
- Auxiliary: organization of production, often partly or wholly outside the firm (through outsourcing and offshoring); generally based on intensive use of ICT.
- Downstream: sales network, postsales assistance.

These activities are not important only for high-tech products. Rather, the importance of each component varies with the particular business considered. For final goods producers, the crucial needs are the establishment of a brand, the organization of production, and the creation of a sales network. For high-tech activities, the creation of the product, particularly through R&D, remains the main route to competitive advantage. For producers of intermediate goods, customers require constant assistance, particularly for firms producing industrial machineries.

We interviewed some firms operating in the traditional sectors of clothing and shoes. The success stories entailed a shift of the business focus away from production toward brand creation and product design while maintaining a coordinating role in production, which was mostly outsourced, often abroad.[13] Out of 800 workers of a firm producing machines for tile making, only 70 were employed in the plant, the rest divided between product design (200) and marketing and administration. The prototypes of successful firms suggest that competitive strength is built outside the factory by workers not directly involved in the production process. We will use this insight in our subsequent empirical analysis: restructuring means a greater reliance on nonproduction workers and consequently entails a reduction of the share of blue-collar workers in the workforce.

In terms of cross-sectoral differences, the process seems to be most intensive for low-tech activities. Most of the high-tech firms did not perceive either the euro or the globalization as a discontinuity in the competitive landscape. For them, in fact, competition focuses mostly on innovation and R&D. For example, an entrepreneur producing electrical machinery said that his firm had a three-year lead over its Chinese competitors in technology and contended that this was the key competitive edge to be maintained, rather than lowering production costs. Another firm in the medical and precision instrument field saw its main competitors as located in Germany and Japan; the strong euro had created the opportunity for an important acquisition in the United States.

For low-tech firms—particularly those operating in the traditional sectors, such as clothing and leather—the change was much more profound. All the entrepreneurs in these sectors stressed that a dramatic change in the competitive environment had occurred with the introduction of the euro. Some had changed their business model radically (see note 13); those who had not were clearly struggling. This anecdotal evidence squares with the results of the previous section: the euro was a greater shock for activities of low-skill content. It also suggests that the lower the technological content of the activity, the sharper the shift away from production is likely to be.

Further, the entrepreneurs do not think that the restructuring process is over. They all believed that the international landscape will keep changing fast in the coming years. Also, changes in the business model depend crucially on the individual histories of the firms. In particular, for family firms (almost all those interviewed could be classified as such), radical change tends to coincide with generational succession. Finally, restructuring itself is an ongoing sequential activity, not a 0/1 event. For example, many firms had been introducing business software—particularly some form of enterprise resource planning (ERP)—but this was mostly done in steps: first by digitalizing accounting, then business-to-business transactions, then production, and so on. In fact, we interviewed firms with very different degrees of penetration of business software. All in all, therefore, we expect

13. An entrepreneur in the shoe sector defined his firm as "a services firm that collects information from the market, elaborates it, designs products and dictates instructions to the other firms on how to produce them." Until 1999, this firm, which now employs 260 workers and only produces the models internally, was a traditional shoemaker that produced for other brands.

restructuring to be a smooth ongoing process rather than concentrated in a short period of time.

3.4.2 Quantitative Evidence from Manufacturing Firms

The increasing availability of data sets with firm-level information has spurred a vast literature on restructuring (Davis, Haltiwanger, and Schu 1996).[14] The basic idea, following the seminal work of Lilien (1982), is that periods of restructuring are characterized by intense factor reallocation and increased dispersion of firms' performance. In fact, when a shock hits the economy, some firms adapt and some do not, so their performance diverges, and factors are reallocated to successful restructurers. In this section, we use the insights from this literature and the case studies reviewed previously to assess the degree of restructuring of the Italian manufacturing sector following the introduction of the euro.

The data come from the Bank of Italy's annual survey of manufacturing firms (INVIND), which is an open panel of around 1,200 firms per year that are representative of manufacturing firms with at least fifty employees. It contains detailed information on firms' characteristics, including industrial sector, nationality, year of creation, number of employees, value of shipments, value of exports, and investment. The questionnaire contains a fixed part and a rotating part used to investigate topics of special interest in the year. The resulting database has been used extensively. (For a description of the database, see, among others, Fabiani, Schivardi, and Trento [2005]; Guiso and Parigi [1999]; and Iranzo, Schivardi, and Tosetti [2008]).

If not all firms are equally successful at restructuring, performance should become more highly dispersed. Following up on the aggregate analysis, we consider productivity, measured as log of sales per worker,[15] and check whether its dispersion increased after the introduction of the euro. Figure 3.5 shows that in fact it did: the cross-firm dispersion of sales per worker goes from around 0.64 in the first part of the 1990s to around 0.70 in the euro period.[16] Moreover, the dispersion increases almost monotonically up to the last available year (2007), suggesting that the process is still very much under way: in fact, if the restructuring wave was over, we would expect dispersion to revert to business-as-usual levels. We have also computed the dispersion of gross operating profits (EBITDA: earnings before interest, taxes, depreciation, and amortization) over value added, drawn from the Cerved data

---

14. This subsection draws on the Master's dissertation of Daniela Puggioni (2008) at the University of Cagliari.

15. Usually, productivity is measured as value added per worker, but this is not available for a sufficiently long time span. However, given that part of the restructuring activity might entail the offshoring of some part of the production process, sales per worker might capture such reorganization of the production chain better.

16. To make sure that results are not driven by outliers, we have also computed various interquartile ranges, finding exactly the same pattern.

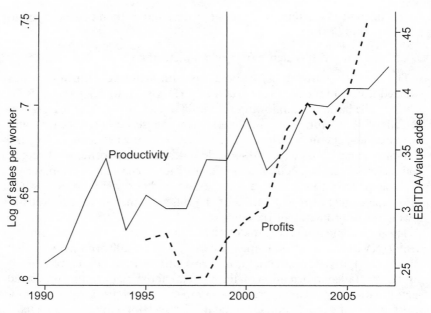

Fig. 3.5   Standard deviation of productivity and profits

Note: Productivity is measured as log of sales per workers (left scale) in the INVIND database. Profitability is EBITDA/value added (right scale) in the Cerved database. In this and the following graphs, a vertical bar is drawn corresponding to 1999, the year of the euro introduction.

set.[17] In fact, Foster, Haltiwanger, and Syverson (2008) show that selection and reallocation are due more to differences in profitability than in productivity. In figure 3.5, we therefore also plot the standard deviation of profits, finding that they follow a similar pattern to productivity.

We next consider reallocation measures based on job flows.[18] The job creation rate (JC) is defined as

$$JC_t = \frac{\Sigma_{f \in E^+} \Delta E_{ft}}{(1/2)(E_t + E_{t-1})},$$

where ΔE_{ft} is the change in employment for firm f at time t, E^+ is the set of firms that expand employment, and E_t is aggregate employment.[19] The job destruction rate (JD) is defined similarly:

17. The INVIND survey does not allow computation of profitability measures. We have therefore used Cerved, a database with balance-sheet information for almost all Italian limited liability companies, available since 1996. Cerved has no information on employment and therefore cannot be used for the other analysis in this section.

18. See Davis, Haltiwanger, and Schu (1996) for a detailed explanation of job flow measures.

19. The normalization by $(1/2)(E_t + E_{t-1})$ rather than E_{t-1} constrains JC between –2 and 2 rather than –1 and ∞. The distribution is symmetric around 0 and easier to interpret graphically.

$$JD_t = \frac{\Sigma_{f \in E^-} |\Delta E_{ft}|}{(1/2)(E_t + E_{t-1})},$$

where E^- is the set of firms that reduce employment; net employment growth is $EG_t = JC_t - JD_t$; and job reallocation is the sum of job creation and destruction, $JR_t = JC_t + JD_t$. Finally, we also construct a measure of excess job reallocation, $ER_t = JR_t - |EG_t|$, which measures the job reallocation in excess of that required to reach a given change in net employment; for example, a sector might be constantly expanding employment and at the same time reallocating production among existing units: ER measures the job flow rate net of that due to sectoral employment expansion.

In figure 3.6, we report JC, JD, and EG. Job destruction peaks in 1993, when employment in the sample contracted by more than 5 percent. After that, both JC and JD remain fairly stable at values between 2 percent and 4 percent. Consistent with the downward trend in manufacturing employment, EG is negative in most years. Job reallocation also peaks in 1993, then reverts to a fairly stable level of around 6 percent. The ER variable shows a modest upward trend since 1998, with a peak in 2000, but again with fairly modest variations. Thus, the traditional measures of restructuring offer little support to the hypothesis of an increase in restructuring after the euro. All the indicators of job reallocation (with the exception of ER) peak in the recession of the early 1990s and then level off. This occurs at

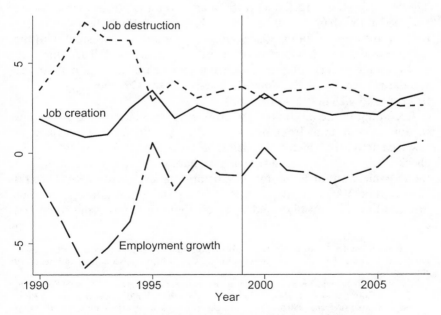

Fig. 3.6   Job creation, job destruction, and net employment growth
Source: Based on INVIND database.

the same time as the increase in productivity and profitability dispersion, which suggests two things. First, the reallocation process induced by the euro has a smooth, ongoing character, especially when compared to that related to the deep recession of 1993; in particular, it seems to have little effect on the reallocation of factors across firms, possibly because of the degree of flexibility of the factor markets. Second, and strictly related, the posteuro restructuring might be of a different type from that of the early 1990s and might require different indicators: in particular, rather than showing up in job flows across firms, it might have induced more within-firm changes in workforce composition.[20]

The case studies suggest that the firms that did well tended to shift from production to upstream and downstream activities, such as R&D, design, marketing, and distribution chains. In terms of workforce composition, this implies that we should see a decrease in the share of blue-collar workers. Their average share decreased from 0.69 in 1990 to 0.62 in 2007 (figure 3.7). This pattern reflects a secular trend, common to all developed economies, but with a clear break around the 1992 devaluation: from 1992 to 1998, the share stays roughly constant at around 0.67. It starts declining rapidly in 1999, falling to 0.62 in 2007. This evidence is consistent with the thesis that the devaluation of 1992 allowed firms to gain cost competitiveness, boosting the relative importance of production. With the euro, this possibility was ruled out, and firms had to adapt their strategy, shifting away from production and therefore reducing the share of blue-collar workers. This interpretation is further corroborated by the analysis of the cross-firm variance in the share of blue-collar workers. Up to 1998, there is no clear trend in the cross-sectional dispersion of this share.[21] Consistent with the hypothesis that the euro has forced a shift away from low-skill activities and that the process has not been uniform across firms, starting in 1999, the standard deviation of the share of blue-collar workers increases steadily, from around 0.18 to 0.21.

According to the insights of the cross-country analysis of the previous section, the shift away from low-skill workers should have been stronger in low-tech activities, which had relied more on competitive devaluations. To check whether this is indeed the case, we have grouped firms according to the Organization for Economic Cooperation and Development (OECD) classification system (OECD 2003), dividing them into four classes: low, medium-low, medium-high, and high tech. Figure 3.8 reports the time series

---

20. Unfortunately, due to the lack of information on entry and exit, we cannot compute the decomposition of productivity growth into the within-firm, between-firm, and net entry components.

21. This graphical evidence is supported by the more formal analysis of Iranzo, Schivardi, and Tosetti (2008), who study the within- and between-firm skill dispersion using the same sample for the period from 1980 to 1997, finding a very stable time series pattern for the cross-firm component of skill dispersion (i.e., no evidence of an increase in dispersion).

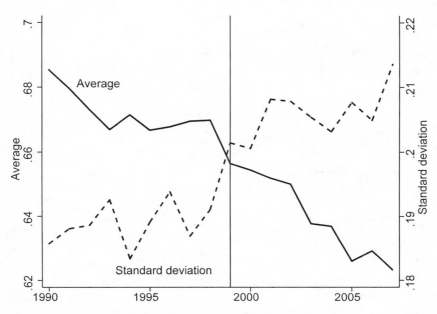

Fig. 3.7   Cross-firm average and standard deviation of the share of blue-collar workers
Source: Based on INVIND database.

for the share of blue-collar workers for the four groups of firms. In general, the paths are similar to the aggregate, with a pause in the decrease after the 1992 devaluation and an acceleration starting in 1999. A clear exception is the group of high-tech firms for which no clear pattern emerges, while the decrease is sharpest among the low-tech firms, which reduced the share of blue-collar workers by around 8 percentage points between 1999 and 2007. A similar picture emerges when considering the cross-firm dispersion in the share of blue-collar workers: again, the largest increases are recorded by low- and medium-low tech firms.

To corroborate the graphical analysis, we have run some diff-in-diff regressions of the following form:

(4) $\text{ShBlue}_{ft} = \alpha_0 + \alpha_1 * \text{LOW}_f * \text{POST}_t + \alpha_2 \text{LOW}_f + \alpha_3 X_{ft} + \text{YEAR}_t + \varepsilon_{ft},$

where ShBlue_{ft} is the share of blue-collar workers in firm f at time t, LOW is a dummy equal to 1 if the firm belongs to the low-tech group, POST is a dummy equal to 1 for the years 1999 to 2007, YEAR is a full set of year dummies, and X_{ft} includes firm size (log of total employment) and four regional dummies (northwest, northeast, center, and south). The LOW dummy controls for fixed group attributes—in particular for the fact that low-tech firms have a higher share of blue-collar workers than other firms;

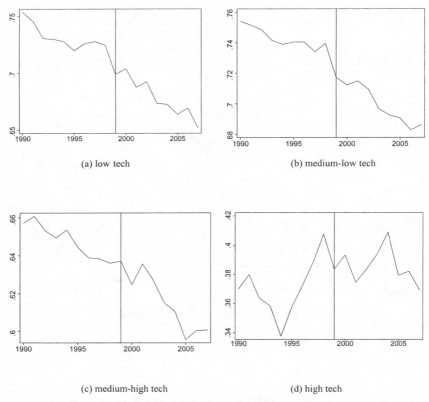

(a) low tech

(b) medium-low tech

(c) medium-high tech

(d) high tech

Fig. 3.8   Share of blue-collar workers by technological intensity
Source: Our elaborations on INVIND database.

the year dummies control for possible time trends. The coefficient α_1 therefore measures the change in the share of blue-collar workers for the firms in the LOW group before and after the euro as a deviation from the change for firms in the control group (firms not in the LOW group). As such, it can be interpreted as the extra effect of the euro on the LOW firms, compared to the control group. The results reported in table 3.10 clearly confirm the graphical analysis. The first column applies only the dummy for the low-tech firms; the control group therefore comprises all other firms. The coefficient indicates the decrease in the share of blue-collar workers has been 3 percentage points greater among low-tech firms than among others since 1999, with a strong statistical significance. In the second column, we also include a MEDIUM-LOW*POST dummy, so now the control group consists of medium-high and high-tech firms. Again, we find that low and medium-low-tech firms decreased the share of blue-collar workers more substantially; the same occurs when we include a dummy for medium-high-tech firms as

Table 3.10   **Share of blue-collar workers**

	Period: 1990 to 2007			Period: 1984 to 1990		
	(1)	(2)	(3)	(4)	(5)	(6)
LOW * POST	−0.031***	−0.031***	−0.072***	0.003	0.004	0.038*
	(0.005)	(0.006)	(0.013)	(0.009)	(0.011)	(0.021)
MED-LOW * POST		−0.019***	−0.059***		−0.006	0.029
		(0.006)	(0.013)		(0.010)	(0.021)
MED-HIGH * POST			−0.050***			0.036*
			(0.013)			(0.021)
LOW	0.076***	0.132***	0.336***	0.073***	0.127***	0.304***
	(0.004)	(0.005)	(0.010)	(0.007)	(0.008)	(0.015)
MED-LOW		0.135***	0.339***		0.135***	0.310***
		(0.004)	(0.010)		(0.007)	(0.014)
MED-HIGH			0.242***			0.215***
			(0.010)			(0.015)
ln(emp)	−0.030***	−0.024***	−0.018***	−0.035***	−0.029***	−0.021***
	(0.001)	(0.001)	(0.001)	(0.002)	(0.002)	(0.002)
Observations	24,143	24,143	24,143	5,142	5,142	5,142
R^2	0.09	0.15	0.20	0.14	0.22	0.32

Note: The dependent variable is the share of blue-collar workers at the level of the firm; ln(emp) is the log of total employment; LOW is a dummy equal to 1 for low-tech firms, and similarly for MED-LOW and MED-HIGH; POST is a dummy equal to 1 for the post-1998 years. Robust standard errors in parentheses.

***Significant at the 1 percent level.
*Significant at the 10 percent level.

well (column [3]). The intensity of the decrease is inversely related to the technological content. Consistent with the findings of the previous section, the effect of the euro on workforce composition decreases monotonically with technological intensity. These results are very robust to changes in the specification. We have also included additional firm controls, such as indicators of productivity, export propensity, and sales (as an alternative measure of size), finding no significant differences in the results.

One important objection to this exercise is that we might be capturing differences in trends in the occupational mix. That is, it might simply be that low-tech firms were already reducing blue-collar workers more intensively before the euro launch. For a limited number of firms, we can reconstruct the technological classification since 1984. To check whether we are picking up differences in trends, we have rerun regression (4) for the period from 1984 to 1990, with the POST dummy equal to 1 for 1988 to 1990 and 0 before. (This splits the sample approximately equally.) If we are simply capturing differences in underlying trends, we should then find that α_1 is negative also in the 1980s, when competitive devaluations were still possible. But columns (4) through (6) of table 3.10 show that if anything, in the 1980s, low-tech firms were actually increasing the blue-collar intensity of the workforce compared to the high-tech ones. These findings are robust to changes in the year of definition of the postperiod and to including years up to 1998. We can conclude that before the euro, low-tech firms used devaluations to regain price competitiveness and intensified their reliance on low-skilled workers; on the contrary, high-tech firms competed mostly in other dimensions and so were increasing the relative skill content of their workforce.

3.4.3   Restructuring and Firm Performance

Was restructuring effective in terms of firms' performance? We measure performance in terms of growth of value added and productivity and rely on a simple cross-sectional empirical specification of the following form:

$$(5) \qquad g_{i,t_0t} = \beta_0 + \beta_1 \times RES_{i,t_0} + \beta_2 X_{i,t_0} + YEAR_{t_0} + \varepsilon_i,$$

where g_{i,t_0t} is the firm's average growth rate of real value added or productivity (value added per employee) in the period t_0t, and t_0 is the first available year for a firm in the sample, starting in 2000. To maximize the number of firms, we do not limit the sample to those that are surveyed both in 2000 and 2005 but also include firms sampled for at least a pair of consecutive years during the period. To net out cyclical effects, we compute the growth rate as the residual of a preliminary regression of the raw growth rate data on year dummies and the initial value of value added or productivity. The starting year is 2000 instead of 1999, because some of our proxies for restructuring take 2000 as the reference year. (The results do not change using 1999.) The variable $YEAR_{t_0}$ is a set of dummies for the first year in which a firm is in the data set; X_{it_0} includes firm size (log of total employment), sectoral dummies at two digits of the NACE revision 1 classification, and the usual four regional dummies, all computed at t_0. We focus on the coefficient of RES, a measure of restructuring activity for which we use different proxies. The first comes directly from the previous analysis and refers to the share of blue-collar workers: here, we check both the initial level of the share (ShBlue) and its average annual change in 2000 to 2006 (ΔShBlue). If the reduced reliance on low-skilled workers has indeed been one of the dominant strategies to regain competitiveness after the introduction of the euro, we should find a negative relationship between this variable and firm performance. There is a clear negative effect of the initial share of blue-collar workers on value added and productivity growth (table 3.11, columns [2] and [5]), while the coefficient of the contemporaneous change in that share is not significantly different from 0 (columns [1] and [4]). The former result confirms the idea that if we control for sectoral differences in technology, firms that focused more on nonproduction activities through a larger share of white-collar workers have performed better. Given the likely smooth and ongoing nature of the restructuring process, it is not surprising that our contemporaneous indicator is not able to fully capture the impact of restructuring on performance.

We then search for a heterogeneous effect of restructuring across sectors.

Table 3.11   **Firm performance and share of blue-collar workers**

	Value added growth			Productivity growth		
	(1)	(2)	(3)	(4)	(5)	(6)
ln(emp)	0.013***	0.016***	−0.001	0.012***	0.017***	0.002
	(0.004)	(0.004)	(0.006)	(0.004)	(0.004)	(0.006)
ΔShBlue	−0.022			0.017		
	(0.072)			(0.052)		
ShBlue		−0.055**	−0.055		−0.094***	−0.035
		(0.023)	(0.036)		(0.020)	(0.035)
Observations	3,042	3,178	1,008	3,044	3,181	1,009
R^2	0.030	0.044	0.063	0.034	0.053	0.076

Note: Regressions are run over the period from 2000 to 2006, except for columns (3) and (6), where the period is 1990 to 1995. The dependent variable is the annual average real growth rate of value added/labor productivity in the two periods; ln(emp) is the log of total employment as of 2000; ShBlue is the share of blue-collar workers over the total number of employees as of 2000; ΔShBlue is the average annual change in the share of blue-collar workers between 2000 and 2006. Robust standard errors in parentheses.
***Significant at the 1 percent level.
**Significant at the 5 percent level.

As pointed out in the previous section, we might expect that when controlling for average sectoral differences in the blue-collar share, firm heterogeneity in performance is more strongly linked to the share in low-tech sectors. The data do not support this thesis, possibly because of a lack of sufficient statistical power. (The coefficient is negative but statistically insignificant.)

We check whether the effect of the blue-collar share on performance is indeed related to the euro by running similar regressions for the period from 1990 to 1995, when Italian firms could rely on devaluation to gain international competitiveness. Over this period, we would expect no role for restructuring, and the results (columns [3] and [6]) show that this is indeed the case.

In the INVIND questionnaire referring to 2006, firms were asked about their business strategies—in particular about significant changes since 2000. The changes refer to significant renewals of the product menu and to greater reliance on branding strategies.[22] We exploit this information in two steps. First, we construct a dummy variable NEWSTRAT that is equal to 1 when a firm claims to have been either changing the product menu or investing more resources in product branding and that is equal to 0 otherwise. As shown in columns (1) and (5) of table 3.12, the dummy variable does have

22. More precisely, firms were asked the following question: "Which of the following statements better describe your strategic behavior during the 2000–06 period? 1 = the firm has not changed strategy; 2 = the firm has changed strategy, mostly by introducing relevant changes in the product menu; 3 = the firm has changed strategy, mostly by investing more resources on its own brand; 4 = the firm has changed strategy, mostly by internationalizing its activity."

Table 3.12   Firm performance and restructuring

	Value added growth				Productivity growth			
	(1)	(2)	(3)	(4)	(5)	(6)	(7)	(8)
ln(emp)	0.017***	0.018***	0.016***	0.016***	0.017***	0.018***	0.016***	0.016***
	(0.005)	(0.005)	(0.005)	(0.005)	(0.005)	(0.005)	(0.005)	(0.005)
NEWSTRAT	0.016*	0.015*			0.013*	0.011		
	(0.009)	(0.009)			(0.008)	(0.007)		
ShBlue		−0.099***		−0.080***		−0.138***		−0.107***
		(0.027)		(0.027)		(0.023)		(0.022)
SMALLCH			−0.004	−0.004			0.001	0.001
			(0.013)	(0.013)			(0.014)	(0.013)
LARGECH			0.119**	0.112**			0.066*	0.057*
			(0.050)	(0.049)			(0.036)	(0.032)
Observations	1,989	1,989	2,159	2,159	1,987	1,987	2,157	2,157
R^2	0.043	0.060	0.058	0.067	0.050	0.087	0.060	0.081

Note: The dependent variable is the annual average real growth rate of value added/labor productivity over the period from 2000 to 2006; ln(emp) is the log of total employment as of 2000; ShBlue is the share of blue-collar workers over the total number of employees as of 2000; NEWSTRAT is a dummy variable equal to 1 if a firm has claimed to have significantly changed its strategy over the 2000 to 2006 period mostly by changing the product menu or by investing more resources in product branding, and it is equal to 0 otherwise; SMALLCH is a dummy variable equal to 1 if a firm's product menu in 2006 results to be slightly (i.e., still falling in a similar sectoral grouping) renewed with respect to what it was in 2000, and it is equal to 0 otherwise; LARGECH is a dummy variable equal to 1 if a firm's product menu in 2006 results to be significantly (i.e., falling in a different sectoral grouping) renewed with respect to what it was in 2000, and it is equal to 0 otherwise. Robust standard errors in parentheses.

***Significant at the 1 percent level.

**Significant at the 5 percent level.

*Significant at the 10 percent level.

a significantly positive effect on performance; the effect also survives the introduction of the share of blue-collar workers (columns [2] and [6]), which indicates that the performance improvement following the new strategy is realized on the top of that coming from the workforce composition. More detailed information on the intensity of the product change is then used to distinguish firms that renewed products within the same sectoral grouping (SMALLCH) from those that started producing products so new as to actually change the productive sector (LARGECH).[23] The control group here consists of firms that between 2000 and 2006 kept on producing almost the same products. As shown in columns (3) and (4) for value added growth and columns (7) and (8) for productivity growth, the strongest boost to performance has come from significant changes in the product menu. As for the blue-collar share, again we find no sectoral heterogeneity in the effect of product change and branding on performance (not reported).

All in all, the evidence of this section indicates that firms that undertook restructuring activities recorded a higher growth of both value added and productivity growth. Although more work will be required to establish a clear causal relation between restructuring and performance, this evidence squares with and complements the results previously discussed in the chapter.

3.5   Conclusion

We have shown that the euro has been accompanied by a process of within-sector reallocation, consistent with the hypothesis that the end of devaluations has forced restructuring in the countries and sectors that had depended most heavily on them. We used productivity growth as an indirect indicator of reallocation. This begs the question of how restructuring actually took place. We therefore use firm-level data for Italy with detailed information on restructuring activity. A series of interviews with entrepreneurs suggested that since the adoption of the euro, firms have shifted their business focus from production to upstream and downstream activities related to R&D, product design, marketing, distribution, and postsale assistance. This search for market power has been stronger in the traditional, low-tech industries. Hard quantitative evidence on a sample of Italian manufacturing firms showed that the process has entailed a reallocation of workers, mainly within rather than across firms, with a decrease in the share of blue-collar workers. Finally, we found that restructuring has improved performance.

---

23. The exact question asked to the firms is as follows: "With respect to your product menu in 2000, now you produce mostly: 1 = the same products; 2 = slightly different products that fall into a similar sectoral category; 3 = products that are so different to fall into a completely different sectoral category."

Appendix

Table 3A.1   Classification of NACE sectors into skill, ICT, and R&D intensity classes

Sector (NACE code in parentheses)	Skill content	ICT content	R&D content
Food products and beverages (15)	MEDIUM LOW	MEDIUM LOW	LOW
Tobacco products (16)	MEDIUM HIGH	MEDIUM LOW	LOW
Textiles (17)	LOW	LOW	LOW
Wearing apparel, dressing (18)	LOW	LOW	LOW
Leather, leather products, and footwear (19)	LOW	LOW	LOW
Wood and products of wood and cork (20)	LOW	LOW	LOW
Pulp, paper, and paper products (21)	MEDIUM HIGH	MEDIUM HIGH	MEDIUM LOW
Printing, publishing, and reproduction (22)	HIGH	MEDIUM HIGH	MEDIUM LOW
Coke, refined petroleum products, and nuclear fuel (23)	MEDIUM HIGH	LOW	MEDIUM HIGH
Chemicals and chemical products (24)	HIGH	MEDIUM HIGH	HIGH
Rubber and plastics products (25)	MEDIUM LOW	LOW	MEDIUM HIGH
Other nonmetallic mineral products (26)	LOW	MEDIUM LOW	MEDIUM LOW
Basic metals (27)	MEDIUM LOW	MEDIUM LOW	MEDIUM LOW
Fabricated metal products (28)	LOW	MEDIUM LOW	MEDIUM LOW
Machinery, n.e.c. (29)	MEDIUM LOW	HIGH	MEDIUM HIGH
Office, accounting, and computing machinery (30)	HIGH	HIGH	HIGH
Electrical machinery (31)	MEDIUM HIGH	HIGH	MEDIUM HIGH
Radio, television, and communication equipment (32)	HIGH	HIGH	HIGH
Medical, precision, and optical instruments (33)	HIGH	HIGH	HIGH
Motor vehicles, trailers, and semitrailers (34)	MEDIUM HIGH	MEDIUM HIGH	MEDIUM HIGH
Other transport equipment (35)	MEDIUM HIGH	MEDIUM HIGH	HIGH
Manufacturing, n.e.c.; recycling (36, 37)	MEDIUM LOW	MEDIUM HIGH	not allocated

Source: Based on EU KLEMS data.

Note: "n.e.c." = not elsewhere classified.

Table 3A.2   **Descriptive statistics, dependent variables (percentage points)**

	Productivity growth			Employment growth		
Country	Mean	Median	Standard deviation	Mean	Median	Standard deviation
Austria	4.2	3.9	2.3	−1.1	−0.9	2.5
Belgium	2.2	1.9	1.5	−1.4	−1.2	1.9
Denmark	1.9	1.2	2.4	−2.9	−2.4	2.9
Finland	4.5	3.2	4.9	−0.5	−0.4	2.8
France	3.6	2.8	4.2	−1.4	−0.9	2.5
Germany	2.6	1.7	3.2	−1.2	−0.6	1.8
Greece	1.7	0.2	4.8	−1.8	−1.0	2.4
Ireland	7.5	6.0	6.2	−1.2	−0.2	4.3
Italy	0.1	0.1	2.2	−0.4	−0.2	1.5
Luxembourg	2.6	1.9	3.9	−0.5	0.6	3.2
The Netherlands	3.1	2.6	2.1	−1.7	−1.2	1.8
Portugal	1.1	0.9	2.1	−1.8	−1.5	1.7
Spain	1.0	0.4	1.3	1.4	1.7	2.6
Sweden	6.6	3.4	10.1	−1.5	−1.3	1.7
United Kingdom	4.4	3.8	2.1	−4.6	−3.5	3.7

Source: Based on EU KLEMS data.

Note: Manufacturing sector. Average growth across sector, weighted with sectoral employment, calculated over the period from 1998 to 2005.

References

Auer, R., and A. Fischer. 2008. The effects of trade with low-income countries on US industry. CEPR Discussion Paper no. 6819. London: Center for Economic Policy Research.

Baldwin, R. 2006. The euro's trade effects. ECB Working Paper no. 594. Frankfurt: European Central Bank.

Bartelsmann, E., S. Scarpetta, and F. Schivardi. 2005. Comparative analysis of firm demographics and survival: Micro-level evidence for the OECD countries. *Industrial and Corporate Change* 14 (3): 365–91.

Bernard, A., J. Jensen, and P. Schott. 2006a. Survival of the best fit: Exposure to low-wage countries and the (uneven) growth of U.S. manufacturing plants. *Journal of International Economics* 68 (1): 219–37.

———. 2006b. Trade costs, firms and productivity. *Journal of Monetary Economics* 53 (5): 917–37.

Bertola, G. 2007. Economic integration, growth, distribution: Does the euro make a difference? University of Turin, Department of Economics. Unpublished Manuscript.

Borenstein, S., J. Farrell, and A. Jaffe. 1998. Inside the pin-factory: Empirical studies augmented by manager interviews. *Journal of Industrial Economics* 46 (2): 123–4.

Bugamelli, M., S. Fabiani, and E. Sette. 2008. The pro-competitive effect of imports from China: An analysis on firm-level price data. Paper presented at the Bank of Italy conference on "Trends in the Italian Productive System," 27–28 November, Rome.

Bugamelli, M., and A. Rosolia. 2006. Produttività e concorrenza estera. *Rivista di Politica Economica* 9/10:55–87.
Buiter, W., and C. Grafe. 2003. Emu or ostrich? In *Submissions on EMU from leading academics,* ed. Her Majesty's Treasury, 23–42. London: Her Majesty's Stationery Office.
Chen, N., J. Imbs, and A. Scott. 2007. The dynamics of trade and competition. University of Lausanne, Faculty of Business and Economics. Unpublished Manuscript.
Davis, S., J. Haltiwanger, and S. Schu. 1996. *Job creation and destruction.* Cambridge, MA: MIT Press.
de Nardis, S., R. De Santis, and C. Vicarelli. 2008. The euro's effects on trade in a dynamic setting. *European Journal of Comparative Economics* 5 (1): 73–85.
European Commission. 1993. *White book of growth, competitiveness and employment.* Brussels and Luxembourg: European Commission.
———. 2008. *EMU@10: Successes and challenges after 10 years of economic and monetary union.* Brussels and Luxembourg: European Commission.
Fabiani, S., F. Schivardi, and S. Trento. 2005. ICT adoption in Italian manufacturing: Firm-level evidence. *Industrial and Corporate Change* 14 (2): 225–49.
Finicelli, A., A. Liccardi, and M. Sbracia. 2005. A new indicator of competitiveness for Italy and the main industrial and emerging countries. *Supplements to the Statistical Bulletin,* vol. 15, no. 66. Bank of Italy.
Foster, L., J. Haltiwanger, and C. Krizan. 2001. Aggregate productivity growth: Lessons from microeconomic evidence. In *New directions in productivity analysis,* ed. E. Dean, M. Harper, and C. Hulten, 303–73. Chicago: University of Chicago Press.
Foster, L., J. Haltiwanger, and C. Syverson. 2008. Reallocation, firm turnover, and efficiency: Selection on productivity or profitability? *American Economic Review* 98 (1): 394–425.
Giavazzi, F., and A. Giovannini. 1989. *Limiting exchange rate flexibility: The European monetary system.* Cambridge, MA: MIT Press.
Guiso, L., and G. Parigi. 1999. Investment and demand uncertainty. *Quarterly Journal of Economics* 114 (1): 185–227.
Iranzo, S., F. Schivardi, and E. Tosetti. 2008. Skill dispersion and productivity: An analysis with employer-employee matched data. *Journal of Labor Economics* 26 (2): 247–85.
Lilien, D. 1982. Sectoral shifts and cyclical unemployment. *Journal of Political Economy* 90 (4): 777–93.
Melitz, M. 2003. The impact of trade on intra-industry reallocations and aggregate industry productivity. *Econometrica* 71 (6): 1695–725.
Omiccioli, M., and F. Schivardi. 2007. Le trasformazioni in atto nel sistema produttivo italiano: Cosa fanno le imprese italiane per competere? Internal Report. Rome: Bank of Italy.
Organization for Economic Cooperation and Development (OECD). 2003. *OECD science, technology and industry scoreboard 2003: Annex 1.* Paris: OECD.
Puggioni, D. 2008. Il processo di ristrutturazione dell'industria manifatturiera italiana. Master's diss., University of Cagliari.
Rajan, R., and L. Zingales. 1998. Financial dependence and growth. *American Economic Review* 88 (3): 559–86.
Timmer, M., M. O'Mahony, and B. van Ark. 2007. The EU KLEMS growth and productivity accounts: An overview. European Union Level Analysis of Capital, Labor, Energy, Materials, and Service Inputs (EU KLEMS) Productivity Report. Available at: http://www.euklems.net.

Comment   Gianmarco I. P. Ottaviano

A decade after the introduction of the euro, studies of the effects of the euro on real and financial variables are flourishing. A couple of years ago, the state of the debate was summarized by *The Economist* (2006) as follows: "In the continuing controversies about Europe's bold experiment in monetary union, there has at least been some agreement about where the costs and benefits lie. The costs are macroeconomic, caused by forgoing the right to set interest rates to suit the specific economic conditions of a member state. The benefits are microeconomic, consisting of potential gains in trade and growth as the costs of changing currencies and exchange-rate uncertainty are removed."

Against this background, Bugamelli, Schivardi, and Zizza consider a specific aspect of the cost-benefit trade-off by looking at the "macro cost" of renouncing to competitive devaluations and the "micro benefit" due to productivity gains through firm restructuring once the competitive boost of devaluations within the euro area has been removed.

Even though the recent financial turmoil has someway stressed also the existence of potentially relevant macroeconomic benefits, the authors' effort remains worthwhile, given that the quantification of the microeconomic effects of the euro is still at an infant stage, mainly due to the lack of quality data at the firm level for several European countries.

In their effort, the key challenge the authors face is how to disentangle confounding factors, as there are several measurable microeconomic effects that the euro may have had. In particular, the literature has highlighted three main categories of microeconomic effects stemming from the reduction of several types of transaction costs. First, there are the effects on trade flows. Through the export participation effect, some firms that were formerly unable to export become active in international markets. Through the market coverage effect, exporters start to serve a larger number of foreign countries. Through the product variety effects, exporters start to sell a larger number of products in foreign markets. Through the export intensity effect, exporters increase the sales of each product in each foreign market in which it is sold. Second, there are the effects on prices. Through the (pure) transaction cost effect, a fall in the costs associated with exporting activities directly translates in lower export prices. Through the procompetitive effect, increased arbitrage opportunities for customers, which are due to lower transaction costs, force firms to reduce their markups and limit their ability to extract value by quoting different prices in different countries (the so-called "pricing to market"). This maps into lower export price levels and lower price dispersion across national markets. Third and last, there are the

Gianmarco I. P. Ottaviano is a professor of economics at Bocconi University.

effects on firm performance. Through intraindustry reallocations, tougher competition forces less-efficient firms to exit (selection). Through intrafirm reallocations, tougher competition forces surviving firms to restructure (restructuring). Hence, even when observed in the data, restructuring, which is the focus of the authors' investigation, may have nothing to do with having foregone the right to devaluate.

The challenge becomes even tougher when one considers that several of the foregoing effects are not specific to the introduction of the common currency but may be the result of other parallel events, such as the broader process of European integration or globalization at large. Hence, restructuring may not only have little to do with the foregone possibility of competitive devaluations but also with the euro altogether.

Unfortunately, all these confounding factors are not discussed in the chapter, which to many readers may cast a methodological shadow on the authors' identification strategy of the restructuring effects of foregone competitive devaluations. Such strategy is based on treatment-versus-control comparisons aimed at identifying the differential impact of the euro between otherwise identical groups. These groups are defined along three dimensions: EU countries inside or outside the euro area, sectors in which devaluations were more or less important for competitiveness before the euro, and low- or high-tech firms. The author's basic idea is: "If the euro has had any effect in terms of restructuring, we expect it to be strongest in the country-sectors that relied more intensively on competitive devaluations"—that is, in countries that were formerly keener to devaluate and in sectors where competition is mainly in terms of prices, as in these sectors, devaluations were more likely to affect competitiveness.

For many readers, it may be hard to see how this treatment-versus-control strategy allows the authors to isolate the specific effects of the euro in terms of foregone devaluations from its effects in terms of lower transaction costs, and to some extent, from the effects of other parallel events. For instance, aren't the country-sector-firms in which the authors look for the effects of foregone devaluations the same in which one would expect the impact of lower transaction costs to be stronger? Aren't such country-sector-firms precisely those in which one would expect growing competition from emerging countries from outside the European Union? Isn't it possible that the "clear break around the 1992 devaluation" has something to do with the single market rather than with the devaluation per se?

References

Economist. 2006. The euro and trade. June 22.

Business Cycles in the Euro Area

Domenico Giannone, Michele Lenza,
and Lucrezia Reichlin

4.1 Introduction

When asked for his opinion in the 1960s on what had been the impact of the French revolution, the Chinese premiere Zhou Enlai famously said, "It's too early to tell."

This might be what will be said about the effects of the European Monetary Union (EMU) on euro area business cycles in 250 years. Indeed, some of these effects may take a long time to manifest themselves, as they result from changes in trade and specialization patterns across the euro area (see, for example, Krugman [1993] and Frankel and Rose [1998]).

However, other effects, such as the loss of flexibility in macroeconomic policies, emphasized, for example, by Feldstein (1998), have more immediate consequences on business cycles, and it should already be possible to identify them at the occasion of the tenth anniversary of the union.

A lot has been written on business-cycle synchronization within the euro area, and a few papers are trying to address how it has been affected by the EMU. The literature, however, is far from being consensual. (In the next section, we review the findings.) Moreover, very little is known about the

Domenico Giannone is professor of economics at the Université Libre de Bruxelles. Michele Lenza is an economist at the European Central Bank. Lucrezia Reichlin is professor of economics at the London Business School.

We would like to thank the editors, Alberto Alesina and Francesco Giavazzi, as well as the seminar participants at the National Bureau of Economic Research conference on "Europe and the Euro" in Milan and "The Euro Area, the Euro and the World Business Cycle" in Aix-en-Provence. We also thank Filippo Di Mauro, Gabriel Fagan, Francesco Mongelli, and in particular, our discussants Tommaso Monacelli and Benoit Mojon. The opinions in this chapter are those of the authors and do not necessarily reflect the views of the European Central Bank. Please address any comments to Domenico Giannone (dgiannon@ulb.ac.be), Michele Lenza (michele.lenza@ecb.europa.eu), or Lucrezia Reichlin (lreichlin@london.edu).

historical characteristics of national and aggregate business cycles in the euro area. One of our objectives is to describe the basic characteristics of real economic activity in the area as a whole and in member countries, as well as the dynamic relations between national cycles over the last forty years. Having formed a view on these features for a sufficiently long historical period (our sample starts in 1970), we then address the question of changes related to the EMU.

We adopt a very conservative and narrow approach. Because we are look-ing for robust results on a topic for which there is little consensus about descriptive statistics, we analyze annual data, which are less affected by mea-surement error than quarterly statistics and are available for all countries for a relatively long time period. Moreover, we look at real data only, because the well-documented changes in nominal variables and the convergence of infla-tion and interest rates that have taken place since the early 1990s, if of signifi-cance, should be reflected in visible changes in the output structure over time. In a way, the establishment of the EMU helps identify broader economic relations without having to define a complex model. Finally, amongst real variables, we focus on gross domestic product (GDP) per capita only, dis-regarding other real indicators, such as labor market or consumption data. This choice is partly motivated by the lack of reliable comparative statistics, but also because unless the omitted real variables have a predictive power for output, output dynamics should reflect changes in different sectors of the real economy.

We first analyze asymmetries in levels of economic activity, and then we look at growth rates to try to identify patterns across countries and over time in the evolution of gaps between each member's growth rate and the euro-wide average.

Then, we study the dynamic relationship between growth rates. We base our analysis on two simple models: one that characterizes the joint output dynamics of the euro area countries and one that studies the euro area aggre-gate cycle in relation to that of the United States, the other large common-currency area in the world.

We first look at the relation between countries' output dynamics and average euro area growth. Precisely, based on the economic structure pre-vailing before 1999 and conditioning on the observed path of euro area growth before and after 1999, we ask whether we would have observed in each country the realized growth observed during the EMU years. We then focus on the euro area aggregate cycle and ask the question of whether the observed growth path in the EMU years could have been expected on the basis of the past distribution and conditioning on external develop-ments. To capture external development, we use as a conditioning variable the observed path of U.S. GDP growth. The choice of U.S. output as a conditioning variable is motivated by the findings in Giannone and Reichlin (2005, 2006) and by some additional results reported here, which show that the dynamic correlation between U.S. and euro area growth is robust and has been stable over time.

Overall, the results of the chapter should reassure the early critics of the EMU. The level of heterogeneity that we have observed over the last ten years is in line with historical experience. Differences between countries are small and the transmission of common shocks rather homogeneous.

On a more pessimistic tone, one of our findings is that the average growth experienced by the euro area as a whole from 1999 to 2006 has been slightly lower than what we would have expected based on its historical relation with the United States. However, the causes of slow growth do not appear to be related to the asymmetric adjustment to shocks emphasized in the discussion that took place ten years ago.

4.2   What Do We Know about the Euro Area Business Cycles?

There is a large empirical literature that describes the characteristics of business cycles and their evolution in Organization for Economic Cooperation and Development (OECD) countries. Most papers, however, don't analyze the total sample of euro area member countries and focus either on large European countries (including also noneuro area nations), the Group of 7 (G7), or a larger number of OECD economies. What we have learned about the euro area business cycles comes from this literature. Next, we summarize the results.

Papers have addressed different questions.

At the beginning of the EMU, there was an effort to collect data on the aggregate euro area economy (Fagan, Henry, and Mestre 2001). With these data, some studies in the first years of the EMU have tried to characterize the euro area aggregate business cycle, both for what concerns the dating of recessions and expansions of levels of economic activity (the so-called classical cycle) and the growth cycle.

Other studies have focused on countries' heterogeneity and look at the synchronization of recessions or use growth rates and filtered data to identify the cross-country pattern of comovements between some components of output or industrial production data. A popular approach has been to identify the relative importance of a common world component in major OECD countries, a European (and/or euro area) component, and in some papers, a regional component. Few of these studies, however, are recent enough to be sufficiently informative on the EMU regime's facts.

Many papers have focused on the issue of structural change. Here, authors have asked whether the degree of synchronization has changed in relation to the exchange rate mechanism (ERM), the Maastricht treaty, and the EMU. Some studies have looked backward and have estimated the degree of heterogeneity of the response to common euro area, European, or world shocks before the inception of the EMU in order to infer on that basis what would have happened as a consequence of the single currency and to evaluate its potential costs.

Finally, some studies have used a variety of methods to characterize the synchronization of turning points of classical cycles focusing on growth rather than on recession episodes.

Because the set of countries, the time period, and the variables used are different across these studies, it is quite difficult to report results in a synthetic way. Following is a review of the findings.

4.2.1 Characteristics of the Euro Area Aggregate Business Cycle: Recessions and Expansions

The first attempt to look at the euro area as a single economy and to date the turning points of its classical cycle has been pursued by the Center for Economic Policy Research (CEPR) dating committee on the basis of judgemental criteria (www.CEPR.org) and with data from 1970 to 2003. Artis, Marcellino, and Proietti (2005) reproduce these data using more formal techniques. The result of these studies is that the timing of euro area recessions is similar to that of U.S. recessions as classified by the National Bureau of Economic Research (NBER; www.nber.org), although euro area turning points lag U.S. ones (see Giannone and Reichlin [2005] for a documentation of this point). None of these studies, however, analyze recent data, and in the euro area sample, no classical recession has been identified so far.

Turning points have also been established on the basis of a cyclical component extracted from many economic activity indicators. This component, the coincident indicator of the euro area business cycle (EuroCOIN), corresponds to a growth-cycle concept and is regularly updated by the CEPR (see www.CEPR.org and Altissimo et al. 2001).

4.2.2 Characteristics of the National Business Cycles

The literature seems to agree that the timing of classical recessions is very synchronized across euro area countries (Artis, Marcellino, and Proietti 2005; Harding and Pagan 2006), although there is no comprehensive analysis of all euro area economies that includes recent years.

In general, evidence on growth rates points to the importance of the world component in the European business cycle (Canova, Ciccarelli, and Ortega 2005; Kose, Otrok, and Whiteman 2003; Monfort et al. 2004). Others have emphasized the strong link between the U.S. and the euro area business cycle (Agresti and Mojon 2001; Canova, Ciccarelli, and Ortega 2005; Del Negro and Otrok 2008; Giannone and Reichlin 2005, 2006).

Papers are less consensual on the identification of a specific euro area or European business cycle over a longer sample. While some studies identify the emergence of a European cycle in the 1990s, some date it back to the 1970s, and others don't find it at all (see the following review).

A different approach has been to look at the relative importance of regional, national, and euro-wide cycles. Forni and Reichlin (2001) and Croux, Forni, and Reichlin (2001), on the basis of data including only a couple of years of the EMU sample, have shown that a regional component—orthogonal to the national one—explains a large component of national European cycles (around 30 percent).

Finally, the European Central Bank (ECB) recently published a report on output growth differentials since 1990 in euro area countries and found that they are small (and comparable with those of U.S. states) but persistent (ECB 2007). The same message comes from a more analytical study by Giannone and Reichlin (2006).

4.2.3 Changes Since the ERM, Maastricht, and the EMU

Evidence on changes of the characteristics of euro area cycles is less consensual. Clearly, with many institutional changes clustered around the early 1990s and a short sample covering the EMU regime, it is hard to come up with robust findings. Artis and Zhang (1997), analyzing cycles before and after 1979 (the beginning of the first ERM), find increased synchronicity since the ERM for countries belonging to the ERM. However, Artis (2003) revisits these findings using data up to 2001 and concludes that on a sample of twenty-three countries, there is no evidence of a European cycle. This again contrasts with the results of Lumsdaine and Prasad (2003) based on seventeen OECD countries (of which ten belong to the euro area and thirteen to Europe) between 1963 and 1994. They find that especially after 1973, there is a clear European business cycle. Helbling and Bayoumi (2003), on the other hand, find little synchronization between G7 growth cycles from 1973 to 2001 and estimate that Germany was more synchronized with Anglo-Saxon countries than with France in that period, although they also find instability over time of cross-country correlations. Focusing on slowdown episodes, however, they point to strong cross-country correlations during recessions.

Two papers use more recent data. On the basis of data up to 2007 on seven euro area and three European noneuro area countries, Canova, Ciccarelli, and Ortega (2008) find that an EU cycle emerges in the 1990s, but this is common to EMU and non-EMU countries. The same authors find that a European cycle was absent until the mid-1980s. Del Negro and Otrok (2008), with data from 1970 to 2005, find no change in average cross-country correlations of euro area business cycles or for the larger set of European countries, while they do detect a decline in G7 average correlations.

4.2.4 Shocks and Propagations

Few studies have tried to assess the propagation of U.S., German, or world shocks across countries on the basis of semistructural or structural models.

Before the establishment of the EMU, Bayoumi and Eichengreen (1992), with a sample of twelve members of the European Union from 1960 to 1988, identify demand and supply shocks on the basis of countries' vector autoregressions (VARs) on output growth and inflation. They identify a core group (Germany, France, Belgium, the Netherlands, and Denmark) whose supply shocks are both smaller and more correlated across neighboring countries, as well as a periphery (the United Kingdom, Italy, Spain, Portugal, Ireland, and Greece) with large and weakly correlated shocks.

Giannone and Reichlin (2006) study the response of output growth of euro area countries to a euro area-wide shock on the basis of the 1970 to 2005 sample. They find that a large part of countries' business cycles is due to common (area-wide) shocks, while idiosyncratic fluctuations are limited but persistent.

Different results, on the other hand, are found by Canova, Ciccarelli, and Ortega (2008). With quarterly data from 1970 to 1993, these authors find no positive spillovers of German shocks to other EMU countries, while, with information up to the ECB creation at the end of 1998, they find a lot of commonalities in the response of EMU countries to German shocks. The same result, according to the authors, holds for the longer-term sample, including the first four years of the EMU.

This review shows that although there is a broad consensus on the synchronization of recessions and expansions on the basis of data on the level of economic activity, the literature is not at all in agreement on the facts of growth cycles—that is, the facts based on either growth rates or filtered data capturing some longer-moving average of growth rates. Results differ, depending on the sample, the method, the data, or the data transformation. These differences in opinions about what are essentially descriptive statistics are surprising. They are partly explained by poor data quality, short samples for the policy regimes of interest, and a lack of robustness with respect to data filtering and statistical methods.

The attempt of our chapter is to reevaluate some of the facts as we try to emphasize robustness. We aim to characterize the features of the euro area cycle for member countries and for the aggregate since 1970 and to compare these characteristics with those of the U.S. cycle. Although our analysis is limited because it mainly focuses on GDP per capita, it covers all euro area countries and a relatively long time span. In the next section, we describe our data set and discuss measurement issues.

4.3   Data

Business-cycle analysis is typically performed with quarterly data. However, to avoid measurement issues, and because our aim is to cover all euro area countries for a period of time—including a few full business cycles— we have made the choice of using annual data. Although we may lose information on short-term dynamics, we consider annual data to be more reliable for the purpose of establishing robust facts on real economic activity.

The quality of quarterly historical data for the euro area is still poor. Moreover, quarterly data are not available for all countries for a sufficiently long sample. (They are harmonized only since 1991.) For some countries, even if available, quarterly data are constructed artificially from annual data.

A way to assess the importance of measurement error is to look at the spectral density of quarterly GDP growth at different frequencies. A series for which measurement error explains a large component of the total volatility should have the bulk of variance concentrated at high frequencies. For the United States, where quarterly data are of relatively good quality, quarterly GDP growth exhibits a peak at business-cycle frequencies and the bulk of the variance at low frequencies. It is interesting to look at Germany for comparison.

Figure 4.1 plots the spectral density for Germany and the U.S. quarterly GDP for the sample from 1970 to 1989.

Clearly, German and U.S. quarterly GDP show a very different frequency

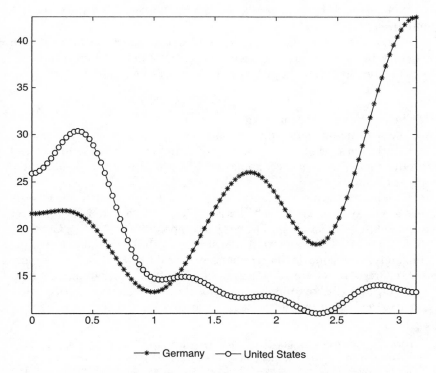

Fig. 4.1   Spectral densities: Germany and the United States, 1970 to 1989

Source: IMF International Statistics for GDP volume; 2000 = 100.

Note: The figure reports the spectral density of quarterly GDP growth in the United States and Germany in the 1970 to 1989 sample. The estimates are computed by using a Bartlett lag window of eight lags.

decomposition of the variance, which indicates large measurement error in the case of Germany. Large concentration of volatility is at frequencies higher than the year, which suggests that by using yearly data, the problem of measurement might be mitigated.

We consider real GDP per capita purchasing power parity (PPP) adjusted, because this facilitates international comparisons on the levels of economic activity. Data are PPP adjusted using 2000 weights. The sample is from 1970 to 2006.)[1]

We consider the twelve countries that composed the euro area until December 2006—before the inclusion of Malta, Cyprus, and Slovenia.

4.4   Euro Area Economic Activity: 1970 to 2006

We begin from descriptive statistics on the level of economic activity. We start from 1970 to form a view on the level of heterogeneity, as it was almost forty years ago—well before the introduction of common EU policies throughout the 1990s and the establishment of the euro in 1999.

Define $y_{i,t}$, $1 = 1, \ldots, 12$ as the log of real GDP per head (times 100) for country i.

Table 4.1 reports the percentage difference between the real GDP of each country and the euro area aggregate in different years and subperiods.

This corresponds to the last term of the expression:

$$y_{i,t} = y_{\mathrm{ea},t} + (y_{i,t} - y_{\mathrm{ea},t}),$$

where $y_{\mathrm{ea},t}$ refers to the euro area.

The last column reports the population weights.

Clearly, the sizes of the gaps are sensitive to the time period and depend on the level of aggregate economic activity, which in turn depends on the phase of the cycle.

Looking at starting conditions in the 1970s, we can heuristically identify two groups of countries. The first is a core group with a level of output per capita close to the average. The core is composed of Italy (IT), Germany (GE), France (FR), Belgium (BE), Austria (AT), the Netherlands (NE), and Finland (FI). Second, in the periphery, we have Portugal (PT), Luxembourg (LU), Greece (GR), Ireland (IE), and Spain (SP). In this group, only Luxembourg started above the average, while the other countries started below the average level of output per capita before the start of the euro.

---

1. The source is OECD, National Accounts. Data are constructed by using national series for GDP in volume at the prices of a common base year (2000) and then by deflating them by PPP for a fixed year (2000). We follow the OECD recommendation of deflating the GDP per-head series by the PPP of a fixed year instead of using the current PPP series. This implies a lack of homogeneity over time but has the advantage of using a price structure that is constantly updated and of protecting against the variance from one year to another of PPP calculations, which is quite large (see Lequiller and Blades [2006]).

Table 4.1   **Real GDP per head: Percentage difference with respect to the euro area**

	1970	1980	1990	1999	2006	1970 to 1998	1999 to 2006	Weights
Germany	5.9816	4.6662	5.2049	5.0789	2.7851	5.1641	2.8321	27.1819
France	6.2354	7.3947	4.5943	1.4335	0.7428	5.5033	1.1018	19.551
Italy	0.1412	3.6302	5.7794	3.2955	−2.0718	3.1775	0.8867	19.2345
Spain	−22.1873	−25.8476	−21.5717	−17.8209	−11.494	−21.7787	−13.2354	13.124
The Netherlands	21.3416	13.73	10.1749	15.4823	16.2235	13.9666	15.5633	5.0325
Greece	−16.6007	−9.9608	−29.4855	−31.271	−13.6088	−19.972	−21.3453	3.459
Belgium	10.7573	12.4221	10.0924	9.4879	11.207	10.9122	10.2991	3.404
Portugal	−60.8551	−54.9653	−45.4417	−38.4188	−42.5336	−50.7258	−39.7879	3.3559
Austria	8.4662	13.6951	13.2693	15.5907	16.1375	13.3786	15.283	2.6414
Finland	−2.3158	1.3018	5.7416	0.7445	11.9744	0.14	6.7632	1.6837
Ireland	−41.8626	−38.9094	−27.5039	3.3636	28.1836	−30.655	22.0886	1.1994
Luxembourg	47.5378	36.8334	59.3318	68.7465	86.1238	51.2636	80.3809	0.1328

Note: The table reports the percentage difference between the euro area and each country in specific periods and on average before and after the inception of the euro. The countries are ordered according to the average population share over the entire period, as reported in the last column.

Note that in comparing levels of economic activity, one should be aware of measurement issues. In particular, if lack of precision in the calculation of purchasing power parities is taken into account, a difference in levels of less than 5 percent between the GDP per head of two different countries should not be considered really significant (Lequiller and Blades 2006). For example, for Greece, recent changes in the construction of the official statistics have produced a series that does not seem to be reliable.[2]

The difference between GDP per capita of countries of the core and periphery, however, is economically significant, because it exceeds 10 percent.

It is interesting to note that the countries in the core group have remained homogeneous throughout the sample, while countries with heterogeneous starting conditions have no general tendency to become closer to the euro area. Differences in levels of economic activity are persistent. Some countries seem to converge, such as Spain; others do not seem to catch up, such as Greece. Ireland, on the other hand, caught up and overshot. Overall, by superficial inspections of these numbers, nothing much seems to have changed since the 1990s. The same findings are in Giannone and Reichlin (2006).

4.5   Business Cycles

Rather than filtering data, we consider annual growth rate. This is partly because business-cycle facts are not robust to different detrending techniques (see, for example, Canova [1998]) and annual growth rates are easily interpretable, and partly because considering any smoother component of growth rates implies extracting a moving average with the consequence of losing points at the end of the sample—which, for the EMU regime, is already quite short.

As each country's growth depends on both euro area developments and its idiosyncratic dynamics, it is useful to consider the following decomposition:

$$\Delta y_{i,t} = \Delta y_{ea,t} + (\Delta y_{i,t} - \Delta y_{ea,t}),$$

where Δ is the difference operator.

The variations in the gap $(\Delta y_{i,t} - \Delta y_{ea,t})$, which is the growth differential with respect to the euro area, represent country-specific business-cycle developments that may originate either in idiosyncratic shocks or in heterogenous reactions to euro area shocks. This is a rough measure of business-cycle heterogeneity.

2. Greek national accounts were revised in September 2006 to take into account underground activity, raising the level of output by about 26 percent. (See International Monetary Fund [2007]).

Table 4.2   **Annual growth rates of real GDP per head**

	Average growth rate		Variance growth rate	
Countries	Pre-EMU	EMU	Pre-EMU	EMU
Euro area	2.24	1.59	2.30	1.27
Germany	2.21	1.30	2.64	1.58
France	2.07	1.50	2.70	1.05
Italy	2.35	0.92**	3.96	2.13
Spain	2.40	2.38	4.62	1.30
The Netherlands	2.03	1.68	2.36	2.47
Greece	1.71	3.80	12.29	0.28***
Belgium	2.20	1.80	3.29	1.37
Portugal	3.04	1.07	14.03	2.68
Austria	2.50	1.66*	3.01	1.30
Finland	2.35	2.99	9.57	1.56
Ireland	3.85	4.69	7.90	5.39
Luxembourg	3.00	3.76	11.48	4.42

Note: The table reports (a) the average real GDP per capita growth rate and (b) the variance of the growth rate of the euro area and the twelve countries we study.
***Significant at the 1 percent level.
**Significant at the 5 percent level.
*Significant at the 10 percent level.

Table 4.2 reports estimates for average growth and its variance. Estimates are computed for different subsamples.

Results are also reported for a test on whether the numbers are significantly different across periods. The test is constructed by comparing the measure computed using the observed post-EMU data and the distribution of the measures we obtained by using block bootstrap over the pre-EMU period. Asterisks indicate that there have been significant changes in our measures after the EMU.[3]

For most countries, the average rate of growth was lower during the EMU period. However, the difference is not significant, except for Austria and Italy. The same is true for the variance, which has decreased everywhere, but significantly only for Greece. (It should be recalled that numbers for Greece are not very reliable.)

Let us now analyze the pattern of heterogeneity. To this end, we consider the quadratic mean of growth differentials and look at its cross-sectional and time series pattern.

The choice of this statistic is motivated by the fact that it has a simple economic interpretation.

Following Kalemli-Ozcan, Sorensen, and Yosha (2001), we assume log

---

3. Statistical significance has been assessed by using block bootstrap, with blocks of two years in length.

utility and define utility in autarky as U^A and utility in a full-risk-sharing equilibrium as U^S. Under normality and the assumption that output is a random walk, we have:

$$U^A[Y_{i,0}(1 + G_i)] = U^S[Y_{i,0}],$$

where $G_i = (1/2\delta)E(\Delta y_{i,t} - \Delta y_{ea,t})^2$ is the permanent increase in output needed to compensate an average consumer in an autarkic country for not being in a full risk-sharing equilibrium, and δ is the intertemporal discount rate.

As noted by Kalemli-Ozcan, Sorensen, and Yosha (2001), under these simplifying assumptions, G_i can be used as a measure of the gains from risk sharing. This is explained as follows. In the extreme case in which the countries that are members of the monetary union are able to fully share risk, only area-wide fluctuations matter, and asymmetries are painless. At the other extreme, if countries are autarkic, they are forced to consume at each point in time what they produce, and asymmetries are painful. How economically important asymmetries are depends on how close we are to autarky.[4]

Notice that the quadratic mean of the growth differential of country i with respect to the euro area, apart from a scaling coefficient, is an estimate of G_i.

We first ask whether our measure of asymmetry is related to the initial (1970s) level of the gaps.

In figure 4.2, we plot the quadratic mean of the growth differential for each member country against the differentials in starting conditions, measured by the gap in GDP per capita in 1970.

Heterogeneity is smaller for those countries that were closer to each other in the 1970s in terms of levels of GDP. (The exception is Finland, which experienced an idiosyncratic period of volatility in the early 1990s related to the banking crisis.) For those countries, the average quadratic growth differential is also small with respect to the variance of GDP growth (see table 4.2).

Because the ratio between the mean of the quadratic gap and the variance of GDP growth is equal to the variance explained by the euro area under the assumption of extreme symmetry (i.e., assuming that the expected growth of each country GDP, given the euro area GDP, is equal to the euro area GDP growth itself), our results suggest that most of the business-cycle fluctuations in countries with similar starting conditions are driven by euro area-wide shocks, which propagate in an homogeneous way.

Let us now look at heterogeneity over time. Has it changed since the 1970s?

---

4. Of course, a measure of the costs of business-cycle asymmetries should be based on data on consumption as well as output. Giannone and Reichlin (2006), for example, use output and consumption data and apply the method proposed by Sorensen and Yosha (1998) to assess the changes in the degree of risk sharing within the euro area over time. They find that risk sharing has increased in the last decade.

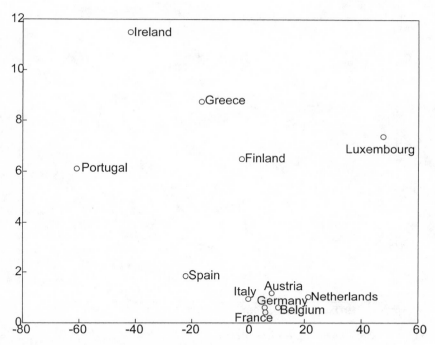

Fig. 4.2   Growth dispersion and starting conditions

Source: OECD, National Accounts.

Note: The figure plots the quadratic mean of the differential in GDP growth in twelve euro area countries (computed in the sample 1971 to 2006) against the gap in 1970 GDP per capita levels in each country with respect to the euro area aggregate.

To this end, we compute the statistics:

$$\frac{1}{2H+1}\sum_{h=-H}^{H}\left[\sum_{i=1}^{12}\omega_{i,t}(\Delta y_{i,t+h}-\Delta y_{ea,t+h})^2\right],$$

where $\omega_{i,t}$ is the share of population in country i relative to the euro area during the year t: at any point in time, this is a measure of cross-sectional dispersion of growth rates across member countries. Countries are weighted according to their size. The measure is temporally smoothed by taking a centered-moving average.

Because population weights are quite constant over time, the measure can be interpreted as the weighted cross-sectional average of the quadratic mean of the gap of the dispersion of GDP growth between member countries and the area average, the economic meaning of which we previously discussed:

$$\sum_{i=1}^{12}\overline{\omega}_i\left[\frac{1}{2H+1}\sum_{h=-H}^{H}(\Delta y_{i,t+h}-\Delta y_{ea,t+h})^2\right],$$

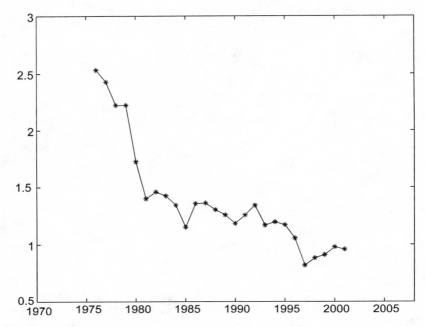

Fig. 4.3   Cross-country growth dispersion

Source: OECD, National Accounts.

Note: The figure reports $[1/(2H + 1)]\sum_{h=-H}^{H} [\sum_{i=1}^{12} \omega_{i,t}(\Delta y_{i,t+h} - \Delta y_{ea,t+h})^2]$, a measure of cross-sectional dispersion of GDP growth rates across member countries of the euro area.

where $\bar{\omega}_i$ is the average population weight of the member country i.

Results are illustrated in figure 4.3.

Cross-sectional dispersion today is less than half of what it was at the beginning of the sample. Dispersion clearly declined in the early 1980s—much earlier than the inception of the EMU, the fiscal and nominal convergence started with the Maastricht treaty, and the acceleration of financial and good market integration witnessed since the late 1980s.[5]

To sum up, asymmetries are very small for countries with a similar level of development and are larger for countries with low GDP per capita relative to the euro area. Asymmetries have declined over time as an effect of decline output volatility in the early 1980s (the Great Moderation). Because asymmetries have changed very little as a consequence of the EMU, the costs of business-cycle heterogeneity associated with it have been small.

5. The reduction in cross-country dispersion in business-cycle fluctuations coincides with a worldwide moderation of business-cycle fluctuations, which took place since the mid-1980s. For an exhaustive documentation of the decline in worldwide volatility, see Stock and Watson (2005).

4.6   A Model of Dynamic Interactions among Member Countries

To go beyond descriptive statistics, we must build a model to study cross-country dynamic interaction in economic activity.

We have chosen to base our analysis on output data only. This is obviously a narrow approach, but it is justified on two grounds.

First, as it is well documented, nominal variables have been converging since the early 1990s to reach similar levels at the end of the decade. This allows the design of a control experiment where real activity in a period of nominal heterogeneity can be compared with real activity with nominal homogeneity, and it is an alternative way to estimate a model for the whole period, including also nominal variables. Therefore, it makes sense to study the dynamic relation amongst real variables only, provided that we try to understand the changes induced by the EMU.

Second, although in principle, other real information such as consumption and external accounts is informative on the effect of the EMU (see Blanchard [2006]; Boivin, Giannoni, and Mojon [2008]; and Lane [2006], among others), heterogeneity in these variables should be reflected in output dynamics, unless they were leading indicators of output. There is no clear evidence, however, that consumption and current accounts have predictive power for GDP.

Our controlled experiment consists of computing the expected path of a member country, conditioning on the pre-EMU correlation structure and on the entire path of the euro area, and then asks whether intraeuro area relations have changed since the EMU.

The model is a VAR on output per capita of twelve countries of the euro area. A VAR is a very general dynamic model that is suitable for describing dynamic correlations. Moreover, a VAR can be estimated with level variables, which allows common trends to be taken into account.

We collect all the time series in a vector $Y_t = (y_{1,t}, \ldots, y_{12,t})'$. We consider the model

$$Y_t = c + A_1 Y_{t-1} + \ldots + A_p Y_{t-p} + e_t,$$

where $e_t \sim \mathrm{WN}(0, \Sigma)$.

With twelve variables and twenty-nine years of data, there are too many parameters to estimate, so we use Bayesian shrinkage and set the shrinkage parameter as in Banbura, Giannone, and Reichlin (2008).[6]

Let us denote the vector of the estimated parameters for the pre-EMU years as $\theta_{\text{pre-emu}}$.

The expectation of GDP per capita for each member country on the basis

---

6. We set the tightness parameter such that the in-sample fit for the euro area growth is the same found with a bivariate VAR with euro area and U.S. GDP.

of pre-EMU data, conditional on the aggregate outcome, that is the entire (pre- and post-EMU) path of area-wide aggregate GDP is:

$$\Delta\hat{y}_{i,t|ea} = E_{\theta_{pre-emu}}[y_{i,t}|y_{ea,70}, y_{ea,71}, \ldots, y_{ea,05}, y_{ea,06}] \text{ for } t = 70, \ldots, 06,$$

where $y_{ea,t}$ denotes the euro area average output per capita. We also compute uncertainty around the conditional expectations, which allows us to assess the statistical significance of the differences between observed euro area and country growth rates and the conditional expectations of the latter.[7]

Notice that $y_{ea,t}$ is approximately equal to $\omega_{1,t}y_{1,t} + \ldots + \omega_{12,t}y_{12,t}$, where $\omega_{i,t}$ is the share of population in country i relative to the euro area during the year t.

Figure 4.4 reports results for core countries. Figure 4.5 provides results for the other group but also includes Finland. The charts report 68 percent and 95 percent confidence intervals around the conditional forecast and realized GDP growth in country i and in the euro area.

Let us first analyze the pre-EMU years, on the basis of which we have estimated the parameters.

What emerges from the figures is that for the countries of the core, uncertainty around the country's forecasts, conditional on observed area-wide developments, is rather limited. Moreover, for each country, realized GDP growth is within the confidence bands around the conditional forecasts. These two facts indicate that country-specific fluctuations are rather limited and that the linkages among those countries and the aggregate are strong.

In addition, for each country, GDP growth is very close to the growth rate of the euro area.

Finally, the individual country's GDP growth forecasts, conditional on the euro area, are not significantly different from the euro area GDP growth itself. This is not only a further indication that asymmetric, idiosyncratic shocks are small, but it also implies that asymmetries in the propagation of shocks are limited.

Let us now look at the conditional forecast for the EMU period derived under the pre-EMU structure.

In general, the realized values are not significantly different from what we would have expected on the basis of euro area-wide developments and the pre-EMU distribution. This suggests that there is no evidence in the breakdown in the interrelationship amongst euro area member countries, although the growth of Austria, Italy, and the Netherlands is at the edge of the 68 percent confidence bands in the most recent period.

For the so-called periphery, the picture is more complex. For countries of this group, GDP growth dynamics are less similar to that of the euro area.

7. The conditional mean is computed using the Kalman filter, and the confidence bands are computed using the Carter and Kohn algorithm. For details, see Giannone and Lenza (2008).

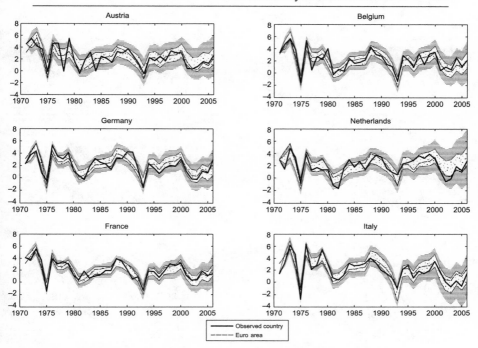

Fig. 4.4   Conditional expectations, given area-wide developments

Source: OECD, National Accounts.

Note: The figure reports GDP growth observed in each country and the euro area GDP growth. In addition, we report upper and lower bounds (black for the 68 percent and gray for the 95 percent confidence bands) for the GDP in each country, conditional to the observation of the euro area GDP. The conditional expectations are computed using the parameters estimated using the sample from 1970 to 1998.

However, uncertainty around the conditional forecast is large, indicating that the linkages between each of these countries and the rest of the euro area have been rather weak. As a consequence of such uncertainty, realized GDP is generally not statistically different from the forecast conditional on the average. This is the case not only in the pre-EMU period but also during the EMU years.

Spain and Portugal are interesting cases, because uncertainty is more in line with that of the core group. However, while in Spain, there is a high degree of similarity with euro area aggregate dynamics, and realized GDP growth in the EMU period is exactly in line with the conditional expectation (in the center of the confidence bands), in Portugal, the forecast conditional on the euro area is more volatile than that of the euro area. Moreover, in Portugal, the realized GDP growth in the EMU period has been systematic in the lower part of the distribution of the forecast conditional on area-wide developments.

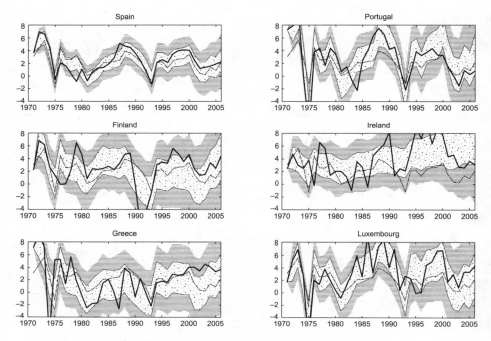

Fig. 4.5   Conditional expectations, given area-wide developments

Source: OECD, National Accounts.

Note: The figure reports GDP growth observed in each country and the euro area GDP growth. In addition, we report upper and lower bounds (black for the 68 percent and gray for the 95 percent confidence bands) for the GDP in each country, conditional to the observation of the euro area GDP. The conditional distributions are computed using the parameters estimated using the sample from 1970 to 1998.

Overall, these results tell us that some idiosyncracies are definitely present, and in general, they have not decreased over time, but they remain confined to the experience of small countries, both before and after the introduction of the common currency. Given the uncertainty, any statement on the real effect of the EMU in these countries is likely to be ill founded.

4.7   The Area-Wide Business Cycle

In table 4.2, we have seen that during the EMU years, all countries of the euro area experienced a relatively low GDP growth. The average growth from 1971 to 1998 was approximately 2.2 percent, while from 1999 to 2006, it was approximately 1.6 percent.

Seven years of data is very little to perform historical comparisons, as the average length of a business cycle is between six and nine years. However, we can perform a conditional exercise similar to the one proposed in the previous section. In that exercise, we forecast each country GDP per capita conditional on the pre-EMU structure and the observed path of euro area-wide growth, while here, we forecast euro area growth, conditional on the pre-EMU structure and on the observed path of U.S. GDP growth. The choice of the United States as a conditioning variable, however, must be justified. To this end, we must show that the relationship between U.S. and euro area GDP growth is tight and stable.

This is a controversial fact. For example, Alesina and Giavazzi (2006) have studied the relation between GDP per capita in the United States and in the largest euro area countries since 1945 and have claimed that after a period of catch-up, the gap stabilized since the 1970s but widened again in the last decade. On the other hand, Giannone and Reichlin (2005, 2006) show that since the 1970s, the euro area business cycle has experienced a stable relation with the cycle of the United States.

Let us report some descriptive statistics on the U.S. and euro area business cycle drawn from Giannone and Reichlin (2005, 2006).

In figures 4.6 and 4.7, we show the level of GDP per head in the two areas of the world and the gap between the levels.

Clearly, the U.S. and the euro area GDP per capita have moved along the same trend since 1970, with a gap that is stationary around a constant. On average, GDP per capita has been 30 percent lower than in the United States, with no sign of catching up. Fluctuations in the gap reflect different duration and amplitude of the two cycles (see Giannone and Reichlin [2005] for details).

Another key characteristic, illustrated in figures 4.8 and 4.9, is that the

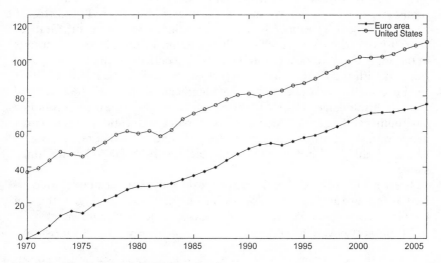

Fig. 4.6   The (log) level of GDP per head

Source: OECD, National Accounts.

Note: The figure reports the log-level of GDP per head in the United States and the euro area in the sample from 1970 to 2006.

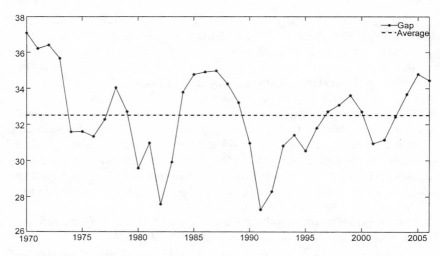

Fig. 4.7   The transatlantic gap

Source: OECD, National Accounts.

Note: The figure reports the difference between the log-levels of GDP per head in the United States and the euro area in the sample from 1970 to 2006.

euro area growth lags the United States. Figure 4.8 plots growth rates of GDP per capita, and figure 4.9 plots its corresponding five-years centered average, where the leading-lagging relation emerges very clearly.

To show that the U.S. leading relation with respect to the euro area is robust, we must also show that U.S. GDP growth is a good predictor of euro area growth. The appendix shows this point by reporting both Granger causality tests (in-sample predictability) and out-of-sample results. Results in the appendix also show that the forecasting performances have not deteriorated with the EMU. This gives further support to the hypothesis that the introduction of the euro has not significantly changed the historical transatlantic linkages. In spite of the relevant changes in the macroeconomic environment (the Great Moderation, German reunification, the euro area inception), the relationship between the U.S. and euro area real economic activity highlighted in Giannone and Reichlin (2005, 2006) has remained stable.

These results suggest that the euro area-U.S. dynamics can be characterized by the euro area rate of growth adjusting itself to the U.S. growth, with the United States not responding to shocks specific to the euro area.[8]

All these results, and particularly the robustness of the out-of-sample

8. Giannone and Reichlin (2005) use the restriction implied by the Granger causality tests to simulate levels of output and to verify whether it is possible to reproduce the properties of the dating of business cycle identified from the data. They find that the model reproduces them with a large degree of accuracy.

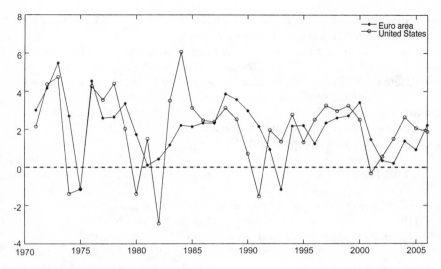

Fig. 4.8   GDP growth rates

Source: OECD, National Accounts.

Note: The figure reports the annual growth rates of GDP per head in the United States and the euro area in the sample from 1971 to 2006.

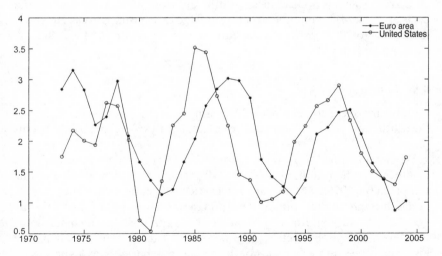

Fig. 4.9   GDP growth rates: five-years centered moving average

Source: OECD, National Accounts.

Note: The figure reports the five-years centered moving averages of annual growth rates of GDP per head in the United States and the euro area in the sample from 1973 to 2004.

forecast, indicate that U.S. GDP is a good candidate as a control variable for the counterfactual exercise on the euro area.

As we did for the countries of the euro area, here, we characterize the joint dynamics of the U.S. and the euro area aggregate by means of a VAR estimated until 1998. With the counterfactual, we would then ask if the latter has changed. Precisely, conditional on the U.S. cycle and the structure of the euro area economy before the start of the EMU, we ask whether we would have expected the growth rate observed between 1999 and 2006.

The VAR is now bivariate with $Y_t = (y_{us,t}, y_{ea,t})$.

This exercise is complementary to the one performed in the previous subsection. There, we kept average euro area as given and explored changes in heterogeneity. Here, we explore changes in the average growth. We ask whether the low growth of the euro area after 1998 should have been expected on the basis of the pre-1999 economic structure in the area and conditional on the present, past, and future realization of the U.S. growth.

Using the same notation as in previous section, we compute the conditional expectation:

$$\Delta \hat{y}_{i,t|ea} = E_{\theta_{pre-emu}}[y_{ea,t}|y_{us,70}, y_{us,71}, \ldots, y_{us,05}, y_{us,06}] \text{ for } t = 70, \ldots, 06.$$

Figure 4.10 illustrates that we would have observed a large part of the slowdown but not all of it. In fact, for each year since the inception of EMU, euro area growth is not significantly different from what is expected on the basis of pre-EMU economic structure and the U.S. business cycle. However, from 2001 to 2005, growth in the euro area is always on the lower side of the confidence bands.

4.8   Conclusions

Contrary to the conjecture of the pessimists and to that of the optimists, the features of euro area business cycles have hardly changed since the beginning of the EMU.

We have identified two groups of countries. The first is composed of EMU members that had similar levels of GDP per capita at the beginning of our sample in the 1970s. These countries have also experienced similar business cycles throughout the sample period, and the establishment of the EMU has not changed this pattern. The second group is composed by member states with levels of economic activity that were more heterogeneous and that have historically been more volatile. For these countries, business cycles have been less correlated with the rest of the euro area throughout the period, and again, no change can be detected with the inception of the single currency.

This story has a remarkable implication. The loss of flexibility in exchange rate and monetary policy had almost no effect on output comovements across countries, even if, as it has been emphasized by many observers, EMU member states have differed from one another for what concerns degree of competitiveness, real interest rates, and other economic characteristics.

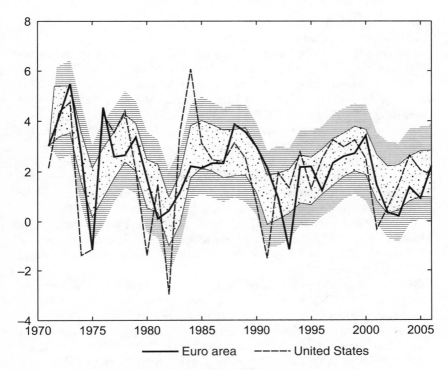

Fig. 4.10   Euro area GDP growth and its conditional expectations

Source: OECD, National Accounts.

Note: The figure reports GDP growth observed in the United States and the euro area. In addition, we report upper and lower bounds (black for the 68 percent and gray for the 95 percent confidence bands) for the GDP growth in the euro area, conditional to the observation of the U.S. GDP. The conditional distributions are computed using the parameters estimated using the sample from 1970 to 1998.

Finally, we have shown that part but not all of the relatively slow growth of the euro area in the first years of the millennium can be attributed to the lagged response to the U.S. cycle.

Appendix

Predictive Relation between the United States and the Euro Area

In this section, we evaluate the forecasting performance of the bivariate U.S.-euro area VAR we used in section 4.7.

Recall that the bivariate VAR was

$$Y_t = A(L)Y_{t-1} + Bu_t,$$

with $Y_t = (y_{us,t}, y_{ea,t})$ and $y_{us,t}$ and $y_{ea,t}$ indicating the log levels of the U.S. and euro area per capita GDP, respectively.

The variable we target is the annualized h-period change of per capita GDP: $(1/h)(y_{i,t+h} - y_{i,t})$, where i = ea, us and h is the forecast horizon, which ranges from one to three years ahead. The full sample is from 1970 to 2006, and we evaluate the forecasting performance of the model in the two samples from 1980 to 2006 and from 1999 to 2006.

The evaluation exercise is out of sample. For each period t, we estimate the bivariate VAR on the available information up to that period and iterate the VAR h times forward to forecast U.S. and euro area GDP h periods ahead. We then update the database recursively until exhaustion of the sample. The VAR model is estimated with one lag—the same specification we used for the exercises in the main text.

We compare the performance of the bivariate VAR with a benchmark of nonforecastability, the random walk model, whose forecast at time t for GDP growth per capita between time t and $t + h$ is the estimated average GDP growth rate until time t.

We also report the outcomes of an AR(1) forecast for both U.S. and euro area per capita GDP for the sake of assessing the contribution in terms of forecasting performance of the transatlantic linkages.

Table 4A.1 can be split into two sections reporting the results for the evaluation samples from 1980 to 2006 and from 1999 to 2006. Results are cast in terms of the ratio of the mean squared forecast error (MSFE) of the bivariate VAR and the AR(1) models with respect to the MSFE of the random walk model.

Starting with the first section of the table, which refers to the 1980 to 2006 evaluation sample, rows from (1) to (3) refer to the three forecast horizons of one to three years ahead. Columns (2) and (3) refer to the euro area, while columns (4) and (5) are analogous for the United States. Notably, columns (2) and (4) report the ratio of the mean squared forecast error of the VAR relative to the random walk model for the euro area and United States, while columns (3) and (5) report the ratio of the autoregressive forecast relative to the random walk model. A number smaller than 1 in the ratios indicates that the VAR or the autoregressive models outperform the random walk.

The second section of the table is analogous to the first for the evaluation sample from 1999 to 2006 and does not need further explanation.

When focusing on the 1980 to 2006 sample, it can first be seen that U.S. GDP per capita helps to forecast GDP per capita in the euro area. The MSFE error of the VAR model, in fact, is about half of the MSFE of the random walk and the AR(1) model at one and two years ahead and is about 70 percent at three years ahead. However, the euro area GDP per capita does not help to forecast U.S. GDP.

Results are qualitatively confirmed in the euro area sample from 1999 to 2006 showing that in particular, the forecasting performance of the bivariate

Table 4A.1   **Evaluation period by region**

| | 1980 to 2006 | | | | 1999 to 2006 | | | |
| | Euro area | | United States | | Euro area | | United States | |
Ratio	VAR/RW	AR/RW	VAR/RW	AR/RW	VAR/RW	AR/RW	VAR/RW	AR/RW
$h = 1$	0.51	0.96	1.24	1.15	0.66	0.81	1.00	1.02
$h = 2$	0.52	1.02	1.29	1.25	0.66	0.83	1.17	1.16
$h = 3$	0.67	1.08	1.48	1.46	0.78	0.94	1.44	1.39

Note: VAR = vector autoregression; RW = random walk; AR = autoregression.

VAR is robust to the changes in the monetary policy regime that came with the inception of the euro area.

References

Agresti, A. M., and B. Mojon. 2001. Some stylised facts on the euro area business cycle. ECB Working Paper no. 95. Frankfurt: European Central Bank.

Alesina, A., and F. Giavazzi. 2006. *The future of Europe: Reform or decline.* Cambridge, MA: MIT Press.

Altissimo, F., A. Bassanetti, R. Cristadoro, M. Forni, M. Hallin, M. Lippi, and L. Reichlin. 2001. EuroCOIN: A real time coincident indicator of the euro area business cycle. CEPR Discussion Paper no. 3108. London: Center for Economic Policy Research.

Artis, M. J. 2003. Is there a European business cycle? CESifo Working Paper no. 1053. Munich: Munich Society for the Promotion of Economic Research.

Artis, M. J., M. Marcellino, and T. Proietti. 2005. Dating the euro area business cycle. In *Euro area business cycle: Stylized facts and measurement issues,* ed. L. Reichlin, 83–93. London: Center for Economic Policy Research.

Artis, M. J., and W. Zhang. 1997. International business cycles and the ERM: Is there a European business cycle? *International Journal of Finance and Economics* 2 (1): 1–16.

Banbura, M., D. Giannone, and L. Reichlin. 2008. Large Bayesian VARs. ECB Working Paper no. 966. Frankfurt, Germany: European Central Bank.

Bayoumi, T., and B. Eichengreen. 1992. Shocking aspects of European monetary unification. NBER Working Paper no. 3949. Cambridge, MA: National Bureau of Economic Research, January.

Blanchard, O. 2006. A macroeconomic survey of Europe. Massachusetts Institute of Technology, Department of Economics. Manuscript, September.

Boivin, J., M. P. Giannoni, and B. Mojon. 2008. How has the euro changed the monetary transmission? NBER Working Paper no. 14190. Cambridge, MA: National Bureau of Economic Research, July.

Canova, F. 1998. Detrending and business cycle facts. *Journal of Monetary Economics* 41 (3): 475–512.

Canova, F., M. Ciccarelli, and E. Ortega. 2005. Similarities and convergence in G-7 cycles. *Journal of Monetary Economics* 54 (3): 850–78.

———. 2008. Did the Maastricht treaty or the ECB creation alter the European business cycle? Unpublished Manuscript. Available at: http://www.eco.unibs.it/~amisano/JEUBES3/political_events_june2008.pdf.

Croux, C., M. Forni, and L. Reichlin. 2001. A measure Of comovement for economic variables: Theory And empirics. *Review of Economics and Statistics* 83 (2): 232–41.

Del Negro, M., and C. Otrok. 2008. Dynamic factor models with time-varying parameters: Measuring changes in international business cycles. Staff Report no. 326. New York: Federal Reserve Bank of New York.

European Central Bank (ECB). 2007. Output growth differentials in the euro area: Sources and implications. *ECB Monthly Bulletin,* April, 73–87.

Fagan, G., J. Henry, and R. Mestre. 2001. An area-wide model (AWM) for the euro area. ECB Working Paper no. 42. Frankfurt: European Central Bank.

Feldstein, M. 1998. The political economy of the European Economic and Monetary Union: Political sources of an economic liability. NBER Working Paper no. 6150. Cambridge, MA: National Bureau of Economic Research, February.

Forni, M., and L. Reichlin. 2001. Federal policies and local economies: Europe and the US. *Journal of Financial Economics* 45 (1): 109–34.

Frankel, J. A., and A. K. Rose. 1998. The endogeneity of the optimum currency area criteria. *Economic Journal* 108 (449): 1009–25.

Giannone, D., and M. Lenza. 2008. Conditional forecasting with large Bayesian VARs. Unpublished Manuscript.

Giannone, D., and L. Reichlin. 2005. Euro area and US recessions, 1970–2003. In *Euro area business cycle: Stylized facts and measurement issues,* ed. L. Reichlin, 83–93. London: Center for Economic Policy Research.

———. 2006. Trends and cycles in the euro area: How much heterogeneity and should we worry about it? ECB Working Paper no. 595. Frankfurt: European Central Bank.

Harding, D., and A. Pagan. 2006. Synchronization of cycles. *Journal of Econometrics* 132 (1): 59–79.

Helbling, T., and T. Bayoumi. 2003. Are they all in the same boat? The 2000–2001 growth slowdown and the G-7 business cycle linkages. IMF Working Paper no. 03-46. Washington, DC: International Monetary Fund.

International Monetary Fund (IMF). 2007. *Greece: Selected issues.* IMF Country Report no. 07/27. Washington, DC: IMF.

Kalemli-Ozcan, S., B. E. Sorensen, and O. Yosha. 2001. Economic integration, industrial specialization, and the asymmetry of macroeconomic fluctuations. *Journal of International Economics* 55 (1): 107–37.

Kose, M. A., C. Otrok, and C. H. Whiteman. 2003. International business cycles: World, region, and country-specific factors. *American Economic Review* 93 (4): 1216–39.

Krugman, P. 1993. Lessons of Massachusetts for EMU. In *The transition to economic and monetary union in Europe,* ed. F. Giavazzi and F. Torres, 241–61. Cambridge: Cambridge University Press.

Lane, P. R. 2006. The real effects of European Monetary Union. *Journal of Economic Perspectives* 20 (4): 47–66.

Lequiller, F., and D. Blades. 2006. *Understanding national accounts.* Paris: Organization for Economic Cooperation and Development.

Lumsdaine, R. L., and E. S. Prasad. 2003. Identifying the common component of international economic fluctuations: A new approach. *Economic Journal* 113 (484): 101–27.

Monfort, A., J.-P. Renne, R. Rueffer, and G. Vitale. 2004. Is economic activity in the

G7 synchronized? Common shocks versus spillover effects. EABCN/CEPR Discussion Paper no. 2. London: Euro Area Business Cycle Network/Center for Economic Policy Research.

Sorensen, B. E., and O. Yosha. 1998. International risk sharing and European monetary unification. *Journal of International Economics* 45 (2): 211–38.

Stock, J. H., and M. W. Watson. 2005. Understanding changes in international business cycle dynamics. *Journal of the European Economic Association,* 3 (5): 969–1006.

Comment on this chapter, by Tommaso Monacelli, can be found on page 447.

5

The Estimated Trade Effects of the Euro
Why Are They Below Those from Historical Monetary Unions among Smaller Countries?

Jeffrey Frankel

Andrew Rose's 2000 paper, "One Money, One Market: Estimating the Effect of Common Currencies on Trade," was perhaps the most influential international economics paper of the last ten years. Applying the gravity model to a data set that was sufficiently large to encompass a number of currency unions led to an eye-opening finding: members of currency unions traded with each other an estimated three times as much as with otherwise similar trading partners. Even if Rose had not included the currency union dummy, his paper would still have been important, because he had bilateral exchange rate variability on the list of variables explaining bilateral trade, and it was highly significant statistically.[1] But the attention grabber was that the currency union dummy had a far larger and highly significant effect—the famous tripling estimate—above and beyond the effect of bilateral variability per se. The Rose paper was of course motivated by the coming of the European Monetary Union (EMU) in 1999, even though estimates were necessarily based on historical data from (much smaller) countries that had adopted currency unions in the past.

Jeffrey Frankel is the James W. Harpel Professor of Capital Formation and Growth at the John F. Kennedy School of Government, Harvard University, and a research associate of the National Bureau of Economic Research.

The author wishes to thank Francesco Giavazzi, Ernesto Stein, and Sylvana Tenreyo for comments and Clara Zverina for research assistance.

1. The finding that a fixed exchange rate in itself also produces a statistically significant increase in bilateral trade has more recently been confirmed by Klein and Shambaugh (2006).

5.1   First Post-1999 Results on Effects of the Euro on European Trade Patterns

By roughly the five-year mark, 2004, enough data had accumulated to allow an analysis of the early effects of the euro on European trade patterns. The general finding was that bilateral trade among euro members had indeed increased significantly but that the effect was far less than the one that had been estimated by Rose on the larger data set of smaller countries. Micco, Stein, and Ordoñez (MSO; 2003) found in a data set of European countries that trade between pairs of the first twelve EMU joiners rose significantly between 1999 and 2002, an estimated 15 percent beyond what could be explained by growth and other factors. The estimates of the euro effect in a larger set of twenty-two industrialized countries ranged from 6 to 26 percent, depending on dummies. The authors expressed a preference for estimates that allowed for pair dummies and produced a somewhat smaller estimate of the effect: 4 to 16 percent.[2] These magnitudes were less than in the Rose studies. As the authors pointed out, however, the effects were both statistically significant and also economically important, which is not bad, considering that the sample covered only the first four years of the EMU, a period in which the euro did not even circulate in currency form.

Other evidence from the first five years confirmed the finding. Bun and Klaassen (2002, 1) updated gravity estimates and found that "the euro has significantly increased trade, with an effect of 4% in the first year" and a long-run effect projected to be about 40 percent. Flam and Nordström (2006) found an effect of 26 percent in the change from 1995 through 1998 to 2002 through 2005. Berger and Nitsch (2005) and De Nardis and Vicarelli (2003) reported similarly positive results. More recently, Chintrakarn (2008) finds that two countries sharing the euro have experienced a boost in bilateral trade between 9 and 14 percent. Overall, the central tendencies of these estimates seem to be an effect in the first few years on the order of 10 to 15 percent.[3]

Thus, the trade effects of monetary union are not entirely limited to small countries. But they are far smaller than the tripling estimated by Rose. The central questions of this chapter are (a) what are the estimated effects,

2. Earlier, the preferred Micco, Stein, and Ordoñez (2002) estimates of "differences in differences" showed that between 1992 and 2001, the boost to intra-EMU trade was about 18 to 35 percent, depending on whether using country-pair dummies or conditioning on the standard gravity variables.

3. Studies with price data have tended to be more mixed, but some confirm that the euro is facilitating arbitrage among the markets of member countries. Looking at price data across pairs of European cities, Rogers (2001, 2002) finds evidence of convergence—but in the 1990s. In the European auto market, Goldberg and Verboven (2001) find gradual convergence over the period from 1970 to 2000. Goldberg and Verboven (2004) nail down EMU per se as a significant determinant of this convergence. Other positive findings come from Allington, Kattuman, and Waldman (2005) and Parsley and Wei (2001). Engel and Rogers (2004) are more negative.

updated at the ten-year mark, and (b) assuming they are similar to the 10 to 15 percent effects estimated by the early studies of euroland, what explains the large gap between the euro estimates and the tripling effects estimated by Rose and others using much larger historical data sets? Is it a matter of lags so that the 10 to 15 percent can be expected to rise gradually over time, eventually reaching levels comparable with those estimated for currency unions that have been around for one hundred years? Or is the currency union effect systematically smaller for large countries than for small countries? Or, is the tripling among the smaller countries merely an artifact of estimation problems associated with endogeneity and omitted variables? Finally, is there some effect (or lack thereof) peculiar to Europe?

5.2   The Critiques

Rose's remarkable tripling estimate has by now been replicated in various forms many times. But no sooner had he written his paper than the brigade to "shrink the Rose effect"[4]—or to make it disappear altogether—descended en masse. These critiques sometimes read to me as "guilty until proven innocent."

It is understandable that a threefold effect was greeted with much skepticism, as this is a very large number. There are five grounds for skepticism, as I classify them. Each of these arguments is potentially potent in the context of assessing the euro's effect on European trade patterns, if for no other reason than the claims that the Rose finding has always been spurious. But the critiques need to be assessed.

The first critique is the proposition that one cannot necessarily infer from cross-sectional evidence what would be the effect in real time of countries adopting a common currency. Most pre-1999 members of currency unions had essentially never had their own national currencies but instead used an external currency, at least since independence. In such cases as Panama or most of the Communaute Financière d'Afrique (CFA) countries in Africa, the currency arrangement goes back more than a century. In other cases, such as the Eastern Caribbean currency area, the currency dates from postwar independence.

Second are allegations of missing variables. The statistical association between currency links and trade links might not be the result of causation running from currencies to trade but might arise instead because both sorts of links are caused by a third factor, such as colonial history, remaining political links, complementarity of endowments, or accidents of history.

---

4. The phrase is from Richard Baldwin (2006). Baldwin's survey of the critiques concludes in the end that there is a Rose effect but that it is probably substantially smaller than a tripling. That is fine with me. If Rose had come up with a 50 percent effect on trade from the beginning, everyone would have considered that very large and important.

Another alleged missing variable is a country's "multilateral resistance" to trade or a more specific measure of remoteness from the rest of the world.

The third critique also concerns causality: the endogeneity of the currency decision. Countries choose as partners for currency links the neighbors with whom they trade the most rather than the other way around. Perhaps the endogeneity of the currency union decision and the simultaneity of other regional trade-promoting forces have been stronger among developing countries than among European countries. In other words, much of the correlation observed for currency unions among other countries may be spurious.

Fourth, the estimated effect on trade simply seems too big to be believable. While this judgment is explicitly a gut reaction, it is widely shared. Furthermore, an influential argument by Van Wincoop to the effect that the question has been misparameterized and that the true effects are substantially smaller seems to support it.

Fifth, Rose's evidence came entirely from countries that were either small (e.g., Ireland, Panama) or *very* small (e.g., Kiribati, Greenland, Mayotte). Thus, it was not clear that the estimates could be extended to larger countries. European economies tend to be large—some, particularly Germany, very large—while the set of non-EMU currency union countries tends to be small—some of them very small. If the currency union effect is substantially more important in small, highly trade-dependent countries, that could readily explain the small estimates for Europe.

While each of these five arguments has some validity, to each there is a better response than one might expect.

5.2.1   Times Series Dimension

First, regarding the time dimension, a logical interpretation is that even if the full comparative statics effect were to obtain in the very long run after a change in regime, they might not show up in the short run due to very substantial lags. That would not be surprising, as we have evidence of long lags in effects on bilateral trade.

Even thirty years may not be the long-run effect. The effect may keep rising for a long time. Panama reports sending more than half its exports to the United States; perhaps one reason is that it has been on the U.S. dollar for over one hundred years.

We know that other gravity influences leave an effect on bilateral trade many decades after the cause has been removed. One piece of evidence is the generally slow speed of adjustment estimated in models with lags.[5] Another important example is the effect that colonial relationships have, even decades after independence, and even after controlling for continu-

---

5. Eichengreen and Irwin (1998). Frankel (1997) discusses lagged effects historically for the cases of FTAs and political unions.

ing linguistic, political, or other links. Consider as an illustration a trivia question: what is Congo's largest trading partner? Not one of its neighbors, nor a large country, as the simple gravity model would lead you to expect; it is Belgium, the old colonial master, with whom ties were abruptly severed fifty years ago.[6] Even when the original reason for a high level of bilateral trade has disappeared, the stock of capital that firms have invested in the form of marketing and distribution networks, brand-name loyalty among customers, and so forth, lives on for many years thereafter. The word *hysteresis* is sometimes applied to this phenomenon, suggesting that the effect is considered to be permanent.

Subsequent research on currency unions using time series data finds that a substantial share of the tripling that Rose had estimated from the cross-sectional data, which is presumably the long-run effect, shows up within a few decades of a change. Using a 1948 to 1997 sample that includes a number of countries that left currency unions during that period, Glick and Rose (2002) find that trade among the members was twice as high in the currency union period as afterward. This suggests that roughly two-thirds of the tripling effect may be reached within three decades of a change in regime. (This reasoning assumes symmetry with respect to entry into and exit from currency unions.)

5.2.2   Omitted Variables

The second objection concerns the possible influence of omitted factors. Rose in fact did a thorough job of controlling for common languages, colonial history, and remaining political links.[7] The large estimated effect of a common currency remains. It seems very possible that there remain other omitted factors (including accidents of history) that influence both currency choices and trade links. Nevertheless, Rose's various extensions of the original research—these robustness tests, together with the time series results (Glick and Rose 2002) and the common use of fixed effects—reduce some of the force of this critique.

The omitted variable that is probably of greatest concern to the critics comes from the influential Anderson and Van Wincoop (2001) paper and is usually called "multilateral resistance term."[8] More concretely, in a cross-

6. Kleiman (1976) finds that about one-quarter of the (two- to four-fold) bias of colonial times remains for countries that have been independent for two decades. Anderson and Norheim (1993) find longer lags in the effects of colonial status. Wang and Winters (1991) and Hamilton and Winters (1992) find significant effects for UK excolonial relationships (though not French) as late as 1984 to 1986.

7. While it is admirable how many factors Rose controls for, I agree with Baldwin (2006) and also Melitz (2001) in regarding as a "nuisance" Rose's persistent habit of calling these "nuisance parameters." These coefficients are of interest in their own right and also help to gauge the persuasiveness of the overall model.

8. Baldwin wants to call it the "relative prices matter" term. It could also be called the "general equilibrium" term.

sectional context, the variable may come down to "remoteness." A country's remoteness is defined as the average distance from all trading partners, a weighted average based on the sizes of the trading partners; it is expected to have a positive effect on trade between a pair of countries, controlling for the more obvious negative effect of the distance between them bilaterally. The authors are a bit fanatical on this point: anyone who omits the relevant terms is not fit to be received in polite society.[9]

The Anderson and Van Wincoop (2001) model is an important contribution, both in serving as a theoretical foundation for the gravity model and in offering an argument that some of the border effects may have been quantitatively overestimated. Rose and Van Wincoop (2001) find that taking multilateral resistance and trade diversion into account should a priori knock the estimated value of the euro on bilateral trade down from tripling to 58 percent (among the original euro members). But the model's insistence on the role of trade diversion may be too doctrinaire. If I understand correctly the aspect of the Anderson and Van Wincoop theory that leads to numerical estimates of the effects of borders and currencies that are sharply reduced in magnitude, it is the property that the elimination of borders or currency differences within a region theoretically entails substantial diversion of trade away from the rest of the world and thus an increase in multilateral resistance. But such trade diversion from currency unions, whatever its basis in theory, is not observed in the data, by and large.[10] Thus, the argument for imposing the constraints from this particular theory may not be as strong as it otherwise would be. Furthermore, even if one goes along with Van Wincoop in imposing the constraint, the currency union term apparently remains high, (a) compared to its standard error, (b) compared to what we all thought ten years ago, and (c) compared to what happens to the free trade agreement (FTA) term when it too is knocked down by imposing the Van Wincoop constraint.

5.2.3   Causality Problems

The endogeneity of a country's choice of exchange regime is perhaps the most intractable problem with the Rose-style estimates. After all, optimum currency area theory suggests that countries should peg if they are small and open and should peg to the partners with whom they trade a lot.[11] El

---

9. I am one of those who long ago included remoteness in some of my gravity estimates (though not all). I devoted two pages to the subject in Frankel (1997, 143–4) and noted that it sometimes makes a difference to the results. The resistance to Canadian-U.S. trade is an example of where it makes a difference: Wei (1996) found that controlling for remoteness helped knock down the home country bias from around 10 to around 3. Another may be the finding of a huge apparent effect of Pacific Islanders adopting the Australian dollar in Nitsch (2001).

10. For example, the United Kingdom does not appear to have lost trade to euroland as a result of the euro; Begg et al. (2003), Frankel and Rose (2002), Frankel (2003), Micco, Stein, and Ordoñez (2003), and Chintrakarn (2008).

11. McKinnon (1963). Among many applications to Central and Eastern Europe is Frankel (2005).

Salvador decided to adopt the dollar because it traded a lot with the United States rather than the other way around. In that case, the Rose finding would be spurious. Controlling for exogenous third factors such as colonial history is a partial correction but not a complete one, because they don't completely determine trade patterns.

One might reasonably ask why the same logic would not apply equally to the decisions by European countries to join the euro. Clearly, the countries that have been most firmly committed to European monetary integration from the beginning (say, Germany, the Netherlands, and Luxembourg) have been those that were the most thoroughly integrated with each other, anyway. Those that have stayed out tend to be those that are less integrated. If this is enough to produce a tripling in the context of other countries, why is the estimated correlation so low in Europe?

Many of the critiques of the Rose results, after pointing out a problem of omitted variables or endogeneity or one of the other legitimate problems, offer a purported way to address it and then report that the currency union effect disappears.[12] My own view is that many of these responses effectively throw out most of the data in the name of addressing the (correctly emphasized) issues of endogeneity or country size. Or, they do something similar: put in a great many dummy variables or fixed effects, often one for every pair of countries. This approach seems these days to be considered not just good econometric practice, but essential; we are told that we are not allowed so much as a peek at evil studies that neglect to do this. But my view is that because the finding of statistical significance arose only when Rose put together a large enough data set for it to show up,[13] there is not that much information gained in reducing the data set sharply and then noticing the loss in statistical significance. Most of the statistical power lies in the cross-country variation. Throw that out, and one may be left with little.

That said, the complete bilateral data set is so large and the statistical relationship is so strong that there is some firepower to spare, and it is worth using some of it to try to get at the problems of endogeneity and missing variables. Including fixed effects for countries and/or years has become standard. The results generally hold up. Adding fixed effects for *pairs* of countries in the basic specification is a bit more problematic, though reasonable as a test for robustness. Rose (2001) himself tried adding pair-fixed effects to his original data set and found that the currency union dummy lost all significance, while he pointed out that it is hard to see how it could have been otherwise, as all the action is in the bilateral cross-section. The same was

12. See Rose (2001) for a reply to one, and for more, see his Web site, available at: http://faculty.haas.berkeley.edu/arose/RecRes.htm#CUTrade.
13. Earlier gravity studies had not found major evidence of currency link effects on bilateral trade, presumably because the data sets were too small to include many examples of countries with institutionally fixed exchange rates: Thursby and Thursby (1987), De Grauwe (1988), Brada and Mendez (1985), and Frankel and Wei (1993, 1995a, 1995b, 1997).

true with Pakko and Wall (2001). Klein (2002), who deliberately focuses on U.S. bilateral data alone, is one of many examples of throwing out enough data until the results become insignificant. Persson (2001) is another, despite the virtues of the matching estimator. When Rose tries Persson's matching estimator on a larger data set, he finds a significant (though smaller) effect (2.6.3).

More persuasive still is a before-and-after study such as that of Glick and Rose. It eliminates the problem that Panama has always (since independence) been on the dollar because it has always traded with the United States, much as Luxembourg has always had a currency union with Belgium (at least since the Latin Monetary Union of 1865) because it has always traded with Belgium. Rather, these results show that when a country enters or leaves a currency link, its bilateral trade responds accordingly. But none of this is to deny that endogeneity remains a likely problem. For example, an evolution in trade patterns may come first, with the currency decision following. In theory, Ireland may have switched its currency allegiance from Britain to the continent in response to shifting trade patterns rather than as a cause of them. Attempting to deal with the endogeneity problem should be a priority.

5.2.4 Implausible Magnitude of the Estimate

Fourth, although those who claim that the tripling number is too large to sound plausible have a point, they tend to neglect two counterarguments. In the first place, the estimated effect of currency unions is on the same order of magnitude as the estimated effects of FTAs, or if anything is larger.[14] When one applies some of the variant estimation strategies, such as the Rose and Van Wincoop reparameterization, so that the estimated effect of currency unions falls, the estimated effects of regional trading arrangements tend to fall in tandem. The point estimates, significance levels, *and necessary methodological qualifications* are comparable across the two kinds of unions: FTAs and currency unions. In the second place, the estimated effects of currency unions are almost as big as the famous estimated effects of borders (home bias)—for example, in the Canadian-U.S. context, which is at least as big as a factor of three.[15] This home bias is surprising but is a fact of life. Something needs to explain it, and there are not very many candidates other than exchange rate variability. Thus, the Rose findings remain a challenge to the traditional views of international economists, who believed that trade

---

14. Baldwin cites approvingly an assertion of Berger and Nitsch (2005) that it is implausible, even crazy, to think that the trade effect of the euro could be as large as the trade effect of the European Union. But this finding is common econometrically. If critics were to apply the same tough standards to both customs unions and currency unions, they would likely find the estimated magnitude at least as large in the latter case as in the former. As traditionally specified, this is a tripling.

15. McCallum (1995), Helliwell (1998), Wei (1996), and Nitsch (2000, 1991).

barriers were far more important than either currency differences or other remaining barrier frictions.

5.2.5   Country Size

The fifth critique is the claim that the result from pre-1999 currency unions are relevant only for small countries, which are highly trade dependent, but are less relevant for larger countries, such as those in Europe. A partial response has been possible all along: there has been no evidence of the monetary union effect varying with size within the available sample. But if one suspects a threshold effect, above which the monetary union effect diminishes, and if one posits that euro members are the first to be big enough to lie above that threshold, then this could explain the gap. The question of whether the largest economies are truly different can only be answered with data from those countries. Fortunately, the euro experiment is now ten years old, and so we should hope to be able to answer the question. But to do so, we will have to expand our view beyond the sort of data set used by Micco, Stein, and Ordoñez (2003), which was limited to European countries, or at most, to the set of industrialized countries, and we will have to nest it within the larger sort of data set used by Rose, which captures trade among all countries.

5.3   Econometric Investigation of the Euro-Rose Gap in Estimated Effects

The tasks addressed in the remainder of this chapter are first, to confirm that the effects of the euro to date, even if statistically significant, are still relatively small, even with the addition of the several extra years of data that are now available, and second—and more importantly—to try to explain the gap. Three candidate explanations for the gap are the most obvious possibilities:

- Time is needed for gradual adjustment.
- Currency union effects for large countries are fundamentally different from those for small countries.
- Earlier estimates from pre-1999 samples of currency unions were biased upward by endogeneity.

5.3.1   Reproduction of Findings for Early Euro Years: Jumping the Gun

We begin by reproducing the results in Micco, Stein, and Ordoñez (2003), who estimated the effect of the euro on trade patterns for a relatively narrow sample: Europe (or alternatively, for all industrialized countries) during the period from 1992 to 2002. Table 5.1 does successfully replicate the results: pairs of euro countries enjoy greater bilateral trade, with a coefficient that first appears suddenly significant in 1998 and then gradually rises in level and significance through 2002 (also see figure 5.1).

Table 5.1   **Recreation of estimated effects on bilateral trade patterns in the first three years of the euro**

	Developed sample		EU sample	
	Coefficient	Standard error	Coefficient	Standard error
EMU2–1993	–0.0176	0.0331	–0.0068	0.0295
EMU2–1994	0.0377	0.0337	0.0246	0.0296
EMU2–1995	0.0512	0.0340	0.0162	0.0297
EMU2–1996	0.0359	0.0345	0.0000	0.0296
EMU2–1997	0.0443	0.0350	0.0175	0.0296
EMU2–1998	0.0981	0.0358***	0.0637	0.0296**
EMU2–1999	0.1166	0.0360***	0.0731	0.0297**
EMU2–2000	0.1036	0.0367***	0.0762	0.0300***
EMU2–2001	0.1351	0.0369***	0.1662	0.0298***
EMU2–2002	0.1544	0.0368***	0.1644	0.0297***
Log of product of real GDPs	1.1382	0.0464***	1.0620	0.0520***
Free trade agreement	–0.0097	0.0188	0.0453	0.0300
EU	0.0095	0.0239	–0.0470	0.0467
EU trend	–0.0008	0.0014	–0.0013	0.0035
Real exchange rate of country 1	–0.1737	0.0453***	–0.1872	0.0627***
Real exchange rate of country 2	–0.2643	0.0518***	0.3738	0.0885***
Observations	2,541		1,001	
Within R^2	0.462		0.671	
Between R^2	0.686		0.784	
Overall R^2	0.684		0.783	

Notes: Recreation of Micco, Stein, and Ordoñez (2003) on their original data sample and methodology (EMU impact on trade: data from 1992 to 2002). Includes year and country-pair fixed effects.

***Significant at the 1 percent level.
**Significant at the 5 percent level.

Why does the effect show up in 1998, the year *before* EMU? It is likely that currency unions, much as FTAs, can start to have substantial effects on trade patterns even before they have formally gone into effect. This pattern is familiar in the data.[16] The most obvious interpretation is that once the negotiations, which typically have been going on for many years, are far enough along that the union appears almost certain to take place, businessmen move quickly to try to establish a position in what is expected to be a large new market opportunity, perhaps to get a "first mover advantage." This argument works best theoretically in the case of markets destined for imperfect competition. But even in perfectly competitive markets, firms might want to get started early if there are transition costs associated with rapid investment in a new market.

16. For example, Frankel (1997).

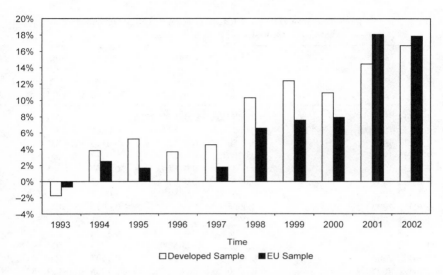

Fig. 5.1   Results from a study of the trade effects in the early years; Micco, Stein, and Ordoñez (2003): EMU impact on trade

Baldwin (2006) regards as suspicious the striking fact that the estimated effect in euroland appears suddenly in 1998, even though EMU did not take effect until January 1999. Even allowing the principle that business percep-tions of imminent monetary union can set the date rather than waiting for 1999, he claims that "right up to . . . March 1998, skeptics doubted that the monetary union would ever become a reality" (52). But statistics from finan-cial markets tend to identify June 1997 as the breakpoint in perceptions.[17] So, it is plausible that businesses had started reacting in a measurable way by 1998.

Next, we updated the results, because another four years of data have become available. We find that the effect of the euro on bilateral trade re-mains highly significant statistically during the years from 2003 to 2006 but that the point estimate is no longer rising. Rather, it appears to have leveled off at approximately 0.1, still very far below the Rose estimates of doubling or tripling. In the EU-only sample, the coefficient on intraeuroland trade rises to a highly significant estimated level of 0.13 to 0.16 in 2001 to 2002 but does not rise any further in 2003 to 2006. In the sample that includes all developed countries, the euro effect becomes significant in 2003 at 0.11 but does not continue its upward trend during 2004 to 2006 (see table 5.2).

17. On June 15, 1997, implied probabilities of joining Germany in EMU in 1999 were 100 percent for Belgium and France and over 70 percent for Finland, Spain, and Portugal (calcula-tions from JP Morgan based on spreads in the interest rate swap market). A similar statistic from Goldman Sachs on the probability of EMU taking place on January 1, 1999, shot up above 75 percent after the Stability and Growth Pact was agreed in June 1997.

Table 5.2   **Update of table 5.1: Creation of estimated effects on bilateral trade patterns in the first eight years of the euro**

	Developed sample		EU sample	
	Coefficient	Standard Error	Coefficient	Standard Error
EMU2–1993	–0.0489	0.0457	–0.0137	0.0352
EMU2–1994	–0.0297	0.0463	–0.0060	0.0352
EMU2–1995	–0.0258	0.0458	–0.0113	0.0352
EMU2–1996	–0.0300	0.0461	–0.0132	0.0352
EMU2–1997	–0.0138	0.0464	0.0007	0.0352
EMU2–1998	0.0315	0.0463	0.0453	0.0352
EMU2–1999	0.0205	0.0468	0.0707	0.0358**
EMU2–2000	–0.0064	0.0469	0.0719	0.0358**
EMU2–2001	0.0650	0.0469	0.1621	0.0355***
EMU2–2002	0.0698	0.0469	0.1306	0.0354***
EMU2–2003	0.1102	0.0469**	0.1334	0.0354***
EMU2–2004	0.1160	0.0467***	0.1507	0.0354***
EMU2–2005	0.0940	0.0469**	0.1385	0.0354***
EMU2–2006	0.0806	0.0481*	0.1450	0.0354***
Log of product of real GDPs	0.6623	0.0378***	0.4090	0.0341***
Free trade agreement	0.0066	0.0163	–0.0669	0.0232***
EU	(dropped)		(dropped)	
EU trend	0.0000	0.0017	–0.0019	0.0015
Real exchange rate of country 1	–0.0184	0.0032***	0.0006	0.0029
Real exchange rate of country 2	–0.0004	0.0027	0.0074	0.0024***
Observations	2,850		1,170	
Within R^2	0.998		0.999	
Between R^2	0.650		0.804	
Overall R^2	0.920		0.929	

Notes: EMU impact on trade: data from 1992 to 2002. Update: euro effect continues strong, 2001 to 2006. Includes year and country-pair fixed effects.
***Significant at the 1 percent level.
**Significant at the 5 percent level.
*Significant at the 10 percent level.

5.3.2   Effect of Size

Table 5.3 investigates whether the effects of monetary union diminish with the size of the countries involved. It adds an interactive size term, computed as the product of the sizes of the respective countries and the dummy variable for currency union membership. The intent is to explore the hypothesis that currency union effects on trade are bigger for small countries than for large countries and that this might explain the relatively smaller effect in Europe. It is true that larger countries experience smaller boosts to intraunion trade: the interactive term is statistically significant. But the effect is still not significant within non-EMU monetary unions. Rather, it appears *within*

Table 5.3   **Currency union effect diminishes with size only *within* EMU but not among other countries**

Log of bilateral trade	OLS Gravity estimates	Fixed effects (Country-pair)
Currency union (CU)	1.1778	−2.8473***
	(2.5491)	(0.5906)
EMU	15.3995**	(dropped)
	(7.5823)	
CU * log product of real GDPs	−0.0172	0.0655***
	(0.0550)	(0.0132)
EMU * log product of real GDPs	−0.2695*	0.0186
	(0.1539)	(0.0310)
Log distance	−0.8772***	0.3096***
	(0.0456)	(0.0106)
Log product of real GDPs	0.7458***	0.1045***
	(0.0123)	(0.0169)
Log product of real GDP/capita	0.0242	1.0935***
	(0.0151)	(0.0160)
Common language	0.2589***	−0.0407**
	(0.0746)	(0.0179)
Common land border	0.0746***	−0.4764***
	(0.1854)	(0.0504)
Regional FTA membership	0.4199***	0.0079
	(0.1669)	(0.0384)
Number landlocked	−0.4382***	0.2127***
	(0.0642)	(0.0152)
Area	−0.1048***	−0.1123***
	(0.0114)	(0.0024)
Common colonizer	0.4360***	0.0715***
	(0.1306)	(0.0285)
Current colony/colonizer	1.7076***	0.4120***
	(0.4883)	(0.0976)
Ever colony/colonizer	0.0731	−1.1098***
	(0.1189)	(0.0407)
Common country	2.4202	(dropped)
	(3.2544)	
Intercept	−23.2333***	−6.7655***
	(0.5598)	(0.6212)
Observations	297,322	297,322
OLS R^2	0.4955	
Within R^2		0.6868
Between R^2		0.0911
Overall R^2		0.2861

Notes: Includes currency union and EMU dummies, interaction variable between currency union and country size, elapsed time variables, and year fixed effects. Standard errors recorded in parentheses. (For OLS regression, standard errors are robust to country-pair clustering.) Based on annual data for 217 countries from 1948 to 2006.

***Significant at the 1 percent level.

**Significant at the 5 percent level.

*Significant at the 10 percent level.

EMU. (The effect of EMU on bilateral trade remains, even after controlling for size.) We need to imbed the sample of European or industrialized countries within a more comprehensive set of countries before we can pass judgment on the claim that size explains the difference in effects.

5.3.3 Imbedding Euro Estimates in a Larger Sample of Countries and Time

To try to nail down the gap between the euro estimates of a 10 to 15 percent effect and the Rose-style estimates of a tripling, it is necessary to imbed the euro data set inside an updated version of the larger cross-country data sets employed by Rose and others. Micco, Stein, and Ordoñez (2003), like some of their competitors, looked only at a set of European countries, or at most, a set of rich countries. When we imbed the data set from tables 5.1 and 5.2 inside the larger data set, we can explicitly control for size and a Europe dummy to try to isolate where the big gap arises.

What follows are step-by-step results leading from Micco, Stein, and Ordoñez (2003) up to the higher results (from the 15 percent effect to the tripling effect; see table 5.4). We pursue the step-by-step analysis in two different dimensions: first, we use the two samples that MSO use (developed countries and EU sample) as well as our full sample at every step to show what difference the sample makes. Second, we start with a sample for 1992 to 2006. (This is the start date of MSO, but their data set stopped at 2001.) We then expand this to our full data set from 1948 to 2006 to see what difference the addition of the earlier observations makes. We also show both fixed effects (with country-pair fixed effects and year effects) and ordinary least squares (OLS; with year fixed effects).

Table 5.5 shows the estimation results, followed by the corresponding figure 5.2, for the first step: the 1992 to 2006 sample with only one dummy for EMU (no EMU-time interactions). We see that the euro effect exceeds 10 percent only when estimated within the EU sample. The estimates for the effect of the EMU on bilateral trade using the full sample or developed country sample are lower—around 6 percent—and they fail to be significant for the full sample. Using OLS instead of fixed effect estimators decreases the effect significantly for the full and developed country samples but increases it to above 30 percent for the EU sample.

Table 5.6 and the corresponding figures that follow (figures 5.3 and 5.4) remain in the 1992 to 2006 sample time frame but add EMU-year interaction terms to the specification so that we can follow the evolution of the euro's effect over time. We can recreate (as we did previously) the MSO results for the developed and EU samples that they used: estimates are significant during the euro period.[18] The effect of the euro on trade rises steadily from 1998, reaching the statistically significant level of 0.15 to 0.17 in 2001 to 2002.

18. The reader should not be confused by the EMU-year interactive effects in the OLS column, which in most years can be taken to be essentially 0. The coefficient to focus on is the

We have added four years to the sample relative to the initial round of studies. The euro effect remains in the same range and remains statistically significant. But it does not continue to increase over the period from 2002 to 2006. For the author, the most surprising finding of this study was the absence of any evidence that the effects of the euro on bilateral trade have continued to rise during the second half of the eight-year history of the euro. This seems counter to historical experience in other countries with lags in bilateral trade effects from both currency union entries/exits and other factors.

The results become less clear when we apply the specification to the full sample of countries. (The effect appears slightly negative for the years from 1993 to 1996, jumps up in 1997, and becomes negative again in 2005 to 2006, but none of these estimates is significant in the full sample.)[19] This might seem to justify the MOS strategy of having confined their estimation to samples of EU and developed countries under the logic that developing countries are too different to be useful. The most important point to note for our purposes, however, is that the coefficient on non-EMU currency unions remains a significant 0.75 (under OLS[20]). The exponential of 0.75 is 2.1, so this is a doubling of bilateral trade. The existence of the gap between small estimates for the euro (not even significant in this sample) and big estimates for other monetary unions is still very much in evidence. But we need a longer time sample if we want to obtain more reliable estimates and sharpen our standard errors.

Table 5.7 and the subsequent figure 5.5 show step 2: we now expand the data set to 1948 to 2006, which covers almost sixty years of data. The graph reveals that a crucial difference between MSO and broader estimates was the sample size. While estimates of the euro's effect on trade continue to linger around 10 to 25 percent for the developed and EU samples that MSO used, they have climbed dramatically to 0.9 to 1.0 for the full sample, which exponentially is 2.5 to 2.7—almost tripling. All these estimates are highly significant now that we have more data with which to work. We have uncovered the possibility that the large gap is an artifact of the largely nonoverlapping historical periods analyzed in the Rose and MOS studies (pre- and post-1999, respectively). Interestingly, the estimated trade effects of the euro are now even larger and more significant than the trade effects of non-EMU currency unions rather than the other way around. Moreover, for those

---

dummy "both countries in EMU," which is a highly significant 0.354. One needs to add this coefficient to the year estimates. Look at the bar charts in the figures to see this. In 1996, the 0.354 coefficient is almost knocked out by the significant negative year effect. Thereafter, it dominates (i.e., 0.354).

19. When we use OLS, estimates are positive only for the developed and EU samples, but they seem strange—for the EU sample, they start rather high in 1993, decrease slightly until 1996, and then take off again until a high in 2004. Only in 1994 to 1997 are they significant.

20. It loses some luster under fixed effects, but this is perhaps to be expected, as there are only fifteen years of observations, and much of the variation in the data is eaten up by fixed effects and interactive year dummies.

Table 5.4   **The effect of currency unions on trade: Does size matter?**

Dependent variable	Log of bilateral trade
A. 1948 to 2006: Fixed effects estimator with country-pair fixed effects	
Currency union	2.661**
	(1.092)
Currency union × log of product of real GDPs	−0.041*
	(0.021)
Free trade agreement	0.113
	(0.069)
Log of product of real GDPs	−1.612***
	(0.018)
Log of product of real GDPs per capita	2.979***
	(0.024)
Currently in colonial relationship	1.032
	(0.815)
Real exchange rate of country 1	0.068***
	(0.005)
Real exchange rate of country 2	0.134***
	(0.012)
Constant	32.558***
	(0.587)
Observations	168,174
Number of identifications	10,739
R^2	0.09
B. 1948 to 2006: Fixed effects estimator with country-pair and year fixed effects.	
Currency union	1.887*
	(1.064)
Currency union × log of product of real GDPs	−0.021
	(0.021)
Free trade agreement	0.436***
	(0.068)
Log of product of real GDPs	0.127***
	(0.044)
Log of product of real GDPs per capita	1.484***
	(0.042)
Currently in colonial relationship	0.811
	(0.794)
Real exchange rate of country 1	−0.029***
	(0.005)
Real exchange rate of country 2	0.073***
	(0.012)
Constant	−28.055***
	(1.534)
Observations	168,174
Number of identifications	10,739
R^2	0.14

Note: Standard errors in parentheses.
***Significant at the 1 percent level.
**Significant at the 5 percent level.
*Significant at the 10 percent level.

Table 5.5 The effect of currency unions on trade: Recreating Mico, Stein, and Ordoñez (2003) with our data (1992 to 2006); EMU dummy only

	Full sample		Developed sample		EU sample	
	Fixed effects	OLS	Fixed effects	OLS	Fixed effects	OLS
Both countries in non-EMU currency union	0.575	0.752	(dropped)	(dropped)	(dropped)	(dropped)
	(0.226)**	(0.214)***				
Both countries in EMU	0.058	-0.017	0.06	-0.014	0.122	0.301
	(0.100)	(0.130)	(0.018)***	(0.095)	(0.014)***	(0.078)***
Free trade agreement (non-EU)	0.155	1.116	0.046	0.013		
	(0.108)	(0.153)***	(0.026)	(0.172)		
Both countries in EU		-0.104		0.344		
		(0.120)		(0.125)***		
European integration trend	0.007	0.042	0.001	-0.003	0.005	0.011
	(0.008)	(0.007)***	(0.001)	(0.005)	(0.002)**	(0.005)**
Log of distance		-1.292		-0.856		-1.125
		(0.023)***		(0.071)***		(0.129)***
Log of product of real GDPs	1.206	1.033	0.648	0.774	0.399	0.667
	(0.019)***	(0.012)***	(0.038)***	(0.026)***	(0.036)***	(0.049)***
Log of product of real GDPs per capita		-0.057		0.38		0.362
		(0.014)***		(0.103)***		(0.121)***
Common language		0.41		0.069		-0.155
		(0.049)***		(0.161)	(0.255)	
Common border		0.789		0.316		-0.036
		(0.117)***		(0.161)		(0.147)
Number of landlocked countries in pair		-0.369		-0.382		-0.657
		(0.034)***		(0.100)***		(0.115)***
Log of product of land areas		-0.08		0.018		0.13
		(0.009)***		(0.030)		(0.055)**

(continued)

Table 5.5   (continued)

	Full sample		Developed sample		EU sample	
	Fixed effects	OLS	Fixed effects	OLS	Fixed effects	OLS
Common colonizer post-1945		0.855 (0.079)***				
Current colony		1.21 (0.552)**				
Ever colony		1.218 (0.132)***		0.521 (0.219)**		0.725 (0.206)***
Real exchange rate of country 1	0.034 (0.004)***	-0.003 (0.006)	-0.019 (0.003)***	-0.048 (0.021)**	0.001 (0.003)	0.005 (0.017)
Real exchange rate of country 2	-0.038 (0.012)***	-0.006 (0.005)	0.002 (0.003)	-0.064 (0.017)***	0.014 (0.003)***	0.005 (0.014)
Constant	-55.992 (0.901)***	-34.46 (0.393)***	-27.1 (2.018)***	-35.659 (2.048)***	-13.113 (1.905)***	-29.645 (2.643)***
Observations	101,128	100,747	2,850	2,850	1,104	1,104
Number of identifications	9,576		190		78	
R^2	0.09	0.69	0.55	0.92	0.77	0.95

Notes: 1992 to 2006: Fixed effects estimator with country-pair and year fixed effects, as well as OLS estimator with year fixed effects. Includes only EMU dummy; no EMU-time interactions. Embedding euro-based samples (with estimated impact on bilateral trade of 15 percent) within larger sample (with much higher estimates): step-by-step breakdown of possible sources of gap. Step 1: Recreate Micco, Stein, and Ordoñez (2003) starting in 1992 (as they do)—both with EMU dummy only and with EMU-time interactions, using our full sample, as well as the developed sample and EU sample that Micco, Stein, and Ordoñez use. Dependent variable: log of bilateral trade. Standard errors in parentheses. Figure 5.2 illustrates the results from this table.

***Significant at the 1 percent level.

**Significant at the 5 percent level.

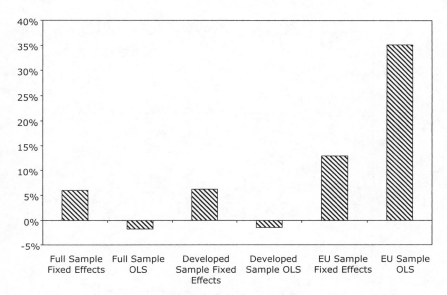

Fig. 5.2   The effect of EMU on trade: Different estimators and samples (1992 to 2006)

concerned with the Van Wincoop view that the gravity specification used here overstates what would be the percentage effect of joining (or leaving) a monetary union, it is worth noting that the estimated coefficient of EMU is larger than that on the European Union or other FTAs, and this is a comparison that stands up with fixed country effects.

There appears to be much useful information from including all sixty years of available data in addition to including developing countries in the entire sample rather than restricting ourselves to post-1992 observations of European or rich countries. Estimates such as those for the coefficients on common border or common language shift substantially when the more complete data set is brought to bear. Only by using the entire sample can we uncover large short-term effects—over 100 percent when using fixed effects estimation. Second, the trade effects in the year before a monetary union formally goes into operation are even larger and apply equally to EMU as to other monetary unions.

Table 5.8 continues the analysis of the full sixty-year data set but now adds interaction effects between EMU and years before and after entry; it does the same for non-EMU monetary unions. We aggregate over each five-year interval in order to cut down on the loss of degrees of freedom, and because it is implausible to think that there are sharp changes between, say, effects in years 19 and 20. The corresponding figures 5.6 and 5.7 show the interaction effects both for non-EMU currency unions and for EMU: the bar with

Table 5.6 The effect of currency unions on trade: Recreating Micco, Stein, and Ordoñez (2003) with our data (1992 to 2006); includes EMU-time interactions

	Full sample		Developed sample		EU sample	
	Fixed effects	OLS	Fixed effects	OLS	Fixed effects	OLS
EMU * 1993	-0.105	-0.192	-0.037	-0.05	-0.019	-0.033
	(0.227)	(0.047)***	(0.041)	(0.029)	(0.047)	(0.039)
EMU * 1994	-0.196	-0.215	-0.032	-0.138	-0.005	-0.182
	(0.245)	(0.098)**	(0.042)	(0.053)***	(0.042)	(0.074)**
EMU * 1995	-0.093	-0.026	-0.027	-0.144	-0.014	-0.203
	(0.237)	(0.102)	(0.042)	(0.052)***	(0.042)	(0.080)**
EMU * 1996	-0.104	-0.064	-0.037	-0.153	-0.026	-0.211
	(0.242)	(0.106)	(0.042)	(0.055)***	(0.042)	(0.079)***
EMU * 1997	0.144	0.144	-0.021	-0.132	-.007	-0.182
	(0.246)	(0.109)	(0.042)	(0.057)**	(0.042)	(0.076)**
EMU * 1998	0.166	0.104	0.034	-0.087	0.046	-0.133
	(0.254)	(0.122)	(0.043)	(0.064)	(0.042)	(0.078)
EMU * 1999	0.212	0.195	0.034	-0.221	0.072	-0.119
	(0.254)	(0.123)	(0.043)	(0.078)***	(0.043)	(0.085)
EMU * 2000	0.163	0.146	0.013	-0.244	0.078	-0.116
	(0.256)	(0.122)	(0.044)	(0.080)***	(0.043)	(0.085)
EMU * 2001	0.046	0.077	0.078	-0.304	0.171	-0.049
	(0.261)	(0.127)	(0.044)	(0.089)***	(0.043)***	(0.086)
EMU * 2002	-0.002	0.045	0.058	-0.329	0.147	-0.072
	(0.261)	(0.131)	(0.044)	(0.091)***	(0.043)***	(0.091)
EMU * 2003	0.112	0.175	0.12	-0.27	0.17	-0.047
	(0.260)	(0.133)	(0.044)***	(0.093)***	(0.043)***	(0.092)

	(1)	(2)	(3)	(4)	(5)	(6)
EMU * 2004	0.105 (0.258)	0.21 (0.131)	0.121 (0.044)***	−0.266 (0.094)***	0.176 (0.043)***	−0.038 (0.095)
EMU * 2005	−0.036 (0.262)	0.016 (0.135)	0.051 (0.044)	−0.331 (0.099)***	0.13 (0.043)***	−0.079 (0.095)
EMU * 2006	−0.118 (0.262)	−0.08 (0.136)	0.028 (0.044)	−0.359 (0.102)***	0.102 (0.043)**	−0.107 (0.100)
Both countries in non-EMU currency union	0.576 (0.226)**	0.752 (0.214)***				
Both countries in EMU		−0.177 (0.155)		0.273 (0.101)***		0.354 (0.109)***
Free trade agreement (non-EU)	0.166 (0.108)	1.117 (0.153)***	0.051 (0.027)	0.026 (0.172)		
Both countries in EU	0.209 (0.183)	−0.069 (0.146)	0.014 (0.031)	0.361 (0.131)***		
European integration trend	0.008 (0.010)	0.035 (0.008)***	0 (0.002)	0.003 (0.005)	0.005 (0.002)**	0.011 (0.004)**
Log of distance		−1.292 (0.023)***		−0.845 (0.071)***		−1.112 (0.135)***
Log of product of real GDPs	1.205 (0.019)***	1.033 (0.012)***	0.645 (0.038)***	0.774 (0.026)***	0.412 (0.036)***	0.669 (0.051)***
Log of product of real GDPs per capita		−0.057 (0.014)***		0.407 (0.104)***		0.39 (0.121)***
Common language		0.409 (0.050)***		0.076 (0.161)		−0.118 (0.259)
Common border		0.79 (0.117)***		0.32 (0.161)**		−0.04 (0.150)
Number of landlocked countries in pair		−0.369 (0.034)***		−0.397 (0.101)***		−0.668 (0.117)***

(continued)

Table 5.6   (continued)

	Full sample		Developed sample		EU sample	
	Fixed effects	OLS	Fixed effects	OLS	Fixed effects	OLS
Log of product of land areas		-0.08 (0.009)***		0.015 (0.030)		0.129 (0.056)**
Common colonizer post-1945		0.855 (0.079)***				
Current colony		1.21 (0.553)**				
Ever colony		1.219 (0.132)***		0.507 (0.220)**		0.701 (0.205)***
Real exchange rate of country 1	0.034 (0.004)***	-0.003 (0.006)	-0.018 (0.003)***	-0.051 (0.021)**	0.001 (0.003)	-0.001 (0.016)
Real exchange rate of country 2	-0.037 (0.013)***	-0.006 (0.005)	0.004 (0.003)	-0.071 (0.017)***	0.013 (0.003)***	-0.007 (0.014)
Constant	-55.96 (0.901)***	-34.464 (0.393)***	-26.966 (2.009)***	-36.249 (2.114)***	-13.838 (1.880)***	-30.58 (2.724)***
Observations	101,128	100,747	2,850	2,850	1,104	1,104
Number of identifications	9,576		190		78	
R^2	0.09	0.69	0.56	0.92	0.78	0.95

Notes: 1992 to 2006: Fixed effects estimator with country-pair and year fixed effects, as well as OLS estimator with year fixed effects. Step 1 including EMU-time interactions (1992 to 2006 sample period). Dependent variable: log of bilateral trade. Standard errors in parentheses. Figures 5.3 and 5.4 illustrate the results from this table.

***Significant at the 1 percent level.

**Significant at the 5 percent level.

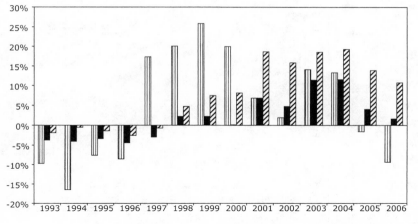

Fig. 5.3   The effect of EMU on bilateral trade; Recreating Micco, Stein, and Or-doñez (2003) with our data: Fixed effects estimators

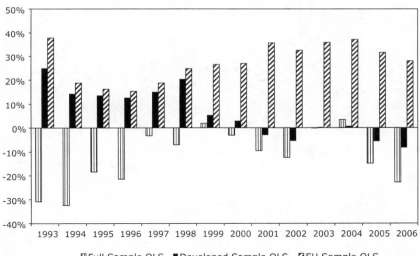

Fig. 5.4   The effect of EMU on bilateral trade; Recreating Micco, Stein, and Or-doñez (2003) with our data: OLS estimators

Table 5.7   The effect of currency unions on trade: Full data from 1948 with EMU dummy

	Full sample		Developed sample		EU sample	
	Fixed effects	OLS	Fixed effects	OLS	Fixed effects	OLS
Both countries in non-EMU currency union	0.746 (0.188)***	0.309 (0.244)	(dropped)	(dropped)	(dropped)	(dropped)
Both countries in EMU	0.93 (0.116)***	1.005 (0.097)***	0.097 (0.014)***	−0.076 (0.094)	0.12 (0.013)***	0.241 (0.077)***
Free trade agreement (non-EU)	0.662 (0.085)***	0.794 (0.184)***	0.057 (0.012)***	0.097 (0.117)		
Both countries in EU		0.042 (0.096)		0.187 (0.076)**		
European integration trend	−0.005 (0.009)	0.009 (0.003)***	−0.005 (0.001)***	−0.005 (0.002)**	0.001 (0.001)	0.006 (0.003)
Log of distance		−1.043 (0.032)***		−0.861 (0.061)***		−1.105 (0.123)***
Log of product of real GDPs	1.592 (0.015)***	0.819 (0.015)***	0.513 (0.020)***	0.795 (0.025)***	0.376 (0.024)***	0.678 (0.050)***
Log of product of real GDPs per capita		−0.009 (0.018)		0.164 (0.094)		0.248 (0.132)
Common language		0.296 (0.067)***		0.011 (0.152)		−0.181 (0.235)
Common border		0.664 (0.139)***		0.337 (0.148)**		0.015 (0.130)

	(1)	(2)	(3)	(4)	(5)	(6)
Number of landlocked countries in pair		-0.391 (0.046)***		-0.448 (0.088)***		-0.64 (0.117)***
Log of product of land areas		-0.071 (0.012)***		-0.006 (0.028)		0.119 (0.056)**
Common colonizer post-1945		0.678 (0.098)***				
Current colony		-0.254 (0.234)				
Ever colony		1.023 (0.142)***		0.529 (0.222)**		0.69 (0.194)***
Same nation		0.457 (0.626)				
Real exchange rate of country 1	-0.071 (0.005)***	-0.006 (0.008)	-0.028 (0.002)**	-0.065 (0.023)***	-0.007 (0.003)**	-0.008 (0.018)
Real exchange rate of country 2	-0.018 (0.012)	-0.001 (0.008)	-0.005 (0.002)*	-0.08 (0.017)***	0.011 (0.002)***	-0.016 (0.014)
Constant	-72.821 (0.713)***	-25.903 (0.499)***	-19.917 (1.050)***	-32.311 (1.750)***	-11.718 (1.264)***	-28.14 (2.465)***
Observations	166,990	166,609	5,130	5,130	1,601	1,601
Number of identifications	10,590		190		78	
R^2	0.13	0.43	0.65	0.92	0.81	0.95

Notes: 1948 to 2006. Fixed effects estimator with country-pair and year fixed effects, as well as OLS estimator with year fixed effects. Includes only EMU dummy; no EMU-time interactions. Figure 5.5 illustrates these results for the sample period from 1948 to 2006. Dependent variable: log of bilateral trade. Standard errors in parentheses.

***Significant at the 1 percent level.

**Significant at the 5 percent level.

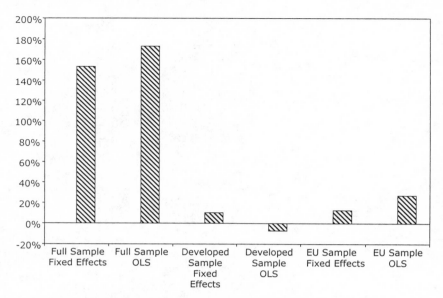

Fig. 5.5   The effect of EMU on trade: Different estimators and samples (1948 to 2006)

horizontal stripes represents the full-sample estimates for non-EMU currency union interactions with "1 yr. prior to CU entry," "1–5 yrs. post," "6–10 yrs. post," "11–15 yrs. post," "16–20 yrs. post," "21–25 yrs. post," and "26–30 yrs. post." The other three bars represent the estimates for the interaction terms of EMU with different years prior and post-EMU entry based on the three different sample sizes (full: vertical stripes; developed: solid black; EU: diagonal stripes). As there are no non-EMU currency unions in the developed sample, we only have the full-sample estimate for the non-EMU currency union interactions with time.

The central puzzle addressed by this chapter, the huge discrepancy between the euro effects to date and other monetary unions, seems to be sharply diminished here. It is true that in the one year prior to monetary union, the apparent effect is huge for noneuro monetary unions and that also in the first five years, it is several times larger. Perhaps reverse causality is a particular problem in these cases. But in years 6 to 10, the difference between EMU and noneuro currency unions is much smaller.

That the trade effects fail to rise in years 6 to 10 relative to years 1 to 5 turns out to apply to other currency unions as much as to EMU—in fact, more so. To help decide whether this is telling us that the long-run effect is reached within five years, we need to look at the out-years for the non-EMU cases (because there are no EMU observations out further than ten years). The long-run effects depend entirely on whether one looks at fixed effects or

Table 5.8   The effect of currency unions on trade: 1948 to 2006 data and currency union and EMU–time interactions

	Full sample		Developed sample		EU sample	
	Fixed effects	OLS	Fixed effects	LS	Fixed effects	OLS
1 year prior to non-EMU currency union entry	1.102	1.823				
	(1.228)	(0.160)***				
1–5 years post-non-EMU currency union entry	0.849	2.36				
	(0.444)	(0.917)**				
6–10 years post-non-EMU currency union entry	−0.048	0.713				
	(0.397)	(1.010)				
11–15 years post-non-EMU currency union entry	−1.049	0.388				
	(0.381)***	(0.843)				
16–20 years post-non-EMU currency union entry	−1.351	0.274				
	(0.376)***	(0.874)				
21–25 years post-non-EMU currency union entry	−1.911	−0.094				
	(0.383)***	(0.383)				
26–30 years post-non-EMU currency union entry	−1.127	0.342				
	(0.383)***	(0.425)				
1 year prior to EMU entry	0.563	0.939	0.074	0.223	0.052	0.23
	(0.234)**	(0.099)***	(0.025)***	(0.069)***	(0.023)**	(0.071)***
1–5 years post-EMU entry	0.018	−0.024	−0.048		−0.049	−0.176
	(0.171)	(0.032)	(0.019)***		(0.017)***	(0.049)***
6–10 years post-EMU entry				0.181		
				(0.042)***		
Both countries in non-EMU currency union	0.907	0.237				
	(0.197)***	(0.264)				

(*continued*)

Table 5.8 (continued)

	Full sample		Developed sample		EU sample	
	Fixed effects	OLS	Fixed effects	LS	Fixed effects	OLS
Both countries in EMU	0.767	1.001	0.115	−0.08	0.169	0.451
	(0.167)***	(0.111)***	(0.019)***	(0.101)	(0.019)***	(0.097)***
Free trade agreement (non-EU)	0.485	0.735	0.078	0.1		
	(0.082)***	(0.182)***	(0.012)***	(0.108)		
Both countries in EU	0.451	0.052	0.1	0.13		
	(0.116)***	(0.109)	(0.012)***	(0.081)		
European integration trend	0.032	0.012	−0.002	−0.007	0.012	0.001
	(0.010)***	(0.004)***	(0.001)	(0.002)***	(0.002)***	(0.003)
Log of distance		−1.045		−0.852		−1.078
		(0.032)***		(0.059)***		(0.117)***
Log of product of real GDPs	0.114	0.823	0.525	0.801	0.401	0.699
	(0.044)**	(0.015)***	(0.019)***	(0.025)***	(0.025)***	(0.046)***
Log of product of real GDPs per capita	1.5	−0.011		0.147		0.256
	(0.042)***	(0.018)		(0.092)		(0.132)
Common language		0.307		0.019		−0.111
		(0.067)***		(0.144)		(0.229)
Common border		0.655		0.348		0.052
		(0.138)***		(0.145)**		(0.135)
Number of landlocked countries in pair		−0.393		−0.494		−0.709
		(0.046)***		(0.084)***		(0.115)***
Log of product of land areas		−0.074		−0.022		0.071
		(0.012)***		(0.027)		(0.048)

	(1)	(2)	(3)	(4)	(5)	(6)
Common colonizer post-1945					0.67 (0.098)***	
Current colony					−0.258 (0.235)	
Ever colony	0.595 (0.170)***		0.499 (0.211)**		1.006 (0.141)***	
Same nation					0.44 (0.623)	
Real exchange rate of country 1	−0.003 (0.017)	−0.007 (0.003)**	−0.069 (0.023)***	−0.027 (0.002)***	−0.007 (0.008)	−0.029 (0.005)***
Real exchange rate of country 2	−0.008 (0.015)	0.012 (0.003)***	−0.085 (0.017)***	−0.003 (0.002)	0 (0.008)	0.073 (0.012)***
Constant	−28.439 (2.548)***	−12.921 (1.336)***	−31.916 (1.721)***	−20.545 (1.037)***	−25.806 (0.495)***	−27.662 (1.537)***
Observations	1,628	1,628	5,326	5,326	168,174	168,174
Number of identifications		91		210		10,739
R^2	0.94	0.80	0.92	0.66	0.43	0.14

Notes: 1948 to 2006: Fixed effects estimator with country-pair and year fixed effects, as well as OLS estimator with year fixed effects. Step 2 including non-EMU currency unions and EMU-time interactions (1948 to 2006 sample period). Dependent variable: log of bilateral trade. Standard errors in parentheses. Figures 5.6 and 5.7 illustrate these results (for fixed effects estimators and for OLS estimators).

***Significant at the 1 percent level.

**Significant at the 5 percent level.

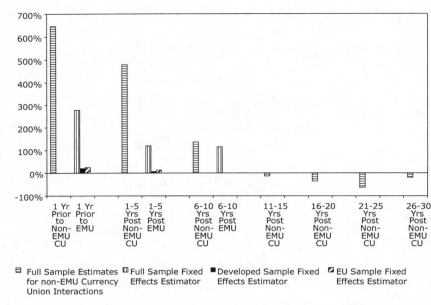

Fig. 5.6   The effect of non-EMU currency unions and of EMU on bilateral trade over time: Fixed effects estimators

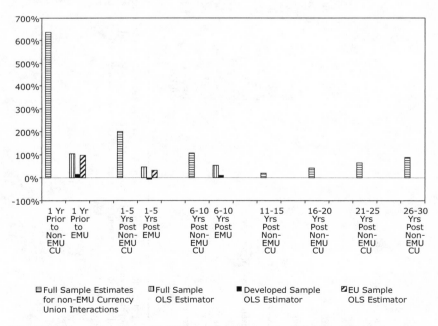

Fig. 5.7   The effect of non-EMU currency unions and of EMU on bilateral trade over time: OLS estimators

simple OLS results. Under fixed effects, the impact of currency unions continues to decline after ten years (and in fact appears to go negative). Perhaps this has something to do with decreasing effects of colonial legacies. When using OLS instead of fixed effects, the estimated effects remain positive throughout the period (but fail to be significant and even at the thirty-year mark do not rise above the effect in the first ten years). We have not thought of a reason for this discrepancy. But there is no evidence here that any of the observed euro-noneuro discrepancy in estimates is due to lags.

5.4   A Natural Experiment to Isolate Causality

The problem of endogeneity is probably the most serious stumbling block in interpreting the Rose findings as a causal relationship between the currency decision and trade patterns. Even when one controls for many other determinants of bilateral trade—geographic, historical, linguistic—one can't escape entirely from the concern that there are missing variables that determine bilateral trade and that the currency regime decision in turn reacts to trade rather than the other way around. The OLS results reported in the previous section may give cause for worry that the high correlations in the year before monetary union and in the five years after are due to reverse causality—that the Eastern Caribbean countries form a currency union because their trade with each other is increasing rather than the other way around.[21]

One way to address the causality problem is with before-and-after case studies. There are a few uniobservational case studies. One example is the case of Ireland. Thom and Walsh (2002) focus on Ireland's abandonment of the pound sterling in 1979; Dwane, Lane, and McIndoe (2006) include also Ireland's adoption of the euro in 1999. There are strong trends in the share of Irish trade, away from the United Kingdom and toward euroland. But it is not possible statistically to discern effects of the two currency changes independently of the effects of Ireland's earlier accession to the European Commission or of the longer-term trend.[22]

Another example is the Czech-Slovak breakup of 1993, which had a substantial negative effect on bilateral trade.[23] It is viewed as more supportive of the Rose effect, apparently because a customs union was retained. But we know that political borders such as the one that divided the new Czech and

21. I have a harder time, however, seeing how such reverse causality could explain the results with fixed effects or the Glick-Rose estimates.

22. The case examined is potentially one of the more important ones, as Ireland is one of the largest countries in the sample of countries that entered or left a currency union in the period between the 1960s and 1999. But the lack of statistically significant findings is probably to be expected, given the other ongoing developments and the very small number of data points.

23. Frankel (1997, 121–2); Fidrmuc, Horvath, and Fidrmuc (1999); Fidrmuc and Fidrmuc (2001).

Slovak Republics at the same time that the two adopted separate currencies have effects at least as large as conventional trade barriers.

As noted, Glick and Rose (2002) put together a huge data set covering the entire postwar period, which includes enough additional examples such as the breaking of the Irish-pound link and the Czech-Slovak link to get statistical significance out of the time series dimension. Indeed, they are able to do so even when including pair-specific dummies, thereby giving up the power in the cross-sectional variation. The beauty of fixed effects is indeed that they take account of time-invariant facts, observed or unobserved; so, Glick and Rose's still-significant results are very persuasive. As usual, the authors try lots of robustness checks. This might have been enough to satisfy the hard-line skeptics.[24]

But it was not. For one thing, most of the Glick and Rose results are not only from small countries but also from instances of currency unions breaking up rather than forming, so one cannot be sure that they apply equally to an example of large countries uniting in a currency union. For another thing, the decision to join a currency union, including the decision by Ireland or Slovenia to join EMU, could be misleadingly correlated with a shift in trade patterns toward continental Europe, either because (a) such a shift is a political goal, encouraged by other means as well, or (b) trade is shifting in this direction for natural economic reasons, and policymakers want to reduce foreign exchange costs for importers and exporters.

It would be useful to try some more real-time experiments. A useful comparison would be among the Nordic countries: Finland (which joined the euro along with the European Union while suffering an exogenous loss of trade with the Soviet Union after 1990), Sweden (which joined the European Union but not the euro) and Norway (which has joined neither). But even if these interesting experiments were to produce the finding that the euro joiners experienced increased bilateral trade with euroland relative to the others, the critics could still plausibly claim endogeneity. Perhaps Finland joined the euro as a result of stronger political commitments to European integration than the others had, and perhaps this commitment is reflected in other trade-reallocating forces that are not the causal result of the euro itself. Another useful experiment would be to compare those Central and Eastern European countries that have chosen to tie their currencies rigidly to the euro, such as Estonia, with those who have opted for flexibility, such as the Czech Republic. It might also be interesting to look at the case of Switzerland, the one country in the heart of Europe never to join the European Union or EMU, despite sharing borders and languages with four countries.

24. I don't agree with the admonishment (e.g., Tenreyro 2001) that they should try all the robustness checks at the same time rather than one by one. One by one is the way to keep the volume of output manageable. Furthermore, I don't see as interesting an algorithm that checks whether trying every possible permutation can eventually produce some equation in which the currency union coefficient loses significance.

We here propose a sort of natural experiment designed to be as immune as possible from this sort of endogeneity argument. The experiment is the effect on bilateral trade of African CFA members of the French franc's 1999 conversion to the euro. The long-time link of CFA currencies to the French franc has clearly always had a political motivation. So, CFA trade with France in the past could not reliably be attributed to the currency link, perhaps even after controlling for common language and former colonial status. But with the advent of the euro, fourteen CFA countries woke up in the morning and suddenly found themselves *with the same currency link to Germany, Austria, Finland, Portugal,* and so forth as they had with France. There was no economic/political motivation on the part of the African countries that led them to an arrangement whereby they were tied to these other European currencies. Thus, if CFA trade with these other European countries has risen, that suggests a euro effect that we can declare causal.

Table 5.9 reports results. The dummy variable representing when one partner is a CFA country and the other is a euro country has a highly significant coefficient of 0.57. Taking the exponent, the point estimate is that the euro boosted bilateral trade between the relevant African and European countries by 76 percent. Table 5.10 looks at the effects over time. The apparent timing of the effect is partly supportive, though only partly. Its gradual rise during the 1980s and then loss of significance after 1991 matches the contemporaneous progress of European monetary integration and the abrupt crisis in the exchange rate mechanism (ERM) in 1992. The somewhat stronger trade results that begin again in 1997 match well the pattern of the final implementation of EMU that we saw among the euro countries themselves. The estimated effect in 1999 is a big 96 percent.[25] The puzzle is the loss of significance in the last two years of the sample, 2005 to 2006.

The version of the CFA experiment reported in tables 5.9 and 5.10 does not control for distance. Distance is a relatively poor proxy for transport costs in the case of Africa, because the exports and imports of many of the countries have to travel routes overland to the nearest port and then by sea around the continent, routes that are far longer than indicated distance as the crow flies. For example, Mali, Niger, and Chad (all three of them members of the CFA zone) are as close to the center of the euro zone as the corners of the euro zone are to each other, and yet their actual transport distances to Europe are high.

We have also tried the CFA natural experiment with the usual control for distance. The results for the case where all the other variables are retained are reported elsewhere.[26] The overall pattern is the same as without distance with respect to time pattern and significance, but the estimated magnitudes are somewhat lower: the coefficient on the dummy representing trade between

---

25. Exp (0.508 + 0.165) = 1.9601.
26. See tables 8a and 8b of Frankel (2009).

Table 5.9   **CFA natural experiment: The impact of EMU on bilateral trade between CFA and EMU members with year interactions, 1948 to 2006**

Dependent variable	Log of bilateral trade
Currency union	1.706***
	(0.385)
EMU	0.917***
	(0.132)
Both countries in European Union	−0.275
	(0.206)
Both countries in CFA franc area (West and Central African)	−0.731*
	(0.438)
One country in CFA franc area, the other in EMU	0.572***
	(0.119)
Log of product of real GDPs	0.812***
	(0.016)
Log of product of real GDPs per capita	−0.026
	(0.019)
Common language	0.355***
	(0.073)
Common land border	2.507***
	(0.134)
Free trade agreement	1.951***
	(0.181)
Landlocked	−0.265***
	(0.049)
Log of product of land areas	−0.106***
	(0.012)
Common colonizer post-1945	0.765***
	(0.106)
Currently in colonial relationship	−0.527**
	(0.230)
Ever in colonial relationship	1.036***
	(0.151)
Same nation/perennial colonies	0.462
	(0.431)
Real exchange rate of country 1	−0.002
	(0.008)
Real exchange rate of country 2	−0.004
	(0.008)
Constant	−34.079***
	(0.456)
Observations	169,561
R^2	0.40

Note: 1948 to 2006: OLS estimator with year fixed effects. Robust standard errors in parentheses, clustered on country-pairs.

***Significant at the 1 percent level.

**Significant at the 5 percent level.

*Significant at the 10 percent level.

Table 5.10   **The impact of EMU on bilateral trade between CFA and EMU members, 1948 to 2006**

Dependent variable	Log of bilateral trade
Currency union	1.710***
	(0.386)
EMU	0.229*
	(0.138)
Both countries in European Union	−0.137
	(0.211)
Both countries in CFA franc area (West and Central African)	−0.726*
	(0.439)
One country in CFA franc area, the other in EMU	0.165
	(0.241)
One country in CFA, one country in EMU × 1980	0.144
	(0.094)
One country in CFA, one country in EMU × 1981	(dropped)
One country in CFA, one country in EMU × 1982	0.024
	(0.082)
One country in CFA, one country in EMU × 1983	0.184*
	(0.097)
One country in CFA, one country in EMU × 1984	0.324**
	(0.130)
One country in CFA, one country in EMU × 1985	0.345***
	(0.121)
One country in CFA, one country in EMU × 1986	0.437***
	(0.135)
One country in CFA, one country in EMU × 1987	0.414***
	(0.151)
One country in CFA, one country in EMU × 1988	0.467***
	(0.141)
One country in CFA, one country in EMU × 1989	0.313**
	(0.151)
One country in CFA, one country in EMU × 1990	0.234
	(0.160)
One country in CFA, one country in EMU × 1991	0.350*
	(0.182)
One country in CFA, one country in EMU × 1992	0.221
	(0.159)
One country in CFA, one country in EMU × 1993	0.186
	(0.164)
One country in CFA, one country in EMU × 1994	0.066
	(0.163)
One country in CFA, one country in EMU × 1995	0.237
	(0.166)
One country in CFA, one country in EMU × 1996	0.079
	(0.158)
One country in CFA, one country in EMU × 1997	0.640***
	(0.226)
One country in CFA, one country in EMU × 1998	0.549**
	(0.222)
One country in CFA, one country in EMU × 1999	0.508**
	(0.222)

(*continued*)

Table 5.10 (continued)

Dependent variable	Log of bilateral trade
One country in CFA, one country in EMU × 2000	0.450**
	(0.223)
One country in CFA, one country in EMU × 2001	0.546**
	(0.223)
One country in CFA, one country in EMU × 2002	0.519**
	(0.226)
One country in CFA, one country in EMU × 2003	0.428*
	(0.233)
One country in CFA, one country in EMU × 2004	0.437*
	(0.235)
One country in CFA, one country in EMU × 2005	0.22
	(0.238)
One country in CFA, one country in EMU × 2006	0.178
	(0.246)
Log of product of real GDPs	0.813***
	(0.016)
Log of product of real GDPs per capita	−0.027
	(0.019)
Common language	0.358***
	(0.073)
Common land border	2.515***
	(0.134)
Free trade agreement	1.940***
	(0.182)
Landlocked	−0.267***
	(0.049)
Log of product of land areas	−0.107***
	(0.012)
Common colonizer post-1945	0.770***
	(0.106)
Currently in colonial relationship	−0.493**
	(0.229)
Ever in colonial relationship	1.004***
	(0.149)
Same nation/perennial colonies	0.46
	(0.433)
Real exchange rate of country 1	−0.003
	(0.008)
Real exchange rate of country 2	−0.006
	(0.008)
Constant	−34.094***
	(0.457)
Observations	169,561
R^2	0.40

Note: 1948 to 2006: OLS estimator with year fixed effects. Robust standard errors in parentheses. Dummy for CFA-EMU country-pairs takes on value 1 from 1999 onward.

***Significant at the 1 percent level.

**Significant at the 5 percent level.

*Significant at the 10 percent level.

CFA members and euro members again rises during the 1980s, loses significance in 1992 (the year of the ERM crisis), comes roaring back with a highly significant 0.78 in 1997 (two years before the first EMU year), stays strong through 2004, and then puzzlingly loses significance in 2005 to 2006. In 1999, CFA countries trade with euro countries an extra 47 percent more than otherwise similar pairs of countries.[27]

The list of explanatory variables has grown rather long. The author has never been very fond of the real exchange rate variables. Further, the dummy "currently in colonial relationship" seems to offer little, either ex ante or in practice, that is not already covered by the dummy "ever in colonial relationship" together with "same nation/perennial colonies." In view of multicollinearity concerns, all three variables are dropped in the final tables reported in this chapter. In table 5.11, the dummy variable representing when one partner is a CFA country and the other is a euro country has a highly significant coefficient of 0.38. Taking the exponent, the point estimate is that the euro boosted bilateral trade between the relevant African and European countries by 46 percent. Table 5.12 looks at the effects over time. The apparent timing of the effect coincides better with the advent of full EMU than before: it is not significant in the 1980s, but as before, it attains in 1997 to 2004 a highly significant effect that is in the vicinity of 50 percent.[28] The puzzle of lost significance in 2005 to 2006 remains.

Overall, it is striking that this natural experiment produces such strong estimates for the trade effects of an exogenous currency link. Evidently, the findings of strong effects from currency links among small countries cannot be entirely attributed to the endogeneity of the decision to form a monetary union.

5.5   Conclusion

This chapter seeks to explain the discrepancy between estimates of the euro's effect on trade among members—about 15 percent in our results, as in those of earlier authors—and estimates of the effects of other earlier currency unions in large samples of countries—on the order of 200 percent. It examines three obvious suspects. First are lags. The euro is still very young. We do find an upward trend in the trade effect during 1999 to 2004, but surprisingly, we find no tendency during 2005 to 2006 for the euro's effect to have risen above the level that it had attained by 2004 (15 percent). Second is size. The European countries are much bigger than most of those who had formed currency unions in the past. But the effect of a currency union does not appear to diminish discernibly with country size. Third is

27. Exp $(0.623 - 0.241) = 1.4652$.
28. In 1999, exp $(0.623 - 0.241) = 1.47$. It is also worth noting that the effect on trade *between* two CFA members is not significantly less than for pairs that belong to other currency unions.

Table 5.11   **CFA natural experiment: The impact of EMU on bilateral trade between CFA and EMU members with year interactions, 1948 to 2006 (with distance but without real exchange rates)**

Dependent variable	Log of bilateral trade
Currency union	0.547*
	(0.300)
EMU	1.198***
	(0.101)
Both countries in European Union	−0.535***
	(0.195)
Both countries in CFA franc area (West and Central African)	−0.268
	(0.398)
One country in CFA franc area, the other in EMU	0.381***
	(0.108)
Log of product of real GDPs	0.769***
	(0.015)
Log of product of real GDPs per capita	0.015
	(0.018)
Log of distance	−0.964***
	(0.035)
Common language	0.203***
	(0.069)
Common land border	0.616***
	(0.154)
Free trade agreement	0.617***
	(0.180)
Landlocked	−0.491***
	(0.048)
Log of product of land areas	−0.082***
	(0.012)
Common colonizer post-1945	0.566***
	(0.106)
Ever in colonial relationship	0.771***
	(0.151)
Same nation/perennial colonies	4.093
	(3.259)
Constant	−24.486***
	(0.521)
Observations	294,182
R^2	0.38

Note: 1948 to 2006: OLS estimator with year fixed effects. Robust standard errors in parentheses, clustered on country-pairs.

***Significant at the 1 percent level.

*Significant at the 10 percent level.

Table 5.12   **The impact of EMU on bilateral trade between CFA and EMU members, 1948 to 2006 (with distance but without real exchange rates)**

Dependent variable	Log of bilateral trade
Currency union	0.553*
	(0.301)
EMU	–0.049
	(0.241)
Both countries in European Union	–0.191
	(0.234)
Both countries in CFA franc area (West and Central African)	–0.274
	(0.398)
One country in CFA franc area, the other in EMU	–0.111
	(0.300)
One country in CFA, one country in EMU × 1980	0.152
	(0.315)
One country in CFA, one country in EMU × 1981	0.114
	(0.287)
One country in CFA, one country in EMU × 1982	0.049
	(0.279)
One country in CFA, one country in EMU × 1983	0.208
	(0.284)
One country in CFA, one country in EMU × 1984	0.359
	(0.286)
One country in CFA, one country in EMU × 1985	0.316
	(0.290)
One country in CFA, one country in EMU × 1986	0.42
	(0.309)
One country in CFA, one country in EMU × 1987	0.334
	(0.297)
One country in CFA, one country in EMU × 1988	0.402
	(0.332)
One country in CFA, one country in EMU × 1989	0.203
	(0.337)
One country in CFA, one country in EMU × 1990	–0.032
	(0.326)
One country in CFA, one country in EMU × 1991	0.236
	(0.332)
One country in CFA, one country in EMU × 1992	0.176
	(0.321)
One country in CFA, one country in EMU × 1993	0.174
	(0.321)
One country in CFA, one country in EMU × 1994	0.053
	(0.321)
One country in CFA, one country in EMU × 1995	0.215
	(0.320)
One country in CFA, one country in EMU × 1996	0.073
	(0.320)
One country in CFA, one country in EMU × 1997	0.683**
	(0.306)
One country in CFA, one country in EMU × 1998	0.626**
	(0.304)

(continued)

Table 5.12   (continued)

Dependent variable	Log of bilateral trade
One country in CFA, one country in EMU × 1999	0.572*
	(0.299)
One country in CFA, one country in EMU × 2000	0.526*
	(0.298)
One country in CFA, one country in EMU × 2001	0.612**
	(0.301)
One country in CFA, one country in EMU × 2002	0.591*
	(0.304)
One country in CFA, one country in EMU × 2003	0.512*
	(0.306)
One country in CFA, one country in EMU × 2004	0.489
	(0.303)
One country in CFA, one country in EMU × 2005	0.31
	(0.306)
One country in CFA, one country in EMU × 2006	0.265
	(0.315)
Log of product of real GDPs	0.769***
	(0.015)
Log of product of real GDPs per capita	0.016
	(0.018)
Log of distance	−0.964***
	(0.036)
Common language	0.201***
	(0.069)
Common land border	0.619***
	(0.154)
Free trade agreement	0.605***
	(0.180)
Landlocked	−0.489***
	(0.048)
Log of product of land areas	−0.082***
	(0.012)
Common colonizer post-1945	0.567***
	(0.106)
Ever in colonial relationship	0.776***
	(0.152)
Same nation/perennial colonies	4.106
	(3.270)
Constant	−24.485***
	(0.521)
Observations	294,182
R^2	0.38

Note: 1948 to 2006: OLS estimator with year fixed effects. Robust standard errors in parentheses.

***Significant at the 1 percent level.
**Significant at the 5 percent level.
*Significant at the 10 percent level.

the endogeneity of the decision to adopt an institutional currency link. Perhaps the high correlations estimated in earlier studies were spurious, an artifact of reverse causality. But we examine the natural experiment of trade between CFA countries and (non-Francophone) euro members and find a strong switch that in this case is unlikely to be the artifact of an endogenous currency decision. In short, we find no evidence that any of these factors explains any share of the gap, let alone all of it.

What we find instead is a surprising new suspect: results reported here suggest that the discrepancy might stem from sample size. If one estimates the effects of the euro versus other monetary unions in a large sample that includes all countries and all years, thereby bringing to bear as much information as possible on questions such as the proper coefficients on common border and common language in a gravity model, then the effect of the euro in the first eight years appears to be large, even comparable with the effect of the other noneuro monetary unions. It is hard to believe, however, that the true effect of the euro has indeed been this large; if intraeuroland trade had doubled or tripled since 1999, we would see it in the raw data and would not need to run a regression. Perhaps it is best to summarize the conclusions of the chapter by saying that each of the three obvious suspects—lags, size, and endogeneity—has an apparent alibi, but the true perpetrator remains at large.

References

Allington, N. F. B., P. Kattuman, and F. Waldmann. 2005. One money, one market, one price. *International Journal of Central Banking* 1 (3): 73–115.

Anderson, J. and E. van Wincoop. 2001. Gravity with gravitas: A solution to the border puzzle. NBER Working Paper no. 8079. Cambridge, MA: National Bureau of Economic Research, January.

Anderson, K., and H. Norheim. 1993. History, geography and regional economic integration. In *Regionalism and the global trading system,* ed. K. Anderson and R. Blackburst. London: Harvester Wheatsheaf.

Baldwin, R. 2006. The euro's trade effects. ECB Working Paper no. 594 Frankfurt: European Central Bank.

Begg, D., O. Blanchard, D. Coyle, B. Eichengreen, J. Frankel, F. Giavazzi, R. Portes, et al. 2003. *The consequences of saying no: An independent report into the economic consequences of the UK saying no to the euro.* London: Commission on the United Kingdom Outside the Euro.

Berger, H., and V. Nitsch. 2005. Zooming out: The trade effect of the euro in historical perspective. CESifo Working Paper no. 1435. Munich: Munich Society for the Promotion of Economic Research.

Brada, J., and J. Mendez. 1985. Economic integration among developed, developing and centrally planned economies: A comparative analysis. *Review of Economics and Statistics* 67 (4): 549–56.

Bun, M., and F. Klaassen. 2002. Has the euro increased trade? TI Discussion Paper no. 2002-108/2. Amsterdam: Tinbergen Institute. Available at: http://www.eabcn .org/research/documents/bun_klaasen02.pdf.

Chintrakarn, P. 2008. Estimating the euro effects on trade with propensity score matching. *Review of International Economics* 16 (1): 186–98.

De Grauwe, Paul. 1988. Exchange rate variability and the slowdown in growth of international trade. *IMF Staff Papers* 35:63–84.

De Nardis, S., and C. Vicarelli. 2003. Currency unions and trade: The special case of EMU. *World Review of Economics* 139 (4): 625–49.

Dwane, C., P. Lane, and T. McIndoe. 2006. Currency unions and Irish external trade. IIIS Discussion Paper no. 189. Dublin: Institute for International Integration Studies, Trinity College.

Eichengreen, B., and D. Irwin. 1998. The role of history in bilateral trade flows. In *The regionalization of the world economy,* ed. J. Frankel, 33–62. Chicago: University of Chicago Press.

Engel, C., and J. Rogers. 2004. European product market integration after the euro. *Economic Policy* 19 (39) : 347–84.

Fidrmuc, J., and J. Fidrmuc. 2001. Disintegration and trade. LICOS Discussion Paper no. 9901. Catholic University of Leuven, LICOS Center for Institutions and Economic Performance.

Fidrmuc, J., J. Horvath, and J. Fidrmuc. 1999. The stability of monetary unions: Lessons from the breakup of Czechoslovakia. *Journal of Comparative Economics* 27 (4): 752–81.

Flam, H., and H. Nordström. 2003. Trade volume effects of the euro: Aggregate and sector estimates. Stockholm University, IIES Seminar Paper no. 746. Institute for International Economic Studies.

Frankel, J. 1997. *Regional trading blocs in the world trading system.* Washington, DC: Institute for International Economics.

———. 2003. The UK decision re EMU: Implications of currency blocs for trade and business cycle correlations. In *Submissions on EMU from leading academics,* ed. Her Majesty's Treasury, 93–105. London: Her Majesty's Stationery Office.

———. 2005. Real convergence and euro adoption in Central and Eastern Europe: Trade and business cycle correlations as endogenous criteria for joining EMU. In *Euro adoption in Central and Eastern Europe: Opportunities and challenges,* ed. S. Schadler, 9–22. Washington, DC: International Monetary Fund.

———. 2009. The estimated trade effects of the euro: Why are they below those from historical monetary unions among smaller countries? Working Paper no. 2009-0008. Harvard University, Weatherhead Center for International Affairs, April.

Frankel, J., and A. Rose. 2002. An estimate of the effect of common currencies on trade and income. *Quarterly Journal of Economics* 117 (2): 437–66.

Frankel, J., and S.-J. Wei. 1993. Trade blocs and currency blocs. NBER Working Paper no. 4335. Cambridge, MA: National Bureau of Economic Research, April.

———. 1995a. Emerging currency blocs. In *The international monetary system: Its institutions and its future,* ed. H. Genberg, 111–43. Berlin: Springer.

———. 1995b. European integration and the regionalization of world trade and currencies: The economics and the politics. In *Monetary and fiscal policy in an integrated europe,* ed. B. Eichengreen, J. Frieden, and J. von Hagen, 202–31. Heidelberg: Springer-Verlag.

———. 1997. Regionalization of world trade and currencies: Economics and politics. In *The regionalization of the world economy,* ed. J. Frankel, 189–226. Chicago: University of Chicago Press.

Glick, R., and A. Rose. 2002. Does a currency union affect trade? The time-series evidence. *European Economic Review* 46 (6): 1125–51.

Goldberg, P. K., and F. Verboven. 2001. Market integration and convergence to the law of one price: Evidence from the European car market. NBER Working Paper no. 8402. Cambridge, MA: National Bureau of Economic Research, July.

———. 2004. Cross-country price dispersion in the euro era: A case study of the European car market. *Economic Policy* 19 (40): 483–521.

Hamilton, C., and L. A. Winters. 1992. Opening up international trade in Eastern Europe. *Economic Policy* 7 (14): 77–116.

Helliwell, J. 1998. *How much do national borders matter?* Washington, DC: Brookings Institution Press.

Kleiman, E. 1976. Trade and the decline of colonialism. *Economic Journal* 86 (343): 459–80.

Klein, M. 2002. Dollarization and trade. NBER Working Paper no. 8879. Cambridge, MA: National Bureau of Economic Research, April.

Klein, M., and J. C. Shambaugh. 2006. Fixed exchange rates and trade. *Journal of International Economics* 70 (2): 359–83.

McCallum, J. 1995. National borders matter: Canada-U.S. regional trade patterns. *American Economic Review* 85 (3): 615–23.

McKinnon, R. 1963. Optimum currency areas. *American Economic Review* 53 (4): 717–24.

Melitz, J. 2001. Geography, trade and currency union. CEPR Discussion Paper no. 2987. London: Center for Economic Policy Research.

Micco, A., E. Stein, and G. Ordoñez. 2002. *Should the UK join EMU?* Washington, DC: Inter-American Development Bank.

———. 2003. The currency union effect on trade: Early evidence from EMU. *Economic Policy* 18 (37): 315–43.

Nitsch, V. 1991. *National borders and international trade: Evidence from the European Union.* Berlin: Bankgesellschaft.

———. 2000. National borders and international trade: Evidence from the European Union. *Canadian Journal of Economics* 33 (4): 1091–105.

———. 2001. *Honey, I shrunk the currency union effect on trade.* Berlin: Bankgesellschaft.

Pakko, M. R., and H. J. Wall. 2001. Reconsidering the trade-creating effects of a currency union. *Federal Reserve Board of St. Louis Review* 83 (5): 37–46.

Parsley, D., and S.-J. Wei. 2001. Limiting currency volatility to stimulate goods market integration: A price based approach. NBER Working Paper no. 8468. Cambridge, MA: National Bureau of Economic Research, September.

Persson, T. 2001. Currency unions and trade: How large is the treatment effect? *Economic Policy* 16 (33): 435–48.

Rogers, J. H. 2001. Price level convergence, relative prices, and inflation in Europe. International Finance Discussion Paper no. 699. Washington, DC: Board of Governors of the Federal Reserve System.

———. 2002. Monetary union, price level convergence, and inflation: How close is Europe to the United States? International Finance Discussion Paper no. 740. Washington, DC: Board of Governors of the Federal Reserve System.

Rose, A. 2000. One money, one market: Estimating the effect of common currencies on trade. *Economic Policy* 15 (30): 7–45.

———. 2001. Currency unions and trade: The effect is large. *Economic Policy* 16 (33): 449–61.

———. 2004. A meta-analysis of the effect of common currencies on international trade. NBER Working Paper no. 10373. Cambridge, MA: National Bureau of Economic Research, March.

Rose, A. K., and E. van Wincoop. 2001. National money as a barrier to trade: The real case for monetary union. *American Economic Review* 91 (2): 386–90.

Tenreyro, S. 2001. On the causes and consequences of currency unions. Harvard University, Department of Economics. Manuscript, November.

Thom, R., and B. Walsh. 2002. The effect of a common currency on trade: Ireland before and after the sterling link. *European Economic Review* 46 (6): 1111–23.

Thursby, J. G., and M. C. Thursby. 1987. Bilateral trade flows, the Linder hypothesis, and exchange risk. *Review of Economics and Statistics* 69 (3): 488–95.

Wang, Z. K., and L. A. Winters. 1991. The trading potential of Eastern Europe. CEPR Discussion Paper no. 610. London: Center for Economic Policy Research.

Wei, S.-J. 1996. Intra-national versus international trade: How stubborn are nations in global integration? NBER Working Paper no. 5531. Cambridge, MA: National Bureau of Economic Research, April.

Comment   Silvana Tenreyro

Background and Summary

In an influential and provocative paper, Andy Rose (2000) reported that sharing a common currency enhanced bilateral trade by more than 200 percent.[1] The paper divided the profession into two camps: believers and skeptics. The latter doubted the plausibility of such a large trade effect and pointed out the futility of attempting to extrapolate the postwar experience of currency unions (made mostly of small and poor countries) to countries adopting the euro. Subsequent work by Micco, Stein, and Ordoñez (2003) using data on the early years of the euro found that the effect of the euro on bilateral trade between euro zone countries ranged from 4 to 10 percent when compared to trade between all other pairs of countries and from 8 to 16 percent when compared to trade among noneuro zone countries.

As the euro marks its tenth anniversary, Frankel's chapter provides a timely opportunity to explain the gap between Rose's and Micco, Stein, and Ordoñez's estimates and to reappraise the effect of the euro on trade.

The chapter argues that the gap between estimates is not caused by any of the usual suspects. In particular, the difference is not caused by (a) lags (or the view that it takes time for currency unions to affect trade patterns); (b) omitted variables (including the Anderson and Van Wincoop multilateral resistance term);[2] (c) reverse causality (trade may lead to the formation of currency unions); or (d) threshold effects (or the view that currency unions can cause large trade increases in countries that are below a certain size or income threshold). Instead, the chapter concludes that the culprit for the difference in estimates is sample size. Indeed, Micco, Stein, and Ordoñez (2003) estimated the euro effect using only post-1992 data. When the whole sample (with all country pairs, going back to the mid-1940s) is used, Fran-

Silvana Tenreyro is a reader in economics at the London School of Economics.

1. With some exceptions, work by other scholars found confirmatory results using postwar data. See early review in Alesina, Barro, and Tenreyro (2002) and Baldwin (2006).

2. See Anderson and Van Wincoop (2002).

kel's chapter finds that sharing the euro is associated with an increase in trade among euro zone countries of between 150 and 170 percent, very close to the tripling effect documented by Rose. The chapter then argues that the large estimates for the euro (150 to 170 percent trade effect) resulting from the extended sample should be preferred.

Comments

Explaining the source of difference in estimates is certainly a welcome contribution. The case in support of the large estimates (from the extended sample), however, is unconvincing. To see why, let us start by looking at figure 5C.1, which shows the exports from euro zone countries to other euro zone countries relative to the aggregate gross domestic product (GDP) of the euro zone.[3] The plot shows that in 1990, the average euro zone country was exporting 12 percent of its GDP to other euro zone countries. The corresponding figure was (just below) 16 percent by the end of the sample.

If the chapter's preferred estimates are correct, the question is then: what would exports have looked like if the euro had not been introduced? This question can easily be addressed using the chapter's estimates. The estimated equation is given by:

$$\ln y_{ijt} = x_{ijt}\beta + \gamma_t \, \mathrm{EMU}_{ijt} + \varepsilon_{ijt},$$

where y_{ij} is bilateral trade between two countries i and j at time t, x_{ijt} is a set of controls, and EMU_{ijt} is a dummy variable that takes on the value 1 if both countries are in the euro zone and 0 otherwise. Hence, predicted bilateral trade flows are given by:[4]

$$\hat{y}_{ijt} = \exp(x_{ijt}\hat{\beta})$$

if at least one of the countries is not in the euro zone, and

$$\hat{y}_{ijt} = \exp(x_{ijt}\hat{\beta} + \hat{\gamma}t) = \exp(x_{ijt}\hat{\beta}) \exp(\hat{\gamma}_t)$$

if both countries are in the euro zone. The factor $\exp(\hat{\gamma}_t)$ is the enhancement effect coming from using the euro. Hence, we can compute the counterfactual bilateral trade flows between euro members in the post-1998 period under the assumption that the euro had not been introduced as:

$$\frac{y_{ijt}}{\exp(\hat{\gamma}_t)},$$

where y_{ij} is *actual* exports between two euro zone members, and the coefficients $\hat{\gamma}_t$, $\{t = 1998 \ldots\}$ are the chapter's (preferred) estimates. Aggregating y_{ijt} over all euro members, we can then compute overall exports from euro

---

3. By euro zone, here, I refer to the eleven countries that adopted the euro in 1999, plus Greece.

4. This ignores heteroskedasticity and other issues raised in Santos-Silva and Tenreyro (2006).

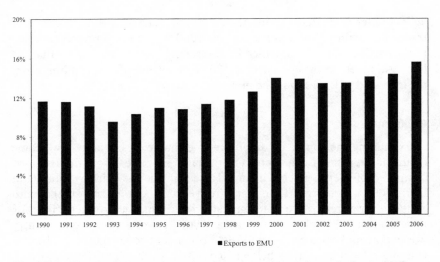

Fig. 5C.1   Exports from euro zone to other euro zone members relative to GDP

Source: Tenreyro's computation using Direction of Trade Statistics (DOTS; International Monetary Fund) and World Development Indicators (WDI; World Bank).

countries to other euro countries as a share of GDP, as in figure 5C.1. Figure 5C.2 shows these counterfactual exports as a share of GDP, together with the actual shares (from figure 5C.1).

As the figure illustrates, the chapter's preferred estimates imply that if the euro had not been introduced, trade shares would have collapsed in 1998. This leaves the reader with two options: either believe that trade shares would have shrank dramatically without the euro or remain skeptical of the large estimates. I could not come up with any substantive reason for a trade fall of such dimensions. Moreover, for the reasons I will later explain, I think the estimation is misspecified, and the biases generated by the misspecification become more severe when the large sample is used.

There are at least two important concerns raised by the estimation approach that the chapter tries to address: endogeneity and sample size. I would like to discuss them in more depth.

Endogeneity: A Natural Experiment

In an almost self-contained section, the chapter argues that endogeneity is not a serious problem in the estimation and therefore not the source of the large estimates. To make this point, the chapter studies bilateral trade patterns between countries in the euro zone and countries in the CFA franc zone.[5] The latter, which were pegging their currency to the French franc

5. The CFA franc zone comprises two different monetary unions: the West African Economic and Monetary Union, which uses the West African franc CFA (where CFA stands for *Commu-*

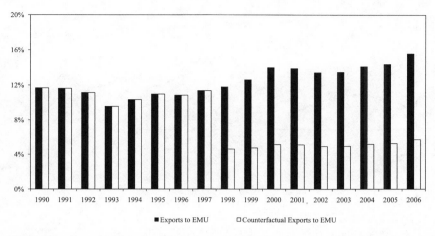

Fig. 5C.2   Actual and counterfactual exports from euro zone to other euro zone members relative to GDP

Source: Tenreyro's computation using DOTS, WDI, and Frankel's (2008) estimates.

before the introduction of the euro, continued to peg their currency to France's—that is, to the euro—after 1999. These countries hence found their currency almost accidentally pegged to that of all other countries in the euro zone. This historical accident is an ideal quasi experiment to evaluate the effect of a strong peg on trade. And it is obviously an important exercise in its own right and is of fundamental value for development macroeconomists. The author should be commended for the idea. As before, however, I would like to comment on the size of the trade enhancement effect.

To gauge the trade impact of the strong peg between the CFA franc and the euro, the chapter introduces a dummy variable that takes on the value 1 if one of the countries is in the CFA franc zone and the other is in the European Monetary Union (EMU; currently or in the future) and 0 otherwise; so, for example, for the pair Italy-Congo, this dummy is always 1. This dummy is then interacted with year dummies from 1980 to 2006 so as to estimate the extra trade between CFA and euro zone country pairs over time. That is:

$$\ln y_{ijt} = x_{ijt}\beta + \gamma_1 \cdot \text{one country in CFA, the other in EMU} \times 1980$$
$$+ \gamma_2 \cdot \text{one country in CFA, the other in EMU} \times 1981$$
$$+ \gamma_3 \cdot \text{one country in CFA, the other in EMU} \times 1982$$
$$\cdots\cdots\cdots\cdots\cdots\cdots\cdots\cdots\cdots\cdots\cdots\cdots\cdots\cdots\cdots\cdots\cdots\cdots$$
$$+ \gamma_{28} \cdot \text{one country in CFA, the other in EMU} \times 2006 + \varepsilon_{ijt}.$$

---

nauté Financiére d'Afrique), and the Economic and Monetary Community of Central Africa, which uses the Central African CFA franc (where CFA stands for *Coopération Financière en Afrique Centrale*).

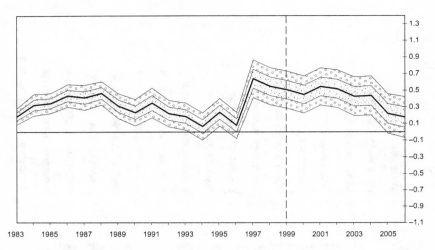

Fig. 5C.3   CFA-euro zone coefficients and standard error bands

As before, the estimated coefficients $\hat{\gamma}_1$ through $\hat{\gamma}_{28}$ relate to the extra trade between a CFA member and a euro zone member (future or current). Figure 5C.3 plots these coefficients together with the one- and two-standard-error bands against time (as reported in the chapter), highlighting the year in which the euro was introduced. Interestingly, trade between these two groups of countries has been historically larger than trade between other country pairs (the coefficients are always positive). The figure also shows a stark increase in trade in 1997. The timing is not perfect for the euro, as trade seems to jump before the actual introduction of the euro; the chapter acknowledges this point straight away but compellingly argues that the effect may have been anticipated as expectations of the euro became more firmly established. However, there is some confusion regarding the magnitude of the effect. The chapter estimates a CFA franc-euro effect of about 70 percent in the post-1997 period (with 70 percent = [exp(0.55) – 1] · 100 percent, where 0.55 is an average of the point estimates of the $\hat{\gamma}$ coefficients over the post-1997 period). The enhancement effect, however, should be computed as the difference between the post- and pre-1997 (or the relevant year) periods, as trade between these two groups was already large in the 1980s. The average $\hat{\gamma}$ coefficient in the pre-1997 period was about 0.35, implying that the enhancement effect could not have been larger than 20 percent (20 percent = [exp(0.55 – 0.35) – 1] · 100 percent). This number is much closer to Micco, Stein, and Ordoñez's estimates than to Rose's, suggesting that endogeneity may have played an important role in Rose's estimates after all. *But this should not distract us from the main finding: the euro has increased trade between CFA franc zone and euro zone countries; this is an unexpected, positive, and important by-product of the euro.*

Sample Size (and the Problems with Zeroes and Heteroskedasticity)

The chapter argues that the gap between 10 and 200 percent in estimates is almost fully explained by sample size. When the full sample (with all country pairs, going back to the mid-1940s) is used, the estimated coefficient on the euro becomes close to 200 percent. As argued earlier, it is impossible to conceive an enhancement effect of such magnitude without making heroic assumptions. Still, it is of academic interest to ask why and how the chapter can obtain such large estimates in the full sample. To understand why, notice that the large-sample specification imposes the same coefficients of the gravity equation to all country pairs over time. The chapter argues that this is a good strategy, as more information is available to pin down the coefficients on other gravity variables. But it is not clear to me why one should do that: coefficients may indeed have changed over time and across countries, and constraining the estimated parameters to be constant could lead to serious misspecification. This adds problems to the already misspecified estimation, which uses the logarithm of bilateral trade, a variable that (a) frequently (in more than 30 percent of the observations) takes the value 0 and (b) is highly hetoreskedastic. Both the presence of zeroes and heteroskedasticity lead to inconsistent estimates in logarithmic specifications, as shown in Santos-Silva and Tenreyro (2006). The larger sample makes the problem of zeroes and heteroskedasticity much more severe, as there is a larger proportion of zeroes in the sample going back to the mid-1940s, and as it includes highly heterogeneous countries, increasing the relevance of heteroskedasticity. In sum, there is every reason to try to avoid the large-sample estimates, unless an appropriate estimator is used. My suggestion is to use the estimator proposed in Santos-Silva and Tenreyro (2006), together with time-varying coefficients on the gravity variables and the euro effect.

Final Remarks

Frankel has written an enjoyable and stimulating article that will give new impetus to the debate over the pros and cons of currency unions.

References

Alesina, A., R. Barro, and S. Tenreyro. 2002. Optimal currency areas. In *NBER Macroeconomics annual,* ed. M. Gertler and K. Rogoff, 301–56. Cambridge, MA: MIT Press.
Anderson, J., and E. van Wincoop. 2003. Gravity with gravitas: A solution to the border puzzle. *American Economic Review* 93 (1): 170–92.

Baldwin, R. 2006. *In or out: Does it matter? An evidence-based analysis of the euro's trade effects.* London: Center for Economic Policy Research.

Micco, A., E. Stein, and D. Ordoñez. 2003. The currency union effect on trade: Early evidence from EMU. *Economic Policy* 18 (37): 315–56.

Rose, A. 2000. One money, one market: Estimating the effect of common currencies on trade. *Economic Policy* 15 (30): 7–46.

Santos-Silva, J. M. C., and S. Tenreyro. 2006. The log of gravity. *Review of Economics and Statistics* 88 (4): 641–58.

A New Metric for Banking Integration in Europe

Reint Gropp and Anil K Kashyap

6.1 Introduction

In this chapter we propose a new approach for assessing banking integration in Europe. The measurement of integration is of considerable policy relevance. For example, the European Central Bank (ECB) mission statement reads: "We in the Eurosystem have as our primary objective the maintenance of price stability for the common good. Acting also as a leading financial authority, we aim to safeguard financial stability and *promote European financial integration*" (italics added). The ECB (2009) defines financial integration by saying "*The market for a given set of financial instruments or services to be fully integrated when all potential market participants in such a market (i) are subject to a single set of rules when they decide to deal with those financial instruments or services, (ii) have equal access to this set of financial instruments or services, and (iii) are treated equally when they operate in the market*" (7).

This definition has direct implications for how banking integration should

Reint Gropp is senior professor of financial economics and taxation at the European Business School and a research associate at the Center for European Economic Research (ZEW). Anil K Kashyap is the Edward Eagle Brown Professor of Economics and Finance at the University of Chicago and a research associate of the National Bureau of Economic Research.

This chapter was presented at the NBER summer institute preconference and the 2nd ZEW conference on banking integration and stability. Comments from participants, especially Massimiliano Affinito and Loretta Mester (discussants), Alberto Alesina, Olivier Blanchard, Ricardo Caballero, and Francesco Giavazzi are gratefully acknowledged. Research assistance by Markus Balzer, Biliana Kassabova, Matthias Köhler, and Marco Lo Duca is gratefully acknowledged. Gropp thanks the DFG (German Science Foundation) for research support and the Goethe University Frankfurt for its generous hospitality. Kashyap thanks the Initiative on Global Markets at the University of Chicago for financial support. The views in this chapter are our own and not necessarily shared by any of the institutions with which we are affiliated. All mistakes are ours alone.

be measured. For instance, the equal access condition presumes that it is profitable for all services to be offered in all markets. This is akin to requiring that if there is demand for a service it must be met everywhere within an economic area at the lowest cost at which it can be provided anywhere within that area. This seems a useful benchmark for bond or wholesale banking markets, but much less relevant for locally provided retail banking services. Unless bank cost structures are identical across local communities some services might not be offered in some locations. This is not informative about financial integration.

The equal treatment provision is also unusual because it includes no efficiency benchmark. As an extreme example, consider the case of a monopolist supplying financial services far above marginal cost. This would satisfy the ECB definition, but clearly would not be efficient, and we doubt it would be viewed as acceptable by policymakers.

The common problem highlighted by both these observations is that market conditions depend on both supply and demand. The ECB definition pays insufficient attention to the supply side of the market. Existing empirical work (as represented by Cabral, Dierck, and Vesala [2002]; Baele et al. [2004]; Adam et al. [2002]; ECB [2009]) also suffers to certain extent from the same criticism.

Previous research assessing integration has been of three varieties. One looks at the extent of cross-border direct retail operations of banks (Gual [2004]; Perez, Salas-Fumas, and Saurina [2005]). These data are tracked by the Bank for International Settlements (BIS) and suggest that while wholesale or money market flows across borders within the euro area are large, retail flows are generally less than 1 percent of total lending. This is taken as evidence against retail banking integration, although most authors would concede that cross-border retail flows do not constitute a necessary condition for retail banking integration to take place. One could easily imagine a financial system in which we would observe a complete absence of cross-border retail flows, but which would be perfectly integrated. For example, the threat of such flows could be enough to ensure perfect integration.

A second indicator is cross-border bank mergers (see most recently Köhler [2007, 2009] for evidence on this and a review of this literature). The absence of such deals, say, in comparison to the number of domestic bank mergers, has also been taken as evidence against retail bank integration. Of course, similar arguments apply in this case, as cross-border retail flows and cross-border mergers are likely to be neither necessary nor sufficient for financial integration to take place.

The third method for detecting integration comes from the study of retail interest rates by Adam et al. (2002). They look at five-year corporate loans and mortgage loans and find lending rates barely converge after 1999. In a partial adjustment model the speed of convergence is only 2 percent per year for corporate rates and 7 percent for mortgage rates. Based on this slow rate of convergence, they conclude that retail banking markets are far from integrated and do not seem to be on a path toward integration.

The ECB's annual financial integration report (2009) reports extensive descriptive information, such as the cross-country standard deviation of interest rates on various bank products to argue that retail bank markets are not integrated. Affinito and Farabullini (2009) show that interest rate dispersion is reduced after controlling for variables reflecting the characteristics of domestic borrowers, such as risk exposure, disposable income, firm size, and so forth. They also demonstrate that price dispersion is larger across the euro area than across regions in Italy. They conclude that "euro area prices appear different because national banking products appear different or because they are differentiated by national factors" (31–32). We argue that this same reasoning implies that interest rate dispersion is a poor guide to judging integration. Indeed, we will present examples that show that interest rate dispersion may be completely unrelated to banking integration.

The starting point for our analysis is a reconsideration of the relevance of the law of one price in this context. We argue that the law of one price in retail banking, the way it has been applied in the previous literature, constitutes neither a sufficient nor necessary condition for retail banking integration. The reason is the high degree of heterogeneity in demand for retail bank products that may arise from differences in tax systems, preferences, risk characteristics, or other demand-side related factors (section 6.2). Once we admit that there are legitimate reasons why demand might differ across markets, then even with a single supply curve prices would differ. Yet these price differences would not represent a failure of integration.

In section 6.3 we propose a new test of retail bank integration in the spirit of Stigler (1963), which we argue constitutes a sufficient condition for banking integration. Our notion of integration presumes new entry and takeovers will lead to a convergence in profitability. This way of looking at integration shifts the focus to looking at barriers to entry and takeovers and to comparisons of profit rates rather than prices of banking products. The remainder of the chapter explores whether integration in this sense holds.

In section 6.4 we describe the data we use to carry the test of our condition. This sample consists of 36,000 observations on banks in France, Germany, Italy, Spain, the United States, and the United Kingdom between 1994 and 2006. The sample includes listed and unlisted banks and also includes many savings and cooperative banks. We show that average profitability varies widely among bank types (listed, unlisted) in Europe, but not in the United States. Further, even within listed and unlisted banks, profitability varies widely across countries in Europe.

In section 6.5 we estimate a partial adjustment model to assess convergence. The logic of our test suggests investigating whether profit rates converge and whether the tendency toward convergence depends on the strength of the market for corporate control. Hence, publicly traded banks should be under different pressure than unlisted banks.

We find this to be the case. Listed banks in Europe and the United States each show a tendency to revert to the average profit rates in their respective areas. The nonlisted commercial banks in the United States that are unusually profitable tend to have these profits competed away—but underperforming nontraded banks do not seem to improve. The profit rates of the unlisted commercial banks in Europe show no tendency to converge to any type of European average; there is some evidence profit rates for unlisted banks converge to a country-specific average. We read these patterns as suggesting the U.S. banking market is reasonably well-integrated, but that the banking market in Europe appears far from being integrated. We close this section with some thoughts on the relationship between the introduction of the common currency in the euro area and banking integration.

Section 6.6 offers some final thoughts on how the results might inform future policy discussions regarding financial integration.

6.2   The Law of One Price Revisited

Intuitively, assessing integration using the law of one price seems appealing. Indeed, for many financial instruments such as government bonds, or high grade corporate securities, checking for the convergence of prices is standard practice. In the case of bank products, however, heterogeneity that invariably is present will undermine this type of comparison. Banks offer highly differentiated products to their customers, which may frequently be tailored toward their specific life circumstances, preferences, risk characteristics, and needs. Unless one accurately controls for these differences, which may very likely systematically differ across countries, the law of one price will not send a clear message regarding the state of integration.

We illustrate this point in two ways. Figure 6.1 shows our understanding of the standard view of financial integration that underlies law of one price tests using generic supply and demand schedules. This characterization presumes that there is a single demand curve (which is common across markets and customers) and different supply curves. The standard view presumes that if we observe more than one price for a similar product (as in the figure with P1, P2, and P3), then this is evidence for market segregation and a lack of integration. In the language of the ECB definition of integration, the equal treatment of customers across markets would not be satisfied since identical customers are facing different prices.

The logic behind the ECB definition would be that the common set of regulatory rules would lead supplier S1 to capture the market, because she or he is the low cost provider of the financial service. So they should supply Q3 and the prevailing market price should be P3. Under these circumstances

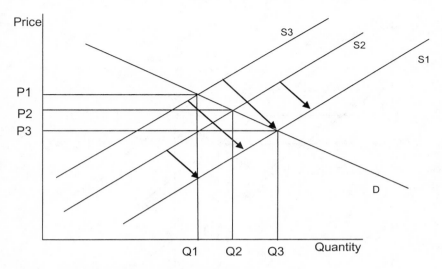

Fig. 6.1   Standard view of financial integration

the law of one price will give an accurate picture of the degree of financial integration.

Now consider figure 6.2. Again, we would observe multiple prices (P1, P2, P3). But in figure 6.2, there is only one supply curve and the observed violation of the law of one price is due to unobserved heterogeneity in demand. The demand variation may be a function of differences in preferences, risk characteristics, or other demand characteristics in different markets (countries). In this case, all of the conditions required under the ECB definition of integration might hold.

Thus, as a purely logical matter, tests for the law of one price implicitly assume that demand for bank's products is homogeneous across markets and products.[1] If there were sufficient harmonization across countries of all the factors that might lead to violations of the preconditions for capital structural irrelevance, then perhaps this assumption might be reasonable.[2] But we know statutory corporate tax rates differ considerably, and effective rates show even larger differences; for instance, Mintz (2006) reports that effective average corporate tax rates in France, Germany, Italy, and Spain are 32.1 percent, 38.1 percent, 30.2 percent, and 23.2 percent. So based purely on

1. For an argument along similar lines, see Perez, Salas-Fumas, and Saurina (2005).
2. One can summarize the necessary conditions for the Modigliani and Miller capital structure irrelevance as requiring that: (a) investors and firms can trade the same set of securities at competitive market prices equal to the present value of their future cash flows; (b) there are no taxes, transactions costs, or issuance costs associated with security trading; (c) a firm's financing decisions do not change the cash flows generated by its investments, nor do they reveal new information about them. See Berk and DeMarzo (2007, chapter 14) for further details.

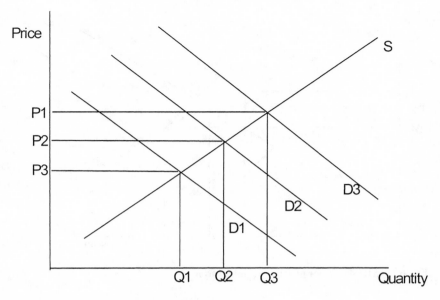

Fig. 6.2   **Alternative view of financial integration**

differences in the tax advantages of interest deductibility, the preference for debt versus equity financing should differ in these countries. Consequently, there is no reason to expect demand for bank loans to be equalized and, hence, prices on bank loans to converge.

On top of the tax issues, the large literature on differences on the effectiveness in corporate governance across countries imply potentially differential benefits of debt financing to control agency costs. These considerations would generate further variation in the demand for debt, and likely the monitoring provided by banks.

Once demand differences are acknowledged, deciding how to describe the state of market integration becomes much more difficult. The well-known literature on price discrimination following from Varian (1985) suggests that prices would likely differ in the presence of cross-market differences in demand. This may or may not entail any efficiency or welfare costs.

One way to see the subtleties involved is to suppose that the ultimate source demand differences can be traced to variation in the costs that different customers face in searching for credit. This seems like a plausible benchmark in the context of many retail bank products. In this case, the large body of research dating back to Salop and Stiglitz (1982) becomes relevant. These models of spatial competition describe conditions under which price dispersion for *identical* goods can arise in equilibrium. In this case, even within countries prices would not converge. Note that in this class of models, financial service firms would enter the market and drive profit rates down to the level of the entry cost. In this case there would be no inefficiencies in the market, despite the price dispersion.

For all these reasons, it seems to us the conditions needed to construct an informative test for integration based on the law of one price are very unlikely to prevail. Hence, we look for a different type of test.

6.3   Return on Assets as a Measure of Bank Integration

Stigler (1963) kicked off a large literature in industrial organization based on the observation that in equilibrium (with well-functioning markets) the expected returns of comparable assets in an economy should be similar. Stigler's empirical work (and all of the subsequent work we have found, such as Fama and French [2000]), has been conducted using nonfinancial businesses. We explore whether the returns on assets of banks across different markets/countries converge and suggest that convergence of profitability is a preferable measure of financial integration to the law of one price.

Convergence would only be expected if the structure of the retail banking industry is such that (a) product markets are contestable and (b) the market for corporate control operates efficiently across markets.[3] While neither of these conditions has received much attention in the discussion over retail banking integration, they seem to be essential preconditions for an integrated equilibrium. More specifically, if these two conditions hold, the implications for the return on assets of banks in different countries are straightforward. If a bank earns rents in a market, the threat of a new entrant should drive down these rents toward the equilibrium value. If a bank underperforms in a market, a more efficient competitor should take this bank over, driving returns on assets up toward the equilibrium value.

We should emphasize that contestability and a functioning market for corporate control are necessary and sufficient conditions for financial integration to take place. For example, consider the hypothetical monopoly supplier that we argued earlier might satisfy the ECB definition of integration. If this monopolist were faced with a threat of takeover (possibly from outside the euro area) and the market was contestable, then the banking services would be provided efficiently at marginal cost. Profits would converge and we would identify the market as integrated. Conversely, if there was not any takeover pressure, or if the market could not be captured by a competitor, then prices might differ across locations and/or be priced above marginal cost. In this case, profits need not converge and we would judge the markets not to be integrated.

Likewise, the models predicated on the Salop and Stiglitz depiction of

---

3. We presume throughout the analysis that all banks can be meaningfully compared. Banks specialize so as to fill very different niches, then the Stigler reasoning breaks down since effectively the banks would not be competing. Hence, we do not control for risk or make any other adjustments to reflect differences in operating practices or strategies.

spatial competition also posit entry as an equilibrating mechanism. In that framework, banks choose where to locate by spreading out so that the profits are competed down to just cover entry costs. Given homogeneity of regulations across the euro area this would also lead to convergence in profits.

Empirically, we look for convergence in the return on assets (ROA) of banks by estimating variants of the classic partial adjustment equation.[4] Under rational expectations we can use realized ex post values as a proxy for expected returns (e.g., Cochrane 2001) and start with a specification of the form

(1) $$\Delta ROA_{it} = \eta + \lambda(ROA_t^* - ROA_{it-1}) + u_i + v_{it}.$$

In what follows, we consider several models of the long-run equilibrium profitability, ROA*. The actual estimating equation is the differenced form of (1):[5]

(2) $$\Delta ROA_{it} = \alpha + \lambda\Delta ROA_t^* - \beta\Delta ROA_{it-1} + w_{it}.$$

In principle, the coefficient on the lagged dependent variable, β, should equal $1 - \lambda$. But as emphasized by Caballero and Engel (2004), the ordinary least squares (OLS) estimate of β is biased toward zero if changes in profitability are lumpy. The intuition for this econometric problem is easiest to see under the extreme case when changes in ROA are always discrete and ROA* is a random walk. In this case, the OLS estimate of β can be deduced by considering four possible terms based on whether the ROA adjusted either at $t - 1$ or t. In three of these cases, there was no adjustment in either or both periods, so that the covariance between the change ROA at time t and $t - 1$ will necessarily be zero. The only time when a correlation is possible is when there is adjustment in consecutive periods. Because the $t - 1$ adjustment would optimally put ROA at its equilibrium value, there would be no way to predict whether the subsequent shocks would involve upward or downward adjustment. So, on average, these two changes will be uncorrelated as well.[6]

Our theory implies that the adjustment mechanism is likely to involve discrete entry and exit decisions, so we would expect the change in profitability to exhibit considerable kurtosis. We show later that this is indeed the case,

---

4. An alternative to using banks' profitability would be to check for convergence in banks' profit or cost efficiency. For a survey of this literature see Hughes and Mester (2008). Below we present results for one alternative measure of bank profitability (ROE).

5. This specification is derived by taking lags of both sides of the equation and taking the difference. The constant term would be zero but as explained in the next footnote, for certain specifications we consider samples where the mean adjustment is nonzero by construction. So we include the constant in all specifications to permit comparisons across specifications.

6. There may be a second problem with estimating equation (2) with OLS; the lagged dependent variable on the right-hand side may be correlated with the error term (Nickell 1981). We discuss some instrumental variables estimates that potentially attend to this concern following.

hence we will infer the adjustment speed from the change in the estimated target for profitability and make no attempt to impose a restriction linking the coefficients on ΔROA^* and the lagged dependent variable.

This reasoning suggests the following (strong) definition of convergence.

Strong definition of integration: The world banking market is integrated if there is a common ROA^* to which all banks converge.

There are many reasons (including regulatory) that banks in the United States and Europe might find it difficult to use the same business model in each location. If that is true then pressure from banks on the different continents driving convergence may be weak.

Hence, we also consider weaker definitions of integration. Our second definition requires that all banks in the European Union (EU) converge to the same equilibrium value of ROA. Hence:

Weak definition of integration: The EU banking market is integrated if there is a common ROA^* to which all EU banks converge.

To clarify the interpretation of the results for integration in the EU, we also study the behavior of U.S. banks. We do this because the U.S. banking market is generally considered to be integrated and (relatively) efficient (although we do test this presumption). Accordingly, we compare both the equilibrium value ROA and the estimated speed of convergence for both U.S. and European banks. We view the U.S. results as providing both a check of our procedure and a quantitative benchmark for the European estimates.

One useful feature of our framework is that it naturally suggests culprits that might be responsible if integration is absent. In particular, besides just estimating equation (2) for all banks, it is informative to check whether the underperforming banks raise their profitability or whether highly profitable banks see declines in profits.[7] If underperforming banks raise their profitability, we would interpret this as evidence in favor of a functioning market for corporate control, forcing them to improve their performance.[8] If highly profitable banks see their profits decline quickly, this would be evidence for contestability in banking markets, in which the threat of entry or actual entry quickly eliminates rents.

These possibilities suggest that it would be useful to conduct the tests controlling for differences in contestability or the effectiveness of corporate governance. This leads us to estimate ROA convergence separately for different

7. We allow the constant in equation (2) for precisely this reason. When estimated on a sample of banks whose ROA is either above or below ROA^* it would make no sense to omit the constant. So to permit comparisons in the full sample estimates, we also allow an intercept.

8. Given that we are estimating continuous, albeit lumpy, adjustment, we think of the main mechanism as the threat of takeover more than a potential takeover itself.

types of banks. Both contestability and the market for corporate control should be fully operational for listed banks, while the threat of a takeover may be considerably weaker for an unlisted bank. Hence, for unlisted banks we would expect much slower ROA convergence from below. We would expect adjustment due to contestability to be similar for unlisted and listed banks; if we find differences here, this would be strong evidence of lack of integration.

Finally, the tests will be conducted deflating profits by the book value of assets (rather than the market value). There are several reasons for this choice. The structure of the European banking sector is one of them. As we show later, the number of listed banks for which we could conceivably calculate market values is low in Europe. By limiting our analysis to these banks we would miss an important share of the European retail banking sector, especially in Germany, where both savings and cooperative banks are important. Indeed, the differences between listed and unlisted banks are themselves informative so that ignoring the nontraded banks would reduce the power of our tests. Moreover, as a practical matter, proper measurement of the market values of banks' assets would require market values of the loan portfolios of banks, which are unavailable. Lastly, the efficiency of stock market valuations would force rates of return measured at market prices to converge, irrespective of the degree of integration. The point of our procedure is to see operating performance (i.e., the cash flows produced by the banks for a given book value of assets) convergences, not whether the stock market functions properly. Hence, our measure is only informative about integration when the analysis is done using book values.

6.4   Data

We confine the study to banks in France, Germany, Italy, Spain, and the United Kingdom, and include U.S. banks as a benchmark. We start with all consolidated and unconsolidated balance sheet data for banks in these countries that are available in the Bankscope database. We first eliminate all banks that are part of the consolidated balance sheet of another bank. We track banks from 1994 to 2006. We also eliminate banks with zero or negative total assets, missing post-tax profits, total customer loans, total deposits, interest earnings, and operating expenses. We drop banks that had fewer than four observations and observations in the bottom or top 2 percent of the change in ROA.

The resulting distribution of bank/year observations is given in table 6.1. About two-thirds of the observations are from EU countries, with Germany accounting for 46 percent of the sample and the United States accounting for just under one-third.

Data on the type of banks are reported in table 6.2. Roughly 40 percent

Table 6.1   **Sample country composition**

Country	Number of banks	Percent
Germany (DE)	17,013	46.61
Spain (ES)	764	2.09
France (FR)	2,720	7.45
Italy (IT)	2,686	7.36
United Kingdom (UK)	1,378	3.78
United States (U.S.)	11,940	32.71
All	36,501	100.00

Table 6.2   **Sample bank type composition**

Bank type	Number of banks	Percent
Commercial bank	15,645	42.9
Savings bank	9,271	25.4
Cooperative bank	11,585	31.7
Total	36,501	100.00

Notes: Bank type is determined based on Bankscope variable "Specialisation (General)." "Commercial bank" include banks classified by Bankscope as bank holding companies, medium- and long-term credit banks, and mortgage banks.

of the sample consists of commercial banks or bank holding companies; below, we group these banks along with the handful of medium-and long-term credit banks and real estate banks into the "commercial bank" category. Of the commercial banks, 60 percent are U.S. institutions.

The banks not counted as commercial are savings or cooperative banks. The location of the savings and cooperative banks across countries is also very uneven. Almost all cooperative banks are either located in Germany (8,813 bank/year observations) and Italy (1,980) bank/year observations) and are extremely small. Savings banks are predominantly located in Germany (5,981 bank/year observations) and the United States (2,414 bank/year observations).

In table 6.3, we present sample statistics for the level and change of ROA. We compute return on assets as the ratio of post-tax profits divided by total assets. The mean return on assets is 0.62 percent, which is somewhat lower than the average value of ROA of 0.8 percent obtained in a very large cross-national sample in Demirguc-Kunt and Huizinga (1998). The distribution is skewed to the right with a median of 0.45 percent. As one would expect, the mean and the median of the first difference of ROA are zero or very close to zero. Importantly, the kurtosis of the change in ROA is 8.12, which suggests that the lumpiness concerns discussed by Caballero and Engel (2004) are quite relevant.

Table 6.3   **Descriptive statistics**

	Mean	Median	Standard deviation	Kurtosis	Number of observations
Return on assets	0.0062	0.0045	0.0058	6.89	36,501
Change in return on assets	0.00003	0	0.0027	8.12	36,501
Return on equity	0.084	0.072	0.059	4.19	36,501
Change in return on equity	−0.0005	−0.0006	0.049	21.18	36,501

Notes: Return on assets is Pre-Tax Profits (Bankscope variable I28) divided by Total Assets (Bankscope variable A61). Return on equity is Pre-Tax Profits (Bankscope variable I28) divided by Total Equity (Bankscope variable L42).

When estimating equation (2) we must construct an estimate of ROA*. The essence of the Caballero and Engel bias argument is that firm-specific proxies for the target level of profitability will still be plagued by the effects of infrequent adjustment.[9] Fortunately, aggregate variables can be used to construct a target measure and in our application, the mean rate of profitability is a natural candidate target. So we will consider various mean rates of profit as the equilibrium target.

Figure 6.3 shows the mean rate of returns for all banks in the sample. It is quite clear that there are substantial differences in profit rates across the counties in our sample. The U.S. profit rates are consistently higher than elsewhere and German rates are consistently lower, and until the last couple of years of the sample the gap between the two does not narrow. Given the different governance mechanisms and profit objectives across banks and the different percentages of bank types across countries, we do not view these differences as particularly informative.

Figure 6.4 breaks out the banks into categories that we find more meaningful. The upper panel shows the ROAs for the publicly traded banks; there are 699 banks, with three-quarters U.S.-based. These banks presumably have a strong profit motive and are potentially taken over if they are poor performers, so that both the necessary preconditions for our test hold for these institutions. The profit rate distribution, especially in the early part of the sample, is quite dispersed. As in figure 6.3, the U.S. banks show

9. Fama and French (2000) build a firm-specific target and use the dividend payout rate, a dummy for dividend paying firms and the ratio of the market value of equity to the book value of equity. Even if we were to ignore the lumpiness issues, these variables would not work well in our context. For example, we have many nonlisted firms so we cannot use the market-to-book ratio. We did not have complete data on dividend payments available either. Virtually all large listed banks pay dividends and for the unlisted ones the data are not available. It is not clear for the cooperative banks whether dividend payments should be thought of in the usual sense (because the banks can pass profits back to their members in other ways, such as through lower fees). Further, we are interested in whether banks converge to a common target, rather than a firm-specific target.

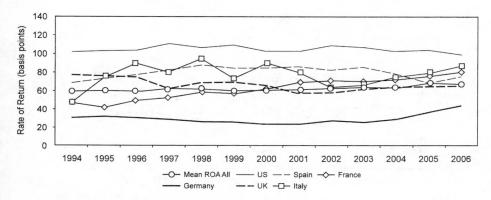

Fig. 6.3   Average ROA for all banks

persistently higher profits than the others. Given the high percentage of U.S. banks in the sample, this makes the mean rate for all the listed banks higher in every year than the average for each of the European countries. As a second point of reference, the heavy line in the figure shows the average for the European countries only. By the last few years of the sample the average profit rates narrowed. For example, in 1996 the range of average profit rates across countries was 91 basis points, and by 2006 the range had shrunk to 54 basis points.

The second panel shows commercial banks that are not publicly traded. These banks are supposed to maximize profits but if they are not doing so it may be costly to acquire control to correct any underperformance. Again, the U.S. banks are noticeably and consistently more profitable than their European counterparts. As a reference, we include the average profit rate for the listed European banks. While the mean for the listed banks is in the middle of the distribution from 2000 onwards, the distribution of profit rates (if anything) is widening slightly over the last six years. While in 1999 the difference in average profit rates of the unlisted European banks was 26 basis points, by the end of the sample the spread was 43 basis points.

The last panel shows the profit rates for savings and cooperative banks. A priori, these banks satisfy neither of our necessary conditions for profit convergence—there are so few of these banks in the United Kingdom that we omit their average from the picture. Recall that most of the banks in the sample are in Germany and the United States and through 2003 the movements in the profit rates in these countries appear to be completely disconnected, before converging somewhat in the last years of the sample. The ROA in the other three countries also narrowed substantially at the end of the sample, but the averages over the prior years were very different.

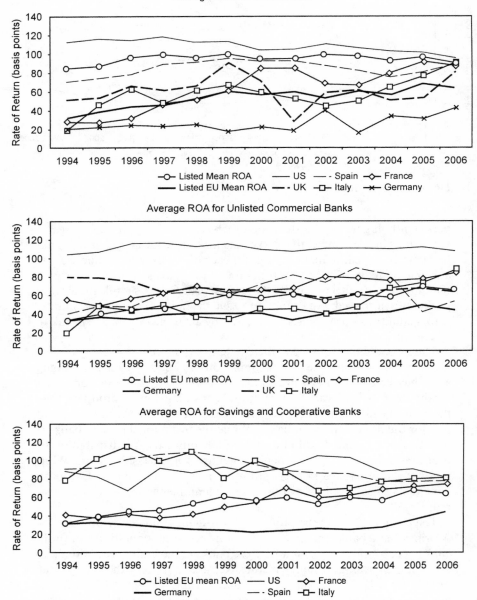

Fig. 6.4 Average ROA listed banks; average ROA for unlisted commercial banks; average ROA for savings and cooperative banks

6.5   Convergence Estimates

6.5.1   Baseline

We turn now to more formal econometric tests to assess convergence based on estimating equation (2) for the three groups of banks in figure 6.4. Because the preconditions involving contestability and corporate control most naturally hold for the listed banks, we begin by estimating the equation for them. The first column in table 6.4 shows that listed banks profit rates move toward the average for all banks in the sample, closing half the gap between their own level of profits and the target each year.[10] Fama and French, in their investigation of nonfinancial firms, estimated the speed of convergence (to a firm-specific mean) to be roughly 0.4. The lagged dependent variable has a significant negative coefficient, which based on the reasoning on Caballero and Engel is not surprising.[11] Consequently, in what follows we ignore the coefficient estimate on the lagged dependent variable and concentrate instead on the implied estimate for λ from the ROA* proxy.

Based on figure 6.4, we know that the average profit rate for the full sample is driven by developments in the United States. Moreover, figure 6.4 also tells us that the average in rate in each of the European countries lies below the sample average in each year. So based on these considerations there are good reasons to doubt the robustness of this initial specification. In the second specification in table 6.4, we drop the U.S. banks and reestimate the equation. This regression confirms the hunch that the European banks are not tracking the overall sample average profit rate. The estimated value for λ is negative and insignificant from zero. Hence, the apparent convergence from the first specification is entirely due to the U.S. banks and there is no evidence that European banks are mirroring their U.S. counterparts. Therefore, the strongest version of integration fails.

The next two specifications in table 6.4 explore weaker tests of convergence, asking whether the U.S. banks' profits move with the average in the United States and whether the European rates move with the European average. Both of these tendencies are present. The U.S. banks' convergence is, if anything, implausibly high, with λ estimated to be 0.85. Taken literally, this implies that virtually all profit differences are eliminated within one year. We suspect that some of this comes from the fact that our sample includes

10. The standard errors are clustered at the bank level throughout our analysis. If instead we cluster by date the standard errors for U.S. samples fall and those for the EU samples tend to rise somewhat.

11. The intuition is as follows. If the adjustment involves discrete actions and the ROA* has a trend, then the periods of inaction will cause the typical change in the actual ROA to be less than the trend. Consequently, the longer the period in between the adjustments, the larger will be the observed action to catch up. Without making specific assumptions on the stochastic process for the trend we cannot calculate the magnitude of this bias.

Table 6.4 ROA convergence

Region	Listed banks				Unlisted commercial banks		Savings banks and coops	
	Overall listed mean	Overall listed mean	U.S. listed mean	EU listed mean	U.S. listed mean	EU listed mean	U.S. listed mean	EU listed mean
Proxy for ROA*	All countries	All countries without U.S.	U.S.	EU	U.S.	EU	U.S.	EU
ΔROA*	0.533***	-0.14	0.849***	0.326**	0.431***	-0.014	1.147***	-0.064**
	(0.075)	(0.166)	(0.102)	(0.134)	(0.101)	(0.082)	(0.136)	(0.030)
ΔROA$_{t-1}$	-0.245***	-0.245***	-0.242***	-0.241***	-0.189***	-0.158***	-0.15***	-0.304***
	(0.019)	(0.049)	(0.196)	(0.048)	(0.2)	(0.022)	(0.026)	(0.011)
Constant	0.00004	0.0004***	0.00009***	0.0003***	0.0001***	0.00006	0.00006	0.000
	(0.00003)	(0.00006)	(0.00003)	(0.00007)	(0.00004)	(0.00005)	(0.00006)	(0.00001)
R^2	0.0706	0.0658	0.0813	0.0697	0.0404	0.0246	0.0544	0.0848
N	5,362	1,198	4,166	1,199	5,377	5,237	2,397	18,125
Number of banks	699	164	535	164	666	721	287	2,184

Notes: Ordinary least squares estimates of equation (2) in the text. Standard errors adjusted for clustering at the bank level in parentheses. Sample is taken from Bankscope as described in the text. The dependent variable is ΔROA$_t$ of bank i. ΔROA$_{t-1}$ is the dependent variable lagged by one period; ΔROA* represents the first difference of the mean of ROA of the regional subsample for different groups of banks as indicated in the table. Bank types (listed, unlisted commercial banks, savings banks, and cooperative banks) are classified using Bankscope variable Specialisation (General).

***Significant at the 1 percent level.

**Significant at the 5 percent level.

*Significant at the 10 percent level.

a period of substantial consolidation in the U.S. banking market, when the largest listed banks took over many of the middle-sized banks that had been prominent prior to the possibility nationwide branching—see Jones and Critchfield (2005) for a survey of overall consolidation trends in the United States.

For the European publicly traded banks, we find significant convergence toward the mean rate for Europe. The estimated value of λ, 0.33, is plausible and significantly lower than the U.S. estimate.[12] Thus, European listed banks do appear to be operating in an integrated market.

Nonlisted banks have prominent market shares in both the United States and Europe. In this sample, the percentage of European bank assets residing in listed banks is 53 percent, while the analogous percentage in the United States is 47 percent in 2006. Therefore, the finding of convergence for listed banks in the EU and United States is not a sufficient statistic for the overall state of market integration. So we next ask whether the nontraded banks are also moving toward the average profit rates for the listed banks.

For the United States the answer is yes. The nonlisted commercial banks show a significant propensity to move toward the average rate of profit for their listed competitors. The estimate for λ is .431, which is significantly below the rate for listed banks. A lower speed of convergence for unlisted banks is not surprising. We expect that in markets where high profits are being earned, competition among unlisted banks and from listed banks would compete down any rents. But, in cases where an unlisted bank is underperforming, taking it over may be much more costly than taking over a poor performing listed bank. This second consideration would lead to a lower average speed of convergence. We explore this conjecture in the next section.[13]

The European results for unlisted banks are strikingly different from the United States. The estimate of λ for unlisted commercial banks is –0.014 and insignificantly different from zero. The corresponding coefficient for savings and cooperative banks is –0.06 and significant at the 5 percent level. Hence, there is no indication that the profit rates of unlisted banks in Europe are tied to profit patterns for listed banks. Hence, even our weak definition of integration fails for unlisted and noncommercial banks in the EU.

---

12. Not surprisingly, the U.S.-listed banks are not converging to the average profit rate of the European banks, nor are the European banks moving toward the average profit rate for the U.S. banks.

13. For completeness, the table also includes information on savings and cooperative banks. Remarkably the profits of savings banks in the United States also tend to converge to the rates of listed banks. The coefficient for λ is 1.15. We find this result surprising and puzzling for at least two reasons. One is that there is abundant evidence that savings banks have a fundamentally different business model than commercial banks, especially large commercial banks (Critchfield et al. 2004). The conventional view is that in the U.S. community banks hardly compete with large commercial banks. Moreover, it is often very difficult to take over community banks. Hence, it is not clear what mechanism would force convergence for these banks.

6.5.2   Further Tests

We next explore whether the mechanisms suggested by our theory appear operative. In particular, we ask whether banks whose profits are above ROA* fall (due to competition) and whether banks with below target profits improve (due to a threat of a takeover). We view these predictions as asymmetric because competition should always be a force to dissipate rents, but taking over or restructuring an underperforming bank is costly. So if corporate governance changes are associated with a high fixed cost, they may be difficult to implement. This is true even for listed banks, as many of the gains of a takeover frequently accrue to the shareholders of the existing firm (e.g., Shleifer and Vishny 1988). Furthermore, cooperative banks may not even have a profit maximization motive, so if they were recording low profits they might have little incentive and no outside pressure to improve. Accordingly, in these tests we study only commercial banks (listed and unlisted) where there is no ambiguity about the management objectives.[14]

We refine the basic predictions about the effects of contestability and corporate governance in two ways. First, we expect all commercial banks (listed or not) to be subject to competitive pressure. Thus, we expect abnormal profits to be competed away for all commercial banks. Second, we expect an asymmetry in the effect of corporate governance, with listed banks being easier to restructure than unlisted banks.

The first two specifications in table 6.5 show the estimates of λ for listed U.S. banks that are below and above ROA*. In both cases, λ is significantly positive, although the estimate for the underperforming banks is implausibly large. The estimates suggest that competitive forces and corporate governance are both operating for these banks.

The next two columns show the analogous estimates for the EU-listed banks. Both the estimates are close to 0.3, and thus effectively the same as the estimate from table 6.4 where the speed of adjustment was restricted to be the same in both directions. The standard errors are now much larger, so we cannot be confident that the estimates are different from zero. Hence, the evidence for contestability and the market for corporate control operating with respect to the EU mean is relatively weak. One potential explanation is that this is a sample size problem: we have data for only about 100 listed banks (and 600 observations) in the EU, as opposed to more than 400 banks (and more than 2,000 observations) in the United States. This accurately reflects the limited number of listed banks in the EU, so there is nothing that we can do about this shortage of data.[15]

---

14. We are ignoring agency problems and corporate governance issues here.

15. It is important to distinguish between the number of listed banks and their market share. In the United States there are hundreds of listed banks. In some European countries, most notably Spain and the United Kingdom, there are a relatively small number of listed banks operating, but their market share exceeds the market share of listed banks in the United

The next pair of estimates shows the results for unlisted U.S. commercial banks. The underperforming banks do not seem to raise their profits. Hence, the pressure on poorly performing unlisted banks to improve performance through the market for corporate control is weaker for unlisted than for listed commercial banks. In contrast, high profit unlisted banks do tend to see their rents competed down (and the estimate is significant at the 1 percent level). This pattern is consistent with the view that competitive forces are operative for these banks even if there are impediments to a functioning market for corporate control.

The final estimates in the table show the results for unlisted EU commercial banks. The estimate for the underperforming banks is insignificantly different from zero, suggesting that they face no pressure to raise profits. The point estimate for the relatively high profit banks is negative (i.e., they tend to move away from the equilibrium value) but insignificantly different from zero, implying that competition pressure is also absent. The failure of underperforming banks to improve is not surprising, but the absence of competitive pressures among unlisted commercial banks is noteworthy. To explore this further we examined whether either finding was due to banks in one individual country. This does not appear to be the case, so we do not report the results; we obtain the same results as shown for the unlisted European banks when we reestimate the regressions omitting each country.

As a final assessment of the unlisted European banks, we reestimate equation (2) using the within-country mean ROA for unlisted commercial banks as ROA*. The results are reported in table 6.6. The first column shows that profits do converge to these country-specific targets profit rates. The estimate for λ is 0.258 and hence is close to the estimate for listed banks (from table 6.3). The next two columns show that both underperforming and high profit banks also converge, although the estimate for the high profit banks is only marginally significant.[16]

When we repeat this test for listed banks we find no convergence; that is, the profits of listed banks in each country do not converge to the average profits of the unlisted banks in that country.[17] Hence, there appears to be incomplete integration between listed banks on the one hand and unlisted banks on the other. Put differently, we do not find any proxy for target

---

States. This points to another potential reason for the weaker estimated convergence among European banks: if these mega-banks are so large that no domestic institutions can acquire them, then the only potential buyers might be outside the country. If so, the fixed costs involve in turning these banks around will be higher for the relevant suitors and the pressure to reform may be weaker.

16. If we repeat this exercise for the cooperative and savings banks in Europe, their ROAs also converge to the within-country mean ROA of cooperative and savings banks. As in the case of the U.S. savings and cooperative banks, the estimated coefficients for these regressions seem implausibly large.

17. To save space we do not show the results, but the point estimate for λ that is analogous to the specification shown in the first column of table 6.6 is 0.16 with a standard error of 0.345.

Table 6.5   Mean reversion for relatively high and low profit banks

	Listed banks				Unlisted commercial banks			
	U.S. listed mean	U.S. listed mean	EU listed mean	EU listed mean	U.S. listed mean	U.S. listed mean	EU listed mean	EU listed mean
Region	U.S. from below	U.S. from above	EU from below	EU from above	U.S. from below	U.S. from above	EU from below	EU from above
Proxy for ROA*								
Adjustment								
ΔROA*	0.922***	0.656***	0.317*	0.273	0.16	0.45***	0.101	−0.244
	(0.144)	(0.129)	(0.169)	(0.207)	(0.145)	(0.133)	(0.083)	(0.158)
ΔROA_{t-1}	−0.254***	−0.151***	−0.274***	−0.165**	−0.197***	−0.115***	−0.113***	−0.146***
	(0.028)	(0.034)	(0.067)	(0.067)	(0.028)	(0.029)	(0.030)	(0.030)
Constant	0.0005***	−0.0004***	0.0006***	−0.00005	0.0007***	−0.0004***	0.0005***	−0.0005***
	(0.00006)	(0.00005)	(0.0001)	(0.0001)	(0.00006)	(0.00006)	(0.00006)	(0.00009)
R^2	0.0901	0.0368	0.0842	0.0352	0.0437	0.0166	0.0127	0.0224
N	2,026	2,140	629	570	2,486	2,891	3,164	2,073
Number of banks	440	403	127	108	525	536	591	502

Notes: Ordinary least squares estimates of equation (2) in the text. Standard errors adjusted for clustering at the bank level in parentheses. Sample is taken from Bankscope as described in the text. The dependent variable is ΔROA_i of bank i; ΔROA_{t-1} is the dependent variable lagged by one period; ΔROA^* represents the first difference of the mean of ROA of the regional subsample for different groups of banks as indicated in the table. "Adjustment from below" and "Adjustment from above" refers to sample splits according to whether ROA of bank i was below or above the respective sample mean ROA* during period t. Bank types (listed or unlisted commercial) are classified using Bankscope variable Specialisation (General).

***Significant at the 1 percent level.

**Significant at the 5 percent level.

*Significant at the 10 percent level.

Table 6.6   **Country-specific mean reversion for unlisted European commercial banks**

	Unlisted commercial banks		
Proxy for ROA*	Country-specific unlisted mean	Country-specific unlisted mean	Country-specific unlisted mean
Region	EU	EU	EU
Adjustment		from above	from below
ΔROA*	0.258***	0.281*	0.184**
	(0.077)	(0.154)	(0.081)
ΔROA$_{t-1}$	–0.156***	–0.140***	–0.117***
	(0.022)	(0.03)	(0.031)
Constant	0.000	–0.0006***	0.0004***
	(0.000)	(0.00008)	(0.00005)
R^2	0.027	0.0217	0.016
N	5,237	2,001	3,236
Number of banks	721	494	603

Notes: Ordinary least squares estimates of equation (2) in the text. Standard errors adjusted for clustering at the bank level in parentheses. Sample is taken from Bankscope as described in the text. The dependent variable is ΔROA, of bank *i*; ΔROA$_{t-1}$ is the dependent variable lagged by one period; ΔROA* represents the first difference of the mean of ROA of the regional subsample for different groups of banks as indicated in the table; ΔROA* represents the first difference of the country-specific mean of ROA for unlisted banks as indicated in the table. "Adjustment from below" and "Adjustment from above" in columns (3) and (4) refers to sample splits according to whether ROA of bank *i* was below or above the respective sample mean ROA* during period *t*. Unlisted commercial banks are identified using Bankscope variable "Listed Institution" and "Specialisation (General)"
***Significant at the 1 percent level.
**Significant at the 5 percent level.
*Significant at the 10 percent level.

profitability that governed both the listed and unlisted European banks, even within countries.

The overall picture that emerges is one of limited bank integration throughout Europe and of incomplete bank integration even within countries in Europe. For the relatively few banks whose shares are publicly traded, profit rates do tend to move in tandem and converge to the EU average rate. But the vast majority of banks are not listed. These banks' profits do not tend to move in step with the listed banks and instead tend to converge only to a country-specific target.

It may be tempting to argue that these results are attributable to the very simple econometric specification that we have used. That the same specifications deliver a very different set of results in the United States suggests otherwise.[18] In the United States the listed banks' profits converge to the

18. We also doubt that the difference in the U.S. and EU results are attributable to other econometric problems. For instance, we know that the coefficient of the lagged dependent variable in regressions of the form as in equation (2) is biased. Phillips and Sul (2003) show that the

average level (although at a much faster rate than in Europe). Likewise, the high profit unlisted banks also see their profits competed away and they converge to the same profit rate as for listed banks. This suggests to us that there is nothing mechanical about our procedure that precludes finding integration in a market.

We use ROA as our baseline measure because given differences in taxes alluded to previously, bank leverage ratios could differ, and hence expected returns on equity could differ.[19] As a robustness check, however, we also reestimated the model using return on equity (ROE) rather than the ROA as our profit measure.

Table 6.7 shows the results for the most noteworthy specifications reported in tables 6.5 and 6.6 with ΔROE_t as the dependent variable and ROE* in place of ROA*. As before, we find convergence for listed banks in both the United States and the European Union and convergence of unlisted banks to the listed ROE* only in the United States. Unlisted banks in Europe do not show any convergence toward the equilibrium ROE. The difference to the results with ROA are mainly in the speed of adjustment of listed banks in the EU, which is now of comparable magnitude to that of listed banks in the United States. We also confirm the finding that underperforming listed banks adjust up and high profit listed banks adjust down in the United States and the EU. For unlisted banks, high profits are competed away in the United States, but underperforming unlisted banks continue to do so. Neither mechanism seems to be operable for unlisted banks in the EU. All of this is consistent with the results for ROA in tables 6.5 and 6.6.

6.5.3 The Role of the Euro

Unfortunately, because we are forced to rely on changes in ROA* to estimate the speed of convergence, our short sample does allow us to generate meaningful pre- and post-euro estimates. So quantifying any changes in the state of integration that have been associated with the introduction of the euro is not possible.[20] Nevertheless, the structure of our test suggests that competition policy and corporate governance reforms will be needed to promote more banking integration. Obviously the common currency does

---

bias that affects the lagged dependent variable can also lead to bias in the coefficient on other variables in the equation. Unfortunately their results suggest that the direction of the bias is a complicated function of several factors, which makes it difficult to determine even the sign of the bias. We reestimated equation (2) using the second lag of ΔROA as an instrument for the lagged dependent variable. This does alter the coefficient on the lagged dependent variable substantially, usually making it closer to zero, but the patterns of convergence across different groups of banks and across regions remain robust to this change in estimation procedure.

19. The ROA, in contrast, may be affected by the degree to which banks have off-balance sheet operations, while ROE would not.

20. The descriptive evidence (section 6.4) shows that mean profit rates of listed banks, and for savings and cooperative banks, converged somewhat across European countries since 2004. We cannot, however, exclude the possibility that the convergence is due to reasons unrelated to the regime shift in monetary policy.

Table 6.7   Robustness: Return on equity

	Listed banks		Unlisted commercial banks		Listed banks		Unlisted commercial banks		Listed banks		Unlisted commercial banks	
Proxy for ROE*	U.S. listed mean	EU listed mean	U.S. listed mean	EU listed mean	U.S. listed mean	U.S. listed mean	U.S. listed mean	U.S. listed mean	EU listed mean	EU listed mean	EU listed mean	EU listed mean
Region	U.S.	EU	U.S.	EU	U.S.	U.S.	U.S.	U.S.	EU	EU	EU	EU
Adjustment from					Below	Above	Below	Above	Below	Above	Below	Above
ΔROE*	0.775***	0.815***	0.353***	0.090	0.663***	0.706***	-0.097	0.534***	0.659***	0.655**	0.047	-0.026
	(0.099)	(0.174)	(0.127)	(0.096)	(0.126)	(0.122)	(0.170)	(0.163)	(0.221)	(0.260)	(0.097)	(0.210)
ΔROE$_{t-1}$	-0.357***	-0.423***	-0.304***	-0.389***	-0.408***	-0.215***	-0.317***	-0.188***	-0.330***	-0.414***	-0.331***	-0.306***
	(0.049)	(0.045)	(0.029)	(0.025)	(0.063)	(0.063)	(0.046)	(0.037)	(0.065)	(0.092)	(0.034)	(0.045)
Constant	0.0005	0.002	-0.0006	0.001	0.005	-0.006***	0.010***	-0.01***	0.015***	-0.014***	0.01***	-0.024***
	(0.0004)	(0.001)	(0.0005)	(0.0007)	(0.0008)	(0.0007)	(0.001)	(0.001)	(0.002)	(0.003)	(0.001)	(0.002)
R^2	0.13	0.17	0.09	0.12	0.15	0.06	0.09	0.03	0.12	0.15	0.09	0.07
N	4,166	1,199	5,377	5,237	2,013	2,153	2,357	3,020	706	493	3,677	1,560
Number of banks	535	164	666	721	445	410	512	555	139	113	663	440

Notes: Ordinary least squares estimates of a modified version of equation (2) in the text; the dependent variable is ΔROE, of bank i; ΔROE$_{t-1}$ is the dependent variable lagged by one period; ΔROE* represents the first difference of the mean of ROE of the regional subsample for different groups of banks as indicated in the table. Standard errors adjusted for clustering at the bank level in parentheses. Sample is taken from Bankscope as described in the text. Bank types (listed, unlisted commercial banks) are classified using Bankscope variable Specialisation (General).

***Significant at the 1 percent level.

**Significant at the 5 percent level.

*Significant at the 10 percent level.

not directly influence either of these factors, so any impact of the euro would be through an indirect channel.

Has the euro had an effect on the ease with which banks can enter markets across countries? At first glance, it is difficult to see how the euro could have had a first-order impact. Regulatory reform during the late 1980s and early 1990s—and in particular the 2nd Banking Directive of 1989—permitted (in theory) the establishment of subsidiaries and branches of any bank residing in the EU in any other EU country. Legally, it eliminated any impediments to cross-country banking and cross-country establishments of branches or subsidiaries within the EU.

What could explain the lack of cross-border contestability in this chapter? Entry can take place through takeovers, the establishment of branches and subsidiaries, or the initiation of direct cross-border operations. In regards to takeovers, Köhler (2009) presents evidence that impediments seem at least, to some extent, to relate to nationalist motives. Köhler shows that opaque merger control procedures significantly reduce the likelihood of foreign ownership of a bank, especially if this bank is large. Opaque procedures permit more discretion by the supervisor or other government authorities in blocking the acquisition of a domestic bank by a foreign bank. Prominent recent examples where authorities seem to have thwarted cross-border transactions include the failed takeovers of Banca Antonveneta and Banca Nazionale de Lavoro by foreign banks in Italy or the French reluctance to permit foreign bidders for Societe Generale.[21] Clearly, if national authorities are able to block cross-border mergers, this may also prevent the market for corporate control from operating efficiently.

In terms of direct cross-border retail business, the common currency may have been helpful. Exchange rate risk has been eliminated and rates and conditions may be easier to compare across countries. Retail flows remain small (ECB 2009), however, although there is a bit of evidence of an increase in cross-border retail activity in the vicinity of some borders (Fidrmuc and Hainz 2008). On balance, it seems that there are likely many factors that impede the contestability of retail banking markets in Europe.[22]

What about the market for corporate control? We already mentioned national objectives that may be an obstacle. There is considerable evidence that following the introduction of the euro money markets have become integrated (ECB 2009), which should have equalized the cost of funds across countries. Combined with the elimination of exchange rate volatility this should facilitate the comparability of rates of returns of banks in different countries. The under- or overperformance of a bank, therefore, can be more

21. See Köhler (2009) for more details on these and other similar episodes involving different countries in Europe.
22. It is plausible that cultural factors as in Guiso, Sapienza, and Zingales (2004) are important, in particular with respect to retail banking services. However, we are not aware of systematic evidence on this and other factors affecting cross-border entry of markets.

easily compared and evaluated. In addition, deeper equity and bond markets permit easier financing of large-scale transactions (ECB 2009). Hence, the euro may have improved the corporate governance of listed banks in the euro area. Martynova and Renneboog (2006) find that nonfinancial cross-border corporate takeovers did increase in the euro area more strongly than domestic takeovers since 1998. Ekkayokkaya, Holmes, and Paudyal (2009) present results that are consistent with increased cross-border competition among bidders for banks in the post-euro era. This is consistent with the rates of ROA convergence among EU-listed banks that we found.

The effect of increasing profit convergence on financial stability is ambiguous ex-ante. The usual trade-off between greater diversification of banks' portfolios (increasing financial stability) and the fact that the similarity of the portfolios may increase overall systemic risk seems to apply (Wagner 2009). The integration among listed banks in the EU that is suggested by our metric is consistent with the evidence in Gropp, Vesala, and L. Duca (2009), who present evidence that cross-border contagion within Europe may have increased among large listed banks.

However, unlisted commercial banks, savings, and cooperative banks constitute about 50 percent of total assets of the banking systems of the major European countries studied here and the retail market share may be even larger. The governance of these banks is not subject to the same mechanisms as the governance of listed banks. The evidence shows that they neither respond to competitive pressures as much as listed commercial banks, nor do these banks face pressure to remedy underperformance through a threat of takeover. These rigidities remain in place, and as far as we can see would be unaffected by the introduction of the common currency.[23]

6.6   Conclusion

This chapter argues that tests conducted in the previous literature for retail banking integration in the euro area may be misleading. The tests are neither necessary nor sufficient conditions for integration and tend to ignore efficiency and equilibrium concepts. We propose an alternative that tries to address these shortcomings and we argue that the convergence of the return on assets of banks may be a superior measure of banking integration in at least two dimensions. One, the return is an equilibrium concept in the sense that it reflects both price and quantity effects, as well as demand and supply aspects. Two, the test we propose also comes with natural diagnostics that help us interpret what might be responsible for a lack of integration.

Estimates from a partial adjustment model suggest that banking markets

---

23. Hartmann et al. (2006) show that the high share of these banks may have had an adverse effect on growth in the euro area, evidence that is consistent with the evidence presented in this chapter.

in the United States and Europe are very different. In the United States, listed and unlisted banks' profits converge toward the same target level of profitability. For both types of banks, if profitability is above average it tends to be pushed back toward ROA*. For unlisted U.S. banks, there is no evidence that underperforming banks are pushed toward an improvement in their performance by a threat of a takeover. Hence, for unlisted commercial banks integration fails even in the United States, due to poor corporate control.

In Europe, only the listed banks appear to be governed by a common ROA*. For unlisted banks, we observed substantial differences across European countries in the mean profitability (figure 6.4) and we find no evidence that unlisted commercial banks converge to a common equilibrium value. Perhaps somewhat surprisingly, we find evidence not only for impediments to a properly operating market for corporate control but also evidence for impediments to competition. For unlisted commercial banks in Europe, rents do not tend to get competed away. This suggests not only impediments to integration across borders among unlisted commercial banks in Europe but also lack of integration within individual countries between listed banks and unlisted banks.

Our approach also highlights the importance to shift attention to mechanisms that permit an effective functioning of the market for corporate control and bank entry in a cross-border dimension. The chapter shows that the large market share of unlisted, savings, and cooperative banks may be an important impediment to banking integration in Europe. Our estimates also suggest focusing more attention on understanding the differences between listed and unlisted banks, and more specifically, seeking to understand why the two groups are so much more different in Europe than in the United States.

References

Adam, K., Jappelli, A. Menchini, M. Padula, and M. Pagano. 2002. *Analyse, compare and apply alternative indicators and monitoring methodologies to measure the evolution of capital market integration in the EU*. Report, Economic Studies on the Internal Market. Brussels: European Commission.

Affinito, M., and F. Farabullini. 2009. Does the law of one price hold in euro-area retail banking? An empirical analysis of interest rate differentials across the monetary union. *International Journal of Central Banking* 5 (1): 5–37.

Baele, L., A. Ferrando, P. Hördahl, E. Krylova, and C. Monnet. 2004. Measuring financial integration in the euro area. European Central Bank (ECB) Occasional Paper no. 14.

Berk, J. and P. DeMarzo. 2007. *Corporate finance*. Boston, MA: Addison Wesley.

Caballero, R. J., and E. Engel. 2004. Adjustment is much slower than you think. Economic Growth Center, Yale University Working Paper no. 865, revised.

Cabral, I., F. Dierck, and J. Vesala. 2002. Banking integration in the euro area. ECB Occasional Paper no. 6.

Cochrane, J. H. 2001. *Asset pricing.* Princeton, NJ: Princeton University Press.

Critchfield, T., T. Davis, L. Davison, H. Gratton, G. Hanc, and K. Samolyk. 2004. Community banks: Their recent past, current performance, and future prospects. *FDIC Banking Review* 16 (3): 1–56.

Demirguc-Kunt, A., and H. Huizinga. 1998. Determinants of commercial bank interest margins and profitability. World Bank Policy Research Working Paper no. 1900, March.

Ekkayokkaya, M., P. Holmes, and K. Paudyal. 2009. The euro and the changing face of European banking: Evidence from mergers and acquisitions. *European Financial Management* 15 (2): 451–76.

European Central Bank (ECB). 2009. *Financial integration in Europe.* Report of the ECB. Frankfurt, Germany: European Central Bank, April.

Fama, E. F., and K. R. French. 2000. Forecasting profitability and earnings. *Journal of Business* 73 (2): 161–75.

Fidrmuc, J., and C. Hainz. 2008. Integrating with their feet: Cross border lending at the German-Austrian border. CESifo Working Paper no. 2279. Munich: Ifo Institute for Economic Research, April.

Gropp, R., J. Vesala, and M. Lo Duca. 2009. Cross-border bank contagion in Europe. *International Journal of Central Banking* 5 (1): 97–139.

Gual, J. 2004. The integration of EU banking markets. Center for Economic and Policy Research (CEPR) Working Paper no. 4212.

Guiso, L., P. Sapienza, and L. Zingales. 2004. Cultural biases in economic exchange. NBER Working Paper no. 11005. Cambridge, MA: National Bureau of Economic Research, December.

Hartmann, P., A. Ferrando, F. Fritzer, F. Heider, B. Lauro, and M. Lo Duca. 2006. The performance of the European financial system. Paper presented at the Conference, Financial Modernisation and Economic Growth in Europe. 28–29 September, Berlin.

Hughes, J., and L. Mester. 2008. Efficiency in banking: Theory, practice, and evidence. Federal Reserve Bank of Philadelphia Working Paper no. 08-1.

Jones, K. D., and T. Critchfield. 2005. Consolidation in the U.S. banking industry: Is the "long, strange trip" about to end? *FDIC Banking Review* 17 (4): 31–61.

Köhler, M. 2007. M&A control as barrier to EU Banking market integration. Centre for European Economic Research (ZEW). Unpublished Manuscript, August.

———. 2009. Transparency of regulation and cross-border bank mergers. *International Journal of Central Banking* 5 (1): 39–73.

Martynova, M., and L. Renneboog. 2006. Mergers and acquisitions in Europe. Tilburg University Finance Working Paper no. 114/2006, January.

Mintz, J. 2006. *The 2006 tax competitiveness report: A proposal for pro-growth tax reform.* C.D. Howe Institute. Available at: www.cdhowe.org/pdf/commentary_239 .pdf.

Nickell, S. 1981. Biases in dynamic models with fixed effects. *Econometrica* 49 (6): 1417–26.

Perez, D., V. Salas-Fumas, and J. Saurina. 2005. Banking integration in Europe. Bank of Spain Working Papers no. 0519.

Phillips, P., and D. Sul. 2003. Bias in dynamic panel estimation with fixed effects, incidental trends and cross section dependence. Cowles Foundation Discussion Paper no. 1438, September.

Salop, S., and J. E. Stiglitz. 1982. The theory of sales: A simple model of equilibrium price dispersion with identical agents. *American Economic Review* 72 (5): 1121–30.

Shleifer, A., and R. W. Vishny. 1988. Value maximisation and the acquisition process. *Journal of Economic Perspectives* 2 (1): 7–20.

Stigler, G. J. 1963. *Capital and rates of return in manufacturing industries.* Princeton, NJ: Princeton University Press.

Varian, H. 1985. Price discrimination and social welfare. *American Economic Review* 75 (4): 870–75.

Wagner, W. 2009. Diversification at financial institutions and systemic crises. *Journal of Financial Intermediation,* forthcoming.

Comment   Loretta J. Mester

Reint Gropp and Anil Kashyap provide a new measure for assessing the degree of integration of European banking markets—in particular, *retail* banking markets. The role of integration and the best way to assess the current state of integration is a particularly relevant question given the ten-year anniversary of the introduction of the euro in 1999 and the current turmoil taking place in financial markets in which banks play a central role. They have produced a thought-provoking chapter that advances the literature.

I will structure my remarks by first discussing the proposed measure in the chapter and then talking about integration more broadly.

Europe has been working toward integrating financial markets for some time. Dermine (2005) reviews some of the major legislative steps toward integration. These include the European Commission White Paper on the Completion of the Internal Market, published in 1985, which called for a single banking license; the Second Banking Directive, 1989, which allowed for cross-border bank branching; the Maastricht Treaty on European Union, 1992; the Directive on Deposit Guarantee Schemes adopted in 1994; the creation of a single currency, the euro, in 1999; and the Financial Services Action Plan of 1999, which laid out a number of initiatives to promote integration of banking and capital markets by 2005.

Before we can assess the benefits of the Gropp and Kashyap measure of integration over others in the literature, we need a definition of integration and a sense of what benefits integration is expected to provide to the economy. According to the European Central Bank (ECB), the aim of financial integration in Europe is to increase the efficiency of the financial system, increase the effectiveness of the monetary policy transmission mechanism,

Loretta J. Mester is Senior Vice President and Director of Research at the Federal Reserve Bank of Philadelphia and adjunct professor of Finance at the Wharton School, University of Pennsylvania.

The views expressed here are those of the author and do not necessarily represent the views of the Federal Reserve Bank of Philadelphia or of the Federal Reserve System. Prepared for the NBER Conference on Europe and the Euro, October 17–18, 2008, at Bocconi University, Milan, Italy.

increase financial stability, and increase economic development, to the extent that the financial system plays an important role in furthering economic development. Increased integration is expected to lead to increased competition, which leads to a lower cost of production and better allocation of savings toward investment.

Gropp and Kashyap (2009) start with the ECB's definition of financial integration. According to the ECB, a financial market is integrated if all potential market participants are subject to a single set of rules when dealing in the financial instrument or service, have equal access to the instrument or service, and are treated equally when operating in the market. The authors add to this definition the idea of efficiency, which is gained if markets are contestable and the market for corporate control is well-functioning.

In designing measures of integration it would be useful if the measures gave some indication of where integration failure has occurred and point policymakers toward actions to remedy impediments. Gropp and Kashyap provide some evidence on this. Much of the focus to date has been on integrating settlement and clearing systems. In my view, more emphasis should be focused on harmonizing regulatory structures. In particular, the recent events in banking markets suggest that retail markets are integrated enough for deposits to flow to markets with higher safety net protections. Harmonizing the supervisory and regulatory structures, deposit insurance systems, procedures for resolving banking failures, and procedures followed in the midst of financial crises would seem to be an important place to focus attention. This is consistent with the ECB's definition of operating with a single set of rules and being treated equally when operating in the market.

It would also be useful if the measures of integration could inform us about what we can expect from integration. Has financial integration been oversold? Are the gains to integration unbounded? Does integration create some costs that have to be weighed against the benefits of integration? Making cross-border transactions more efficient is a benefit, as more economic activity occurs across borders, but such efficiency also carries a cost in unstable times, especially if the regulatory structures across borders are not harmonized. Can we develop measures that relate integration to the *net* benefits?

The literature on integration has mainly focused on three other types of metrics: (a) cross-border retail operations of banks—flow measures; (b) cross-border bank mergers; and (c) retail interest rate convergence. The ECB has developed a number of metrics for assessing the degree of integration across several market segments of the financial system, including money, bond, equity, and banking markets. These metrics are available in the ECB's report on Financial Integration in Europe (the first report was published in March 2007 and the second in April 2008). The conclusion of the latest report is that the degree of integration varies across market segments. The money market is highly integrated, helped by integration of the high-value payment systems across countries and the recent introduction of the TAR-GET2 system for wholesales payments. Government and corporate bond markets, and even equity markets, have a considerable degree of integration, aided by the development of securities clearing and settlement systems. Wholesale banking markets have become more integrated; retail banking markets in Europe remain fragmented.

The ECB (2008) report provides indicators on retail banking in three categories: (a) cross-border presence indicators like dispersion in the number of bank branches and subsidiaries and volume of assets across euro area countries, and number and value of cross-border M&As; (b) price-based indicators like convergence of retail interest rates; and (c) quantity-based indicators like diversification of deposit and loan amounts across countries. According to the ECB report, from 2001 to 2007, the median share of banking assets of foreign subsidiaries increased from 8.8 percent to 14.4 percent of total banking assets, but the median share of assets of foreign branches decreased slightly over time to about 2.0 percent in 2007. Thus, most of the assets of the euro area banks in other euro area countries are still held in subsidiaries rather than in branches. The number of cross-border M&As has been less than the number of within-country M&As in the banking industry, but there has been an increase in euro area cross-border M&A transactions in terms of value since 2003. The dispersion of interest rates on loans to households for consumption purposes has remained relatively high and has tended to increase in recent years.

Gropp and Kashyap (2008) critique the interest rate metrics used in the literature, arguing that these are inappropriate measures because there is so much heterogeneity in demand in retail banking products across markets. Unless this heterogeneity is adequately controlled for, one should not expect the prices of retail products to be the same across markets. They argue that the law of one price does not hold because of this heterogeneity. But an alternative view is that if we adequately defined the product, the law of one price holds, but it holds for the individual products' characteristics (hedonic pricing), and so the convergence test is difficult to implement. Presumably the heterogeneity they are thinking about is fundamental—for example, differences in search costs, which mean that even within a single market we would not expect a single price—and not due to different regulatory conditions or rules across countries. If price differences are due to different rules under which financial systems operate across countries, we would not want to forgive such differences in assessing the degree of integration—that is, they would be an indicator of a lack of integration.

Instead of focusing on price, Gropp and Kashyap focus on bank profitability—they measure the degree of convergence of bank profit levels to the average profit level across countries. This is perhaps easier to implement, since it assumes banks choose their product characteristics appropriately to maximize profits. Their metric gets at the idea of efficiency, one of the goals of integration. In particular, they relate integration to level of entry and exit barriers; that is, to contestability. The logic of the Gropp and Kashyap measure is straightforward: With low barriers to entry and a well-functioning market for corporate control (which implies low barriers to exit), high-cost banks (and therefore low-profit banks) would be driven out of the market, and banks would not be able to exert any market power over pricing. Thus, bank profitability would converge across banks as integration increases. To the extent that there is profit dispersion, it means there are barriers to entry and/or exit—and hence, almost by definition, low levels of integration.

The authors look for convergence by estimating a partial adjustment equation of the form:

$$\Delta ROA_{it} = \alpha + \lambda ROA_t^* - \beta ROA_{it-1} + w_{it},$$

where ROA is the book value of return on assets and ROA* is long-run equilibrium profit. They define strong integration if there is a common ROA* to which the profit rates of all banks in the world converge and weak integration if there is a common ROA* to which the profit rates of all European Union banks converge. The equation is estimated for several different groups of banks separately: listed banks, unlisted banks, savings and cooperative banks, U.S. banks, EU banks, banks with ROA $>$ ROA*, and banks with ROA $<$ ROA*. These latter two groups can give us some information on whether competitive forces are at work—are returns to high-profit banks being competed away—and whether the market for corporate control is working—are inefficient banks being driven from the market? The ROA* is proxied by the average ROA for the group of banks investigated. Integration is measured by the coefficient λ. As λ approaches 1, adjustment is instantaneous; as λ decreases, adjustment is slower.

The authors find that there is high convergence in the United States, limited retail bank integration in Europe for listed banks but none for unlisted banks or savings and cooperative banks, competitive forces at work but not corporate control at work for unlisted U.S. banks, and neither competitive forces nor corporate control at work for unlisted European banks. (The authors obtain qualitatively similar results when they perform a robustness test using book-value return on equity as the measure of profitability.)

I think the authors' test, with its focus on profitability, is a good alternative to those in the literature, but it also has some implementation difficulties. In particular, I believe the definition of profitability used in the implementation has several drawbacks. First, it is a book-value measure of profits. They give two reasons for using book values. First, the number of listed banks for which market values are available in Europe is low. Second, they say that efficiency in stock market valuations would be misleading about integration. I do not understand that argument. Consider two banks that operate in markets that are not integrated for banking but do have integrated equity markets. If one bank were more efficient than the other, investors would bid up the stock market value of the efficient bank. That is, the market values would diverge even though the stock market is efficient. Presumably the stock market valuations would not converge if there were differences in the profitabilities of the banks regardless of the efficiency of the stock market. It seems preferable to use the measure most reflective of bank profits, and that would seem to be market value.

Another problem with the book-value measure is that it also ignores risk-taking. At its heart, banking is about handling risk, and the amount of risk to take on is a choice of bank management. Banks' comparative advantage follows from their unique capital structure—they obtain private information from deposit histories, which is useful in monitoring loan risk (Mester, Nakamura, and Renault 2007). Banks are able to pool deposits and loans to reduce liquidity risk and credit risk by diversification. Their capital structure, which includes demandable deposits, and its role in the payments system means banks are subject to regulation. Banks wanting to limit the costs of financial distress might limit risk-taking, while banks wanting to exploit the safety net might increase risk-taking. The risk choice is endogenous and risk-taking influences banks' production decisions, including the mix of assets they choose, asset quality, off-balance-sheet activities (some of which are used for hedging), capital structure, debt maturity, and resources allocated to risk management. All of these decisions affect cost and profitability (see Hughes, Mester, and Moon 2001; Hughes et al. 1999). If bank managers care about risk, they may trade off higher expected profit for lower risk when producing banking services, but they may also care about higher moments of the distribution of profits (e.g., profit volatility). Lower profit-lower risk production plans may result in higher value than higher profit-higher risk production plans—discounted present value depends on risk through the discount rate applied to profits and high risk might lead to financial distress, which imposes costs. Bank managers choose production plans that maximize their utility; these plans imply a subjective probability distribution of profits. Each production plan is linked to a subjective, conditional probability distribution of profit by the managers' beliefs about the probability distribution of future economic states and about how these states interact with production plans to generate profit. Given these beliefs, a bank's choice of production plan is equivalent to a choice of a conditional probability distribution of profit. If there are no agency problems, then bank managers choose the production plan that maximizes the market value of the firm.

It seems to me that to assess integration we need to account for risk-taking on the part of the banks. We would want to look at convergence in market values of banks for those that are traded and risk-adjusted profits for those that are unlisted. For example, if we saw two banks operating with the same level of profits, but one chose an ex-ante riskier portfolio than the other, would we want to conclude there was integration? These banks would be operating on very different points on the risk-expected return frontier. To the extent that we are interested in differences in efficiency across banks, we might think about using direct measures of profit and cost efficiency rather than profit levels. This might be preferable, since it might point us toward where failures of integration are coming from—is it the cost side or the revenue side?

Let me finish my remarks by discussing whether we are asking too much from integration. Europe has been working toward integration for a long time. Integration benefits can happen only if integration leads to increased competition in the financial services industry. From the metrics in the literature and in this chapter we can tell whether integration is increasing, but we do not get a sense of what is achievable—how far can integration go? There are some reasons to be cautious here. First, there is some debate in the literature about whether retail banking markets are contestable or not. Xavier Vives (1991) argues that retail banking markets may not meet the criteria for contestability because of barriers to entry, including branch networks and economies of scale and switching costs. It could be that one of the reasons integration has been slower in the retail banking markets than in other financial services segments is due to these higher barriers to entry.

Second, despite the lower barriers to entry across U.S. banking markets, there appear to be continuing differences in efficiency across banks. Thus, expectations of the gains from integration on the efficiency side may be exaggerated. Berger and Mester (1997) find that cost inefficiency averages about 13 percent and profit inefficiency averages 50 percent, suggesting large differences in efficiency across banks in the United States, and much of the differences are unexplained—twenty-five explanatory variables explain only about 7 percent of the variance of measured cost efficiency and about 35 percent of the variance in measured profit efficiency.

Third, while integration raises the number of potential competitors who can exert discipline, evidence from the bank merger literature raises the question of whether bank mergers are value-enhancing or driven by empire building. Corporate control problems in banking can exist because the relationship between bank owners (stockholders) and bank managers is a principal-agent relationship, and the ways of controlling the behavior of bank managers may not be totally effective. Hughes et al. (2003) find that asset acquisitions are associated with worse performance when banks have entrenched management but better performance when management is not entrenched.

Fourth, one of the mechanisms for achieving integration is the market for corporate control. But recent research shows that there are differences in the notion of a corporation's purpose across countries; for example, whether it is there for the shareholders or whether it is for all the stakeholders-shareholders, employees, bondholders, and customers (see Allen, Carletti, and Marquez 2007). These differences also mean there will be differences in corporate governance structures across countries, which may limit what is achievable by integrating banking product markets.

Finally, while integration offers potential efficiency gains, the interaction between financial integration and financial stability is not straightforward. More integration could increase financial stability via diversification of default risk, but it could also increase the possibilities for systemic risk and contagion. This potential cost needs to be recognized. Harmonizing the rules of engagement across markets would help limit this potential cost—and at the same time increase integration. The current financial crisis underscores the importance of participants facing the same rules across markets—one of the facets of the ECB definition of integration. But even though a great amount of progress has been made on harmonizing the regulatory structures across the countries of Europe, some differences remain. In particular, as we have seen, the actions taken in the midst of a crisis differ across the countries, especially when, ex-ante, there has not been a well-articulated process to follow. There can be conflicts of interest across regulatory bodies that have national interests. The financial crisis has illuminated the differences in the government safety net—deposit insurance and lender-of-last-resort functions—that remain across countries. In the United States, even with harmonized banking regulation, there are potential conflicts of interest across the multiple supervisory bodies (Office of the Comptroller of the Currency [OCC], Office of Thrift Supervision [OTS], Federal Reserve, Federal Deposit Insurance Corporation [FDIC]), and there is more separation between regulation of different segments of the financial services industry. In Europe there are differences in where responsibility for the bank supervisory activities lie—in the central bank or another body. This is probably not important in normal economic circumstances, but it might be during financial crises when the ability of the central bank to obtain information from the supervisory authorities in a timely manner becomes crucially important and the credibility the central bank has gained in monetary policy might be transferable to its handling of financial instability.

I want to thank the authors for their thought-provoking chapter. I do believe their proposed new metric is a contribution to the literature and has the potential to be easier to implement and more informative about integration. I would suggest trying to incorporate risk into the measure. Regarding the integration literature more broadly, I would recommend that it bring some focus to the potential costs of integration and ways to address those costs. This would help calibrate what we should expect to gain from further integration. Those further gains may come less from increased efficiency and more from reductions in systemic risk and increased coordination across countries when there is a crisis.

References

Allen, F., E. Carletti, and R. Marquez. 2007. Stakeholder capitalism, corporate governance, and firm value. Wharton Financial Institutions Center Working Paper no. 07-39, August.

Berger, A. N., and L. J. Mester. 1997. Inside the black box: What explains differences in the efficiencies of financial institutions? *Journal of Banking and Finance* 21 (July): 895–947.

Dermine, J. 2005. European bank integration: Don't put the cart before the horse. Institut Européen d'Administration des Affaires (INSEAD) Unpublished Manuscript, October.

European Central Bank (ECB). 2008. *Financial integration in Europe.* Report of the ECB. Frankfurt, Germany: European Central Bank, April.

Gropp, R., and A. K. Kashyap. 2009. A new metric for banking integration in Europe. NBER Working Paper no. 14735. Cambridge, MA: National Bureau of Economic Research, February.

Hughes, J. P., W. Lang, L. J. Mester, and C.-G. Moon. 1999. The dollars and sense of bank consolidation. *Journal of Banking and Finance* 23 (February): 291–324.

Hughes, J. P., W. Lang, L. J. Mester, C.-G. Moon, and M. Pagano. 2003. Do bankers sacrifice value to build empires? Managerial incentives, industry consolidation, and financial performance. *Journal of Banking and Finance* 27 (3): 417–47.

Hughes, J. P., L. J. Mester, and C.-G. Moon. 2001. Are scale economies in banking elusive or illusive? Evidence obtained by incorporating capital structure and risk-taking into models of bank production checking accounts and bank monitoring. *Journal of Banking and Finance* 25 (December): 2169–2208.

Mester, L. J., L. Nakamura, and M. Renault. 2007. Transactions accounts and loan monitoring. *Review of Financial Studies* 20 (May): 529–56.

Vives, X. 1991. Banking competition and European integration. In *European financial integration,* ed. C. Mayer and A. Giovannini, CEPR, 9–31. Cambridge: Cambridge University Press.

Why the European Securities
Market Is Not Fully Integrated

Alberto Giovannini

7.1 Introduction

Economists have often used the concept of integration to measure international efficiency. Integration is estimated with similar methods both in goods markets and in financial markets. The method typically adopted is that of sizing deviations from the law of one price: researchers identify identical assets and determine whether they are traded at the same price in different countries. In finance, this method is especially useful, since in financial markets certain assets can in some cases be replicated through appropriate combinations of other assets.[1] The study of deviations from the law of one price is a useful device to identify where distortions are, and is routinely carried out, also by official institutions. In the euro area, the European Central Bank (ECB) publishes reports on the integration of financial markets that apply these methods.[2]

However, the measure of deviations from the law of one price has limitations. First, it is often the case that identical assets cannot be found, and therefore the law of one price cannot apply. In these cases researchers resort to equilibrium pricing models, so that the hypothesis of integration gets to be merged with the hypothesis that the pricing model is correct. In addition, when the analysis becomes very detailed (in general-equilibrium analysis a good is defined not only by its nature but also by time and place) the test of

Alberto Giovannini is the chief executive officer of Unifortune Asset Management.

1. The classic case is interest rate parity: a Eurodeposit loan in a given currency can be replicated through a combination of spot and forward foreign exchange transactions and a Eurodeposit loan in another currency.

2. See European Central Bank (2007).

the law of one price loses power. Therefore, it is not appropriate to rely only on the law of one price to determine the degree of integration and efficiency of financial markets.

An alternative method to discuss integration, which is the starting point of this chapter, is to ask whether similar or identical assets are traded in different markets or in the same market, and what defines a financial marketplace. Consider the case of the European Union (EU) or, more narrowly, of the euro area, and consider securities for simplicity. Can we say that in the EU or the euro area securities markets are integrated? Macroeconomists would tend to believe that it should be the case, based upon two observations: first, throughout the EU there is freedom to trade securities among the different member states; and, second, in the narrower euro area there is no foreign exchange risk, so the comparison of different asset prices is straightforward and the last barrier to securities trade is gone. Yet, as I show in this chapter, the actual picture of European securities markets is very different. This discrepancy is due to the fact that the basic implicit tenet that allows to associate freedom of trade with perfect integration is full competition and absence of distortions: both conditions are not verified in practice.

This chapter explains what a single, fully integrated securities market is, and why we do not have it yet in Europe. I argue that any market, including a securities market, is defined by the arrangements put in place to ensure delivery of goods and of payments to the counterparties in each trade (posttrading arrangements). An analysis of these arrangements is the most reliable way to obtain an accurate assessment of the extent to which there is integration in a geographic area like the EU or the euro area. In the chapter I analyze posttrading arrangements in the EU and discuss their reform, whose objective is to obtain a single EU securities market.

In section 7.2, I describe the two pillars of posttrading, clearing and settlement, and the actors that perform these functions. In section 7.3 I explain where the current status quo in European securities markets comes from. Section 7.4 takes up the question of financial reform: is there a case for intervention in securities markets to induce integration? In section 7.5 I describe the reform strategy that is under way in the EU, and its accomplishments so far, which are rather disappointing. In section 7.6 I analyze the political economy of this financial reform, to provide an explanation of the slow pace of reform. Section 7.7 contains a few concluding remarks.

7.2   What Are Clearing and Settlement?

It is now commonplace to use the word "plumbing" when referring to clearing and settlement. Indeed, clearing and settlement are plumbing in more than one way. First, they are the little-visible infrastructures that make certain the receipt of securities by the buyer and the receipt of the cash (or other means of payment) by the seller. Following, I will present a more detailed description of what is needed to ensure these simple things to take place. These infrastructures, like plumbing, permit the working of financial markets. Clearing and settlement are plumbing also in the sense that the little glamorous community of professionals involved in these activities is, to say the least, not very visible, either in the financial press or in the public discourse. The little visibility is in part explained by the very dry, technical nature of the work they carry out. Yet it is not justified by the importance of the infrastructure. The volume of economic transactions handled by clearing and settlements providers is mind-boggling: in 2006, the Depository Trust & Clearing Corporation (DTCC) settled more than $1.5 quadrillion (1 quadrillion equal 1,000 trillion; i.e., 1 million billions) of securities transactions,[3] while Euroclear's turnover in the same year was "a mere" €450 trillion.[4] A failure of the clearing and settlement system can have major economic impact. Some of the most important financial crises in recent decades have been accompanied or caused by clearing and settlement problems: the Herstatt crisis and the 1987 U.S. stock market collapse are the best-known examples. For these reasons, whenever financial turmoil is in the horizon, authorities, who are well aware of the importance of clearing and settlement, immediately take initiatives to ensure that clearing and settlement can continue sufficiently smoothly: this was especially evident in the eve of the year 2000, as well as when financial markets were disrupted in the wake of the September 11, 2001 attacks on New York City.

To effect a securities transaction the following steps need to be taken (figure 7.1 reports a more detailed but identical functional analysis):

- Verification of the transaction or settlement details: an essential prestep of clearing.
- Clearing: the establishment of the credits and debits, of securities and amounts due, which can be done in a bilateral (counterparty clearing), or multilateral (central counterparty clearing) way. Different clearing arrangements can produce different settlement flows. For example, a counterparty clearing arrangement may compute the net payments due as a result of the sum of the transactions between two counterparties over a prespecified period. In a central counterparty clearing system, the central counterparty becomes the other side of all bilateral transaction, thus netting all flows in its books. Notice that in central counterparty clearing the central counterparty needs to assess and control the risk it takes from all counterparties (to maintain the integrity of the netting process in its books).
- Settlement: it is the delivery of the securities and the payment of funds between the buyer and seller. This involves securities depositories (Central Securities Depositories [CSDs] or International Central Securities

---

3. See http://www.dtcc.com/about/business/index.php, May 2008.
4. Norman (2007).

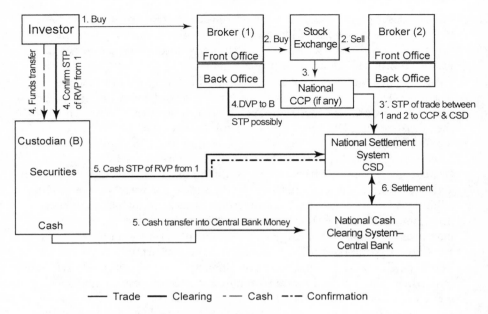

Fig. 7.1   Flows and costs in a domestic transaction
Source: The Giovannini Group (2001).

Depositories [ICSDs]), which, among other functions, hold the securities and carry out the notary function, ensuring that all securities paid equal securities received, so that the integrity of the outstanding stock is preserved. The payment of funds is typically effected via a banking/payments system.

A number of observations are useful at this point.

1. Clearing and settlement need to work well together, since errors in clearing produce errors in settlement. Yet they are separable functions. More importantly, the volume, and therefore the risk, of actual settlement operations are determined by clearing: a clearing process that produces extensive netting of bilateral transactions results in a minimum of settlement instructions.

2. It is evident that the functions I just described are the core of a market. Indeed, I argue that these functions actually *define* a marketplace, since they define the confines and the mechanics of transactions: a market is defined by the arrangements to get the goods and the money delivered—that is, the posttrading arrangements—not by trading arrangements. This point is confirmed by the fact that, if economic actors are free to do so, they often come up with different trading venues, which fulfill different functions (e.g.,

by selecting different points in the liquidity/transparency frontier). This is not the case of clearing and settlement: multiple clearers may exist, but only because they are bundled to other services (typically, trading: see the U.S. experience with derivatives exchanges, for example).

3. The most important fact about the production of clearing and settlement services is that their only inputs are information, as well as the use of computing and communication services. Unlike many other processes in finance, there is no human input in the actual process of posttrading: no decisions to be taken, no judgment of risk and expected returns, no analysis. All of these valuable inputs stay out of clearing and settlement per se, but are of course essential in the design of clearing and settlement systems. Thus, I conclude that these processes are as close to zero marginal cost production functions as you can get in finance. On the other hand, there are huge technical difficulties and considerable risks to be assessed in the design (and setup) of a clearing and settlement system.

4. There are several important functions that are contiguous to clearing and settlement. Here I list just some examples:

- Custody, the actual holding of securities, is the closest function to settlement; indeed, settlement is carried out by custodians.
- Securities lending is a way to oil the settlement process. A custodian, or an entity in charge of settlement, knows who is long a given security and who is short; it can then match the longs and shorts through securities loans, thus minimizing the disruptions to the settlement process that arise from fails. In addition, securities lending for purposes other than the smooth working of the settlement process requires access to a settlement system; intermediaries in the securities lending market can use information on the settlement process to improve their brokerage services.
- All the typical global custodian (or prime brokerage) services, including securities valuation, securities lending (for the purpose of establishing short positions), and cash lending.
- Other services (often carried out by global custodians) associated with corporate actions (dividend payments, annual general meeting [AGM] voting and securities registration, share capital increases, etc.).
- Last, but not least, trading. For example, a stock exchange that offers posttrading services can provide so-called straight-through processing, which facilitates and simplifies stock trading for its customers.

It is apparent that the contiguity of various financial services to the core clearing and settlement functions gives rise to economies of scope. These in turn create incentives for a relatively wide spectrum of actors to compete for the clearing and settlement market. This last point is examined in more detail, with reference to the experience in Europe, in the next section.

7.3   Evolution of the Posttrading Market in Europe

The entities providing trading and posttrading services had been traditionally structured as mutual companies—that is, customer-controlled firms—or government-owned entities. Di Noia (2000), following Hansman (1996), claims that the mutual nature of financial infrastructure companies came from the monopolistic nature of the business. If a firm is a monopolist, to be user-owned minimizes distortions. Similarly, a monopoly owned by the state will charge prices in accordance to the objectives of the state. Often, the monopoly status of the firms was sanctioned by law, both in the case of trading (concentration rules) and posttrading (see the Giovannini Group 2001). Financial infrastructure firms in each country were also managed with a keen eye to the efficiency of the country's financial marketplace: in a number of European countries there have been committees, often called "financial marketplace" whose aim was to coordinate regulators, users, and providers of infrastructure services in the interest of the market as a whole. It is not surprising that such committees could easily transform into defenders against foreign competition when trading in financial assets became liberalized among European countries. This point is discussed in greater detail following.

National financial markets in Europe were largely isolated and national infrastructures were designed to cater exclusively to domestic users. This led to the birth of entities whose sole function was to provide services to international investors. Capital controls in the United States and Europe led to the development of the so-called Eurobond market, where bonds denominated in currencies other than that of the issuer, namely the U.S. dollar, were sold mainly to international investors (i.e., investors with international securities accounts). In 1968 Morgan Guaranty set up Euroclear in Brussels. Euroclear started to settle transactions in Eurobonds without physical delivery of the bonds: the bonds were kept in the same physical place, and transactions simply led to book entries reassigning the bonds to the new owners. This was the first international central securities depository (ICSD). Shortly afterwards, Cedel was founded in Luxembourg by seventy-one banks from eleven countries, with the same mission as Euroclear.[5]

The coexistence of national infrastructures with a growing international infrastructure has characterized European financial markets in the following years. However, this coexistence progressively became competition as a result of two major phenomena: the liberalization of international financial transactions—a by-product of the creation of the Single European Market—and the introduction of the euro, which eliminated an important barrier across the different European financial markets (namely, exchange risk).

---

5. See Norman (2007) for the best description of the history of posttrading in Europe.

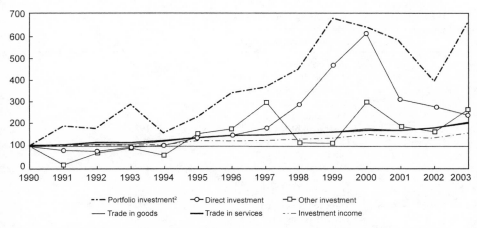

Fig. 7.2   Trends in international trade and investment components, OECD, 1990 = 100, current prices
Source: Bertrand (2006).

The events in Europe were a kind of enhanced version of global developments in financial markets. Since the beginning of the 1990s international portfolio investment has boomed: see, for example, the data for the Organization for Economic Cooperation and Development (OECD) reported in figure 7.2. As a result, infrastructure providers have felt keener competitive pressures from abroad, and have started to react to them. A very noticeable manifestation of this reaction has been a wave of demutualizations or privatizations of the exchanges, often in tandem with privatizations of the posttrading platforms. Table 7.1 reports a list of exchanges that abandoned the mutual governance structure, with the respective dates. There are a few reasons for this: the first, mentioned by Aggarwal (2002), is the increased competition among stock exchanges, requiring faster and more efficient decision making (it is claimed that a mutual company has a more cumbersome decision process than a common stock company). In particular, the decision process leading to alliances may be facilitated in a common stock setting as opposed to a mutual setting. In addition, the presence of potential conflicts of interest between the stock exchanges and their users (intermediaries) may call for a more diverse ownership structure, and more autonomous management.[6] Finally, a common stock structure may make it easier to raise capital, because it allows reaching out to a much wider universe of potential investors.

Stock exchanges claim that demutualization has led to higher profits

6. Yet, as is the case of Italy, the privatization of the stock exchange, the central securities depository, and the central counterparty resulted in intermediaries holding shares of the privatized companies, some sort of hybrid or artificial mutual structure, thus actually creating a setting vulnerable to the potential conflicts mentioned previously.

Table 7.1   **Exchange demutualizations**

Demutualized exchanges	Year
Stockholm Stock Exchange	1993
Helsinki Stock Exchange	1995
Copenhagen Stock Exchange	1996
Amsterdam Stock Exchange	1997
Borsa Italiana	1997
Australian Stock Exchange	1998
Iceland Stock Exchange	1999
Simex	1999
Athens Stock Exchange	1999
Stock Exchange of Singapore	2000
Hong Kong Stock Exchange	2000
Toronto Stock Exchange	2000
London Stock Exchange	2000
Deutsche Borse	2000
Euronext	2000
The Nasdaq Stock Market	2000
Chicago Mercantile Exchange	2000

Source: Aggarwal (2002).

(hence greater efficiency). Verifying this claim is beyond the scope of this chapter. However, I note that in connection with the wave of demutualization there has been an a dramatic increase in trading volumes, which in good part is due to factors other than the marketing efforts of the exchanges. Table 7.2 reports turnover data for a list of European exchanges. The 60 percent increase in trading revenues between 2000 and 2007 is remarkable, considering that the seven-year period starts—in the year 2000—at the peak of the equities bubble, a time when equity transactions were commensurably high.

In Europe, the twin revolutions, liberalization and monetary union, had the simple effect to increase the demand for cross-country transactions within the euro area. More importantly, together with an increase in actual demand for cross-border transactions, there was a universal feeling that cross-border business would skyrocket. Therefore, liberalization and monetary union made the existing infrastructure for financial markets obsolete, as I will explain more in detail in the next section.

7.4   Financial Market Reform: The Case of Europe's Clearing and Settlement

Figure 7.3 reports the graphic analysis of a cross-border transaction. The figure illustrates that the same functions can be, and are, carried out by different actors, a point already mentioned earlier. In particular, international settlement can be carried out through an ICSD or through an agent

Table 7.2   **Turnover at European exchanges**

Exchange	2000 Total turnover (€)	Exchange	2007 Total turnover (€)
Athens Exchange	117,166	Athens Exchange	122,364
Borsa Italiana	1,013,633	Borsa Italiana	1,680,200
Budapest Stock Exchange	13,091	Budapest Stock Exchange	34,610
Cyprus Stock Exchange	10,919	Cyprus Stock Exchange	4,193
Deutsche Börse	2,296,156	Deutsche Börse	3,144,150
Euronext	2,533,295	Euronext	4,086,811
Irish Stock Exchange	15,734	Irish Stock Exchange	99,550
Ljubljana Stock Exchange	707	Ljubljana Stock Exchange	3,439
London Stock Exchange	4,943,465	London Stock Exchange	7,544,970
Luxembourg Stock Exchange	1,822	Luxembourg Stock Exchange	176
Malta Stock Exchange	200	Malta Stock Exchange	65
OMX Nordic Exchange Copenhagen	101,216	OMX Nordic Exchange	1,321,807
OMX Nordic Exchange Stockholm	526,244	Oslo Børs	399,054
Oslo Børs	75,159	Prague Stock Exchange	36,581
Spanish Exchanges (BME) Madrid	660,785	Spanish Exchanges (BME)	2,160,321
SWX Swiss Exchange	692,258	SWX Swiss Exchange	126,748
Warsaw Stock Exchange	21,054	Warsaw Stock Exchange	63,876
Wiener Börse	10,497	Wiener Börse	94,489
Total	13,033,399	Total	20,923,404

Source: Federation of European Stock Exchanges (FESE): http://www.fese.be/en/?inc=art&id=4.

bank, or via the services of a global custodian or, finally, through a link between the domestic and foreign central securities deposit (CSD). As a result, all of these institutions are currently competing for the same cross-border business in Europe.

What is the attraction of the cross-border business? Not only, as I argued previously, is cross-border business expected to be the growth segment in the EU market, but also the unit revenues from servicing cross-border securities transactions are orders of magnitude higher than those for the equivalent domestic transactions. This result is documented in various studies. The studies mostly resort to unit revenues because prices for posttrading services have the following two features: (a) they are not publicly available information, and (b) they are widely different across users (typically users with more market power get discounts).[7] The Giovannini Report (2001) illustrates data studied by the Center for European Policy Studies (CEPS), which compares unit revenues of ICSDs with unit revenues of domestic CSDs, after adjusting for netting. This method is based on the hypothesis that ICSDs business is mainly cross-border (the income statements used for the comparison are from 2000). Table 7.3 reports the results of this experiment. They are strik-

7. The disparity of prices across users is puzzling given the standardized nature of these services, which are mostly carried out by computers.

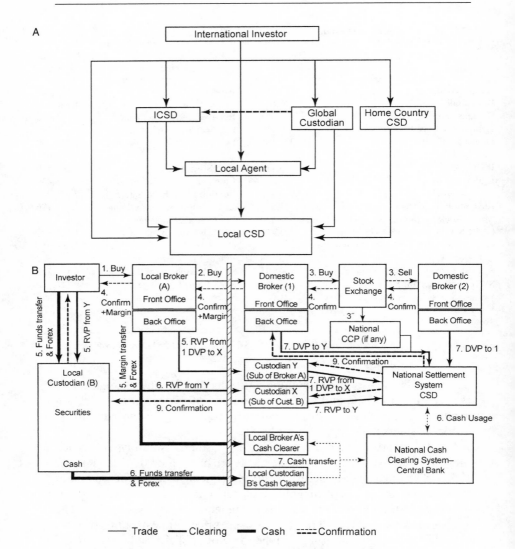

Fig. 7.3   *A,* **A nondomestic transaction;** *B,* **Instruction flows in a cross-border transaction**

Source: The Giovannini Group (2001).

ing: the unit revenue from cross-border transactions is more than ten times the same from domestic transactions. This result, published in 2001, was never seriously disputed by any researcher or service provider in the post-trading industry.

Another authoritative study, by NERA (2004), compares posttrading costs actually using pricing schedules supplied by service providers. The

Table 7.3   Operating income per transactions in selected CSDs (figures in euro)

	Organization	Operating income (€)	Transactions (prenetting)	OPINC/ Transaction (€)	Transactions (postnetting)	OPINC/ transaction
ICSD	Euroclear Bank	360,590,000	11,000,000	32.78	11,000,000	32.78
ICSD	Clearstream Luxembourg	401,175,000	12,000,000	33.43	12,000,000	33.43
DK	VP	27,122,013	6,800,000	3.99	6,800,000	3.99
DE	Clearstream Frankfurt	268,745,000	125,000,000	2.15	125,000,000	2.15
ES	SCLV	45,758,000	11,000,000	4.16	11,000,000	4.16
GR	CSD	47,805,161	21,973,933	2.18	21,973,933	2.18
FR	Euroclear France	144,968,647	135,000,000	1.07	41,000,000	6.60
FR	Clearnet France	125,448,000				
IT	Monte Titoli	22,175,332	126,395,972	0.18	8,783,635	2.52
PT	Interbolsa	14,205,395	8,654,761	1.64	8,654,761	1.64
SE	VPC[b]	43,125,089	14,633,242	2.95	14,633,242	2.95
UK	CREST[a]	143,446,634	58,816,750	2.44	58,816,750	2.44
EU	EU	1,644,565,272	531,874,658	2.86+	319,662,321	5.14
	EU (excl. ICSDs)	882,800,272	508,874,658	1.49+	296,662,321	2.98
ICSD	SIS	103,231,065	17,745,900	5.82	17,745,900	5.82
US	DTCC++	638,261,727	1,387,500,000	0.46	230,271,931	2.77

Sources: CEPS using data from national CDSs, Clearstream and Euroclear; the Giovannini Group (2001).

Notes: Number of transactions: Prenetting: Postnetting data provided where applicable. Transactions should be single-counted. However, this is not as straightforward as it appears. The number of Clearstream Frankfurt above is single-counted stock-exchange trades only. *Operating income:* Taken from profit-and-loss accounts of CSDs, as figures in the CSDs annual reports. The figures are from 2000 unless otherwise stated. *Exchange rates:* If data is not originally in euro, the following exchange rates have been used: 1€= US$0.924; 1€ = DKr7.45; 1€ = SKr 8.45; 1€ = £0.69. *CCPs:* If a CSD does benefit from netting then the operating income of that CCP has been included (Clearnet France, NSCC). It has not been possible to determine the operating income of Banca d'Italia's L.d.T. +: Per transaction operating income (excluding the income of Clearnet). *++DTCC:* If subtract interest income, the DTCC's discount policy makes expenditures exceed revenues. The share of interest income (11 percent of total income) has therefore been subtracted from the discount as well. This produces an operating income of €638m. *ICSDs:* Banking revenues are core income for ICSDs, as their services are different from other CSDs. The banking revenues of Euroclear Bank, on the other hand, are largely excluded in the annual statement of Euroclear. This is due to an agreement relating to the exit of JP Morgan from Euroclear.

[a] Daily average multiplied by 250 working days.

[b] Värde papperscentralen AB (VPC) settlement income amounted to €15.2 million in 2000. The remaining two-thirds of total operating income is mainly made up of issuance income, which is not a core activity of a CSD. The total figure has been included, however, as it has not been possible to verify whether other EU CSDs also have issuance income.

conclusions of that study are broadly in agreement with those previously reported: "For an exchange-traded equity transaction settled on a net basis, the cost in the US is around €0.10, in the UK, Italy and Germany the cost is in the range of €0.35 to €0.85." (NERA 2004, 87). The study also states, ". . . a standard cross border trade settled through an ICSD can cost €35 or more" (87).

At the root of these price differences there is the added complexity of cross-border transactions: a cross-border transaction can involve as many as eleven intermediaries and fourteen instructions between parties (The Giovannini Group 2001). This complexity is due to the simple fact that EU markets are separate entities, from a legal and regulatory standpoint. As a result, these markets have developed different conventions and technical standards. The complexity therefore arises from the need to bridge separate markets.

At first blush this complexity—and the various risks it gives rise to— cannot explain a price differential of the order of 10 to 1. To my knowledge, nobody has ever attempted the steep task of quantifying the effects of market fragmentation on the actual costs of posttrading services. The general belief, supported by the few valuations of the business providing international clearing services that have surfaced (Norman [2007], for example, cites some), is that the profitability of cross-border services is, at the price levels mentioned previously, very high. It is, however, to be expected that it will decrease as a result of increasing volumes of transactions and an increasingly crowded marketplace. Indeed, since the aforementioned studies, a number of developments indicate that the ratio of cross-border to domestic costs has decreased: the latest estimate that has been informally cited is, to my knowledge, 4:1, a number that is still frighteningly high.

Hence, the sense in which the European financial market has got obsolete infrastructure is that it may be described as a juxtaposition of national monopolies that have been historically isolated from one another: a far cry from an efficient, integrated market. Should this be sufficient ground for a public initiative? Consider the fundamental factors driving the evolution of markets. Financial markets make heavy use of communication and information technologies.[8] As a result, the primary driver of progress is progress in communication and information technologies, one that has been very fast in recent decades. In the presence of competition, it is to be expected that the dramatic changes brought about by technical progress in information and communication would be transforming the way financial markets perform their basic functions. The regulatory framework designed to support these functions would need to change to reflect the new way such functions are performed.

---

8. The basic functions of financial markets are the facilitation of assets trades, the allocation of resources over time and space, the trading of risk, the provision of information on the value of investment assets, and the solution or principal-agent problems. These functions require as inputs people and information.

Should regulators and lawmakers take the lead in this transformation process, or should they just accommodate the effects of the strong forces of change mentioned previously?

In general, as well as in this case, the role of government authorities is justified on economic grounds by the presence of market failures, which are phenomena that prevent the normal market mechanism to reach an efficient allocation of resources. An additional condition for government intervention to be justified is that it is effective; that is, it actually identifies and eliminates the market failures. It is useful to concentrate on the market failures that are to be expected in posttrading:

- Coordination failures: the service providers along the posttrading value-chain need to coordinate their actions. The equilibrium may not be the optimal one when providers do not internalize the effects of other participants' reactions to their own decisions (Nash equilibrium).
- Technology, and in particular near-zero marginal costs in information processing, may give rise to a single supplier. If it is a for-profit business it will, in absence of regulation, practice monopoly pricing.
- In addition, market or monopoly power will induce for-profit suppliers to practice price discrimination as well as service bundling. A number of services offered in competitive markets will be bundled to the service offered in a monopoly regime, to protect the former from competition.

This reasoning applies in a domestic financial market. In an international setting, market failures are trivially represented by barriers that prevent, or make more difficult, the provision of posttrading services cross-border.

The Giovannini Group (2001) provided an analysis of barriers to the provision of cross-border posttrading services. These barriers justify the presence of the complex systems of cross-border securities settlement previously described, which give rise to those very large cost differences. The barriers are listed in table 7.4.

An analysis of the list of barriers reveals that they are the result not of conscious protectionist attitudes, but just of a history of separated national financial markets. For example, the use of communication standards that differ from country to country (barrier 1), the presence of different rules governing corporate actions (making it cumbersome and costly to access a market from abroad, barrier 3), the differences in operating hours and settlement deadlines (barrier 7, making, together with barrier 4, difficult to connect different settlement systems) and the differences in standard settlement periods (barrier 6) were not the result of protectionism, just historical accident. The list contains barriers caused by technical standards and conventions, which can be regarded as private-market rules. There are also barriers caused by laws and regulations. For example, barriers 13, 14, and 15 pertain to different legal treatment of interest in securities and they are also the result of history, not protectionism. The same is true for the barriers

Table 7.4   The fifteen barriers identified by the Giovannini group

Number	Barrier
1	Differences in IT standards and interfaces
2	National restrictions on the location of clearing and settlement
3	Differences in rules and processes relating to corporate actions
4	Absence of intraday finality between systems
5	Impediments to remote access
6	National differences in settlement periods
7	National differences in operating hours/settlement deadlines
8	Differences in issuance practice
9	National restrictions on location of securities
10	National restrictions on activity of primary dealers and market makers
11	Domestic withholding tax regulations serving to disadvantage foreign intermediaries
12	Transactions taxes collected through a functionality integrated into a domestic settlement system
13	Absence of a EU-wide framework for the treatment of interests in securities
14	National differences in the legal treatment of bilateral netting for financial transactions
15	Uneven application of national conflict of law rules

associated with different systems of taxation. In addition, certain provisions like those granting monopoly power to domestic posttrading infrastructures (see, for example, barrier 2 on restrictions on the location of clearing and settlement and barrier 10 on primary dealer restrictions) are probably not inspired by protectionism, but by the desire to allow the maximum exploitation of the benefits of economy of scale, by avoiding fragmentation of posttrading services.

Therefore, the analysis of barriers seems to suggest that things that are efficient in domestic markets become the source of fragmentation in an international setting. This, however, is not the only problem: the technology used to deliver posttrading services is characterized by near-zero marginal costs, therefore there are potential distortions when this technology is managed for profit by entities that are large enough to be able to affect market prices.

In summary, the combination of barriers to efficient cross-border posttrading with an industry structure characterized by national monopolies, in turn justified by the technology to deliver posttrading services, appear to be the necessary conditions for government initiative. The existence of necessary conditions raises the question of the most effective initiatives that government can take. In practice, governments are constrained by the institutional setting of their decision making. In particular, in the European Union there is a complex interaction between the EU Commission and national governments, which has shaped and crucially affected the reform initiatives.

7.5 The European Commission's Reform Strategy and Its Performance So Far

The most straightforward strategy for reform of the posttrading infrastructure in the EU would have been to coordinate consolidation of the different providers: the different segments of the posttrading functions could have been horizontally integrated across the different EU member countries, to achieve the scale that is the necessary condition for lower costs. However, while this strategy ensures—by its very nature—the achievement of an efficient outcome, it leaves aside the presence of the barriers to cross-border business mentioned in the previous section. If consolidation occurs in the absence of barrier's removal, the cost of cross-border business will remain higher than the cost of domestic business. In addition, a top-down strategy is vulnerable to the problems of government involvement in business decisions, with potential costly errors.

An alternative strategy is truly opening markets; that is, to eliminate all barriers to cross-border trading, and let the structure of the industry evolve on its own. In this case a situation like the one studied by Krugman (1994) would be created: when trade is opened among national monopolies, the one with the lowest average cost (and presumably lowest prices) progressively takes over the whole integrated market, because it is able to charge the lowest price throughout, and by gaining ever larger market shares, it maintains and improves its pricing advantage over competitors. In Krugman's simple description it is assumed that national monopolists have identical technologies. If that was the case, letting the markets produce the Krugman outcome would not be a particularly useful exercise, although in practice the single EU-wide supplier would not emerge as the entity that progressively erodes to zero the market power of the smaller competitors, but rather would be formed through mergers, a faster and quicker way to gain the scale that allows the lowest costs. What would justify a hands-off approach that limits itself to the elimination of all barriers to trade is the presence of different know-how and skills. A competitive game would presumably be a more efficient device to make the better technologies and know-how emerge, although the cost advantages of the larger players at the time of market opening would still distort the outcome.

The EU Commission decided to follow the logic presented previously. It embraced the view that the elimination of the barriers is the starting point of reform and that authorities should stay out of the process of consolidation that should be expected as a result of the elimination of barriers. In a Communication issued in 2004 (EU Commission 2004), the Commission stated that the priorities were:

1. Liberalization and integration of existing securities clearing and settlement systems.

2. Application of competition policy.

3. Adoption of a common regulatory and supervisory framework including questions of definitions.

4. Adoption of appropriate governance arrangements.

To achieve them, it decided to embark on the following:

- To draw up a Directive on clearing and settlement which addressed questions of (a) rights of access and choice, (b) a common regulatory framework, and (c) governance.
- To set up the a consultative and monitoring Group, called CESAME (Clearing & Settlement Advisory and Monitoring Experts 2008) with the mandate to organize the removal of the so-called private sector barriers and advise the Commission on public sector barriers.
- To establish a group to advise on reforms in the taxation area.
- To establish a group to advise on reforms in the legal area.

The Commission added rights of access, a regulatory framework, and governance among the areas where it would legislate because it recognized that granting access to nondomestic providers is the precondition for market liberalization, that regulatory issues would be raised with respect of the risks that intermediaries in charge of posttrading would be allowed to take (in the interest of the safety of the system as a whole), and that, given that the industry has at least a tendency to converge toward a (natural) monopoly, it would be important that the governance of the providers at least to some extent limit the incentives that a monopolist manager has to maximize its own profits, thus increasing costs and charges for its customers.[9] Taxation and legal issues are part of the list of barriers, but since they require action that requires heavier involvement of national government, the choice of separate working groups allows conducting the work with this different style.

The members of CESAME were (together with representatives from the Commission Directorate-General for the Single Market [DG Markt], which chaired the group, and representatives from the Directorate General for Competition [DG Comp]) top officials from the European Central Bank and the Bank of England, and the chairman of CESR, the Committee of European Securities Regulators. The industry representatives were from a number of banks involved in posttrading services, the national CSDs and ICSDs, stock exchanges, and associations representing industry groups involved in clearing and settlement. There were, however, no representatives of those most directly affected by the high costs of posttrading services, like final investors and asset managers. In addition, the representatives for the various providers and industry groups were, with few exceptions, people working full-time in Brussels on relations with the Community institutions.

The function of CESAME was to act as an information clearinghouse: it

---

9. See EU Commission Communication (2004) for a discussion of this.

had to inform the financial community as a whole of the initiatives undertaken to remove the barriers related to technical standards and market conventions, for which governments had no direct role to play. It also had to receive inputs from financial markets on making the process of removing barriers related to technical standards and conventions speedier and more effective. It had to provide information to government authorities and the Commission in the first place on aspects related to its own activities in the liberalization of the posttrading market and, of course, it had to inform the market on how such initiatives were progressing. The idea was that this mechanism, supported by a skilled and competent secretariat from DG Markt, would ensure a more democratic process; that is, a process where authorities would be less vulnerable to capture from private interests. In addition, this mechanism was meant to provide coordination among the many different actors involved in posttrading: knowing that a certain set of reforms would take place, the different actors would make investment decisions under the maintained hypothesis that in a given interval of time the EU market would be much more integrated—thus bringing about an efficient aggregate outcome and avoiding losses due to misdirected investment decisions.

In summary, the process for reform designed by the EU Commission apparently addressed all the market failures that have emerged in the analysis: from simple coordination failures in standard setting and in investment planning to the barriers to cross-border integration and the implications for having monopolistic suppliers of posttrading services.

The CESAME had its first meeting in July 2004. It had some of its work already cut out for itself: the Giovannini Group (2003) had laid out a plan for reform that included a list of responsible entities to coordinate action for each barrier and a timetable and sequencing order. These devices were meant to ensure consistency among the different initiatives and to provide incentives for speedy action. The CESAME essentially adopted the process design described in the Giovannini Group (2003). The timetable is reproduced in figure 7.4. It shows that the maximum time required for the elimination of barriers was estimated to be three years. The figure also highlights that separation of responsibilities (which entities were to be considered to take the responsibility for the initiatives designed to remove each barrier) was such that most work had to be done by authorities, as it pertained to regulations and laws, which can only be changed or cancelled by entities that have the power to do so: parliaments and governments.

Four years after the first meeting of CESAME, which officially kicked off the reform process, the original mandate of the group is over.[10] Has the process delivered what had been promised? Evaluating progress in the removal

---

10. Members of the group prepared a report (CESAME 2008) containing detailed descriptions of all initiatives and progress. After the expiry of the mandate of CESAME, the Commission has decided to reform the group to carry on the unfinished work.

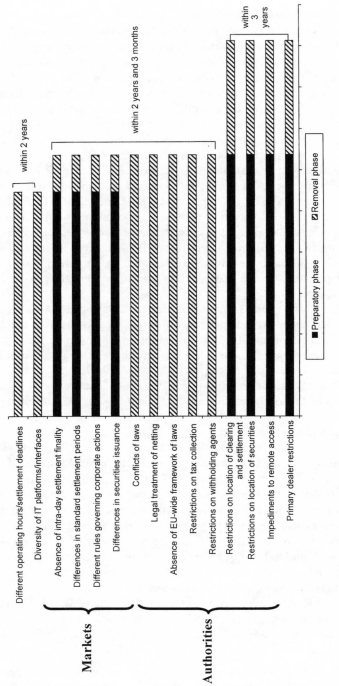

Fig. 7.4   Timetable for the elimination of barriers

of cross-country posttrading barriers is not straightforward, because the reforms in technical standards, conventions, rules, regulations, and laws are nonlinear. In the case of technical standards and conventions, after new templates have been identified and proposed, their adoption is up to the free decisions of market participants. The process is nonlinear because it is characterized by coordination equilibria (the behavior of each actor depends on the behavior of the other actors). Similarly, there are nonlinearities in the case of new rules, regulations, and laws, even though, once new rules, regulations, and laws are issued, they are immediately adopted, by definition. With these caveats in mind, an analysis of the state of affairs does not lead those who laid out the reform strategy to congratulate themselves.

Table 7.5 summarizes the progress.[11] Of the fifteen barriers originally identified, only two have been dismantled. The reforms of standards and conventions (required to remove the private sector barriers) have proceeded in order, but in some cases extremely slowly, so that after four years not even the preparation phase is completed. The changes in regulations and laws required to remove public-sector barriers are even less advanced: in most cases there has been study, in some cases proposals, but little or no action from the Commission and national governments.

This very significant discrepancy between outcome and expectations could in part be due to wrong expectations: has the time to completion of the reforms been estimated to be too optimistic? While the work carried out between 2004 and 2008 has unearthed a number of details and issues that were not foreseen before the start, the expected time to completion of the reforms was drawn by a number of professionals both from the financial industry and the EU Commission: it was aggressive but not unrealistic. Hence, the disappointing outcome of the reform process has to be found elsewhere.

The most significant deviation from the initial plan is the decision by Commissioner McCreevy not to draft a directive. The 2004 Communication envisaged the production of a directive, whose objective was to gather together the reforms of regulations needed to remove most of the public-sector barriers. McCreevy's decision was taken at the end of an extremely drawn out discussion and preparation phase, which included a very vocal debate between two camps in favor and against the directive, some statements from the European Parliament on the desirability of legislation, and a very thorough cost-benefit analysis of legislation ("Impact Assessment").

While the Commission 2004 Communication made it very clear what the contents of a directive would be, debaters in favor and against argued their views only about certain details. Among the most vocal entities in favor of a directive were banks involved in the asset servicing business (which includes posttrading services), coordinated by BNP Paribas around a group that

---

11. The table draws from CESAME (2008).

Table 7.5   **Progress in the elimination of barriers**

Number	Barrier	What happened	Dismantled? If no, when?
1	Differences in IT standards and interfaces	New SWIFT protocol	No. 2011
2	National restrictions on the location of clearing and settlement	MiFID Code of Conduct	No
3	Differences in rules and processes relating to corporate actions	New standards being finalized	No
4	Absence of intraday finality between systems	Standards finalized	No. 2008
5	Impediments to remote access	Some progress in MiFID. Code of Conduct	No
6	National differences in settlement periods	No progress	No
7	National differences in operating hours/settlement deadlines	New standards	No. 2008
8	Differences in issuance practice	Coordination in issuance and distribution by numbering agencies	Yes
9	National restrictions on location of securities	Being studied by ad-hoc Legal group	No
10	National restrictions on activity of primary dealers and market makers	Under consideration by Commission	No
11	Domestic withholding tax regulations serving to disadvantage foreign intermediaries	Ad hoc fiscal group has identified problems and proposed solutions	No
12	Transactions taxes collected through a functionality integrated into a domestic settlement system	Ad hoc fiscal group has identified problems and proposed solutions	No
13	Absence of a EU-wide framework for the treatment of interests in securities	Being studied by ad-hoc Legal group	No
14	National differences in the legal treatment of bilateral netting for financial transactions	Collateral directive solves the problem.	Yes
15	Uneven application of national conflict of law rules	Being studied by ad-hoc Legal group	No

called itself the "Fair & Clear" group.[12] Their argument was that a directive was necessary essentially to clarify that the business of securities lending by CSDs had to be subject to the same restrictions as those imposed on banks. Their concern was that CSDs would use their control of the final settlement function (recall that settlement is complete only when the central securities depositories accounts have been updated) to subsidize more lucrative asset servicing business, like securities lending. Hence, banks in the asset servicing business wanted a directive to contain the competitive threat from CSDs, and in particular Euroclear.

By contrast, the camp against the directive was populated by a variety of entities: first and foremost Euroclear, but also Europarliamentarians worried that a directive would become hostage to special interests (see, notably, the positions of Theresa Villiers, who was Rapporteur on posttrading in 2004) and some very influential representatives from the London financial community (like, for example, Sir David Walker and Sir Nigel Wicks, also Deputy Chairman of Euroclear). In general, those who argued against a directive pointed to two things: a directive would take too much time to be produced (the consensus view is that the time to produce a directive is four years), and a directive would be distorted by special interests (in other words, the EU political process is seriously faulty).

The decision not to issue a directive was, in my opinion, the key mistake at the root of the lack of progress in the removal of barriers related to rules, regulations, and laws. It was a mistake for the simple reason that rules, regulations, and laws not consistent with an integrated posttrading market can only be changed by new rules, regulations, and laws: since this reform has to be coordinated across Europe, a directive appears to be the natural tool to achieve the task. Commissioner McCreevy apparently did not recognize this point. He justified his decision with his general aversion to lawmaking: he said that laws have to come in only when the private sector fails to get things done according to the desired plan.[13] Instead of a directive, McCreevy took the initiative to coordinate the signing (in November 2006) of a code of conduct by the stock exchanges, the clearinghouses, and the CSDs. The code contained commitments toward price transparency, access and interoperability, and service unbundling. This was a welcome initiative—as many national monopolies have in the past actively used complex and opaque pricing systems, bundling strategies, and restrictive practices to maximize their profits—but in no way could it represent a substitute for what a directive was meant to do. Indeed, the code does not remove regulatory barriers, such as, for example, the requirement of a license for remote access.

Similarly, the Markets in Financial Instruments Directive, which sets the principle of freedom of choice of posttrading venues, does not remove

---

12. See Fair & Clear (2004).
13. See McCreevy (2006).

legal barriers to consolidations or prevent the protection of national champions.[14]

The hypothesis presented in this chapter is that the slowdown of financial market integration described before is not the result of individuals' initiatives, even though those are the proximate causes. The reason why the reform did not occur is that all national governments and the EU Commission were not of the opinion that such a reform would be a serious priority, and that this opinion was informed by market participants in pursuit of their interests. In the next section, I try to uncover the political economy of financial market reform.

7.6   Why Has Integration Not Been Delivered?
The Political Economy of Financial Reform

The history of the European Union is characterized by some bold reforms in economic institutions that have had a major impact on societies and living standards. Among these, monetary union stands out as a huge, successful reform that has been carried out relatively quickly. From the perspective of political economy, monetary union appears very interesting. Elsewhere (Giovannini 1992) I have argued that monetary union was a reform for which gainers and losers were not clearly identified groups. This stands in contrast with other international liberalizations, like trade reforms, where gainers are all consumers and exporters and losers are those working in import-competing industries. The financial industry stood to gain from new opportunities but to lose from the closing down of foreign exchange market "while forex traders were obviously and vocally against their bosses, and in general the broker-dealer community was supportive of the project, as it saw its benefits in terms of potential new business." (Graham Bishop, private conversation with the author, July 25, 2008).

In the presence of a vacuum of political forces for or against, a reform like monetary union is subject to two kinds of forces: on one side, elites that see the economic benefits of the reform can push it through the political process with relative ease because they do not have to fight with the political influence of the sectors negatively affected by the reform, as in the case of trade liberalization. On the other side, the national currency lends itself to becoming a symbol for other objectives. For example, those who stand to lose from liberalization in general may seek to stop the process by derailing monetary union. Because the national currency is a highly visible symbol, and because the complexities of a monetary union are not immediately clear to everybody, strategies of this kind may actually work.[15] On balance, it appears that

---

14. See Turing (2008).
15. See, for example, the debate that surrounded the Swedish referendum on the single currency.

in most countries the reform has gone through relatively smoothly and that those exploiting it for other purposes have been few.

A reform of posttrading that facilitates the creation of a single, integrated clearing and settlement platform has potentially a very large positive economic impact on the countries involved.[16] The positive impact of an integrated capital market is not easy to estimate through the standard static analysis: Hotelling triangles are hard to estimate (since supply and demand elasticities in the case of securities trading can be very large indeed). In addition, the interesting and relevant economic effects are not those measured through partial equilibrium analyses of the securities markets, but stem from the effects that a single, integrated securities market has on capital formation and risk-taking in the EU economies as a whole. This is a very difficult problem to address. The EU Commission has valiantly taken up this task in its impact assessment, and has produced estimates on the incremental impact of the reform on EU-wide gross domestic product (GDP), with a permanent increase ranging between 0.2 percent and 0.6 percent. An analysis of these estimates is beyond the scope of this chapter. It suffices here to point out that, as several authors have noted, there is abundant historical evidence on the nexus between an efficient financial system and economic performance: see, for example, Rajan and Zingales (2003). Thus, the desirability of the reform is, among the informed public, easy to accept. The difference between this reform and monetary union is that the integration of financial markets infrastructure is below the radar screen of parliamentarians because it is an arcane topic, just like plumbing. Indeed, even within the EU Commission recognition of the importance of the post-trading infrastructure has arrived late: the so-called Financial Services Action Plan, a comprehensive strategy aimed at creating an integrated and efficient EU financial system, in its initial versions, did not contain any mention of the urgency of reforming posttrading, which turns out to be the precondition for any meaningful integration of markets. The Economic and Financial Committee of the EU launched a research program on the importance of financial markets infrastructure after hearing a presentation of the Giovannini Group (2001).[17]

Hence, like monetary union, the reform of posttrading is one that informed people think brings large benefits, although these benefits are not easy to explain and not understood by the larger public. In addition, the individuals who will stand to lose from the reform are hard to identify: there may be a number of people who are made redundant by the creation

16. See the Impact Assessment prepared by the staff of DG Markt: EU Commission (2005).

17. In that presentation I argued that the state of financial markets in Europe was like that of a country after a war: everybody is happy to be free, governments declare the start of peace, but nothing works and the situation is as miserable as during the war. Similarly, allowing free trade of securities in the EU was not any reason for complacency, since European financial markets were hopelessly fragmented.

Table 7.6   Schematic of economic incentives to reform

	Status quo	Reform
Users: Intermediaries, investment managers	Pay high costs, though costs are passed through	Lower costs. Gains from new business opportunities are there but not so visible
Suppliers: for-profit market infrastructures	High profit margins, relatively low volumes, protected market share	High volumes, low margins, potential prize of becoming the sole supplier, or sanction of being taken over

of an integrated and efficient posttrading platform in the EU, but these people normally do not have political representation. Hence, the standard political-economic analysis does not apply. In what follows, I try to highlight a number of effects that I have observed that may help explain the outcome so far.

In table 7.6 I summarize the economic incentives of the two classes of interest groups for the status quo and reform. As mentioned previously, the users' community, which is aware of the costs of posttrading, is the community of intermediaries, securities trading houses (broker-dealers), and investment managers. This group does not suffer directly from the costs of posttrading as it is able to pass this cost along to their customers. Since the cost is a system-wide cost, it does not produce a disadvantage to any one institution. Financial intermediaries have some interest in lower trading costs, especially as they would give rise to more business opportunities, though these opportunities are not immediately apparent. Therefore, the opportunity cost of no reform is not very high for the users' community.

Now consider suppliers. Under the status quo suppliers have low volumes in cross-border business, but very high unit revenues. In an integrated market, volumes are presumably much higher, and there is the potential of becoming the sole supplier in every zero marginal cost segment of the business. Of course, there is also the risk of losing the competitive game in the bigger market. Hence, suppliers would either resist integration or try to influence the reform process in a way that advantages their own chances of becoming the winner-take-all.

Resistance to integration has been evident in recent years. One manifestation of it has been the development of so-called "financial-marketplace" committees in various EU countries. Until recently, these committees have worked with the explicit aim of maintaining and fostering the business of the national financial market, typically around the national stock exchange. The strategies followed by the financial-marketplace committees, which often included government authorities playing the role of observers or coordinators, were to make the domestic market somehow different from foreign markets, making it somehow special. In other words, the strategy was to erect various regulatory, convention, and other barriers to foreign competition.

This strategy is fraught with what I call the fallacy of localism. Local financial markets are, more than international financial markets, populated by medium and small intermediaries that can use their size to their own advantage. They are physically closer to customers and through specialization they can reach excellence in certain areas of the financial business. By their nature, small intermediaries cannot sustain large fixed costs. Now consider two alternative structures for the EU financial market. The first structure, like the present, is characterized by a sum of largely isolated, though accessible, national markets. The markets are isolated because they are characterized by standards, conventions, and regulations that are specific to each one. An alternative structure is one where standards, conventions, and regulations pertaining to all markets are the same, so that the EU can be considered a truly single marketplace. Under both market structures investors and issuers would want to take full advantage from the possibility of accessing all markets. However, under the first structure, few intermediaries would have the resources needed to allow their clients to access all EU national markets. Indeed, for each market, intermediaries would have to deploy the resources that are needed to perform all procedures specific to that market. With twenty-five EU member states, this cost becomes prohibitive to any medium-small intermediary. By contrast, under the alternative market structure, there would be no additional cost to access other markets because there would not be any procedures that are specific to that market. This example illustrates the fallacy of localism. Those policymakers that create national financial marketplaces with the aim of protecting domestic (small- and medium-size) intermediaries, are not taking into account that all people want and/or need access to all markets. In fact, the financial marketplace policies end up crowding out small and medium financial intermediaries in favor of large, multinational intermediaries that are able to exploit their size to finance the fixed costs needed to give all their clients access to all domestic markets. In conclusion, strategies that are designed to protect domestic financial intermediaries end up giving them a competitive disadvantage, as long as there remains freedom to trade financial assets and freedom to establish financial businesses in different EU countries.

Another factor affecting the reform process is the technical nature of the subject combined with the role of clearing and settlement at the core of the financial markets. The fundamental dilemma of policymakers is that they have to set rules on issues that they do not know firsthand, or on which they have partial information. The functions of liquidity transformation and risk trading (which is accomplished through leverage) performed by financial markets make them inherently fragile, prone to multiple equilibria and excess volatility. Thus, financial market reform is an area of policy-making where the dilemma presents itself in very stark form. On one side, the subject matter is highly technical and complex, with many implications, some difficult to predict; on the other side, wrong decisions may raise especially serious risks: an inappropriate reform may create additional instabilities with potentially very large economic costs. The result is that policymakers involved in financial market reform are especially vulnerable to regulatory capture: they are particularly sensitive to ideas and suggestions of practitioners in the field, who are also interested parties.

Finally, and related to the point made before, I have one observation about consultative reforms. As described above, CESAME was designed to provide information to industry actors, policymakers, and the users' community at large, and through the dissemination of information, to act as a coordinating device. The virtual absence of the users' community was evident in CESAME. In addition, regular industry representatives were in most cases individuals, within companies or associations, in charge of institutional relations (managing relations with policymakers and regulators, often based full-time in Brussels), and therefore not directly involved in the technicalities of posttrading. In these conditions, the risk that industry interests are overrepresented is higher.

In summary, the political economy of the reform of EU financial market infrastructure has the following characteristics:

- Like monetary reform, it is an arcane subject with little genuine political appeal.
- Like other forms of international liberalizations, the gainers are disperse and largely unaware of what is going on, let alone the potential gains of the reform.
- The industry of financial markets infrastructure is not all against reform, but many actors feel threatened by it (many protected markets would disappear).
- The intensely technical nature of the reform hinders the power of initiative of authorities.
- The consultations process allows de facto overrepresentation of posttrading industry interests.

These conditions would lead to predictions that broadly match the actual outcome so far: reform has been very slow; all fundamental aspects of reform, that is, the legal and regulatory framework that would allow true consolidation and integration of posttrading service providers, are still to start in a significant way. In other words, since the interest groups with relatively more effective influence on policymaking are ambivalent about the gains from liberalization (some certain market advantages would be lost), and since policymakers are not under pressure to move forward—and may well be concerned about undesired and unforeseen effects of reform—progress has been very slow. In the concluding section I will try to identify some lessons on the appropriate design of mechanisms to manage a reform process in financial markets.

7.7   Concluding Remarks

After the introduction of the single currency, the construction of a truly integrated and liquid securities market appears in the natural development in the EU, and a worthwhile objective for its impact on financial intermediation and the efficiency of EU economies. The creation of a single EU securities market is proving a much harder task than those who conceived it initially envisaged. This chapter has discussed the lack of progress in the reform of financial market infrastructure in the EU.

To explain why the pace of reform has, so far, been much slower than expected, I have highlighted a number of issues. First, the EU financial market status quo is very complex. There are a multitude of different standards, conventions, rules, regulations, and laws, which coexisted easily in a condition of very limited cross-border financial activity, but have become a huge hindrance as cross-border transactions are allowed and are needed. With this kind of initial conditions, a reform plan requires a complex, concerted action that involves public and private actors alike, from all countries involved in the reform. In this process, legacy players (the current providers of posttrading services) are by necessity crucial actors. Under the status quo legacy players enjoy stable market shares (mainly due to regulatory frameworks that enforce their monopoly rights in the countries where they are based) and high profitability to cross-border business. Because of this, it would not be expected that legacy suppliers would welcome bold reforms that would in a sweep dramatically increase competition among providers in all countries.

The EU Commission and national governments have all recognized the importance of reform, but have made very little progress in the long list of initiatives that they originally laid out for themselves. I argue that lack of leadership by government authorities is the main cause of the insignificant progress so far. The main cause of governments' lack of leadership is difficult to identify. My hypothesis is that it is the result of the combination of two sets of factors:

1. The distribution of economic payoffs: each of the existing providers faces the threat of decreased protection and increased competition, while those who certainly stand to gain (final investors) are unaware of the reform, let alone of its benefits.

2. Government authorities' reform task is highly complex and delicate: the perception of risks is heightened and their tendency to rely on the advice of legacy providers is increased; this condition needs to be contrasted to monetary union, where the vast majority of the knowledge on the technicalities and the economic impact of the reform resided with central banks, which are public authorities and are not driven by profit motives.

Under these conditions, it is unlikely that government authorities would push hard for reform: indeed, developments so far are consistent with this hypothesis; the key actions that were expected of EU lawmakers have yet to occur.

Looking back at the history of the attempt of reforming European financial markets infrastructure it is natural to ask whether, with the benefit of hindsight, the design of the reform mechanism could be improved in any way. As mentioned before, in 2004 the Commission stated its intentions to draw up a Directive on clearing and settlement that addressed questions of rights of access and choice, a common regulatory framework, and governance. If the process to issue the directive had started then, now it would be at a very advanced stage, if not completed. In the complex interaction between the work of government authorities and that of the private sector, as described in this chapter, it cannot go unnoticed that the private sector's motivations to push ahead crucially depends on authorities' revealed preferences: if the authorities' actions do not match the strategy that they themselves have laid out, private market participants may not believe in the reform's momentum.

Alternatively, more top-down initiatives aimed at consolidating the fundamental functions of clearing and settlement—like facilitating the creation of an EU-wide clearing platform and a single CSD—could still be feasible though much more difficult to put in place, as the interests of those private suppliers that want to drive this consolidation may be at odds with these projects. The experience of the Target 2-Securities project of the European Central Bank (which provides a securities' settlement functionality with central bank money) is a good illustration of this difficulty. Even though the project is moving ahead, it has been subject to heavy criticism by the industry, which has waged a campaign to discredit it. However, even if top-down strategies were to become more feasible, the requirement of an appropriate legal and regulatory framework, which presupposes new rules and laws to be issued by national authorities, does not go away.

I would like to conclude with a note of optimism: even though progress has been disappointingly slow, the direction of reform has been broadly correct and, in particular, the project to create an integrated and efficient securities market in Europe is understood and shared by an ever-larger number of people. These are important and encouraging achievements, which do not preclude, at any moment, an acceleration of the pace of reform.

References

Aggarwal, R. 2002. Demutualization and corporate governance of stock exchanges. *Journal of Applied and Corporate Finance* 15 (1): 105–13.

Bertrand, A. 2006. Possible use of CPIs for globalisation indicators and investment protection analysis. Paper presented at the International Conference on CPIs, Bank of Spain. 1–2 March.

Center for Excellence in Science and Mathematics (CESAME). 2008. The work of the Clearing and Settlement Advisory and Monitoring Experts Group. Report. Brussels: CESAME.

Di Noia, C. 2002. Customer-controlled firms: The case of financial exchanges. In *Capital markets in the age of the euro,* ed. G. Ferrarini, K. J. Hopt, and E. Wymeersch. Kluwer.

European Central Bank. 2007. *Financial integration in Europe,* March. Frankfurt: ECB.

EU Commission. 2004. *Clearing and settlement in the European Union—The Way Forward.* Communication from the Commission to the Council and the European Parliament, COM(2994) 312 final, 28.4.2004.Brussels. Directorage General for the Internal Market

———. 2005. Draft working document on post-trading. Unpublished manuscript. Available at: http://ec.europa.eu/internal_market/financial-markets/docs/clearing/draft/draft_en.pdf.

Fair & Clear. 2004. Contribution to the communication on clearing and settlement in the european union—The way forward. Unpublished manuscript. Paris, BNP Paribas.

Giovannini, A. 1992. EMU: What happened? Exploring the political dimension of optimum currency areas. In *The monetary future of Europe,* ed. G. de la Dehesa, A. Giovannini, and R. Portes. London: CEPR.

Hansmann, H. 1996. *The ownership of enterprise.* London: The Belknap Press of Harvard University Press.

Krugman, P. 1994. *Rethinking international trade.* Cambridge, MA: MIT Press.

McCreevy, C. 2006. Clearing and settlement: The way forward. Speech presented to the Economic and Monetary Affairs Committee of the European Parliament, July 11.

NERA Economic Consulting. 2004. *The direct costs of clearing and settlement: An EU-US comparison,* City Research Series no. 7. London: Corporation of London.

Norman, P. 2007. *Plumbers and visionaries—Securities settlement and Europe's financial market.* London: John Wiley & Sons, Ltd.

Rajan, R., and L. Zingales. 2003. *Saving capitalism from the capitalists.* New York: Crown Business.

The Giovannini Group. 2001. *Cross-border clearing and settlement arrangements in the European Union.* Brussels: European Commission, November.

———. 2003. *Second report on EU clearing and settlement arrangements.* Brussels: European Commission, April.

Turing, D. 2008. After Giovannini—A new agenda for clearing and settlement. Clifford Chance, LLP. Unpublished manuscript, May.

Comment   Richard Portes

Having read Alberto Giovannini's chapter, I feel I have crossed a barrier: I finally understand clearing and settlement (C&S), if not the complicated plumbing, at least the underlying issues. Europe has "Polish plumbers"

Richard Portes is professor of economics at London Business School, founder and president of the Centre for Economic Policy Research (CEPR), and a research associate of the National Bureau of Economic Research.

(just not enough of them), in the American election campaign we saw "Joe the plumber," and securities markets everywhere have plumbing. It is very important.

But it is difficult. Even "Joe the plumber" did not have a proper license, and I certainly do not. Alberto acknowledges the "technical nature of the subject"—he even calls it "arcane"—but he then proceeds to inflict it on us, just because it is so important. The chapter gives a great description and analysis of C&S processes, of industry structure and its evolution.

The main message is that the key to reform is the political economy of obstacles to reform—identifying the rents and who earns them, and trying to counteract the resulting lobbies. The chapter argues that we cannot rely on the market participants to generate reform unaided. We need a top-down solution: for example, Big Bangs (major securities market liberalizations) have always been imposed against the wishes of market participants, most of whom then benefited, however, from consequent huge increases in turnover.

Reforming C&S is a major step in achieving financial integration. But how should we *define and measure* financial integration? My preferred perspective relies on the *law of one price (LOP):* assets generating identical cash flows should command the same return regardless of the domiciles of issuer and asset holder. Thus, cross-border flows of assets are neither necessary nor sufficient for integration. The LOP may hold without any flows at all; and cross-border flows may not equalize returns if there are cross-country differences in institutions' monopoly power. Nevertheless, we do look at quantities as well as prices: levels of *cross-border financial market activity.*

Another definition of financial market integration comes from the European Central Bank (ECB). Not surprisingly, it takes a more institutional perspective, saying that the market for a given set of financial instruments and/or services can be regarded as fully integrated if all potential market participants with the same relevant characteristics have the following:

1. Face a single set of rules when they decide to deal with those financial instruments and/or services.

2. Have equal access to the aforementioned set of financial instruments and/or services.

3. Are treated equally when they are active in the market.

Alberto's definition is very different from either. He defines a "market" by "the arrangements put in place to assure delivery of goods and of payments to the counterparties in each trade." This sees the market as posttrading, not trading itself, and this is his criterion for financial integration in a region—seamless, competitive posttrading. I find this rather idiosyncratic and surely *too narrow*—even Alberto slips into talking about exchanges, about "national financial markets" in the conventional sense. And sometimes he distinguishes between a market and its "infrastructure" ("plumbing"). Moreover, the definition is not quantitative. This is a problem when making intertemporal comparisons or trying to assess the effect of monetary union.

Taking a broader perspective, we can see that in addition to problems of C&S, many other obstacles can hinder financial integration: capital controls; different tax codes; accounting and auditing differences; different bankruptcy laws; different requirements of different regulatory authorities (e.g., consumer protection rules) that entail that financial institutions have to market different products across countries; weaknesses in judicial enforcement of contracts; the market structure of exchanges; and restrictive practices. The single market programme (SMP) and Financial Services Action Plan (FSAP) have attacked many of these barriers, however, and technological advances and market forces have mitigated their effects.

Thus, home bias in equity markets is falling, especially in the European Monetary Union (EMU). Cross-border equity holdings have risen even more than the global expansion of cross-border activity. Returning to the LOP, we find significant euro area convergence in equity returns and a declining relative influence of U.S. markets on euro area equity markets. Other evidence of equity market integration includes the often-remarked switch from country to sectoral portfolio strategies and the development of pan-euro area index benchmarks (Dow Jones Stoxx, etc.).

We also see falling home bias in the bond markets and considerable integration of the euro area bond markets. Euro area corporate bond market integration is clear from the minimal role of country effects in determining yield spreads. Moreover, effective bid-ask spreads in the euro area corporate bond markets are now actually lower than in the United States (Biais et al. 2006).

Government bond market integration has been driven by competition (governments can no longer rely on a captive domestic investor base, so they must eliminate causes of market segmentation). But Treasuries and Debt Management Offices try to maintain liquidity in their own securities through various restrictive practices, often aided by primary dealers (Dunne et al. 2006). *Perfect* substitutability probably requires "joint and several liability", and that will not come for many years. Common issuance, however, is not infeasible, and the primary dealers have worked out detailed proposals. But there is strong resistance to common issuance, coming in part from the European Central Bank, for reasons that are not entirely clear. Still, *there is a lot of substitutability arising from having only a single futures contract at each maturity*—that is, a single benchmark (the Bund contract is used for hedging at the ten-year horizon).

Regression results from gravity models, in the spirit of Portes and Rey (2005), find that cross-border bond investment is 197 percent larger among euro area member countries than between other country pairs. Cross-border bond holdings increased 90 percent among euro countries from 1997 to

2004, over and above what a range of other variables can explain (Lane 2005). Common membership of the euro area raises bilateral portfolio equity holdings by 45 percent according to Coeurdacier and Martin (2007), and by 62 percent according to Lane and Milesi-Ferretti (2005). And as further evidence of financial market integration, the Feldstein-Horioka effect has vanished within the European Union (Jappelli and Pagano 2008).

The conclusion I draw from this is that although reform of C&S is slow, the obstacles to efficient C&S have not impeded significant progress in cross-border financial integration in the European Union. Much as I sympathise with Alberto Giovannini's frustration, much as I would like to see the vested interests overcome and the rents disappear, I am pleased to see that markets and regulators are having considerable effects nevertheless.

References

Biais, B., F. Declerc, J. Dow, R. Portes, and E.-L. von Thadden. 2006. *European corporate bond markets: Transparency, liquidity, efficiency*. London: Center for Economic Policy Research.

Coeurdacier, N., and P. Martin. 2007. The geography of asset trade and the euro: Insiders and Outsiders. Discussion paper no. 6032, Center for Economic Policy Research.

Dunne, P., M. J. Moore, and R. Portes. 2006. An empirical analysis of transparency-related characteristics of European and U.S. sovereign bond markets. CBFSAI Research Technical Paper no. 9/RT/06. Dublin: Central Bank & Financial Services Authority of Ireland.

Jappelli, T., and M. Pagano. 2008. Financial market integration under EMU. CSEF Working Paper no. 197. Naples: Centre for Studies in Economics and Finance, University of Naples Federico II.

Lane, P., and G. M. Milesi-Ferretti. 2005. The international equity holdings of euro area investors. IIIS Discussion Paper no. 104. Dublin: Institute for International Integration Studies.

Portes, R., and H. Rey. The determinants of cross-border equity flows. *Journal of International Economics* 65 (2): 269–96.

The Euro and Fiscal Policy

Antonio Fatás and Ilian Mihov

8.1 Introduction

The creation of a single currency in Europe has been accompanied by some major changes in the institutional setting for fiscal policy. In this chapter we ask whether the new institutional framework has led to a change in the conduct of fiscal policy in the members of the euro area. The run-up to the launch of the euro was already difficult and driven by the strict criteria defined by the Maastricht treaty. Because this was a process driven by entry requirements, limited attention was paid to the long-run optimality of these conditions. With the introduction of the euro in January 1999 the issues became broader and moved from a matter of debate in the academic profession to a real-time challenge for policymakers. Within the first years of the European Monetary Union (EMU), the framework for fiscal policy embedded in the Stability and Growth Pact (SGP) has been subjected to many criticisms and has certainly failed to provide a credible framework for the conduct of fiscal policy. Although the pact was intended to be conducive to an environment of discipline, coordination, and stability, its constraints became binding for several countries and presented challenges to macroeconomic stability and to the credibility of the pact at the very early years of the EMU.

Antonio Fatás is the Portuguese Council Chaired Professor of European Studies and professor of economics at INSEAD. Ilian Mihov is the Novartis Chair of Management and Environment and professor of economics at INSEAD.

We are indebted to Alberto Alesina and Francesco Giavazzi for very useful comments on earlier drafts of the chapter, as well as to Roberto Perotti (our discussant). We are also grateful to the participants at the NBER Conference on Europe and the Euro in Milan, October 17–18, 2008, for their feedback on the chapter.

We review the behavior of fiscal policy after the introduction of the euro in several dimensions: procyclicality, volatility, coordination, and the role of automatic stabilizers. We characterize how the common currency and the constraints associated with the Stability and Growth Pact have shaped fiscal policy among the members of the union. The focus of the chapter is not so much in providing yet another discussion on the merits and the faults of the Stability and Growth Pact and how it could be reformed. We are after characterizing the behavior of fiscal policy and understanding whether, from the perspective of the euro and monetary policy, there should be any strong concerns about this behavior. Is the European Central Bank (ECB) being hurt by the behavior of fiscal policy? Does monetary policy have to compensate for the poor behavior of fiscal policy? In that sense, we see our analysis as taking place at the aggregate level more than at the national level. Nevertheless, given that there are no fiscal policy decisions taking place at the level of the monetary union, we also report results related to the behavior of fiscal policy at the national level.

Our results show that despite the significant change in the institutional setting, the cyclical behavior of fiscal policy in the euro area is mildly procyclical and has not changed much since the introduction of the new currency. In contrast, U.S. fiscal policy has become distinctly countercyclical over the period 1999 to 2007. We also document that there has been a broad-based decline in the volatility of discretionary fiscal policy in all major economies. This decline is quite substantial for the euro area and is present in the majority of the member states. Furthermore, the discrepancy of fiscal policy across euro area countries—measured by the dispersion of cyclically-adjusted balances—has decreased threefold since 1999.

The chapter is organized as follows. In the next section (8.2) we provide an assessment of the debates around fiscal policy as well as an overview of the academic literature. In section 8.3 we characterize the behavior of fiscal policy at the euro level and we compare it to policy dynamics in the United States and other Organization for Economic Cooperation and Development (OECD) economies. Section 8.4 asks the question whether the correct cyclical measure is the output gap or output growth. In section 8.5 we discuss coordination of fiscal policies, and section 8.6 concludes.

8.2   The Debates on Fiscal Policy

The fiscal framework of the Maastricht treaty and the introduction of the euro generated a renewed interest in fiscal policy and in the design of institutions that promote good policies. The first problem in the analysis of the recent experience in the euro area comes from the observation that it is difficult to reach a consensus on what constitutes good fiscal policy and what should be the appropriate policy stance, given economic conditions. Our approach is to focus on a set of particular behaviors of fiscal policy that have been analyzed previously in the literature and that can be linked potentially to a broad set of theoretical frameworks that study biases in fiscal policy.

We characterize the performance of fiscal policy authorities and the environment in which they operate along three main dimensions: (a) Long-term sustainability of fiscal policy; (b) the behavior of fiscal policy over the business cycle; (c) volatility (i.e., changes in fiscal policy that are exogenous to the cycle). Implicitly, we assume that good fiscal policy must be sustainable, possibly countercyclical (but also could be acyclical), and it should not be a significant source of volatility.

We start with an overview of the debates on these topics and a brief review of the academic literature. We also offer a short discussion of the rules and institutions designed to constrain fiscal policy discretion. The analysis is framed in the context of EMU. In the next section we empirically characterize each of the fiscal policy behaviors we describe here.

8.2.1   Sustainability of Fiscal Policy

Long-term sustainability is central to the institutional setting of fiscal policy in EMU and one of the biggest concerns of both policymakers and academics. For emerging markets, confidence in the sustainability of government budgets has direct effects on interest rates and economic performance. Many of the deepest crises in these countries have been characterized by large increases in the risk premium or defaults on government debt.

In developed countries, the concerns started with the increase in government debt levels in the mid-1970s, and while these levels have stabilized or have even gone down in recent years, the uncertainty of the consequences of future demographic changes has kept the debate alive.

The difficulty of governments to produce sustainable budgetary plans became known in the academic literature as the deficit bias of governments (Persson and Svensson 1989; Alesina and Tabellini 1990). This deficit could be due to the common pool problem or the strategic behavior of politicians in power as they tie the hands of the new elected governments or it could be simply a sign of short-sightedness of policies (for a survey of the theoretical literature see Persson and Tabellini [2001]).

In the EMU context, the Maastricht treaty identifies sustainability as the most important bias to deal with in the context of a single-currency area. What is the economic rationale for such a concern in a monetary union? Unsustainable fiscal policy may generate excessive macroeconomic volatility, which in turn will complicate the goal of the central bank in maintaining stability within the EMU. The potential tension between fiscal and monetary authorities is present in any economy, but these tensions might be more relevant for a monetary union where fiscal policy is decentralized and coordination might be more difficult or simply not in the interest of national governments.

This view has been articulated explicitly by the ECB in their statements where the "sustainability of public finances" is seen as the main goal of the fiscal framework. And the logic is that "sound fiscal policies and a monetary policy geared to price stability are fundamental for the success of a Monetary Union. They are prerequisites for macroeconomic stability and cohesion in the euro area" (Statement of the Governing Council of the ECB, March 21, 2005).

Under extreme circumstances, unsustainable fiscal policy plans can lead to a deterioration of credibility and the expectation that monetary policy will bail out governments by creating unexpected inflation. In the context of a shared currency it can be that this bias becomes stronger as governments do not internalize the consequences of their behavior on the credibility of the common currency. This could create externalities in terms of credibility or simply through interest rate channels. Although this is a possibility, the academic literature does not reach a consensus either on whether these externalities matter or on their size.

While sustainability relates to the long-term behavior of fiscal policy, it is connected in many ways to the discussions around business cycle stabilization policies. The lack of discipline in fiscal policy can make the macroeconomic management of the economy difficult. First, from a dynamic point of view, if governments face debt levels that are unsustainable, they will have very little room to use automatic stabilizers in bad times so all the pressure will fall on monetary policy to smooth the business cycle. As such, a combination of high deficits and procyclical fiscal stance amplifies economic fluctuations because it reduces the effectiveness of automatic stabilizers (as argued by Melitz [2000] and Perry [2003]). Second, unsustainable plans will have to turn into sustainable ones by fiscal consolidations that are likely to have a short-term effect on the economy. Finally, high debt levels lead to higher interest rate and lower investment and growth (Mankiw and Elmendorf [1999] provide a survey of the empirical literature). Of course, a deterioration of macroeconomic performance might not have a direct impact on the conduct of monetary policy but there is, however, the argument that favorable macroeconomic conditions can make the running of monetary policy easier from a political point of view. For example, in the presence of inflationary pressures, fiscal prudence will reduce the need to increase interest rates.

There is yet another connection between sustainability and the cyclical stance of fiscal policy; one that is related to the design and implementation of budgetary plans. When it comes to the discussions on what constitutes a sustainable fiscal policy, there is the need to measure, characterize, and monitor annual budgets. Because of the short-term fluctuations in budgets due to automatic stabilizers, there is the need to capture the structural balance in a given year; that is, the budget balance adjusted for cyclical changes. Without a proper understanding of how fiscal policy behaves over the business cycle, it is impossible to provide long-term guidance to budgetary plans.

This has been one of the major difficulties of the implementation of the limits on deficits and debt of the Maastricht treaty. While they were based on simple principles of sustainability, there were endless discussions on the special circumstances that had led to balances that did not corresponded with the projected levels. The 2005 reform of the Stability and Growth Pact allowed for a more flexible interpretation of the limits that takes into account the cyclical position of the economy. There is, however, no consensus on how this adjustment needs to be made and some see this flexibility as a relaxation of the constraints.

In summary, although the main concern of the EMU fiscal policy framework was long-term sustainability, the implementation of the rules have led to debates that have focused much more on the cyclical behavior of fiscal policy. We now turn to this debate.

8.2.2   Fiscal Policy Stance and Management of Business Cycles

Although there is a large body of theoretical literature on fiscal policy, it is difficult to provide an easy characterization of what the appropriate behavior of fiscal policy over the business cycle should be. A starting framework could be one of tax smoothing, as in Barro (1979). Within that framework we can find a pattern of cyclical fluctuations of the budget as distortionary taxes are kept constant and the balance has to absorb changes in other revenues or expenditures or changes in taxes that follow the stochastic properties of the cyclical shocks (as in Chari, Christiano, and Kehoe [1994]). Within the context of Keynesian models, and under the assumption that consumers are liquidity-constrained, it is expected that governments run deficits during bad times and surpluses during good times, as this policy will help to stabilize the economy.

From the perspective of monetary policy, high deficits can lead to inflationary pressures and might force the ECB to keep interest rates higher than what they otherwise would be. Of course, it has to be that these high deficits take place at a time when they are not needed, which leads to the discussion on what is the appropriate stance of fiscal policy during the cycle. This is relevant for economies where fiscal and monetary policies are decided at the same level but it might become more acute when we have a scenario of a monetary union. The decentralized nature of national budgets can make the coordination of policies more difficult.

Beyond the theoretical discussions, the issue of the cyclicality of fiscal policy has received much attention in the empirical literature. There is strong evidence that fiscal policy tends to be less countercyclical than what normative models suggest. In fact, in many cases, fiscal policy is procyclical, which will exacerbate the business cycle and makes the conduct of monetary policy more difficult. Theories explaining this behavior point to increases in spending in good times that exceed the increase in tax revenues. Most Latin American economies, for example, display procyclical fiscal policy as documented in Gavin and Perotti (1997) and explained in terms of the voracity effect in Tornell and Lane (1999). The evidence for OECD and European economies is somewhat mixed. There is some evidence of pro-cyclical behavior, but in most cases, policy is either acyclical or only slightly countercyclical. Lane (2003) and Wyplosz (2005) present evidence on the cyclical properties of fiscal policy for this group of countries. More recent studies corroborate these results (e.g., Kaminsky, Reinhardt, and Vegh 2004). Alesina, Campante, and Tabellini (2007) also discuss similar evidence and present alternative political economy theories of this behavior.

When analyzing the cyclical behavior of fiscal policy it is important to understand that fiscal policy is a combination of automatic stabilizers and discretionary policy. Many of the aforementioned papers deal with discretionary changes but we cannot forget that for most countries the majority of cyclical changes in budgets are a result of automatic stabilizers.

The role of automatic stabilizers is one that has received little attention in the literature. In the case of EMU, the assumption is that they are influenced by tax codes and spending rules that have not been affected by the limits on deficits and debt. Many studies about automatic stabilizers take a public finance perspective and attempt to measure the elasticity of different fiscal components to the cycle. For example, Auerbach and Feenberg (2000) study the size of the automatic stabilizers in the United States to conclude that they have been quite stable despite changes in tax rates.

From a macroeconomic point of view, the effects of automatic stabilizers have been linked to the size of governments. The reason for this link is the empirical regularity presented in Galí (1994) and confirmed in Fatás and Mihov (2001), that large governments display less volatile business cycles. The logic is that the size of the governments is related to the safety network provided by governments. There is some evidence that this robust empirical regularity has gotten weaker in recent years as some governments have reduced their size, which has not resulted in a more volatile economy (see Debrun, Pisany-Ferry, and Sapir 2008). One potential explanation for the weakening of the link between government size and volatility is that recent declines in government size have happened in components that are inconsequential for macroeconomic volatility. The reduced-form nature of the empirical analysis does not provide a deeper insight into the sources of the reduced role of government size for macroeconomic stability.

8.2.3   Volatility

Fiscal policy can be a source of business cycles. When governments implement changes in fiscal policy for political reasons or, more generally, for reasons that are not driven by economic conditions, then these changes will lead to fluctuations in output and consumption. In principle, such policies may have a negative effect on the economy if they simply add volatility, which in some cases may slow down growth. The effects of fiscal policy shocks has received much attention after the work of Blanchard and Perotti (2002), Fatás and Mihov (2001), and Burnside, Eichenbaum, and Fisher (2004). The origin of these changes has been associated to the political business cycle. While the evidence is mixed, there is some recent support for the presence of an electoral cycle among some economies (Drazen 2000). The macroeconomic consequences of volatility in fiscal policy as well as its institutional origin has been documented in Fatás and Mihov (2003, 2007), where the aggressive use of discretion in fiscal policy has been shown to generate macroeconomic volatility and lower growth.

The issue of volatility has not been a major concern in the EMU context, but we will still study it empirically to see if there is any evidence of changes in the use of discretionary fiscal policy. It is possible that the absence of national currencies has changed the incentives of governments to engage in policies that lead to a political business cycle.

8.2.4   Rules, Institutions, and Fiscal Policy in the Context of EMU

The 1992 Maastricht treaty recognized the importance of providing a framework for fiscal policy in EMU and established limits to deficits and debt in order to "avoid excessive government deficits" (Article 104c). At the same time it defined an Excessive Deficit Procedure in case of violations. The main goal of this fiscal framework was to ensure the sustainability of public finances among members of the European Monetary Union and provide the necessary credibility to the currency. The implementation of this principle was done through a ceiling on deficits and debt as percentage of gross domestic product (GDP). These ceilings were defined independently of the business cycle, although there could be exceptional circumstances under which a country could go above those limits.

The Stability and Growth Pact (1997) developed the original ideas of the Maastricht treaty into a set of more detailed rules and processes to ensure budget discipline and enforcement. With the Stability and Growth Pact there is a slight change in the focus and motivation of the framework. From the narrow goal of ensuring sustainability of the Maastricht treaty, there is a broader need to "strengthen the surveillance of budgetary positions and the surveillance and coordination of economic policies." From a process point of view, the Pact included the creation of an early-warning mechanism through the preventive arm and emphasis on medium-term budgetary plans.

As a condition for entry in the single currency area, the limits on deficits and debt had a large impact on fiscal positions. The run-up to EMU saw a large decline in budget deficits among all candidates. Once EMU started there was a clear sign of fiscal fatigue that, combined with the slowdown of 2002, led to several countries being above the agreed ceilings. While growth rates were low in those years, they were not low enough to qualify as a "severe economic downturn." As countries breached the limits on budget deficits it became clear that the enforcement mechanisms of the SGP were not credible. This opened a broad debate on the merits of the current system among policymakers and academics. It is difficult to provide an exhaustive review of this literature but Buti and Sapir (2002), Galí and Perotti (2003), Fatás et al. (2003), Blanchard and Giavazzi (2004), Brunila, Buti, and Franco (2001), and Buiter and Grafe (2002) provide a review of the early years as well as proposals to modify the stability and growth pact. More recent reviews include von Hagen (2005) and Wyplosz (2005).[1] This debate led to a proposal to amend the principles of the Stability and Growth put forward by a report of the Economic and Financial Affairs Council (ECOFIN) in March 2005, which was later endorsed by the European Council.

The modifications introduced in 2005 allowed for more flexible interpretations of the limits on deficits, including adjustments for cyclical conditions. These changes were criticized by many, including the ECB, as an attempt to relax the constraints that governments faced and a failure to address the real problems with the current fiscal policy framework. The fact that the European economies witnessed healthy growth rates in the years that followed eased the tensions imposed by the limits on deficits. What remains unclear is how the new rules, which provide much more room for the interpretation of what constitutes an excessive deficit, will work in the years to come as the euro economies enter a recessionary environment and deficits are likely to be above the established ceiling. It is likely that we will return to the debate about the trade-off that exists between simple rules that might be seen as inappropriate or short-sighted, and the necessary flexibility to deal with idiosyncratic conditions in each country. The evolution of the Stability and Growth Pact has been toward flexibility, which has been welcomed by governments, but there are well-founded concerns that the added flexibility has relaxed the constraints of the system to a point that they have become irrelevant. This is very much linked to the academic debate about rules versus institutions. Even if we accept that there is a need to restrict governments and fiscal policy, are numerical rules the right way to do so or can we design a set of budget processes and institutions that can ensure the proper behavior of fiscal policy by using (good) judgment? Wyplosz (2005) and Fatás et al. (2003) argue that establishing checks on the budgetary process through independent committees might generate a superior outcome relative to simple numerical rules.

8.3   Fiscal Policy in the Euro Area

To start the empirical assessment of fiscal policy, we first take the perspective of the ECB as it tries to manage the economic conditions of the euro

---

1. This debate is also linked to the earlier academic literature on the effects of budget-balance constraints of U.S. states (Alt and Lowry 1994; Poterba 1994; von Hagen 1992; Alesina and Bayoumi 1996). There is also a broader literature on the connection between budgetary processes and fiscal outcomes (Poterba and von Hagen 1999).

area and has to deal with the euro area fiscal policy stance. This euro fiscal policy stance is the result of a collection of decentralized national fiscal policies. Each of these policies is decided independently and they react to national economic conditions but this is, in principle, irrelevant to the conduct of monetary policy that is only concerned with the aggregate of the euro countries. For this reason we also look at data at the level of individual countries.

When we look at fiscal policy at the national level, we are interested in the same characterization of fiscal policy, but the issues that arise are slightly different. National governments are worried that in the absence of monetary policy they need to be more aggressive in the use of fiscal policy as a way to smooth the business cycle. This is even more relevant in the European context where mobility of labor is very limited. Has this happened? Or have the constraints on deficits and debt limited the flexibility available to fiscal policy?

A second source of costs for national economies could be associated to interest rate effects of fiscal policies in other countries. As all countries share a common currency, there could be a spillover from deficits in the other members of EMU via the interest rate (or the premium associated to the euro currency, if it had an effect on the credibility of the ECB). This raises the issue of coordination and the extent to which national fiscal policies take into account what is happening in other countries or at the European level.

8.3.1   Sustainability of Fiscal Policy

Figure 8.1 shows the evolution of the debt to output ratio for the euro area, the United Kingdom, and the United States.[2] The evolution of this ratio for the euro countries shows an increasing trend until the mid-1990s. There is a clear downward trend that starts at this point. This trend was also followed by the United States and the United Kingdom until 2001 to 2002. The trend in the euro area has been interpreted before as a clear sign of the discipline that the entry conditions imposed on all members.[3]

Figure 8.2 provides more insights on these trends by looking at structural budget balances, which are measured as the cyclically adjusted balance as a percentage to potential output (using the OECD methodology). The decade of the 1970s as well as late 1980s and early 1990s showed high deficits for all countries in the sample. By the early 1990s there was a growing need to tackle these deficits as levels of government debt increased in several

2. Figure 8.1 reports gross government debt. It might be more appropriate to look at net liabilities, which in the case of the United States stand at about 44 percent of GDP, while in Europe they are closer to 47 percent. However, although the levels are different, the dynamics of the net and gross liabilities for the three countries in the figure are very similar.

3. Of course, one can construct explicit measures of sustainability by calculating the required tax rate, which ensures that public debt does not explode (given assumptions on future interest rates and output growth). Blanchard (1993) reviews some of the proposals for such "indicators of sustainability."

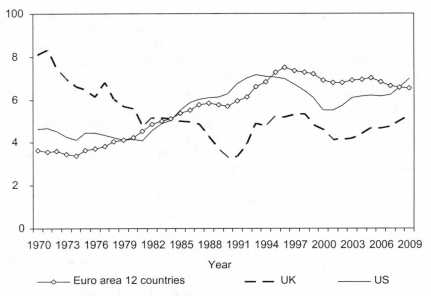

Fig. 8.1   Gross government debt (percentage of GDP)
Notes: Data are from the OECD Economic Outlook. The series for the UK are gross government financial liabilities as a percentage of GDP. For the euro area the series are gross government financial liabilities (Maastricht definition) as percentage of GDP. Data for 2008 and 2009 are forecasts.

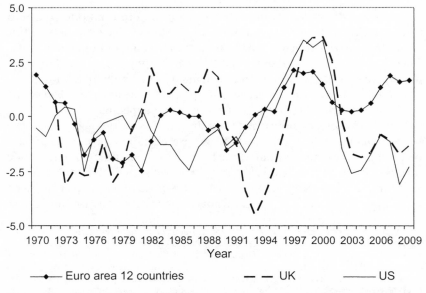

Figure 8.2   Cyclically-adjusted budget balance as a percentage of potential output
Notes: Data are from the OECD Economic Outlook. Data for 2008 and 2009 are forecasts.

countries. This effort started in the mid-1990s, which coincides with the adoption of the Maastricht Treaty among European countries. Therefore, for EMU countries, the fiscal consolidation efforts that were necessary because of the high debt levels were reinforced by the limits on budget deficits and debt that were being created as a condition for entry into the single-currency area.

During this period of fiscal consolidation all major economies, with the exception of Japan, behaved in a very similar way: structural budgets were brought up closer to balance or even to surplus. The improvement in the euro area budget balance is not as large as in the case of the United Kingdom and the United States but it is also true that the worsening of the balances as a result of the economic slowdown of 2001/2003 is much more pronounced in the United States and the United Kingdom than in the euro area. For the euro countries, 1997 represents an inflexion point as the adjustment of structural deficits clearly slows down right at the time when entry decisions for EMU are made. The euro structural balances improve again after 2003/2004, which coincides with a period of faster growth rates.

8.3.2   The Reaction of Fiscal Policy to Macroeconomic Conditions

To be able to interpret the stance of fiscal policy we need to separate the cyclical component from the structural one. Separating the cyclical from the structural component of fiscal policy is not an easy task and it is possibly one of the most controversial issues in the academic literature. Not only are there some practical issues related to estimating the cyclical behavior of fiscal policy, because of endogeneity, but there is also the broader debate on how to characterize the business cycle itself. Before we look at the data it is good to do a simple taxonomy of the different concepts of fiscal policy we want to measure.

From a methodological point of view, we can think of fiscal policy as a combination of three elements:

1. *Automatic stabilizers:* this is the reaction of fiscal policy to business cycles and it is a result of the tax code and spending rules that link budgetary components to changes in GDP.

2. *Endogenous discretionary fiscal policy:* it includes changes in fiscal policy taken in response to changing economic conditions. These changes are discretionary in the sense that they are not coded in tax or spending laws.

3. *Exogenous discretionary fiscal policy:* here we include changes in fiscal policy that are not related to economic conditions. They can be driven by political considerations (e.g., elections) or, in the case of European countries, by the conditions set by the Maastricht treaty.

From a conceptual point of view, it might be difficult to separate these three components. For example, governments that are trying to implement a reduction in their debt levels (as it has been the case for most of these countries during recent years) might wait for a favorable economic environment to implement their adjustment policies. This could be seen as an endogenous change in fiscal policy but it is not directly motivated by the economic cycle.

From an econometric point of view, we can summarize the behavior of fiscal policy by using a fiscal policy rule such as

(1) $$\mathrm{Bal}_t = \alpha + \beta \, \mathrm{Cycle}_t + \lambda \, \mathrm{Debt}_{t-1} + \phi \, \mathrm{Bal}_{t-1} + \varepsilon_t,$$

where "Bal" is a measure of fiscal policy, and "Cycle" is a variable that captures the state of the economy. "Debt" is gross government debt as percentage of GDP.[4] The logic of this rule is that fiscal policy is a function of the level of debt (the parameter λ can be seen as related to the indicators of sustainability) as well as a function of the current state of the cycle (captured by β). Any change in fiscal policy that is not directly related to the state of the economy or the level of debt will be part of the residual, which we will identify with exogenous discretionary fiscal policy.

There are two alternative approaches to estimating this policy rule: if fiscal policy is measured as the actual budget balance then the parameter β captures both the automatic stabilizers and the endogenous changes in discretionary fiscal policy. If instead we use a cyclically-adjusted measure of the budget balance on the left-hand side, the parameter β is reflecting the endogenous response of fiscal policy to the business cycle.

8.3.3   The Endogenous Response of Fiscal Policy to the Cycle

We start by looking at the behavior of cyclically-adjusted balances as a measure of the discretionary response of governments to the business cycle. We use the structural balances constructed by the OECD. For details on this methodology see Girouard and Andre (2005). The drawback of this methodology is that it heavily relies on the process to extract the cyclical component out of fiscal policy that requires strong assumptions on potential output, cyclical elasticities of different fiscal variables, and could potentially create a bias in the results. Blanchard (1993) and Mohr and Morris (2007) discuss the potential drawbacks of cyclically-adjusted measures of fiscal policy.[5]

From an econometric point of view there could be a problem of endogeneity when it comes to the estimation of the aforementioned policy rule. To deal with this problem we use instrumental variables as previously proposed by Galí and Perotti (2003) and Alesina, Campante, and Tabellini (2007). There are cases where we discuss how the instrumental variables (IV) results

---

4. The inclusion of debt in fiscal policy rules is advocated among others by Favero and Giavazzi (2007).

5. Generally speaking, the elasticities used to adjust the budget balance assume that the cyclical adjustment is happening mostly through revenues and not spending (see Girouard and André 2005). There is, however, evidence that spending also adjusts to the cycle in a counter-cyclical manner (Melitz 2006).

relate to the ordinary least squares (OLS) estimates because we feel that the OLS estimates might provide a useful perspective. The instruments for the output gap are one lag of their own output gap as well as the current value of the U.S. output gap. For the United States we use the lag of own output gap as well as the lag of the output gap of the euro area.[6]

Table 8.1 presents the results. The top panel shows the estimates for the euro area as well as three large countries that we use as benchmarks of comparison. The reason for comparing the euro area to these three countries is that they are the largest three countries with similar level of GDP per capita and therefore the closest benchmark we can find. The bottom panel shows the estimates for each of the individual EMU countries as well as seven additional economies, for the purpose of benchmarking. We present the results of estimating equation (1) both by instrumental variables and OLS.

We note first that the coefficient on debt in all cases is positive, as expected. Among the first four countries, the largest coefficient is in the United States, followed by the United Kingdom and the euro area. The coefficient for Japan is several times lower than the coefficients for other countries. It is hard to reach strong conclusions just from the size of this coefficient but fiscal policy in the United States, United Kingdom, and in the euro area seem to be more responsive to concerns of sustainability.[7] If we look at the results of the individual countries, the coefficient on debt remains positive for all countries with the exception of New Zealand (when estimated by OLS). There are large variations in this coefficient. If we ignore Luxembourg, that displays a very large coefficient. We find the largest coefficients in Italy and outside of the euro area.

If we now look at the cyclical behavior of the balance (the coefficient β), comparing the OLS and IV estimates reveal that, for many of the countries, OLS estimates for the parameter are lower than the instrumental variables ones. In principle, one might have expected the opposite. The OLS estimates are likely to be biased downwards because fiscal policy expansions (decrease in the budget balance) are likely to lead to increases in output. This reverse causality is likely to lower the OLS estimates of the cyclical elasticity of fiscal policy (the parameter β), but our results point in the opposite direction.

If we focus on the top panel of the table, and regardless of the estimation method, the euro area displays the most procyclical policy out of this group, in contrast with the United States, that shows acyclicality or mild

6. Our instrumenting strategy assumes that the U.S. gap does not react contemporaneously to developments in other countries, while output in other countries is influenced by the U.S. output gap. Under this assumption current foreign gaps will be inappropriate instruments for the U.S. gap and therefore we use the lagged euro gap as an additional instrument for the U.S. reaction function.

7. Of course, a positive coefficient may also capture that once debt becomes low, fiscal policy becomes expansionary.

Table 8.1 Fiscal policy reaction function

	Gap		Debt ($t-1$)		CAB ($t-1$)		R^2
	Coefficient	s.e.	Coefficient	s.e.	Coefficient	s.e.	
	A. (IV estimates, no break); Dependent variable: Cyclically-adjusted balance						
EURO area 12 countries	−0.222	(0.063)***	0.014	(0.007)**	0.732	(0.078)***	
Japan	−0.043	(0.138)	0.005	(0.007)	0.904	(0.071)***	
United Kingdom	−0.174	(0.142)	0.016	(0.034)	0.833	(0.099)***	
United States	−0.004	(0.113)	0.031	(0.015)**	0.778	(0.106)***	
Austria	0.053	(0.104)	0.025	(0.012)**	0.521	(0.126)***	
Belgium	−0.156	(0.223)	0.040	(0.015)**	0.706	(0.125)***	
Finland	0.151	(0.115)	0.032	(0.015)**	0.664	(0.119)***	
France	−0.193	(0.108)	0.009	(0.006)	0.674	(0.165)***	
Germany	−0.269	(0.115)**	0.017	(0.012)	0.674	(0.087)***	
Greece	−0.331	(0.457)	0.030	(0.011)**	0.567	(0.125)***	
Ireland	−0.234	(0.206)	0.005	(0.012)	0.832	(0.056)***	
Italy	−0.399	(0.133)***	0.066	(0.015)***	0.472	(0.104)***	
Luxembourg	0.044	(0.201)	0.987	(0.488)	0.274	(0.184)	
Netherlands	−0.308	(0.163)	0.004	(0.018)	0.766	(0.163)***	
Portugal	−0.188	(0.080)**	0.043	(0.040)	0.337	(0.121)**	
Spain	−0.078	(0.089)	0.036	(0.014)**	0.832	(0.112)***	
Denmark	0.620	(0.315)	0.041	(0.010)***	0.632	(0.110)***	
Sweden	1.003	(0.377)**	0.053	(0.021)**	0.407	(0.218)	
Australia	0.021	(0.197)	0.052	(0.017)***	0.851	(0.106)***	
Canada	0.106	(0.079)	0.051	(0.013)***	0.725	(0.077)***	
New Zealand	0.901	(0.640)	0.004	(0.031)	0.032	(0.462)	
Norway	−0.110	(0.151)	0.056	(0.042)	0.959	(0.068)***	
Switzerland	0.095	(0.141)	0.077	(0.029)**	0.473	(0.221)	

B. (*OLS estimates, no break*); *Dependent variable: Cyclically-adjusted balance*

EURO area 12 countries	-0.145	(0.061)**	0.016	(0.006)**	0.721	(0.076)***	0.82
Japan	-0.042	(0.100)	0.005	(0.007)	0.904	(0.069)***	0.78
United Kingdom	-0.196	(0.127)	0.017	(0.032)	0.837	(0.095)***	0.67
United States	0.133	(0.065)**	0.028	(0.014)	0.770	(0.103)***	0.69
Austria	-0.014	(0.087)	0.022	(0.011)	0.523	(0.126)***	0.49
Belgium	-0.199	(0.124)	0.038	(0.014)**	0.711	(0.123)***	0.91
Finland	0.232	(0.084)**	0.034	(0.015)**	0.601	(0.096)***	0.71
France	-0.127	(0.083)	0.009	(0.006)	0.652	(0.151)***	0.49
Germany	-0.240	(0.118)	0.017	(0.012)	0.681	(0.092)***	0.80
Greece	-0.388	(0.228)	0.029	(0.012)**	0.562	(0.114)***	0.76
Ireland	-0.219	(0.121)	0.006	(0.012)	0.832	(0.057)***	0.88
Italy	-0.195	(0.126)	0.065	(0.014)***	0.510	(0.104)***	0.92
Luxembourg	-0.033	(0.168)	0.968	(0.478)	0.311	(0.186)	0.62
Netherlands	-0.191	(0.164)	0.007	(0.019)	0.704	(0.163)***	0.51
Portugal	-0.161	(0.067)**	0.036	(0.040)	0.356	(0.119)***	0.42
Spain	-0.079	(0.072)	0.036	(0.014)**	0.832	(0.110)***	0.87
Denmark	0.467	(0.125)***	0.040	(0.010)***	0.669	(0.105)***	0.83
Sweden	0.699	(0.255)**	0.050	(0.018)**	0.537	(0.155)***	0.75
Australia	0.070	(0.117)	0.052	(0.018)***	0.833	(0.092)***	0.77
Canada	0.100	(0.070)	0.051	(0.013)***	0.727	(0.076)***	0.91
New Zealand	0.364	(0.143)**	-0.009	(0.019)	0.394	(0.238)	0.65
Norway	-0.013	(0.127)	0.048	(0.040)	0.997	(0.064)***	0.93
Switzerland	0.014	(0.106)	0.068	(0.027)**	0.535	(0.212)**	0.81

Note: Robust standard errors (s.e.) in parentheses.

***Significant at the 1 percent level.

**Significant at the 5 percent level.

counter-cyclicality. The U.K. results are closer to that of the euro area while Japan is closer to the United States. The procyclicality of the euro area is confirmed when looking at the individual euro countries. The majority display negative coefficients, some close to –0.4 (Italy). In contrast, for the non-euro countries (and with the exception of Norway), the coefficients are all positive and in some cases large (Sweden and New Zealand).

Another important insight from this table is that many of the coefficients on the output gap are not significant. This was also the case in Galí and Perotti (2003). In some sense, this could be expected given that the cyclically-adjusted balance has been constructed by purging the cyclical component from the budget balance. However, the method used is not simply an econometric one but one that relies on information on elasticities of the different fiscal components. So as long as governments engage often, and in the same direction, in fiscal policy decisions that are discretionary and related to the cycle, we should expect these coefficients to be significant. The fact that the coefficients are not significant could be an indication that this is not a behavior that we observe often. It could also be that the behavior is not consistent: maybe in some years fiscal policy behaved procyclically and in others countercyclically.

One of the questions that academics as well as policymakers are concerned about is whether policy in the euro countries has changed as a result of the introduction of the euro. Here we need to be very careful as we will be looking at very short time series when we split the sample into two. There are two possible ways of splitting the sample: in 1992 when the Maastricht treaty was approved and governments started dealing with limits on budget deficits, even if they were just entry conditions, and 1999 when the limits are actually enforced and there is a single monetary policy. We will show in the main text of the chapter the results where we split the sample in 1999 but we have also produced results splitting the sample in 1992 that are not included in this chapter but are available upon request.

Table 8.2 presents the results of estimating the policy rule in table 8.1 by allowing different elasticities before and after 1999.[8] Overall, there is a clear pattern of policies becoming more countercyclical after 1999. Among the top four large countries, the United States shows the largest change toward countercyclical policy.[9] While in the first sample policy looks mildly procyclical, it becomes very countercyclical after 1999. In the euro area there is practically no change in the coefficient between the two periods.

If we look at the individual EMU countries, when comparing the pre- and post-1999 samples we do not see any clear direction of change—in six countries policy has become less procyclical, while in the other six countries

---

8. We only include in this table the IV results. The OLS estimates show a similar pattern.

9. For the United Kingdom the change is even more dramatic in the IV estimates, but the standard errors are very large and the OLS estimates do not confirm this large shift in policy.

Table 8.2 Fiscal policy reaction function (IV estimates, with a break in 1999); Dependent variable: Cyclically-adjusted balance

	Gap before 1999		Gap after 1999		p-value: Equality	Debt (t − 1)		CAB (t − 1)	
	Coefficient	s.e.	Coefficient	s.e.		Coefficient	s.e.	Coefficient	s.e.
EURO area 12 countries	−0.218	(0.077)***	−0.206	(0.120)	0.94	0.016	(0.008)	0.736	(0.089)***
Japan	−0.072	(0.143)	0.280	(0.648)	0.60	0.015	(0.009)	0.840	(0.083)***
United Kingdom	−0.186	(0.148)	5.713	(7.710)	0.45	0.011	(0.039)	0.680	(0.259)**
United States	−0.035	(0.133)	1.326	(0.267)***	0.00	0.033	(0.016)**	0.700	(0.071)***
Austria	−0.002	(0.118)	−0.059	(0.257)	0.84	0.019	(0.016)	0.485	(0.134)***
Belgium	−0.120	(0.283)	−0.223	(0.223)	0.81	0.060	(0.027)**	0.519	(0.221)**
Finland	0.128	(0.105)	0.829	(0.517)	0.19	0.028	(0.018)	0.658	(0.150)***
France	−0.196	(0.116)	0.155	(0.206)	0.09	0.014	(0.011)	0.640	(0.181)***
Germany	−0.212	(0.142)	−0.305	(0.217)	0.74	0.038	(0.019)	0.637	(0.113)***
Greece	−0.429	(0.578)	0.166	(0.833)	0.50	0.031	(0.012)**	0.606	(0.154)***
Ireland	−0.174	(0.180)	−0.291	(0.574)	0.86	0.024	(0.029)	0.815	(0.066)***
Italy	−0.435	(0.157)***	−0.153	(0.257)	0.41	0.069	(0.017)***	0.453	(0.134)***
Luxembourg	0.549	(0.545)	0.646	(0.410)	0.87	0.712	(0.491)	−0.116	(0.278)
Netherlands	−0.458	(0.228)	−0.246	(0.182)	0.43	0.050	(0.030)	0.587	(0.207)**
Portugal	−0.119	(0.088)	−0.211	(0.159)	0.65	0.065	(0.059)	0.158	(0.177)
Spain	−0.088	(0.085)	−0.951	(0.451)**	0.08	0.047	(0.016)***	0.629	(0.153)***
Denmark	0.699	(0.320)**	−0.242	(0.299)	0.02	0.040	(0.011)***	0.630	(0.114)***
Sweden	1.118	(0.401)***	0.662	(0.401)	0.30	0.057	(0.024)**	0.372	(0.238)
Australia	0.170	(0.224)	−2.014	(1.748)	0.21	0.049	(0.026)	0.755	(0.207)***
Canada	0.129	(0.086)	−0.553	(0.586)	0.25	0.051	(0.014)***	0.784	(0.107)***
New Zealand	0.629	(0.420)	1.122	(0.641)	0.53	0.002	(0.068)	−0.022	(0.414)
Norway	0.091	(0.141)	−0.280	(0.487)	0.48	0.063	(0.050)	0.894	(0.082)***
Switzerland	−0.105	(0.156)	−0.023	(0.143)	0.69	0.044	(0.028)	0.470	(0.246)

Note: Robust standard errors (s.e.) in parentheses.

***Significant at the 1 percent level.

**Significant at the 5 percent level.

policy has become more procyclical. Formal tests as indicated by *p*-values signal that there is no evidence of a statistically significant shift in the cyclicality of fiscal policy in the euro area. Of all countries in the sample, we only find two where there is a statistically significant change in fiscal policy cyclicality. In the case of the United States, policy becomes more countercyclical; in the case of Denmark policy becomes more procyclical.

To some it might look like a surprise that the euro area fiscal stance is clearly procyclical given that we have seen in recent years an improvement in the budget balance during a period (post-2003) where the economy displayed increasing growth rates. It might also look like these results contradict those in other papers that show acyclical or even countercyclical fiscal policy for euro countries (e.g., Alesina, Campante, and Tabellini 2007). It is important to emphasize that the results in tables 8.1 and 8.2 are based on the cyclically-adjusted budget balance, so we are ignoring automatic stabilizers.[10] Our methodology is the one used by Galí and Perotti (2003). Their results are closer to ours, but still there is a difference when it comes to the euro area, where we are showing that fiscal policy is much more procyclical. Their estimates for the cyclicality of fiscal policy at the aggregate level are coming from estimating regression (1) for each of the countries and then aggregating the coefficients across countries. We are looking at the whole euro area without taking into account individual behavior. In addition, our sample is longer and all these factors could explain the differences in results.

To understand better the strong procyclicality of fiscal policy of the euro area, we have plotted the change in the cyclically-adjusted budget balance against the output gap for the years between 2000 and 2007. This is not exactly what is in our regression where we have the level of the balance on the left-hand side but the coefficient on the lagged value is high (although lower than one), plus it is quite common in the literature to look at changes in fiscal policy stance (see European Economy [2008] or Alesina, Campante, and Tabellini [2007]).

Figure 8.3 plots these two variables for the euro area and figure 8.4 does the same thing for the United States. The difference between the two plots is shocking. While for the United States there is a clear positive correlation signaling strong countercyclical policy, for the euro area we see exactly the opposite, a strong negative correlation. The evolution of the euro fiscal stance is marked by decreasing balances after 2000, which reflect the relaxation of fiscal policy after the launch of the euro, a sign of fatigue after the strong pre-1998 decrease in deficits to qualify for membership to EMU. After the recession of 2002/2003 and despite the existence of a negative

10. Table 8A.1 in the appendix shows the results of regressing the primary balance on the output gap. In that case, we observe acyclicality (if we use IV estimates) or even countercyclicality (OLS) for the euro area, consistent with previous results in the literature.

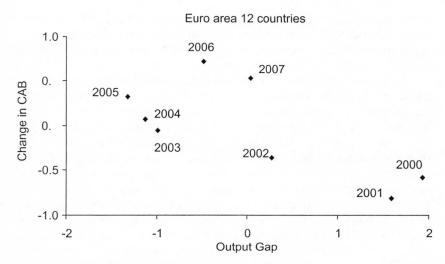

Fig. 8.3   **Fiscal policy stance and the output gap: Euro area**

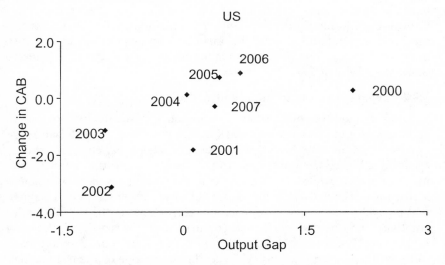

Fig. 8.4   **Fiscal policy stance and the output gap: United States**

output gap, there is an improvement in the structural balance that again represents procyclical policy. This improvement is due to two reasons: first, some of the euro countries were caught in levels of deficit that were too close to 3 percent (or above 3 percent) and they had little room to adjust their fiscal policies. Second, and this is especially true in 2005, tax revenues increased faster than what many governments expected. One interpretation is that the tax elasticities were larger than normal. Some of this could be due to composition effects such as an increase in profits as a share of GDP during these years (see European Commission 2007). These increases in revenues and elasticities were assumed to be permanent by governments and led to increases in spending or decreases in taxes that in the years that followed (2006 and 2007) led to a structural balance that remained too low despite the improvement in the cyclical condition of the economy. This reading of the behavior of fiscal policy during these eight years reveals that some of it is due to special circumstances (such as the effects of the launch of the new currency) but it is also difficult to avoid a sense that the fiscal policy framework did not work as expected. While our sample finishes in 2007, as we are writing this chapter we are witnessing once again a recession, and one that is affecting all advanced economies. While it is too early to reach conclusions about the extent to which fiscal policy will be used, so far the United States has shown once again a more aggressive response of fiscal policy to deteriorating economic conditions with projected deficits for the years to come that are much larger than the ones we see in European countries. The differences in policy seem to be related more to different views on the effectiveness of fiscal policy (and the long-term costs of implementing large fiscal policy stimulus) than to the limits imposed by the Stability and Growth Pact. Many European countries are planning deficits in excess of the 3 percent limit and some of the non-euro European countries that are not subject to this limit are also being more conservative than the United States (e.g., Sweden).

8.3.4   Digging Deeper: Spending and Taxes

To understand the source of changes in policy elasticities, we now look at the behavior of cyclically-adjusted spending and taxes. Tables 8.3 and 8.4 replicate the results of table 8.2 but where the dependent variable is either the cyclically-adjusted spending or taxes. In the euro area, spending has become more procyclical while taxes have become more countercyclical. The same is true for the United States and Japan.[11] Consistent with previous claims that procyclicality is driven by spending (Gavin and Perotti 1997; Tornell and Lane 1999), we find that in most countries spending is procyclical. Only Finland and France have changed their policies toward more countercyclicality in the past ten years, as evidenced by the p-value of the test for the equality of the coefficients before and after 1999.

Tax revenues in some countries have also become or have remained procyclical. However for the euro area, Japan, U.K., and U.S. tax revenues signal countercyclical policy stance in recent years. The move is particularly pronounced in the case of the United States, where several expansionary tax

11. For the United Kingdom, as in table 8.2, we see a large change toward countercyclicality in both taxes and spending. But the large coefficients and standard errors, together with the fact that the OLS results produce very different results, makes the interpretation of these changes very difficult.

Table 8.3   Fiscal policy reaction function (IV estimates, with a break in 1999); Dependent variable: Cyclically-adjusted spending

	Gap before 1999		Gap after 1999			Debt $(t-1)$		Spending $(t-1)$	
	Coefficient	s.e.	Coefficient	s.e.	p-value: Equality	Coefficient	s.e.	Coefficient	s.e.
EURO area 12 countries	0.037	(0.090)	0.138	(0.061)**	0.42	−0.013	(0.008)	0.905	(0.051)***
Japan	0.027	(0.065)	0.275	(0.135)	0.10	−0.018	(0.006)***	1.012	(0.040)***
United Kingdom	−0.166	(0.072)**	−2.884	(3.360)	0.42	0.006	(0.016)	0.642	(0.136)***
United States	−0.023	(0.066)	0.055	(0.073)	0.34	−0.038	(0.012)***	1.108	(0.064)***
Austria	0.015	(0.104)	−0.073	(0.139)	0.64	−0.020	(0.026)	0.997	(0.092)***
Belgium	0.262	(0.120)**	0.297	(0.150)	0.86	−0.018	(0.006)***	0.970	(0.045)***
Finland	−0.026	(0.073)	−0.713	(0.060)***	0.00	−0.088	(0.025)***	1.156	(0.064)***
France	0.157	(0.095)	−0.092	(0.056)	0.03	−0.024	(0.010)**	0.987	(0.036)***
Germany	−0.449	(0.939)	0.303	(0.211)	0.47	−0.050	(0.046)	0.774	(0.256)**
Greece	0.342	(0.373)	−0.819	(1.134)	0.33	0.001	(0.020)	0.932	(0.109)***
Ireland	0.264	(0.236)	0.049	(0.209)	0.59	−0.042	(0.041)	1.145	(0.071)***
Italy	0.213	(0.116)	0.064	(0.156)	0.45	−0.056	(0.016)***	1.160	(0.062)***
Luxembourg	0.286	(0.506)	0.085	(0.258)	0.74	−0.247	(0.513)	0.549	(0.406)
Netherlands	0.138	(0.124)	0.023	(0.107)	0.52	−0.041	(0.014)***	0.955	(0.048)***
Portugal	0.270	(0.080)***	0.105	(0.087)	0.20	0.039	(0.048)	0.678	(0.093)***
Spain	0.199	(0.050)***	0.122	(0.249)	0.77	−0.015	(0.013)	0.882	(0.075)***
Denmark	−0.207	(0.247)	−0.158	(0.065)**	0.85	0.008	(0.038)	0.881	(0.161)***
Sweden	−0.142	(0.081)	−0.268	(0.290)	0.69	−0.046	(0.014)***	0.986	(0.056)***
Australia	−0.322	(0.151)**	0.903	(0.745)	0.11	−0.019	(0.022)	0.788	(0.083)***
Canada	−0.002	(0.088)	0.506	(0.387)	0.21	−0.044	(0.014)***	1.048	(0.051)***
New Zealand	−0.483	(0.926)	1.774	(1.268)	0.32	0.026	(0.111)	1.809	(0.807)
Norway	−0.153	(0.117)	−0.097	(0.151)	0.77	−0.024	(0.022)	0.836	(0.073)***
Switzerland	−0.070	(0.155)	0.011	(0.121)	0.69	0.003	(0.050)	0.737	(0.373)

Note: Robust standard errors (s.e.) in parentheses.

***Significant at the 1 percent level.

**Significant at the 5 percent level.

Table 8.4   Fiscal policy reaction function (IV estimates, with a break in 1999); Dependent variable: Cyclically-adjusted tax receipts

	Gap before 1999		Gap after 1999		p-value: Equality	Debt (t − 1)		Taxes (t − 1)	
	Coefficient	s.e.	Coefficient	s.e.		Coefficient	s.e.	Coefficient	s.e.
EURO area 12 countries	−0.148	(0.079)	0.012	(0.156)	0.42	0.001	(0.006)	0.734	(0.092)***
Japan	0.010	(0.084)	0.853	(0.313)**	0.01	0.002	(0.008)	0.877	(0.066)***
United Kingdom	−0.210	(0.122)	2.043	(3.309)	0.50	0.052	(0.027)	0.755	(0.085)***
United States	0.050	(0.060)	1.162	(0.246)***	0.00	0.048	(0.011)***	0.578	(0.076)***
Austria	0.140	(0.128)	0.047	(0.153)	0.68	0.023	(0.020)	0.861	(0.123)***
Belgium	0.125	(0.170)	0.111	(0.152)	0.96	0.000	(0.009)	0.928	(0.125)***
Finland	0.157	(0.093)	0.141	(0.545)	0.98	0.016	(0.025)	0.940	(0.112)***
France	−0.166	(0.164)	−0.044	(0.196)	0.67	0.014	(0.013)	0.833	(0.086)***
Germany	1.049	(1.107)	0.238	(0.423)	0.57	0.038	(0.047)	0.704	(0.451)
Greece	−0.437	(0.421)	−0.707	(0.568)	0.65	0.037	(0.015)**	0.592	(0.186)***
Ireland	−0.031	(0.328)	−0.233	(0.266)	0.70	0.005	(0.038)	0.822	(0.189)***
Italy	−0.192	(0.155)	−0.516	(0.242)**	0.29	0.026	(0.025)	0.859	(0.123)***
Luxembourg	0.409	(0.541)	0.367	(0.213)	0.93	0.121	(0.383)	0.392	(0.234)
Netherlands	−0.031	(0.181)	−0.103	(0.144)	0.78	−0.034	(0.018)	0.902	(0.050)***
Portugal	0.184	(0.105)	−0.102	(0.087)	0.07	0.056	(0.045)	0.666	(0.090)***
Spain	0.115	(0.090)	−0.308	(0.362)	0.29	−0.010	(0.015)	0.847	(0.088)***
Denmark	0.430	(0.187)**	−0.282	(0.288)	0.03	0.057	(0.018)***	0.623	(0.086)***
Sweden	0.305	(0.134)**	0.132	(0.341)	0.63	0.017	(0.013)	0.787	(0.104)***
Australia	−0.305	(0.242)	−1.293	(1.124)	0.41	0.022	(0.025)	0.929	(0.114)***
Canada	0.075	(0.063)	−0.008	(0.419)	0.85	0.019	(0.012)	0.843	(0.088)***
New Zealand	0.711	(0.390)	0.371	(0.463)	0.68	−0.072	(0.068)	0.801	(0.188)***
Norway	−0.004	(0.116)	0.690	(0.233)***	0.01	−0.008	(0.028)	0.709	(0.111)***
Switzerland	−0.198	(0.190)	0.275	(0.128)	0.04	0.107	(0.062)	0.099	(0.336)

Note: Robust standard errors (s.e.) in parentheses.

***Significant at the 1 percent level.

**Significant at the 5 percent level.

packages introduced in the beginning of the 2000s coincided (deliberately or not) with a negative output gap in the U.S. economy. From tables 8.3 and 8.4 we can conclude that the increase in countercyclicality in the United States over the past ten years is coming from the revenue side rather than from the spending side.

It is also possible that the changes in the reaction of cyclically-adjusted tax receipts over the past ten years in some countries signal that the elasticities used in adjusting budgetary variables have changed. Indeed, recently the European Commission has started paying special attention to time varying elasticities, as documented in European Economy (2007).

8.3.5   Automatic Stabilizers

We now look at the automatic stabilizers component of fiscal policy. In table 8.5 we rerun the previous regression by using as dependent variable the component of fiscal policy that is linked to automatic stabilizers. This is measured as the difference between the actual and the cyclically-adjusted budget deficit. The regressions are estimated by OLS as they recover the log-linear relationship between the gap and automatic stabilizers used by the OECD in the process of adjusting budget to automatic changes in revenues and spending. This exercise produces very different results. First of all, the coefficient on the cycle now becomes clearly significant, as one would expect. In addition, the coefficients for the euro area now show clearly the countercyclical nature of fiscal policy. When comparing the euro area with the United States, we see that the size of the coefficient, in absolute value, is higher for the euro area. One potential reading of this comparison is that European countries have stronger automatic stabilizers built in and they have less need to use countercyclical discretionary measures. This is consistent with the fact that European governments have larger governments and that the size of governments have been associated to the significance of automatic stabilizers. (Galí 1994; Fatás and Mihov 2001).

The coefficients on the gap are closely related to the elasticities used by the OECD to derive the cyclically-adjusted budget balance. The OLS regression should uncover the weighted average of all elasticities (direct taxes, indirect taxes, social security payments, etc.) with the weights being given by the significance of each category in the overall budget. Since the OECD uses time-invariant elasticities, there is no point in searching for time-variation in these coefficients. The R^2 also shows that the errors in this estimation are quite small, which implies that indeed this manipulation uncovers relatively well a weighted-average estimate of the tax and spending elasticities used by the OECD.

The results at the national level confirm the ones for the euro area. Coefficients are positive and highly significant. Coefficients in the euro area vary from a low 0.3 (Greece) to a high of 0.65 (Germany), while in the United States and the United Kingdom these coefficients are 0.29 and 0.39,

Table 8.5   **Automatic stabilizers (OLS estimates)**

	Gap		Constant		
	Coefficient	s.e.	Coefficient	s.e.	R^2
EURO area 12 countries	0.464	(0.005)***	0.021	(0.009)**	1.00
Japan	0.267	(0.012)***	−0.014	(0.021)	0.95
United Kingdom	0.391	(0.021)***	−0.011	(0.033)	0.94
United States	0.293	(0.013)***	0.000	(0.020)	0.95
Austria	0.430	(0.015)***	0.011	(0.034)	0.95
Belgium	0.582	(0.046)***	0.042	(0.082)	0.83
Finland	0.460	(0.010)***	−0.194	(0.046)***	0.98
France	0.439	(0.016)***	0.001	(0.028)	0.94
Germany	0.647	(0.062)***	0.334	(0.094)***	0.82
Greece	0.307	(0.019)***	0.012	(0.020)	0.94
Ireland	0.410	(0.012)***	−0.010	(0.033)	0.98
Italy	0.378	(0.019)***	−0.071	(0.032)**	0.93
Luxembourg	0.423	(0.026)***	0.013	(0.061)	0.96
Netherlands	0.534	(0.036)***	−0.015	(0.068)	0.88
Portugal	0.333	(0.010)***	0.077	(0.036)**	0.98
Spain	0.422	(0.013)***	−0.023	(0.044)	0.97
Denmark	0.503	(0.034)***	0.016	(0.064)	0.85
Sweden	0.522	(0.022)***	−0.108	(0.044)**	0.96
Australia	0.339	(0.017)***	−0.008	(0.025)	0.91
Canada	0.370	(0.013)***	−0.055	(0.021)**	0.97
New Zealand	0.417	(0.007)***	0.047	(0.015)***	0.99
Norway	1.518	(0.268)***	11.656	(1.194)***	0.57
Switzerland	0.392	(0.014)***	−0.197	(0.035)***	0.98

Note: Robust standard errors (s.e.) in parentheses.
***Significant at the 1 percent level.
**Significant at the 5 percent level.

respectively. Thus, in the euro area the increase of the gap by 1 percent generates a budget surplus of about 0.46 percent, while in the United States, the surplus goes up only by 0.29 percent.

One question that emerges from this discussion is whether automatic stabilizers lead to lower output volatility. In figure 8.5 we use the elasticities reported in table 8.5 and we plot them against output volatility (in logarithm). The correlation is quite clear—countries like Germany, the Netherlands, and Belgium, with high elasticity of the budget with respect to the output gap, exhibit low levels of output volatility. The relationship between elasticities and volatility is statistically significant, with a slope estimate of −3.3. This implies that an increase in elasticity by 0.1 leads to a reduction in output volatility by about 30 percent. As we mentioned before, there is no time variation in these elasticities as they assumed to be constant in the construction of the cyclically-adjusted balance. At the same time recent research has shown that the empirical relationship between gov-

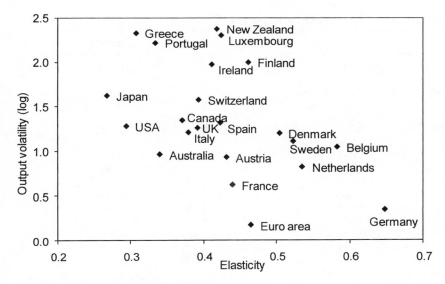

Fig. 8.5   **Output volatility and automatic stabilizers**

ernment size and the volatility of GDP seems to have become weaker (as documented in Debrun, Pisany-Ferry, and Sapir [2008]). The fact that the relationship has become weaker is an indication that there have been changes in the effectiveness of automatic stabilizers that have also weakened the link between the size of the government and their smoothing effect. Given that the close link between government size and automatic stabilizers, it seems important to review the assumption of time-invariant elasticities. If one finds that elasticities have changed, then researchers will be able to construct better measures of the structural balance. If, on the other hand, it turns out that elasticities have not changed, then the link between government size and stabilization has become indeed weaker, which will lead to review of the desirability of having large governments. Larger governments, as much as they might be able to provide a cushion to business cycle fluctuations, can be associated with crowding out and lower growth.

8.3.6   The Use of (Exogenous) Discretionary Fiscal Policy

To establish whether exogenous discretionary policy has become more aggressive since 1999, we calculate the volatility of the residuals from equation (1). Table 8.6 compares the volatility of discretionary policy before and after EMU as well as with the United States, United Kingdom, and Japan. We show volatilities calculated using a fiscal policy rule with a break in 1999. What is evident from the previous numbers is that the euro area has the lowest standard deviation of the residual, so the size and frequency of fiscal policy exogenous "shocks" is much smaller than for the other countries.

Table 8.6   Volatility of the residuals

Country	Before 1999	After 1999
EURO area 12 countries	0.304	0.146
Japan	1.096	2.543
United Kingdom	1.845	0.899
United States	0.641	0.135
Austria	0.792	1.123
Belgium	1.658	0.927
Finland	1.811	1.062
France	0.517	0.171
Germany	0.713	0.492
Greece	2.729	1.461
Ireland	0.904	2.784
Italy	1.416	0.415
Luxembourg	0.628	0.953
Netherlands	1.189	0.798
Portugal	1.379	0.961
Spain	0.625	0.457
Denmark	1.377	1.200
Sweden	3.017	1.082
Australia	0.613	0.711
Canada	1.018	0.409
New Zealand	0.109	0.281
Norway	1.466	1.399
Switzerland	0.219	0.308

We also see a decrease in the volatility over time. The fact that the volatility is lower for the euro area should not be a surprise as this is an aggregate of national fiscal policies and it is difficult to think about coordinated changes in fiscal policy. It might be that we observe such changes of policies at the national level but they are not synchronized and therefore vanish when we aggregate all the countries. However, and as we have seen in the previous section, we do observe some significant changes in fiscal policy at the euro level. So one potential reading of these results is that European countries are less willing to engage in discretionary changes in fiscal policy. It is possible that this decline in aggressiveness is due to the increased monitoring of national fiscal policies by the European Commission. On the margin, changing fiscal stance for reasons unrelated to the state of cycle has become more difficult, as any change is carefully scrutinized by the Commission. Potentially this is only a partial explanation, as the volatility in the United States has declined even faster than in the euro area.

When we look at individual countries, most euro countries display low volatility of exogenous discretionary policy, which is consistent with what we found for the aggregate of the euro countries. We also see that this volatility has decreased in the second half of the sample for all countries with the exception of Austria, Ireland, and Luxembourg. Outside of the

EU-15, only Canada and the United States show substantial reduction in policy volatility.

8.4   Does Fiscal Policy React to Output Growth or to the Output Gap?

Both in the construction of the cyclically-adjusted balance, as well as in the estimation previously reported, there is an assumption that fiscal policy reacts to the output gap. There are two issues: first, the reported gap might be a noisy and biased estimate of the actual gap. Second, fiscal authorities might be more concerned with growth rather than the gap.

We can illustrate the difficulty in interpreting regression results by redoing figures 8.3 and 8.4 (euro area and U.S. correlation between cyclically-adjusted balances and the cycle) by using the output growth rate instead of the gap as a measure of the cyclical position of the economy. Figures 8.6 and 8.7 plot the change in the structural balance against real growth for the euro area and the United States. It is interesting that while for the United States the picture looks very similar to the previous plot, for the euro area we now see a much less clear picture. While the years 2000 and 2001 show procyclical fiscal policy, in the years that follow 2002 through 2007 we see a positive slope, signaling acyclical or countercyclical policy. This is very different from what we saw in figure 8.3, using the output gap, where euro fiscal policy was clearly procyclical.

The comparison between figure 8.3 and figure 8.6 opens the door for a different interpretation of our results. There is still no doubt that U.S. fiscal policy is more countercyclical (and in a consistent manner) than the euro one. But whether the euro fiscal policy has been countercyclical or procyclical (or has switched from one to the other) remains an open question. The European Commission uses the output gap as the cyclical indicator to assess

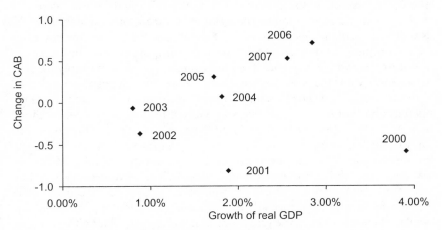

Fig. 8.6   Fiscal policy stance and output growth: Euro area

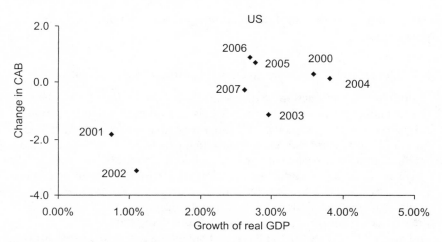

Fig. 8.7   Fiscal policy stance and output growth: United States

the stance of fiscal policy, but it might be that politicians care more about growth and react to the output growth rate.

There is even a deeper issue: current practice in removing the cyclical component of the budget balance uses as a starting point the automatic reaction of fiscal variables to the output gap. That is the case for the measures we have used in this chapter and produced by the OECD or the structural balance used by the European Commission. What if in fact tax revenues react more closely to the growth rate of output rather than to the gap? If this is the case, then many of the results in the literature have to be reinterpreted. To evaluate this possibility, we run a "race" between the gap and output growth. In table 8.7 our dependent variable is the primary balance as percent of GDP, while the key regressors are the growth rate of real GDP and the output gap.

The results are quite interesting. With the exception of Denmark and Sweden, in all countries where we have significant coefficients the key variable is output growth and not the output gap. Importantly, in the euro area the gap enters with a negative, albeit insignificant, coefficient (implying procyclicality), while the growth rate enters with a significant positive coefficient (countercyclicality). The estimates imply that the primary balance—which includes both automatic stabilizers and structural balances—reacts more readily to output growth rather than to the output gap. At this point, the only thing that we can do is to raise a warning flag. To reestimate the results in the previous tables we need first to decompose the balance into cyclical and structural components by using elasticities with respect to output growth and not the output gap. Furthermore, it is quite conceivable that certain fiscal variables respond to the gap (e.g., unemployment benefits), while others respond to the growth rate (tax revenues). And although this task lies beyond the scope of the chapter, table 8.7 is still useful in both

Table 8.7   Fiscal policy reaction function: gap vs. growth (OLS estimates, no break). Dependent variable: primary balance

	Gap		Output growth		Debt $(t-1)$		Primary balance $(t-1)$		R^2
	Coefficient	s.e.	Coefficient	s.e.	Coefficient	s.e.	Coefficient	s.e.	
EURO area 12 countries	-0.114	(0.169)	0.463	(0.157)**	0.016	(0.034)	0.657	(0.193)***	0.86
Japan	0.015	(0.089)	0.283	(0.121)**	0.010	(0.008)	0.877	(0.068)***	0.81
United Kingdom	0.029	(0.128)	0.179	(0.135)	-0.006	(0.025)	0.728	(0.084)***	0.66
United States	0.153	(0.084)	0.375	(0.085)***	0.026	(0.014)	0.808	(0.085)***	0.79
Austria	0.214	(0.115)	0.101	(0.162)	0.025	(0.012)**	0.526	(0.126)***	0.53
Belgium	-0.018	(0.154)	0.296	(0.186)	0.042	(0.011)***	0.729	(0.114)***	0.90
Finland	0.221	(0.118)	0.458	(0.118)***	0.008	(0.017)	0.685	(0.092)***	0.84
France	0.047	(0.091)	0.372	(0.090)***	0.013	(0.005)**	0.495	(0.113)***	0.69
Germany	-0.192	(0.220)	0.628	(0.143)***	0.004	(0.022)	0.617	(0.265)**	0.76
Greece	-0.228	(0.229)	0.101	(0.149)	0.025	(0.012)**	0.571	(0.162)***	0.72
Ireland	-0.239	(0.131)	0.329	(0.131)**	0.008	(0.012)	0.783	(0.082)***	0.90
Italy	0.001	(0.128)	0.158	(0.159)	0.066	(0.013)***	0.532	(0.103)***	0.92
Luxembourg	0.366	(0.249)	-0.061	(0.279)	1.059	(0.523)	0.290	(0.183)	0.72
Netherlands	0.065	(0.266)	0.417	(0.191)**	-0.006	(0.021)	0.562	(0.235)**	0.67
Portugal	0.018	(0.084)	0.141	(0.129)	0.082	(0.029)***	0.406	(0.121)***	0.59
Spain	-0.021	(0.111)	0.354	(0.187)	0.013	(0.015)	0.842	(0.082)***	0.91
Australia	0.084	(0.152)	0.364	(0.144)**	0.031	(0.021)	0.830	(0.091)***	0.83
Canada	0.190	(0.082)**	0.334	(0.066)***	0.057	(0.012)***	0.703	(0.074)***	0.93
Denmark	0.714	(0.247)***	0.221	(0.218)	0.036	(0.010)***	0.691	(0.112)***	0.87
New Zealand	0.828	(0.409)	-0.091	(0.379)	-0.003	(0.023)	0.285	(0.262)	0.83
Norway	0.138	(0.203)	0.691	(0.245)***	0.087	(0.074)	0.736	(0.133)***	0.70
Sweden	1.058	(0.306)***	0.044	(0.251)	0.05	(0.017)***	0.527	(0.130)***	0.86
Switzerland	0.225	(0.193)	0.163	(0.202)	0.084	(0.035)**	0.441	(0.180)**	0.84

Note: Robust standard errors (s.e.) in parentheses.

***Significant at the 1 percent level.

**Significant at the 5 percent level.

raising the issue and in pointing out that the disparity of findings in the literature might be due to the difference in the cyclical indicator used to evaluate the behavior of fiscal policy. It is certainly worth considering in future work an alternative adjustment based on the growth rate. See Blanchard (1993) for an in-depth discussion of the alternative adjustment methods.

8.5   Coordination of National Fiscal Policies: Is There a Euro-Wide Fiscal Policy Stance?

In the previous sections of the chapter we looked both at the behavior of fiscal policy for the aggregate of the twelve euro countries as well as for each of the countries. Although there is no government behind the behavior of the euro aggregate, it is simply the collection of twelve individual policies; these individual policies have been designed within the institutional framework of the Maastricht treaty and the Stability and Growth Pact so the idea of Euro-wide fiscal policy is not entirely meaningless. The framework has possibly introduced some commonalities across national fiscal policies. For example, the run-up to the euro launch led to fiscal consolidation efforts for many of the governments. In addition, the interpretation and implementation of the Stability and Growth Pact has led to increasing emphasis on coordination of national fiscal policies. This coordination of national fiscal policies runs contrary to the intuition that with a common monetary policy, fiscal policy should behave in an even less coordinated fashion as it needs to deal with idiosyncratic national shocks. In this section we look at national fiscal policies and ask the question of whether we have seen any move toward coordination or synchronization. Figure 8.8 plots the annual standard deviation of the structural budget balance across euro countries and compares it to the same measure for the non-euro countries in the sample.[12] Since 1999, there is a clear trend toward less dispersion among the euro countries that is not evident for the rest of the countries. This trend can be the result of proactive coordination but it could also be the outcome of some countries being close or above the limits established for budget deficits.

The trend toward more similar structural balances might be a result also of synchronization of business cycles. Indeed, figure 8.9 shows that the dispersion of the output gap has been declining steadily since the early 1990s. Interestingly, however, this trend is visible both for the euro area and for the group of the non-euro area countries. If we compare now figures 8.8 and 8.9, it seems that there is more to the synchronization of fiscal policy stances across euro countries than just synchronization of business cycles.

Finally, figure 8.10 reports synchronization of fiscal policy by looking

---

12. Norway is excluded from this calculation because of the high volatility of the budget stemming from fluctuations in oil prices.

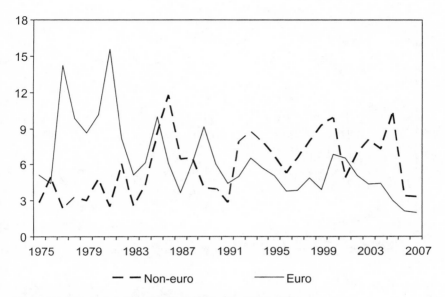

Fig. 8.8 Dispersion of cyclically-adjusted budget balances
Note: Standard deviation across countries in percent.

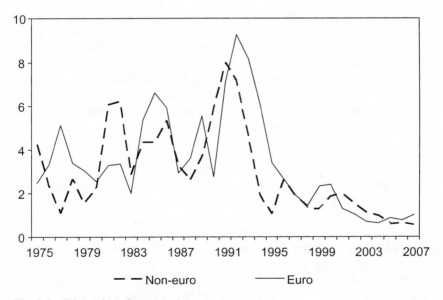

Fig. 8.9 Dispersion of output gaps
Note: Standard deviation across countries in percent.

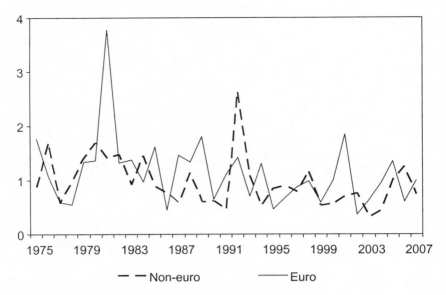

Fig. 8.10   Dispersion of exogenous discretionary fiscal policy

at the exogenous component. We measure the dispersion (using standard deviation) of the residuals from equation (1) across both euro and non-euro countries. In this case we see that there is a very small downward trend for both samples. We already know that the typical size of these shocks has decreased over the sample period, so this could simply be due to the fact that we see fewer and smaller changes in discretionary fiscal policy and, therefore, an increase in synchronization for many countries. Of course, this need not be the case, as it is possible that many large and coordinated changes in fiscal policy lead to a small cross-country standard deviation.

8.6   Concluding Remarks

The 1992 Maastricht treaty recognized the importance of providing a framework for fiscal policy in EMU and established limits to deficits and debt in order to "avoid excessive government deficits" (Article 104). At the same time it defined an Excessive Deficit Procedure in case of violations. The Stability and Growth Pact (1997) developed the original ideas of the Maastricht treaty into a set of more detailed rules and processes to ensure budget discipline and enforcement. The principles of the Stability and Growth pact were later amended by a report of the ECOFIN council in March 2005 that was later endorsed by the European Council.

This is the environment under which fiscal policy has been conducted in the euro area, an environment that has been a source of criticisms and debates. Some have seen these limits as unnecessary constraints on national fiscal policy at a time when it was needed the most, with negative consequences on the macroeconomic performance of these economies. For those who had to implement the constraints and procedures (European Commission) or those who were supposed to care about them (ECB), the rules have not provided an easily enforceable system and the outcome has been far from what the system was designed for. Fiscal consolidation has not been large enough and national policies have continued to display many of the prior biases (such as procyclicality).

In this chapter we have provided a characterization of fiscal policy at the euro and the national levels and used countries outside of the euro area as benchmark. Our goal was not to propose an alternative fiscal policy framework but more to validate or disprove the conventional wisdom about how fiscal policy has behaved and the extent to which the EMU fiscal policy framework has affected that behavior.

Overall, our results have shown that the behavior of fiscal policy in the euro area has not been too different from what we have seen in other countries and that the introduction of the euro has not led to a significant change. The fear that fiscal policy would become less disciplined because governments would not internalize the cost of "bad" fiscal policy in the absence of national currencies is not validated by our results. There is also very little evidence that the fiscal policy stance at the national level has gotten worse. Although cyclically-adjusted balances still show some tendency to be procyclical for some countries in the euro zone, it is still true that the automatic stabilizers do most of the countercyclical adjustment in the union. The other positive reading of our results is that governments have not abused their discretion and that the size of frequency of politically motivated fiscal policy changes has decreased among the European economies.

Coordination of fiscal policies has received much recent attention by the European Commission as a way to justify the strong surveillance mechanisms that they impose on national countries. The notion of coordination is sometimes linked to that of economic convergence but this link is theoretically not founded, as we should expect the opposite: as countries have abandoned monetary policy, there is a stronger need to rely on fiscal policy as an automatic stabilizer. Of course, if business cycles become more synchronized, we will see coordination but there is no need to impose that coordination as one lets automatic stabilizers run their course. This is indeed what our results show. But it also seems that there is something beyond business cycle synchronization since a similar decline in dispersion for the countries outside the euro zone has not been met with a decline in the dispersion of their structural balances. Other measures of fiscal policy, those that also include the discretionary component, do not show any tendency to become less coordinated. If any, there seems to be more coordination and synchronicity at that level, which supports the view that governments have not taken advantage of the euro fiscal framework to push different political agendas through the use of fiscal policy.

Our analysis of the euro-wide aggregates provided us with the perspective that the ECB and monetary policy have about fiscal policy. In some sense, it could be argued that this is the relevant dimension in which to discuss fiscal policy in the euro area. As much as national fiscal policies can show biases and behaviors that are not optimal, when it comes to monetary policy and the currency, what matters is the behavior of fiscal policy at the aggregate level (of course, the aggregate is made out of the sum of all the national fiscal policies, so their understanding can still provide very useful insights).

When looking at the euro-wide fiscal policy we see a behavior that is different from what we have seen in the United States. Fiscal policy is more procyclical in the euro area than in the United States (where it is strongly countercyclical), but it is also true that the automatic stabilizers are larger in the euro zone. In addition, and this should be welcomed by the ECB, fiscal policy is less volatile at the euro level when it comes to exogenous changes, those that are not motivated by the economic environment.

Last but not least, it is important to emphasize that many of the findings in the literature are sensitive to the cyclical indicator used in the regression analysis. In this chapter we show that the primary balance reacts more readily to the growth rate of real output rather than to the output gap. Reassessing the construction of cyclically-adjusted variables might lead to significant changes in the way that researchers view fiscal policy stance in the OECD economies.

Appendix

Table 8A.1   **Fiscal policy reaction function**

	Gap		Debt $(t-1)$		Primary balance $(t-1)$	
	Coefficient	s.e.	Coefficient	s.e.	Coefficient	s.e.
A. Dependent variable: Primary balance (IV estimates, no break)						
EURO area 12 countries	−0.006	(0.103)	0.020	(0.011)	0.657	(0.143)***
Japan	−0.004	(0.145)	0.005	(0.007)	0.901	(0.082)***
United Kingdom	0.041	(0.143)	−0.003	(0.030)	0.728	(0.110)***
United States	0.099	(0.141)	0.038	(0.018)**	0.695	(0.118)***
Austria	0.316	(0.109)***	0.027	(0.013)**	0.481	(0.133)***
Belgium	−0.048	(0.249)	0.035	(0.013)**	0.756	(0.126)***
Finland	0.285	(0.213)	0.037	(0.018)**	0.676	(0.173)***
France	0.083	(0.162)	0.011	(0.007)	0.577	(0.203)***
Germany	0.025	(0.128)	0.021	(0.016)	0.570	(0.119)***
Greece	−0.436	(0.466)	0.022	(0.012)	0.604	(0.148)***

Table 8A.1   (continued)

	Gap		Debt ($t-1$)		Primary balance ($t-1$)	
	Coefficient	s.e.	Coefficient	s.e.	Coefficient	s.e.
Ireland	−0.242	(0.210)	0.005	(0.014)	0.910	(0.058)***
Italy	−0.123	(0.117)	0.065	(0.014)***	0.493	(0.096)***
Luxembourg	0.427	(0.194)	1.009	(0.473)	0.266	(0.207)
Netherlands	−0.070	(0.261)	0.017	(0.020)	0.793	(0.228)***
Portugal	−0.010	(0.090)	0.068	(0.036)	0.442	(0.151)***
Spain	0.015	(0.100)	0.036	(0.012)***	0.841	(0.102)***
Denmark	1.016	(0.298)***	0.047	(0.008)***	0.579	(0.086)***
Sweden	1.217	(0.434)***	0.051	(0.016)***	0.474	(0.188)**
Australia	0.309	(0.239)	0.058	(0.019)***	0.745	(0.105)***
Canada	0.339	(0.107)***	0.062	(0.014)***	0.653	(0.078)***
New Zealand	1.022	(0.390)**	−0.001	(0.024)	0.201	(0.237)
Norway	−0.002	(0.284)	0.129	(0.082)	0.743	(0.149)***
Switzerland	0.396	(0.163)**	0.115	(0.018)***	0.318	(0.160)
B. Dependent variable: Primary balance (OLS estimates, no break)						
EURO area 12 countries	0.156	(0.105)	0.025	(0.011)**	0.545	(0.145)***
Japan	0.086	(0.104)	0.005	(0.007)	0.883	(0.079)***
United Kingdom	0.074	(0.132)	−0.002	(0.024)	0.726	(0.083)***
United States	0.342	(0.082)***	0.033	(0.016)	0.650	(0.107)***
Austria	0.265	(0.094)***	0.025	(0.012)**	0.506	(0.130)***
Belgium	0.100	(0.127)	0.042	(0.011)***	0.725	(0.111)***
Finland	0.498	(0.141)***	0.027	(0.017)	0.533	(0.114)***
France	0.177	(0.105)	0.011	(0.007)	0.532	(0.144)***
Germany	0.092	(0.130)	0.024	(0.016)	0.540	(0.119)***
Greece	−0.194	(0.199)	0.025	(0.012)**	0.612	(0.124)***
Ireland	−0.112	(0.121)	0.013	(0.013)	0.923	(0.064)***
Italy	0.084	(0.114)	0.069	(0.014)***	0.491	(0.098)***
Luxembourg	0.328	(0.168)	0.999	(0.458)	0.321	(0.214)
Netherlands	0.206	(0.236)	0.019	(0.020)	0.599	(0.219)**
Portugal	0.042	(0.072)	0.085	(0.028)***	0.402	(0.142)***
Spain	0.071	(0.095)	0.032	(0.011)***	0.815	(0.103)***
Denmark	0.903	(0.128)***	0.041	(0.009)***	0.618	(0.083)***
Sweden	1.096	(0.260)***	0.051	(0.016)***	0.517	(0.119)***
Australia	0.383	(0.139)**	0.057	(0.020)***	0.720	(0.090)***
Canada	0.360	(0.094)***	0.063	(0.013)***	0.646	(0.073)***
New Zealand	0.741	(0.100)***	−0.005	(0.021)	0.339	(0.181)
Norway	0.162	(0.202)	0.100	(0.073)	0.704	(0.128)***
Switzerland	0.304	(0.132)**	0.108	(0.015)***	0.386	(0.150)**

Note: Robust standard errors (s.e.) in parentheses.

***Significant at the 1 percent level.

**Significant at the 5 percent level.

References

Alesina, A., and T. Bayoumi. 1996. The costs and benefits of fiscal rules: Evidence from U.S. states. NBER Working Paper no. 5614. Cambridge, MA: National Bureau of Economic Research, June.

Alesina, A., F. Campante, and G. Tabellini. 2007. Why is fiscal policy often procyclical. Weatherhead Center for International Affairs, Harvard University. Working Paper no. 2007-15.

Alesina, A., and G. Tabellini. 1990. A positive theory of fiscal deficits and government debt. *Review of Economic Studies* 57 (3): 403–14.

Alt, J., and R. Lowry. 1994. Divided governments, fiscal institutions, and budget deficits: Evidence for the states. *American Political Science Review* 88 (December): 811–28.

Auerbach, A. J., and D. Feenberg. 2000. The significance of federal taxes as automatic stabilizers. *The Journal of Economic Perspectives* 14 (3): 37–56.

Barro, R. J. 1979. On the determination of the public debt. *Journal of Political Economy* 87 (5): 940–71.

Blanchard, O. 1993. Suggestions for a new set of fiscal indicators. In *The New political economy of government debt,* ed. H. A. A. Verbon and F. A. A. M. van Winden, 307–25. Amsterdam: Elsevier Science Publishers.

Blanchard, O., and F. Giavazzi. 2004. Reforms that can be done: Improving the SGP through a proper accounting of public investment. Center for Economic Policy Research (CEPR) Discussion Paper Series no. 4220.

Blanchard, O., and R. Perotti. 2002. An empirical characterization of the dynamic effects of changes in government spending and taxes on output. *Quarterly Journal of Economics* 117 (4): 1329–68.

Brunila, A., M. Buti, and D. Franco. 2001. Introduction. In *The stability and growth pact,* ed. A. Brunila, M. Buti, and D. Franco, 1–22. Hundsmills: Palgrave.

Buiter, W., and C. Grafe. 2002. Patching up the pact: Some suggestions for enhancing fiscal sustainability and macroeconomic stability in an enlarged European Union. CEPR Discussion Paper Series no. 3495.

Burnside, C., M. Eichenbaum, and J. Fisher. 2004. Assessing the effects of fiscal shocks. *Journal of Economic Theory* 115 (1): 89–117.

Buti, M., and A. Sapir. 2002. *EMU and economic policy in Europe: The challenge of the early years.* Northampton, MA: Edwrd Elgar.

Chari, V. V., L. Christiano, and P. Kehoe. 1994. Optimal fiscal policy in a business cycle model. *Journal of Political Economy* 102 (4): 617–52.

Debrun, X., J. Pisany-Ferry, and A. Sapir. 2008. Government size and output volatility: Should we forsake automatic stabilization? IMF Working Paper no. 08/12. Washington, DC: International Monetary Fund, May.

Drazen, A. 2000. *Political economy in macroeconomics.* Princeton, NJ: Princeton University Press.

European Central Bank (ECB). 2005. Statement of the Governing Council on the ECOFIN Council's report on improving the implementation of the Stability and Growth Pact. Press release, 21 March.

European Commission. 2007. Public Finances in EMU—2008. Brussels: European Commission, Economic and Financial Affairs.

Fatás, A., and I. Mihov. 2001. Government size and automatic stabilizers. *Journal of International Economics* 55 (1): 3–28.

———. 2003. The case for restricting fiscal policy discretion. *Quarterly Journal of Economics* 118 (4): 1419–47.

————. 2007. Policy volatility, institutions and economic growth. Institut Européen d'Administration des Affaires (INSEAD). Unpublished Manuscript, Fontainebleau, France.

Fatás, A., A. H. Hallet, A. Sibert, R. Strauch, and J. von Hagen. 2003. Stability and growth in Europe: Towards a better pact, *Monitoring European integration*. CEPR report, Monitoring European Integration Series no. 13. London: CEPR.

Favero, C., and F. Giavazzi. 2007. Debt and the effects of fiscal policy. Bocconi University, IGIER (Innocenzo Gasparini Institute for Economic Research) Working Paper no. 317.

Galí, J. 1994. Government size and macroeconomic stability. *European Economic Review* 38 (1): 117–32.

Galí, J., and R. Perotti. 2003. Fiscal policy and monetary integration in Europe. *Economic Policy* 18 (37): 533–72.

Gavin, M., and R. Perotti. 1997. Fiscal policy in Latin America. In *NBER Macroeconomics Annual,* ed. B. S. Bernanke and J. J. Rotemberg, 11–60. Cambridge, MA: MIT Press.

Girouard, N., and C. André. 2005. Measuring cyclically-adjusted budget balances for OECD countries. OECD Economics Department Working Paper no. 434. Paris: OECD Economics Department.

Kaminsky, G., C. Reinhart, and C. A. Vegh. 2004. When it rains it pours: Procyclical capital flows and macroeconomic policies. NBER Working Paper no. 10780. Cambridge, MA: National Bureau of Economic Research, September.

Lane, P. R. 2003. The cyclical behavior of fiscal policy: Evidence from the OECD. *Journal of Public Economics* 87 (12): 2661–75.

Mankiw, N. G., and D. W. Elmendorf. 1999. Government debt. In *Handbook of macroeconomics*, vol 1C, ed. J. B. Taylor and M. Woodford, 1615–63. Amsterdam: Elsevier.

Melitz, J. 2000. Some cross-country evidence about fiscal policy behavior and consequences for EMU. *European Economy* 2:3–21.

————. 2006. Non-discretionary and automatic fiscal policy in the EU and the OECD. In *Fiscal surveillance in EMU: New issues and challenges,* ed. S. Deroose, E. Flores, A. Torrini, and P. Wierts, Hundsmills: Palgrave.

Mohr, M., and R. Morris. 2007. Uncertainty in measuring the underlying budgetary position and fiscal stance,. Unpublished manuscript.

Perry, G. 2003. Can fiscal rules help reduce macroeconomic volatility in the Latin America and the Caribbean region? World Bank Policy Research Working Paper no. 3080.

Persson, T., and L. Svensson. 1989. Why a stubborn conservative would run a deficit: Policy with time-inconsistent preferences. *Quarterly Journal of Economics* 104 (2): 325–45.

Persson, T., and G. Tabellini. 2001. Political institutions and policy outcomes: What are the stylized facts? CEPR Discussion Paper Series no. 2872, London.

Poterba, J. 1994. State responses to fiscal crises: The effects of budgetary institutions. *Journal of Political Economy* 102 (4): 799–821.

Poterba, J., and J. von Hagen. 1999. *Fiscal institutions and fiscal performance.* Chicago: University of Chicago Press.

Tornell, A., and P. Lane. 1999. The voracity effect. *American Economic Review* 89 (1): 22–46.

von Hagen, J. 1992. Budgeting procedures and fiscal performance in the European communities. Commission of the European Communities, DG II Economic Papers 96.

———. 2005. Fiscal rules and fiscal performance in the EU and Japan. CEPR Discussion Paper no. 5330.
Wyplosz, C. 2005. Fiscal policy: Institutions versus rules. *National Institute Economic Review* 191 (January): 70–84.

Comment   Roberto Perotti

This is an interesting and well-written chapter that presents a useful overview of fiscal policy issues and some interesting results. In these comments I will focus on what I regard as the two most important empirical questions studied in the chapter: (a) is fiscal policy more or less countercyclical in Europe than in the United States? and (b) has the euro plus the Growth and Stability Pact induced a more procyclical (less countercyclical) behavior of fiscal policy in European Monetary Union (EMU) countries?

On the first issue, the answer of the chapter is clear, and confirms both existing empirical results and common wisdom on the difference between Europe and the United States: "discretionary" fiscal policy seems more countercyclical in the United States, "automatic stabilizers" more countercyclical in Europe. The authors present convincing empirical evidence on this effect, and support it with equally convincing robustness analysis. I do not have much to add on this point.

On the second issue, obviously it is hard to base any conclusion on less than ten years of data, but even leaving this problem aside, I think the verdict is still open, and hard to reach. As the authors point out in section 8.4, following the discussion at the conference, the problem is well illustrated by a comparison of figures 8.3 and 8.6: while discretionary fiscal policy in the euro area seems procyclical if evaluated against the output gap, it appears countercyclical if evaluated against the growth rate of gross domestic product (GDP).

Note that this issue in turn involves two fundamentally different underlying issues. The first is, what is the appropriate variable to cyclically adjust the budget? Suppose that a certain expenditure item changes automatically, by law, in response to the output gap; then the appropriate variable to cyclically adjust this expenditure item is the output gap. Similarly, the appropriate variable is output growth if by law an expenditure or revenue item moves with the change in the level of output. In reality, things are even more complex, because the reference level for cyclical adjustment (potential output or last year's output) is not defined by law.

But even assuming we have taken a stance on the appropriate reference

Roberto Perotti is professor of economics at Bocconi University and a research associate of the National Bureau of Economic Research.

level of output in doing the cyclical adjustment, this is different from the question: "to what variable do policymakers react when setting discretionary fiscal policy?" Here I would surmise that the reasons for using the output gap in monetary policy reaction functions are more compelling than in fiscal policy reactions functions. Monetary authorities understand and use the concept of output gap; fiscal policymakers (therefore including congressmen when voting on the budget) typically do not know, do not understand, and do not use the concept of output gap; they react to GDP growth.

A second explanation for the results on the cyclical behavior of discretionary fiscal policy (and at the same time an illustration of the perils of drawing inference from 8 data points) is ideology and fatigue. Comparing figures 8.3 and 8.4, it is clear that the results are heavily influenced by two years. The euro area result in figure 8.3 depends heavily on 2000 and 2001, two good years in terms of gap, when, however, many governments relaxed their discretionary fiscal policy following several years of budget cuts enacted to qualify for the EMU. Conversely, the U.S. results are heavily influenced by 2001 and 2002, two years of low output gap in the United States, when taxes were cut and spending increased, due in part to the ideology of the new administration and in part to exogenous foreign policy events.

How Central Bankers See It
The First Decade of European
Central Bank Policy and Beyond

Stephen G. Cecchetti and Kermit L. Schoenholtz

9.1   Introduction

Otmar Issing: "There was a clear view from a number of outside observers that we would fail and that it would be a disaster in any respect."

As late as 1997, less than a year before the European Central Bank (ECB) was scheduled to come into existence, there was widespread skepticism about whether the European Monetary Union (EMU) would begin on schedule as a broad union and, in some quarters, whether it would happen at all. Yet here we are a full decade after the advent of EMU and today there are fifteen countries where the euro is legal tender. The twenty-one members of the Governing Council of the ECB make monetary policy for a region of 320 million people with a gross domestic product (GDP) of roughly €9 trillion. And it is hard to find major fault with what they have done over the past decade.

In this chapter, we begin with a brief history of the challenges that faced

Stephen G. Cecchetti is Economic Adviser and Head of the Monetary and Economic Department at the Bank for International Settlements, a research fellow at the CEPR, and a research associate of the National Bureau of Economic Research. Kermit L. Schoenholtz is an adjunct professor at New York University Stern School of Business.

This chapter was prepared for the NBER conference "Europe and the Euro," 17–18 October 2008, Milan, Italy. It is traditional to use the introductory footnote to thank colleagues who contributed comments and advice. In this case, there were dozens of people without whom we could not have written this chapter. First, seventeen senior officials sat for interviews that their staffs helped organize; second, Citigroup facilitated interview transcription; third, several economists helped with data and filled in parts of the history (notably, Jose Luis Alzola); and finally, the editors of this volume spurred us to write this chapter. To all of them we extend our heartfelt thanks. We also would like to thank Alberto Alesina, Vitor Gaspar, and Francesco Giavazzi for comments on an earlier draft, and Malcolm Spittler of Citigroup for his excellent research assistance.

the people who forged the policies of the ECB in its first decade. What tests did these central bank pioneers face as the European Monetary Institute was transformed into the ECB on 1 June 1998? With hindsight, it is fair to say that the preparations were a success in nearly every way. The ECB was able to conduct monetary policy operations immediately without a major misstep. The original Governing Council's interest rate decisions were sound, overcoming a lack of data and models that would have panicked most people. While communication at the start may not have been as smooth as some people wished, it improved over time. Looking back, nearly every possible contingency that the ECB actually faced was anticipated and successfully addressed, reflecting careful preparation and unusual foresight.

Our task does not stop at recounting the past. Looking forward, we go on to ask what the likely challenges are for the next decade. The ECB is an evolving institution that is changing in unique ways. The euro area continues to expand. Enlargement could bring ten additional members into the monetary union over time—and more if the European Union itself grows. Each of these countries has its own language, cultural traditions, and social norms. Adding them to the euro system affects decision making and communication, as well as policy itself.

Beyond increasing its size, the ECB faces challenges in retaining public support for its own policies and in promoting the structural reforms needed to increase the flexibility of member economies. Regional economic divergences *within* a country may create problems, but they are unlikely to be as severe as the political difficulties that the ECB is likely to face should the economies of the various countries in the euro area experience dramatically different economic fortunes for extended periods. Furthermore, as we look forward, prosperity in Europe does not depend on monetary policy alone. The decisions by member governments have an important impact on what the ECB can and cannot achieve.

Finally, there is the question of financial stability. Here, the ECB position as a pan-euro area financial institution is unique. While the Governing Council has clear control over the combined balance sheet of the central banks in the euro system (those of the National Central Banks plus that of the ECB itself), it does not have regulatory or supervisory authority. And unlike the United Kingdom, where regulation and supervision resides in a single institution, financial oversight in the euro area is at the national level and *each country is different.*

In drafting this history, we have benefited from many studies that analyzed ECB policy, from its rate-setting patterns to its effectiveness in securing price and economic stability to its communication efforts. The ECB itself has been an excellent source, reflecting its admirable penchant for self-assessment.[1]

---

1. The *Monetary Policy of the ECB,* first published in 2001 and revised in 2004, as well as Issing et al. (2001) are early examples of comprehensive explanations and assessments.

But there is no shortage of outside reviews and critiques.[2] Furthermore, we now have nearly a decade of data with which to characterize the economic outcomes of ECB policy.

However, our unique advantage arises from a series of seventeen extended interviews conducted between June 2007 and February 2008 with a range of current and former ECB policymakers, and with other policymakers and scholars who viewed the evolution of the ECB from privileged vantage points outside the institution. The questionnaire that we employed as a basis for the interviews forms appendix A of this chapter. Appendix B reports the prominent themes in response to these questions. Abbreviated biographies of the interviewees are in appendix C.

The ground rules for our interviews were straightforward: we asked each interviewee to review and correct an edited transcript of the interview, adding or deleting anything they wished. While we have used their responses to inform our judgment and understanding, all direct quotes in either the main text or the footnotes have been approved by the interviewees. We are very grateful for their generous support, especially considering that our interviews were conducted during the financial crisis that began in August 2007.

The remainder of this chapter proceeds as follows. This introduction is followed by a brief discussion of the initial conditions in 1998 and the challenges that participants expected as the monetary union was getting under way. In section 9.3, we move to a more detailed discussion of the construction of the ECB's operational framework, including the creation of the euro area money market as well as the initial implementation of the policy and communication strategies. We then proceed to an evaluation of ECB policy performance in the first decade of monetary union in section 9.4. We provide a brief discussion of the euro area inflation experience, as well as the stresses and strains created by various aspects of the policy strategy. Section 9.5 looks to the future. Here, we report on the key challenges that our interviewees foresee over the second decade of EMU. Enlargement and financial stability are the issues that are clearly on people's minds, so that is where we focus most of our attention. Section 9.6 concludes.

While we base nearly everything that we write on the series of interviews we conducted, the narrative that follows (including any errors or faulty judgments) is our own. We include extensive quotes in the form of footnotes to provide a sense of why we have drawn the conclusions that we have.

---

2. A list would start with the *Monitoring the European Central Bank* series published by the Center for Economic Policy Research in London, and include analysis from the Observatorio del Banco Central Europeo in Madrid as well as the Center for European Policy Studies in Brussels.

9.2   Initial Conditions

Jean-Claude Trichet: "The main challenge we saw was to transfer to the new currency what had been promised: namely, that it would be as confidence inspiring, as credible, and as good a store of value as the previous national currencies had been."

The European Central Bank (ECB) came into existence on June 1, 1998—replacing its predecessor, the European Monetary Institute (EMI). At the start of 1999, the ECB took over monetary control in the initial eleven countries of the euro area.

The ECB was a new and unprecedented institution without a track record, but it was not born in a vacuum. The treaty of Maastricht provided for its independence from governments and established a hierarchical mandate for ECB policy with price stability as the top priority.[3] Because any alteration of the treaty requires unanimous support of the member states of the European Union, this mandate remains widely perceived as immutable. While the ECB began with only a few hundred employees, it drafted a significant portion of its staff from national central banks (NCBs) which, together with the ECB, form the euro system.

Nevertheless, the policy tests facing the ECB at its inception were numerous and daunting. Section I, part a, of appendix B identifies the most prominent concerns that our interviewees perceived when the ECB began. From this list, it is evident that the ECB faced an extraordinary challenge as it sought to inherit from the start the credibility of its most successful predecessor central banks.[4] There also were great risks, as there would be no honeymoon or grace period. Any significant rise of inflation expectations or of inflation risk premia in the run-up to EMU might have branded policy a failure even *before* the ECB began to exercise monetary control.

By day one, the new central bank needed to promote the development of a euro area-wide money market in which it could operate. The euro system needed to determine which matters would be centralized within the ECB, and which would be delegated to the NCBs for execution or oversight. There was concern whether the powerful NCB governors—and their large staffs—would overwhelm the ECB, and potentially undermine the euro area focus of the new central bank.[5] While the EMI had narrowed the options for the

---

3. The treaty allows the region's finance ministers to negotiate an international agreement (such as a fixed-exchange rate regime) that could theoretically override ECB monetary independence. So far, however, there has been no such proposal, let alone indications of consensus among finance ministers to alter the floating-rate regime.

4. Axel Weber: "The biggest challenge for the newly-founded euro system—operating without a track record—was to gain credibility in financial markets and among the citizens of Europe."

5. Six members of the ECB Executive Board would join eleven NCB Governors in the initial Governing Council. While exaggerated by the inclusion of NCB operational personnel, the NCB workforce was about 100 times larger than that of the ECB at the ECB's inception. At

policy strategy, the ECB had only seven months in 1998 to consider specific alternatives (principally inflation or monetary targeting), to specify the strategy in detail (including the operational methodology), and to prepare the apparatus for making decisions and communicating. In doing so, it lacked the timely data and reliable models of the euro area that modern central bankers rely on in making policy rate decisions. Moreover, the structural changes induced by the creation of the euro—which favored a rapidly integrating financial market and economy—meant fundamental uncertainty about the monetary transmission mechanism. In a virtually unique manner, at the start the ECB had to manage a currency that did not exist in notes or coin.

Also, the ECB was to begin operations in an environment of overt skepticism.[6] Some observers anticipated currency disturbances reminiscent of the Exchange Rate Mechanism (ERM) crises even after the start of EMU (see, e.g., Garber 1999).[7] Prior to EMU, it was common among prominent economists to conclude that the euro area's lack of labor mobility and of a mechanism for fiscal burden-sharing made it a suboptimal currency area that would be prone to country-level divergences in activity, employment, and fiscal balances (see Feldstein [1997] or Obstfeld [1998]).

Against this background, the broad membership of EMU—which included several formerly high-inflation countries—raised doubts about credibility: would the euro area yield curve be an amalgam of EMU member yield curves, or would it mimic those with the most favorable inflation track records (such as Germany, Benelux, and France)? The former outcome might even have prompted speculation about secession from EMU, however difficult. Similarly, would cross-country yield spreads be so wide as to cast doubt on EMU's sustainability?

Finally, it was unclear at the outset to what extent monetary union would promote European political union, or even whether fiscal and supply-side reforms could keep pace with monetary and financial integration. The EMU's most extreme critics viewed it as a political device to secure bureaucratic mastery over Western Europe, rather than as a means of promoting euro area welfare.[8]

---

end-2007, ECB employment had trebled from its end-1998 level of 450, but was still only a fraction of NCB staff.

6. Andrew Crockett: "A few years before the start most observers would not have believed you if you'd told them there would be twelve members, or at least eleven and soon twelve, at the beginning of monetary union."

7. Vitor Gaspar: "People worried about the possibility of turbulence in the foreign exchange markets."

8. See, for example, Connolly (1995). With regard to the ECB, Connolly writes: "But if the ECB *is* ever created, it will certainly not act in a disinterested way in the interest of the Community as a whole, simply because there is no such thing as the Community interest. Either it will act in French interests or it will not. If it does, then Germany will destroy it, putting an end to fifty years of a 'European Germany.' If it does not, then it might well destroy France" (391).

9.3   An Operational Framework

Otmar Issing: "What really shocked me [when I arrived] was the lack of any reasonable information (data, etc). We were preparing monetary policy for totally uncharted waters."

Alexandre Lamfalussy: "I feared that they would have technical problems of all kinds. Ultimately, I was wrong. The implementation went extraordinarily smoothly."

Vitor Gaspar: "An explicit strategy was clearly necessary to ensure the internal cohesion of the decision-making bodies of the ECB. It also was necessary to have a consistent framework which would enable the bank to communicate to a very diverse set of constituencies."

In light of these initial conditions, how would the ECB secure the goal of price stability and the subsidiary goals established by the treaty?

9.3.1   A Single Money Market

No ECB policy using interest rates as a tool could be implemented effectively without the existence of a deep, efficient euro area money market. Such a market did not exist before EMU. From a technical perspective, the euro system introduced a real-time gross settlement system, TARGET, as the foundation for a single market for overnight liquidity at the start of the ECB. The system had to be fully functional by January 4, 1999 when the ECB conducted its first open-market operation.[9] Interviewees who were involved in these preparations recalled concern about the lack of time for testing and worries that any operational failure would significantly damage the reputation of the ECB and the single currency even before it got going. There was at least one brief occasion in the spring of 1999 when money markets seemed slow to react to policy developments, but TARGET has been viewed as an extraordinary achievement, bringing about a near-instant integration of the national markets for overnight liquidity. Further evolution of TARGET over the years (including the November 2007 introduction of TARGET II) built effectively on this success.

In contrast, several interviewees viewed the public reaction to the 2002 introduction of euro notes and coin as the ECB's greatest self-made disappointment in its first decade. From a technical perspective, this enormous logistical process went more quickly and smoothly than many had expected. Most of the legacy currency was replaced within a matter of weeks rather than months, and there were no notable disruptions of retail activity. Official

---

9. Christian Noyer: "The greatest concern was to be sure to start operations effectively on the 4th of January 1999. If we wanted to have a single money market functioning in euros, we needed absolutely to have the TARGET system working to enable banks to exchange liquidity and the central bank to intervene. We needed the system working from the start to enable us to provide liquidity to the market."

estimates indicate that the changeover boosted the price level on average by 0.12 percent to 0.29 percent (Eurostat 2003).[10] However, as the ECB subsequently observed, this modest one-off price adjustment prompted an unanticipated (albeit temporary) rise of inflation expectations in some countries that may have contributed to doubts about EMU in the public mind. (Various explanations of this phenomenon may be found in the essays collected in Del Giovane and Sabbatini [2008] as well as in Dzuida and Mastrobuoni [2007]). Some policymakers still wonder whether a more aggressive communication effort would have anticipated and blunted these doubts.[11]

9.3.2 Objectives and Strategy

Prior to the start of operations, the ECB stated a quantitative definition of price stability: inflation of less than 2 percent as measured by the Harmonized Index of Consumer Prices (HICP). Some outside observers criticized this goal as asymmetric (in contrast with the inflation level or bandwidth objectives commonly used by inflation-targeting central banks). Concerns about goal asymmetry appeared particularly acute amid the deflation scare earlier in this decade. In 2003, following a broad policy review, the ECB clarified its numerical objective, but did not alter it substantively—it was restated as "less than, but close to 2 percent." Since that time, the ECB's announced goal has not changed, and objections to its asymmetry have waned. In part, that may reflect the judgment of some observers that the actual target is roughly symmetric around 2 percent (see Galí et al. 2004). The ECB's response to the record 2008 overshoot of its target appears consistent with that view.

In October 1998, the ECB announced the "two-pillar" strategic framework that included a focus on monetary developments (Pillar I) and on all other factors affecting the economic and inflation outlook (Pillar II). The official policy review in 2003 left these two pillars in place, but described the approach in a more eclectic (and less mechanical) fashion that focused on the use of the monetary pillar as a "cross-checking" device in which monetary analysis utilizes a broad array of financial variables. Galí et al. (2004) characterized the 2003 shift as a deemphasis of M3 growth that made clear that "money growth is not an alternative policy target" (18).

There is a voluminous literature studying this unique framework, which would seem to be neither fish (inflation targeting) nor fowl (monetary targeting). Much of the analysis from outside the ECB has criticized the monetary

10. Popular claims that official measures understate the price impact of the changeover have not been supported by subsequent analysis (see Del Giovane and Sabbatini 2008).

11. According to Eurobarometer 58 (2003), 77 percent of euro area respondents judged that prices had been "rounded up" during the conversion to the euro. Ignazio Angeloni: "None of us thought at the beginning that a key problem would come from the introduction of the euro bank notes and coins (rather than from the 1999 introduction of the euro). . . . Specifically, I refer to the impact of the introduction of the euro on retail prices and to the effect on expected inflation and perceived inflation in particular."

pillar as superfluous in securing price stability under a flexible inflation-targeting framework; Svensson (2000) quipped that the first pillar was really just a brick in the second pillar. One early study argued that the negative correlation between monetary signals and policy rates in some periods confirms that the ECB "ignores the monetary pillar" (see Begg et al. 2002, 20). A later analysis expressed doubt that policy decisions would have been any different had been there no "explicit role for money" (see Galí et al. 2004, 59).

In contrast, ECB analysis has focused on establishing the importance of monetary developments for price stability over a horizon longer than that of most economic forecasts. The ECB officials, such as Issing (2003), also have suggested that monetary developments can help policymakers anticipate threats to price stability from asset price bubbles. Nevertheless, ECB policymakers have been obliged to account for sustained overshoots of monetary aggregates beyond reference values that have not appeared linked to price developments. This pattern has tended to downgrade the perceived policy importance of such overshoots and has reinforced doubts about the monetary pillar on the part of many skeptics. It remains distinctly possible that the modest signal-to-noise ratio of monetary developments eventually could erode the credibility of a central bank that emphasizes its reliance on information from monetary analysis.

However one may view the lingering debate about the two pillars, as Issing (2006b) emphasizes, critics underestimate the historical utility of the hybrid strategy in securing for the ECB from its inception the credibility of its most effective predecessor, the Bundesbank. Failure to do so at the start could have been extremely costly, if not irretrievable. By its nature, the ECB must communicate to a more diverse public than virtually any central bank. Even in the distant future, the differences in languages, traditions, institutions, and legal systems across EMU members are unlikely to disappear. In Germany—which represented one-third of EMU economic activity at the start—the association of low inflation with Bundesbank monetary targeting in the public mind probably warranted an ECB emphasis on euro area monetary developments as a means to anchor inflation expectations. Achieving this desired continuity required a consistency of objectives and communication mechanisms suited to the unique historical circumstances. Looking forward, it remains to be seen whether the ECB's low-inflation reputation will spur it over time to simplify the policy strategy while keeping inflation expectations well-anchored.[12]

9.3.3   Communications

Otmar Issing: "Translation was, of course, linguistically always very good, but the same words and phrases may seem different against the back-

---

12. For example, Papademos (2006) describes how the two pillars eventually could merge into one.

ground of different historical experiences. For example, one colleague once said to me, 'Otmar, we have a paragraph containing three times a reference to price stability. I think this is too much for this argument. In my country, if you say three times why you seek price stability, it weakens your argument.' And my argument was, if in Germany it's only two times, they say, 'Oh, is the ECB less stability oriented than the Bundesbank?'"

In the course of linking its communication strategy with its objectives and instruments, the ECB developed innovative mechanisms for communication to compensate for constraints that differentiate it from other large central banks. Like most modern central banks, the ECB views transparency both as a goal in itself—necessary for accountability in a democratic society—and as a means to make its policies more effective.[13] It is now a commonplace that central bank policy is transmitted to the economy through forward-looking financial markets, so that clear objectives, a systematic approach to analysis and decisions, and timely public statements are indispensable.

Yet the ECB has also been keen to shield individual members of the Governing Council from pressures to pursue national, rather than euro area, policy goals. The concern, which appeared particularly acute at the start of EMU but remains notable today, is that domestic politics could make Council members less inclined to support policies that would be in the best interests of the euro area, but not necessarily optimal for their home countries. For this reason, the ECB eschews the publication of minutes that would detail Council members' statements or votes.[14] The ECB's alternative—the immediate post-meeting press conference held by its President—narrows the information loss due to the lack of detailed minutes, while accelerating the diffusion of the consensus judgment.[15]

As with other major central banks, ECB communications is a work in progress characterized by a trend toward greater transparency. Some interviewees noted that, in the early years, failure to synchronize public statements by Governing Council members occasionally contributed to confusion.[16] Jansen and de Haan (2004) show that NCB Presidents "made at least as many statements" in the early years as the Executive Board, but also indi-

---

13. Lucas Papademos: "What matters for the effectiveness of communication is to explain as clearly as possible the decisions taken and the policy being implemented in relation to the central bank's objective and strategy. It is essential to explain how the monetary policy stance contributes to the achievement of the objective. The more transparent and convincing a central bank is about the consistency of its actions with its objective and strategy, the greater the effectiveness of its policy." See also European Central Bank (2006b).

14. Fabrizio Saccomanni: "[P]ublication of minutes would be taken in Europe as an excuse to speculate about national preferences regarding monetary policy. We have to be careful not to create unnecessary problems of sensitivity at the national level."

15. Sirkka Hämäläinen: "From the very beginning, I have seen the press conference as the best way to communicate."

16. Sirkka Hämäläinen: "Communication and public statements of the members of the Governing Council (the Board members included) were not initially always fully synchronized and thus monetary policy messages sent to markets were somewhat confusing."

cate that the frequency of contradictions in statements about interest rates declined over time. The observed decline in the implied volatility of options on short-term futures also suggests that ECB communication with markets has become more effective (see ECB 2006a).

Other changes also reflect the maturing of the institution (including its data set and models): for example, the ECB began to publish its semiannual staff economic forecasts in December 2000, subjecting internal views to wide external scrutiny. More broadly, the ECB has developed an active dialogue with the public regarding its practices and their evolution. The ECB seminars, conferences, and official participation in outside programs like the ECB Watchers' Conference promote an exchange of ideas with academicians, market practitioners, and others. In the official sector, the ECB also pursues active communication through frequent parliamentary testimony and routine contact with the Eurogroup, Economic and Financial Affairs Council (ECOFIN), and the European Commission.[17]

At least one recent study by Eijffinger, Geraats, and van der Cruijsen (2006) compares the level of ECB transparency favorably with that of other central banks.[18] Our own judgment, which coincides with the consensus of interviewees, is that there is no single "best practice" with regard to transparency and communication.[19] Communication is about language and gesture, both of which depend on tradition and history. Effective signaling under constraints requires a thorough understanding of how the signals will be received (which may differ across languages and cultures) and also about which signals could distort the incentives of policymakers and thereby undermine the benefits of transparency. In the words of John Taylor, "More talk does not mean more transparency." At the same time, the ECB's tendency to describe its decisions as unanimous may understate the nature and vigor of important Governing Council debates, thereby diminishing the ability of observers to make an informed judgment about policy and sustaining skepticism about ECB communications more generally.

A key question that arises frequently today is whether central banks should announce an expected path of future policy rates. Ultimately, to maximize the effectiveness of monetary policy, the signals and means of signaling need to be consistent with a central bank's objectives and strategy.

17. Jean-Claude Trichet: "I have to explain regularly and tirelessly all over Europe that I am as frequently in Brussels with the European Parliament as Ben Bernanke and Alan Greenspan appears and appeared before Congress, perhaps even a little bit more frequently. . . . I invited twice a month the President of the college of Ministers of Finance (the Eurogroup) to attend the Governing Council meeting of the ECB. . . . I am, myself, invited every month to attend the meetings of the Ministers of the euro area. Three times a month, there is physical contact between the ECB's Governing Council and the executive branches and the Commission."

18. However, public perceptions of ECB transparency may be less favorable: see Eijffinger and van der Cruijsen (2007).

19. Philipp Hildebrand: "The notion that you could somehow hold up the Norwegian model or the Swedish model or the Swiss model as the right model for the ECB strikes me as slightly naïve."

Such announcements systematically reinforce policy goals through rapid market adjustments. At the same time, excessive concreteness that surpasses the ability of policymakers to reliably anticipate future developments can be counterproductive. For these reasons, it is far from clear that publication of an expected future policy rate would be optimal for all central banks (which have different objectives and constraints) or on all occasions for a particular central bank (which may face periods of heightened uncertainty).[20]

The same judgment could be applied to the use of "code words" to signal policy intentions. Codes are imperfect signals at best, and typically relate only to near-term policy prospects, which may be of least importance in the formulation of critical long-run market expectations. Rather, these expectations depend sensitively on the transparency and reliability of the central bank's reaction function, along with an understanding of the evolution of prices and the economy.

The role of signaling in the monetary transmission mechanism highlights how important it is for central banks to understand markets and their policy responses. Central bankers know that any slavish response to market expectations runs the risk of creating price level or inflation indeterminacy. At the same time, equilibrium in markets requires that the expectations of market participants and central bank decision makers coincide. Consequently, to make their policies most effective, central banks need to understand how markets behave and how to affect expectations without diminishing market incentives for price discovery.

In the case of the ECB, we suspect that the lack of direct financial market experience on the part of most Governing Council members may have complicated this task. The first decade record is filled with outside complaints about ECB communication with financial markets. Much of this criticism underestimates the political constraints under which a multinational organization such as the ECB functions and the challenge of communicating with so many diverse constituencies. Nevertheless, a greater presence of senior ECB leaders with financial market (rather than central bank) experience might have sped the evolution of the central bank's communications.

9.3.4 Data, Models, and Policy Analysis

Over the first decade of EMU, the ECB has made enormous strides in developing data for and models of the euro area economy, as well as advancing the frontiers of policy analysis. In the early years of EMU, the lack of consistent, timely euro area-wide data added sharply to policy uncertainty about the current state of the economy. Even near the end of 2000, for example, published euro area output gap estimates of official institutions

---

20. For a view calling on the ECB to announce an explicit rate path, see Geraats, Giavazzi, and Wyplosz (2008). For a counterargument from a member of the Governing Council, see Weber (2007).

differed by nearly 1 percentage point, with the Organization for Economic Cooperation and Development (OECD) figure standing at –0.3 percent, while the European Commission published an estimate of –1.2 percent. Moreover, recent readings show very large revisions to these "real-time" estimates—the current OECD measure of the euro area output gap in 2000 is +1.2 percent, while the Commission's is +1.9 percent.[21] The structural changes induced by EMU added to uncertainty, while the lack of models for the economy as a whole sharply limited the ability of policymakers to be forward-looking.

Perhaps as compensation, the decision-making process at the ECB allocated until recently a significant role to the Chief Economist in setting the stage for policy rate decisions. The likely effect was to enhance attention to the limited supply of timely aggregate data relative to the abundant supply of anecdotes in policy making, helping to narrow the grounds for policy debate. As a result, the "proposal power" inside the Governing Council may have been of greatest importance in the early years of EMU, precisely when the shortage of data and forecast models was most acute.

Today, there are still important gaps in the availability of timely euro area data, although progress depends largely on advances outside the ECB.[22] At the same time, the ECB has developed a forecasting apparatus that is state-of-the-art in the central banking world and—as previously mentioned—routinely publishes its staff projections. In addition, the broad research program of the ECB has reached a status that puts it at the frontier of applied policy analysis alongside the best research efforts of other leading central banks and academic institutions.

9.3.5   Euro System—A Constitutional Pact

The Maastricht treaty's map for the governance of the ECB and the euro system is a complex one. How can the region's central bankers actually make decisions and divide labor? From the point of view of monetary policy, a key question was whether policy determination would be truly euro area oriented, or if it would reflect some ambiguous compromise arising from the pursuit of national interests? With fifteen NCB governors and six Executive Board members serving on the initial Governing Council, it is natural

21. For comparison, the average of the output gaps in the year 2000 reported in the IMF *World Economic Outlook* of October 2000 (2007) for France, Germany and Italy was –1.2 percent (+1.4 percent).

22. For example, employment data are available in the United States within days of each reporting month, but only seventy-five days after the end of a reporting quarter in the euro area. Similarly, GDP data with breakdowns are available in the euro area at $t + 65$ days, compared to $t + 31$ days in the United States. And, in some euro area countries, harmonized index of consumer prices (HICP) flash estimates only recently became available. It is up to the national statistical agencies and Eurostat to change this, not the ECB. For a discussion of plans for improvement, see the report of the Economic and Financial Committee (2007) that was endorsed by the ECOFIN Council.

to wonder whether community interests might have been overwhelmed by national ones. At least one study examined (and rejected) the hypothesis that median voting of Council members sensitive to their domestic inflation conditions accounted for policy patterns in the ECB's early years (see Alesina et al. 2001).

Our interviews revealed unanimity among ECB insiders that country-specific factors were irrelevant in the policy rate-setting process even at the start of EMU. Having feared a greater role for national interests, some interviewees reported reacting with surprise and satisfaction at that time.[23] Others suggested that the long process of preparing for EMU—including joint preparatory work at the EMI—had fostered a broad consensus among euro area central bankers about the objectives and implementation of monetary policy that underpinned the ECB's behavior.[24]

Interviewees also indicated that operational matters resulted in less willingness to don a "euro area hat." For example, efforts to streamline the euro system—which would affect the locus of some operations and employment—were more likely to inspire national concerns. Perhaps not surprisingly, in 2007 the euro system had fifteen local mints accredited for production of euro notes, compared to only two mints in the United States.[25]

Nevertheless, the euro system has successfully addressed many critical questions requiring a judgment about how to divide labor between the ECB and the NCBs. Monetary policy operations are at the top of this list. Policy is set by the ECB and implemented by the NCBs with their local counterparties using contractual arrangements based on national laws. The ECB lays down the guidelines for open market operations—such as the single list of collateral acceptable for repo—and instructs the NCBs about the size of operations, but the NCBs conduct the operation. Unlike the U.S. Federal Reserve system, there is no single locus (such as New York) for open market operations. Operations coordinated in this decentralized manner require sophisticated information and communication technology that did not exist in the early history of the Federal Reserve.[26]

23. Hans Tietmeyer: "[The decision-making process] was smoother than I anticipated, because I thought that the different traditions and structures of the national central banks could play a diverging role, and that at least some governors could be tempted to feel themselves primarily as representatives of a national area. But especially at the governors' level, there was a relatively broad-based common feeling from the beginning."

24. Sirkka Hämäläinen "To me, it was quite clear that after those many years of working together it was natural to expect it to be very smooth."

25. For a discussion of euro note printing, see European Central Bank (2007a). It is worth mentioning that some Federal Reserve District Banks, despite their eighty-four-year historical advantage over the euro system, sustain branch operations that may no longer serve a clear economic purpose.

26. Christian Noyer: "We have a center, but the operations are made in the national central banks. We don't need to concentrate actions geographically (in contrast to the U.S. example in New York) because we have been born in a time of highly sophisticated telecommunication networks and computer systems, so it's easy to do that without concentrating the operations."

9.4   The First Decade of Performance

Axel Weber: "I think the success is the high degree to which price stability has been achieved. . . . Long-term inflation expectations have been stable and low and anchored at the level defined as price stability."

Hans Tietmeyer: "From the beginning, the ECB was seen inside and outside the euro area as independent and credible."

Fabrizio Saccomanni: "The euro is now considered to be an important currency with a global role."

Timothy Geithner: "[S]ince the ECB has been setting monetary policy, it has not produced a sustained period of subpar growth; the euro area has not experienced greater volatility of economic growth; and there has certainly not been any erosion of inflation performance. These may not be the only measures of central bank credibility, but they suggest that the ECB is performing well."

A review of the euro area outcomes in the first decade of the ECB yields a positive appraisal of ECB monetary policy, particularly in light of the extraordinary initial conditions from which policy evolved.

9.4.1   Inflation Record

The inflation record is straightforward. Over the period since 2001 (assuming that ECB policy typically affects prices with a lag of about two years), HICP inflation has averaged 2.3 percent, modestly above the ECB's official target of "less than, but close to 2 percent." During that period, headline inflation ranged from a trough of 1.6 percent in 2004 to a recent peak of 3.7 percent amid a record oil price shock. For comparison, in the pre-EMU period 1991 to 1998, headline inflation averaged 2.6 percent and ranged from 0.8 percent to 5.0 percent.[27] Even in Germany, which boasts the preeminent pre-EMU inflation track record, inflation has been lower and far more stable in EMU: under the Bundesbank, German inflation averaged 3.4 percent from 1965 to 1998 (with a standard deviation of 3.4 percent), while German inflation since 2001 has averaged 1.8 percent (with a standard deviation of only 0.6 percent).

The stability of euro area inflation can be seen in the broad decline of its rolling standard deviation during the ECB years (see figure 9.1). Other nominal variables, such as GDP, display a similar pattern. This remarkable steadiness is consistent with the evidence of reduced inflation persistence in many countries, including the largest euro area members (see Cecchetti et al.

27. Euro area core inflation as measured by the HICP excluding energy and raw food averaged 1.8 percent from 2001 to 2007, remaining within the 1 percent to 2 percent range in seventy-one of eighty-six months. By contrast, from 1991 to 1998, core inflation averaged 2.9 percent and was in the 1 percent to 2 percent range only twenty-eight out of ninety-six months.

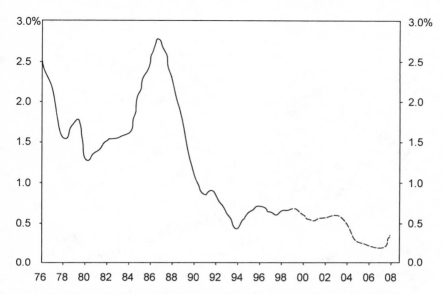

Fig. 9.1   Five-year moving standard deviation of annual HICP inflation, 1976–2007

Sources: European Central Bank, Eurostat, and authors' calculations.

2008). Yet this phenomenon should *not* be attributed primarily to external factors. Indeed, the treaty's mandate and ECB commitments likely helped to embed this stability in long-term inflation expectations at an early stage.

Even prior to EMU, long-term government bond yields had converged to levels consistent with low euro area-wide inflation, rather than to some weighted average of the yields of the high and low inflation countries (see figure 9.2). By the start of EMU, the euro area yield curve also appeared consistent with that of the yield curves of the lowest-inflation countries (see figure 9.3).

This profound market confidence also is evident in the stability of inflation survey data, which has been anchored very close to the ECB's objectives. For example, the ECB's Survey of Professional Forecasters' mean projection of long-term inflation has been stuck, with the exception of a single quarter, in a tiny 1.8 percent to 2.0 percent range since the survey began in 1999.[28] Even the oil price shock of 2007 to 2008 so far has failed to dislodge these expectations, while surveys of long-term inflation expectations in the United States have crept to the highest levels in more than a decade.

In light of the trying economic circumstances of the past decade, the

28. Andrew Crockett: "In some respects, the credibility of the ECB could be said to be even greater than that of the Federal Reserve. Inflationary expectations in the United States are further away from the so-called comfort zone of the Fed than European inflationary expectations are away from the ECB's target."

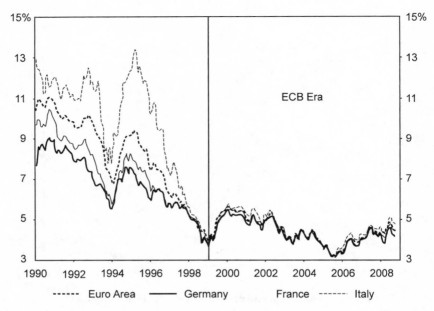

Fig. 9.2   Ten-year government yields, January 1990–March 2008
Source: Ecowin.

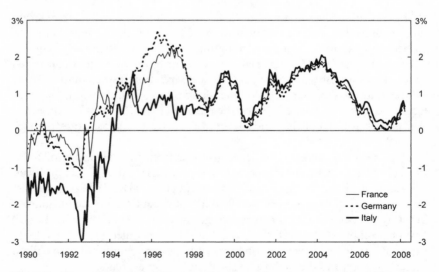

Fig. 9.3   Slope of selected yield curves (ten-year minus two-year govt. yields), January 1990–March 2008
Sources: Ecowin and authors' calculations.

achievement of low and stable inflation in the euro area most likely reflects good monetary policy, not good fortune. Several factors make this assessment compelling. First, since its inception, the euro area experienced large (and occasionally record) price shocks from developments in energy, commodity, and currency markets—not unlike the Great Inflation episode. Second, the economy's persistent rigidities resulted in a low level of potential growth.[29] Third, the loss of country-level monetary independence eliminated a potential remedy for idiosyncratic shocks. Fourth, rather than benefiting from fiscal reforms, the region exhibited fiscal fatigue (partly reflected in the relaxation of the euro area's fiscal compact—the Stability and Growth Pact, or SGP). Finally, the ECB endured repeated interventions by various regional politicians that might have weakened the credibility of a central bank less ardently committed to independence and price stability.[30]

Some outside observers have criticized the ECB for exceeding its inflation objective, and for not resetting its objective in line with actual practice on the occasion of the 2003 policy review (see Galí et al. 2004). During the deflation scare, others suggested that the target was set too low to allow for efficient cyclical and competitive adjustments in some regions without favoring a disruptive decline of prices and wages (see European Economic Advisory Group 2003). Our own judgment is that while the lingering asymmetry of the ECB's objective may not be optimal, in the absence of any credible deflation threat it is unimportant. It seems fair to conclude that the ECB has been very successful—at least until 2008—in keeping inflation stably close to its goal over the first decade. Considering the uncertainties and doubts that preceded the ECB's existence, EMU skeptics must view this achievement as stunning. More important, low nominal bond yields and reasonably stable wage-setting in the face of record commodity price shocks confirm that capital and labor markets have confidence in the ECB's low-inflation commitment.

9.4.2   Dividends of Price Stability

Consistent with the Great Moderation literature, Cecchetti et al. (2008) note that the stabilization of euro area inflation has been associated with a continued low level of output volatility compared to the Great Inflation

---

29. The following comment of Hans Tietmeyer is representative of views expressed by the majority of our interviewees: "My real disappointment relates to the domestic policies of some national governments, especially regarding inappropriate fiscal reforms and not creating appropriate conditions for more dynamic and flexible markets."

30. On this point, our interviewees were unanimous: on no occasion did the ECB alter policy as a result of strains with European politicians. Lucas Papademos: "My colleagues and I are very attached to the principle of central bank independence. Appropriate monetary policy decisions are best taken within an institutional framework that effectively safeguards this independence. Attempts by political leaders to influence ECB decisions will either have no effect or they may be counterproductive."

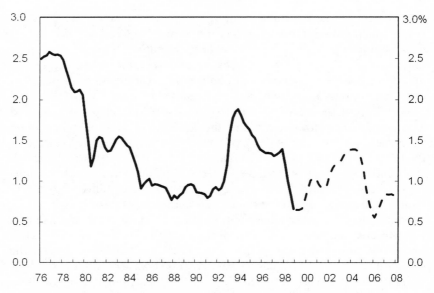

Fig. 9.4   Five-year moving standard deviation of real GDP, 1976–2007
Source: European Central Bank and authors' calculations.

period (see figure 9.4). As just mentioned, the plethora of shocks that hit the euro area economy in this period appears to undermine claims that this outcome is merely a result of good fortune. The largest shocks include the bursting of the global equity bubble, global recession, terrorist attacks, war in Iraq, a deflation scare that triggered unusually low global policy rates, and large currency swings. Yet the low level of euro area GDP volatility compares favorably even with the widely acknowledged U.S. example (see figure 9.5). Under the ERM regime of the early 1990s, large changes in the value of the U.S. dollar had occasionally created stresses across European bond markets and cross-exchange rates that added to output volatility. The single currency regime appears to have counteracted such stresses. We agree with Cecchetti, Flores-Lagunes, and Krause (2006) that improved policy under the ECB shifted the euro area to a better trade-off between the variability of inflation and the variability of output.

By securing price stability, ECB policy contributed indirectly to many other advances in euro area welfare. One example is the progress in capital markets and the financial system. Government bond markets appear to have been largely integrated at a very early stage in EMU. Legal and other obstacles still inhibit the integration of some markets, especially for corporate equities. However, the rapid expansion of markets for corporate bonds and for many derivative instruments over the past decade partly reflected the stable euro area economic environment. The breadth and depth of

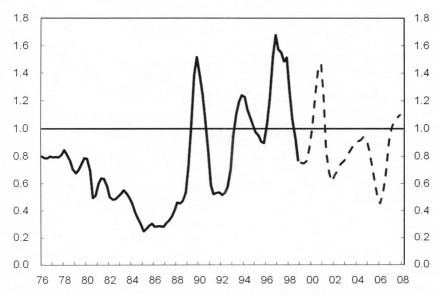

Fig. 9.5   Real GDP volatility—ratio of euro area to United States, 1976–2007
Sources: European Central Bank, U.S. Bureau of Labor Statistics, and authors' calculations.

these markets facilitate the efficient allocation of savings in the region. The gradual evolution toward banking integration also contributes to regional efficiency.

9.4.3   Monetary Pillar: Did It Matter?

One issue that may affect future policy strategy is the performance of the monetary pillar in the first decade.[31] Compared to the 4.5 percent reference value for M3 growth set at the start of EMU, M3 growth averaged 7.4 percent since 2000 and exceeded the reference value in eighty-eight out of ninety-seven months (see figure 9.6). Because the overshoot did not prevent the ECB from achieving a high degree of price stability, one may safely conclude that it did not prompt the ECB to become overly restrictive.

From this pattern, it is clear that the ECB's use of its monetary pillar has been far from mechanical. The ECB policymakers, notably Issing (2004) and Stark (2006), have emphasized that the prominent role of money in their strategy aims at underscoring policy's "medium-term orientation," while taking account of the potential links between money and credit growth and asset price bubbles. The ECB staff research (Fischer et al. 2006) discusses

31. Alexandre Lamfalussy's comment is representative of the views inside the ECB in the early days: "I have always been in favor of the two-pillar approach in terms of strategy. I use economic analysis and then cross check it by examining the monetary aggregates."

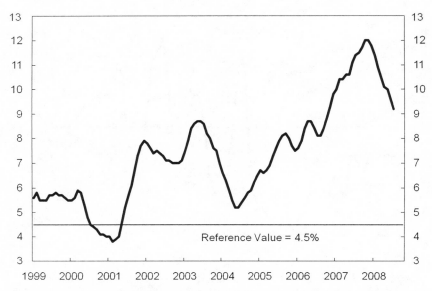

Fig. 9.6   Annual growth of M3 (three-month centered moving average), 1999–2007
Source: European Central Bank.

the complex and evolving analysis that the central bank devotes to monetary developments as a "cross check" for other inflation indicators.

However, the complexity of the procedure—which involves the estimation of underlying trends in monetary aggregates adjusted for portfolio shifts—likely makes any policy response to monetary developments less predictable. Without adjustments to the aggregates, money-based forecasts typically overpredicted inflation, while the adjustments may be large and occur with some time lag. In turn, market uncertainty about the ECB's response may reduce the effectiveness of policy, because ECB behavior is less likely to be reinforced by market anticipations. For example, Andersson, Hansen, and Sebestyén (2006) found euro area bond markets to be insensitive to news about M3 announcements. To the extent that the ECB actually responded to monetary news, the response appears to have been received in the euro area bond market as an unanticipated policy disturbance, despite the prominent role of the monetary pillar. In this sense, the pillar has yet to be defined in an operational manner that elicits market understanding.

9.4.4   Currency Considerations

The performance of the ECB cannot be divorced from the role of the new currency, which instantly became the world's second-most important store of value and means of payment and has continued to rise in importance since inception.

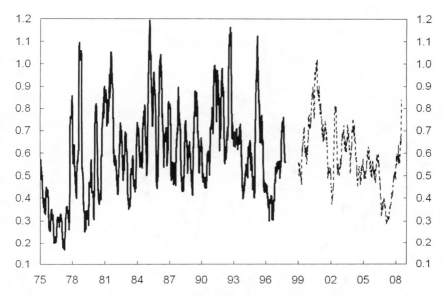

Fig. 9.7   Three-month moving standard deviation of euro/US$ and DM/US$ exchange rates, January 1975–March 2008

Sources: ECB, Federal Reserve, and authors' calculations.

The fluctuations of the foreign exchange value of the euro during its first decade of life are surely relevant for future policy strategy. Prior to EMU, some observers expected that the reduced importance of the currency for euro area-wide activity would downgrade its impact on policy, hinting that currency volatility versus the dollar would rise compared to, say, the Deutsche Mark. In fact, there is little direct evidence of increased volatility (see figure 9.7). Taking January 1999 as a base of 100, movements in the real euro/dollar exchange rate have been large, ranging from an index trough of 83 in 2008 to a peak of 139 in 2001, but the order of magnitude of these swings does not appear out of line with patterns in some earlier periods (see figure 9.8).

Broadly speaking, the ECB in its first decade has been as inclined to intervene directly in currency markets as the Federal Reserve (or U.S. Treasury); which is to say, not very.[32] From an operational and international coordination perspective, our interviewees highlighted the flexibility that the ECB demonstrated in joint operations to support the euro in its early years. Yet direct market intervention was rare: multilateral intervention occurred only once (on September 22, 2000), when there was a clear sense that the euro was undervalued. While unilateral intervention may have taken place on other

32. See Bini-Smaghi (2007) for a discussion of euro system intervention policy.

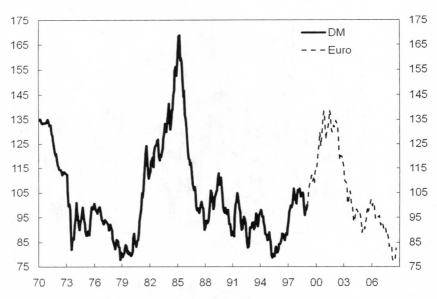

Fig. 9.8   Inflation-adjusted euro/US\$ and DM/US\$ exchange rates (January 1999 = 100), 1970–February 2008

Sources: Deutsche Bundesbank, European Central Bank, U.S. Bureau of Labor Statistics, and authors' calculations.

occasions, we are aware of only one instance (on November 3, 2000) that was reported in the ECB's *Monthly Bulletin.* Verbal intervention was more frequent, but one study viewed early statements by ECB officials as merely adding to currency volatility, with little persistent impact on the exchange rate (see Jansen and de Haan 2003). In recent years, ECB officials occasionally have jawboned in an attempt to slow the euro's rise, but have not capped the climb. In real, trade-weighted terms against a broad range of currencies, the euro has appreciated by about 5 percent from its start in 1999 and by 28 percent from its trough in November 2000.

9.4.5   Disappointments: Outside the ECB

The most frequently expressed disappointments about the euro area in its first decade have nothing to do with ECB monetary policy per se: namely, the lack of structural and fiscal reforms and the lack of concomitant progress toward political union.[33] Many of our interviewees contrasted the European Union's ambitious Lisbon Agenda with the scattered, desultory character of actual supply-side reforms and the frequency of backsliding.

---

33. An indicative quote comes from our interview with Edward George: "[T]he problem is not the functioning of monetary union in a narrow sense, but the performance of the wider economy given the lack of political consensus that I think you need for successful economic management."

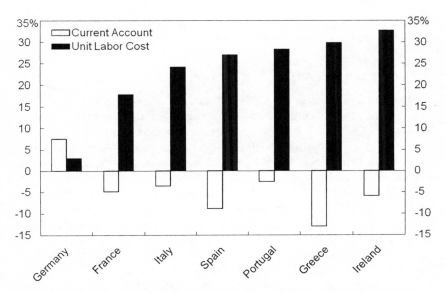

Fig. 9.9   Selected EMU members: Changes in current account balances (share of GDP) and unit labor costs (percent), 2007 vs. 1998
Source: EU Commission Ameco database.

Some expressed concern that the region's low potential growth would lead observers to blame the ECB because of the need for policy to tighten even at early stages of recovery. Judgments about fiscal policy have been less negative than pre-EMU skeptics feared, but the lack of consolidation in some high-debt countries remains notable, especially amid renewed divergence between several national economies (see figure 9.9). The relaxation of the SGP and the decentralization of the region's fiscal arrangements only add to doubts about coordination and the prospects for future consolidation.

In contrast to what many EMU advocates anticipated, there is little doubt that progress toward political union has not kept pace with monetary union.[34] From the ECB's perspective, this pattern complicates efforts to secure broad popular support. In a democratic society, public backing is critical to ensure the independence of a central bank over the long term. While the Maastricht treaty provides the ECB with a very strong foundation, the ECB lacks the natural constituency that the most credible national central banks typically enjoy, especially when confronted by politicians with a shorter horizon. The ECB's efforts to communicate help to build that popular support, but this

34. Axel Weber: "Regarding disappointments, in contrast to my initial expectation as an outside observer, the creation of EMU did not have a significant impact on further political unification in Europe. The catalytic role of the euro, not just in financial markets but also in the political sphere, was something that I expected to gain some stronger momentum in the first ten years. Looking back, it hasn't."

process may take decades and will almost certainly be less rapid than in a period of speedier progress toward political union.[35]

9.5   The Challenges Ahead

Over the next decade, the ECB will face many of the policy challenges common to all major central banks. From time to time, we expect that it will: (a) reassess and refine the strategy employed to secure its treaty-mandated objectives; (b) improve its models of the euro area economy, taking account of structural changes induced by the integration of Europe and by trends such as global economic and financial integration; (c) advance the frontiers of research and central bank practice to understand how asset prices and other financial developments should be integrated into policy decisions; (d) regularly reassess the outlook for price developments and recalibrate its policy stance consistent with its objectives and strategy; (e) manage liquidity as a lender of last resort when crisis threatens; (f) communicate its understanding and its policy thrust to the public at large to foster accountability and make policy effective; and (g) cooperate with policymakers outside the euro area to address issues of mutual interest, ranging from financial stability to exchange rate developments to the operation of official international financial intermediaries. These issues are of great interest, and the ECB likely will make important contributions to global "best practice," while also benefiting from the successes of other central banks.

In the remainder of this chapter we focus on challenges for the ECB that *differ* substantively from those facing other major central banks. The concerns identified by our interviewees as likely to pose special challenges for the ECB exhibit some variation, but two stand out: (a) enlargement, and (b) the complex framework for addressing financial instability. A variety of other matters received attention, but less broadly. These include the need to develop and secure a popular basis for the ECB, the need to manage a low-growth region facing competitiveness challenges and regional divergences, difficulties of fiscal coordination, and potential conflict over currency matters with ECOFIN, among others. We address each of these in turn.

9.5.1   Enlargement

Jean-Claude Trichet: "We are 27 countries in the European Union. In the euro area, we are 15. Of the 27, 25 have no opt-out clause. The challenge is to progressively absorb all the newcomers: none of them has an opt-out clause. At the same time it is imperative to preserve the credibility of the euro area as a whole by strictly respecting the conditions of entry, the Maastricht criterion."

---

35. Philipp Hildebrand: "[T]he big challenge for the ECB remains that it does not have a natural (or national) constituency in the population."

Otmar Issing: "It was extremely important to have an automatic rule which determines who will vote when. That rotation rule is in place and can be applied when the number of members reaches 21. Discussion rules can be changed anytime. New people will find reasonable solutions."

Lucas Papademos: "As the euro area expands and the number of Governing Council members increases, it may be more efficient to take decisions by voting rather than by forging a consensus as is presently the case."

Enlargement will affect the euro area and the ECB in many ways. By virtually any metric, it will add to the region's diversity (whether the focus is on language, culture, or legal systems). From an economic perspective, a twenty-five-country currency area will form the world's largest in terms of GDP, with a population of about 500 million, compared to around 300 million in the United States. The ratio of per capita incomes between the richest and poorest members would widen to nearly 13 from less than 4, based on recent data (see figure 9.10).[36] The speed of integration of product, labor, and financial markets may quicken, accelerating structural change. And each new euro area member will bring with it a new fiscal agent and a parliament. Among other things, this expansion will increase incentives for free-riding, thereby complicating any constitutional changes that would require unanimity.

Naturally, the need to assess the preparedness of prospective members will repeatedly revive the issues that confronted the European Council ahead of EMU: What degree of convergence has been achieved, and what is needed to satisfy the treaty's provisions? Although we did not explicitly pose this question, our interviewees reported no reason to expect that convergence prerequisites would be relaxed in the future.

Against this background, the ECB has established a set of voting rules—essentially a rotation structure for NCB governors that resembles the voting practices of the U.S. Federal Open Market Committee. In this sense, the ECB is well ahead of other political structures in the European Union—including the European Council and the ECOFIN—that also may experience stress as their membership becomes larger and more diverse.

Nevertheless, in the absence of further reforms, enlargement threatens to make the ECB less nimble.[37] The large number of voting parties (capped at twenty-one in December 2002), and the larger number of potential discussants in the Governing Council (which includes nonvoting Governors), will tend to complicate decision making. If increased membership makes policy debates interminable, it may not take long for the Governing Council to

36. This calculation excludes Luxembourg, which has the euro area's highest income per capita.

37. Philipp Hildebrand: "Making the institution function well as it enlarges will be a very big challenge. As the membership increases, at some point, there will be an inevitable need to look at institutional reform to make sure the organization can remain nimble and effective."

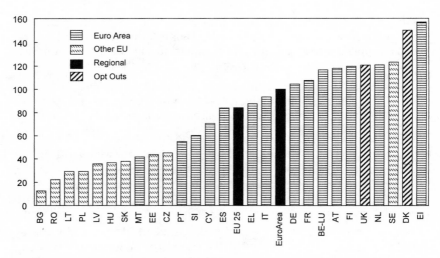

**Fig. 9.10   European union: Per capita income by country (euro area average =
100), 2007**
Source: IMF.

adopt mechanisms for speeding discussion. Over time, efficiency considerations likely will boost pressures to shift from a "consensus" model to a
voting model for making policy choices.[38]

The committee process, which still requires Frankfurt visits by NCB staff
to achieve consensus and make decisions outside of the narrow arena of
policy rate determination, poses a greater challenge. Innovative approaches
that delegate authority (or monitoring responsibilities) to subgroups that
do not include all twenty-five national representatives may become more
frequent. One past example of such cooperation has been the development
of TARGET II undertaken by a subset of NCBs and then distributed to the
euro system as a whole.

Yet it remains to be seen whether an increasingly diverse membership will
be prepared to delegate authority across a broader set of tasks. How will the
enlarged membership affect the consensus on issues such as the quantitative
definition of price stability or on the policy strategy? How will ECB decision practices evolve? How will membership of the Executive Board evolve
to reflect enlargement? Will it become more difficult to reach consensus on
the appointments of top ECB officials? Will trends toward economic divergence for some existing euro area members intensify or diminish as membership rises? How will the difficulty of coordination among twenty-five
fiscal agents affect monetary policy? Will a larger number of more diverse

38. The possibility of a future shift toward a voting model was mentioned by more than
one interviewee.

members exposed to idiosyncratic shocks raise the chances of a national fiscal crisis, widen market yield spreads, and, in the extreme, lead to a test of the Maastricht treaty's "no-bailout" provisions?

Enlargement will be a particular challenge in the area of communication. Even today, no other central bank faces the task of communicating with the public at large in fifteen different countries. While the presence of NCB governors at the ECB is helpful, it is far from a panacea. As our interviewees observed, speaking to local governments or populations is fundamentally different than communicating with financial markets. As we noted earlier, the lack of synchronization in this effort in the early years of the ECB may have created market confusion on occasion. Regardless of their current cyclical circumstances, diverse national histories may prompt different constituencies to view identical policy statements as accommodative or restrictive. If the longest-run challenge of the ECB is to secure a popular base, as several interviewees suggest, then enlargement only intensifies that challenge.[39]

Against this background, we do not expect the ECB to publish minutes, detail the statements or votes of Council members, or announce an expected policy rate path anytime soon. However, policymakers may choose to consider other means of reporting on policy-related discussions that better reveal the range of Council views without inviting invidious political attacks against individuals. For example, information about the evolving strength or weakness of the policy consensus could affect forward-looking financial markets in a fashion that would enhance the effectiveness of policy.

Of course, the EU itself may expand beyond its current membership of twenty-seven. We expect that new entrants to the EU will wish to join the euro area at an early stage to secure the benefits of its credibility. Consequently, the enlargement challenge is both unique and open-ended.

9.5.2   Financial Stability

Jaime Caruana, "When I was going to Frankfurt as a central banker, my role was clear. I had to vote for the best monetary policy for the euro zone. When I participated in financial stability discussions, my role was clear: as the Spanish banking supervisor, my mandate in the Spanish law was to defend the Spanish banking system. I was accountable to the Spanish Parliament. Fortunately, protecting the Spanish banking system was consistent with protecting the European one, but I think that introducing some balance, some European mandate would be better."

---

39. Beyond enlargement per se, several interviewees expressed concern that politicians and the public at large would forget how difficult life was before monetary union. Ignazio Angeloni: "Over time, I think that people will start forgetting the benefits and the advantages of belonging to the euro. They will forget how difficult it was to manage their own currencies. I am talking about particularly those that had unstable exchange rates. They will forget the times of high interest rates due to currency challenges. And they will start thinking that perhaps without the euro they can be better off. Unavoidably, I think there will be political elements in national politics that will try to exploit anti-euro public opinion sentiments."

Christian Noyer: "We need to have the same rules. Even if we had a single supervision authority, it would not solve the problem simply because there are differences in the regulations. The single authority would have to implement 15 different legislations of regulation. Unifying the rules is certainly the first thing to do."

Axel Weber: "We need an evolving European structure of banking supervision. When the banks become more international, more pan-European, so will banking supervision. This is an evolution that will become more important in the future."

Jean-Claude Trichet: "At this stage, what we are calling for is a close relationship—intimate cooperation between the banking surveillance authorities themselves, and very close links with the central bank, including a full transfer of information."

Our questionnaire (drafted in the spring of 2007) highlights concerns about the euro area's framework for financial stability that predated the global crisis that began in August 2007. At this writing, that crisis is testing the industrial world's stability apparatus more broadly, intensively, and persistently than any prior experience in the postwar period, and certainly far beyond what any simulation or diagnostic stress test likely would achieve. As a result, the crisis has revealed important strengths of the euro area stability mechanisms, but has not reduced our unease about vulnerabilities in this framework.

Because these concerns are largely shared by our interviewees, we are confident that the ECB will seek aggressively to approach "best practice" in this area, as it has in other matters. However, continued progress toward financial integration, in the context of a fragmented and complex stability framework, probably makes this goal the most important as well as the most difficult one for the ECB over the next decade. Failure to advance the stability framework—which is a task that goes far beyond the limits of what the ECB alone can achieve—could involve large costs for the region as a whole and could reduce the competitiveness of euro area financial centers.

In the area of liquidity provision as a lender of last resort, recent experience has highlighted important ECB successes. In August 2007, the ECB boosted liquidity supply early and aggressively to counter sharp increases in funding rates as banks turned cautious and alternative private sources of funding shut down. The ECB's Bagehot-style marginal lending facility (MLF, designed to cap overnight rates in normal times) can be viewed as an automatic mechanism for calming liquidity fears in a crisis.[40] In order

---

40. Vitor Gaspar: "If you look at the functioning of the ECB's marginal lending facility and you compare with the prescriptions from Bagehot on the functioning of the lender of last resort, there should be no need for any ambiguity concerning the lender of last resort function. The lender of last resort is simply subsumed within the regular functioning of the operational framework." See also Gaspar (2006).

to deliver liquidity effectively, the ECB utilized the broad flexibility that it enjoys with respect to assets that it may accept as collateral or acquire outright, including a variety of asset-backed securities.[41] Beginning in December 2007, the ECB also cooperated with other central banks, including playing a role in distributing dollar liquidity to banks in its region.

As term euro rates surged, the ECB was compelled to engage in fine-tuning operations that supplied an extraordinary volume of liquidity, suggesting that intermediaries became reluctant in the crisis to use the anonymous MLF. The ECB's actions also did *not* prevent term money market spreads from widening in a persistent fashion once the crisis began in earnest. Unlike the Swiss National Bank, for example, the ECB did not alter its overnight rate target to stabilize term money market rates. The effect has been a tightening of money market conditions that policymakers did not explicitly seek.

Yet the ECB could have avoided this outcome (by lowering policy rates) if it had wished to do so. The ECB's willingness to tolerate a rise in term money market rates (and to consider *increasing* the key rate on repurchase agreements) highlights the extent to which it has distinguished between the provision of crisis liquidity and the setting of policy rates. Moral hazard concerns still would arise if the ECB appears compelled to compensate for uncertainty about systemic vulnerabilities by generous liquidity provision. Even so, it seems fair to conclude that the ECB's tool kit for liquidity supply has been crisis-tested and satisfies current "best practice" standards among central banks.

At the same time, other, potentially more troubling aspects of the euro area stability framework have been brought to light in this episode.[42] In contrast to liquidity matters—which lie clearly within the ECB's mandate—solvency matters are addressed exclusively by national institutions, which may have different views about what constitutes a systemic threat and about how and when public resources should be employed.[43] The fact that there is no euro area fiscal agent means that burden-sharing across nations would be a challenge should a large (truly European, rather than national) institution become unstable. In many, but not all, euro area countries, the NCB is the banking supervisor, but few NCBs also supervise nonbank financial institutions or securities markets.[44] Rules for supervision are made at the country level, and have not been fully aligned across the euro area despite

41. See European Central Bank (2006a) for a description of collateral rules. We note that the Federal Reserve's liquidity-supply mechanisms have evolved during the crisis to become more like the ECB's both in terms of acceptable collateral and the range of counterparties.

42. For a view that regulatory competition contributed to recent financial excesses, see Tabellini (2008).

43. Several interviewees expressed concern about the difficulty in identifying insolvency.

44. It also remains to be seen how the ECB and an NCB, which implements any lending to specific institutions, would balance the needs for overall monetary control and for liquidity supply to a troubled institution should its requirements be large.

the existence of some common financial directives. It is even conceivable that conflicts could arise between the national mandates of some NCB governors in their role as supervisors and the mandate imposed by the Maastricht treaty in their role as members of the ECB Governing Council.[45]

As our interviewees stressed, there is little or no political will to replace this fractured supervision and crisis management framework with a more centralized one. In fact, it is not even clear that the presence of a single supervisor would successfully resolve the time-sensitive information and coordination problems that are inherent in financial crises.[46] At present, even the largest financial institutions typically still have an identifiable national home, while mid-sized and small institutions usually operate locally and can be monitored by an expert familiar with local conditions and traditions. Finally, no supervisor anywhere has the means to address the costs of insolvency.[47]

Against this background, many interviewees favored a gradual, long-term shift toward greater supranational supervision, particularly as financial integration advances. However, there was a strong practical consensus that, for the foreseeable future, the ECB should aim to help the existing highly decentralized system become sufficiently effective so that it can act as one in a crisis.

Crisis management in a decentralized system is a daunting challenge that will require the cooperation and support of many policymakers—including legislatures—to limit the potential damage to the euro area from a financial crisis. In this context, the ECB has sought to cooperate closely with European supervisors to ensure the timely flow of information to decision makers in a crisis.[48] Even when the supervisory function is performed by an NCB—directly ensuring the euro system's involvement—the timely flow of information necessitates a well-defined set of procedures and practices that are understood in advance. For example, the central bank's reputation could

45. In the recent crisis, there was one potential institutional risk that reportedly was conveyed to the ECB only *after* the risk had subsided and shortly before it became public.

46. While there was substantial disagreement among the interviewees over the desirability of a pan-European regulator, even those in favor of consolidation expressed doubts that such an institution would come into existence anytime soon. Several respondents did suggest a certain inevitability in the process. Jaime Caruana: "I stated publicly when I was [at the Bank of Spain] that either we would find a system that works like a one-regulator system in Europe, or we will end up having one regulator in Europe."

47. Fabrizio Saccomanni "There is obviously great concern by political leaders that they may be confronted with a 'European' financial crisis of which they know nothing and for which they might be required to bear a financial burden that would involve taxpayer money." Andrew Crockett: "It is not clear what would happen in the event that a substantial-sized European financial institution got into life-threatening trouble." Jean-Claude Trichet. "There is no taxpayer money at the level of Europe as a whole."

48. Alexandre Lamfalussy: "In crisis management situations, the flow of information is extraordinarily important and there is a natural tendency of each group who possess information to hold it back as long as feasible. That's instinct: Hand it over only when necessary. This is not helpful, so here we might have a problem."

be put at risk if an insolvent institution were able to exploit the marginal lending facility (even temporarily) because the ECB lacked knowledge of the circumstances.

In recent years, the ECB has helped prepare for episodes of financial instability by promoting cooperation among supervisors and the central bank.[49] The Committee of Bank Supervisors, which meets at the ECB, is one example. The ECB also has been a party to Memorandums of Understanding (MoUs) with supervisors and fiscal agents that promote cooperative behavior and help clarify responsibilities in a crisis. Also, the ECB has cooperated with supervisors in simulation exercises or stress tests to prepare officials for a crisis. Going forward, the ECB can seek to promote a unified, best-practice approach among supervisors in collecting and assessing information about the institutions under their purview. Such a common methodology—akin to the guidelines and materials developed by the Federal Reserve for the supervisors in its District Banks—would appear to be a prerequisite for efficient information flow in a crisis.[50]

The ECB, like any lender of last resort, has to be concerned lest its preparations and plans for addressing crises prompt moral hazard. Even so, some interviewees thought that the complexity and decentralization of the stability framework favored the development of a "handbook" for crisis response, combined with clarity about the chain of command in a crisis. Agreement on such a structure would require the mutual assent of many parties, because it is not set in law as a euro area standard. Without it, however, policymakers may not know who is in charge. Moreover, the lack of accountability would diminish the incentives to manage effectively. The task of balancing such preparations and crisis flexibility against moral hazard risks is difficult even where the crisis chain of command is clear, but seems even greater where it is not.

Managing a future crisis also could be complicated by differing national legal mechanisms and procedures. For example, euro area members have different practices with regard to deposit insurance, bankruptcy, and even court procedures. There also is no common approach for early public intervention in the case of a troubled financial institution, such as the procedures for "prompt corrective action" in the United States or the proposed "special resolution regime" in the United Kingdom.[51] A credible threat of early intervention creates incentives for financial institutions to guard their capital and thereby limits systemic risks. Early intervention rules also could reduce

---

49. See the relevant articles in the *ECB Bulletin* (2004b and 2007a).

50. In a recent assessment of the financial stability framework, the euro system concludes that "supervisory convergence is a key objective." See ECB (2007b).

51. For details of the United Kingdom's proposed special resolution regime, see Bank of England, HM Treasury, and Financial Services Authority (2008). When asked whether an early intervention scheme was needed in the euro area, Jaime Caruana responded that there is a clear need for "some kind of early intervention system where the rules are clear and you know that you have to act rapidly at the beginning."

"home-host" strains that may arise when banks compete in other national markets by narrowing the uncertainty of host supervisors about the workout procedures and the availability of capital in a crisis. As U.K. policymakers learned from the Northern Rock episode, the lack of an early intervention mechanism can leave policymakers with a painful choice between acquiescing to heightened systemic threats from a bank run or to moral hazard-inducing bailouts of shareholders, debt holders, and management.

Naturally, enlargement will add to the complexity of the euro area stability framework. Accordingly, the ECB also may wish to encourage prospective new members to implement best-practice rules and procedures in this area as they prepare for accession to the single currency.

9.5.3   Other Distinguishing Challenges

Otmar Issing: "What is unique for the ECB is the complex environment. For any central bank, be it the Bundesbank, Banque de France, or the Federal Reserve, the support of the people is crucial. But, the ECB still is a young institution, and the euro area is very complex, not least due to the language and communication problem."

Sirkka Hämäläinen: "There are many signs of weaker political commitment: unwillingness to meet the commitments of the Stability and Growth Pact, attacks on the independence of the ECB, or the lack of measures for structural improvements. Monetary policy needs strong political support to be effective."

Enlargement and financial stability are not the only issues that are likely to affect the ECB differently over the coming decade. The list of unique challenges identified by our interviewees is substantial, and includes popular attitudes toward the central bank, potential for regional divergences in a low-growth region, coordination with fiscal agents, response to currency disturbances, personnel selection, and operational efficiency. In this section we briefly discuss a few of these.

Broadening the Popular Base

Before the Maastricht treaty was enacted, critics sometimes spoke of a "democratic deficit" to describe a perceived lack of grassroots support for and involvement in the political (and monetary) integration that European leaders sought to realize. This legacy, combined with the complexity of euro area and European governance, boosts the importance of ECB transparency and accountability. Over the long term, no central bank can operate in a truly independent fashion without a modicum of popular support for its objectives and methods. In the case of the ECB, the broader the popular support, the more its policies are likely to appear credible and resilient (and, as a consequence, prove effective).

As previously highlighted, the ECB uses many means to address its diverse constituencies and to garner support. Going forward, if necessity is the mother of invention, the ECB is likely to be at the forefront in improving central bank communications, because the challenges that it faces are notably greater and more enduring than at other central banks. As our interviewees emphasized, communication in multiple languages and across cultures and traditions is inherently complex, and will become increasingly so as the euro area enlarges. Some national politicians also may view the ECB as an easy target, because it lacks a national constituency that would raise the political costs of ECB-bashing.[52] At some stage, effective ECB policy will conflict with the short-term interests of particular countries or their policymakers. Reduced momentum toward political integration in Europe also exposes the ECB to potential backlash against policy centralization, even when changes in the economic environment—such as increased financial integration—favor coordinated responses.[53]

Suboptimal Currency Area

Critics of the Maastricht treaty bemoaned the lack of European fiscal and labor market flexibility long before the ECB was established. If anything, the track record of EMU's first decade has resulted in less economic and fiscal divergence than many observers, including some interviewees, had feared. However, risks remain because potential growth is low, labor markets are relatively rigid, and there is little scope for fiscal burden-sharing. Moreover, as Papademos (2007) describes, some countries—including Greece, Italy, and Portugal—exhibit divergent trends in the growth of unit labor costs that appear to diminish their competitiveness. Widening current account imbalances are a symptom of this competitiveness problem (see figure 9.9).

The ECB cannot alter its policy rate for the purpose of limiting economic divergence or to boost growth sustainably above potential. Nevertheless, both divergence and low potential growth add to the strains associated with stability-oriented monetary policy, making ECB policies less popular and less credible.[54] In the extreme, economic divergences can prompt a regional fiscal crisis that might test untried portions of the Maastricht treaty, such as the "no bailout" clause. While such a test currently seems a remote possibility, it cannot be ruled out over the long run.

Coordination with Fiscal Agents

In the first decade of EMU, contrary to pessimistic expectations, there were no fiscal crises, and the excessive deficit procedures that began in reces-

---

52. Philipp Hildebrand: "Politicians face a relatively low cost for attacking the ECB compared to the cost they would face in attacking a similarly credible national central bank."

53. Axel Weber: "I think politicians very often forget the merits and the advantages of having independent central banks guaranteeing price stability and have not lived in periods where they see the downside effects of high inflation on the economy."

54. Ignazio Angeloni: "If [cyclical and inflation] divergence persists, it could present problems. I regard these potentially as political risks, political strains."

sion mostly have been wound down as deficits narrowed cyclically. However, the willingness of fiscal policymakers to relax the Stability and Growth Pact strongly hints at fiscal fatigue. Despite some consolidation, three countries (Belgium, Greece, and Italy) still have gross general government debt ratios in excess of 80 percent of GDP. More importantly, officials have expressed concern about the threat of fiscal unsustainability in some countries as the euro area population ages.[55]

At this stage, there remains little reason to predict an acute challenge, but it is not difficult to imagine circumstances in which difficulties might arise. For example, the threat of a debt deflation could place an excessive burden on monetary policy to secure price stability without coordinated fiscal support. Achieving coordination among fifteen or more fiscal decision makers (or even among a handful of large-country decision makers) makes the ECB's potential challenge more complex than that of other major central banks.[56]

We view the likelihood of a sustained, open conflict between monetary and *aggregate* fiscal policy as remote. As Sargent and Wallace (1981) famously showed a quarter of a century ago, such a conflict can undermine the inflation credibility even of a resolute central bank. Fortunately, there is little reason to anticipate such a clash. For example, recent Eurobarometer polls suggest that when inflation rises, popular awareness helps underpin the ECB's objective of price stability.[57] And despite evidence of fiscal fatigue over the past decade, peer pressure among fiscal policymakers has helped to limit the kind of post-EMU fiscal slippage that many skeptics anticipated.

Against the background of diverging competitiveness, a somewhat more likely (if still highly improbable) scenario would be a rise of market disturbances caused by the loss of confidence in a (group of) fiscal agent(s). Would such a fiscal crisis also threaten the stability of the regional financial system (say, by weakening institutional balance sheets and the credibility of national deposit insurance schemes)? The notable decline of home country bias in euro area debt after EMU almost surely has reduced "concentration risk" in the financial system (see Issing 2006a). Nevertheless, no central bank can afford to ignore the potential linkages between fiscal and financial instability. Consequently, it would be surprising if the ECB became less inclined to advocate fiscal prudence as it seeks to secure price stability.

---

55. Of current EMU members, a recent European Commission report (2007) that addresses fiscal sustainability and aging populations cited Greece and Portugal as "high-risk" cases. Only Austria, Finland, and the Netherlands were "low risk."

56. Timothy Geithner: "They never resolved fundamentally what was going to be the framework of discipline on the fiscal side."

57. Asked to name the two most important issues facing their country, the share of persons in the euro area identifying rising prices or inflation jumped to 26 percent in the autumn of 2007 (making it the second item on the list), up from 16 percent a year earlier (and a 16 percent average of the previous three years).

Exchange Rate Considerations

The euro depreciated considerably in the early years of EMU. However, the ECB has never faced an exchange rate crisis similar to the one in the United States in the late 1970s: (a) a plunging currency; (b) rising inflation expectations; and (c) sharply weakening long-term financial markets. This may reflect another dividend of the ECB's anti-inflationary credibility. However, over the next decade, it is easy to imagine the combination of a continued unwinding of the large current account imbalances that have characterized the global economy over the past decade and an upward revaluation of currencies in some large emerging economies. Discontinuities in this process could test the ECB's ability to work cooperatively with other central banks to limit disturbances in other financial markets and (thereby) to secure economic and price stability.

The key issues for the euro area will be to clarify who decides currency policy and what circumstances, if any, merit currency intervention. The ECB's track record now provides considerable confidence that these issues will be addressed successfully in the future. But the Maastricht treaty's allocation of authority for setting the currency regime to finance ministers leaves lingering uncertainties.

Other Matters

We close by mentioning without elaboration three additional challenges that surfaced in our interviews. First, some interviewees pointed to the loss of political will toward European integration as a potential source of added complexity in matters ranging from enlargement to financial stabilization. Second, there was concern that the generational turnover of leadership at the ECB in coming years will focus attention not only on the competence and diversity of new Executive Board members (and senior staff), but also on the potential for rigidities with respect to country representation. While the treaty's mandate for ECB autonomy is very powerful, turnover also creates a risk that politicians least supportive of the ECB would promote candidates less zealously independent. Third, there was the hope that the pace of progress toward operational efficiency will reveal the ECB's ability to overcome national resistance to productivity-enhancing consolidation (e.g., in reducing the large number of physical mints).

9.6   Conclusions

John Taylor: "The biggest success has been to set it up from scratch, to deal with the inherent difficulties of communication and different traditions, and to have a policy apparatus which is basically working well in terms of interest rate decisions, et cetera. That has to be viewed as a major achievement. It's the first time anything like that has been done."

Philipp Hildebrand: "I sometimes have the impression that the ECB has more credibility than it gives itself credit for."

In reflecting on the first decade of European Monetary Union we are reminded of the story of the Vasa, the Swedish warship to which a museum is devoted in Stockholm.[58] In an effort to build a symbol of Sweden's burgeoning naval power, King Gustavus II Adolphus ordered the construction of a large and elaborate ship. No expense was spared. To accommodate the seventy-two cannons cast for it, the Vasa was built with two gun decks rather than the usual one. The result was a massive, top-heavy, and unstable ship that the King nevertheless ordered to set sail on August 10, 1628. The Vasa sank almost immediately after encountering its first stiff breeze less than two kilometers from port.

There are two morals to the story of the Vasa. First, governments occasionally arrange large, prestigious projects that fail infamously. And second, experts do not like to convey bad news to kings or ministers about their pet projects. In the ECB's case, the Maastricht treaty ventured where no vessel had gone before, but it has worked well. That success presumably is owed to the design and the crew, not to the lack of turbulence.

Our ECB interviewees rightly express pride and satisfaction in their accomplishment. Literally thousands of people worked diligently for years to make monetary union not only a reality, but a success. It is difficult to find major fault with the operational framework or the monetary policy decisions of the first decade of EMU.

Indeed, with the broader perspective of time, many of the criticisms that have been addressed at the ECB appear ancillary in light of the euro area's track record of low and stable inflation and reasonably stable economic growth. The ECB focused effectively on price stability, while maintaining its treaty-mandated independence. Critics acknowledge that the two-pillar strategy did *not* prompt the ECB to become overly restrictive for any sustained period, despite persistent overshoots of the monetary reference value. And it is doubtful that ECB goal asymmetry is prompting a sustained rise of long-term inflation expectations, as some observers anticipated.

Naturally, policy strategy, implementation, and communication should be routinely reviewed, and there is always room for improvement. Some outside observers have suggested that the ECB missed a key opportunity in 2003 to make greater progress toward best practice. Our own view is that the ECB leadership has demonstrated an open attitude to proposals for reform—including recommendations in the areas of strategy and communications—provided that the proposals adequately reflect the complex political constraints under which the ECB operates.

Ultimately, with successes come new challenges. For the euro system, our

---

58. For details of the Vasa's history and the museum, see http://www.vasamuseet.se/InEnglish/about.aspx.

interviewees highlighted two: enlargement and financial stability. On the first, we see the constant addition of new countries as a tremendous challenge for both communication and policy setting itself. As the euro area expands, the addition of new constituencies that speak different languages and have different customs and histories will complicate communication further. In addition, the more countries there are, the more likely that real divergence at the national level will arise. Also, dramatically different productivity and labor market performance would place substantial stress on monetary union.

Once everything is said and done, the issue of financial stability seems paramount to us. The key problem is one of information and coordination during a crisis, as well as harmonization of procedures. It is extremely unlikely that Europe will create a supranational supervisory authority to complement the ECB in the foreseeable future. In the absence of such a new organizational structure the majority of interviewees anticipated that the current one would need to work *as if* it were a single entity.

Returning to the accomplishments of the first decade of monetary union, our interviewees were unanimous in their conclusion that the ECB has many more successes than disappointments to its credit. We agree.

Appendix A

Questionnaire

The following questionnaire was drafted in June 2007 and formed the basis for all of our interviews. In every case, we sent the questionnaire with our initial letter requesting an interview. We clearly stated in that letter that we would be happy to omit any question that the interviewee did not wish to answer. In one case, we discussed the questions with the interviewee in advance and agreed on some changes, which are noted in the footnotes.

I.   Policy in the First Decade of Monetary Union

a. Thinking back to 1998, what did you anticipate would be the biggest policy challenges? Now, nearly a decade later, what do you think the biggest policy challenges were? How did your policy goals evolve over time?

b. What were the ECB's most important policy successes and disappointments?

c. How has the decision-making process of the Governing Council evolved? How do the decision processes under the Duisenberg and Trichet presidencies compare? Has the process been smoother or more complicated than initially expected?[59]

59. For some of the interviewees we substituted the following question: How has the decision-making process of the Governing Council evolved over time?"

d. On occasion, the relationship between the ECB and the political leaders of selected euro area countries has been strained. How have these developments affected ECB policy determination?

II.   Policy in the Second Decade of Monetary Union

a. Looking forward, what is the biggest challenge facing the euro area over the next decade?
b. Are the ECB's challenges different from those facing a "mature" central bank?
c. Communication policy is a work in progress for many central banks. Which of the world's central banks do you believe is at the frontier of best practice in communication policy? What aspects of that central bank's policy would you single out as worthy of emulation elsewhere? How do you see the ECB's communication policy evolving over the next few years?
d. Some observers express concern about the difficulties facing the ECB in personnel matters. How does the role of nationality in personnel selection affect confidence in the ECB and its governance?[60]

III.   Financial Stability

a. Does the euro area face any unusual challenges in promoting financial stability?
b. Does the lack of direct responsibility for regulatory and supervisory matters create any obstacle for the ECB in pursuing its financial stability objective?
c. What is the biggest challenge for policy coordination in a crisis? What legal, regulatory, or behavioral obstacles remain for effective coordination?

Appendix B

Common Themes

Following is a summary of the themes that emerged from our interviews. For each question, we looked for similarities in the responses of the interviewees. Beyond that, we have used our judgment in creating the list. The following results should not be interpreted as implying agreement or consensus among the interviewees.

---

60. This question was omitted for some interviewees.

I. Policy in the First Decade of Monetary Union

a.   Thinking Back to 1998, What Were the Challenges?

Strategy, Instruments, Communications were all open issues
Unprecedented experiment with little time to prepare
No track record (untested operational framework)
Absence of data at the outset
Uncertain transmission mechanism
Challenge of anchoring inflation expectations and creating credibility
Potential conflict between the ECB and the NCBs
Worries about fiscal policy and the Stability and Growth Pact
Concern that entry of many countries would destabilize EMU
Skepticism of external observers that the project would succeed
Challenge of creating a virtual currency initially
Euro area was not an optimal currency area—one size does not fit all
Structural inflexibility in the euro area economies
Difficulties created by enlargement
Hindsight: Goals were stable; optimal currency area fears were overdone;
    communication challenge underestimated

b.   Important Successes and Disappointments

Successes

Rapid establishment of credibility and stable goals (mandate + legacy)
Overcame external shocks (not just luck)
Major advances in data collection and forecasting
Transparent policy strategy, especially the quantitative definition of price
    stability
Excellent track record: low inflation, stable inflation expectations, and low
    inflation volatility
Cooperation between the ECB and the NCBs
No major errors in interest rate setting
An effective decision-making apparatus
Operational success in liquidity provision in crisis and foreign exchange
    intervention
Successfully guarded institutional independence from start
Effective international cooperation
Rapid money market integration; deep bond market integration
Euro has become a leading world currency
Consolidation of European banking and financial integration
2003 reform: altered communication strategy and use of policy framework
The euro yield curve was the best legacy yield curve at start

Avoided deflation panic
Effective personnel selection

Disappointments

No internal disappointments
Lack of fiscal and structural reforms (thereby sustaining low potential growth)
Teething problems in communication strategy
Introduction of coins and notes leads to substantial perceived inflation
Pace of financial integration was not what had been hoped
Little impact on political unification that some proponents hoped would come
Lack of understanding of ECB's role vis-à-vis national governments, the NCBs, and the European Commission
Inflation sometimes above 2 percent
Lack of a framework for financial stability
Some signs of divergence

c.   Has the Decision-Making Process Evolved?

No major changes in decision-making process
Effective decision-making apparatus, including the role of the staff
Proposal power of Chief Economist at the start
No national arguments on monetary policy
Early consensus on the policy strategy
Eclectic, careful vetting of policy
Consensus does not mean unanimity
Evidence of rapid decisions in crises
EMI prep aided consensus
Evolution of the communication style
Less effective cooperation on banking and national economic policy
Infrastructure decisions more problematic

d.   Have Politicians Had an Impact?

Little or no impact of pressure on decisions
Successfully established and maintained institutional independence
Easy to resist pressure from one country
Treaty protects ECB well
Political debate reflects traditional differences
Political influences can cause volatility and confusion
Pressures arise from lack of popular support for ECB
ECB as a cheap target

II.   Policy in the Second Decade of Monetary Union

a.   What are Biggest Challenges Looking Forward?

Maintaining popular support
Multi-national communications
Enlargement (the agreed upon voting system will help)
Maintain price stability in a credible regime
Financial stability
Real divergence
Fiscal and structural issues
Loss of political will (slow financial integration)
EU growth trend (competitiveness and dynamics)

b.   Is ECB Mature?

Most problems similar to those of other central banks
Enlargement
Multicountry
Selection of next President and Vice President key
Transmission Mechanism still uncertain
Financial Stability
Federal System/Multiple Fiscal Agents
Issues outside conventional monetary policy

c.   Is There Best Practice in Communication?

No "one size fits all"
Communication policy is by its nature evolutionary
ECB transparency and accountability are high; there is no need for major
    change
Communication is necessarily shaped by history, language, diverse con-
    stituency
More talk does not mean more transparency
Two pillars aided at start, but for how long?
Successes: quantitative definition of price stability
Press conference as substitute for minutes
Not publishing votes promotes "euro area" thinking
Would an inflation target be clearer?
Enlargement adds to communication challenge
Naïve to cite small-country central bank strategy as a model for ECB

d.   Nationality of the Board?

Nationality irrelevant for staffing
High standard of personnel achieved

Favorable comparison to other international organizations
Nationality of Executive Board members is key; need wider rotation
What happens if United Kingdom enters?

III.   Financial Stability

a.   Unusual Challenges in Financial Stability?

Greatest contribution to financial stability is continued price stability
Liquidity provision is a joint ECB/NCB responsibility
Ex-ante crisis management creates moral hazard
Bailouts have to be done by national governments with public funds
Financial regulatory process is in flux with overlapping jurisdictions in
    Europe, EU, euro area
Relationship among markets in different countries in flux
Various committees and MoUs promote cooperation, but the mechanism
    is complex
Euro system Marginal Lending Facility follows the Bagehot procedures
Common collateral framework makes the Lender of Last Resort operate
    more efficiently
There remains the danger of perpetuating insolvency through central bank
    lending
The key to crisis management is timely information exchange
Supervision needs to evolve with financial integration
Burden-sharing challenge rises with financial integration
Contrast: NCB Governor role in monetary policy versus role in financial
    stability
Pragmatic approach: European Secretariat
Early intervention needed (better incentives for market *plus* reduction of
    home/host stresses)
Real test will come with a solvency crisis in a recession
Decentralization creates a challenge in distinguishing illiquidity from insol-
    vency
Lack of coordination could threaten competitiveness of European financial
    centers?

b.   Lack of Regulatory and Supervisory Authority

Supranational supervisor not necessary—complex coordination is a sub-
    stitute
Doctrine: Close relationship between ECB and supervisory authorities
Exchange of information identified as key
Requires protocols to aid information flow under stress
NCBs provide relationship with counterparties
There may be an evolution toward more supranational approach?

National mandate, culture, practices, law, hinder supervisors from working
   as one
Political resistance to European supervision
ECB can see unusual borrowing by an institution
Reforms needed not just for institutional design: Crisis handbooks, exercises

c. Policy Coordination in Crisis?

Multiparty coordination difficult
Burden-sharing not centralized
Long evolution ahead
Greater diversity of circumstances and sophistication
Collateral regime insufficient with insolvency
Euro system lacks a clear New York Fed style liquidity desk
CB as natural leader in crisis (source of liquidity)

Appendix C
Brief Biographies of Interviewees

We interviewed seventeen high-level current and former officials, the
majority of whom were directly involved in the creation of the monetary
union. We sent out twenty-two interview requests. Two were declined; two
agreed to interviews but we were unable to schedule them; and in one case
we received no response.

Following, we provide a very brief biographic sketch of each interviewee.
In order to conserve space, we focus on the experience that is most relevant
for our purposes. A complete biography of any of these people would run
for pages. The date of the interview is in parentheses.

Dr. Ignazio Angeloni (September 13, 2007): From September 1998 to
December 2002, Dr. Angeloni was Deputy Director General in the Direc-
torate Research at the European Central Bank. Prior to that he was at the
Bank of Italy. At the time of the interview, Dr. Angeloni was Director for
International Financial Relations at the Italian Treasury.

Dr. Jaime Caruana (November 1, 2007): From 2000 to 2006, Dr. Caruana
was Governor of the Bank of Spain, during which time he also served as
Chairman of the Basel Committee on Banking Supervision (2003 to 2006).
Prior to joining the Bank of Spain, Dr. Caruana held various positions in the
Spanish Treasury. At the time of the interview, Dr. Caruana was Counsel-
lor and Director of the Monetary and Capital Markets Department at the
International Monetary Fund.

Sir Andrew Crockett (October 30, 2007): From 1994 to 2003, Sir Andrew
was the General Manager of the Bank for International Settlements. Prior

to that, he held various positions at the Bank of England. At the time of the interview, Sir Andrew was President of JP Morgan Chase International.

Dr. Vitor Gaspar (August 29, 2007): From September 1998 to December 2004, Dr. Gaspar was the Director-General Research at the European Central Bank. Prior to that he was Director of the Research and Statistics Department of Bank of Portugal and Director of Economic Studies at the Portuguese Ministry of Finance. At the time of the interview, Dr. Gaspar was Acting Director of the Bureau of European Policy Advisors at the European Commission.

President Timothy F. Geithner (November 16, 2007): Since 2003, Mr. Geithner has been President of the Federal Reserve Bank of New York and Vice Chairman of the Federal Open Market Committee. He also serves as Chairman of the Committee of Payment and Settlement Systems. Prior to joining the Federal Reserve, Mr. Geithner held leading positions at the International Monetary Fund and the U.S. Treasury, where he was Under Secretary for International Affairs from 1999 to 2001.

Lord Edward George (January 9, 2008): From 1993 to 2003, Lord George was Governor of the Bank of England, where he worked for his entire career beginning in 1962. At the time of the interview, he was a member of the House of Lords.

Dr. Sirkka Hämäläinen (October 9, 2007): From 1998 to 2003, Dr. Hämäläinen was a member of the Executive Board of the European Central Bank. From 1992 to 1998, she was Governor of the Bank of Finland.

Vice Chairman Philipp M. Hildebrand (January 28, 2008): Since 2003, Dr. Hildebrand has been a member of the Governing Board of the Swiss National Bank, and was named Vice Chairman in 2007. Prior to joining the Swiss National Bank, he held various positions in private financial institutions.

Prof. Dr. Otmar Issing (June 29, 2007): As a member of the Executive Board of the European Central Bank from June 1998 to May 2006 Professor Issing was responsible for the Directorates General Economics and Research. From 1990 to 1998 he was a member of the Board of the Deutsche Bundesbank with a seat in the Central Bank Council. From 1988 to 1990 he was a member of the Council of Economic Experts in Germany. At the time of the interview, Professor Issing was President of the Center for Financial Studies at the University of Frankfurt.

Baron Alexandre Lamfalussy (November 6, 2007): From 1994 to 1997, Baron Lamfalussy was the founding President of the European Monetary Institute. Prior to that, he held various positions at the Bank for International Settlements, including serving as General Manager from 1985 to 1993. At the time of the interview, Baron Lamfalussy was Professor emeritus at the Catholic University of Louvain.

Governor Christian Noyer (February 27, 2008): Since 2003, Mr. Noyer has been Governor of the Banque de France. From 1998 to 2002, he was the founding Vice President of the European Central Bank. Prior to joining the ECB, Mr. Noyer held leading positions at the French Treasury and Finance Ministry.

Vice President Lucas D. Papademos (November 15, 2007): Since 2002, Dr. Papademos has been Vice President of the European Central Bank. Prior to taking his current position, beginning in 1994, he was Governor of the Bank of Greece.

Dr. Fabrizio Saccomanni (November 6, 2007): Since 2006, Dr. Saccomanni has been Director General of the Bank of Italy. From 2003 to 2006, he was Vice President of the European Bank for Reconstruction and Development. Prior to that, Dr. Saccomanni held a variety of positions at the Bank of Italy.

Prof. John B. Taylor (January 25, 2008): Professor Taylor is the Mary and Robert Raymond Professor of Economics at Stanford University and the Bowen H. and Janice Arthur McCoy Senior Fellow at the Hoover Institution. He has been a member of the faculty at Stanford University since 1984. During that period, Professor Taylor also has served as a member of the President's Council of Economic Advisers (1989 to 1991) and as Under Secretary of the Treasury for International Affairs (2001 to 2005).

Prof. Dr. Hans Tietmeyer (October 9, 2007): From 1993 to 1999, Prof. Tietmeyer was President of the Deutsche Bundesbank. At the time of the interview, he was inter alia President of the European Business School, International University, Schloss Reichartshausen, Germany.

President Jean-Claude Trichet (December 14, 2007): Since 2003, Mr. Trichet has been President of the European Central Bank. Prior to assuming his current position, he was Governor of the Banque de France starting in 1993, Under Secretary of the Treasury starting in 1987, and Counsellor of the President of the Republic until 1981.

President Axel A. Weber (October 10, 2007): Professor Weber has been President of the Deutsche Bundesbank since April 2004. Prior to that he was Professor of International Economics at the University of Cologne and a member of the German Council of Economic Experts.

References

Alesina, A., O. Blanchard, J. Galí, F. Giavazzi, and H. Uhlig. 2001. *Defining a macroeconomic framework for the euro area: Monitoring the European Central Bank 3.* Washington, DC: Center for Economic Policy Research.

Andersson, M., L. J. Hansen, and S. Sebestyén. 2006. Which news moves the euro area bond market? European Central Bank (ECB) Working Paper no. 631, May.

Bank of England, Her Majesty's Treasury and Financial Services Authority. 2008. *Financial stability and depositor protection: strengthening the framework.* Consultation document, January.

Begg, D., F. Canova, P. De Grauwe, A. Fatás, and P. R. Lane. 2002. *Surviving the slowdown: Monitoring the European Central Bank 4.* Washington, DC: Center for Economic Policy Research.

Bini-Smaghi, L. 2007. The exchange rate policy of the Euro. Speech at the Annual Meeting Association Française de Sciences Economiques La Sorbonne. 21 September, Paris.

Cecchetti, S. G., A. Flores-Lagunes, and S. Krause. 2006. Has monetary policy become more efficient? A cross-country analysis. *Economic Journal* 116 (4): 408–33.

Cecchetti, S. G., P. Hooper, B. Kasman, K. L. Schoenholtz, and M. W. Watson. 2008. *Understanding the evolving inflation process.* U.S. Monetary Policy Forum Report no. 1, Rosenberg Institute, Brandeis International Business School and Initiative on Global Financial Markets, University of Chicago Graduate School of Business.

Connolly, B. 1995. *The rotten heart of Europe: The dirty war for Europe's money.* London: Faber and Faber.

Del Giovane, P., S. Fabiani, and R. Sabbatini. 2008. What's behind "inflation perceptions"? A survey-based analysis of Italian consumers. In *The Euro, inflation, and consumers' perceptions: Lessons from Italy,* ed. P. Del Giovane and R. Sabbatini, 157–98. Berlin: Springer-Verlag.

Del Giovane, P., and R. Sabbatini, eds. 2008. *The Euro, inflation, and consumer's perceptions: Lessons from Italy.* Berlin: Springer-Verlag.

Dzuida, W., and G. Mastrobuoni. 2007. The Euro changeover and its effects on price transparency and inflation. Kellogg School of Management, Northwestern University. Unpublished Manuscript, July.

Economic and Financial Committee. 2007. *EFC 2007 status report on information requirements in EMU.* ECFIN report, October.

Eijffinger, S. C. W., P. M. Geraats, and C. A. B. van der Cruijsen. 2006. Does central bank transparency reduce interest rates? Center for Economic Policy Research Working Paper no. DP5526, March.

Eijffinger, S. C. W., and C. A. B. van der Cruijsen. 2007. Actual versus perceived central bank transparency: The case of the European Central Bank. Tilburg University, Discussion Paper no. 2007-78, October.

Eurobarometer, various issues, European Commission.

European Central Bank. 2004a. Developments in the EU framework for financial regulation, supervision and stability. *ECB Monthly Bulletin,* November: 81–93.

———. 2004b. *The Monetary policy of the ECB,* 2nd ed. Frankfurt: European Central Bank.

———. 2006a. *The implementation of monetary policy in the Euro Area: General documentation on Eurosystem monetary policy instruments and procedures.* Frankfurt: European Central Bank.

———. 2006b. The predictability of the ECB's monetary policy. *ECB Monthly Bulletin,* January: 51–61.

———. 2007a. Circulation and supply of euro banknotes and preparations for the second series of banknotes. *ECB Monthly Bulletin,* October: 101–7.

———. 2007b. Review of the Lamfalussy framework: Eurosystem contribution. Available at: http://www.ecb.int/pub/pdf/other/lamfalussy-review2007en.pdf.

———. 2007c. The EU arrangements for financial crisis management. *ECB Monthly Bulletin,* February: 73–84.

European Commission, *European Economy,* various issues.

European Commission. 2007. *European Economy, public finances in EMU* 3 (June). Report of the European Commission.

European Economic Advisory Group at CESifo. 2003. Executive Summary. In

Report on the European economy 2003. Munich: Ifo Institute for Economic Research.

Eurostat. 2003. May 2003 euro-zone annual inflation down to 1.9%. *Euro-Indicators News Release 69/2003,* 18 June.

Feldstein, M. 1997. The political economy of the European economic and monetary union: Political sources of an economic liability. *Journal of Economic Perspectives* 11 (4): 23–42.

Fischer, B., M. Lenza, H. Pill, and L. Reichlin. 2006. Money and monetary policy: The ECB experience 1999–2006. ECB Working Paper, November.

Galí, J., S. Gerlach, J. Rotemberg, H. Uhlig, and M. Woodford. 2004. *The monetary policy strategy of the ECB reconsidered: Monitoring the European Central Bank 5.* Washington, DC: Center for Economic Policy Research.

Garber, P. M. 1999. The TARGET mechanism: Will it propagate or stifle a stage III crisis? *Carnegie-Rochester Conference Series on Public Policy* 51 (1): 195–220.

Gaspar, V. 2006. Bagehot and Coase meet the Single European Market. European Commission. Unpublished manuscript, October.

Gaspar, V., and A. K. Kashyap. 2006. Stability first: Reflections inspired by Otmar Issing's success as the ECB's chief economist. NBER Working Paper no. 12277. Cambridge, MA: National Bureau of Economic Research, June.

Geraats, P., F. Giavazzi, and C. Wyplosz. 2008. *Transparency and governance: Monitoring the European Central Bank 6.* Washington, DC: Center for Economic Policy Research.

International Monetary Fund (IMF). *World economic outlook,* various issues.

Issing, O. 2003. Monetary and financial stability: Is there a trade-off? Speech presented at the Conference, Monetary Stability, Financial Stability, and the Business Cycle. 28–29 March, Bank for International Settlements, Basle, Switzerland.

———. 2004. Financial integration, asset prices, and monetary policy. Speech presented at the Symposium, Capital Markets and Financial Integration in Europe. 10 May, Frankfurt, Germany.

———. 2006a. Globalization, EMU and the euro. Speech presented at the Conference, Globalization: Opportunities and Challenges for the World, Europe and Austria. 22 May, Vienna, Austria.

———. 2006b. The ECB's monetary policy strategy: Why did we choose a two pillar approach? Paper presented at the Conference, The Role of Money: Money and Monetary Policy in the Twenty-First Century, European Central Bank. 10 November, Frankfurt, Germany.

Issing, O., V. Gaspar, I. Angeloni, and O. Tristani. 2001. *Monetary policy in the euro area: Strategy and decision-making at the European Central Bank.* Cambridge: Cambridge University Press.

Jansen, D.-J., and J. de Haan. 2003. Statements of ECB officials and their effect on the level and volatility of the euro-dollar exchange rate. Munich Society for the Promotion of Economic Research. CESifo Working Paper no. 927, April.

———. 2004. Look who's talking: ECB communication during the first years of EMU. Munich Society for the Promotion of Economic Research. CESifo Working Paper no. 1263, August.

Obstfeld, M. 1998. EMU: ready or not? Princeton Essays in International Finance, no. 209, July.

OECD Economic Outlook, various issues.

Papademos, L. 2006. The role of money: Money and monetary policy in the twenty-first century. Speech at the Fourth ECB Central Banking Conference. 9 November, Frankfurt, Germany.

———. 2007. Inflation and competitiveness divergences in the euro area countries:

Causes, consequences and policy responses. Speech presented at the Center for Financial Studies of the University of Frankfurt Conference, The ECB and its Watchers IX. 7 September, Frankfurt, Germany.

Sargent, T. J., and N. Wallace. Some unpleasant monetarist arithmetic. 1981. Federal Reserve Bank of Minneapolis, *Quarterly Review* (Fall). Available at: http://www.minneapolisfed.org/research/QR/QR531.pdf.

Stark, J. 2006. The role of money: Money and monetary policy in the twenty-first century. Speech presented at the fourth ECB Central Banking Conference. 9 November, Frankfurt, Germany.

Svensson, L. E. O. 2000. The first year of the eurosystem: Inflation targeting or not? *American Economic Review* 90 (2): 95–99.

Tabellini, G. 2008. Why did bank supervision fail? VOX website, 19 March. Available at: http://www.voxeu.com/index.php?q=node/994.

Weber, A. 2007. How should central banks signal their intentions regarding future interest rates? Presented at the Center for Financial Studies of the University of Frankfurt Conference, The ECB and its Watchers IX. 7 September, Frankfurt, Germany. Available at: www.ifk-cfs.de/fileadmin/downloads/events/ecbwatchers/20070907ecb_weber.pdf.

Comment   Pervenche Berès

First of all, I would like to thank Cecchetti and Schoenholtz for their in-depth chapter, taking into account that among seventeen interviews, sixteen were conducted with central bankers. Before anything else, let me tell you that I share their general positive appraisal of the first decade of the European Central Bank (ECB), and maybe especially of the last year. I welcome the fact that the euro has brought stability and fostered economic integration in the euro area, even if internal economic divergences have not diminished enough and productivity has not developed satisfactorily.

Reacting on their chapter, I suggest coming back on key issues to be further explored for the discussion, especially concerning the main challenges ahead.

First, I would like to come back to the ECB's operational framework. Together with Werner Langen, from the Economic and Monetary Committee of the European Parliament, I have drafted a report, *EMU@10: The First Ten Years of Economic and Monetary Union and Future Challenges* (Berès and Langen 2008), following the communication of the Commission last spring. The report addresses many elements of this debate; it was voted in ECON and November 2008 in plenary session. I will now discuss the chapter with elements on monetary policy that are developed in our report.

As regards the definition of price stability, the ECB aims at inflation rates of below, but close to, 2 percent over the medium term. We consider that

Pervenche Berès is the Chairwoman of the Committee on Economic and Monetary Affairs of the European Parliament.

this definition should be examined in the context of increased heterogeneity of the euro area and the need to ensure financial stability. The presentation points out that this would be a good monetary policy, I would, however, specify add in good times, where all central bankers could follow a line of price stability that was eased by the prevailing condition of globalization, with a strong pressure on consumer good prices that was based on outsourcing. Let us not forget that the objective of price stability can be achieved effectively only if the root causes of inflation are properly addressed. And let us keep in mind that article 105 of the EC Treaty also assigned to the ECB the task of supporting the general economic policies of the Community, even though I believe it will become more difficult now for the ECB to argue that the best way to achieve this broader task is price stability. Here and there, the issue of who should set the definition of price stability or the inflation target is also discussed. The question is whether the Council and the European Parliament could or should be involved in such a discussion.

We are also of the opinion that the ECB should move toward a direct inflation targeting regime where a point inflation target is supplemented by a range of permitted fluctuations around the target rate, and should make public its inflation forecasts. This should not preclude paying attention to the dynamics of monetary aggregates in order to avoid new asset bubbles, even if asset bubbles can be better addressed by proper regulation than by monetary policy.

We also stress the necessity of exploring possible improvements in the procedure for appointing the members of the ECB's executive board before 2010. We agree with Cecchetti's and Schoenholtz's view that it is important that a variety of backgrounds be represented among executive board members: I would mention academic or professional experience, and background in the economic, monetary, and financial sector. But let me admit that as regards this nomination procedure and its practice, I have two strong regrets. One is that the Council merely rubberstamps the proposals made by the Member States when they come from a big country and by doing so, does not exert one of its important decision powers related to the shaping of monetary policy. The second one is that the EP is only consulted, contrary to the power it has regarding the appointment of Commissioners and the U.S. Congress has vis-à-vis the Fed.

On transparency and accountability, I regret that your chapter does not make mention—at least once—of the European Parliament, and surprisingly enough, you do not discuss "accountability," but rather "communication" issues. The regular reports of the ECB to Parliament, in particular to its Committee on Economic and Monetary Affairs, as well as the regular ex-change of views with the Pr President of the ECB constitute a monetary dialogue and contribute to the transparency of monetary policy. It improves the accountability of the ECB vis-à-vis the citizens of the Union. I am moreover in favor of stronger public debate on the future common monetary and currency policies in the euro area as part of the convergence process. The truth is that the shaping of the ECB's accountability is an original one, since there is no euro zone country or constituency. Because of this, it could not be shaped on the basis of the previous German model, where the Bundesbank was accountable to the country and its citizens. It does not completely follow the U.S. model either, where the Fed is closely accountable to the Congress (that has nomination powers and can change the statute of the Fed).

A second issue to be further explored is the question of enlargement. I regard an enduring and successful expansion of the euro area as a major challenge for the coming years, whereby both institutional standards for the ECB and the decision-making process of the ECB have to be adapted to this change. Moreover, the rotation model has to take into account the economic weight of the individual member States.

In this context, I draw attention to our calls for an ECB executive board of nine members, thus replacing the system existing now and avoiding the even more complex solution decided upon for the future, with the enlargement of the euro area. This has been the EP's position for years, since the ECB has imposed to the Council its ideas about the future rotation system.

Just a word on the conditions of enlargement: if equal treatment of the Member States in the euro area and Member States wishing to join must be ensured, long-term stability of the euro area must be regarded as an aim of common interest. Enlargement and stability must go hand in hand.

On communication, a topic that is stressed several times in your chapter, I indeed share the view that communication is of utmost importance to prepare the introduction of the euro in the Member States planning to join the euro area; I would add that communication on the enlargement of the euro area is also important for all Member States in the euro area. But if you realize that the ECB celebrated the tenth anniversary of the euro on the 1st of January 2009 and that the citizens were celebrating the fifth anniversary of coins and notes on the 1st of January 2007, you can measure the gap in terms of communication.

The major issue is the challenge of financial stability, as stated by Cecchetti and Schoenhotz. The papers seem to open space for a certain confusion between the need for EU regulation and supervision. In reality, the single EU regulator already exists; what is lacking in this field is a coherent implementation of the regulation and an EU supervision.

I believe that the EU urgently needs to enhance its supervision structure, taking into account the specific role of the ECB. The European Parliament has been extremely active on this issue. An initiative report from the Economic and Monetary Committee with recommendations to the Commission on Lamfalussy follow-up and the future structure of supervision has just been voted in plenary session last month.

A "Europeanization" of the financial supervision structure, financial market transparency, effective competition rules, and appropriate regulation is necessary in the medium term, in order to improve crisis management and cooperation between the European System of Central Banks, supervisory authorities, governments, and market participants. An integrated, comprehensive (covering all financial sectors), consistent, and coherent supervisory framework starting with a balanced approach in regulating the cross-border spread of financial risk on the basis of harmonized legislation would decrease compliance costs in the case of multijurisdiction activities. In recent different reports, the Parliament calls on the Commission to put forward proposals for revising the existing supervisory architecture along those principles. If we want to have a two-step approach, what is needed is to start with an upgrade of the three level-three committees and then to move toward a European system of national supervisors along the lines of the European System of Central Banks (ESCB). In any solution, the role of the ECB will need to be increased and defined so as to ensure and define a good articulation between a macro and a micro prudential approach.

Finally, let me briefly refer to topics that we cannot develop here, because time is limited, but that are worth mentioning. Of course, as Cecchetti and Schoenholtz have mentioned, many disappointments of the first decade come from "outside the ECB." I can only echo this point. But we need to recall that they are not the only ones responsible for this situation. We have already mentioned the lack of initiative or involvement when it comes to nominations to the board or to supervision issues. But it could also be said regarding the way the Council up to now has used its powers regarding exchange rates or the power to speak at the Council of governors meeting, where the absence of the Council results in Jean-Claude Trichet being the only one to speak on wages but also on the level of public spending. I agree that future challenges concern not only the ECB, but structural and fiscal reform, as well as economic governance.

In particular, I am convinced that the European Monetary Union (EMU) policy agenda for the next decade will be marked by the challenges presented by the recent financial market turmoil and its implications for the real economy. I note in this context that Member States within the euro area are better equipped to face major shocks than in the past thanks to the common monetary policy and reforms carried out in recent years. However, in the interest to largely combat economic slowdown and high inflation, I would suggest:

- A coordinated response at the EU level, based on common understanding of the problems and common follow-up measures while accepting some national specificities.
- Ambitious and adjusted National Reform Programmes and their committed implementation, including strong dialogues with social partners.

- Fully and timely implementation of the Financial Services roadmap, including follow-up actions and increased effectiveness of supervision to the ongoing financial turmoil.
- Completing the tools used for designing monetary policy by the thorough analysis of factors that influence the stability and functioning of the financial system.
- A proactive European reaction within international fora, notably at the Financial Stability Forum (FSF) and International Monetary Fund (IMF) and the increase of common political decision-making processes.
- Organizing the European voice within the G8 and reflecting on its role as a more efficient worldwide economic decision-making body while adjusting it to the consequences of globalization and more dominant worldwide acting financial markets.

In conclusion, I would like to underline that more needs to be done to reap the full benefits of EMU and to strengthen citizens' understanding and commitment to the ECB and the single currency.

I recall that during the first decade of EMU, Parliament has done a huge amount of work to ensure more transparency and democratic accountability of the ECB. In the background of the financial crisis, the European Parliament is currently playing an active role, on legislative or nonlegislative files, to help build adequate answers to the challenges that face the ECB, in particular in the area of financial stability.

Reference

Berès, P., and W. Langen. 2008. *EMU@10: The first ten years of Economic and Monetary Union and future challenges.* Economic and Monetary Committee of the European Parliament. Report, November.

Reevaluating Swedish Membership in the European Monetary Union
Evidence from an Estimated Model

Ulf Söderström

10.1 Introduction

When the Swedish government negotiated the treaty of accession to the European Union in 1993 and 1994, the negotiations did not include an exemption to the third stage of the Economic and Monetary Union (EMU). In contrast to Denmark and the United Kingdom, which did obtain such exemptions, Sweden is therefore required by EU law to join EMU and adopt the euro as soon as the convergence criteria specified in the Maastricht treaty are fulfilled. Nevertheless, the Swedish Parliament (the Riksdag) decided in 1997 that Sweden would not join the Exchange Rate Mechanism (ERM) of the European Monetary System, and the Swedish central bank (Sveriges Riksbank) has followed a policy of inflation targeting with a flexible exchange rate since 1993. As a consequence, in the assessments made by the European Commission prior to the launch of EMU in 1999 and every two years since 2000, Sweden has been judged not to fulfill the criterion regarding exchange rate stability, which requires the member state to participate in the ERM (now the ERM II). Sweden, therefore, is a member state with a

Ulf Söderström is a researcher in the Monetary Policy Department of Sveriges Riksbank, the central bank of Sweden.

This chapter was prepared for the NBER conference on "Europe and the Euro" in October 2008. I am grateful for comments from, and discussions with, Carlo Altomonte, Carlo Favero, Nils Gottfries, Steinar Holden, Lars Jonung, Thomas Lindblom, Anders Vredin, an anonymous reviewer, and the editors, Alberto Alesina and Francesco Giavazzi. I also thank seminar participants at Sveriges Riksbank and Uppsala University, and participants at the NBER conference. And I am indebted to Malin Adolfson and Jesper Lindé for help with the estimated open economy model. The views expressed in this chapter are solely the responsibility of the author and should not be interpreted as reflecting the views of the Executive Board of Sveriges Riksbank.

See page 440 for Carlo A. Favero's comment on this chapter and the following chapter.

derogation from the third stage of EMU, but is not exempted from participation.[1] A national referendum on Swedish participation in EMU was held in September 2003, and the result was a rejection of membership with 56 percent of the electorate voting against and 42 percent voting in favor. As a consequence, the Riksdag decision of 1997 remains in force, and Sweden remains outside EMU.

Ten years after the launch of EMU, I revisit the question of the potential costs and benefits for Sweden of joining the monetary union. I first (in section 10.2) return to the report of the Calmfors Commission, the government commission assigned to study the consequences of EMU membership in 1995 and 1996. I summarize the main conclusions of the Commission, and provide an updated evaluation of the arguments made in the report. Some of these arguments speak more strongly in favor of Swedish EMU membership today than in 1996, while others more clearly speak against membership.

I then take a broad look at European business cycles (in section 10.3) and discuss the comovement between the Swedish and European economies. I show that European business cycles are closely correlated with each other, suggesting that business cycles in Europe are largely driven by common shocks. Although the large EMU member countries show stronger comovement with the euro area, Sweden tends to be at least as strongly correlated with the euro area as some EMU members (for instance, Finland), and more closely correlated than Norway and the United Kingdom. This evidence indicates that membership in EMU would not be very costly for Sweden, and not more so than for some current EMU members.

Next, I present evidence from an estimated model of the Swedish economy. I discuss in section 10.4 the importance of country-specific shocks for Swedish business cycle fluctuations since 1993, and I study the source and effects of fluctuations in the exchange rate. In contrast to the evidence in section 10.3, the estimated model suggests that country-specific shocks are an important source of Swedish business cycle fluctuations, and therefore that participation in the monetary union may be costly. On the other hand, the model interprets most fluctuations in the exchange rate as caused by shocks to the exchange rate risk premium, rather than endogenous movements that help the economy adjust after disturbances to other sectors in the economy. As such risk premium shocks induce inefficient volatility in the macroeconomy, the benefits of having a flexible exchange rate may be small, speaking in favor of EMU membership (which to a large extent would eliminate exchange rate fluctuations, as the EMU countries represent around 60 percent of Swedish trade).

---

1. The assessments also conclude that Swedish legislation concerning the financial independence of the Riksbank and the Riksbank's integration into the European System of Central Banks (ESCB) is not consistent with the Maastricht treaty and the statutes of the ESCB and the European Central Bank (ECB).

I then (in section 10.5) use the model for a counterfactual experiment to evaluate what would have been the consequences for the Swedish economy if Sweden had joined EMU in January 1999. The simulations predict that Swedish membership in the monetary union might have led to slightly higher gross domestic product (GDP) growth and inflation, but also higher volatility in GDP growth. Furthermore, EMU membership might have implied higher inflation in 2004 and 2005, when inflation was exceptionally low in Sweden. However, the effects of EMU membership are not dramatic, reflecting the strong comovement of the Swedish and euro area economies in the last decade.

The model is silent on many relevant issues. I discuss some of these in section 10.6; for instance, the impact of EMU on economic integration and labor markets, and whether Sweden has lost political influence in the EU by not participating in EMU. Finally, I conclude in section 10.7 that, perhaps unsurprisingly, the evidence presented here is not conclusive about the whether the costs or the benefits of Swedish EMU membership dominate. These conclusions may, however, be sharpened by the outcome of the current financial crisis.

10.2   The Calmfors Commission

Ahead of the Riksdag decision in 1997 concerning Swedish membership in EMU, the Swedish government appointed a commission (the "Calmfors Commission") to analyze the consequences of EMU and of Swedish membership in the monetary union. The Commission, composed of five economists and three political scientists, was appointed in October 1995 and delivered its report in October 1996 (see Calmfors et al. 1996).

The Commission argued that monetary union would lead to small efficiency gains due to reduced transaction costs and exchange rate uncertainty and increased competition, speaking in favor of Swedish membership. However, these gains needed to be weighed against the adverse effects of large country-specific disturbances that could have severe consequences if they were not counteracted by independent monetary policy and exchange rate policy. While these large disturbances normally would not be an important problem, the Commission argued that independent monetary policy could be an important insurance against such extreme events.

An important argument in favor of Swedish EMU membership was deemed to be the potential loss of political influence within the EU if Sweden were to stay outside the monetary union.

All in all, the final assessment of the Commission was that the economic arguments did not favor participation, while the political arguments were in support of membership, but that the arguments against membership in 1999 were stronger than those in favor. Therefore, the Commission concluded that while Sweden should aim at future membership in the monetary union, it would be better not to join EMU in the first wave of 1999.[2]

The Commission listed four main reasons for its conclusion:

1. The EMU membership would be risky with the then-high level of unemployment, as the economy would be particularly vulnerable to adverse shocks. After a long period with an unemployment rate around 2 to 3 percent, the Swedish unemployment rate had increased quickly to above 9 percent during the recession in 1992 and 1993, and remained at this level until the late 1990s. (See also figure 10.3.)

2. The already precarious fiscal situation also made membership risky, as fiscal measures would need to carry a larger burden of stabilization policy within the monetary union, and a deterioration of the government finances would need to be followed by drastic countermeasures to satisfy the rules of the Stability and Growth Pact. The ratio of government debt to GDP was close to 75 percent in 1995 and 1996, and the government deficit amounted to 9 percent and 7 percent of GDP in 1994 and 1995, respectively. Again, this difficult fiscal situation was partly caused by the recession in the early 1990s.

3. To ensure legitimacy among the electorate, the commission saw a need for a broad public debate concerning the monetary union before a definitive decision was taken. There had not been any extensive debate of EMU before the referendum concerning EU membership in 1994, as EMU membership was seen as an issue separate from EU membership.

4. The fact that only a subset of EU members were likely to join the monetary union, and, in particular, not Denmark and the United Kingdom, implied that the potential economic gains of membership seemed small, while the costs of staying outside in terms of lost political influence seemed limited. In 1996, many observers expected that only a small core of EU member states (consisting of Germany, France, the Benelux countries, Austria, and perhaps Finland and Ireland) would be able to qualify for EMU membership.

The Commission stressed that its assessment of membership would be positively affected if unemployment were to fall and the fiscal situation stabilized. At the same time, the Commission feared that staying outside EMU might lead to a loss of credibility for the Swedish currency, leading to increased short-term interest rates and a continued large spread between Swedish and EMU long-term interest rates.

When revisiting the issues more than ten years later, some arguments seem to speak more strongly in favor of Swedish membership in EMU,

---

2. One member of the Commission dissented from this conclusion, arguing that the costs of monetary union would be large also in the longer term, and that Sweden should not join the monetary union in the future. See Reservation (statement of dissenting opinion) by Gottfries in Calmfors et al. (1996).

while other arguments speak more strongly against. First, the EMU project must be deemed as a great success. More countries than expected joined in 1999, and although Denmark is not an EMU member, it maintains a fixed-exchange rate against the euro, and its monetary policy shadows that of the European Central Bank (ECB). The ECB has established credibility for a low inflation policy, and the euro has become a major currency, probably more important than the individual currencies taken together. The gains in terms of economic integration also seem fairly large, perhaps larger than expected in 1996 (see section 10.6). Second, since 1996, unemployment has fallen considerably in Sweden (to around 6 percent in September 2008), and the fiscal situation has been stabilized (government debt in 2007 was around 40 percent of GDP and the government ran a surplus of around 3.5 percent of GDP). Thus, Sweden today seems less vulnerable to adverse shocks than in 1996. Finally, there do not seem to have been any large country-specific disturbances to the Swedish economy, so the gains from independent monetary policy may have been small. While the last point is not particularly strong, as independent monetary policy may turn out to be of crucial importance in the future, the other arguments suggest that the case for EMU membership may be stronger today than in 1996.

There are, however, also arguments that speak more strongly against EMU membership today. First, the Commission's fears about a loss in credibility for Swedish monetary policy and the Swedish currency never materialized. As we will see next, Swedish long-term interest rates have converged substantially toward European rates, although not to the same extent as those in the EMU member countries. Second, the recent literature does not find strong support for the proposition that Sweden has lost political influence within the EU (see section 10.6). And third, while there was a broad public debate about Swedish EMU membership ahead of the referendum in 2003, public opinion seems to be largely against membership.[3]

All in all, the events of the past ten years help to gain perspective on some of the important issues concerning Swedish membership in EMU that were discussed by the Calmfors Commission. However, at this stage it is not clear whether the case for membership has become stronger or weaker. The remaining sections will therefore cover many of these issues in more detail.

10.3   European Business Cycles

In this section I give an overview of the convergence of business cycles in Europe. The purpose is to give a broad view of the similarities of the

---

3. According to Statistics Sweden, since 2004 around 50 percent of the Swedish population have been against EMU membership while 35 to 40 percent have been for membership. However, a more recent poll by Sifo Research International (in October 2008) suggests that the balances may have shifted somewhat in favor of membership, with 47 percent against and 42 percent for.

Swedish and euro area business cycles, and thus the possible consequences for Sweden of joining the monetary union, and to compare with other European countries that have chosen different strategies in their relationship with the EU and the EMU. I thus compare Swedish data with those of the euro area as a whole and three groups of countries. The first group contains the four largest euro area member countries: France, Germany, Italy, and Spain. The second group consists of three Nordic countries: Denmark, which is a member of the EU but not of EMU, although it maintains a fixed exchange rate against the euro within ERM II; Finland, which is a member of EMU; and Norway, which remains outside the EU. Finally, I include in the comparison the United Kingdom, which like Sweden is a member of the EU, but neither of EMU nor ERM II.[4]

To evaluate convergence and the effects of EMU, I compare data from two subsamples: the period before EMU from 1994 to 1998, and the period after the launch of EMU from 1999 to 2007.[5] The data were collected from various sources; see the appendix for details.

I study the properties of business cycles in the selected countries in terms of the average level and volatility of a number of business cycle indicators in the different countries and their correlation with the euro area: GDP growth and the GDP gap (the percent deviation of GDP from trend); the rate of unemployment; the consumer price index (CPI) inflation rate; short-term (three-month) and long-term (ten-year) interest rates; and the nominal and real exchange rates.

The data are presented in figures 10.1 through 10.8, while tables 10.1 through 10.3 show sample means, standard deviations, and correlations with the euro area for the two subperiods. The main impression is that there is strong comovement of business cycles across Europe. Most countries experienced an expansion in 1997 to 2000 with high growth, increasing output gaps, and falling unemployment. This period was followed by a contraction in 2001 to 2003, with low growth, falling output gaps, and increasing unemployment, but since around 2003, most countries have experienced a gradual expansion of economic activity. At the same time, inflation and interest rates fell dramatically from the early 1990s until around 1999, after which they have been stabilized at low levels. In particular, long-term interest rates have converged strongly since the early 1990s, and in particular after 1999 (with the possible exception of Norway and the United Kingdom).[6] Also Swedish interest rates (short- and long-term) have converged toward the EMU rates,

---

4. The case of the United Kingdom is analyzed in detail in chapter 11 in this volume by DiCecio and Nelson.

5. I choose 1994 as the starting point for the pre-EMU sample to avoid the turbulent years in the early 1990s in Sweden and many other European countries.

6. Ehrmann et al. (2007) study in detail the convergence of interest rates within the euro area.

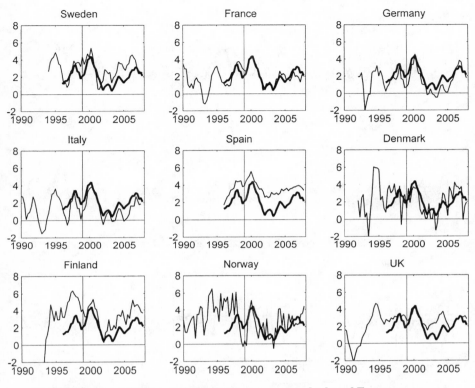

Fig. 10.1   Annual GDP growth rate in the euro area and selected European economies, 1990–2007

Source: OECD.

Notes: Four-quarter GDP growth rate in euro area (thick line) and selected European countries (thin line). Percent per annum. The vertical line represents the launch of EMU in January 1999.

less so than in the EMU member countries and Denmark, but more than in Norway and the United Kingdom.

Table 10.1 shows that most countries have experienced lower average GDP growth, unemployment, and short- and long-term interest rates in the post-EMU period than before 1999, while inflation has been low throughout the sample period. On average, Sweden has experienced higher GDP growth, lower unemployment, and lower inflation than most euro area countries in both sample periods. Table 10.2 shows that Sweden, along with Italy, Spain, and the other Nordic countries, has tended to have more volatile business cycles than the three large economies (Germany, France, and the United Kingdom) and than the euro area at large.

As for business cycle correlations, table 10.3 shows that the Swedish GDP

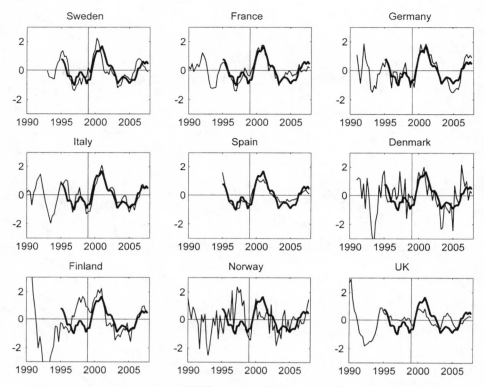

Fig. 10.2   GDP gap in the euro area and selected European economies, 1990–2007
Source: OECD.

Notes: Percent deviation of GDP from trend in euro area (thick line) and selected European countries (thin line). The trend was calculated by the author using the Hodrick-Prescott filter over the entire sample and a smoothing parameter of 1,600. The vertical line represents the launch of EMU in January 1999.

growth and GDP gap are fairly strongly correlated with its euro area counterparts, with correlation coefficients above 0.70 after 1999. Although the Swedish business cycle correlation with the euro area is weaker than those of the largest euro area members, France, Germany, Italy, and Spain (which often have correlation coefficients around 0.9), the business cycle in Sweden seems more strongly correlated with the euro area than in Norway and the United Kingdom, and the correlation is similar to that in Denmark and Finland.

To summarize, European business cycles are closely correlated with each other, and the Swedish business cycle is no exception. Although the large EMU members show even stronger comovement with the euro area, Sweden tends to be at least as strongly correlated with the euro area as some EMU members (for instance, Finland), and more closely correlated than Norway

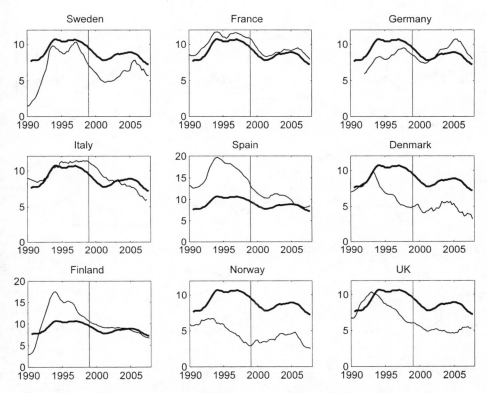

Fig. 10.3   Unemployment rate in the euro area and selected European economies, 1990–2007

Source: OECD.

Notes: Standardized unemployment rate in euro area (thick line) and selected European countries (thin line). Percent per annum. The vertical line represents the launch of EMU in January 1999.

and the United Kingdom. This evidence suggests that European business cycles are to a large extent driven by common shocks. If this is the case, then membership in EMU would not be very costly for Sweden, and not more so than for some current EMU members. However, before drawing this conclusion, we take a further step by using an estimated model to study the importance of country-specific shocks relative to foreign shocks for the Swedish economy.

10.4   The Role of Country-Specific Shocks and Exchange Rate Volatility for Macroeconomic Fluctuations

The traditional arguments against monetary union rest on two assertions. First, independent monetary policy is helpful to stabilize the economy after

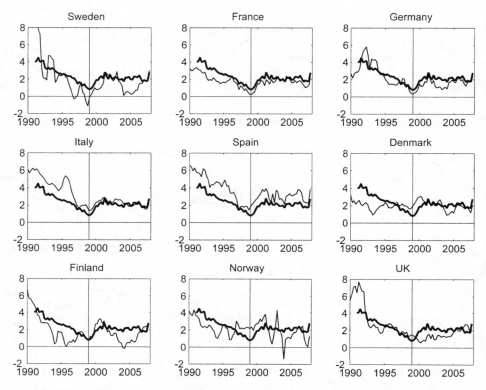

Fig. 10.4   CPI inflation rate in the euro area and selected European economies, 1990–2007

Source: OECD.

Notes: Four-quarter CPI inflation rates in euro area (thick line) and selected European countries (thin line). Quarterly averages of monthly data, percent per annum. The vertical line represents the launch of EMU in January 1999.

country-specific (or "asymmetric") shocks. Such shocks could therefore be costly in a monetary union where the common central bank would not adjust policy sufficiently, as it focuses on stabilizing the union-wide economy. Second, exchange rate movements help to stabilize the economy after shocks. For instance, the economy will recover more easily after a contractionary shock if the exchange rate is allowed to depreciate, something that will not be possible within a monetary union. Both arguments are more important for a small open economy such as Sweden, which would carry a small weight within the monetary union and where exchange rate movements have a strong effect on the economy.

The importance of the first argument depends on the prevalence of country-specific shocks: the more important are these shocks for the domes-

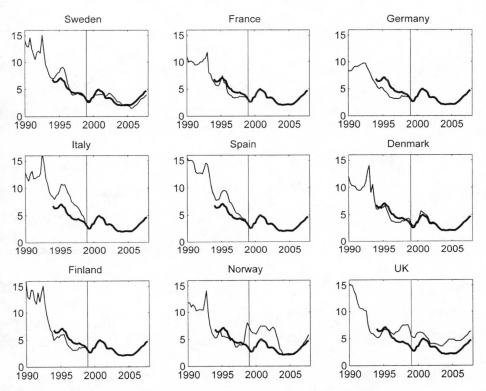

Fig. 10.5   Short-term interest rate in the euro area and selected European economies, 1990–2007

Source: OECD.

Notes: Three-month interest rates in euro area (thick line) and selected European countries (thin line). Quarterly averages, percent per annum. The vertical line represents the launch of EMU in January 1999.

tic economy, the more critical is independent monetary policy. However, the evidence from section 10.3 suggests that common shocks may be more important than country-specific shocks for European business cycles. The validity of the second argument rests on the notion that the nominal exchange rate adjusts appropriately after shocks. But exchange rate movements are known not to be very strongly linked to fundamentals (see, for instance, Obstfeld and Rogoff [2001]). If exchange rate movements are driven mainly by idiosyncratic shocks (for instance, to the foreign exchange risk premium), they may induce additional volatility rather than help the economy to adjust after shocks.[7]

In this section, I try to shed more light on these issues by studying the

7. This argument is emphasized by several of the contributions in Jakobsson (2003).

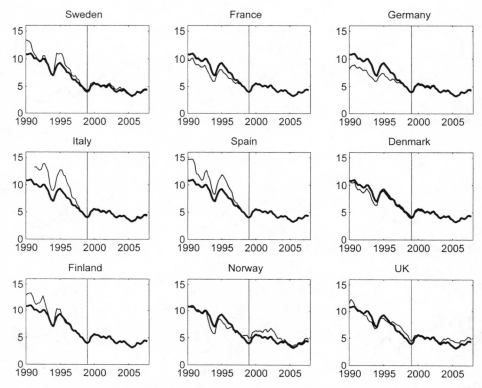

Fig. 10.6   Long-term interest rate in the euro area and selected European economies, 1990–2007

Source: OECD.

Notes: Ten-year government bond yield in euro area (thick line) and selected European countries (thin line). Quarterly averages, percent per annum. The vertical line represents the launch of EMU in January 1999.

importance of shocks for the Swedish economy in a model of a small open economy developed and estimated on Swedish data by Adolfson et al. (2007) and Adolfson et al. (2008).[8]

10.4.1   A Model of a Small Open Economy

The model used for these exercises is a Dynamic Stochastic General Equilibrium (DSGE) model with optimizing agents and rational expectations. The model economy consist of four groups of agents: households, firms, the government, and the foreign economy. *Households* maximize utility over an infinite horizon. They consume a basket of domestically produced

8. Adolfson, Laséen, et al. (2007) provide a more detailed nontechnical description.

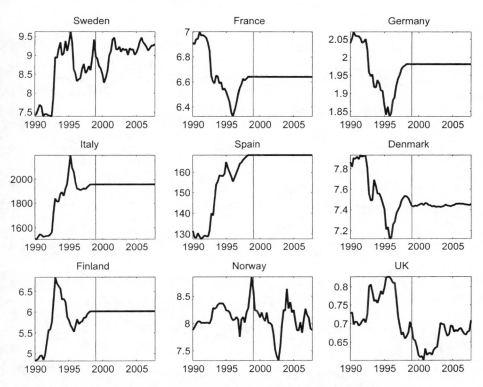

Fig. 10.7   Nominal exchange rate against the ECU/euro in selected European economies, 1990–2007

Source: FRED data base, Federal Reserve Bank of St. Louis.

Notes: Domestic currency price of ECU/euro. Quarterly averages of daily data. The vertical line represents the launch of EMU in January 1999.

goods and imported goods, which are supplied by domestic and importing firms, respectively. Households save in domestic and foreign currency-denominated nominal bonds, but must pay a premium on foreign bond holdings, a premium that depends on the domestic economy's net foreign asset position and an idiosyncratic shock. Households also own the capital stock, which they rent to domestic firms, and they decide the rate of capital accumulation given costs of adjusting the rate of investment. Finally, households supply a differentiated labor service under monopolistic competition and staggered wages.

The choice between domestic and foreign bond holdings implies that domestic and foreign interest rates are linked by an uncovered interest rate parity (UIP) condition. However, the premium on foreign bond holdings leads to an exchange rate risk premium that generates short-run deviations

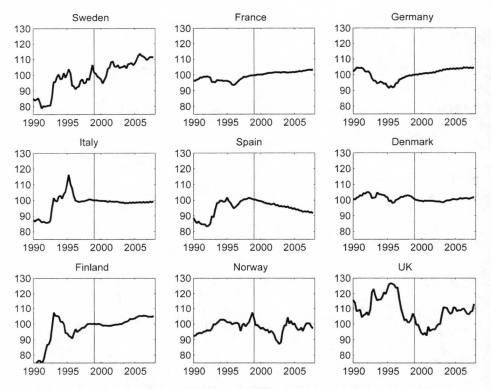

Fig. 10.8   Real exchange rate against the ECU/euro in selected European economies, 1990–2007

Sources: Author's calculation based on data from the FRED data base, Federal Reserve Bank of St. Louis (nominal exchange rates), and OECD (consumer prices).

Notes: Nominal exchange rate (domestic currency price of ECU/euro) deflated by the consumer price level. Quarterly averages, 1999 = 100. The vertical line represents the launch of EMU in January 1999.

from the fundamental value of the exchange rate determined by UIP. Idiosyncratic shocks to this risk premium generate volatility in the exchange rate and therefore inefficient fluctuations in the economy.

There are three types of *firms*—in the domestic, import, and export sectors—that produce differentiated goods under monopolistic competition and set prices in a staggered fashion. Domestic firms either produce consumption or investment goods. Staggered prices on imports and exports imply that exchange rate pass-through to both import and export prices is incomplete in the short run. Thus, changes in the exchange rate do not immediately feed through to import and export prices, but only after a gradual process of price changes.

The *government* spends resources on consuming part of the domestic

Table 10.1   Sample mean of selected business cycle indicators

Sample	Euro area	Sweden	France	Germany	Italy	Spain	Denmark	Finland	Norway	U.K.
(a) GDP growth										
1994–1998	2.2[a]	3.1	2.2	1.8	1.8	3.4[a]	3.2	4.3	4.1	3.2
1999–2007	2.1	3.1	2.1	1.5	1.4[b]	3.6	2.0	3.3	2.3	2.7
(b) Unemployment										
1994–1998	10.4	9.2	11.3	8.7	11.1	17.5	6.2	14.2	4.7	7.7
1999–2007	8.4	6.0	9.0	8.8	8.5[b]	10.3	4.7	8.8	3.8	5.1[b]
(c) CPI inflation rate										
1994–1998	2.1	1.1	1.4	1.7	3.3	3.2	2.0	1.0	1.9	2.1
1999–2007	2.0	1.3	1.6	1.5	2.2	3.0	2.1	1.5	1.9	1.5
(d) Short-term interest rate										
1994–1998	5.4	6.0	4.7	4.0	7.9	6.9	4.8	4.3	5.1	6.5
1999–2007	3.2	3.1					3.4		4.9	4.9
(e) Long-term interest rate										
1994–1998	7.0	7.9	6.3	6.0	8.8	8.2	6.9	7.1	6.6	7.3
1999–2007	4.4	4.6	4.4	4.3	4.6	4.4	4.5	4.4	5.2	4.8

Note: Quarterly data, 1994:1–2007:4, except [a] 1996:1–1998:4, [b] 1999:1–2007:3.

Table 10.2 Standard deviation of selected business cycle indicators

Sample	Euro area	Sweden	France	Germany	Italy	Spain	Denmark	Finland	Norway	U.K.
(a) GDP growth										
1994–1998	0.73[a]	1.18	1.01	0.82	1.22	0.95[a]	1.75	1.22	1.89	0.64
1999–2007	1.04	1.16	0.99	1.39	1.24[c]	0.72	1.50	1.28	1.38	0.64
(b) GDP gap										
1994–1998	0.54[b]	0.87	0.59	0.55	0.77	0.72[b]	0.88	1.07	1.17	0.34
1999–2007	0.76	0.81	0.71	1.04	0.85[c]	0.52	1.12	1.05	0.83	0.42
(c) Unemployment										
1994–1998	0.25	0.72	0.30	0.55	0.31	1.63	1.09	2.01	1.05	1.20
1999–2007	0.55	0.88	0.63	1.05	1.44[c]	1.37	0.66	0.98	0.68	0.38[c]
(d) CPI inflation rate										
1994–1998	0.61	1.17	0.53	0.64	1.28	1.23	0.22	0.59	0.63	0.45
1999–2007	0.43	0.87	0.51	0.55	0.41	0.59	0.56	0.95	1.12	0.55
(e) Short-term interest rate										
1994–1998	1.19	1.96	1.36	0.87	2.00	1.94	1.16	1.10	1.16	0.74
1999–2007	0.94	0.87					1.07		2.07	0.84
(f) Long-term interest rate										
1994–1998	1.59	2.15	1.18	0.95	2.81	2.52	1.31	1.86	1.00	1.11
1999–2007	0.65	0.74	0.64	0.61	0.65	0.70	0.72	0.70	0.98	0.38
(g) Nominal exchange rate[d]										
1994–1998		4.52	1.52	2.56	4.14	2.53	1.93	3.63	2.71	9.43
1999–2007		3.27					0.15		3.42	4.89
(h) Real exchange rate										
1994–1998		4.09	1.89	2.80	4.83	1.97	1.65	3.24	2.33	9.75
1999–2007		4.90	0.94	1.58	0.55	2.56	0.86	2.43	3.85	6.34

Note: Quarterly data, 1994:1–2007:4, except [a]1996:1–1998:4, [b]1995:1–1998:4, [c]1999:1–2007:3. [d]1999 = 100.

Table 10.3   Correlation coefficient of selected business cycle indicators with euro area counterpart

Sample	Sweden	France	Germany	Italy	Spain	Denmark	Finland	Norway	U.K.
(a) GDP growth									
1996–1998	0.77	0.84	0.80	0.73	0.88	-0.02	0.79	-0.09	0.80
1999–2007	0.70	0.89	0.93	0.93[a]	0.89	0.70	0.85	0.50	0.71
(b) GDP gap									
1995–1998	0.84	0.80	0.76	0.79	0.91	0.19	-0.31	-0.19	0.78
1999–2007	0.74	0.89	0.95	0.92[a]	0.93	0.73	0.84	0.52	0.66
(c) Unemployment									
1994–1998	0.86	0.80	-0.15	-0.50	0.78	0.61	0.73	0.69	0.67
1999–2007	0.50	0.87	0.47	0.47[a]	0.58	0.74	0.63	0.58	0.07[a]
(d) CPI inflation rate									
1994–1998	0.79	0.85	0.75	0.84	0.96	0.18	-0.29	-0.48	0.64
1999–2007	0.52	0.85	0.80	0.65	0.75	0.01	0.25	0.10	0.09
(e) Short-term interest rate									
1994–1998	0.95	0.96	0.81	0.86	0.94	0.89	0.92	0.24	-0.53
1999–2007	0.79	1.00	1.00	1.00	1.00	0.99	1.00	0.73	0.67
(f) Long-term interest rate									
1994–1998	0.99	0.99	0.98	0.99	0.99	0.99	0.97	0.93	0.94
1999–2007	0.94	1.00	1.00	1.00	1.00	0.99	1.00	0.93	0.83

Note: Quarterly data, 1994:1–2007:4, except [a]1999:1–2007:3.

good, collects taxes from households, and sets monetary policy. The fiscal surplus/deficit plus the seigniorage are transferred back to the households in a lump sum fashion. Monetary policy is delegated to an independent central bank that sets the interest rate according to a Taylor (1993)-type interest rate rule. In particular, the one-period nominal interest rate is set as a function of current and past CPI inflation, the deviation of current and past GDP from trend, and the real exchange rate and the interest rate in the previous quarter. In addition, there is a shock to the interest rate rule that captures temporary deviations from the systematic behavior of monetary policy.

Finally, as Sweden is a small open economy, the *foreign economy* is assumed to be independent of the Swedish economy, so foreign inflation, output, and the foreign interest rate follow an exogenous vector autoregressive (VAR) model. The foreign variables are trade-weighted averages of foreign data.

In total, the model describes the evolution of twenty-seven variables, fifteen of which are observable. The model also includes twenty-one different exogenous disturbances: one is a nonstationary global technology shock common to the domestic and foreign economies, nine shocks are specific to the domestic economy (including a stationary technology shock), three originate in the foreign economy, seven are related to monetary and fiscal policy, and the remaining shock is to the foreign exchange risk premium. The model is rewritten in terms of stationary variables, log-linearized around its steady state, and then estimated by Adolfson, Andersson, et al. (2007) on quarterly data from 1980 until the third quarter of 2005, with a structural break in the first quarter of 1993, as Sweden moved from a fixed-exchange rate regime to a regime with an inflation target and a flexible exchange rate. I here present results pertaining to the period starting in 1993.

10.4.2 The Sources of Macroeconomic Fluctuations

To analyze the relative importance of different shocks in the estimated model, I decompose the volatility of key variables—annual domestic and CPI inflation, annual GDP growth, the annualized short-term interest rate, and the real exchange rate—at different horizons into the fraction caused by each shock. I then study these variance decompositions to see (a) what has been the relative importance of domestic shocks for overall volatility; and (b) what has been the relative importance of exchange rate shocks for volatility in the exchange rate and in the economy at large.

The results are reported in table 10.4.[9] First, section (a) shows the total forecast error variance (in percentage points) in each variable at different horizons. The dynamics of the model implies that most of the volatility appears after four quarters, and the real exchange rate is more volatile and persistent than the other variables.

---

9. The variance decompositions are calculated from impulse responses to each shock. In the calculations I exclude a shock to the inflation target, as this has been constant since 1993.

Table 10.4   Variance decomposition in estimated model

Horizon (quarters)	Domestic inflation	CPI inflation	GDP growth rate	Short-term interest rate	Real exchange rate
(a) Variance					
1	0.71	0.51	0.48	0.23	5.52
4	1.00	0.89	0.97	0.25	23.57
20	0.02	0.11	0.08	0.05	3.23
40	0.01	0.02	0.01	0.02	0.61
(b) Fraction due to domestic shocks					
1	99.4	95.2	83.5	35.0	19.6
4	90.6	54.6	66.2	53.7	15.2
20	35.8	32.0	45.8	66.2	74.1
40	68.3	71.2	59.4	71.1	73.3
(c) Fraction due to foreign shocks					
1	0.3	1.3	5.0	0.9	3.7
4	4.9	15.6	17.2	16.1	11.2
20	29.3	23.9	19.1	18.1	1.1
40	30.2	8.8	9.3	28.2	22.2
(d) Fraction due to exchange rate shock					
1	0.3	2.8	1.4	1.8	75.4
4	3.9	27.0	12.3	21.2	71.7
20	34.0	43.1	31.9	15.6	24.6
40	0.0	19.0	29.7	0.1	4.0
(e) Fraction due to policy shocks					
1	0.0	0.7	10.2	62.4	1.3
4	0.6	2.8	4.4	9.0	1.9
20	0.9	0.9	3.2	0.1	0.2
40	1.5	1.0	1.6	0.7	0.4

Notes: This table reports the forecast error variance of key variables (in percentage points) in the estimated model at different horizons and the fraction of this variance (in percent) that is due to different sets of shocks. The GDP growth rate and the inflation rates are four-quarter rates, all data are expressed as percent per annum. The shock to the time varying inflation target was excluded from the calculations; the policy shocks include shocks to monetary policy (to the interest rate rule) and to fiscal policy (to tax rates and government expenditure).

Section (b) reveals that shocks originating in the domestic economy account for much of the variability in domestic variables at all horizons. In the short run, domestic shocks account for 55 to 95 percent of the volatility in CPI inflation, 65 to 85 percent of the volatility in GDP growth, and 35 to 55 percent of the volatility in the short-term interest rate. Also, at longer horizons domestic shocks account for most of the volatility of all variables. Shocks originating in the foreign economy in section (c), on the other hand, account for between 15 and 25 percent of the volatility of CPI inflation volatility, GDP growth, and the short-term interest rate. Thus, although the analysis in section 10.3 suggested the existence of an important common component in the Swedish and euro area business cycles, the estimated model finds that country-specific shocks are two to three times more important than foreign shocks for Swedish business cycle fluctuations.

There are reasons to be careful when interpreting these results. Justiniano and Preston (2006) argue that models of small open economies such as the one used here are not very successful in capturing the influence of foreign variables. While the common nonstationary technology shock in our model increases the influence of foreign shocks relative to their model, our model still does not seem to capture all comovement of the domestic and foreign economies. For instance, the model implies an unconditional contemporaneous correlation between domestic and foreign output growth of 0.19, while in the data used to estimate the model this correlation is 0.54; the correlation of domestic and foreign inflation is 0.05 in the model and 0.29 in the data; and the interest rate correlation is 0.16 in the model but 0.86 in the data. While the inflation correlation in the data is inside a 95 percent probability interval around the model correlations, the correlations of output and the interest rate are not. Thus, the model may well overestimate the importance of domestic shocks relative to foreign shocks.

Comparisons with vector autoregressive (VAR) models estimated on Swedish data give mixed support for this view. In a background study for the Calmfors Commission, Jansson (1997) studied the importance of country-specific shocks in an estimated VAR model using data from eleven European countries over the period from 1960 to 1994. He found that country-specific shocks accounted for 75 to 80 percent of fluctuations in Swedish GDP as well as in the GDP deflator, with the remaining 20 to 25 percent being due to common (that is, foreign) shocks. In comparison, country-specific shocks accounted for merely 25 to 30 percent of GDP fluctuations in the core EMU countries (Austria, Belgium, France, Germany, and the Netherlands), but 93 percent in Finland and Ireland. This evidence is consistent with the results in section (b). On the other hand, Lindé (2003) studies a VAR model of the Swedish economy estimated over the more recent period from 1986 to 2002. He reports that foreign shocks account for 45 to 55 percent of fluctuations in Swedish domestic inflation and GDP, in particular at low frequencies. This evidence thus assigns a less important role to country-specific shocks than do the open economy model and the evidence of Jansson (1997), also suggesting that the open economy model underestimates the influence of foreign shocks on the Swedish economy.

We now turn to the importance of shocks to the exchange rate. Section (d) of table 10.4 shows that such shocks account for a large fraction of the volatility in the real exchange rate (above 70 percent at short horizons), but also 25 to 45 percent of medium-term volatility in CPI inflation (which to some extent is directly determined by exchange rate movements), 15 to 30 percent of GDP growth volatility, and 15 to 20 percent of interest rate volatility at medium-term horizons. Thus, exchange rate movements do help to stabilize the economy after disturbances in other sectors, as close to 30 percent of the volatility in the real exchange is due to endogenous responses to other shocks. However, the remaining volatility in the exchange rate is due to inefficient fluctuations in the exchange rate risk premium, which act to destabilize the Swedish economy, and these shocks are responsible for a significant portion of Swedish business cycle fluctuations.[10]

The evidence presented here thus gives a mixed view of the costs and benefits of monetary union. On the one hand, the estimated model suggests that country-specific shocks are an important source of Swedish business cycle fluctuations, and therefore that independent monetary policy is imperative in order to stabilize the economy. (There is reason, though, to suspect that the model overestimates the influence of country-specific shocks.) On the other hand, exchange rate fluctuations are mainly driven by inefficient shocks to the exchange rate risk premium, which are responsible for a large portion of macroeconomic volatility, implying that the benefits of a flexible exchange rate may be small.[11]

10.5 What If Sweden Had Joined EMU in 1999? A Counterfactual Experiment

A strength of the estimated model is that it is based on the optimizing behavior of private households and firms, and the estimated parameters reflect structural features of the economy, such as preferences and technology, which in principle should be independent of the behavior of monetary and fiscal policy. We can, therefore, use the model to perform counterfactual policy experiments without being vulnerable to the Lucas (1976) critique.[12]

Thus, in this section I use the model to evaluate what would have been the consequences if Sweden had joined EMU at the outset in January 1999. The discussion in section 10.3 showed that the Swedish economy is fairly well aligned with the euro area, suggesting that membership in EMU might not have had important consequences for Sweden. On the other hand, the evidence presented in section 10.4 showed that country-specific shocks have

10. In chapter 11 in this volume, DiCecio and Nelson argue that shocks to the exchange rate risk premium may be endogenous responses to fundamentals rather than inefficient disturbances. The estimated model used here, however, interprets all such movements as inefficient disturbances to the exchange rate.

11. For the United Kingdom, HM Treasury (2003) reports that most movements in the exchange rate between the British pound and the euro have been stabilizing; that is, movements in response to other shocks. This conclusion is based, first, on the fact that the sterling exchange rate largely has moved in the appropriate direction with respect to the position of the U.K. business cycle relative to foreign economies, and second, on evidence from an estimated VAR model where exchange rate shocks have a negligible impact on output, prices, and interest rates in the U.K.

12. Recently, however, Chari, Kehoe, and McGrattan (2009) and Faust (2008) have criticized such a strong structural interpretation of DSGE models.

been the main source of business cycle fluctuations in Sweden since 1993, suggesting that EMU membership might be costly. The counterfactual experiment can help us balance these conflicting views.

10.5.1   A First Impression

For a first informal impression, figure 10.9 shows the monetary policy interest rate, the rate of GDP growth, and the CPI inflation rate in Sweden and the euro area since 1999. The horizontal lines in panel (c) represent the Riksbank's tolerance band from 1 to 3 percent around its 2 percent inflation target.

Initially, in 1999 and early 2000, GDP growth was higher and inflation lower in Sweden than in the euro area, and on balance, monetary policy was slightly more contractionary in Sweden. As inflation and GDP growth picked up in the euro area, the ECB increased the interest rate more aggressively than the Riksbank in 2000, and kept a more contractionary policy

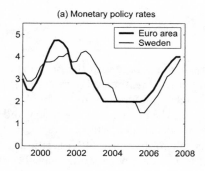
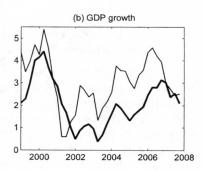
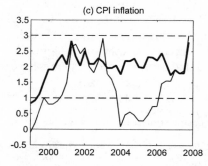

Fig. 10.9   Monetary policy rate, GDP growth rate, and CPI inflation rate in the euro area and Sweden, 1999–2007

Sources: European Central Bank, Sveriges Riksbank, and OECD.

Notes: ECB refinancing rate and Sveriges Riksbank repo rate, quarterly averages of daily data; Four-quarter GDP growth rate, quarterly data; Four-quarter CPI inflation rate, quarterly averages of monthly data. Percent per annum. The horizontal lines in panel (c) represent the Riksbank's tolerance band around its 2 percent inflation target.

until the end of 2001. The recession that started in 2001 was more long-lived in the euro area than in Sweden, necessitating a more aggressive monetary expansion by the ECB, with the Riksbank following about a year later when inflation started falling in Sweden. The higher rate of inflation in the euro area also made the ECB tighten monetary policy earlier and more aggressively in 2006 and 2007. Consequently, monetary policy was more contractionary in Sweden than in the euro area throughout 2002 and 2003, but more expansionary in 2005 to 2007. In general, the two interest rates have followed similar cycles, but the euro area interest rate has tended to lead the Swedish interest rate.

Panel (b) shows that although fluctuations in GDP growth have been closely correlated, the GDP growth rate has been higher in Sweden than in the euro area in almost every quarter since 1999 (with the exception of the 2001 contraction). At the same time, inflation in panel (c) has typically been lower (and more volatile) in Sweden than in the euro area. In particular, the Swedish CPI inflation rate was below 1 percent (the lower bound of the Riksbank's tolerance band) in 1999 and 2000 and in 2004 and 2005.

Due to the uncertain lags in the transmission of monetary policy, it is difficult to say how Swedish membership in EMU from 1999 would have affected the behavior of GDP growth and inflation in Sweden. The ECB's more contractionary monetary policy in 2000 and 2001 might have been appropriate in the boom experienced in Sweden in 2000, and the more expansionary policy in 2002 and 2003 might have dampened the brief downturn in 2003 and increased inflation somewhat in 2004 and 2005, when inflation in Sweden was exceptionally low. However, with slightly longer transmission lags, a more contractionary monetary policy in 2000 and 2001 might have deepened the downturn in 2003, with even lower inflation as a consequence.

10.5.2   Evidence from the Estimated Model

To construct a more rigorous counterfactual experiment I use the estimated model to analyze the possible effects of Swedish EMU membership from 1999 until 2005.[13] In particular, I impose the euro area short-term interest rate instead of the Swedish interest rate and simulate the model starting from the actual situation in the fourth quarter of 1998, feeding in the estimated historical series of the disturbances (excluding those to monetary policy and the exchange rate). I thus obtain model predictions of what would have been the development of the Swedish economy if the interest rate had followed the ECB interest rate since January 1999.[14]

---

13. The experiment ends in the third quarter of 2005 as this is the last observation used when estimating the model.

14. If the model had been estimated on Swedish and euro area data, it would have been natural to simply set the Swedish interest rate equal to the foreign interest rate, implying that the exchange rate would have been fixed (assuming that there were no risk premium

To impose the ECB interest rate on the model, I follow two different strategies. In the first strategy, I introduce shocks to the estimated monetary policy rule so that the interest rate coincides with the ECB interest rate. This exercise manages to exactly mimic the ECB policy, but it assumes that these deviations from the estimated policy rule are unexpected by private agents, and so it does not capture the effects of systematic monetary policy. That is, private agents expect the Riksbank to follow the estimated Swedish policy rule, but are surprised in every period by the fact that Sweden is in fact a member of EMU.

As an alternative strategy, I instead respecify the monetary policy rule in the model so that it responds also to the rate of nominal exchange rate depreciation and fluctuations in the foreign economy (the current level and three lags of foreign output, inflation, and interest rate). I then find the coefficients in this monetary policy rule that best match the behavior of the ECB interest rate since 1999.

Before presenting the results of these two experiments, figure 10.10 compares the model predictions of the short-term interest rate, GDP growth, domestic inflation, and CPI inflation with the estimated monetary policy rule. We note that the model tends to underpredict GDP growth in 2001 to 2004, while capturing fairly well the movements in domestic and CPI inflation.[15]

Introducing Counterfactual Monetary Policy Shocks

Panels (a) and (b) of figure 10.11 show the interest rate when introducing the counterfactual monetary policy shocks in the estimated interest rate rule, and the implied shocks needed to mimic the ECB interest rate. These shocks are not particularly large: their standard deviation is 7 basis points, and the largest shock is 14 basis points. For comparison, the standard deviation of monetary policy shocks in the estimated model is 10 basis points. Fairly small shocks are thus required to make the Swedish interest rate mimic the ECB interest rate.

Figure 10.12 shows the predicted development of GDP growth, domestic inflation, and CPI inflation with the counterfactual monetary policy shocks.

---

shocks). However, the foreign variables in the model represent trade-weighted averages of foreign data, where the euro area (including Denmark) only represents around 60 percent. Therefore, this strategy is not possible. Furthermore, as the trade-weighted exchange rate would have fluctuated in ways that are difficult to predict even if Sweden had been an EMU member, I do not study the consequences of EMU membership for the exchange rate.

15. The deviations of GDP growth and inflation from the actual data are due to measurement errors introduced when estimating the model. Without these measurement errors, the model would have perfectly matched the actual data, as these data were used in the estimation. See Adolfson et al. (2008) for details. Note also that the data for the GDP growth rate in figure 10.10 are slightly different from those in figures 10.1 and 10.9. The data in figure 10.10 are seasonally adjusted data obtained from Statistics Sweden, while those in the earlier figures are unadjusted data obtained from the OECD.

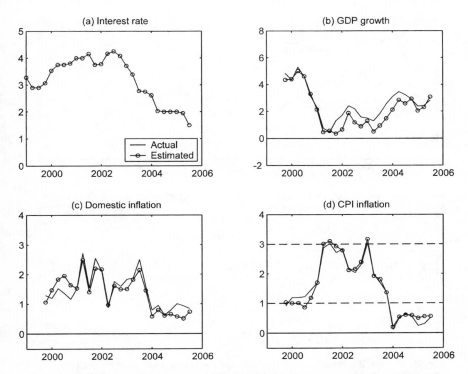

Fig. 10.10   The Swedish economy 1999–2005 according to actual data and the estimated model

Notes: Average quarterly data, four-quarter GDP growth rate, and inflation rates, percent per annum. The horizontal lines in panel (d) represent the Riksbank's tolerance band around its 2 percent inflation target.

Even if the required shocks are fairly small, the effects are nevertheless reasonably large. With the ECB interest rate, Swedish GDP growth would have been slightly lower in the 2000 and 2001 recession (due to the more contractionary monetary policy), but higher in the period from 2002 to 2003 (after a more expansionary policy). The CPI inflation would have been higher in 2000, lower in 2001, and higher in 2002 to 2005. In particular, the ECB policy would have kept Swedish CPI inflation more closely within the Riksbank's tolerance band of 1 to 3 percent in 2004 and 2005.

On average, this exercise suggests that EMU membership would have raised Swedish GDP growth by around 0.1 percentage points per year and inflation by around 0.25 percentage points; see sections (b) and (c) of table 10.5. Inflation would also have been less volatile under the ECB policy with no effects on the volatility of GDP growth.

Under this scenario, EMU membership would thus have been unambiguously beneficial for Sweden.

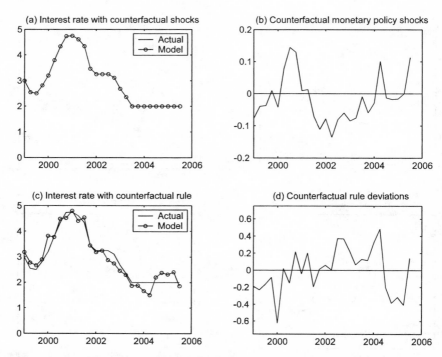

Fig. 10.11   ECB interest rate 1999–2005 and the interest rate in the models with counterfactual monetary policy shocks or a counterfactual monetary policy rule
Note: Average quarterly data, percent per annum.

Imposing a Counterfactual Monetary Policy Rule

Panels (c) and (d) of figure 10.11 instead show the interest rate obtained with the counterfactual policy rule. In this case it is not possible to perfectly mimic the ECB interest rate, and occasionally there are large deviations of the counterfactual interest rate from the ECB interest rate. Nevertheless, the counterfactual interest rate follows the same cyclical patterns as the ECB interest rate, and, as shown in figure 10.13, it implies the same qualitative effects of EMU relative to the Swedish interest rate: more contractionary monetary policy in 2000 and 2001 and 2004 and 2005 and more expansionary policy in 1999 and 2001 to 2004. Figure 10.13 shows that the counterfactual rule (which captures the systematic effects of monetary policy) has a stronger effect on the economy than the rule with the counterfactual shocks in figure 10.12, and as shown in panel (d) of table 10.5, GDP growth is substantially more volatile with the counterfactual rule. The overall patterns are similar, however. The counterfactual rule model predicts that GDP growth would have been lower than the actual growth rate in 2000 and early 2001, but higher in late 2001 and early 2002 and in late 2003 and early 2004,

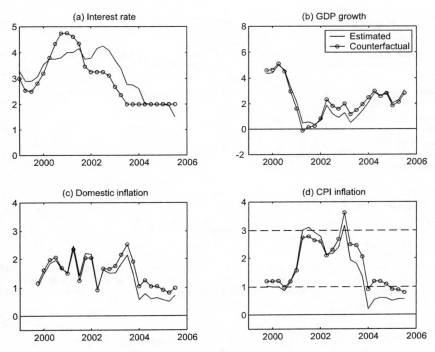

Fig. 10.12   The Swedish economy 1999–2005 according to the estimated model and the model with counterfactual monetary policy shocks

Notes: Average quarterly data, four-quarter GDP growth rate, and inflation rates, percent per annum. The horizontal lines in panel (d) represent the Riksbank's tolerance band around its 2 percent inflation target.

similar to the model with counterfactual shocks. Also, the counterfactual rule model implies that CPI inflation would have been lower in 2000 and 2001 but higher in 2002 to 2005. Finally, the ECB policy would have kept inflation within the target range in 2004 and 2005, but in this case, inflation would have been far below the lower bound in 2000.

This counterfactual experiment thus gives a more ambiguous, but largely negative, picture: EMU membership would have increased average GDP growth only marginally (by 0.05 percentage points), but increased its volatility substantially (by around 0.25 percentage points), and the effects on inflation would have been small on average.

10.5.3   Going Forward

The model was estimated by Adolfson, Andersson, et al. (2007) using data only up until the third quarter of 2005, so it cannot make any predictions about the development in more recent years. Nevertheless, going back to figure 10.9, we see that inflation in both economies has picked up in 2007,

Table 10.5   **Properties of actual data and simulated model data, 1999–2005**

Horizon (years)	Short-term interest rate	GDP growth rate	Domestic inflation	CPI inflation
(a) Data				
Mean	3.18	2.61	1.46	1.53
Standard deviation	0.83	1.26	0.59	0.95
(b) Estimated model				
Mean	3.18	2.17	1.39	1.55
Standard deviation	0.83	1.42	0.60	0.97
(c) Model with counterfactual monetary policy shocks				
Mean	2.96	2.28	1.56	1.79
Standard deviation	0.95	1.41	0.50	0.82
(d) Model with counterfactual monetary policy rule				
Mean	2.96	2.23	1.96	1.56
Standard deviation	0.97	1.68	0.68	0.92

Notes: This table reports the mean and standard deviation of key macroeconomic variables in actual data, the estimated model, and two models with counterfactual paths for the short-term interest rate. Original data are measured as quarterly averages, the GDP growth rate and the inflation rates are four-quarter rates, all data are expressed as percent per annum.

and more recently (in October 2008) reached 4.0 percent in Sweden and 3.2 percent in the euro area. At the same time GDP growth has slowed down to 0.9 percent in Sweden and 1.4 percent in the euro area in the second quarter of 2008 (according to the Organization for Economic Cooperation and Development [OECD]). As shown in panel (a), the ECB started increasing its interest rate already in late 2005, and until late 2007, the ECB interest rate was 50 to 75 basis points above the Riksbank rate. Had we been able to continue our experiments through 2007, the model with the ECB interest rate might therefore have predicted lower inflation but also lower GDP growth in Sweden in 2007 and 2008 than has been the case in practice.

10.6   Additional Issues

The estimated model used in the counterfactual experiments was developed to explain the effects of monetary policy on the economy and the interplay between monetary policy and private sector behavior. However, it is largely silent on many other possible consequences of EMU membership. Therefore, in this section I briefly discuss some of these issues.

10.6.1   Fiscal Policy and the Stability and Growth Pact

Fiscal policy in EMU member countries is constrained by the possibility of sanctions if the rules specified in the Stability and Growth Pact are violated. These rules require government debt to be below 60 percent of GDP

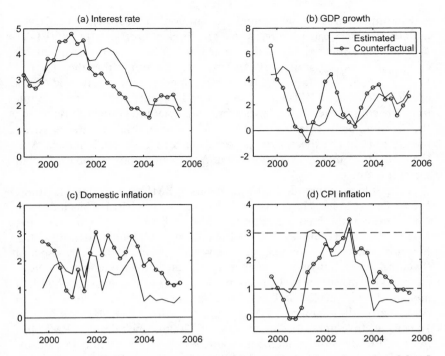

Fig. 10.13   The Swedish economy 1999–2005 according to the estimated model and the model with a counterfactual monetary policy rule

Notes: Average quarterly data, four-quarter GDP growth rate, and inflation rates, percent per annum. The horizontal lines in panel (d) represent the Riksbank's tolerance band around its 2 percent inflation target.

and the deficit in the government's finances to be below 3 percent of GDP. Would these restrictions on fiscal policy have had important implications for Sweden as an EMU member? Probably not. According to Eurostat, Sweden had in 2007 a government surplus of 3.6 percent of GDP and a gross debt-to-GDP ratio of 40.4 percent. And in the period since 1999, the largest government deficit in Sweden has been 1.2 percent of GDP (in 2002) and the largest debt ratio 65.6 percent of GDP (in 1999). According to the assessments made by the European Commission, Sweden has therefore always fulfilled the criterion of fiscal sustainability, so the Stability and Growth Pact would likely not have constrained fiscal policy if Sweden had joined EMU in 1999.

10.6.2   Economic Integration

An important motivating factor behind the creation of EMU was to enhance economic integration within the European Union and thus increase competition and economic efficiency. Many studies have also tried to measure the impact of EMU on economic integration, such as international trade patterns, financial market integration, and foreign direct investment (FDI).

While the estimated model does take into account the short-run effects of monetary policy on imports and exports, it assumes that the long-run trade shares are constant, and therefore is unable to make any predictions about the effects of EMU membership on long-run trade patterns. Similarly, the counterfactual exercises mimic financial integration by removing the premium on foreign bond holdings for Swedish residents. But financial integration can be expected to happen also in other financial markets. And the model is completely silent on the impact of monetary union on foreign direct investment.

A large literature has measured the effects of EMU on international trade. Most of these studies have shown that the creation of EMU has increased trade between the member countries, although the exact estimates vary. Micco, Stein, and Ordoñez (2003) estimate that EMU increased trade within the euro area by 13 percent per year between 1999 and 2002. They also find that the introduction of the euro increased trade between members and non-members by an average of 8 percent per year.[16] A more recent study by Flam and Nordström (2007c) finds that intra-euro area trade has increased by 26 percent after the creation of EMU, and trade with non-EMU members by 12 percent. In a literature survey, Baldwin (2006) concludes that EMU has increased trade between members countries by between 5 and 15 percent, with a best estimate of 9 percent, while trade with non-EMU members has increased by around 7 percent.[17]

Thus, there is no evidence of trade diversion: most studies show that trade with non-EMU members has also increased as an effect of the introduction of the euro. Swedish trade has therefore already seen increased trade flows due to EMU, and according to Baldwin (2006), the additional gains from EMU membership may be modest. Flam and Nordström (2007b), on the other hand, argue that Swedish trade with the EMU countries would have been 13 percent larger in 2002 to 2005 if Sweden had been a member of EMU, implying that the costs of staying outside the monetary union may have been large.

Empirical studies also suggest that financial markets have become more integrated as a consequence of EMU. De Santis (2006) estimates that portfolio flows (in equity and bonds) among euro area countries increased significantly due to EMU, thus contributing to enhanced regional financial integration and risk-sharing, in addition to the elimination of exchange rate risk. (See also Lane [2006a, 2006b].) Similarly, Coeurdacier and Martin (2007) argue that EMU significantly reduced transaction costs for equity and bonds inside the euro area for all investors, but twice as much for investors from

---

16. See also chapter 5 in this volume by Frankel.
17. Melitz (2005) argues that the effect is probably closer to 15 percent than the 9 percent favored by Baldwin (2006).

EMU member countries than for non-EMU investors. Thus, EMU led to a diversion effect in that EMU countries purchase less equity from non-EMU countries. This evidence suggests that the launch of EMU may have relocated portfolio holdings from Sweden to the EMU member countries, and that Sweden might experience an increase in international portfolio inflows and outflows as a consequence of EMU membership, thus enhancing the efficiency of portfolio diversification.

As for foreign direct investment (FDI), De Sousa and Lochard (2006) estimate that EMU has stimulated FDI within the euro area: FDI stocks have increased by around 20 percent within EMU, and FDI flows have increased much more. They find no evidence of an investment diversion effect: the United Kingdom, Denmark, and Sweden have not experienced a fall in FDI inflows, but rather seem to have experienced a positive effect of EMU. In contrast, Flam and Nordström (2007a) do not find any effects of EMU on FDI, but instead argue that the effects on FDI are due to the Single Market. Nevertheless, both studies imply that the gains from Swedish membership in EMU in terms of FDI would be small.

10.6.3   Labor Markets and Wage Formation

Labor mobility could act as an adjustment mechanism in the presence of country-specific shocks in a monetary union. Compared with, say, the United States, labor mobility is fairly low between European countries. There are many reasons for this; for instance, language and cultural differences, incompatibilities between bureaucracies, and welfare systems (including pension systems). However, labor mobility is low also within European countries, suggesting that other factors are also important.

Unfortunately, data on labor mobility across countries are not readily available. As a proxy, U.S. Department of Labor, Bureau of International Labor Affairs (2002) reports that the average share of movers in the population in the 1990s was 7 percent in the European Union but 16 percent in the United States. The share also varies considerably across EU countries, from around 2.5 percent in Italy to above 15 percent in Finland. Likewise, data from the OECD and the U.S. Census Bureau show that the fraction of foreign workers in the total labor force is typically below 10 percent in European countries, while it is around 15 percent in the United States. There is some evidence that labor market reforms have become more frequent after the establishment of monetary union, mainly in the direction of deregulation of labor markets (see, for instance, Bertola and Boeri [2002]), although it is unclear whether the reforms were an effect of monetary union (see Duval and Elmeskov [2005] or chapter 2 in this volume by Alesina, Ardagna, and Galasso). Nevertheless, it seems unlikely that labor mobility across EMU member states will be sufficient to eliminate the effects of country-specific shocks. Also, it is unlikely that the pace of labor market reform would accelerate significantly as a consequence of Swedish EMU membership.

A second issue related to labor markets regards the effect of monetary union on wage formation. In theory, monetary union may either increase or decrease wage restraint. On the one hand, trade unions may internalize the effects of wage demands on inflation and monetary policy to a smaller extent in a monetary union than before, as the effects on union-wide inflation and monetary policy become weaker. This mechanism would imply that wage demands become stronger within a monetary union. (See Soskice and Iversen [1998] and Cukierman and Lippi [2001] who build on insights from Calmfors and Driffill [1988].)

On the other hand, trade unions in a monetary union may take into account the effects of wage demands on their country's competitiveness to a larger extent, as lost competitiveness cannot be regained by exchange rate depreciation or devaluation. Therefore, wage coordination and restraint may increase, especially in the traded sector. (See Holden 2003, 2005.)

Posen and Popov Gould (2006) estimate that wage restraint has increased in almost all euro area members after the launch of EMU. However, wage restraint increased also in Sweden and the United Kingdom in the early 1990s, suggesting that the effect may be largely due to the increased credibility of monetary policy, rather than to the creation of EMU per se. Wage restraint is also small throughout the period in Germany, where monetary policy credibility was strong also before EMU. Thus, if wage restraint depends mostly on the credibility of monetary policy, EMU membership would be unlikely to affect wage restraint in Sweden, where Sveriges Riksbank currently enjoys strong credibility for its monetary policy.

10.6.4   Political Influence

One possible cost of staying outside EMU, stressed by the Calmfors Commission, could be the potential loss of political influence within the EU. For instance, euro area finance ministers regularly meet with the Eurogroup on the day before meetings of the Economic and Financial Affairs Council (ECOFIN), and outsiders may fear that many important issues may be settled within the Eurogroup before the Council meeting.

Recent research casts some light on this issue. Adler-Nissen (2008) conducted interviews with Danish and British EU representatives. She reports that many Danish representatives felt that being outside EMU constrained their possibilities to advance Danish interests within the EU, and that various strategies were needed to compensate for this constraint. Other studies instead suggest that being outside EMU is not a decisive disadvantage within the European Council. Lindahl and Naurin (2003) and Naurin (2007) conducted interviews with working group representatives in the European Council to study the cooperation patterns within the EU. Their results show that the most popular cooperation partners were Germany, France, and the United Kingdom, with Sweden, the Netherlands, and Denmark following closely, in spite of their small weights in the final voting procedures. Similarly, Tallberg (2008) reports evidence on the EU bargaining power based on interviews with present and former heads of government and top officials. He reports that, again, Germany, France, and the United Kingdom exert the greatest influence in Council negotiations. When asked directly, 79 percent of the respondents in the study by Lindahl and Naurin (2003) replied that different countries' decision to join or stay outside EMU does not matter at all for the cooperation pattern. Consequently, while this is not a settled issue, the available evidence suggests that there are no strong political disadvantages for Sweden of remaining outside EMU.

10.7   Final Remarks

After the referendum in 2003 and the strong rejection of the euro, the question of Swedish membership in EMU disappeared from the political agenda. The major political parties agreed that at least two parliamentary elections would be needed before the issue could be taken up for serious consideration again. Thus, EMU membership is not likely to appear on the agenda until after the elections of September 2010.

Ten years after the launch of EMU, the present chapter nevertheless offers an analysis of the pros and cons of Swedish membership. The evidence presented here is not conclusive about whether participation in EMU would be beneficial or costly for the Swedish economy, but the analysis suggests that the consequences of Swedish membership in EMU since the launch in 1999 would not have been dramatic. To some extent, this result probably reflects the fact that the last ten years have been a relatively calm period for the world economy, without any large disturbances to the Swedish nor to the euro area economy. At least this was the case until mid-2007. The outcome of the current financial crisis could lead to sharper conclusions about the potential costs and benefits of EMU.

Sweden came into the crisis in a strong position, with low unemployment and solid government finances. The Riksbank has eased monetary policy more aggressively than the ECB, leading to lower short-term interest rates. Also, interbank rates have been lower in Sweden than in the euro area. And in contrast to many European countries (including EMU member countries and the Nordic countries), Swedish long-term bond yields have not increased relative to Germany, but are currently lower than in Germany.

The Swedish currency has, however, taken a serious blow, and more so than in many other small open economies. Since mid-2008, the Swedish krona has depreciated by around 20 percent against the euro, and by 23 percent in trade-weighted terms. Partly this can be explained by the aggressive monetary easing, but much of this weakening seems to be disconnected from fundamentals.

The weak exchange rate has led to renewed calls for joining the monetary union, and the outcome of the crisis could have important effects on public opinion in Sweden vis-à-vis EMU. The Swedish decision in 1994 to become a member of the European Union was influenced by the deep recession in the early 1990s, coupled with a banking crisis and the European exchange rate crisis in 1992 and 1993. If the Swedish economy were to suffer strong adverse effects of the crisis in spite of its apparent strength, then public opinion may well shift and participation in EMU could become reality sooner than expected. If, on the other hand, Sweden were to come out of the crisis better than the euro area, then Swedish participation in the monetary union might be postponed for a long time. In any case, the present study could be used as a starting point for a renewed debate on possible membership in the third stage of the Economic and Monetary Union.

Appendix

Data Definitions and Sources

GDP: Gross domestic product, constant prices, 2000 = 100. Source: OECD.

Unemployment: Standardized unemployment rate, all persons, seasonally adjusted, percent. Source: OECD.

Consumer prices: Euro area: Harmonized index of consumer prices, all items, 2000 = 100. Other countries: Consumer price index, all items, 2000 = 100. Source: OECD.

Short-term interest rate: Euro area: Three-month EURIBOR; Sweden: Ninety-day treasury bill yield; France: Three-month PIBOR; Germany: Three-month FIBOR; Italy: Three-month interbank deposit rate; Spain: Three-month interbank loan rate; Denmark: Three-month uncollateralized interbank rate; Finland: Three-month HELIBOR; Norway: Three-month NIBOR; United Kingdom: Three-month mean LIBID/LIBOR. All rates percent per annum. Source: OECD.

Long-term interest rate: Ten-year government bond yield, percent per annum. Source: OECD.

Nominal exchange rate: Noon buying rates in New York City for cable transfers payable in foreign currencies, quarterly averages of daily data. Source: Federal Reserve Bank of St. Louis.

Real exchange rate: Nominal exchange rate deflated by consumer price index, 1999 = 100.

Monetary policy rate: Quarterly averages of daily data. Source: European Central Bank, Sveriges Riksbank.

References

Adler-Nissen, R. 2008. The diplomacy of opting out: A Bourdieudian approach to national integration strategies. *Journal of Common Market Studies* 46 (3): 663–84.

Adolfson, M., M. K. Andersson, S. Laséen, J. Lindé, and A. Vredin. 2007. Modern forecasting models in action: Improving macroeconomic analyses at central banks. *International Journal of Central Banking* 3 (4): 111–44.

Adolfson, M., S. Laséen, J. Lindé, and M. Villani. 2007. RAMSES: A new general equilibrium model for monetary policy analysis. *Sveriges Riksbank Economic Review* 2: 5–39.

———. 2008. Evaluating an estimated New Keynesian small open economy model. *Journal of Economic Dynamics and Control* 32 (8): 2690–721.

Baldwin, R. 2006. *In or out: Does it matter? An evidence-based analysis of the euro's trade effects.* Center for Economic Policy Research Report.

Bertola, G., and T. Boeri. 2002. EMU labour markets two years on: Microeconomics tensions and institutional evolution. In *EMU and economic policy in europe: The challenge of the early years,* ed. M. Buti and A. Sapir, 249–80. Northampton, MA: Edward Elgar.

Calmfors, L., and J. Driffill. 1988. Bargaining structure, corporatism, and macroeconomic performance. *Economic Policy* 3 (6): 13–61.

Calmfors, L., H. Flam, N. Gottfries, M. Jerneck, R. Lindahl, J. H. Matlary, E. Rabinowicz, A. Vredin, and C. Nordh Berntsson. 1996. *Sverige och EMU,* SOU 1996:158, EMU-utredningen. Published in English as *EMU: A Swedish perspective.* New York: Kluwer Academic Publishers, Springer Verlag, 1997.

Chari, V. V., P. J. Kehoe, and E. R. McGrattan. 2009. New Keynesian models: Not yet useful for policy analysis. *American Economic Journal: Macroeconomics* 1 (1): 242–66.

Coeurdacier, N., and P. Martin. 2007. The geography of asset trade and the euro: Insiders and outsiders. Discussion paper no. 6032, Center for Economic Policy Research.

Cukierman, A., and F. Lippi. 2001. Labour markets and monetary union: A strategic analysis. *Economic Journal* 111 (473): 541–65.

De Santis, R. A. 2006. The geography of international portfolio flows, international CAPM and the role of monetary policy frameworks. Working Paper no. 678, European Central Bank.

De Sousa, José, and J. Lochard. 2006. Does the single currency affect FDI? A gravity-like approach. University of Paris 1-Panthéon-Sorbonne. Unpublished Manuscript.

Duval, R., and J. Elmeskov. 2005. The effects of EMU on structural reforms in labour and product markets. Working Paper no. 438, Economics Department, OECD.

Ehrmann, M., M. Fratzscher, R. S. Gürkaynak, and E. T. Swanson. 2007. Convergence and anchoring of yield curves in the euro area. Working Paper no. 817, European Central Bank.

Faust, J. 2008. DSGE models in a second-best world of policy analysis. Johns Hopkins University. Unpublished Manuscript.

Flam, H., and H. Nordström. 2007a. The euro and single market impact on trade and FDI. Institute for International Economic Studies, Stockholm University. Unpublished Manuscript.

———. 2007b. Euron och utrikeshandeln: Hur mycket handel förlorar Sverige arligen? *Ekonomisk debatt* 35 (5): 16–30.

———. 2007c. Explaining large euro effects on trade: The extensive margin and vertical specialization. Institute for International Economic Studies, Stockholm University. Unpublished Manuscript.

HM Treasury. 2003. The exchange rate and macroeconomic adjustment. EMU Study.

Holden, S. 2003. Wage-setting under different monetary regimes. *Economica* 70 (278): 251–65.

———. 2005. Monetary regimes and the coordination of wage setting. *European Economic Review* 49 (4): 833–43.

Jakobsson, U., ed. 2003. *Därför euron. Tio ekonomer om den gemensamma valutan.* Stockholm: Ekerlids.

Jansson, P. 1997. How large is the risk of asymmetric shocks for Sweden? *Swedish Economic Policy Review* 4 (2): 447–86.

Justiniano, A., and B. Preston. 2006. Can structural small open economy models account for the influence of foreign disturbances? Columbia University. Unpublished Manuscript.

Lane, P. R. 2006a. Global bond portfolios and EMU. *International Journal of Central Banking* 2 (2): 1–23.

———. 2006b. The real effects of European monetary union. *Journal of Economic Perspectives* 20 (4): 47–66.

Lindahl, R., and D. Naurin. 2003. Gemenskap, utanförskap och inflytande i EU:s ministerråd. Working Paper no. 03/2, Centrum för Europaforskning vid Göteborgs universitet (CERGU).

Lindé, J. 2003. Monetary policy shocks and business cycle fluctuations in a small open economy: Sweden 1986–2002. Working Paper no. 153, Sveriges Riksbank.

Lucas, R. E. 1976. Econometric policy evaluation: A critique. *Carnegie-Rochester Conference Series on Public Policy* 1: 19–46.

Melitz, J. 2005. Comments on Richard Baldwin, "The euro's trade effects." Paper presented at ECB Conference, What Effects Is EMU Having on the Euro Area and Its Member Countries? 16–17 June, Frankfurt.

Micco, A., E. Stein, and G. Ordoñez. 2003. The currency union effect on trade: Early evidence from EMU. In *EMU: Assessing the impact of the euro,* ed. R. Baldwin, G. Bertola, and P. Seabright, 23–64. Blackwell Publishing.

Naurin, D. 2007. Network capital and cooperation patterns in the working groups of the council of the EU. Working Paper no. 2007/14, Robert Schumann Center for Advanced Studies, European University Institute.

Obstfeld, M., and K. Rogoff. 2001. The six major puzzles in international macroeconomics: Is there a common cause? In *NBER Macroeconomics Annual 2000,* ed. B. S. Bernanke and K. Rogoff, 339–411. Cambridge, MA: MIT Press.

Posen, A. S., and D. Popov Gould. 2006. Has EMU had any impact on the degree of wage restraint? Working Paper no. 06-6, Institute for International Economics.

Soskice, D., and T. Iversen. 1998. Multiple wage-bargaining systems in the single European currency area. *Oxford Review of Economic Policy* 14 (3): 110–24.

Tallberg, J. 2008. Bargaining power in the European Council. *Journal of Common Market Studies* 46 (3): 685–708.

Taylor, J. B. 1993. Discretion versus policy rules in practice. *Carnegie-Rochester Conference Series on Public Policy* 39: 195–214.

U.S. Department of Labor, Bureau of International Labor Affairs. 2002. Labor market in the 21st century: Skills and mobility. Proceedings of a Joint United States and European Union Conference.

Euro Membership as a U.K. Monetary Policy Option
Results from a Structural Model

Riccardo DiCecio and Edward Nelson

11.1 Introduction

In June 1999, a poll taken of London-based economists indicated that 65 percent believed that the United Kingdom would join the euro area by 2005.[1] A decade later, not only has U.K. participation in monetary union not taken place, but such a development no longer seems to be the question of "when, not if" that it once appeared. While euro entry has faded as a likely prospect for the United Kingdom, the decade of coexisting European Central Bank (ECB) and Bank of England monetary regimes has provided a firmer picture of the differences between the two regimes and of the likely effect that monetary union would have on U.K. economic performance. The analysis that follows uses a structural open economy model to evaluate the effect that becoming a euro area member would have on the U.K. economy.

Our discussion in section 11.2 provides a background to the debate on European monetary union in the United Kingdom. Section 11.3 discusses some of the economic arguments that have been raised on both sides of the euro adoption debate. Section 11.4 describes the main properties of the

Riccardo DiCecio is an economist at the Federal Reserve Bank of St. Louis. Edward Nelson is a senior economist at the Federal Reserve Board.

Presented at the NBER conference "Europe and the Euro," Bocconi University, Milan, October 16–17, 2008. We thank the conference organizers, Francesco Giavazzi and Alberto Alesina, and Carlo Favero, Richard Portes, Ulf Söderström, and other conference participants, as well as an anonymous referee, for comments on earlier drafts. We are indebted to Christopher Erceg, Christopher Gust, and David López-Salido for providing code. Charles Gascon, Luke Shimek, and Faith Weller provided research assistance. The views expressed in this chapter are those of the authors and should not be interpreted as those of the Federal Reserve Bank of St. Louis, the Federal Reserve System, or the Board of Governors.

1. See MacRae (1999).

model, which is given in detail in the appendix. Section 11.5 provides simulation results for alternative policies. Section 11.6 concludes.

11.2   The United Kingdom and European Economic and Monetary Union

The issue of economic and monetary union has been a long-standing—though until the late 1980s only a sporadic—part of the debate about the implications of the United Kingdom's integration into the European Union. The successful negotiations for U.K. entry into the European Economic Community (EEC, now the European Union) during 1970 to 1972 coincided with the EEC's consideration of the Werner Report[2] proposals for economic and monetary union. In fact, the first instance of the term "euro" being used to describe the putative union currency appears to have been in a discussion in the U.K. press during that period.[3] The United Kingdom seemingly affirmed its commitment to economic and monetary union in joint statements with EEC members in 1972, 1974, 1985, and 1989. But since 1974, U.K. policymakers have expressed reservations about economic and monetary union, which were finally made official with the securing of an "opt-out" clause in 1991 that was executed in 1997.

The United Kingdom did not join the European Communities until January 1, 1973. At a Paris summit in 1972, however, Prime Minister Edward Heath had endorsed the concept of economic and monetary union, with a 1980 deadline. In October 1972, Alec Douglas-Home, the Foreign Secretary in the Heath Government, listed European Monetary Union (EMU) as a priority in the U.K. government's agenda for the EEC (Associated Press 1972). But after a change of government and a further Paris summit in 1974, the official position on monetary union changed. Prime Minister Harold Wilson said he "did not find anyone in Paris . . . who believed there was the remotest possibility of economic and monetary union by 1980," adding that there was "not a hope in hell . . . of EMU taking place in the near future."[4] Elsewhere in his statement, Wilson appeared to suggest that EMU was undesirable in principle even without the 1980 timetable, but he acknowledged that the 1974 summit communiqué had "made EMU a long-term objective." The wording of the communiqué specifically referred to EMU as an "ultimate goal," though Wilson explained to his cabinet colleagues that, despite signing the communiqué, "I made it clear it was a goal we do not share."[5] This discrepancy foreshadowed the pattern in the 1980s, where the United

2. Commission of the European Communities (1970).
3. The *Oxford English Dictionary (OED)* online (www.oed.com) gives a 1971 U.K. press discussion as the first use of the term "euro." But we have been unable to verify this, as the citation details given in the *OED* appear to be faulty.
4. Wilson, in House of Commons *Debates,* December 16, 1974, pages 1127 and 1139.
5. Wilson speaking on December 12, 1974, quoted in Castle (1980, 249).

Kingdom would cosign affirmations of the EMU goal, only to express qualifications in an unwritten or unofficial form.

For the rest of the 1970s, EMU receded as an issue. The EEC's Study
Group on the Role of Public Finance (European Commission 1977, 11)
noted, "Monetary union, on which much has been written, is . . . a long
way off and will probably have to await major developments in the political,
monetary and fiscal fields." A step in this direction was the European Monetary System (EMS), in particular its exchange rate mechanism (ERM),[6]
which the United Kingdom contemplated joining as a founding member in
1978 and 1979. At the time, however, the exchange rate mechanism was not
perceived as part of a formal plan for monetary union. For example, a 1978
U.K. parliamentary committee noted that the EMS proposal was "far from
being a major step on the way to European Economic and Monetary Union,"
and that the Werner proposals for monetary union had been "agreed . . . but
subsequently abandoned" (Expenditure Committee 1978, X).

The lull in progress toward European economic and monetary union was
broken in 1985 with agreement on a single market. This involved the United
Kingdom and other EEC members signing a treaty amendment referring to
economic and monetary union as a goal. The United Kingdom under Prime
Minister Margaret Thatcher further joined in Madrid (1989) and Dublin
(1990) summit declarations endorsing a process that would culminate in
economic and monetary union. In explaining her apparent endorsement of
EMU on occasions like these, Thatcher said in 1990 that her definition of
EMU was "economic and monetary cooperation."[7]

In 1990 Thatcher came out unambiguously against monetary union,
declaring the United Kingdom's own currency (the pound sterling) its
"greatest expression of sovereignty."[8] Disagreement over EMU played a
key role in her forced resignation. Thatcher's successor, John Major, was not
opposed unconditionally to EMU but took the key step of securing for the
United Kingdom the option not to participate in monetary union. At the
Maastricht summit in December 1991, Major obtained an opt-out provision
as a condition of U.K. participation in the Maastricht treaty. The opt-out
pertained to "Stage 3" of economic and monetary union; that is, the stage
at which the union amounted to a single currency.

The likelihood of the United Kingdom joining in monetary union receded
further with the collapse of its membership of the exchange rate mechanism
in 1992 and the perceived success of domestic monetary policy in the early
years of inflation targeting (1992 to 1997). For the 1997 general election,

6. The "ERM" terminology only became prevalent in U.K. policy debates starting in mid-
1989; in most of the pre-1989 discussions within the United Kingdom, the term EMS was used
to refer to the exchange rate mechanism.

7. Thatcher, interview with *Sunday Times,* October 15, 1990, stored at www.margaret
thatcher.org.

8. Thatcher, in House of Commons *Debates,* October 30, 1990, page 874.

both major political parties were committed to a policy of seeking referendum approval before any final decision to enter monetary union could be formalized. Shortly after its election in 1997, the Blair Government "committed the U.K. to the principle of joining the single currency" (HM Treasury 2003b, 1), but made any recommendation of actual entry (and hence a referendum) conditional on the *five economic tests* being passed. The five economic tests are:[9]

1. Are business cycles and economic structures compatible so that we and others could live with euro interest rates on a permanent basis?
2. If problems emerge[,] is there sufficient flexibility to deal with them?
3. Would joining EMU create better conditions for firms making long-term decisions to invest in Britain?
4. What impact would entry into EMU have on the financial services industry?
5. In summary, will joining EMU promote higher growth, stability, and a lasting increase in jobs?

The U.K. Government determined in 1997 and 2003 that these tests had not been satisfied, and so did not proceed to a referendum on U.K. membership of the euro area. (See especially HM Treasury [2003a].)

The prospect of the United Kingdom becoming a member of the euro area now seems remote. Good macroeconomic performance from 1997 to 2007, the related consolidation of the inflation targeting regime, and the move to even greater seniority within the U.K. government of critics of membership (most notably Gordon Brown's move from Chancellor of the Exchequer to Prime Minister) have all been factors reducing the likelihood of euro adoption.

Let us consider, however, the five economic tests and the extent to which our following analysis can bear on them. Question 4 is an industry-level question not easy to answer with a macroeconomic model, while 3 and aspects of 5 cover questions more suitably answered with a model that accounts for changes in long-term economic growth. We therefore consider those questions most suited to a macroeconomic analysis: the interrelated questions 1 and 2, as well as the "stability" aspect of test 5. These were also the aspects of the five economic tests that the U.K. authorities (in HM Treasury 2003b) stressed that the United Kingdom had not met. We interpret these tests as jointly amounting to a test of whether monetary union improves upon or is at least competitive with the existing U.K. monetary policy regime (inflation targeting) in contributing to macroeconomic stabilization.

Before outlining our modeling strategy for investigating this question, we

9. Given in HM Treasury (2003b, I), but originally stated (with some variation in wording) by the government in 1997.

consider some key aspects of the economic debate on the United Kingdom's place in EMU.

11.3   The Economic Debate over the Merits of Monetary Union

Some early discussions of the United Kingdom's position in the European Union took monetary union as an eventual implication of movement to a single trading market. For example, Lionel Robbins stated in 1971, "I do not think that in the end a common market, just like that, can function well if there is not something like a common money."[10] In 1991, former Prime Minister Edward Heath said that "any economist" would say that once the European Union became a single market (in 1992), "there was no alternative to a single currency."[11] These positions, have, however, not had an enduring influence, and the merits of monetary union for the United Kingdom are now seen as an issue separable from the merits of membership in the European Union.

As already noted, a major element of the opposition to European Monetary Union has taken the form of opposition to the perceived loss of political sovereignty, and some adherents to that political argument regard it as a sufficient condition for rejecting monetary union even if euro membership could be shown to be desirable on economic grounds. This seemed to be the stand taken by several members of the conservative governments over the 1990s—see Stephens (1997, 309–15)—but that position was decisively renounced as government policy when in 1997 the Blair Government appealed exclusively to economic merits as the criteria for entry.

The most important implication of monetary union for economic management was identified by Prime Minister Wilson's observation in 1974 that union "would mean one central bank, one central currency . . . [E]very country would have to pursue exactly the same policy with that single currency. . . ." Wilson argued, therefore, that it was an "illusion" to believe that monetary union would occur.[12] While Wilson's *conclusion* proved to be a flawed prediction for much of the European Union, his discussion of the main economic implications of monetary union did anticipate much of the subsequent debate. This debate takes as a starting point the acceptance that a single macroeconomic or demand management (specifically, monetary) policy is implied by union, and aims to establish whether the associated loss of flexibility for the U.K. economy is outweighed by economic benefits of membership. The debate on euro membership, therefore, combines two long-lasting themes in U.K. policy debates: the desirable degree of economic

10. Robbins, in House of Lords *Debates,* July 28, 1971, page 450.
11. Heath, in House of Commons *Debates,* November 21, 1991, page 459.
12. Wilson, in House of Commons *Debates,* December 16, 1974, pages 1127–28.

integration with "Europe," and whether the United Kingdom should give up its freedom to have its own monetary policy.[13]

Many of the details of the economic debate on U.K. membership have been concerned with exchange rate behavior. Euro adoption would mean the end of a regime in which the U.K. pound sterling floats against the euro. Much of the discussion of Buiter (1999), Minford (2002), and Artis and Ehrmann (2006) centers on the issue of whether the exchange rate, when allowed to float, adapts efficiently to shocks, or if it instead fails to respond to fundamentals in a stabilizing manner, and so (ceteris paribus) magnifies macroeconomic variability. Such a way of framing the issue happens to understate the benefits for a country of monetary policy autonomy. For it is certainly not the case that the benefits of monetary autonomy are absent if the exchange rate is driven by nonfundamental factors. Irrespective of what factors drive the exchange rate, a floating rate confers on the central bank autonomy in determination of the amount of base money in existence and so the ability to use domestic short-term interest rates as a policy instrument. This benefit does not depend on a well-behaved exchange rate. It is completely ensured by Phillips and Investment and Saving equilibrium (IS) curves that have standard properties (i.e., with aggregate demand sensitive to real short-term interest rates—possibly indirectly via a term-structure connection to long rates, and with prices adjusting gradually to aggregate demand, so that a Phillips curve that becomes vertical in the long run describes inflation dynamics). So for the exchange rate to respond to "fundamentals" is not a necessary condition for a floating exchange rate to be desirable. In relation to this point, Corsetti, Dedola, and Leduc (2007) present a model where the exchange rate fails completely to adhere to fundamentals, yet the monetary policy strategy followed by the U.K. authorities in preference to monetary union—that is, focusing on a consumer price index (CPI) inflation target alongside a floating exchange rate—is optimal.

Nevertheless, it is true that *one* possible benefit of a floating rate is its potential ability to contribute to stabilization. The debate on whether the exchange rate provides this stabilizing role in practice can be represented by reference to a standard uncovered interest parity condition (see e.g., Woodford 2001, 308):

$$(1) \qquad q_t = E_t q_{t+1} - [(R_t - E_t\pi_{t+1}) - (R_t^* - E_t\pi_{t+1}^*)] + \psi_t,$$

where asterisks denote other-economy values, q_t is the log real exchange rate, R_t is the domestic short-term nominal interest rate in quarterly units, π_t is quarterly inflation, and ψ_t is an exogenous time varying risk premium (i.e.,

---

13. Debates on the second issue predate the creation of any version of the European Union. Indeed, one of the pioneer Keynesians, Richard Kahn, argued, "If Keynes can be said to have devoted his life to anything, it is to liberating internal policy from the domination of external factors" (Kahn 1956, 113). Milton Friedman made a similar assessment of Keynes' contribution (Friedman 1983).

a shock to the uncovered interest rate parity [UIP] condition). There is wide agreement that, in practice, the real exchange rate and the nominal exchange rate move in the same direction in the short run under floating exchange rate regimes. Therefore, claims about whether the nominal exchange rate performs a stabilizing function can be mapped into similar claims about the short-run behavior of q_t.

The view that a floating exchange rate helps macroeconomic stabilization can be broken into two elements. First, different shock patterns or different structure in the home economy, relative to the other economy, might lead to the "natural interest rate" differing across economies. To the extent that stabilization of the home economy's output gap and its aggregate inflation rate require adjustment of nominal interest rates to levels different from those prevailing in the other economy, this adjustment can be accomplished because exchange rate flexibility allows interest rates to differ across economies—i.e., q_t and $E_t q_{t+1}$ are free to move to satisfy the UIP condition if monetary policy moves domestic real and nominal interest rates away from the corresponding other-economy values. Second, fluctuations in the risk premium ψ_t may occur for reasons of economic fundamentals, and the efficient response might be a nominal exchange rate reaction rather than a reaction of domestic interest rates. With a floating nominal exchange rate, this can occur, and this kind of adjustment has, for example, often been argued to describe the Australian dollar's reaction to the 1990s Asian market crises. Monetary union, however, precludes an adjustment along these lines of the domestic economy and of the nominal exchange rate.

The advocacy of euro membership for the United Kingdom in Buiter (1999) does not use an explicit model, but Buiter's analysis implicitly assumes away the model elements that deliver the scenarios described in the preceding paragraph. Buiter (1999, 30) essentially rules out the first case in his statement that "in a rather small and open economy like the U.K., monetary policy works primarily (even if not reliably) through the exchange rate." The position that the exchange rate channel is the main channel through which monetary policy operates in an open economy is very restrictive. It is true that the Mundell-Fleming model and some modern optimization-based models remove the real interest rate from the list of variables that the home-country central bank can influence in the short run.[14] But this result does not hold in models in which the aggregate consumer price index is sticky (e.g., models where imports are intermediates alone and final goods prices are sticky, as in McCallum and Nelson [1999]; or models where imports are final goods but are priced sluggishly, as in Monacelli [2005]). And it is not obvious that the domestic channel of monetary policy is negligible in open economy models in general. In other words, a portion of aggregate real

---

14. See Woodford (2007) for a discussion of the capacity of the central bank to influence real rates in optimizing open economy models.

spending may be sensitive to the real interest rate rather than just the real exchange rate, so this component of aggregate demand can be affected by any monetary policy that can influence real interest rates even if monetary policy's impact on the exchange rate is unreliable. Work done with explicitly optimization-based open economy models with nominal rigidities in general does not support the notion that, in an open economy, monetary policy ceases to work through any channel other than the exchange rate. Thus, Faia and Monacelli (2008, 745), while concluding that "the nature of optimal monetary policy in an open economy emerges as fundamentally different from the one of a closed economy," do not deny a domestic monetary policy channel, domestic real short-term interest rates appear in their consumption Euler equation in the usual manner, so monetary policy can influence aggregate demand via this "domestic" channel if it is able to affect domestic short-term real interest rates in the short run.

The existence of a substantial domestic spending channel of monetary policy seems to be widely accepted for the analysis of the United Kingdom, and the Bank of England's official descriptions of its view of monetary policy transmission include a prominent domestic channel (see, e.g., Bank of England [1999]). Moreover, the U.K. Treasury's assessment of the costs and benefits of euro adoption emphasized the different arrangements for mortgage lending across the United Kingdom and euro area, a comparison that would be irrelevant if no domestic channel of monetary policy existed.[15] The record of U.K. monetary policy episodes also suggests that aggregate demand and inflation do respond to monetary policy actions even when the behavior of the exchange rate does not appear to be in keeping with the direction expected from a monetary policy change: for example, tightenings in 1976 and 1989 were followed by contractions in aggregate demand, even though the sterling exchange rate depreciated for protracted periods. The predominant conclusion from theory and evidence is that domestic channels of monetary policy are present and substantial, so, as suggested previously, floating exchange rates confer on the central bank the ability to determine nominal aggregate demand and the inflation rate, even if the exchange rate *channel* cannot be relied upon.

In opposition to the second position, the euro entry advocates have argued that the UIP shock ψ_t is not a fundamental shock; rather, it reflects an inefficiency or "noise" created by the foreign exchange market, and so any movement it tends to induce in q_t is undesirable. By analogy with the cost-push shock in large dynamic stochastic general equilibrium (DSGE) models (see especially Smets and Wouters [2005, 163]), the UIP shock is, according to this argument, a friction that distorts prices and moves the

---

15. See HM. Treasury (2003a). The Treasury emphasized the fact that in the U.K. mortgage interest rates are predominantly adjustable, while in the euro area they are often fixed. See Rubio (2009) for an investigation of this distinction in a general equilibrium model.

economy further away from its efficient allocation, and is not a shock to which real variables would respond in an efficient flexible-price equilibrium. This argument leads to Buiter's (1999) position that it is desirable to abolish the sterling/euro foreign exchange market by imposing monetary union. Then the condition $R_t = R_t^*$ is an identifying feature of a monetary union. The nominal exchange rate is removed as a variable. To the extent that UIP shocks owe their existence to the market for nominal foreign exchange, the elimination of that market removes UIP shocks from the model. Monetary union is, in that case, materially different from both floating-exchange rate and fixed-exchange rate environments.

The view of critics of monetary union is that union does not remove UIP shocks; instead, it changes the way that they create pressures. Blanchard (1997, 288), for example, argues that "while a common currency will indeed eliminate exchange rate crises, it will not eliminate the underlying reason for such crises—namely, the fact that different interest rates, as well as adjustments in exchange rates, are needed. . . ." Elimination of a floating nominal exchange rate, according to this view, removes a convenient means with which to adapt to the pressure of UIP shocks. Absent floating exchange rates, the pressure of such shocks might be felt in other economic relationships. For example, the pressure formerly felt as UIP shocks might now manifest itself as an increase in the variance of shocks to the IS equation.

All in all, the a priori arguments that led to Buiter's (1999) conclusion that the case for euro adoption by the United Kingdom was "overwhelming" do not seem compelling, as modern open economy models produce many counterexamples. It is desirable instead to consider an explicit structural model that embeds and quantifies many of the model elements underlying the debate on monetary union. We do this in section 11.4.

11.3.1   The Sterling Appreciation

The United Kingdom experienced a "strong pound" period starting in 1996 and continuing during nearly a decade of the euro's existence (see figure 11.1). This period has been said to demonstrate the defects of floating exchange rates as an arrangement for the United Kingdom. It has been emphasized by critics of floating that the sterling appreciation is difficult to trace to economic fundamentals (see, e.g., Cobham 2006). The recent sudden reversal of the pound appreciation, at a time of worldwide contraction in the financial services business, is said by euro membership advocates to demonstrate further the disadvantage of the United Kingdom's exercise of its opt-out from euro participation. Proponents of U.K. participation contend that the strong pound shifted U.K. employment from the exchange rate-sensitive manufacturing sector to the financial services sector, and that the latter increase in employment has proved to be ephemeral.

In our view, however, this episode does not provide unambiguous evidence against the advantages claimed for floating exchange rates. In particular, the

Fig. 11.1   U.K./euro area exchange rate, 1990–2008 (pound sterling received per euro)
Source: Haver/OECD.

case made by membership proponents neglects the major contribution to macroeconomic stabilization that U.K. monetary policy made during the strong-pound period of 1996 to 2007. Monetary Policy Committee decisions had a favorable effect during the period of stagnant or falling manufacturing output and industrial production indices from 1997 to 2007. In 1990 to 1992, the United Kingdom had a fixed exchange rate and no monetary policy autonomy; during this earlier episode of an overvalued pound, contraction proceeded in both the manufacturing sector and aggregate economic activity. In 1997 to 2007, by contrast, the strong pound was associated with stagnant or declining indexes of industrial and manufacturing production, but also with continuous and respectable growth in real gross domestic product (GDP). This is brought out in figure 11.2, which plots annual-average data (from International Financial Statistics [IFS]) of U.K. industrial production and U.K. real GDP for 1990 to 2007. We would argue that, by concentrating on the stabilization of macroeconomic aggregates, the Monetary Policy Committee over this period managed to stop the manufacturing contraction from being associated with aggregate economic contraction. The reason behind its ability to do this was the United Kingdom's monetary policy autonomy, which neither a monetary union nor fixed-exchange rate would have permitted.

As for the rapid end of the strong pound era in 2008, this can be seen as a stabilizing development. By stimulating net exports, the turnabout in

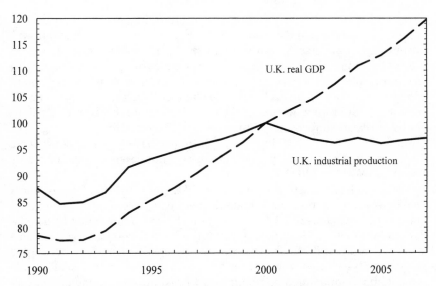

Fig. 11.2   Indexes of industrial production and real GDP, United Kingdom, 1997–2007 (index 2000 = 100)
Source: Haver/IFS.

sterling behavior lessened the implications for U.K. aggregate output and employment of the downturn in the U.K. financial services business. The floating pound has also allowed the Monetary Policy Committee (MPC) to ease monetary policy vigorously relative to euro area policy—a room to move dramatically exemplified by the MPC's 150-basis point cut in the U.K. Bank Rate in November 2008, and by its adoption of quantitative easing in 2009.

11.4   A Structural Model for Considering Monetary Union Questions

The model we use is the two-country open economy model of Erceg, Gust, and López-Salido (EGL) (2007). This model has several major attractions for the study of the United Kingdom's monetary policy options. First, the model is based on optimizing behavior, so consideration of alternative monetary regimes (in either the U.K. economy or the euro area) is a natural and legitimate experiment. In particular, we can explore CPI inflation targeting and monetary union as U.K. monetary policy options. Second, the model is flexible enough to allow the two economies to be asymmetric in several important dimensions: for example, relative size, technology, shock specification, and degree of nominal rigidity (for both prices and wages). This flexibility allows us to determine the impact of monetary union in the presence of different economic structures (and different shock processes) in the United Kingdom and the euro area. Third, Erceg, Gust, and López-Salido (2007) show that the model allows the domestic real interest rate and output gap to be affected substantially by domestic shocks, so there is a nontrivial "domestic" channel despite the presence of openness. This means that our results do not depend on the caricature that U.K. monetary policy effectiveness relies on an exchange rate channel. Fourth, the model can be adjusted to allow for a portion of the volume of imports to be intermediate goods. We can therefore use a feature that was advocated for optimizing open economy models by McCallum and Nelson (1999), and found convenient for the analysis of monetary policy in open economies by Erceg (2002) and Smets and Wouters (2002).

As the model has been laid out in detail in Erceg, Gust, and López-Salido (2007), we simply summarize its main elements here, presenting key equations in an appendix. Households' consumption choice is represented by a standard Euler equation. Government spending in each country is exogenous and is the source of an IS shock. The production function features labor input, an exogenous technology shock specific to each economy, and a fixed-capital stock. Labor is immobile across countries. Firms and workers enter the goods and labor markets, respectively, with a degree of monopoly power and with Calvo-style obstacles to adjustment of the offered prices for their goods and labor services. These contracts are augmented by dynamic indexation: all wage contracts are scaled up by the prior period's wage inflation rate; all price contracts, by prior price inflation. In our estimated version of the model, imports are final consumer goods. The prices of imports are flexible.

11.4.1   Specification and Estimation

We assume that the home economy's size is 20 percent that of the other economy, in order to give the model a "United Kingdom = home economy; euro area = other economy" interpretation. We set the steady-state share of government spending in GDP to 0.33 in the United Kingdom, 0.338 in the euro area. The import share of GDP for each economy is intended to capture the degree of each economy's trade with one another. We make the share 13.5 percent for the United Kingdom; together with the relative sizes of the economy, this implies a 2.7 percent import share for the euro area. The latter takes such a low value because we are neglecting non-U.K. imports into the euro area, given the model's two-economy structure. We fix the exchange rate elasticity of traded goods at EGL's baseline value of 1.5 and the steady-state wage markup in both economies at 50 percent. The discount rate (β) is set at 0.9925, the intertemporal elasticity of substitution is set at $1/\sigma = 1/2$, and the inverse of the Frisch elasticity of labor supply assumed to be $\chi = 5$.

While we estimate the intertemporal elasticity of substitution for consumption and the labor supply elasticity of households using U.K. and euro area data, we constrain the estimate of each parameter to be the same across the two economies.

The monetary policy rule specification is similar but not identical across economies. For the United Kingdom, the monetary policy rule has the short-term nominal interest rate response in a smoothed manner to the lagged four-quarter retail price inflation rate (which we use as the empirical measure for the United Kingdom of consumer price inflation, π_C) and to lagged detrended log output y_t:

$$(2) \quad R_t^{U.K.} = \rho_R R_{t-1}^{U.K.} + (1-\rho_R)\gamma_\pi (0.25 \times (\pi_{C,t-1}^{U.K.} + \pi_{C,t-2}^{U.K.} + \pi_{C,t-3}^{U.K.} + \pi_{C,t-4}^{U.K.}))$$
$$+ (1-\rho_R)\gamma_y y_{t-1}^{U.K.} + e_{Rt}^{U.K.}.$$

Here constants are suppressed, and the monetary policy shock e_{Rt} is assumed to be an AR(1) process. Other than lagging the variables one more period, this specification is a restricted version of the policy rule estimated for the United States by Rotemberg and Woodford (1997), and also follows their use of log-linearly detrended real GDP as the variable to which the authorities respond. Again paralleling Rotemberg and Woodford's specification, the previous reaction function delivers a "long-run" rule of the Taylor form. Our modeling of policymaker behavior using this simple three-parameter rule requires justification in light of Favero's (2001, 237) position that "a strategy closer to the spirit of intertemporal optimization seems more appropriate" in the estimation of policy rules. The use of a simple rule can be defended both on practical grounds—the EGL model is too large for the implied optimal-policy conditions to deliver rules tractable enough for econometric estimation—and for reasons of realism—the inflation variable that U.K. policymakers over our sample concerned themselves with was a CPI-like concept, not the combination of wage inflation and domestic-goods price inflation that the EGL model would tend to suggest targeting.

For the euro area, a similar policy rule specification is estimated, though with no constraint that the estimated responses, or the AR(1) parameter and innovation variance for the shock, be the same as in the United Kingdom. An important qualification is that for the euro area we assume that the inflation variable that enters the rule is the (annualized) one-period lagged quarterly GDP deflator inflation rate (as opposed to the lagged four-quarter CPI-type rate in the U.K. case). The deflator inflation rate is assumed to enter the rule even though it is the Harmonized Index of Consumer Prices (HICP) aggregate that we use as an observable in obtaining our estimates following (where it is used to correspond, for the euro area, to the model's consumer price index). The assumption that euro area policy responds to deflator inflation follows Smets and Wouters (2005).[16]

Each economy has Phillips curves for wage and for price adjustment.

---

16. The United Kingdom is the "rest of world" for the euro area in the two-economy model we are using. Assuming a euro area monetary policy response to deflator inflation captures (more than would an assumption of a policy response to consumer prices), the notion is that euro area policy does not respond to U.K. inflation when the United Kingdom is outside the monetary union.

Each Phillips curve has its own univariate AR(1) shock term. The remaining shocks in the model are two real shocks for each economy—government spending and technology—and a shock that we add to the EGL model, namely a shock to the UIP condition, so that the UIP condition in our model resembles equation (1). The two real shocks for each economy (four in total) and the UIP shock are assumed to be AR(1) processes. Because asymmetry of shocks is a central issue for the debate on monetary union, the stand we take on correlations of shocks is important. We allow the government spending shock to be correlated across economies and the technology shock to be correlated across economies. This cross-correlation is allowed for by empirical estimation of cross-correlations of the shock innovations. We constrain the monetary policy and Phillips curve shocks to be uncorrelated across economies.

The data used in model estimation are, for each economy, detrended logs of per capita consumption, output, and the quarterly real wage (with consumer prices used to deflate nominal wages); (consumer/retail) price inflation for each economy; the nominal U.K. Treasury bill rate; the euro area short-term nominal interest rate; and the change in the nominal exchange rate. Logs of output, consumption, and the real wage are detrended over 1980 to 2005. The U.K. data are described in DiCecio and Nelson (2007).[17] Euro area data come from the ECB's Area-Wide Model database (see Fagan, Henry, and Mestre 2001) and other ECB sources. The sterling/euro exchange rate is from Haver/IFS. Population data are from Haver, the ECB, and (for the United Kingdom) the Office of National Statistics.

We estimate the model by Bayesian likelihood methods (see Smets and Wouters 2003, 2007) on the sample period 1981 Q1 to 2005 Q4,[18] and report parameter estimates in tables 11.1 to 11.3. The posterior estimates indicate a standard amount of price stickiness (around twice-a-year price adjustment, other than the adjustment occurring via the indexation term) for both economies. But there is little estimated wage stickiness. For the euro area, this result is puzzling in light of estimates such as those of Smets and Wouters (2003). One of the simulation experiments that we undertake following allows for more wage rigidity in the euro area. For both economies, the rule estimates indicate substantial interest rate smoothing, a long-run response to inflation close to 1.5, and an output response somewhat below the value (0.5/4 = 0.125) associated with the Taylor rule.

17. In addition to the U.K. variables described there, we have nominal wages for the United Kingdom among our observables. Nominal wages for the United Kingdom consist of total compensation (Office of National Statistics series dtwm.q), divided by aggregate employment (series bcaj.q).

18. Starting estimation in 1981 allows the overhaul of doctrine that took place in U.K. economic policy-making in the late 1970s, documented in Nelson (2009), to make itself felt in changed monetary policy responses to the state of the economy. As a related matter, omitting pre-1980 observations from the sample helps avoid inclusion in estimation many of the substantial breaks in means, trends, and variances from the 1970s to the 1980s in the U.K. data (documented, for example, by Stock and Watson [2002]; Benati [2008]; Boero, Smith, and Wallis [2008]; and Surico [2008]).

Table 11.1   **Bayesian estimates of EGL (2007) model on U.K. and euro area data: Estimation period 1981 Q1–2005 Q4, structural and monetary policy rule parameters**

Parameter interpretation	Prior Mean (Standard deviation)	Posterior Mode	Mean	5%, 95%
Price adjustment probability, U.K.	0.5000 (0.1000)	0.5161	0.5289	0.4461, 0.6132
Wage adjustment probability, U.K.	0.5000 (0.1000)	0.1294	0.1417	0.0977, 0.1851
Price adjustment probability, euro area	0.5000 (0.1000)	0.4720	0.4954	0.4066, 0.5923
Wage adjustment probability, euro area	0.5000 (0.1000)	0.1102	0.1287	0.0800, 0.1790
Labor supply elasticity (both economies)	2.0000 (0.7500)	4.0525	4.0833	3.2859, 4.8279
Intertemporal elasticity of consumption (both economies)	1.5000 (0.3750)	3.2325	3.2495	2.8352, 3.6897
Interest smoothing, U.K. policy rule	0.7500 (0.1000)	0.4544	0.4609	0.3444, 0.5782
Inflation response, U.K. policy rule	1.5000 (0.2500)	1.6423	1.6874	1.5032, 1.8676
Output response, U.K. policy rule	0.1250 (0.0500)	0.1116	0.1193	0.0792, 0.1627
Interest smoothing, euro area policy rule	0.7500 (0.1000)	0.7896	0.7926	0.7585, 0.8296
Inflation response, euro area policy rule	1.5000 (0.2500)	1.2744	1.3197	1.1741, 1.4565
Output response, euro area policy rule	0.1200 (0.0500)	0.0845	0.0917	0.0460, 0.1358

Notes: The estimated probabilities of wage and price adjustment are the probability that *no* discretionary adjustment is allowed this period (in which case a default adjustment takes place of indexation to the previous period's inflation rate of the index in question). Beta distribution prior used for these probabilities; normal distribution prior used for the other parameters.

Table 11.2   **Bayesian estimates of EGL (2007) model on U.K. and euro area data: Estimation period 1981 Q1–2005 Q4, shock autogressive processes**

Parameter interpretation	Prior Mean	Posterior Mode	Mean	5%, 95%
AR(1) parameter, U.K. technology	0.8500	0.9485	0.9302	0.8788, 0.9797
AR(1) parameter, U.K. wage Phillips curve shocks	0.8500	0.9218	0.8523	0.7185, 0.9952
AR(1) parameter, U.K. monetary policy shocks	0.8500	0.4752	0.4795	0.3648, 0.5992
AR(1) parameter, U.K. IS shocks	0.8500	0.9802	0.9760	0.9594, 0.9984
AR(1) parameter, U.K. price Phillips curve shocks	0.8500	0.9924	0.9872	0.9754, 0.9984
AR(1) parameter, UIP shocks	0.8500	0.9391	0.9265	0.8792, 0.9753
AR(1) parameter, euro area technology	0.8500	0.8147	0.7694	0.6271, 0.9049
AR(1) parameter, euro area wage Phillips curve shocks	0.8500	0.9218	0.8548	0.7248, 0.9956
AR(1) parameter, euro area monetary policy shocks	0.8500	0.2482	0.2563	0.1773, 0.3356
AR(1) parameter, euro area IS shocks	0.8500	0.9471	0.9388	0.9120, 0.9643
AR(1) parameter, euro area price Phillips curve shocks	0.8500	0.9882	0.9789	0.9608, 0.9983

Note: Beta prior distribution used throughout (with standard deviation 0.1000).

With the partial exception of the monetary policy shocks, which have only moderate autocorrelation, all the estimated shocks in the model are strongly persistent. In particular, the UIP shock is highly serially correlated. This autocorrelation combines with the estimated innovation variance to give an unconditional standard deviation for the UIP shock of about 0.5 percent, a surprisingly modest value.

Table 11.3   Bayesian estimates of EGL (2007) model on U.K. and euro area data:
                    Estimation period 1981 Q1–2005 Q4, innovation covariance estimates

	Prior (%)	Mode (%)	Mean (%)	5%, 95%
A. Standard deviation of innovations				
Technology, U.K.	0.100	1.049	1.126	0.899, 1.361
Technology, euro area	0.100	0.620	0.714	0.528, 0.912
Government spending, U.K.	0.100	0.760	0.775	0.673, 0.879
Government spending, euro area	0.100	0.610	0.620	0.518, 0.718
Monetary policy rule, U.K.	0.100	0.213	0.217	0.190, 0.244
Monetary policy rule, euro area	0.100	0.148	0.149	0.129, 0.170
UIP disturbance	0.100	0.165	0.189	0.129, 0.248
Price Phillips curve shocks, U.K.	0.100	1.045	1.049	0.728, 1.346
Price Phillips curve shocks, euro area	0.100	0.915	0.898	0.626, 1.140
Wage Phillips curve shocks, U.K.	0.100	0.046	0.078	0.024, 0.149
Wage Phillips curve shocks, euro area	0.100	0.046	0.117	0.022, 0.241
B. Cross-economy correlations of innovations				
Technology	0.000	0.159	0.149	–0.018, 0.311
Government spending	0.000	0.233	0.226	0.050, 0.406

Notes: Inverse gamma distribution prior used for estimation of standard deviations (panel A); uniform distribution with zero prior used for estimation of correlations (panel B).

There is considerable asymmetry in the real shocks facing each economy, with the correlation between innovations to technology being below 0.2 and that between government spending innovations being below 0.3. This is consistent with previous evidence for European economies. For example, Söderström (chapter 10, this volume) argues that "asymmetric shocks seem to be important for the Swedish economy," while Artis and Ehrmann's (2006) vector autoregression (VAR) analysis suggests that German and U.K. real shocks may even be negatively correlated.

A serious question is raised about empirical open economy DSGE models by Justiniano and Preston (2006). They argue that estimated (small) open economy structural models understate the contribution of international shocks to an open economy's economic fluctuations. In their empirical example of the United States and Canada, the U.S. shocks in combination contribute about two-thirds to Canadian output fluctuations in an identified VAR, but to less than 10 percent of Canadian output variation in the estimated DSGE model. We have looked at the impact on our results of this problem by comparing our estimated open economy structural model for the euro area and the United Kingdom with an identified VAR including data for the two economies. The VAR is a four-lag system consisting of a major subset of the variables we use in estimation of the structural model: namely, output growth, inflation, and interest rates for both economies, as well as the change in the nominal exchange rate. The VAR-identified shocks are obtained with a Choleski decomposition, with euro variables ordered first, followed by the exchange rate, followed by the U.K. variables, and the ordering of the variables within each block being: interest rate, output growth, and inflation. This identified VAR delivers an estimated contribution of foreign shocks (including the exchange rate shock) to U.K. output growth variability of 32.7 percent. The contribution of foreign shocks (including the UIP shock) to U.K. output growth variation in the estimated structural model is 29.9 percent. The results differ from Justiniano and Preston's in two respects. First, for the identified VAR, the estimated foreign contribution to domestic economic variability is more modest in our example—and this is despite the fact that we do, and Justiniano and Preston do not, include the exchange rate shock among the foreign shocks. Second, in moving to the structural model, we do not find a dramatically smaller contribution of foreign shocks' contribution to domestic economic fluctuations. In that sense, the understatement problem for our euro area/U.K. structural model is less serious than that found by Justiano and Preston (2006) for their open economy model of the United States and Canada. But this finding is subject to the proviso that, as noted previously, we categorize exchange-rate shocks in both the VAR and structural models as foreign shocks. It is true that most of the foreign contribution to U.K. output variation in our structural model comes from this source, whereas in the VAR, the shocks to the euro area variables form the bulk of the foreign influence on U.K. output growth.

11.5   Simulation Experiments

In this section we present illustrative results from simulations of the model. We consider three assumptions about model structure, starting with the estimated model as the baseline.

11.5.1   Baseline Case

In the baseline case in table 11.4, we compute U.K. economic performance using the estimated model under different monetary policy rules: historical policy and monetary union. We focus on variability of output, CPI inflation, and the short-term nominal interest rate. We acknowledge that open economy models like those used in this chapter frequently do not justify a monetary policy focus on aggregate CPI inflation, and direct attention instead to domestic goods inflation or to a combination of domestic goods and wage inflation. But CPI inflation is bound to be a key variable in a study of U.K. policy options. That is, the inflation rate is focused upon in the U.K. current policy framework and so is a key variable to consider in judging the merits of U.K. entry into monetary union.

Historical policy uses the U.K. and euro area interest rate rules set out in the estimated model. The mode values in tables 11.1 to 11.3 are taken to be the model estimates. When we consider monetary union, the historical U.K. policy rule is dropped in favor of $R_t^{U.K.} = R_t^{EA}$ (where "EA" denotes euro area), and since the United Kingdom is then a euro area member, the euro

Table 11.4   Simulation results

	Standard deviation (%) of United Kingdom		
	CPI inflation (annualized)	Output gap	Nominal interest rate (annualized)
A. Baseline model (Common structure to both economies)			
Historical rules	4.76	3.33	5.11
Monetary union (UIP shocks continue)	4.02	3.19	2.67
Monetary union (UIP shocks vanish)	3.87	3.19	2.57
B. Model with greater wage flexibility in United Kingdom			
Historical rules	4.78	3.34	5.12
Monetary union (UIP shocks continue)	17.66	4.82	2.58
Monetary union (UIP shocks vanish)	17.53	4.81	2.49
C. Model with U.K. imports predominantly intermediates			
Historical rules	4.71	2.72	5.32
Monetary union (UIP shocks continue)	5.05	2.64	2.72
Monetary union (UIP shocks vanish)	4.96	2.64	2.62

area output and price aggregates that enter the euro area policy rule include the corresponding U.K. series. The price aggregate is assumed to be a log-linear combination of the non-U.K. and U.K. economies' output deflators. Subject to these augmented definitions of the aggregates, the interest rate policy rule assumed for the monetary union is the same as that estimated empirically for the euro area: smoothing of 0.79, a response to lagged quarterly inflation that implies a 1.27 "long-run" response, and a response to lagged detrended output that implies a 0.085 "long-run" reaction.[19]

Historical policy in our parameterized model gives, as reported in table 11.4, standard deviations of 4.8 percent for inflation, 3.3 percent for the output gap, and 5.1 percent for the nominal interest rate. The alternative regime of monetary union is considered with and without UIP shocks. When UIP shocks are present, they act in a way that does not disturb equality of interest rates across economies; instead, UIP shocks effectively become a second IS shock and so a source of disturbance to output demand. According to table 11.4, monetary union reduces output gap variability and does so irrespective of the assumption about the presence of UIP shocks. Improvement in U.K. inflation stabilization does occur with monetary union but is somewhat dependent on whether union eliminates UIP shocks. The standard deviation of U.K. inflation falls if UIP shocks vanish. Nevertheless, even when UIP shocks are present, their effect on the results is not dramatic, apparently because our estimates imply a fairly modest variance for this class of shock.

---

19. The monetary policy shock autocorrelation and variances for the policymaker in the monetary union are also those estimated in tables 11.2 and 11.3 for the euro area.

11.5.2   Wages Relatively More Flexible in the United Kingdom

Estimates of a dynamic general equilibrium model for the United Kingdom in DiCecio and Nelson (2007) suggested that U.K. nominal rigidity was concentrated in prices, rather than spread across wages and prices equally. This finding is roughly reflected in our estimates here as well. But it is puzzling that we also find that the probability of wage adjustment is quite rapid in the euro area too, in contrast to estimates such as those of Smets and Wouters (2003). In light of this, we now consider an alternative parameterization of the EGL model in which wages are more flexible in the United Kingdom than in the euro area. Specifically, we raise the degree of nominal rigidity in the euro area above its estimated value. It is now assumed that the probability that wages are not reoptimized is 0.60 in the euro area.

We report the simulation outcomes in the middle set of results (section B) in table 11.4. When there is no monetary union, the standard deviations of U.K. series are virtually unchanged from those under the baseline parameterization. Because the only change in parameterization is to the degree of euro area wage rigidity, the results make economic sense; they reflect the notion that floating exchange rates can insulate the domestic economy from divergences across economies in the degree of nominal rigidity. The loss of the exchange rate mechanism and of an own-economy interest rate rule now seem to have visible costs; U.K. inflation stabilization worsens drastically under monetary union when compared to that under the historical U.K. monetary policy rule, regardless of whether UIP shocks are present. The magnitude of the difference in inflation variability implied by historical rules and that implied by monetary union is very large in table 11.4, and may be questioned. The difference would likely be more modest if, for example, we had assumed a more modest divergence between U.K. and euro area nominal rigidity.[20] We would not give credence to the quantitative magnitude of the results from this model setting. But, qualitatively, the results illustrate the possibility that nominal exchange rate movements help compensate for differences in nominal rigidities across countries.

As in the previous set of results, U.K. interest rate variability does decline when there is monetary union. Thus, embrace of monetary union appears to confer on the United Kingdom more stable interest rates, but these are accompanied by a rule that is directed at aggregates of which U.K. variables make up only a modest portion. Furthermore, the mismatch of contract durations across economies means that rules that are successful at stabilizing euro area inflation are less effective at stabilizing U.K. fluctuations. The result is greater U.K. macroeconomic instability.

Monetary policy is less volatile in the sense that interest rate volatility declines when the United Kingdom joins the union; it gives up a domes-

---

20. Equally, we found that making the discrepancy in nominal rigidity across the two economies larger than that used in figure 11.2 worsens the variability of U.K. inflation.

tic policy rule that was associated with less smooth interest rate behavior. But inflation outcomes become more volatile for the U.K. economy. What appears to be happening is that the less volatile rate behavior is destabilizing for U.K. inflation because of the major mismatch in nominal rigidity; that is, the interest rate should be more volatile, or should be responding in a different way to shocks than what is implied by the euro rule, if the objective is to insulate the U.K. economy from the effects of nominal rigidity.[21] The damage done by the imposition of the euro area rule overwhelms one beneficial effect on inflation variability arising from euro wage patterns. This beneficial effect is that the relatively greater euro area wage stickiness by itself should be helpful for U.K. inflation stabilization by stabilizing U.K. import price inflation. This partial effect seems to dominate when the difference in wage stickiness across economies is a little less than what we are using in the table.

11.5.3   Intermediate Goods Predominant

We revert our settings of wage rigidity to the estimates in tables 11.1 through 11.3 in order to consider a third model variant. Wilson (1976) and Allsopp, Kara, and Nelson (2006) argue that, for U.K. inflation analysis, it is appropriate to model all imports as intermediate goods. With this formulation, imports enter the model alongside labor in the production process to yield final consumption goods. We consider a parameterization of the EGL model that allows for this view of imports' role to predominate. In the baseline parameterization, 100 percent of imports were final consumer goods; now, by contrast, 90 percent of imports are assumed to be intermediate goods and only 10 percent to be final goods.[22] We repeat the policy experiments with this alternative setting of the model in the final three rows of table 11.4. Monetary union appears to worsen inflation performance somewhat—even when UIP shocks are absent—and to reduce the variability of the output gap and the interest rate.

When imports are primarily intermediates, exchange rate variations have a less automatic connection to CPI variations; the fraction of the CPI that is flexible and linked tightly to the exchange rate is small. Under these conditions, extinguishing exchange rate variations is less likely to deliver improved inflation performance, if this also entails giving up the ability to manipulate domestic interest rates.

---

21. Output gap variability falls under union. In a closed economy sticky-price model with no Phillips curve shocks and no indexation, this reduction would by itself imply that policymakers had succeeded in removing the effects of nominal rigidity; it would necessarily be associated also with lower inflation variability. But this implication does not carry over to the present model. Because there are several sources of nominal rigidity in the open economy model we use, as well as Phillips curve shocks, the stability of the UK output gap is not a reliable index (as it is in a sticky-price closed economy model) of the effects of nominal rigidity, so CPI inflation is destabilized by the euro rule despite the accompanying improved stability of the gap.

22. The intermediate technology is that in EGL (2007), including a one-third weight on imports.

11.6   Conclusions

We have considered euro area membership as a U.K. monetary policy option by studying the effect of monetary union under various parameterizations of the Erceg, Gust, and López-Salido (2007) model. One issue in determining whether monetary union contributes to an improvement in U.K. macroeconomic stabilization is the status of the UIP, or foreign exchange risk premium, shock. Much hangs on whether the elimination of the sterling/euro exchange market will be associated with the suppression of UIP shocks, which have been thought to be a major source of exchange rate variation. Suppose these shocks stand in for pressures that the economy needs to adjust to whether it is part of a monetary union or not. Then if the United Kingdom joined the euro area, UIP shocks, instead of vanishing, would continue to make themselves felt via different channels. Our results suggest that monetary union may increase inflation variability if UIP shocks do not disappear at the inception of monetary union. This effect is detectable even though, according to our estimates, UIP shocks are actually only a modest inherent source of exchange rate variation.

We also affirmed that if the differences in the degree of nominal wage rigidity across the United Kingdom and the euro area are sufficiently large, U.K. inflation variability under monetary union is higher than that achievable under monetary policy autonomy. Finally, we found that the improvement in U.K. economic stability under monetary union also diminishes if imports from the euro area are modeled as primarily intermediates instead of finished goods.

Appendix

The Erceg, Gust, and López-Salido (EGL) Model Setup

The EGL (2007) setup, as applied here, consists of twenty-five equations determining the following twenty-five endogenous variables (with real variables in log-deviation form):

$$[c_t^j, y_t^j, l_t^j, c_{D,t}^j, m_{C,t}^j, \pi_t^j, \pi_{C,t}^j, \pi_{w,t}^j, p_{CD,t}^j, \zeta_t^j, R_t^j, \rho_t, \tau_t, s_t], j = \text{U.K., EA,}$$

where EA denotes "euro area."

The consumption bundles in each economy consist of the aggregates:

$$c_t^j = (1 - \omega^j)c_{D,t}^j + \omega^j m_{C,t}^j, \quad j = \text{U.K., EA,}$$

where c is total consumption, c_D is consumption of domestically produced output, and m_C denotes imported consumption goods. The two-economy structure implies that $\omega^{\text{U.K.}} = \upsilon\omega^{\text{EA}}$.

Production functions take the form:

$$y_t^j = z_t^j + l_t^j, \quad j = \text{U.K., EA,}$$

so that output (expressed as a log deviation from its steady-state value) is equal to the sum of the technology shock, z, and log labor input, l.

The resource constraints imply:

$$y_t^j = c_t^j, \quad j = \text{U.K., EA.}$$

There is a risk-sharing condition:

$$\sigma\left(c_t^{\text{UK}} - \frac{g_C^{\text{UK}}}{1-g_C^{\text{UK}}} g_t^{\text{UK}} \right) = \rho_t + \sigma\left(c_t^{\text{EA}} - \frac{g_C^{\text{EA}}}{1-g_C^{\text{EA}}} g_t^{\text{EA}} \right),$$

where ρ_t is the real exchange rate, and the g's are IS shocks.

The intertemporal Euler equation for household consumption in the euro area is

$$\sigma\left(c_t^{\text{EA}} - \frac{g_C^{\text{EA}}}{1-g_C^{\text{EA}}} g_t^{\text{EA}} \right) = \sigma\left(E_t c_{t+1}^{\text{EA}} - \frac{g_C^{\text{EA}}}{1-g_C^{\text{EA}}} E_t g_{t+1}^{\text{EA}} \right) - \left(R_t^{\text{EA}} - E_t \pi_{C,t+1}^{\text{EA}} \right)$$

where $(R - \pi_C)$ is the euro area short-term real interest rate (measured in consumption units).

The demand functions for imported consumer goods are given by:

$$m_{C,t}^{\text{UK}} = c_{D,j}^{\text{UK}} - \eta\tau_t.$$

$$m_{C,t}^{\text{EA}} = c_{D,t}^{\text{EA}} + \eta\tau_t.$$

Wages are governed by the relations:

$$\frac{\xi_w^j\left[1+\chi(1+\theta_w)/\theta_w\right]}{(1-\xi_w^j)(1-\beta\xi_w^j)}[\pi_{w,t}^j - \pi_{w,t-1}^j - \beta(E_t\pi_{w,t+1}^j - \pi_{w,t}^j)]$$

$$= \left[\chi l_t^j + \sigma\left(c_t^j \frac{g_C^j}{1-g_C^j} g_t^j \right) + \mu_{w,t}^j - (\zeta_t^j - p_{CD,t}^j) \right], \quad j = \text{U.K., EA,}$$

where π_w is nominal wage inflation, $(\zeta - p_{CD})$ is the log real wage in consumption units (i.e., the log real wage in output units, ζ, adjusted for the log aggregate relative price of consumer goods in terms of output, p_{CD}), and μ_w is a wage markup shock. The parameters θ_w (common across economies) and ξ_w (different across economies), respectively, denote the steady-state wage markup and the degree to which households are not given clearance to reoptimize nominal wages.

Price inflation is driven by the Phillips curve:

$$\pi_t^j - \pi_{t-1}^j - \beta(E_t\pi_{t+1}^j - \pi_t^j) = \frac{(1-\xi_p^j)(1-\beta\xi_p^j)}{\xi_p^j}(\zeta_t^j - z_t^j) + \mu_{p,t}^j$$

$$j = \text{U.K., EA,}$$

where π is the GDP deflator inflation rate, the probability ξ_p indexes the degree of nominal price stickiness, and μ_p is a price markup shock.

The percent change in the real wage (in output units) is simply the difference between wage and price inflation,

$$\zeta_t^j - \zeta_{t-1}^j = \pi_{w,t}^j - \pi_t^j, \quad j = \text{U.K., EA.}$$

The prices of consumption relative to output are connected to the terms of trade as follows:

$$p_{CD,t}^{UK} = \omega^{UK}\tau_t,$$

$$p_{CD,t}^{EA} = -\omega^{EA}\tau_t.$$

The growth rate of consumer prices (relative to output prices) can be written as the spread between consumer price and output price inflation:

$$p_{CD,t}^j - p_{CD,t-1}^j = \pi_{C,t}^j - \pi_t^j, \quad j = \text{U.K., EA.}$$

The real exchange rate has the following relation to the terms of trade:

$$\rho_t = (1 - \omega^{UK} - \omega^{EA})\tau_t.$$

The following uncovered interest rate parity condition (in real terms) holds:

$$E_i\tau_{t+1} - \tau_t = (R_t^{UK} - E_t\pi_{t+1}^{UK}) - (R_t^{EA} - E_t\pi_{t+1}^{EA}) + \text{euip}_t,$$

where euip_t is the UIP shock.

The percent change in the nominal exchange rate can be expressed as:

$$s_t - s_{t-1} = \tau_t - \tau_{t-1} + \pi_t^{UK} - \pi_t^{EA}.$$

In the case of no monetary union, we assume the monetary policy rules take the form:

$$R_t^{UK} = \rho_R^{UK} R_{t-1}^{UK} + (1-\rho_R^{UK})\left(\frac{\gamma_\pi^{UK}}{4}\sum_{j=1}^{4}\pi_{C,t-j}^{UK} + \gamma_{t-1}^{UK} y_{t-1}^{UK}\right) + e_{Rt}^{UK},$$

$$R_t^{EA} = \rho_R^{EA} R_{t-1}^{EA} + (1-\rho_R^{EA})(\gamma_\pi^{EA}\pi_{t-1}^{EA} + \gamma_y^{EA} y_{t-1}^{EA}) + e_{Rt}^{EA},$$

the e_{Rt} being AR(1) monetary policy shocks.

The eleven exogenous stochastic processes $[z^j, g^j, \mu_w^j, \mu_p^j, e_R^j, \text{euip}]$ are each assumed to follow AR(1) laws of motion.

The preceding outline features imports only as final consumer goods. Erceg, Gust, and López-Salido (2007) also present a version of their model with some imports being intermediates. We use a version of this model, making the assumption that some imports into the U.K. economy are used for production, in our section C experiments in table 11.4.

References

Allsopp, C., A. Kara, and E. Nelson. 2006. United Kingdom inflation targeting and the exchange rate. *Economic Journal* 116 (512): F232–F244.

Artis, M., and M. Ehrmann. 2006. The exchange rate: A shock-absorber or source of shocks? A study of four open economies. *Journal of International Money and Finance* 25 (6): 874–93.

Associated Press. 1972. Briton predicts European nuclear buildup. *Baltimore Sun.* October 14.

Bank of England. 1999. *The transmission mechanism of monetary policy.* London: Bank of England.

Benati, L. 2008. The "Great Moderation" in the United Kingdom. *Journal of Money, Credit and Banking* 40 (1): 121–47.

Blanchard, O. 1997. *Macroeconomics.* Upper Saddle River, NJ: Prentice Hall.

Boero, G., J. Smith, and K. F. Wallis. 2008. Modelling UK inflation uncertainty, 1958–2006. Paper presented at the Robert F. Engle Festschrift Conference. 21 June 2008, San Diego, California.

Buiter, W. H. 1999. Optimal currency areas: Why does the exchange rate regime matter? With an application to UK membership in EMU. Available at: http://www .nber.org/%7Ewbuiter/scotland.pdf. November.

Castle, B. 1980. *The Castle diaries: 1974–76.* London: Weidenfeld and Nicolson.

Cobham, D. 2006. The overvaluation of sterling since 1996: How the policy makers responded and why. *Economic Journal* 116 (512): F185–F207.

Commission of the European Communities, Working Party on Economic and Monetary Union. 1970. *Interim report on the establishment by stages of economic and monetary union in the community.* Brussels: European Communities.

Corsetti, G., L. Dedola, and S. Leduc. 2007. Optimal monetary policy and the sources of local-currency price stability. NBER Working Paper no. 13544. Cambridge, MA: National Bureau of Economic Research, October.

DiCecio, R., and E. Nelson. 2007. An estimated DSGE model for the United Kingdom. *Federal Reserve Bank of St. Louis Review* 89 (4): 215–32.

Erceg, C. 2002. The choice of an inflation target range in a small open economy. *American Economic Review: Papers and Proceedings* 92 (2): 85–89.

Erceg, C., C. Gust, and J. D. López-Salido. 2007. The transmission of domestic shocks in the open economy. NBER Working Paper no. 13613. Cambridge, MA: National Bureau of Economic Research, November.

European Commission. 1977. *Report of the study group on the role of public finance in European integration, volume 1: General report.* Brussels and Luxembourg: Commission of the European Economic Communities.

Expenditure Committee, House of Commons. 1978. *First report from the Expenditure Committee: The European Monetary System.* London: Her Majesty's Stationery Office.

Fagan, G., J. Henry, and R. Mestre. 2001. An area-wide model (AWM) for the euro area. ECB Working Paper no. 42. Frankfurt: European Central Bank.

Faia, E., and T. Monacelli. 2008. Optimal monetary policy in a small open economy with home bias. *Journal of Money, Credit and Banking* 40 (4): 721–50.

Favero, C. A. 2001. *Applied macroeconometrics.* Oxford: Oxford University Press.

Friedman, M. 1983. The Keynes Centenary: A monetarist reflects. *The Economist.* June 4.

HM Treasury. 2003a. Convergence. In *UK membership of the single currency: An assessment of the five economic tests,* ed. HM Treasury, chapter 1. Available at: www.hm-treasury.gov.uk.

HM Treasury. 2003b. Executive summary. In *UK membership of the single currency: An assessment of the five economic tests,* ed. H.M. Treasury. Available at: www .hm-treasury.gov.uk.

House of Commons, U.K. Parliament. *Parliamentary Debates*, various issues. Also available at http://hansard.millbanksystems.com/.

House of Lords, U.K. Parliament. *Parliamentary Debates*, various issues. Also available at http://hansard.millbanksystems.com/.

Justiniano, A., and B. Preston. 2006. Can structural small open economy models account for the influence of foreign disturbances? Columbia University, Department of Economics. Unpublished Manuscript.

Kahn, R. F. 1956. Lord Keynes and the balance of payments. *The Listener.* May 10. Reprinted in *selected essays on employment and growth,* ed. R. F. Kahn, 113–23. Cambridge: Cambridge University Press, 1972.

MacRae, P. 1999. Poll: U.K. given 65 per cent chance of joining euro. *Reuters News.* June 7.

McCallum, B. T., and E. Nelson. 1999. Nominal income targeting in an open-economy optimizing model. *Journal of Monetary Economics* 43 (3): 553–78.

Minford, P. 2002. *Should Britain join the euro? The chancellor's five tests examined.* London: Institute of Economic Affairs.

Monacelli, T. 2005. Monetary policy in a low pass-through environment. *Journal of Money, Credit and Banking* 37 (6): 1047–66.

Nelson, E. 2009. An overhaul of doctrine: The underpinning of U.K. inflation targeting. *Economic Journal* 119 (538): F333–68.

Rotemberg, J. J., and M. Woodford. 1997. An optimization-based econometric framework for the evaluation of monetary policy. In *NBER macroeconomics annual 1997,* ed. B. Bernanke and J. Rotemberg, 297–346. Cambridge, MA: MIT Press.

Rubio, M. 2009. Fixed and variable-rate mortgages, business cycles and monetary policy. Working Paper no. 903. Banco de España, February.

Smets, F., and R. Wouters. 2002. Openness, imperfect exchange rate pass-through and monetary policy. *Journal of Monetary Economics* 49 (5): 947–81.

———. 2003. Monetary policy in an estimated SDGE model of the euro area. *Journal of the European Economic Association* 1 (5): 1123–75.

———. 2005. Comparing shocks and frictions in US and euro area business cycles: A Bayesian DSGE approach. *Journal of Applied Econometrics* 20 (2): 161–83.

———. 2007. Shocks and frictions in US business cycles: A Bayesian DSGE approach. *American Economic Review* 97 (3): 586–606.

Stephens, P. 1997. *Politics and the pound: The Tories, the economy and Europe.* London: Papermac.

Stock, J. H., and M. Watson. 2002. Has the business cycle changed, and why? *NBER macroeconomics annual 2002,* ed. M. Gertler and K. S. Rogoff, 159–218. Cambridge, MA: MIT Press.

Surico, P. 2008. Monetary policy shifts and inflation dynamics. Working Paper no. 338. London: Bank of England.

Wilson, T. 1976. Effective devaluation and inflation. *Oxford Economic Papers* 28 (1): 1–24.

Woodford, M. 2001. Monetary policy in the information economy. In *Economic policy for the information economy,* ed. Federal Reserve Bank of Kansas City, 297–370. Kansas City, MO: Reserve Bank of Kansas City.

———. 2007. Globalization and monetary control. NBER Working Paper no. 13329. Cambridge, MA: National Bureau of Economic Research, August.

Comment   Carlo A. Favero

Introduction

Söderström (chapter 10, this volume) and DiCecio and Nelson (chapter 11, this volume) provide (different) counterfactual evidence on the effects of European Monetary Union (EMU) membership for Sweden and the United Kingdom based on small open economy dynamic stochastic general equilibrium (DSGE) models. Söderström estimates a small open economy model of the Swedish economy with twenty-seven variables (fifteen observables) and twenty-one exogenous shocks: one nonstationary technology shock common to foreign and domestic economies, nine shocks specific to the domestic economy (including a stationary technology shock), three foreign economy shocks, seven monetary and fiscal policy shocks, and a foreign exchange risk premium shock. DiCecio-Nelson use an Erceg, Gust, and Lopez-Salido (2007) model setup with twenty-five equations determining twenty-five endogenous variables and eleven shocks: two technology, two Investment and Saving equilibrium (IS) shocks, two wage markup shocks, two price markup shocks, one uncovered interest rate parity (UIP) shock, and two monetary policy shocks. The main results of the two exercises are that asymmetric shocks have been important for fluctuations in the Swedish economy, but the exchange rate has acted to destabilize rather than stabilize the economy; monetary union does not make a great difference for the United Kingdom, especially if UIP shocks are not zeroed but are transformed in additional demand shocks. Rather than concentrating on specific aspects of the two simulation exercises, I shall devote my discussion to the common general framework adopted here: small open economy DSGE models. In particular, I shall challenge such framework by estimating a small empirical model, a cointegrated vector autoregression (VAR), and by pointing out stark differences in the implications of cointegrated VAR and small open economy DSGE for the working of the economies with particular reference to the relative role of domestic and foreign shocks in explaining gross domestic product (GDP) fluctuations.

Challenging Small Open Economy DSGE Models

One of the main results in Söderström is that domestic shocks explain most of the forecasting variance of output at both short and long horizon. The first column of table 11C.1 reports the results in table 10.4 in (Söderström showing that domestic shocks explain 83.5 percent of the forecasting variance of Swedish GDP at the one-quarter horizon; this share declines

Carlo A. Favero is professor of economics at Bocconi University.

Table 11C.1   **Fraction of GDP forecasting variance due to domestic shocks**

Horizon	DSGE	SW GDP FEVD Bivariate cointegrated VAR EA-SW	EA GDP FEVD[a] Bivariate cointegrated VAR US-EA	CAN GDP FEVD[b] Monetary VAR US-CAN
1	83.5	70.1	65	100
4	66.2	41.5	38	26
20	45.8	20.8	8	25
40	59.4	14.4	4	—

[a]Giannone, Lenza, and Reichlin (2008)
[b]Cushman and Zha (2007)

with the horizon, but very slowly, to reach the value of about 60 percent at the ten-year horizon.

This is a rather common result in small open economy DSGE models (see, for example, Justiniano and Preston [2006]). We challenge this result by identifying domestic and foreign shocks in a much simpler framework. Following the empirical model of common fluctuations of U.S. and euro area GDP proposed by Giannone, Lenza, and Reichlin (chapter 4, this volume), we consider the following bivariate cointegrated VAR for euro area (log of) real GDP, y_t^{EA}, and Swedish real GDP, y_t^{SW}:

$$\Delta = A(L)\Delta z_{t-1} + \alpha\beta' z_{t-1} + \alpha\gamma t + Bu_t ,$$

$$z_t = \begin{bmatrix} y_t^{EA} \\ y_t^{SW} \end{bmatrix} \alpha = \begin{bmatrix} 0.01 \\ (0.02) \\ -0.08 \\ (0.03) \end{bmatrix}$$

$$\beta' = \begin{bmatrix} 1 - 0.40 \\ (0.19) \end{bmatrix}.$$

The application of the Johansen (1995) procedure to the bivariate system produces the following results: (a) there is a single common stochastic trend between y_t^{EA} and y_t^{SW} (the null hypothesis of at most no cointegrating vector is rejected, while the null of at most one cointegrating vector cannot be rejected); and (b) y_t^{SW} is the only variable that reacts to disequilibria.

This evidence on the long-run behavior of the system leads to a natural identification of the two structural shocks hitting the system as a global (permanent) one and a local (temporary) one. The resulting forecasting error variance decomposition (FEVD) reported in column (2) of table 11C.1 leads to results very different from that of the small open economy DSGE model.

In fact, the local shock dominates over short horizon but gets progressively dominated by the global shock that eventually explains the entire FEVD of the Swedish output.

This pattern of variance decomposition for the small open economy is typical of empirical VARs. We report in column (3) the results in Giannone, Lenza, and Reichlin analyzing fluctuations of U.S. and euro area GDP, while column (4) reports the results of the joint analysis of the Canadian and U.S. GDP by Cushman and Zha (1997).

What Is Going On?

The stark contrast between the evidence based on empirical VARs—data consistent and driven by a very limited (and very sensible) set of identifying restrictions—and that produced by small open economy DSGE models raises an interesting question on the possible sources of such discrepancy. Justiniano and Preston (2006) evaluate whether an estimated, structural, small open economy model of the Canadian economy can account for the substantial influence of foreign-sourced disturbances identified in numerous reduced-form VAR studies. The analysis shows that the benchmark model implies cross-equation restrictions that are too stringent when confronted with the data, yielding implausible parameter estimates. Appropriate choice of ad hoc disturbances can relax these cross-equation restrictions and therefore capture certain properties of the data and yield plausible parameter estimates. This success is qualified by the model's inability to account for the transmission of foreign disturbances to the domestic economy: less than 1 percent of the variance of output is explained by foreign shocks.

If the inability to account for the transmission of foreign disturbances is a symptom of misspecification, what are the main dimensions along which the model can be misspecified?

We consider a number of potential sources of misspecification.

First is modeling of the exchange rate. In the swedish model adopted by Söderström, the foreign economy is taken as exogenous and therefore modeled as a small independent VAR; therefore, the main source of transmission of shocks between the two economies is the exchange rate, S, which is modeled as follows:

$$E_t \Delta S_{t+1} = \frac{1}{(1-\phi)}(R_t - R_t^*) - \frac{1}{(1-\phi)} RP_t + \varepsilon_{rp,t}$$

$$RP_t = \phi \Delta S_t - \phi a_t, \quad (S)$$

a_t: net foreign asset position.

Unfortunately, $\varepsilon_{rp,t}$ turns out to be a near-unit root process. In fact, it has a persistence parameter of 0.93 in DiCecio-Nelson and in Adolfson et al. (2008). This implies that the residual term almost entirely explains

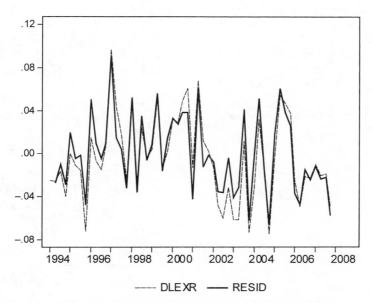

Fig. 11C.1   **Actual values and residuals from the exchange rate equation**

exchange rate fluctuations. We report in figure 11C.1 ΔS_{t+1} and $\varepsilon_{rp,t}$ for Swedish data.

Figure 11C.1 shows rather eloquently that the structural determinants of $E_t \Delta S_{t+1}$ play a rather minor role.

The second factor that can be missed by small economy DSGE models is comovement between asset prices (independent from exchange rate fluctuations). We report in figure 11C.2 comovements between GDP growth, bond markets, and stock markets in the euro area (EA), Sweden (SW), the United Kingdom (UK), and the United States (US; all variables defined in local currency).

The figure shows that international comovements in asset prices are at least as strong as comovement in real GDP growth; in fact, financial markets could be the sources of the common shocks driving common GDP fluctuations. Understanding the sources of common asset price fluctuations leads naturally to investigate a further factor invariably omitted, or at most taken as constant, in the DSGE model: the risk premium (see Rudebusch, Sack, and Swanson [2006]). To have a visual impression of the strength of the international comovement in this variable, we report in figure 11C.3 the time series of the spread between the yield to maturity of Italian and German ten-year government bonds (SP_ITBD) and the (rescaled to match mean) spread between ten-year fixed interest rates on swaps denominated in U.S. dollar and the yield to maturity of ten-year U.S. government bonds.

Figure 11C.3 clearly shows the presence of a comovement between the

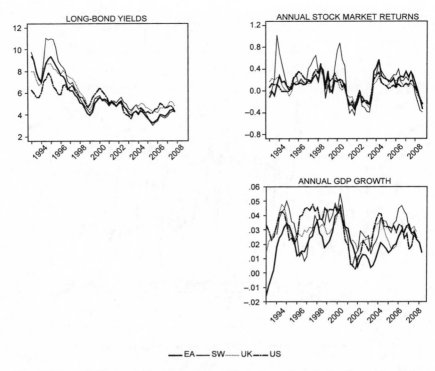

Fig. 11C.2 GDP growth, bond markets, and stock markets in the Euro Area (EA), Sweden (SW), United Kingdom (U.K.) and the United States (U.S.)

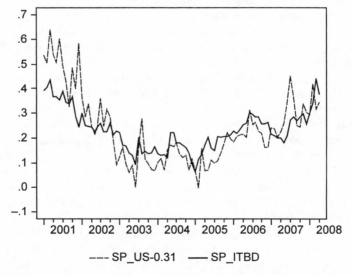

Fig. 11C.3 Spread between the yield to maturity of Italian and German ten-year government bonds (SP_ITBD) and the (rescaled to match mean) spread between ten-year fixed interest rates on swaps denominated in U.S. dollar and the yield to maturity of ten-year U.S. government bonds

relative perceived risk of Italian and German government sectors and the relative perceived risk of the U.S. banking sector and U.S. government sector that clearly calls for the insertion of a common time-varying world factor in the determination of global asset prices.

References

Adolfson, M., S. Laseen, J. Linde, and L. E. O. Svensson. 2008. Optimal monetary policy in an operational medium-sized DSGE model. NBER Working Paper no. 14092. Cambridge, MA: National Bureau of Economic Research, June.

Erceg, C., C. Gust, and J. D. López-Salido. 2007. The transmission of domestic shocks in the open economy. NBER Working Paper no. 13613. Cambridge, MA: National Bureau of Economic Research, November.

Cushman, D. O., and T. Zha. 1997. Identifying monetary policy in a small open economy under flexible exchange rates. *Journal of Monetary Economics* 39 (3): 433–48.

Johansen, S. 1995. *Likelihood-based inference on cointegration in the vector autoregressive model.* Oxford: Oxford University Press.

Justiniano, A., and B. Preston. 2006. Can structural small open economy models account for the influence of foreign disturbances? Columbia University, Department of Economics. Unpublished Manuscript.

Rudebusch, G. D., B. P. Sack, and E. T. Swanson. 2006. Macroeconomic implications of changes in the term premium. Working Paper no. 46. Federal Reserve of San Francisco, November.

Comment on Chapter 4*

Tommaso Monacelli

Introduction

This nice paper contains three main ideas. First, the euro area business cycle is less dispersed than it used to be. Second, it does not seem that the euro has contributed in any way to this change. Third, the euro area business cycle is the U.S./global business cycle. This is therefore a paper with a minimalist view on the role of the euro on the euro area business cycle.

My first reaction after reading the paper was: could we really expect any different result? We know since Baxter and Stockman (1989) that, at least in developed countries, exchange rate regimes are almost irrelevant to the characteristics of the business cycle. If anything, we should expect that in a currency area, the inability to use the nominal exchange rate as a tool to induce a fast and correct adjustment of relative prices should lead to a higher relevance of country-specific shocks. Hence the paper should be interpreted not only as suggesting that it is too soon to tell, but more broadly as a confirmation of the Baxter-Stockman view of the quasi-irrelevance of exchange rate regimes for the business cycle.

The authors find that the euro area business cycle is less dispersed than it used to be. They attribute this outcome to the Great Moderation, but their proof is informed a little bit too much by eyeballing the situation. The idea seems to be the following. Suppose there are no shocks in any economy of the area. This implies zero volatility in all countries, and therefore zero dispersion. However, the Great Moderation refers to a concept of absolute volatility, whereas the reduction in the dispersion of the volatility is a relative concept: in other words, volatility must have dropped more in some coun-

*This chapter begins on page 141.
Tommaso Monacelli is associate professor of economics at Bocconi University.

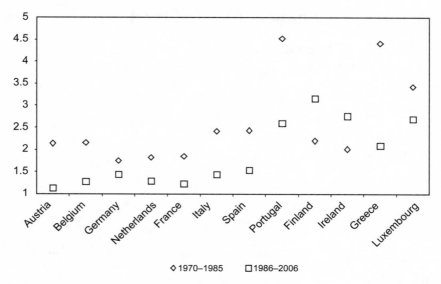

Figure 4C.1   Standard deviation of GDP growth

tries relative to others to induce a fall in the dispersion of business cycles. Figure 4C.1 compares, for each country of the euro area, the standard deviation of GDP growth across two subsamples:[1] 1970–1985, and 1986–2006. We see the volatility moderation at work, but we also see some heterogeneity. The Great Moderation has been particularly strong in Portugal and Greece, and less so in Italy and Spain. There is very little evidence of the Great Moderation in Germany, whereas Ireland and Finland experienced the opposite, a Great Amplification rather than moderation. It is legitimate to think that the transition to the euro (rather than the euro per se) did have some effect here. Despite the euro being a common enterprise, it obviously produced differential effects across countries. But why exactly did these differential effects occur? Was it because some countries had to forcefully reduce nominal exchange rate volatility? Was it because the unpredictable component of monetary policy was minimized in those countries? Or was it instead because a better-anchored monetary policy during the transition also produced relatively more macroeconomic stability? Surprisingly, we do not know much about this indirect effect of the euro, neither from theory nor from any empirical analysis.

Figure 4C.2 displays the correlation of GDP growth in country i with GDP growth in country j, for all $j \neq i$, and averaged across j. This is a measure, computed over ten-year rolling windows, of the comovement of GDP

1. The GDP data are annual PPP adjusted, and have been kindly provided by the authors.

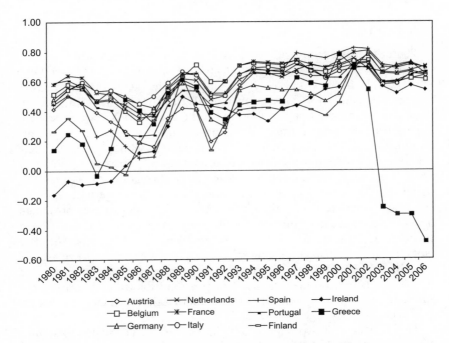

Figure 4C.2   Rolling correlation of GDP growth with remaining euro area countries (average)

growth of country *i* with the rest of the area. We clearly see evidence of convergence, especially for the countries of the so-called periphery (Portugal, Ireland, Greece, and Spain). Yet we also see that this convergence process is by no means coincident with the introduction of the euro, but progressed gradually from the early 1980s on.[2]

While it may seem almost conventional wisdom that a process of convergence in business-cycle comovement started much earlier than the introduction of the euro, it is less easy to come up with a well-identified explanation. Some usual suspects quickly come to mind: was it trade or was it financial integration? Was it policy convergence instead? Or rather, was it simply good luck? Identifying the appropriate explanation would require an extensive empirical analysis that is virtually absent in the literature. Here, however, I would like to make the following simple point. Choose your favorite usual suspect as an explanation of the convergence in business cycles in the euro area: the existing theory would not be very helpful.

2. Notice the breakdown in the correlation of GDP growth in Greece with the rest of the area, due to a deep unsynchronized recession in the early 1990s.

Suspect I: Trade

There is strong empirical evidence that higher trade enhances cofluctuations (Frankel and Rose [1998]; Clark and van Wincoop [2001]; Otto
et al. [2001]). In Kose and Yi (2006), doubling the median trade intensity
increases bilateral cross-correlation of GDP growth by 0.06 in OECD countries. The problem, though, comes with the theory. It is very difficult to
generate a link between trade and comovement within standard dynamic
equilibrium models (Kose and Yi [2001]). If asset markets are complete
(and even if productivity shocks are correlated across countries), a higher
trade intensity leads to a lower cross-country correlation of output. The
idea is that increased openness enhances the swings in international relative prices (terms of trade), thereby exacerbating the negative comovement
across countries. Here comes a double irony. First, lower transport costs
(symbolizing globalization) make the problem worse, because they are
isomorphic to increasing openness. Second, if one increases the elasticity
of substitution between domestically produced and imported goods, the
problem gets even worse. The irony here is that it is trade theorists—not
international macroeconomists—who think that that elasticity of substitution is particularly high.

There are at least two options to fix this problem. The first is to assume
financial autarky, but this is obviously unrealistic. The second is vertical
specialization of production. Vertical specialization occurs when countries
specialize in only particular stages of a good's production sequence. Yi
(2003) shows that vertical specialization explains a substantial share of the
increase in world trade after World War II. Vertical specialization is certainly
a phenomenon that has widely characterized the increase in trade within
the euro area in the past twenty-five years. Although this concept has found
very limited application in the business cycle literature, it seems a promising avenue to strengthen the ability of standard models to generate realistic
cross-country comovement.

Suspect II: Financial Integration

Financial integration (FI) is an alternative potential candidate to explain
the business-cycle convergence observed in the euro area over time. The
existing empirical evidence suggests that FI enhances cofluctuations (Imbs
[2004]). However, once again, theory is not particularly helpful. A standard
two-country dynamic general equilibrium (DGE) model with complete
international financial markets (as in Backus et al. [1994]) would predict
that stronger financial integration leads to a lower international correlation
of output. Intuitively, access to complete asset markets allows the diversify-
ing of idiosyncratic (country-specific in this case) risk. Hence generating
stronger cofluctuations endogenously via stronger international risk-sharing

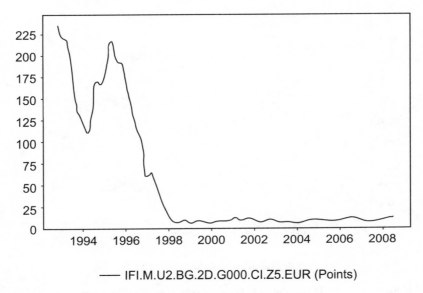

——— IFI.M.U2.BG.2D.G000.CI.Z5.EUR (Points)

Figure 4C.3   **Dispersion in ten-year bond yield spreads**
Source: European Central Bank

is a challenge for open-economy DGE models. At the same time, empirically, it is not completely clear whether the euro area has become fully financially integrated. It is obvious that it has, if one looks at the government bonds market. Figure 4C.3 displays the dispersion in the ten-year government bonds spreads across euro area countries, and shows a dramatic decline in the past fifteen years.

When one looks at credit markets, though, the picture is far less clear. Figure 4C.4 shows, for instance, the cross-country dispersion in (comparable) mortgage loan rates in the euro area countries. The degree of dispersion is still sizeable and, surprisingly, has even increased substantially over time. In general, it is widely acknowledged that large differences remain among the institutional characteristics of mortgage markets in the euro area. This is particularly relevant for the centralized transmission mechanism of monetary policy in the euro area.[3]

Suspect III: Policy Integration (PI) versus Good Luck

Figure 4C.5 gives a dramatic visual impression of how striking the process of monetary policy convergence has been in the euro area. Was policy integration per se in any way responsible for the observed degree of conver-

3. See Calza et al. (2008).

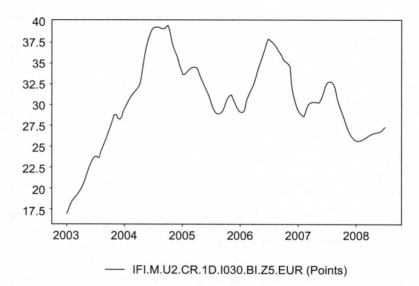

— IFI.M.U2.CR.1D.I030.BI.Z5.EUR (Points)

Figure 4C.4   **Dispersion in five-to-ten-year mortgage loan rates**
Source: European Central Bank

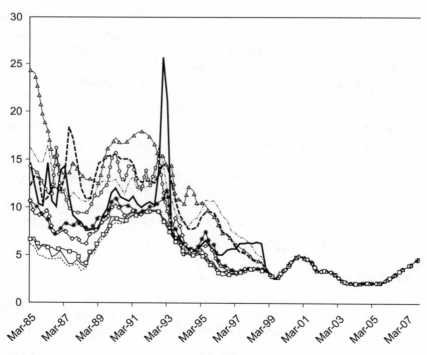

Figure 4C.5   **Short-term interest rates in the euro area**

gence in business cycles in the euro area? Surprisingly, we know very little about this issue. One thing we know, though, is that answering this question requires the virtues of a fully structural DGE model, and we have made substantial progress on this front recently.[4]

Armed with these tools, it would seem particularly urgent to pursue a research agenda that we could summarize in the following questions: (i) Does PI lead to stronger cofluctuations (and has this actually happened in the euro area)? (ii) Is it "convergence per se" or is it "convergence to good policy"? (iii) Has policy integration contributed to the Great Moderation in Europe, as well as to the differential impact of the Great Moderation in different countries (as argued above)? (iv) Can we disentangle policy integration from simple good luck?

Conclusions

This paper presents a series of key facts that characterize the business cycle in the euro area. It argues convincingly that the euro per se is unlikely to have produced any form of convergence in business cycles. At the same time it leaves two fundamental questions still open: (i) What was the cause of the convergence? (ii) Can theory help us to differentiate among alternative hypotheses? I have tried to argue that addressing the latter question is more difficult than may have been anticipated, and that progress on this front remains limited. As Europeans, we should not be particularly proud.

References

Backus, D., P. J. Kehoe, and F. E. Kydland. 1994. Dynamics of the trade balance and the terms of trade: The J-curve? *American Economic Review* 84:84–103.
Baxter, M., and A. C. Stockman. 1989. Business cycles and the exchange-rate regime: Some international evidence. *Journal of Monetary Economics* 23 (3): 377–400.
Calza, A., T. Monacelli, and L. Stracca. 2008. Mortgage markets, collateral constraints and monetary policy: Do institutional factors matter? Bocconi University and ECB.
Clark, T. E., and E. van Wincoop. 2001. Borders and business cycles. *Journal of International Economics* 55:59–85.
Frankel, J. A., and A. K. Rose. 1998. The endogeneity of the optimum currency area criteria. *Economic Journal* 108 (449): 1009–25.
Imbs, J. 1999. Co-fluctuations. London Business School. Unpublished Manuscript.
———. 2004. Trade, finance, specialization, and synchronization. *Review of Economics and Statistics* 86 (3): 723–34.
Kose, M. A., and K.-M. Yi. 2001. International trade and business cycles: Is vertical specialization the missing link? *American Economic Review* 91 (2): 371–75.

---

4. See for instance Smets and Wouters (2007).

————. 2006. Can the standard international business cycle model explain the relation between trade and comovement? *Journal of International Economics* 68: 267–95.

Otto, G., G. Voss, and W. Luke. 2001. Understanding OECD output correlations, RDP 2001–05. Reserve Bank of Australia.

Smets, F., and R. Wouters. 2007. Shocks and frictions in U.S. business cycles: a Bayesian DSGE approach. *American Economic Review* 97 (3): 586–606.

Yi, K.-M. 2003. Can vertical specialization explain the growth of world trade? *Journal of Political Economy* 111 (1): 52–102.

Contributors

Alberto Alesina
Department of Economics
Harvard University
Cambridge, MA 02138

Silvia Ardagna
Department of Economics
Littauer Center 206
Harvard University
Cambridge, MA 02138

Pervenche Berès
European Parliament
Bâtiment Altiero Spinelli, 14G206
60, rue Wiertz/Wiertzstraat
B-1047 Brussels, Belgium

Matteo Bugamelli
Bank of Italy
Via Nazionale 91
00184 Rome, Italy

Stephen G. Cecchetti
Monetary and Economic Department
Bank for International Settlements
Centralbahnplatz 2
4002 Basel, Switzerland

Riccardo DiCecio
Federal Reserve Bank of St. Louis
P.O. Box 442
St. Louis, MO 63166-0442

Barry Eichengreen
Department of Economics
University of California, Berkeley
549 Evans Hall 3880
Berkeley, CA 94720-3880

Antonio Fatás
INSEAD
Boulevard de Constance
77300 Fontainebleau, France

Carlo A. Favero
IGIER, Università Bocconi
Via Salasco 5
20136 Milan, Italy

Martin Feldstein
National Bureau of Economic
    Research
1050 Massachusetts Avenue
Cambridge, MA 02138-5398

Jeffrey Frankel
Kennedy School of Government
Harvard University
79 John F. Kennedy Street
Cambridge, MA 02138

Vincenzo Galasso
IGIER, Università Bocconi
Via Roentgen 1
20136 Milan, Italy

Domenico Giannone
European Central Bank
Kaiserstrasse 29
D-60311 Frankfurt am Main, Germany

Francesco Giavazzi
Department of Economics
Bocconi University
Via Roentgen 1
20136 Milan, Italy

Alberto Giovannini
Unifortune Asset Management
    SGR SpA
Via Donizetti 53
20122 Milan, Italy

Reint Gropp
European Business School
Rheingaustrasse 1
65375 Oestrich-Winkel, Germany

Otmar Issing
Center for Financial Studies
Goethe Universität Frankfurt
House of Finance
Grüneburgplatz 1
D-60323 Frankfurt, Germany

Anil K Kashyap
Booth School of Business
University of Chicago
5807 S. Woodlawn Avenue
Chicago, IL 60637

Michele Lenza
European Central Bank
Kaiserstrasse 29
D-60311 Frankfurt am Main, Germany

Loretta J. Mester
Federal Reserve Bank of Philadelphia
10 Independence Mall
Philadelphia, PA 19106-1574

Ilian Mihov
INSEAD
1 Ayer Rajah Avenue
Singapore 138680

Edward Nelson
Federal Reserve Bank of St. Louis
P.O. Box 442
St. Louis, MO 63166-0442

Gianmarco I. P. Ottaviano
Bocconi University
Via Roentgen 1
20136 Milan, Italy

Roberto Perotti
IGIER, Universitá Bocconi
Via Roentgen 1
20136 Milan, Italy

Richard Portes
London Business School
Regent's Park
London NW1 4SA England

Lucrezia Reichlin
London Business School
Regent's Park
London NW1 4SA England

Fabiano Schivardi
Faculty of Political Science
Cagliari University
Viale S. Ignazio 78
09123 Cagliari, Italy

Kermit L. Schoenholtz
Stern School of Business
New York University
44 West Fourth Street, seventh floor
New York, NY 10012

Ulf Söderström
Sveriges Riksbank
SE-103 37 Stockholm, Sweden

Silvana Tenreyro
Department of Economics
London School of Economics
Houghton Street
London WC2A 2AE England

Roberta Zizza
Bank of Italy
Via Nazionale 91
00184 Rome, Italy

Author Index

Subject Index